PEARSON

mycanadiancommunicationlab™

Save Time.

Improve Results.

More than 6 million students have used a Pearson MyLab product to get a better grade.

MyCanadianCommunicationLab is an all-in-one learning and testing environment for mass communication. The easy-to-navigate site provides a variety of resources, including

- An interactive Pearson eText
- Audio and video material to view or listen to, whatever your learning style
- Personalized learning opportunities—YOU choose what, where, and when you want to study
- Self-assessment tests that create a personalized study plan to guide you on making the most efficient use of study time

To take advantage of all that MyCanadianCommunicationLab has to offer, you will need an access code. If you do not already have an access code, you can buy one online at **www.mycanadiancommunicationlab.ca.**

Pearson eText

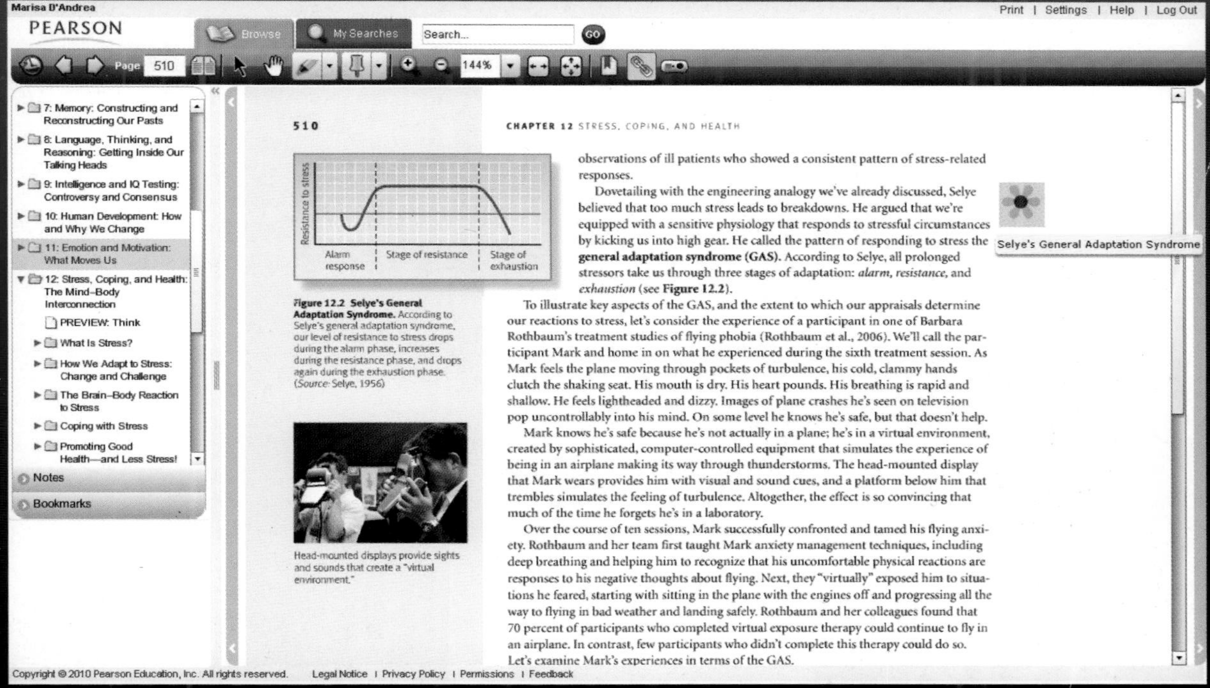

Pearson eText gives students access to the text whenever and wherever they have access to the internet. eText pages look exactly like the printed text, offering powerful new functionality for students and instructors.

Users can create notes, highlight text in different colours, create bookmarks, zoom, click hyperlinked words and phrases to view definitions, and choose single-page or two-page view.

Pearson eText allows for quick navigation using a table of contents and provides full-text search. The eText may also offer links to associated media files, enabling users to access videos, animations, or other activities as they read the text.

Videos and Interactivities

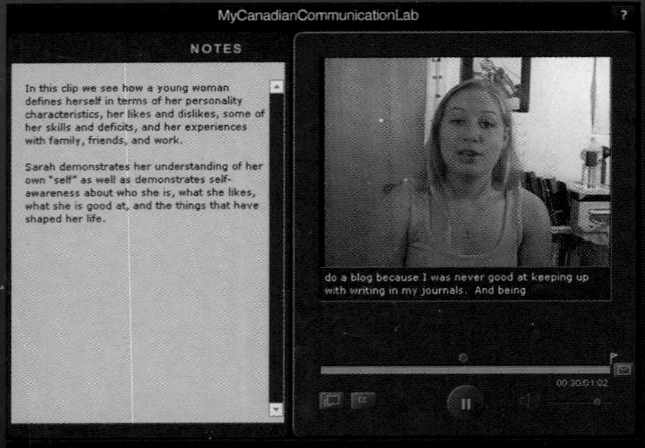

You are presented with video clips of scenarios and examples to help fine-tune your communication skills. Annotations help place the information in context, while follow-up questions provide an opportunity for you to apply your learning.

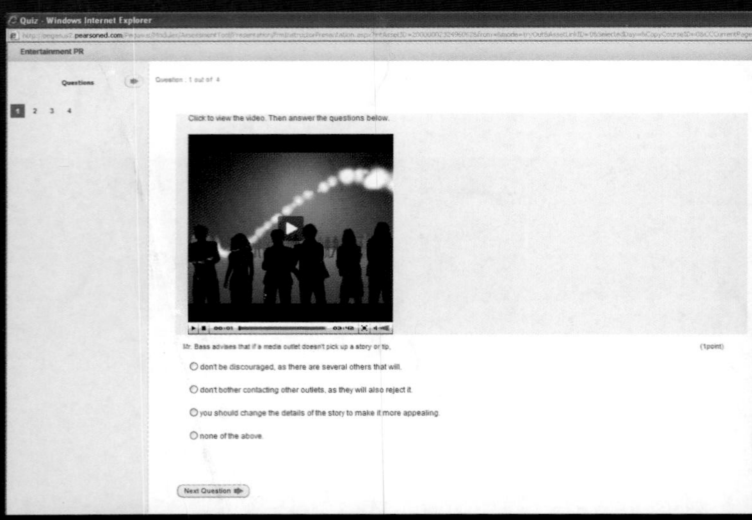

Quizzes and practice tests help you interact with the concepts in the text, learn by applying those concepts, and better prepare for exams.

Save Time. Improve Results. **www.mycanadiancommunicationlab.ca**

John Vivian WINONA STATE UNIVERSITY Peter J. Maurin MOHAWK COLLEGE OF APPLIED ARTS AND TECHNOLOGY

THE MEDIA OF MASS COMMUNICATION

Sixth Canadian Edition

Pearson Canada
Toronto

Library and Archives Canada Cataloguing in Publication

Vivian, John
The media of mass communication / John Vivian, Peter J. Maurin.—6th Canadian ed.

Includes bibliographical references and index.
ISBN 978-0-205-71175-8

1. Mass media—Textbooks. I. Maurin, Peter II. Title.

P90.V58 2011 302.23 C2010-906309-0

ISBN 978-0-205-71175-8

Vice-President, Editorial Director: Gary Bennett
Editor-in-Chief: Ky Pruesse
Acquisitions Editor: David S. Le Gallais
Sponsoring Editor: Carolin Sweig
Marketing Manager: Lisa Gillis
Senior Developmental Editor: Paul Donnelly
Project Manager: Marissa Lok
Production Editor: Susan Broadhurst
Copy Editor: Susan Broadhurst
Proofreader: Suzanne Needs
Compositor: MPS Limited, a Macmillan Company
Photo Researcher: Indu Arora
Art Director: Julia Hall
Cover and Interior Designer: Quinn Banting
Cover Image: Corbis

For permission to reproduce copyrighted material, the publisher gratefully acknowledges the copyright holders listed on page 314, which is considered an extension of this copyright page.

1 2 3 4 5 15 14 13 12 11

Printed and bound in the United States of America.

Brief Contents

Contents

11 Public Relations 164

12 Advertising 181

13 Media Research 199

Preface

Don't blink. If you do, the landscape of the media of mass communication will have morphed and warped into a new reality. The rapidity of change in the mass media and in the world in which the media function necessitated this sixth Canadian edition of *The Media of Mass Communication*. This edition is our effort to provide the most up-to-date package possible to accompany your course. The book is more than a snapshot, though. You will find the sixth Canadian edition of *The Media of Mass Communication* a foundation for strengthening understanding of the mass media. More firmly rooted in principles and foundations, you will find yourself in good stead for staying atop of difficult-to-anticipate changes that are coming quickly to both Canadian and American media even as you read this.

New to This Edition

Another reason for this new sixth Canadian edition comes from our experiences as teachers. We are always searching for new ways to present material in our classes. This revision includes improvements ranging from little things such as word choices, examples, and illustrations to major things such as a stronger emphasis on themes, new topics, and new features to help you pull everything together. Here are some of the key changes.

CURRENT ISSUES

Mass media have had a role, not altogether an exemplary one, in public awareness about the global warming crisis. You will learn about it in this edition. The changing role of the internet in our lives is a recurrent theme. So is the decline of traditional media, particularly magazines and books, but also the troubled future for television and radio as we know them. You will find discussions on gaming as an emerging media vehicle for advertising. There also is new discussion on dilemmas posed by the phenomenal rise of blogging and online activities such as Facebook, Twitter, and YouTube. This edition is as current as we could make it.

GLOBAL EMPHASIS

You will find significantly increased attention to the mass media of China, the Middle East, India, and Columbia, which is essential to an understanding of evolving relationships in political realities and the global marketplace.

CHAPTER REORGANIZATION

The first three chapters—Mass Media Literacy, Mass Media Technology, and Entertainment—set the stage for developing an understanding of the study of mass media. The next nine chapters each focus on a specific media of mass communication. The final five chapters are more issue oriented, and concentrate on diverse topics such as Media Research, Media Law and Ethics, Media Effects, Global Mass Media, and Mass Media and Governance.

NEW PEDAGOGICAL FEATURES

We like to think of this as a pedagogy-enhanced edition. In addition to the features that previous users have enjoyed, we've added some new ones, such as Learning Ahead checklists, Learning Check questions, and links to online assets to help you become the best student you can be.

UPDATED CASE STUDIES

The case studies have been enhanced with questions and activities. Several new case studies are included on Second Life, Magazines on the Internet, Podcasting Evolution, and Is the Internet Changing the Government-Media Landscape?

UPDATED MYCANADIANCOMMUNICATIONLAB

mycanadiancommunicationlab

www.mycanadiancommunicationlab.ca New features in this interactive and instructive online solution help foster student understanding of media literacy and make learning fun! New online videos illustrate chapter content, including "A Day in the Life," which focus on individuals working in the media. Icons in the text direct you to various features and activities on related topics.

Using This Book

This edition retains many of the popular features that have helped your predecessors master the subject, as well as introducing some new ones.

- **Media in Theory.** Chapters open with theoretical questions that lay the foundation for issues explored later in the chapter.
- **Learning Ahead checklists.** Each chapter begins with learning goals to help you guide your thoughts as you read through the chapter.
- **Study Previews.** These previews will help you prepare for the material ahead. Each major section begins with a preview of the concepts that will be covered there.
- **Learning Checks.** Questions peppered throughout the chapters help you be sure that you've grasped the main points.
- **Running Glossary.** Glossary definitions are provided in the margins, on the same page that the name or concept is introduced in the text.
- **Case Studies.** These case studies illustrate an issue discussed in the chapter. Each also includes questions and activities to help deepen your media literacy.
- **Media People.** This feature introduces personalities who have had a major impact on the media or whose story illustrates a major point in media history.
- **Media Timeline.** This updated feature helps you see the sequence of important media events and to put the events discussed in each chapter in historical context.
- **Tables.** Tables help you see certain facts about the mass media at a glance.
- **Questions for Critical Thinking.** These questions ask you to use your imagination and critical-thinking abilities to restructure the material.
- **Keeping Up to Date.** These sections list professional and trade journals, magazines, newspapers, and other periodical references to help you keep current on media developments and issues. Most of these periodicals are available in college and university libraries.
- **For Further Learning.** Now collected at the end of the book, this section offers a selected bibliography, organized by chapter, of additional readings. Included are seminal and leading current works.

Supplements

INSTRUCTOR'S RESOURCE CD-ROM

This resource CD-ROM includes the following supplements for instructors:

INSTRUCTOR'S RESOURCE MANUAL (IRM)

This manual is designed to ease time-consuming demands of instructional preparation, to enhance lectures, and to provide helpful suggestions to organize the course. The IRM contains helpful teaching resources and lecture enrichment, including outlines, synopses, and glossaries.

TEST ITEM FILE (TIF)

The test bank includes multiple choice, true/false, matching, fill-in-the-blank, short answer, and essay questions.

POWERPOINT PRESENTATION PACKAGE

The PowerPoint slides created for this text outline the key points in each chapter and are ideal for lecture presentations.

These supplements are also available for downloading from a password-protected location on Pearson Education Canada's online catalogue, at **vig.pearsoned.ca**. See your local Pearson sales representative for details.

MYTEST

MyTest for *The Media of Mass Communication*, Sixth Canadian Edition, from Pearson Education Canada, is a powerful assessment generation program that helps instructors easily create and print quizzes, tests, exams, and homework or practice handouts. Questions and tests can be authored online, allowing instructors ultimate flexibility and the ability to efficiently manage assessments at any time, from anywhere. Please visit **www.pearsonmytest.com** to access MyTest.

MYCANADIANCOMMUNICATIONLAB

www.mycanadiancommunicationlab.ca This is where students and media connect. MyCanadianCommunicationLab is an interactive and instructive online solution for mass communication courses that combines multimedia, video, activities, research support, tests, and quizzes to make teaching and learning fun!

mycanadiancommunicationlab

COURSESMART

CourseSmart is a new way for instructors and students to access textbooks online any time, from anywhere. With thousands of titles across hundreds of courses, CourseSmart helps instructors choose the best textbook for their class and give their students a new option for buying the assigned textbook as a lower cost eTextbook. For more information, visit **www.coursesmart.com**.

TECHNOLOGY SPECIALISTS

Pearson's Technology Specialists work with faculty and campus course designers to ensure that Pearson technology products, assessment tools, and online course materials are tailored to meet your specific needs. This highly qualified team is dedicated to helping schools take full advantage of a wide range of educational resources, by assisting in the integration of a variety of instructional materials and media formats. Your local Pearson Education sales representative can provide you with more details on this service program.

Acknowledgments

The Canadian author and publisher would like to thank the following reviewers who provided feedback and support during the development of this project:

Stephen Crocker, Memorial University
Lyle Cruikshank, Dawson College
Aliaa Dakroury, University of Ottawa
Kelly Egan, Ryerson University
Kelly Henley, St. Clair College
Timothy Jacobs, Okanagan College
Uldis Kundrats, Nipissing University
David Newman, Simon Fraser University
Roman Onufrijchuk, Simon Fraser University
Kevin Schut, Trinity Western University
Richard Sutherland, University of Calgary
Linda Warren, Niagara College

The Canadian author would also like to thank the remarkable staff at Pearson Education: Carolin Sweig, Suzanne Schaan, Paul Donnelly, and Marissa Lok. A special note of thanks to editor Susan Broadhurst, whose thorough and painstaking editing has made me a better writer and communicator.

Also, much thanks to John Vivian of Winona State University for providing the Canadian author with wonderful material to work with when adapting the text for the Canadian market.

Keeping Current

To you, the student, we want to emphasize that this book is a tool to help you become more intelligent and discerning as a media consumer. If you plan on a media career, the book is intended to orient you to the courses that will follow in your curriculum. This book, though, is only one of many tools for staying on top of the subject for many years to come. A feature at the end of every chapter, Keeping Up to Date, has tips on how to keep current even after your course is over.

—John Vivian and Peter J. Maurin

To Harold Vivian, my father,
who sparked my curiosity about the
mass media at age five by asking what
was black and white and read all over.

And to Elaine Vivian, my mother,
who nurtured this curiosity by keeping
the house stocked with books, magazines
and reading material of every sort.

J. V.

To my soulmate, Kim; thank you for all your
love, patience and understanding over the last
"twenty-five-plus" years. To my kids, Sonja and
Joshua. You are each gifted in your own way;
thank you for letting me be both your dad and
your friend. And always remember I love you more . . . .

This book is also dedicated to
the memory of my mother
and father, Peter and Blanka Maurin.

P. J. M.

Mass Media Literacy

1

Canada's Media Guru Marshall McLuhan's ideas and commentaries on the role and effects of the mass media are still as popular today as they were in the 1960s. His theories make up part of the "Toronto School" or "Canadian School" of communication.

LEARNING AHEAD

- More than most people realize, we are awash in a mass media environment.
- Media literacy begins with an awareness of our media environment.
- Communication through mass media has profoundly affected human existence.
- Mass media's role in binding people together is changing with more media choices.
- Profit potential drives mass media behaviour in a capitalistic environment.

MEDIA IN THEORY

Theories on How the Media Work

Media scholars have devised several ways to dissect and analyze the mass media. These include the ideas of the so-called "Toronto School" or "Canadian School" of communication, which embodies the ideas of Harold Innis and Marshall McLuhan. Both men were determinists; they argued that the physical form of communication would determine the psychological and social outcome.

Marshall McLuhan: The Medium Is the Message

Marshall McLuhan

Marshall McLuhan Canadian who claimed the medium is the message.

hot media Print media, which require more intimate audience involvement.

Marshall McLuhan examined how we perceive media messages: looking not only at the content of the message but also at the form of the message. McLuhan's model divides media into hot and cool categories. Books, magazines, and newspapers are **hot media** because they require a high degree of thinking to use them. To read a book, for example, you must immerse yourself to derive anything from it. You must concentrate and tune out distractions. The relationship between you and the medium is intense—or hot. The same is true of magazines and newspapers, which require the audience to participate actively in the communication process.

In contrast, some media allow the audience to be less actively involved, even passive. These are **cool media**. Television, for example, requires less intellectual involvement than do the hot media. In fact, television requires hardly any effort. When radio is played mostly as background, it doesn't require any active listener involvement at all. It's a cool

cool media Media that can be consumed passively.

medium. Radio is warmer, however, when it engages listeners' imaginations, as with radio drama.

Are movies hot or cold? In some ways, movies are like television, with simultaneous visual and audio components. But there are essential differences. Movies involve viewers completely. Huge screens command the viewers' full attention, and sealed, darkened movie-house auditoriums shut out distractions. On a hot–cool continuum, movies are hot. But what about a movie played at home on television? Cool.

Harold Innis: Time and Space

Harold Innis Canadian whose communication model was based on bias in communication.

bias in communication Theory that media can have a bias for time and space.

Harold Innis was a political economist at the University of Toronto whose communication model was based on what he referred to as **bias in communication.** This bias had effects in both time and space.

This analysis of time and space bias was examined in some detail in *Empire and Communications*, a book published in 1950. This book included a historical look at forms of communication that have helped in the rise and fall of civilizations. Innis's study reported on life from ancient Egypt up to and including North American society in the 1940s. His hypothesis was that the type of social organization in all of these different societies was signified by the types of media that each used to communicate important information. In turn, those media were directly related to how those in power kept power through their "monopolies of knowledge."

By Innis's way of thinking, this communication bias is linked to the media of choice during each historical period and by each civilization. For example, stone and clay have a bias for time; that is, they can last a long time due to their material composition, and therefore can be passed down from generation to generation. Societies using these "time-based" media, according to Innis, were hierarchical and decentralized and based on tradition. On the other hand, paper has a bias for space; it's light and can be passed around from person to person. Cultures using this medium were less hierarchical and more centralized and more commercial than earlier civilizations. In short, media that were light and fast favoured control over space, while heavy, slow, and face-to-face media were better suited to keeping cultures stable over time.

LEARNING CHECK

- What makes "hot" media different from "cool" media? How
- Does digital technology have a bias for "time" or "space"?

MEDIA PEOPLE Marshall McLuhan

Marshall McLuhan

Born in Edmonton in 1911, Canadian communication theorist Marshall McLuhan taught at Assumption College in Windsor (now the University of Windsor) and at St. Michael's College at the University of Toronto. In 1954 he founded *Explorations,* a journal devoted to the analysis of popular media and culture. McLuhan is also the patron saint of *Wired* magazine.

While the phrase "the medium is the message" is the most popular "McLuhanism," he did have some other theories on media, including his attention-grabbing things to say on various aspects of mass media. For example:

- "Television is a serious medium, it's an inner oriented medium, you are the vanishing point, it goes inside you, you go on an inner trip, it is the prelude, the vestibule to LSD."
- "All news is fake. It's pseudo-event. It's created by the medium that is employed. Newspaper news has nothing to do with TV news."
- "Advertising is a service industry that provides its satisfactions quite independent of the product, and people are increasingly tending to get their satisfactions from the ad rather than the product."

Media Ubiquity

STUDY PREVIEW We swim in an ocean of mass communication, exposed to media messages during 68.8 percent of our waking hours. So immersed are we in these messages that we often are unmindful of their existence, let alone their influences.

Media Exposure

Mass media are pervasive in modern life. According to the **Canadian Radio-television and Telecommunications Commission (CRTC)**, Canadians listen to one of 1191 radio stations, watch one of 707 television services available, and also surf the internet or play online games for about two hours each day. The Canadian Newspaper Association (CNA) reports that 4.3 million papers are published daily in Canada.

mass media Strictly speaking, mass media are the vehicles through which messages are disseminated to mass audiences.

Canadian Radio-television and Telecommunications Commission (CRTC) It ensures that Canadians are seen and heard on Canadian media.

So awash are we in mass media messages that most of the time we don't even think about them. Scholars at Ball State University in Indiana found that people are intentionally involved in a media activity, such as watching television or browsing the internet, during 30 percent of their waking hours—almost five hours a day. Much of this media exposure is passive or, as McLuhan would argue, cool. In the 21st century, mass media are essential in most of our daily lives and are sometimes like the air around us: ubiquitous but invisible. They go unnoticed and are taken for granted.

Concurrent Media Usage

Incredible as it may seem, the Ball State study found that besides five hours of media involvement a day, people average more than an additional six hours with the media while doing something else. That's an additional 39 percent of our waking hours. This includes half-watching television while cooking dinner or catching a billboard while commuting. All tallied, the media are part of our lives about two-thirds of the time we're not sleeping—68.8 percent to be precise. Perhaps we need the rest.

Mass media have become so integrated into people's lives that **media multi-tasking** is no chore. The Ball State researchers found that roughly one-third of the time people spend with mass media involves simultaneous contact with two or more other media. This includes reading a newspaper with one ear tuned to a television program, listening to the radio with the other ear, and simultaneously surfing the internet. For the entire report, go to http://www.bsu.edu/news/article/0,1370,--36658,00.html.

media multi-tasking Simultaneous exposure to messages from different media.

mass communication Technology-assisted process by which messages are sent to large, faraway audiences.

Strictly speaking, the media exposure tracked in the Ball State study was not all mass communication. By definition, **mass communication** is the technology-assisted transmission of messages to mass audiences. The Ball State study included technology-assisted one-on-one communication such as instant messaging and email, which primarily are forms of interpersonal communication. The fact, however, is that distinctions between mass communication and some interpersonal communication are blurring. Video gaming, for example, can be a solo activity. Video gaming can also be interpersonal, with two people playing together or apart.

Also, video gaming can be a mass activity with dozens or theoretically thousands, clearly making it a form of mass communication. By lumping technology-assisted communication and mass media communication together, the Ball State data merely reflect the emerging reality that we are living a media-saturated existence.

Inventory of Devices Media devices abound as part of our personal landscapes. How does your own inventory compare with this well-stocked dorm room?

LEARNING CHECK

- Are you surprised at the Ball State University study on the amount of time people spend both consciously and unconsciously with mass media?
- What are your own patterns and habits of using mass media?

Inescapable Symbiosis

Marketplace of Ideas In his tract *Areopagitica* in the 1600s, English thinker John Milton made an eloquent case for free expression. Milton's idea was that individuals can use their power of reasoning to improve their situation and come to know great truths by exchanging ideas freely. The mass media are the primary vehicle for persuasive discourse.

Except perhaps when we backpack into the remote wilderness, most of us have a happily symbiotic dependence on mass media. We depend on media. And media industries, of course, depend on having an audience. What would be the purpose of a radio station, for example, if nobody listened?

Personal Dependence Most days, the most-listened-for item in morning newscasts is the weather forecast. People want to know how to prepare for the day. Not knowing that rain is expected can mean getting wet on the way home or not allowing extra time if the roads are slick. For most us, modern life simply wouldn't be possible without media. We need media for news and information; for entertainment, amusement, and diversion; and for the exchange of ideas.

Information Information takes many forms. For example, advertising offers information to help consumers make intelligent decisions. However, the most visible information delivered by mass media is news. People look to newscasts and newspapers, even Jon Stewart and Rick Mercer, to know what's going on beyond the horizon. If not for the mass media, people would have to rely on word of mouth from travellers to know what's happening in Iraq, in Hollywood, or on Parliament Hill in Ottawa.

Entertainment Before mass media came into existence in the mid-1400s, people created their own diversion, entertainment, and amusement. Villagers got together to sing and swap stories. Travelling jugglers, magicians, and performers dropped by. What a difference mass media have made since then.

Persuasion People come to conclusions on pressing issues by exposing themselves to competing ideas in what's called the **marketplace of ideas**. In 1644 the thinker-novelist John Milton eloquently stated the concept of the value of competing ideas: "Let truth and falsehood grapple; whoever knew truth put to the worse in a free and open encounter." Today more than ever, people look for truth by exposing their views and values to those of others in a mass media marketplace. Milton's mind would be boggled by the volume of information available. Consider the diversity: talk radio, newspaper editorial pages, blogs, anti-war songs on iTunes, and social networking.

marketplace of ideas The concept that a robust exchange of ideas, with none barred, yields better consensus.

The most obvious persuasion that the mass media carry is advertising. People look to ads to decide among competing products and services. What would you know about Nikes or iPods if it weren't for advertising to which you exposed yourself or heard about from a friend who saw or heard an ad?

Media Dependence Not only do people in their contemporary lifestyles need mass media, but the industries that have built up around these media need an audience. This is the interdependence, the symbiosis. To survive financially, a publishing house needs readers who will pay for a book. A Hollywood movie studio needs people at the box office or video store. Media companies with television, radio, newspaper, and magazine products cannot survive financially unless they can deliver to an audience that advertisers want to reach. Advertisers will buy time and space from media companies only if potential customers can be delivered.

LEARNING CHECK

- Why do people need mass media today? And why do mass media need people?
- What is the role of persuasion in a democratic society such as Canada?

Media Literacy

STUDY PREVIEW Understanding mass media begins with a factual foundation. Added layers of sophistication of understanding come from knowing the dynamics that shape media content and their effects. This allows us to assess media issues intelligently.

Watch
ABC's *Nightline*: "My Space, My Vote?"

Hierarchy of Media Literacy

By literacy, people usually mean the ability to read and write. Literacy also can mean command of a specific discipline such as history or physics. **Media literacy** is possessing the knowledge to be competent in assessing messages carried by mass media. Media literacy is essential in this Age of Mass Communication that envelops our lives from dawn to dusk, cradle to grave.

media literacy Competence in or knowledge about the mass media.

Factual Foundation A sophisticated understanding of a subject, whether carpentry or rocket science, begins with basic factual knowledge and vocabulary. So does media literacy. While philosopher John Milton was a brilliant philosophical thinker, he would need to learn the word *radio*, something not yet invented during his lifetime. He would also need to learn how to work the switches, buttons, and knobs for on/off, volume, and channel selection—just as you did at some point. The foundation for media literacy is a factual foundation.

Explore

How do you become more media literate?

Media Dynamics In our media-saturated environment, the more we know about media dynamics, the better equipped we are to make sense of our world. Understanding the dynamics that shape media content is one of these levels. Economics, as an example, explains a lot about media behaviour. To survive, a media company needs to build an audience either for direct sale, as with a book, or to attract advertisers, as with television.

Besides economics, personalities can be a dynamic that shapes media content. Producers decide who makes it on *The Rick Mercer Report*, and who doesn't. At book publisher HarperCollins, the owner of the parent company sometimes decides what book to push and what book to cancel. For that reason alone, we need to know what makes Rupert Murdoch tick. As the media baron who controls HarperCollins' parent company, Murdoch sometimes micromanages the decision on what books are published.

Government regulations and laws are another dynamic. The CRTC governs broadcast media in Canada and imposes Canadian content regulations on Canadian radio and television stations. In turn, each media industry has its own set of guidelines for ethical and professional content.

Media Effects With the mass media so omnipresent in our lives, we must bear some imprint from so much exposure. How much? Everybody, it seems, has an opinion. Undoubtedly you've heard people talk about the latest violent crime and blame television or the movies or video games. The media are easy targets when it comes to blame. The fact, however, is that we know far less about media effects than we need to. Scholarship on media effects is less conclusive than the conventional wisdom of uninformed conversational banter would have it.

Only through media literacy can we proceed together to weed out truly dangerous media effects from those that are disturbing perhaps but inconsequential. There is no shortcut to media literacy if we are to come up with intelligent public policies on the mass media. Nor is there an alternative to media literacy for us as individuals to make well-informed media choices.

Media Issues Public dialogue on today's great social, political, economic, and cultural issues by which we will define our future as a society requires keen levels of media literacy. Unless we can connect the dots in both related and disparate fields, we are impossibly handicapped in sorting through complex media issues. Think about media bashing, including accusations of treason levelled against early American news reports that the Iraq War was not going well. What do the political theorists say? What does the U.S. constitution say? Consider those ads for sugar-laden breakfast cereals aimed at kids. What do developmental psychologists say? What do ethicists say about the morality of advertising as a driving force in what media companies produce? Put another way, if the media industries are capable of reshaping society, do they therefore have a responsibility to provide quality in content?

LEARNING CHECK

- What is media literacy? Why is it important?
- Give examples of elements in the hierarchy of media literacy.

Media Awareness

Most of our media exposure is invisible or at least unnoticed at a conscious level: the background music at the mall, the advertising blurb on a pen, the overblown menu description accompanied by a photo of a stacked-higher-than-life burger. Many media messages blur into our landscape as part of the environment that we take for granted. One measure of media literacy is awareness of the presence of media messages.

Message Form Fundamental media literacy is the ability to see the differences in how various media are able to communicate messages. This is the essence of McLuhan's "the medium is the message" hypothesis. McLuhan used the metaphor of a light bulb to explain his idea. He argued that while everyone notices the content of the light bulb (the light it provides), no one notices the form, that is, the bulb itself. The same holds true for content in the context of the media. People notice the content of the media (a speech on radio, a comedy on television) but not the medium that transmits the message. McLuhan came to believe that the characteristics of the medium influence how we perceive the message. This also helps us understand the limitations of each medium. Someone who criticizes a movie for departing from the particulars of the book on which it's based may well lack sufficient media literacy to recognize that a 100-minute movie cannot possibly be true to a 90 000-word novel.

Message versus Messenger Once there was a monarch, as the story goes, who would behead the bearer of bad news. The modern-day media equivalent is faulting a news reporter for telling about a horrible event or criticizing a movie director for rubbing your face in an unpleasant reality. Media literacy requires distinguishing between messages and the messenger. A writer who deals with the drug culture is not necessarily an advocate. Nor necessarily is a rapper who conjures up clever rhymes for meth.

Motivation Awareness Intelligent use of the mass media requires assessing the motivation for a message. Is a message intended to convey information? To convince me to change brands? To sour me on a candidate? The answer usually requires thinking beyond the message and identifying the source. Is the message from a news reporter who is trying to be detached and neutral about the subject? Or is the message from a group with a political agenda? It makes a difference.

Traditions The past informs our understanding of the present. A long-standing tradition in journalism in both Canada and the United States is that the news media should serve as a watchdog on behalf of the people against government corruption.

As well, media literacy requires an understanding of other traditions. The role of mass media in China, for example, flows from circumstances and traditions radically different from those in Western democracies. Even among democracies, media performance varies. For example, news reporting about criminal prosecutions in Canada is much more restrained than similar reporting in the United States.

Media Myth The fact is that the oft-heard conventional wisdom that media violence begets real-life violence has never been proven, despite hundreds of serious studies by social scientists. In fact, no matter how cleverly criminal defence attorneys have tried to blame violent behaviour on video gaming, television, or movies, the courts have consistently rejected this argument. This is not to say that there is no link between violence in the media and violence in real life. Rather, it's to say that a simple, direct lineage has yet to be confirmed. To separate real phenomena from conjecture and nonsense requires media literacy.

LEARNING CHECK

- Give examples of media awareness as indicators of media literacy.
- How do media myths impede attaining a high level of media literacy?

Human Communication

STUDY PREVIEW Mass communication is a process that targets technologically amplified messages to massive audiences. Other forms of communication pale in comparison in their ability to reach great numbers of people.

Interpersonal Communication

When people talk to each other, they are engaging in **interpersonal communication.** In its simplest form, interpersonal communication occurs between two people who are physically located in the same place. It can also occur, however, between specific individuals on a social networking site or who send text messages to each other.

interpersonal communication Usually involves two people face to face.

There comes a point when the number of people involved reduces the intimacy of the communication process. That's when the situation becomes **group communication.** Your professor lecturing to your class is an example of group communication. So is updating your status on Facebook for all your friends to see.

group communication Involves more than two people; in person.

Mass Communication

Fundamental to media literacy is recognizing the different forms of communication for what they are. Confusing interpersonal communication and mass communication, for example, only muddles any attempt to sort through important and complex issues.

Mass communication involves sending a message to a great number of people at widely separated points. Mass communication is possible only through technology, whether it be a printing press, a broadcast transmitter, or an internet server.

mass communication Technology-assisted process by which messages are sent to large, faraway audiences.

The massiveness of the audience is a defining characteristic of mass communication.

Distance The mass audience is beyond the communicator's horizon, sometimes thousands of kilometres away. This is not the case with either interpersonal or group communication. Even technology-assisted group meetings via satellite, video conferencing, or social networking sites, although they connect faraway points, are not mass communication but a form of group communication.

Audience The mass audience is eclectic and heterogeneous. With sitcoms, for example, the television networks seek mega-audiences of disparate groups: male and female, young and old, liberal and right-wing, devout and nonreligious. Some media products, such as a bridal magazine, narrow their focus. But a bridal magazine's intended audience, although primarily young and female, is still diverse in terms of ethnicity, income, education, and other kinds of other measures. It still is a mass audience.

Feedback The mass audience generally lacks the opportunity for immediate **feedback.** In interpersonal communication, a chuckle or a punch in the nose right then and there is immediate feedback. With most mass communication, response is delayed—a letter to the editor, a cancelled subscription. Even an 800-call to a television news quiz is delayed a bit and is certainly less potent than a punch in the nose. Also, the recipient of an emailed message doesn't necessarily read it right away.

feedback Response to a message.

LEARNING CHECK

- Can you give examples of personal, group, and mass communication besides those cited here?
- Is a football cheerleader with a megaphone a mass communicator? How about someone meeting via a video conference?

Media and Society

STUDY PREVIEW With the advent of radio, people from coast to coast found themselves bound culturally as never before. Later, television networks added to the cultural cohesion. That mass audience of yesterday, however, is fragmenting. Media companies cater increasingly to niches, not the whole.

Watch
ABC's *NightLine*: "The Media and Disasters"

Unification

Media literacy can provide an overview of mass media's effects on society and culture. The most sweeping effect of mass media has been as a cultural unifier.

Print Media The mass media bind communities with messages that become a shared experience. History is peppered with examples. When John Bayne Maclean founded *The Busy Man's Magazine* (now known as *Maclean's*) in 1905, readers throughout Canada had something in common. So do readers of their hometown newspaper.

Radio Early in the 20th century, Canadian politicians saw radio not only as a way to promote entertainment but also as a tool to unite the country. In its early days, Canadian radio succeeded in uniting the country in a way that had never been done before. On July 1, 1927, Canada's 60th birthday, the Canadian National Railway's network of telephone and telegraph lines joined orchestras in several Canadian cities from Halifax to Vancouver through its 23 private radio stations across the nation. About 5 million people in Canada and the United States tuned in to the Diamond Jubilee broadcast.

Television Later, the television networks became major factors in Canada's national identity. Audiences of unprecedented magnitude converged on the networks, all broadcasting the same homogenous cultural fare.

Through most of the 20th century, the most successful mass media companies competed to amass the largest possible audiences. The media, especially those dependent on advertising revenue, had a largely homogeneous thrust that simultaneously created, fed, and sustained a dominant monoculture. Historically, the role of mass media as a binding influence is most clear in news coverage of riveting events. Think of 9/11. Think of Hurricane Katrina or the BP oil spill in the Gulf of Mexico. Even the Grey Cup or Stanley Cup finals can unify Canadians.

Internet The most recent example of a medium that can unite people is the internet. Online communities unite people with a common interest or passion. This unification can take many forms, such as joining a Facebook or MySpace group, participating in an online forum, or subscribing to an online newsletter or RSS.

Moral Consensus

The mass media contribute to the evolution of what society regards as acceptable or as inexcusable. Consider Canadian news coverage of political scandals, such as the 2004 sponsorship scandal or the 2009 Ethics Committee hearings into the business relationship between former Prime Minister Brian Mulroney and German businessman Karlheinz Schreiber. On a lesser scale, media coverage of pro golfer Tiger Woods and his "transgressions" in late 2009 were also based in morality. At many levels, the mass media are essential to the ongoing process of society identifying its values.

You might ask whether the media, in covering controversy, are divisive. The short answer is no. Seldom do the media create controversy. For the most part, media merely cover it. Thorough coverage, over time, helps to bring about societal consensus—sometimes for change, sometimes not. For example, the majority once opposed legalizing abortion. Today, after exhaustive media attention, a majority belief has emerged that abortion should be available legally in a widening array of circumstances. Moral debates, conducted almost entirely through mass media, cover many fundamental issues, such as gun control, gay marriage, and government budget priorities.

Fragmentation

The idea that the mass audience is the largest number of people who can be assembled to hear mass messages is changing. Most media content today is aimed at narrow, albeit often still large, segments. This phenomenon is called **demassification**.

demassification Media's focus on narrower audience segments.

This demassification process, the result of technological breakthroughs and economic pressures, is changing the mass media dramatically. Radio demassified early, in the 1950s, replacing formats designed to reach the largest possible audiences with formats aimed at specific sectors of audience. Magazines followed in the 1960s and 1970s, and today most consumer magazines cater only to the special interests of carefully targeted groups of readers. Now, with dozens of television program services available via cable or satellite in most households, television also is going through demassification.

Accelerating Demassification

Media demassification accelerated in the 1980s with technology that gave the cable television industry the ability to deliver dozens of channels. Most of these channels, while national, took the demassified course of magazines and geared programs to audience niches: sports fans, food aficionados, speed freaks. The term **narrowcasting**, as opposed

narrowcasting Seeking niche audiences, as opposed to broadcasting's traditional audience-building concept.

CASE STUDY

What Role Do the Canadian Media Play?

Ian Morrison is patriotic about Canadian radio and television—so patriotic that in 1985 he helped to create Friends of Canadian Broadcasting, a voluntary organization of 60 000 Canadian households whose main goal is to ensure that Canadians have access to high-quality Canadian media.

Friends of Canadian Broadcasting is a strong supporter of the CBC and the CRTC, and monitors private Canadian broadcasters, such as CTV and Global, to ensure that they invest money in Canadian productions. A Pollar poll commissioned by Friends of Canadian Broadcasting in 2009 suggests that many Canadians share the same beliefs:

- 88 percent of Canadians agree that "as Canada's economic ties with the United States increase, it is becoming more important to strengthen Canadian culture and identity"
- 67 percent believe that Canada's level of public broadcaster funding is insufficient to maintain a unique and vibrant Canadian culture and identity
- 76 percent rate CBC programming as good or better than good
- 83 percent believe that the CBC is important in protecting Canadian identity and culture while 81 percent believe that the CBC is one of the things that helps to distinguish Canada from the United States

According to Morrison, "Patriotism and democracy are values that we care about. Telling Canadian stories establishes a sense of belonging as a distinct country on the northern half of the continent. Democracy is highly influenced by the diversity and integrity of programming."

Friends of Canadian Broadcasting has a clear agenda: to support a healthy Canadian media industry that will help in cultural transmission. Morrison believes that Canadian media provide excellent news and documentary-style programming. However, he says that in a perfect world, English-language Canadian television would provide "good shelf space for Canadian fiction programming. At least two hours a night from Monday to Wednesday nights—as much as the French-language system now provides."

Friends of Canadian Broadcasting claims that "while it would have been easier to follow the movie theatre model—let the market rule—Canadian content laws have given great Canadian artists a chance to get their start in our market. Canadian content has delivered on so many fronts." Writing about Canadian musicians such as Barenaked Ladies and the Tragically Hip, the organization says: "As a consequence to their art form, many of their songs remind us of our shared history."

Ian Morrison

DEEPENING YOUR MEDIA LITERACY

Explore the Issue

Go to www.friends.ca/Get_Involved/campaigns to find out about Friends of Canadian Broadcasting's latest battle regarding Canadian media.

Dig Deeper

With Canada becoming closer economically to the United States, should our media play a larger role in developing our identity? Surf the internet to find opinions on both sides of the argument.

What Do You Think?

What aspects of media literacy and awareness need to be addressed in any discussion of Canadian content on Canadian media?

Contrary to Ian Morrison's views, should we as Canadians simply let the "marketplace" rule what we watch and listen to? What are the implications of doing that?

to broadcasting, entered the vocabulary for media literacy. Then a wholly new technology, the internet, offered people more alternatives that were even narrower.

What has demassification done to the media's role as a contributor to social cohesion? Some observers are quick to link media fragmentation with the political polarization within Canada. Clearly there are cultural divides that have been nurtured if not created by media fragmentation. For example, musical taste is defined today by generational, racial, ethnic, and socioeconomic categories, contrary to the homogenizing of tastes that radio fostered at the national level in its heyday in the 1930s and 1940s. At the same time, there remain media units that amass huge audiences in the traditional sense. Even in the slow summer months, CTV easily draws 1 million viewers to *CSI*. And the *Toronto Star*, with a weekly circulation of more than 2 million, is by far the largest daily newspaper in the country.

A great drama of our times is the jockeying of the mass media for audience in an unpredictable and fast-changing media landscape. In pursuit of audience, whether mass or niche, media companies are experimenting with alternative platforms for delivering content that will find a following or keep a following. Movies aren't only at the multiplex these days; they are also on iPods. CTV/ABC's *Desperate Housewives* isn't only on prime time but is also downloadable. *The Globe and Mail* is online. CBC News has multiple online platforms.

LEARNING CHECK

- Historically, what was the effect of mass media's seeking the largest possible audiences?
- What triggered media demassification? Why is this significant?
- Are mass media today a force of unification or division in society?

Media Economics

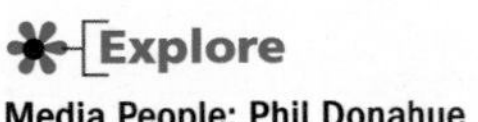

Media People: Phil Donahue

STUDY PREVIEW With few exceptions, North American mass media are privately owned and must turn a profit to stay in business. These economic realities are potent shapers of media content.

Revenue Streams

Media literacy requires an understanding of the dynamics that shape media content. In a capitalistic environment, economics is the primary driver of the behaviour of media companies. With rare exceptions, media companies are businesses whose success is measured by their owners in profits. In short, capitalism rewards enterprises that generate profits. This means producing products that people are willing to buy in enough quantity and at a sufficient price to meet and, if successful, exceed expenses.

Advertising Revenue Advertisers pay the mass media for access to potential customers. From print media, advertisers buy space; from broadcasters, they buy time.

Book publishers once relied solely on readers for revenue, but that has changed somewhat. Today, book publishers charge for film rights whenever a book is turned into a movie or a television program. In doing so, publishing houses now profit indirectly from the advertising revenue that television networks pull in from broadcasting movies.

Movies have also come to benefit from advertising. Today, in addition to box office revenues, moviemakers pick up advertising revenue directly by charging commercial companies to include their products in the scenes they shoot, a technique called product placement.

Circulation Revenue Although some advertising-supported mass media, such as network television, do not charge their audiences, others do. When income is derived from the audience, it's called circulation revenue. *Maclean's* may cost $4.95 at the corner store, but little if any of this charge ends up with Rogers, the magazine's parent company. Distribution is costly, and distributors all along the way take their cut.

Direct audience payments have emerged in recent years in broadcasting. Cable and satellite subscribers pay a monthly fee. Audience support is the basis of subscription television such as commercial-free TMN or HBO Canada. Noncommercial broadcasting, including provincial educational broadcasters such as Saskatchewan's SCN and Ontario's TVO, rely heavily on viewer contributions.

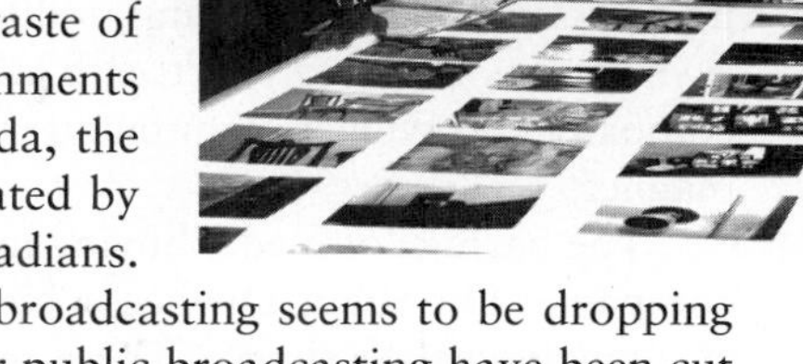

Media Convergence The CSI franchise is co-produced and distributed by Canada's Alliance Atlantis. The success of the company in producing and distributing winning media content was one reason why it was purchased by CanWest Global (now owned by Shaw) in 2007.

Government Subsidies While the idea of government support for the mass media might seem to some a waste of public money, both the U.S. and Canadian governments support some form of public broadcasting. In Canada, the Canadian Broadcasting Corporation (CBC) is mandated by the government to promote Canadian culture to Canadians. In the 21st century, government support for public broadcasting seems to be dropping off, as both Canadian and U.S. government funds for public broadcasting have been cut drastically in the last few years.

Corporate Structures

Another dynamic for media literacy is the corporate structure within which media products exist. Giant corporations with diverse interests have consolidated the mass media into relatively few hands.

Media Chains We are in an era of Big Media, with more cross-ownerships than most people realize. Today most media operations with names that consumers recognize are parts of giant corporations. This trend toward **conglomeration,** sometimes referred to by Canadian writers as "concentration of ownership," involves a process of mergers, acquisitions, and buyouts that consolidates the ownership of the media into fewer and fewer companies. These companies are often "multi-platform" chains, meaning that the company has interests in a number of media. This is known as **convergence.**

conglomeration The combining of companies into larger companies.

convergence Early 21st-century model of media cross-ownership. Converged companies typically own print, broadcast, and internet holdings.

How extensive is convergence in Canada? Consider the following information on the seven media rivals that have established themselves as the major players in Canada:

- Bell Canada Enterprises (BCE) isn't just the phone company. Rather, it's a multimedia company whose major holdings include CTV, Bell Internet, and the CHUM Radio Network.
- Shaw Media, based in Calgary, is another multimedia powerhouse. In addition to being a cable and satellite provider, it purchased the broadcasting assets of CanWest in 2010.
- Quebecor owns TVA (the largest television network in Quebec), Sun Media (the second-largest Canadian newspaper group), and the Canoe.ca website. The company also has interests in 12 publishing houses and Vidéotron, a chain of video rental stores. In 2010, the CRTC gave Quebecor the green light to launch Sun TV News, a 24-hour all news channel.
- Rogers Media has interests not only in cable TV distribution but also in programming with Sportsnet. In publishing, it owns *Maclean's, Chatelaine,* and *Flare* magazines. In addition to all of this, Rogers has a strong presence in wireless communication and owns the Toronto Blue Jays.
- Corus Entertainment's diverse interests include radio stations in western Canada, Ontario, and Quebec. Its television holdings include YTV, Teletoon, and CMT (Country Music Television).
- Astral is another Canadian company, with assets that include The Movie Network, HBO Canada, Teletoon, and a number of radio stations across the country.
- Postmedia Network purchased the publishing arm of CanWest in 2010. It publishes 10 daily newspapers in Canada, including the *National Post.* It also owns Postmedia News, a national news agency.

The deep pockets of a wealthy corporate parent can see a financially troubled media unit, such as a radio station, through a rough period, but there is a price. In time, the corporate parent wants a financial return on its investment and pressure builds on the station to generate more and more profit. This would not be so bad if the people running the radio station loved radio and had a sense of public service, but the process of conglomeration often doesn't work that way. Parent corporations tend to replace media people with career-climbing, bottom-line managers whose motivation is looking good to their supervisors in faraway cities who are under serious pressure to increase profits. In radio, for example, management experts, not radio people, end up running stations and the quality of media content suffers.

Capitalist Environment The structure of American and Canadian mass media is a money-driven system. Executives who don't deliver profits are replaced. If profits lag, investors pull their financing, reducing the capital available for operations and growth. Investors as a group don't care whether their money is in the stock of a mass media company or a widget manufacturer. The investment with the greatest profit potential is a magnet.

The barrage of media buying in 2009 and 2010 illustrates this point. The reason that companies like Shaw, Quebecor, and BCE purchased controlling interest in Canadian television channels is simple. These companies now control both the content providers and the means to distribute that content, whether via cable, satellite, the internet, or mobile devices. In 2010, Astral and Rogers entered into an agreement that gave Rogers customers on demand, online access to Astral's television content. The new business model is to offer consumers access to their favourite content anywhere, at any time, and on the mobile device of their choice. This trend is likely to continue.

Ben Bagdikian A critic of media consolidation.

Nobody begrudges a company making a profit, but at what cost? Media critics such as **Ben Bagdikian** argue that concentrated media ownership and convergence affect the diversity of messages offered by the mass media. Speaking at the Madison Institute in New Jersey, Bagdikian portrayed conglomeration in bleak terms: "They are trying to buy control or market domination not just in one medium but in all the media. The aim is to control the entire process from an original manuscript or new series to its use in as many forms as possible. A magazine article owned by *the company* becomes a book owned by *the company*. That becomes a television program owned by *the company*, which then becomes a movie owned by *the company*. It is shown in theatres owned by *the company*, and the movie sound track is issued on a record label owned by *the company*, featuring the vocalist on the cover of one of *the company* magazines. It does not take an angel from heaven to tell us that *the company* will be less enthusiastic about outside ideas and production that it does not own, and more and more we will be dealing with closed circuits to control access to most of the public."

LEARNING CHECK

- Why have media chains and conglomerates come into being?
- Who owns your daily newspaper? Your favourite local radio station? The dominant local television station? How can you access their content?

Chapter 1 Wrap-Up

How do you become more media literate?

Two-thirds of our waking hours are spent consciously or subconsciously with the mass media. We can be oblivious to their effects unless we cultivate an understanding of how the media work and why. This understanding is called media literacy. Media literacy begins with a factual foundation and becomes keener with an understanding of the dynamics that influence media messages. There are degrees of awareness, including abilities to understand and explain media behaviour and effects and to identify significant media issues.

Most media behaviour, including demassification, can be explained by economics. Advertising, a significant driver of media behaviour, has gravitated to media products that deliver audiences consisting of the advertisers' most likely customers—not blanket mass audiences but niche audiences. An important issue with regards to advertising-funded media is whether he who pays the piper calls the tune. In other words, does the advertiser have control over or an influence on content? The problem is that the economic structure of many media companies creates a conflict between serving the interests of their advertisers and serving the interests of their audiences. Having two masters is problematic.

Questions for Critical Thinking

1. Do your own media habits differ from what the Ball State University study suggests, which is that media exposure is a dominant ingredient in the daily lives of most people?
2. What were your strengths in media literacy at the start of your current course? Did you have any gaps in your media literacy?
3. Some people are confused by the terms *cool media* and *hot media* because, in their experience, radios and television sets heat up and newspapers are always at room temperature. What is the other way of looking at hot and cool media?
4. Mass media have had tremendous effects on shaping society and culture. Describe how these dynamics have worked throughout history.
5. For better or worse, how do economics, including media ownership, shape mass media content?

Keeping Up to Date

Newsmagazines, including *Maclean's*, *Time*, and *Newsweek*, cover mass media issues more or less regularly. So do the *National Post*, *The Globe and Mail*, *The New York Times*, *The Wall Street Journal*, and other leading newspapers.

The *Journal of Communication* and the *Canadian Journal of Communication* are quarterly scholarly publications.

2 Mass Media Technology

LEARNING AHEAD

- Mass communication is a technology-based process.
- Mass production of the written word became possible with movable metal type.
- Chemistry is the technological basis of movies.
- Mastery of the electromagnetic spectrum led to radio and television.
- Orbiting satellites and fibre optics have improved media efficiency.
- Traditional media products and new products are emerging from digital technology.
- Models help to explain the technology-driven process of mass communication.

Media Melding Distinctions between and among media are blurring with delivery devices that combine text, audio, and visuals, including moving images.

MEDIA IN THEORY

Understanding the Role of Technology

One defining characteristic of mass communication is its reliance on technology. People can communicate face to face, which is called **interpersonal communication**, without technological assistance. For centuries people communicated in large groups, as in town hall meetings and concert halls, without microphones—just the human voice, albeit sometimes elevated to extraordinary volume. For mass communication, however, with audiences much more far-flung than those in the largest auditorium, machinery is necessary.

interpersonal communication Usually communication by two people face to face.

Watch

Watch ABC's 20/20: "The Popularity of Instant Messaging and Its Impact on Grammar"

Media technology, the product of human invention, exists in several forms, each one distinctive. Around each of these technologies, industries have been built that are closely allied with each specific technology:

- *Printing technology*. The printing press, dating to the 1440s, spawned the book, newspaper, and magazine industries. After centuries, each still exists in the media landscape.
- *Chemical technology*. Photography and movies have relied on chemical technology throughout most of their history.
- *Electronic technology*. The first of the electronic media, sound recording, actually preceded the widespread use of electricity but quickly became an electrically powered medium. Radio was electrical early on. Television was electronic from the get-go.
- *Digital technology*. Traditional mass media all adapted to digital technology, to varying degrees, beginning in the first decade of the 21st century, but the industries built on the original printing, chemical, and electronic forms remain largely distinctive.

MEDIA TIMELINE Media Technology

1446 Johannes Gutenberg devised movable metal type, permitting mass production of printed materials.

1455 Johannes Gutenberg printed the first of his bibles using movable type.

1690 Ben Harris printed *Publick Occurrences*, the first newspaper in the English colonies.

1741 Andrew Bradford printed *American Magazine* and Benjamin Franklin printed *General Magazine*, the first magazines in the English colonies.

1844 Samuel Morse's telegraph device helped the print media to get the word out.

1876 Alexander Graham Bell patented his telephone shortly before another inventor, Elisha Gray.

1877 Thomas Edison, with help from Montreal's Emile Berliner, introduced the phonograph, which could record and play back sound.

1888 William Dickson devised the motion picture camera.

1906 Canada's Reginald Fessenden broadcast to ships at sea via radio.

1927 Philo Farnsworth invented the tube that picked up moving images for live transmission, which we know now as the television.

1969 The U.S. Department of Defense established the computer network that would become the internet.

1988 Marshall and Eric McLuhan published *Laws of Media.*

2001 Apple introduced the iPod.

2002 Canada's Research in Motion (RIM) introduced its BlackBerry, the first "smart phone."

2003 Virtual media were introduced to the masses.

2004 Facebook, the social media pioneer, made its debut.

2007 Apple unveiled its smart phone, the iPhone.

2010 Google introduced Nexus One, its entry into the smart phone market

Publishing companies such as HarperCollins still produce books. CBC TV is still on the air. The newest distinctive medium built on digital technology is the internet. Even as companies built on older technologies have rushed to find ways to capitalize on this new medium, the internet itself has created entirely new categories of media companies. Think of Wikipedia, Facebook, and Google. Meanwhile, printed and bound books are still with us, as are television channels, Paramount Pictures, and commute-time radio in the car.

Canadian communication theorist Marshall McLuhan believed that we should ask questions about the impact of any new technology. In his book *Laws of Media*, published posthumously in 1988 and co-written by his son Eric, McLuhan introduced his so-called "tetrad of media effects." According to McLuhan, to fully develop one's media literacy, one needs to ask the following four questions about any new technology:

- **What does this medium enhance or extend?** For example, the iPod enhances our enjoyment of music by making it more portable and allows us to create our own playlists and subscribe to podcasts.
- **What does this medium make obsolete?** Because it can be personalized, the iPod has made life difficult for radio. People can now create their own playlists of favourite songs and don't need to rely on traditional radio for music. It also could be argued that iPods, which use MP3 technology, have started to make CDs obsolete.
- **What does this medium retrieve?** Whether intentionally or not, the iPod resurrected the single as a way to market music. People began buying individuals songs instead of entire albums.
- **What does this medium reverse into?** The dark side of personalized music listening is illegal music download and piracy. While friends have shared music for years, digital technology makes it easy to make perfect copies of music you didn't pay for.

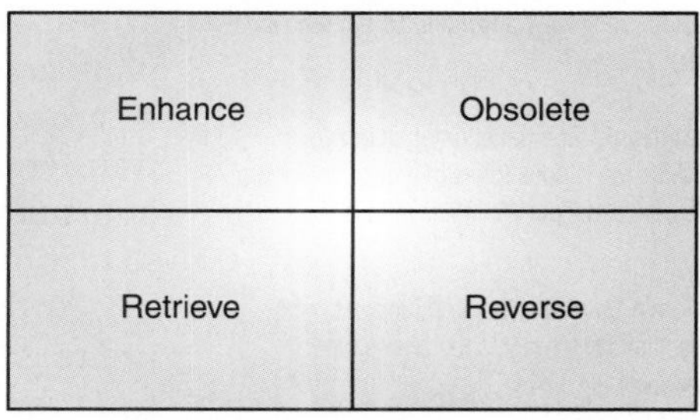

Figure 2.1 **McLuhan's Tetrad of Media Effects**

LEARNING CHECK

- What are the four primary technologies on which mass media are built?
- What are the four parts to McLuhan's tetrad of media effects?

Movable Metal Type
Johannes Gutenberg melted metals into alloys that he cast as individual letters, then arranged them in a frame the size of a page to form words, sentences, and whole passages. Once a page was full, the raised letters would be inked and a sheet of paper pressed onto them to transfer the impression.

Printing

STUDY PREVIEW With the invention of movable metal type in the mid-1440s, suddenly the written word could be mass-produced. The effect on human existence was profound. Incorporating photographic technology with printing in the late 1800s gave printed products a new impact.

Movable Metal Type

Although printing can be traced back a couple thousand years to eastern Asia, an invention in the mid-1440s made mass production of the written word possible for the first time. The innovation was **movable metal type.** A tinkerer in what is now the German city of Mainz, **Johannes Gutenberg,** was obsessed with melting and mixing metals to create new alloys. He came up with the idea of casting the individual letters of the alphabet in metal and then assembling them one at a time into a page for reproduction by pressing paper onto the raised, inked characters. The metal characters were sturdy enough to survive the repeated pressure of transferring the inked letters to paper—something not possible with the carved wood letters that had been used in earlier printing.

In time, industries grew up around this technology, each producing print media products that are still with us today: books, magazines, and newspapers. But historically, the impact of Gutenberg's invention was apparent much earlier. Printing with Gutenberg's new technology took off quickly. By 1500, printing presses were in place throughout Europe. Suddenly, civilization had the mass-produced written word.

Watch

Gutenberg Printing Press Recreation

movable metal type Innovation that made the printing press an agent for mass communication.

Johannes Gutenberg Metallurgist who invented movable metal type in the mid-1440s.

Gutenberg's Impact

Gutenberg's impact was transformational. Scientists who earlier had carried on time-consuming handwritten correspondence with colleagues now could print their theories and experiments for wide dissemination.

Modern science thus took form. Religious tracts could also be mass-produced, as could materials containing serious challenges to religion. The growing quantity of printed materials fuelled literacy and, slowly, a standardization in written languages. What Gutenberg begat can be called the Age of Mass Communication, but his innovation also spurred Western civilization into the ongoing Age of Science and Age of Reason. Civilization hasn't been the same since.

LEARNING CHECK

- What was the link between Gutenberg and the scientific revolution of the 1600s and 1700s?

Print-Visual Integration

Although visuals are not a mass medium, photography increased the communicative power of the printed word in the late 1800s. Experiments at Cornell University in the 1870s led to technology that could mass-produce images in books, newspapers, and magazines. This new technology, pioneered by **Frederick Ives,** was the **halftone.** Ives divided a photograph into a microscopic grid, each tiny square having a raised dot that registered a separate tonal grey from a photograph—the bigger the dot, the more ink it would transfer to the paper and the darker the grey. At the typical reading distance of 35 cm, the human eye can't make out the grid, but the eye can see the image created by the varying shades of grey. Although crude, this was the first halftone.

Frederick Ives Invented the halftone in 1876.

halftone Reproduction of an image in which the various tones of grey or colour are produced by dots of ink of various sizes.

Steve Horgan Adapted halftone technology for high-speed newspaper presses.

At the New York *Daily Graphic*, **Steve Horgan** adapted Ives's process to high-speed printing. In 1880, the *Daily Graphic* published a halftone image of Shantytown, a break from the line drawings that were the newspaper's original claim to distinction. Ives later improved on Horgan's process and visual communication joined the Age of Mass Communication.

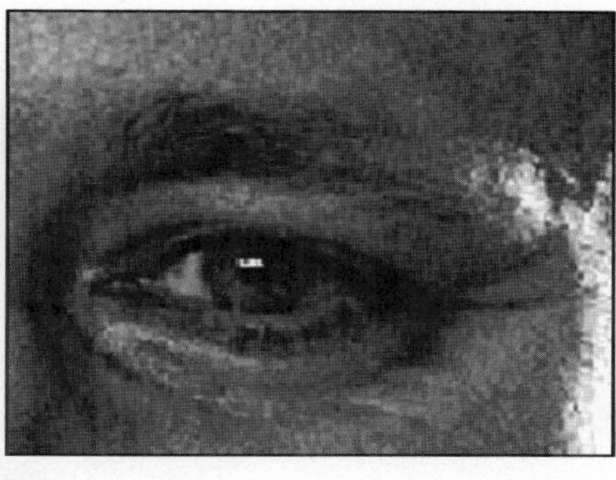

Halftone The halftone process, invented by Frederick Ives, uses dots of various sizes to transfer ink to paper. The dots are invisible except under close examination. At a reading distance, however, the bigger dots leave a darker impression and the smaller dots leave a lighter impression.

Magazines, notably the early ***National Geographic***, also experimented with halftones. When **Henry Luce**, the founder of *Time* magazine, launched *Life* magazine in 1934, photography moved the magazine industry into new visual ground. The oversized pages and slick, super-white paper gave the photographs published in *Life* an intensity not possible with newsprint. *Life* captured the spirit of the times photographically and demonstrated that a wide range of human experiences could be recorded visually. Both real life and *Life* could be shocking. In 1938, a *Life* feature on human birth was so shocking for the time that censors succeeded in banning the issue in 33 cities.

National Geographic A magazine that pioneered the use of visuals.

Henry Luce Magazine innovator whose *Life* exploited photographs for their visual impact.

LEARNING CHECK

- Using a newspaper picture, show how halftones give the illusion of a photograph.

Chemistry

STUDY PREVIEW Historically, photography is rooted in chemistry. Movies also drew on chemical technology but evolved along a separate path.

Photography

The 1727 discovery that light causes silver nitrate to darken was a breakthrough in mass communication. Scientists dabbled with the chemical for the next century. Then, in 1826, **Joseph Níepce** found a way to capture and preserve an image on light-sensitive material. Photography, a chemical process for creating and recording a visual message, was born. The technology was sufficiently established by the 1860s to create a new type of historical archive. Teams of photographers organized by **Mathew Brady** created an incredible visual record, much of it horrific, of the U.S. Civil War.

Joseph Níepce Discovered how to preserve a visual image on light-sensitive material.

Mathew Brady Created a photographic record of the U.S. Civil War.

Over the next half-century, technology developed for reproducing photographs on printing presses. Brady's legacy was issued in book form. Emotional advertisements promising lifelike images of "soldiers dashing and flags flying and horses leaping all over" stirred sales. The time was right and hundreds of thousands of copies were sold to

Mathew Brady

Visual Impact With new technology in the late 1800s that could produce photographs on printing presses, newspapers and magazines suddenly had new potency in telling stories. The potential of photography to send printed media in a new direction was illustrated with painfully gory battlefield scenes from the Civil War. Mathew Brady is the photographer.

a generation of Civil War veterans and their families. By the time World War I began, however, the market was saturated. Also, people had new gruesome photographs from the European front. New grisliness replaced the old.

As well, a new application of photographic chemistry—the motion picture—was maturing.

LEARNING CHECK

- Explain this assertion: Photography and words are not mass media but are essential for the media to exploit their potential.
- How did Mathew Brady build public enthusiasm for photography in mass communication?

Watch

Movie Palaces

Movies

persistence of vision Phenomenon that fast-changing still photos create the illusion of movement.

The motion picture, a late-1800s development, was rooted in chemistry as well. The new media linked the lessons of photography to the recognition of a phenomenon called **persistence of vision.** It had come to be recognized in the late 1800s that the human eye retains an image for a fraction of a second. If a series of photographs captures motion at split-second intervals, those images, if flipped quickly, will trick the eye into perceiving continuous motion. For most people the illusion of motion begins with 14 photos per second.

William Dickson Developed the first motion picture camera.

George Eastman Developed celluloid film.

Cameras At the research labs of prolific inventor and entrepreneur Thomas Edison, **William Dickson** developed a camera that captured 16 images per second. It was the first workable motion picture camera. Dickson used celluloid film perfected by **George Eastman,** who had popularized amateur photography with his Kodak camera. By 1891, Edison had begun producing movies.

Lumière brothers Opened first motion picture exhibition hall.

Projectors Edison's movies were viewed by looking into a box. In France, the **Lumière brothers** Auguste and Louis brought projectors to motion pictures. By running the film in front of a specially aimed, powerful light bulb, the Lumières projected movie images onto a wall. In 1895, they opened an exhibition hall in Paris—the first movie house. Edison recognized the commercial advantage in projection and patented a projector that he put on the market the next year.

LEARNING CHECK

- How are photography and motion pictures similar? How are they different?
- How does persistence of vision work?

Electronics

STUDY PREVIEW Electricity transformed people's lives beginning in the late 1800s with dazzling applications to all kinds of activities. The modern music industry sprang up around these new systems for recording and playing back sound. Radio and television, both rooted in electricity, were among the technologies around which new industries were created.

Watch

Thomas Edison (1847–1931)

Watch

Sound Recording

Electricity as Transformational

The harnessing of electricity had a profound impact on life beginning in the late 1800s. The infrastructure for an electricity-based lifestyle was wholly in place half a century later when massive projects, such as the Sir Adam Beck Hydroelectric Power Stations built near Niagara Falls, Ontario, were launched to produce electricity for a general public hungry to power new gadgets. During this period, inventors and tinkerers came up with entirely new media of mass communication.

For two centuries mass media had comprised only the print media, primarily books, newspapers, and magazines. In the span of a generation, people found themselves marvelling at a dizzying parade of inventions ranging from the light bulb to streetcars. Among the new delights were phonographs, radio, and then television.

Recordings

Sound recording did not begin as an electronic medium. The first recording machine, the **phonograph** invented by Thomas Edison in 1877, was a cylinder wrapped in tinfoil that was rotated as a singer shouted into a large metal funnel. The funnel channelled the vibrations against a diaphragm, which fluttered and thus cut grooves into the rotating tin. When the cylinder was rotated in a playback machine, a stylus picked up sound from the varying depths of the groove. To hear the sound, a person placed his or her ear next to a megaphone-like horn and rotated the cylinder.

phonograph First sound recording and playback machine.

Inherent in Edison's system, however, was a major impediment to commercial success: a recording could not be duplicated, let alone mass-produced. In 1887, Montreal's **Emile Berliner** introduced a sturdy metal disk to replace Edison's foil-wrapped cylinder. From the metal disk Berliner made a model and then poured thermoplastic material into the mould. When the material hardened, Berliner had a near-perfect copy of the original disk—and he could make hundreds of them.

Emile Berliner Invented machine to mass-produce sound recording.

Those early machines eventually incorporated electrical microphones and electrical amplification for reproducing sound. These innovations, mostly by **Joseph Maxwell** of Bell Laboratories in the 1920s, had superior sensitivity. To listen, it was no longer a matter of putting an ear to a mechanical amplifying horn that had only narrow frequency responses. Instead, loudspeakers amplified the sound electromagnetically.

Joseph Maxwell Introduced electrical sound recording in the 1920s.

LEARNING CHECK

- Why would be it be a mistake to call Thomas Edison's first sound recording and playback machine an instrument of mass communication?
- How would you rank the importance of Thomas Edison, Emile Berliner, and Joseph Maxwell in the history of sound recording? Why?

Electromagnetic Spectrum

The introduction of electricity into mass communication occurred with the **telegraph**. After experimenting with sending electrical impulses by wire for more than a decade, **Samuel Morse** convinced the U.S. Congress to spend $30 000 to string electricity-conducting wires 66 kilometres from Washington to Baltimore. In 1844, using his code of dots and dashes, Morse sent the famous message "What hath God wrought." Although telegraph messages basically were communication from Point A to Point B, the way was opened for applying electricity to explicitly mass communication—perhaps even without wires. The telegraph was also a key element in the development of newspapers.

telegraph Electricity-enabled long-distance communication, used mostly from Point A to Point B.

Samuel Morse Inventor of the telegraph in 1844.

Wireless The suggestion of wireless communication was inherent in a discovery by Granville Woods in 1887 of a way to send messages to and from moving trains. Railway telegraphy, as it was called, reduced collisions. Although the invention was intended for electric trains, which drew their power from overhead lines and on-ground rails, Woods's work also posed the question: Could communication be untethered?

Heinrich Hertz Demonstrated the existence of radio waves in 1887.

Guglielmo Marconi Transmitted the first wireless message in 1895.

Watch

Guglielmo Marconi

For hundreds of years, scientists had had a sense that lightning emitted invisible but powerful electrical waves. The word *radi*, from the Latin *radius*, was used because these waves rippled out from the electrical source. A German scientist, **Heinrich Hertz**, confirmed the existence of these waves in 1887 by constructing two separate coils of wire several feet apart. When electricity was applied to one coil, it electrified the other. Thus electricity indeed could be sent through the air on what soon were called Hertzian waves.

A young Italian, **Guglielmo Marconi** became obsessed with the possibilities of the electromagnetic spectrum and built equipment that could ring a bell by remote control—no strings, no wires, just turning an electromagnetic charge on and off. In 1895, when he was 21, Marconi used his wireless method to transmit codes for more than a mile on his father's Bologna estate. Then, on December 12, 1901, Marconi stood on Signal Hill, Newfoundland, and received the Morse code signal for the letter "S" from Cornwall, England. Marconi patented his invention in England, and his mother, a well-connected Irish woman, arranged British financing to set up the Marconi Wireless Telegraph Company. Soon after, ocean-going ships were equipped with Marconi radiotelegraphy equipment to communicate at sea, even when they were beyond the horizon—something that had never been possible before. Marconi made a fortune. Many feel that Marconi is the father of telegraphy, while a Canadian, Reginald Aubrey Fessenden, is the father of radio.

In 1906, a message was sent across the Atlantic. That year, Lee de Forest, a promoter who fancied himself an inventor, created what he called the audion tube to make voice transmission possible. Some say Canadian inventor Reginald Fessenden, who was born in Knowlton, Quebec, should take the credit for the technology for voice transmission. Regardless, it was Fessenden who broadcast the first radio program, also in 1906. From Brant Rock, Massachusetts, where he had a laboratory, Fessenden played the violin, sang "O Holy Night," and played an Ediphone recording of Handel's *Largo*. This shocked wireless operators on ships at sea. Instead of the dots and dashes of Morse code, suddenly there was music. Len Arminio, a journalism professor at Ontario's Loyalist College, refers to Fessenden as "broadcasting's overlooked genius." De Forest, however, stole the limelight with broadcasts from the Eiffel Tower and other stunts. In 1910, de Forest clearly demonstrated radio's potential as an entertainment medium with a magnificent performance by the tenor Enrico Caruso from the New York Metropolitan Opera House. But it was Fessenden who realized the dream of broadcasting voices through the air.

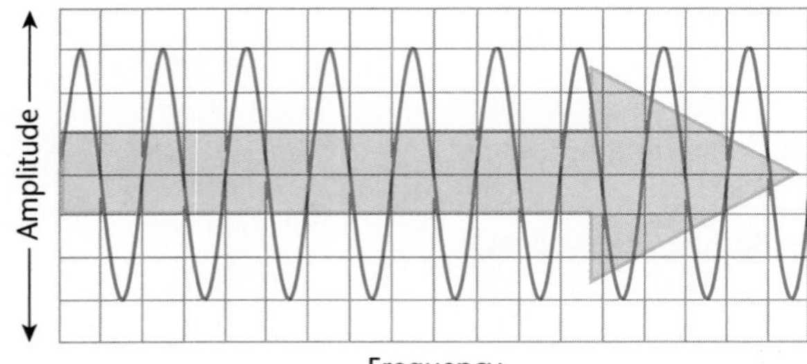

Radio Waves If you could see electromagnetic waves, they would look like the cross-section of a ripple moving across a pond except they would be steady and unending.

Reginald Fessenden Canadian Reginald Fessenden competed with Marconi in the early days of radio technology.

LEARNING CHECK

- How was the telegraph a precursor of radio?
- Marconi's wireless was based on what scientific and technical breakthroughs?
- How did Fessenden improve on Marconi's innovation?

Television For most of its history, dating to experimental stations in the 1930s, television used the airwaves somewhat like radio does. But the technology of television, to capture movement visually for transmission, involved drastically different concepts. Physicists at major universities and engineers at major research labs had been toying for years to create "radio with pictures," as early television was called. However, it was a south Idaho farmboy, **Philo Farnsworth**, who, at age 13 while out plowing the field, came up with a concept that led to his invention of television.

Philo Farnsworth Inventor of television.

Watch

Philo Farnsworth

While plowing the fields, back and forth in rows, the young Farnsworth had an epiphany. Applying what he knew about electricity from science magazines and tinkering, he envisioned a camera-like device that would pick up light reflected off a scene, with the image being sent radio-like to a receiver that would convert the varying degrees of light in the image and zap them one at a time across stacked horizontal lines on a screen, back and forth so rapidly that the image on the screen would appear to the human eye as real as a photograph. And then another electron would be zapped across the screen to replace the first image, with images coming so quickly that the eye would perceive them as motion. Farnsworth called his device an **image dissector**, which literally was what it did.

image dissector First device in early television technology.

Like motion picture technology invented 40 years earlier, television froze movement at fraction-of-a-second intervals and played them in fast sequence to create an illusion that, like movies, capitalized on the persistence-of-vision phenomenon. Unlike movies, Farnsworth did not do this with photographic technology. Television uses electronics, not chemicals, and images recorded by the camera are transmitted instantly to a receiving device, called a *picture tube*, or to a recording device for later transmission.

Although Farnsworth had sent the first television picture, from one room in his San Francisco apartment to another, in 1927, the complexities of television technology delayed its immediate development. So did national survival while Americans focused on winning World War II. By the 1950s, however, a radio-like delivery infrastructure for television was in place.

LEARNING CHECK

- Philo Farnsworth called his invention an image dissector. How were images dissected?
- What is the role of persistence of vision in television technology?
- How is persistence of vision employed differently in television and movies?

New Technologies

STUDY PREVIEW Satellite and fibre optic technologies in the late 1900s improved the speed and reliability of delivering mass messages. These were backshop developments that were largely invisible to media consumers. Plainly visible, though, was the related advent of the internet as a new mass medium.

Orbiting Satellites

More than 50 years ago the Russians orbited *Sputnik*, the first human-made satellite. The accomplishment ignited a rush to explore space near Earth and technology surged. Weather forecasting became less intuitive, more scientific, and many times more accurate. With geopositioning signals from satellites, maps had new, everyday applications that only Spock could have imagined. Communication was transformed too, with signals being bounced off satellites for a straight-line range that far exceeded anything possible with the existing network of ground-based relay towers located every 16 or so kilometres apart.

geosynchronous orbit Orbit in which a satellite's period of rotation coincides perfectly with Earth's rotation.

Arthur C. Clarke Devised the concept of satellites in geosynchronous orbits for communication.

Telstar First communication satellite.

uplink A ground station that beams a signal to an orbiting communication satellite.

downlink A ground station that receives a signal relayed from a communication satellite.

For communication, the key to using satellites was the **geosynchronous orbit.** This was a concept of science fiction author **Arthur C. Clarke**, who also was a serious scientist. Clarke figured out in 1945 that a satellite 35 900 kilometres above the equator would be orbiting at the same speed as Earth's rotation, thus always being above the same point below on Earth—an ideal platform for continuous service to pick up signals from Earth stations and retransmit them to other Earth stations. It was like a 35 900-kilometre-high relay tower. With only one relay, not hundreds, signals would move faster and with more reliability. The **Telstar** communication satellite, launched in 1960, took the first telephone signals from **uplink** stations on Earth, amplified them, and returned them to **downlink** stations. Television networks also used Telstar.

LEARNING CHECK

- What was the genius of Arthur C. Clarke as a mass communication futurologist?
- How does a geosynchronous orbit work?

Back to Wires

landline Conventional telecommunication connection using cable laid across land, typically buried or on poles.

cable television Television transmission system that uses cable rather than an over-the-air broadcast signal.

Even as possibilities with satellites were dazzling scientists, the old reliable of mass communication—the wire, sometimes called a **landline**—was in revival. Interestingly, **cable television** arrived in Canada before the first Canadian television station, perhaps reflecting our desire for American programming. An experiment with redistributing U.S. antenna signals in 1952 in London, Ontario, marked the start of cable television in Canada. Later that year, cable companies were also established in Vancouver and Montreal.

The role of the cable industry changed in 1975 when the Time Inc. media empire put HBO on satellite as a programming service for local cable companies. With exclusive programming available to subscribers, cable suddenly was hot. More cable programming services, all delivered by satellite, came online. By the mid-1980s, TSN, CNN, MuchMusic, and other new Canadian programming was available only through cable operators and not "over the air."

fibre optic cables Thin, flexible fibres of glass capable of transmitting light signals.

Meanwhile, Corning Glass had developed a cable that was capable of carrying light at incredible speeds—theoretically, 299 000 kilometres per second. The potential of these new **fibre optic cables**, each strand carrying 60 000 messages simultaneously, was not lost on the telephone industry. So fast was the fibre optic network that the entire *Oxford English Dictionary* could be sent in just seconds. Soon hundreds of crews with backhoes were replacing copper wires, which had constituted the backbone of telephone communication, with fibre optic cables. Coupled with other new technologies, notably digitization of data, the new satellite-based and fibre optic landline communication systems enabled the introduction of a new medium: the internet.

LEARNING CHECK

- What has been the effect of geosynchronously orbiting satellites on the television industry?
- What technologies transformed the cable television industry beginning in the 1970s?

Digital Integration

STUDY PREVIEW Digital technology has brought efficiency to almost every aspect of humans' lifestyles, including products from traditional mass media companies. A wholly new medium, the internet, is built entirely on binary digital signals.

Semiconductor

semiconductor Silicon chip that is used in digitization.

Researchers at AT&T's Bell Labs knew they were on to something important for telephone communication in 1947. Engineers Jack Bardeen, Walter Brattain, and William Shockley had devised glasslike silicon chips—pieces of sand, really—that could be used to respond to a negative or a positive electrical charge. The tiny chips, called **semiconductors**,

Jack Bardeen, Walter Brattain, and William Shockley

Nobel Winners The 1956 Nobel Prize went to the inventors of the semiconductor. They had devised tiny, low-cost crystals that could be used as switches to transmit data that had been converted to binary codes of 0s and 1s. Digital communication followed, with innovations that led to today's global communication networks.

functioned very rapidly as on-off switches. With chips, the human voice could be reduced to a stream of digits—1 for on, 0 for off—and then transmitted as rapid-fire pulses and reconstructed so quickly at the other end of the line that the sound was like the real thing. Bardeen, Brattain, and Shockley won a Nobel Prize.

Watch

A Day in the Life: **"Xeko"**

Little did they realize that they had laid the groundwork for revolutionizing not just telephonic communication but all human communication.

Bell Labs then took digital on-off binary signals to a new level. By breaking messages into pieces and transmitting them in spurts, Bell suddenly, in 1965, could send multiple messages simultaneously. People marvelled that 51 calls could be carried at the same time on a single line. The capacity of telephone systems was dramatically increased without a single new kilometre of wire being laid.

The potential of the evolving technology was no less than revolutionary. Not only could the human voice be reduced to binary digits for transmission but so could text and even images. Futurologists asked: "Who needs paper?" Might digitization even replace the still newfangled technology of television that had flowed from Philo Farnsworth's pioneering work?

Digitization, alas, did not replace Gutenberg-based print media, and the core media industries are still pigeonholed easily into their traditional categories: books, newspapers, magazines, movies, sound recordings, radio, and television. However, the technology did spawn new media industries built around the new technologies. America Online was in the first generation. Now Google, MySpace, Facebook, and YouTube are leaders.

LEARNING CHECK

- What has proved to be the significance of binary digital signalling?
- How have traditional media industries been affected by binary digital signalling?

Internet Origins

The U.S. military saw potential in digitized communication for a noncentralized network. Without a central hub, the military figured that the system could sustain itself in a nuclear attack. The system, called ARPAnet, short for Advanced Research Projects Agency Network, was up and running in 1969. At first, the network linked contractors and universities so that military researchers could exchange information. In 1983, the National Science Foundation, whose mandate is to promote science, took over and involved more universities, which tied their own internal computer-based communication systems into the larger network. As a backbone system that interconnected networks, the term **internet** fit.

internet A high-capacity global telephone network that links computers.

Media Convergence

The construction of a high-capacity network in the 1990s, which we call the internet, is emerging as the delivery vehicle of choice for any and all media products. The technological basis, called **digital**, is distinctive. Messages—whether text, audio, image, or a combination—are broken into millions of bits of data. The bits are transmitted one at a time over the internet, which has incredibly high capacity and speed, then reassembled for reception at the other end. The process is almost instantaneous for text, whose digital bits of data are small and easily accommodated. Audio and visual messages can take longer because far more data bits are required to reconstruct a message at the reception point. A digitization revolution, called **media convergence**, is in progress.

digital Technology through which media messages are coded into 1s and 0s for delivery transmission and then decoded into their original appearance.

media convergence Melding of print, electronic, and photographic media into digitized form.

Distribution The internet has an unmatchable efficiency in delivering messages. In contrast, a newspaper company needs a fleet of trucks and drivers for predawn runs from the production point to intermediate distribution points. Magazine companies rely on the postal system. Book publishers have massive inventories, which require expensive warehousing, and then high shipping costs. Although books, newspapers, and magazines have not vanished from the media landscape, these companies are shifting to delivering at least some of their content via the internet. Individuals themselves can post videos on YouTube and use other social media to become both distributors and consumers of media content.

Devices With a single device, consumers can pick up media content whatever its origin. The device can be a desktop computer, a laptop, an iPod, a BlackBerry or a Kindle. What these devices have in common is an internet connection. Often, these devices can also be used to either create or consume media content.

Distinctions Digitization and media convergence is breaking down old distinctions. Newspaper people increasingly talk about being in the news business, not the newspaper business. Radio people do likewise, talking about being in the music business, not the radio business. The new emphasis is on content. Consumers acknowledge this underlying shift. Instead of reading a newspaper, for example, more people talk about reading news. Instead of watching television, people watch a sitcom. This makes sense as digital devices supplant Gutenberg print technology and combine radio, television, movie, and recording reception appliances into single devices.

Production For almost a century, print media publishers have recognized their inherent disadvantage in production costs. Printing presses for a big-city daily newspaper require millions of dollars in investment. In contrast, as publishers see it, albeit simplistically, their broadcast counterparts merely flick a switch. But with digitized delivery, the broadcast equivalent of a printing press, even transmitter and tower maintenance seem hopelessly expensive. Production costs for newspaper content can be cut drastically with internet delivery.

Democratization The relatively low cost of internet production and delivery may have its greatest impact in broadening the sources of media content. Almost anybody can afford to create messages for internet delivery and, theoretically, reach everyone on the planet who has a reception device. In contrast to a generation ago, the price of entry into the mass media is no longer millions of dollars for production facilities and millions more for start-up costs, including costs for personnel. Ask any blogger or garage band. Media moguls are struggling to identify ways to maintain their dominance. We are in a turbulent environment of change that's still playing out but that has been described—perhaps with prescience, perhaps prematurely—as the democratization of mass communication.

CASE STUDY

Crossroads of Real and Virtual Life

Launched in 2003, Second Life is a virtual world of more than 8.5 million members worldwide. They call themselves residents. Second Life is just one of the many virtual worlds inspired by Neal Stephenson's novel *Snow Crash* and other books associated with the cyberpunk literary movement.

Second Life facilitates all kinds of real-world activities for residents. Opportunities include actual monetary gain, fundraising, political activism, social networking, dancing, job searches, gambling, and worship. By creating an individual "avatar," residents navigate their virtual existence in the look and body of their own making. They develop online skills to create virtual buildings, vehicles, and machines that can be traded or sold to support the Second Life economy. These skills can also be carried over to their real-world existence.

The virtual audience of Second Life presents a multitude of opportunities for real-world mass communication. Successful media companies such as Dell and Warner Brothers have issued news releases in Second Life. Reuters employs an "in-world" correspondent to cover daily events in the metaverse. The online newsletter *Second Opinion* keeps residents informed of the latest news and virtual economy while *AvaStar* provides members with a lively tabloid. Real-world politicians have taken advantage of this new media outlet by hosting campaign headquarters, taking political polls, and holding press conferences in Second Life.

The virtual media platform created by Second Life residents has captured the attention of many organizations traditionally reliant on social media for their marketing, public relations, and advertising. Only time will tell if this new virtual audience is worth their investment.

Make Believe So immersed are avatars in Second Life that it's becoming the advertising platform du jour. Everybody, it seems, wants to be there. CNN and Reuters have established Second Life news bureaus.

DEEPENING YOUR MEDIA LITERACY

Explore the Issue

Go to www.secondopinion.com to read the latest news in Second Life.

Dig Deeper

How is the news within the virtual world of Second Life different from your local community news? Is the virtual audience any different from a physical audience?

What Do You Think?

How do issues or events taking place in Second Life have an impact on the real world? How do you think Second Life will affect mass media in the future?

LEARNING CHECK

- What are the primary print media? What are the primary electronic media?
- Have electronic media replaced print media?
- What is the future for major mass media?

Watch
ABC's *i-CAUGHT:* "Second Life"

Technology and Mass Communication

STUDY PREVIEW Theorists have devised models to help understand and explain the complex and mysterious technology-dependent process of mass communication. But many models, now more than 50 years old, have been outdated by rapid changes in technology. These changes have added more complexity and mystery to how mass communication works.

Lasswell Model

Harold Lasswell Devised the narrative communication model.

channel The medium through which a message is sent to a mass audience.

effect The consequence of a message.

Scholars got serious about trying to understand how mass communication works in the 20th century. Theories came and went. One of the most useful explanations, elegant in its simplicity as an overview, was articulated in the 1950s by Yale professor **Harold Lasswell.** It is a narrative model that poses four questions: Who says what? In which **channel**? To whom? With what **effect**?

With his reference to *channel*, Lasswell clearly differentiated his model as not just another model for human communication. His channel component clearly made his model one of mass communication technology. Lasswell's channel was a technology-defined mass medium: a book, a movie, a television program.

The Lasswell model is easy to apply. Pick any media message, say, Al Gore's documentary *An Inconvenient Truth*:

- **Who says what?** Gore told a story based on expert testimony and recorded evidence about global warming. His message was that global warming is a human-accelerated phenomenon that threatens Earth as a habitat for life as we know it.
- **In which channel?** The documentary itself was a movie. Also, it was distributed widely in video form for home and group audiences. There also was a book bearing the same title.
- **To whom?** Although unfriendly critics tried to dismiss the work as intended for penguins, the movie's video and book quickly became bestsellers.
- **With what effect?** Public attention quickly embraced the notion that it was possible for human beings, acting quickly, to counter the deterioration of Earth as a habitable planet.

LEARNING CHECK

- How does the Lasswell model of mass communication differ from models for interpersonal communication, such as communication between friends conversing face to face?
- Find a bylined newspaper article that discusses a breakthrough on a recent controversial issue. Then apply the four steps in the Lasswell communication process to the article.

Values and Limitations of Models

Deepening Your Media Literacy: What impedes your understanding?

For all of their usefulness, models of mass communication fall short, far short, of capturing the complexities occurring in our media systems. The volume of messages is incalculable. The word *zillions* comes to mind. What we do know about the volume is that it's increasing rapidly. Nobody has come up with a model to portray the overlays and interplay of all of the content moving through the mass media.

All models—whether of ships, planes, or automobiles—have the same deficiency. By definition, a model is a facsimile that helps us to see and understand the real thing. But no model shows everything. An aircraft engineer, for example, can create a model of an airplane's propulsion system. Although essential to illustrating how the plane will be powered, a model of its propulsion system doesn't illustrate the plane's aesthetic features, or its ventilation system, or its electrical system, or any of hundreds of other important features. Engineers are able to overlay various models to show connections and interrelations—which itself is a major challenge—but this is far short of what it would take to illustrate all that is going on. It's the same with communication: Too much is occurring at any given nanosecond. So, like all models, mass communication models are useful illustrations but limited because there is far more to what's happening than can be reduced to a schematic.

Different models illustrate different aspects of the process. That the process is too complex for a single model to convey it all is clear from the Lasswell model. As sweeping as it is, the Lasswell model is far less than a detailed framework for understanding how mass communication works, but it is a starting point.

LEARNING CHECK

- What are the advantages and disadvantages of any model?
- Can complex phenomena like mass communication be reduced to a model?

MEDIA PEOPLE Steve Jobs

Working in a garage, Steve Jobs and a buddy built an over-the-top desktop computer, which became the foundation for Apple Computer. No wonder, when people think of Jobs, they think of computers. Think again. Jobs, now a multi-billionaire in his fifties, has positioned Apple at the convergence point of computers and television and a whole lot of other media channels.

Jobs's latest breakthrough, in 2002, was the iPod portable music device, which triggered a transformation of music retailing and the music industry. The device morphed into the video iPod in 2005, whose first version could store 150 hours of video downloads from the internet.

Meanwhile, Jobs, who ran both Apple and Pixar Animation Studios, known for the blockbuster movies *Toy Story* and *Finding Nemo*, sold Pixar to Disney ABC for an incredible US$7.4 billion. The deal made Jobs the largest Disney shareholder and put Jobs on the Disney board of directors.

While Disney and Pixar were still negotiating the merger, Jobs pushed for ABC content to be made available for the video iPod. Negotiations took only three days, unbelievably fast by usual business standards. Mickey Mouse and Goofy features from Disney archives immediately were available on video iPods at a download cost of $1.99. So were episodes of ABC's *Desperate Housewives* and *Lost*. Executives at competing television networks saw no choice but to sign on, despite worries about eroding their historic monopoly on distributing programs through their local affiliates.

Incredible new technologies are forcing basic changes. The familiar territory of industry infrastructures that have been in place since the mid-1900s is in profound transition. What's ahead? A shakeup like nothing before.

Steve Jobs The ongoing technical and corporate convergence of the mass media is epitomized in Jobs's linking computers and the internet through his position at Apple, with his role in movies through Disney and Pixar, and with the revolution he stirred in the music industry with the iPod and iTunes store.

WHAT DO YOU THINK?

1. In what ways will the new technology affect the basic function of mass communication?
2. What changes would you make to Lasswell's basic model to account for changes in technology?

Concentric Circle Model

One of the most useful models from the late 20th century was conceived by Ray Hiebert, Donald Ungurait, and Thomas Bohn. It is a series of concentric rings with the source of the message at the centre. The source encodes information or an idea, which then ripples outward to the outermost ring, which is the receiving audience. In between are several elements unique to the mass communication, including gatekeepers, a technologically based medium, regulators, and amplification. The model creates a framework for tracking the difficult course of a message through the mass communication process. In effect, the model portrays mass communication as an obstacle course.

Media People: Steve Jobs

Medium Hiebert, Ungurait, and Bohn, aware that media affect messages, put the label *mass media* on one of their rings. Media make a difference. A message that lends itself to visual portrayal, such as a comedian's sight gag, will fall flat on radio. The medium is indeed critical in ensuring that an outward-rippling message makes its way to the goal—an effect that Hiebert, Ungurait, and Bohn placed at the outermost ring.

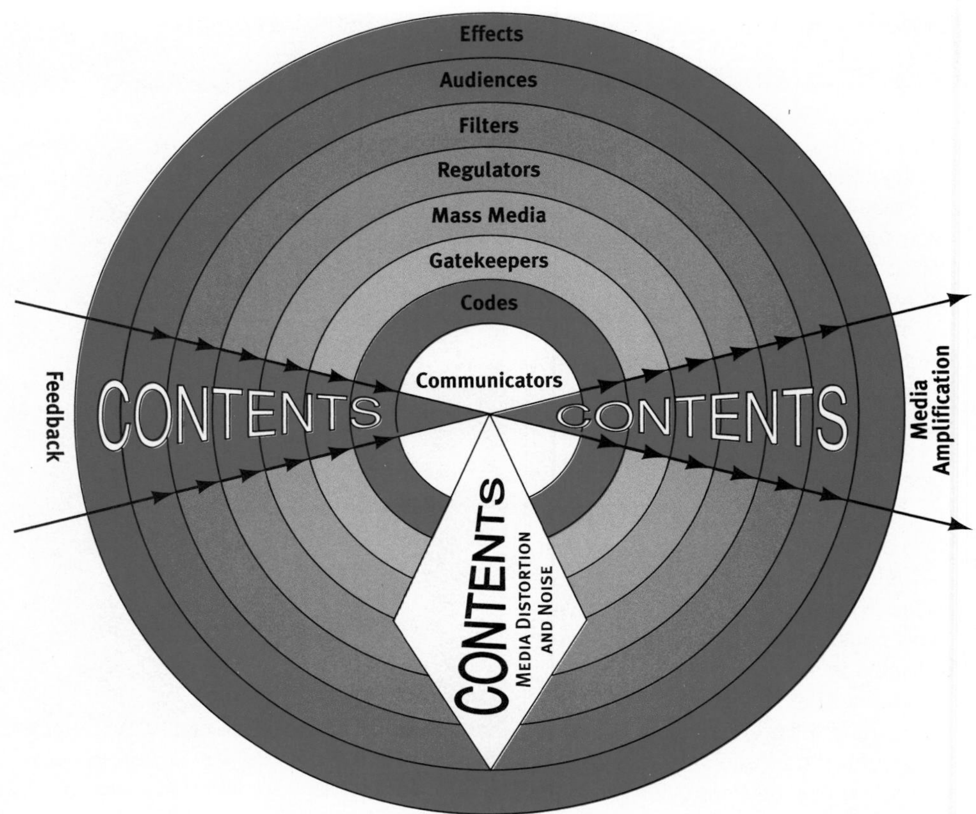

Figure 2.2 Concentric Circle Model The concentric circle model illustrates a great number of obstacles for a mass-communicated message to reach an audience. These include obstacles in the technology, including coding for transmission. It's a detailed model that acknowledges that the media amplify messages, which can compound their effects. Feedback is shown, too. In mass communication, feedback usually is muted and almost always is delayed.

Amplification Important in understanding mass communication is knowing how a mass medium boosts a message's chance of reaching an audience and having an effect. Radio exponentially increases a commentator's audience. A printing press amplifies a message in the same way. Indeed, it's the **amplification** made possible by media technology that sets *mass* communication apart from chatting with a neighbour or making a class presentation.

amplification Giving a message to a larger audience.

Message Controls Most mass communication involves a team, usually dozens of people, sometimes hundreds. Consider a video of a terrorist attack shot by a Canadian Press photographer in Iraq. The video passes through a complex gatekeeping process, with editors, packagers, producers, and others making decisions on how much of the rough footage ends up in distribution to television stations—or whether the images will be broadcast at all. **Gatekeepers** are media people who make judgments on what most merits inclusion in what is sent to networks, stations, and website operators.

gatekeepers Media people who influence messages en route.

Gatekeeping is an unavoidable function in mass communication because there is neither time nor space for all of the messages that might be passed through the process. Gatekeepers are editors who decide what makes it through their gates and in what form.

Like gatekeepers, **regulators** can affect a communicator's messages substantially. Institutions that try to influence mass-communicated messages before they reach the audience are regulators. In Canada, broadcasters are regulated by the CRTC, while advertising is governed by the Competition Act, which is administered and enforced by Canada's Competition Bureau. Regulators in the mass communication process also include pressure groups. In Canada, the Friends of Canadian Broadcasting lobbies for more Canadian content on our airwaves and more funding for Canadian television and movies.

regulators Nonmedia people who influence messages.

There are also gatekeeper-regulator hybrids in the mass communication process. Media trade and professional organizations influence media content. Ethics codes of the Canadian Broadcast Standards Council (CBSC), a self-regulatory body made up of industry professionals, have had wide influence on what Canadians hear and see on our airwaves. Canadian advertisers have guidelines from Advertising Standards Canada, while the Radio-Television News Directors Association of Canada is a self-governing body for broadcast journalists.

Are organizations like the CBSC gatekeepers or regulators? Composed of media people, they would seem to be gatekeepers, but because they do not operate on the front line (that is, they do not make content decisions directly), they have many characteristics of regulators. They are, in fact, gatekeeper-regulator hybrids that institutionalize peer pressure among media people to influence media content.

The regulation process can be heavy-handed. China, for example, has insisted that media companies comply with vaguely defined but stridently enforced bans on subjects that the government sees as challenges to its authority. Although this is censorship, Google, Yahoo! and other transnational media companies eager to profit from access to potentially huge Chinese audiences have chosen to comply.

In-Process Impediments If speakers slur their words, the effectiveness of their messages is jeopardized. Slurring and other impediments to the communication process before a message reaches the audience are called **noise**. In mass communication, based as it is on complex mechanical and electronic equipment, the opportunities for noise interference are countless because so many things can go wrong.

noise Impediment to communication before a message reaches a receiver.

Mass communicators themselves can interfere with the success of their own messages by being sloppy. This is called **semantic noise**. Sloppy wording is an example. So is slurring. **Channel noise** is something that interferes with message transmission, such as static on the radio, or smudged ink on a magazine page, or a faulty microphone on a television anchor's lapel. An intrusion that occurs at the reception site is **environmental noise**. This includes a doorbell interrupting someone reading an article, which distracts from decoding. As would shouting kids, who distract a television viewer.

semantic noise Sloppy message crafting.

channel noise Interference during transmission.

environmental noise Interference at the reception site.

Deciphering Impediments Unwittingly, people who tune in to mass messages may themselves interfere with the success of the mass communication process. Such interference is known as a **filter**.

filter Receiver factor that impedes communication.

If someone doesn't understand the language or symbols that a communicator uses, the communication process becomes flawed. It is a matter of an individual lacking enough information to decipher a message. This deficiency is called an **informational filter**. This filter can be partly the responsibility of the communicator, whose vocabulary may not be in tune with the audience. More often, though, filters are a deficiency in the audience.

informational filter Receiver's knowledge limits that impede deciphering symbols.

There also are physical filters. When a receiver's mind is dimmed with fatigue, a **physical filter** may interfere with the communication process. A drunk whose focus fades in and out suffers from a physical filter. Mass communicators have little control over physical filters.

physical filter Receiver's alertness that impedes deciphering symbols.

Psychological filters also interfere with communication. Conservative evangelist James Dobson and Parkinson's sufferer Michael J. Fox, for example, likely would decode a message on stem cell research far differently.

psychological filter Receiver's state of mind that impedes deciphering symbols.

The Hiebert, Ungurait, and Bohn model was incredibly useful in diagramming the process of mass communication, until new technologies ushered in the internet and transformed a lot of mass communication. Twentieth-century models quickly became, well, so old.

LEARNING CHECK

- What are the similarities and differences in the processes of interpersonal and mass communication?
- What mechanisms, short of censorship, does government use to influence media messages?

Semiotics

The semiotic school of thought looks at the creation of meaning in communication. Technology brings us media messages, but the individual makes sense of the meaning. To understand what semiotics is and what signs are, it is important to see how the French semiotician Roland Barthes expanded on the work of Swiss linguist Ferdinand de Saussure. For de Saussure, the sign is composed of a signifier and a signified, as shown in the figure on next page.

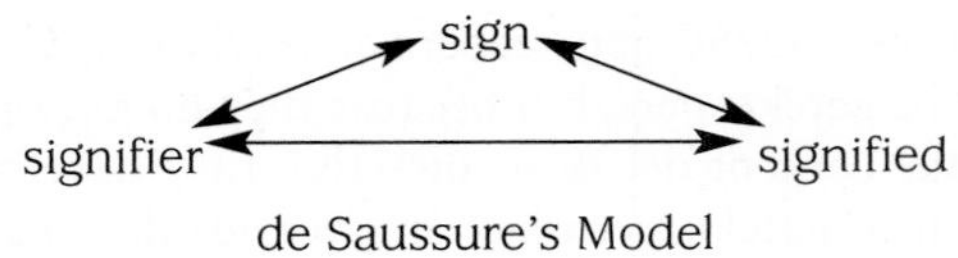

de Saussure's Model

For example, the words *maple leaf* constitute a sign. This sign is composed of a signifier, the letters in the words "m-a-p-l-e-l-e-a-f," and its signified, the mental concept of leaves from a maple tree that accompanies the words. Together, the signifier and signified form the sign of the "maple leaf." The relation between the signifier and its signified is entirely arbitrary. The words *maple leaf* denote what they do solely because of the linguistic conventions of the English language.

Denotation and Connotation

Barthes took this idea of signification one step further. For Barthes, there is not only one level of signification (the mental concept of "maple leaf"), but two: first-order and second-order signified. He called these levels of meaning denotation and connotation, respectively. Barthes's conceptualization of signs is shown in the figure below.

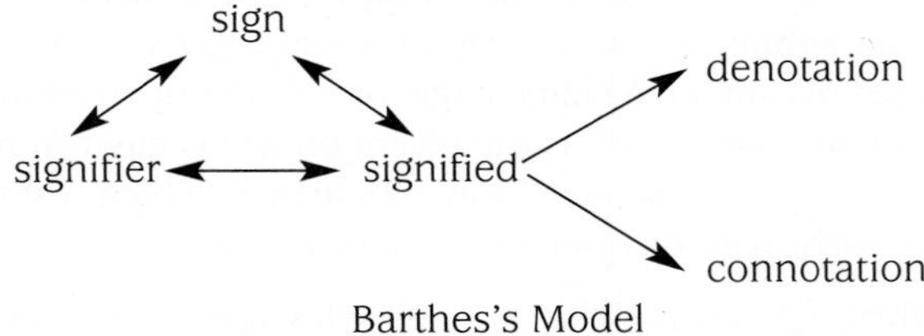

Barthes's Model

Denotation is the same as de Saussure's idea of the signified. It is what Barthes calls the simple, everyday meaning in the sign. For example, "maple leaf" signifies, or denotes, a type of leaf from a particular tree. But it can also mean many other things. There is a difference in its connotation, which deals with an additional level of meaning. For example, a maple leaf can signify Canada, or an NHL team, as well as a leaf from a maple tree. For Barthes, this second-level meaning is a vehicle for cultural ideology. It's only because we are Canadian that the maple leaf signifies Canada to us. Hockey fans will interpret a maple leaf as signifying the team from Toronto. The multitude of meanings that can be associated with a sign is also arbitrary and depends largely on cultural conventions. That's what semiotics looks at—the many different types of meanings that are created by cultural influences.

By analyzing the relationship between denotation and connotation in popular culture, Barthes believed that hidden ideologies (or what he called "mythologies") could be uncovered. A myth can also be defined as a culture's belief system.

C.S. Pierce Classified signs into different categories.

icons Signs that look like what they signify.

index A sign that is connected to what it signifies.

symbol A sign that has an arbitrary connection to what it signifies.

Not all signs are created equal. Communication theorist **C.S. Pierce** designed a way to classify signs according to their level of connotation or denotation. Pierce divided signs into three categories: **icons, indexes,** and **symbols**.

- Icons are signs that resemble what they represent because the signifier looks like what is signified. For example, a map of Canada is an icon of Canada because it looks like the geographic layout of the country. A picture of Arkells is an icon of the Canadian music group. If the sign is denotative and not connotative, it is an icon.
- An index is directly related to what it represents. A popular example of an index is smoke, which usually indicates that there is a fire. Smoke is an index of fire because smoke has a connection with fire. An index is a mixture of connotation and denotation. Smoke by itself is largely denotative, but it connotes something else: fire. A Mountie's hat is also an index; it not only is a hat but also has come to represent an RCMP officer. The late Prime Minister Pierre Trudeau always wore a rose in his lapel. The rose became an index of Trudeau.
- A symbol is a sign that is entirely connotative because there is no clear connection between the signifier and the signified. Words are symbolic of what they represent. The Canadian flag, the fleur-de-lys, and the beaver are all Canadian symbols. They don't look like Canada, but they have all become symbolic of various aspects of our culture. Symbols develop their meaning over time through convention. The meaning given to symbols is arbitrary and can change.

Linear Communication

Point A → Point B

The telegraph moves messages from Point A to Point B. The sender controls the message.

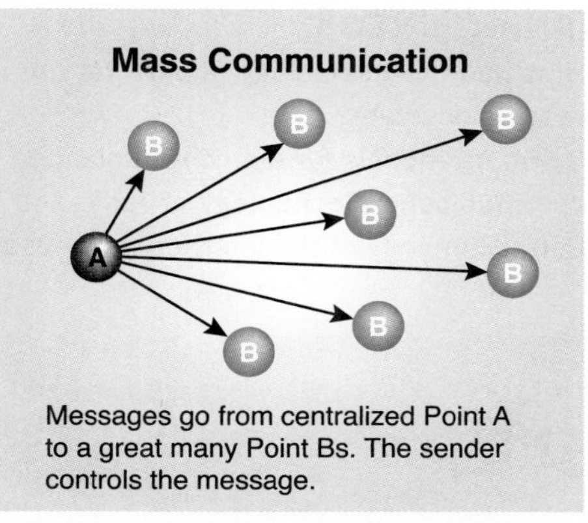

Messages go from centralized Point A to a great many Point Bs. The sender controls the message.

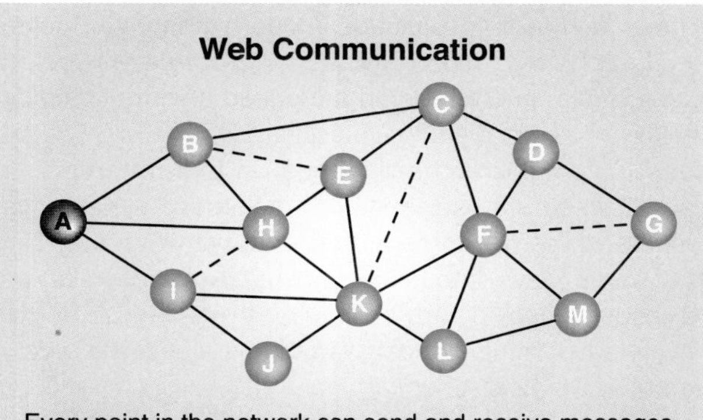

Every point in the network can send and receive messages. The recipient has access to every transmission point and controls what is received.

Figure 2.3 **Points Model** Web communication shifts much of the control of the communication through the mass media to the recipient, turning the traditional process of mass communication on its head.

LEARNING CHECK

- What are the differences between denotation and connotation?
- What plays a bigger role in how we decode messages: personal interpretation or cultural definitions?

21st-Century Models

Scholars again are at work on devising models to help explain the new mass communication. Clearly, the coding of internet messages has become largely automated. There are no typesetters or press operators. Nor are there broadcast control room engineers. Gatekeeping is minimal. Bloggers blog unfettered. The closest that Facebook comes to editing are anonymous campus monitors whose controls are so light-fingered as to be almost nonexistent. Regulators? Governments have scratched the surface on transnational copyright issues, but largely the governments of Western countries have dallied in trying to apply old regulation models to the internet.

In part, the problem is that the heart of the technology for the internet is decentralized. There are no central sources that can be regulated—no newsrooms, no production centres, no presses. In some ways it's a free-for-all. One useful way to envision the internet is to think of old telegraph communication in the 1800s, in which messages went from Point A to Point B. In the 1900s, technology ushered in an explosion of mass communication. Radio, for example, picked up on the mass communication model of print media. Messages went from a single Point A to many recipients: magazine readers in the millions, radio listeners in the millions, and television viewers in the millions. That was the process that Hiebert, Ungurait, and Bohn's concentric circle model captured so well.

In the 21st century, with the internet, every Point A is theoretically reached by every Point B and C and also Points X, Y, and Z. It's not a linear Point A to Point B. Nor is it a message emanating from Point A to multiple points. It's a web of interactive messages reaching an incalculable number of points, which in part is why the term *World Wide Web* came to be.

ABC's *Good Morning America*: "Emmy Censorship"

LEARNING CHECK

- How has the technology underlying the internet rendered early mass communication models obsolete?
- Compare models for the communication technology of the telegraph in the 1800s, the communication technology of radio and television in the 1900s, and the communication technology of the internet in the 21st century.

Chapter 2 Wrap-Up

Mass communication is unique among various forms of human communication because it cannot occur without technology. These technologies include modern printing. Books, newspapers, and magazines are rooted in printing technology. Motion pictures are rooted in chemical technology. Sound recording, radio, and television are called electronic media for a reason. The latest media technology is binary digital signals.

The mass communication process is complex and mysterious. In their attempts to understand the process, scholars have devised a broad range of models and schematics and invented terminology to explain some of the phenomena they observe when they dissect the process. Although useful in some ways, modelling the mass communication process leaves many questions and issues open to further inquiry. If we had all of the answers to how the process works, every advertising campaign would be a success, every book a bestseller, and every television pilot the next *American Idol*.

PEARSON **mycanadiancommunicationlab**

Visit **www.mycanadiancommunicationlab.ca** for access to a wealth of tools and resources that will enhance your learning experience. Features include the following:

- Personalized Study Plan
- Videos
- Activities
- Pearson eText–and much more!

Questions for Critical Thinking

1. Why is an understanding of the basics of technology important in the study of mass communication? Why is mass communication dependent on the technology that delivers media content?
2. What were the early effects of Gutenberg's movable type on civilization? Can you speculate on what our culture would be like without Gutenberg's invention?
3. Photography and movies are both rooted in chemical technology, but one is a mass medium and the other is not. Explain this distinction using this paradigm: A photograph is to a book what a script is to a movie.
4. The digital technology underlying the internet is changing the industries that were built around older mass media. What are these changes? Will traditional media companies as we know them survive?
5. What are the strengths of the Lasswell mass communication model, the concentric circle model, and McLuhan's Four Laws of Media? What are their inadequacies?

Keeping Up to Date

Newsmagazines, including *Maclean's*, *Time*, and *Newsweek*, cover mass media issues more or less regularly. So do the *National Post*, *The Globe and Mail*, *The New York Times*, *The Wall Street Journal*, and other leading newspapers. To keep up with issues in technology, there's *Wired*.

Entertainment

3

Jerry Bruckheimer The signature cinematic feature of his movies and television shows, including *CSI*, is the pace. Because of Bruckheimer, editing has become faster; shots average 2 to 3 seconds, compared to 8 to 11 seconds only 20 years earlier.

LEARNING AHEAD

- Mass media technology has magnified the audience for storytelling and entertainment.
- Pure performance and mediated performance are different.
- Mass media powerfully extend the reach of literature.
- Technology has accelerated music as a social unifier.
- Mass media feed an insatiable demand for sports.
- Gaming has become a mass medium, with advertisers pursuing gamers.
- Mass media have championed the right of adult access to sexual content.
- Quality of mass media entertainment is compromised by factory-style production.
- Mass media often fall short in elevating cultural sensitivity.

MEDIA IN THEORY

The Bruckheimer Effect

There's no doubt that the mass media are a source of entertainment for most North Americans. One of the architects of a good deal of content is Jerry Bruckheimer, who has produced fast-paced films like *The Rock*, *Con Air*, *Pearl Harbor*, *Pirates of the Caribbean*, *National Treasure*, and *Black Hawk Down* as well as films about people who made a difference like *Remember the Titans* and *Veronica Guerin*.

Before 1980, the average shot in a mainstream film lasted 8 to 11 seconds, according to film scholar David Bordwell. In Bruckheimer's *Top Gun*, made in 1986, the shots shrank to 3 to 4 seconds. In 1998's *Armageddon*, they were 2 to 3 seconds. Jeanine Basinger, historian and chair of film studies at Wesleyan University in Middletown, Connecticut, says that Bruckheimer may have been the first filmmaker to understand how quickly audiences can assimilate images and their meaning: "Bruckheimer movies are the opposite of what his critics say. They're not mindless—they engage a different part of the mind." Some also might argue that the fast-paced editing pioneered by Bruckheimer is a variation of Marshall McLuhan's adage that the medium is the message.

Not many people can make the leap from movies to television, but Bruckheimer brought his action-packed brand to shows like *CSI* and its spinoffs, the *Amazing Race* reality show, and *Without a Trace*. Bruckheimer says that he just wants to keep the story moving, and to do that he "takes the air out," just as in his movies, although he likes being able to develop a character through a season's worth of shows.

Bruckheimer came to Hollywood in 1972 with a degree in psychology and a successful career as an advertising art director. In 2003, his films earned $12.5 billion in worldwide box-office receipts. Bruckheimer is "able to make the world's best B movies without condescending to the audience," *Time*'s Joel Stein says. "His instinct for what excites audiences is eerily perfect." "We are in the transportation business," says Bruckheimer. "We transport audiences from one place to another." And he does it at high speed.

Through the mass media, including Bruckheimer's works, people can escape everyday drudgery, immersing themselves in a soap opera, a murder mystery, or pop music.

The pervasiveness of all of these entertainment choices is not always a good thing, according to some theorists who say that a plethora of information and access to ideas and entertainment can induce information anxiety. Even a relatively slender weekday edition of *The New York Times* contains more information than the average person in the 17th century was likely to come across in a lifetime, according to Richard Saul Wurman in his book *Information Anxiety*.

information pollution Media deluge people with information and no sense of order or priority.

While educated people traditionally have thirsted for information, the quantity has become such that many people feel overwhelmed by what is called **information pollution**. We are awash in it and drowning, and the mass media are a factor in this.

media-induced passivity Media entice people away from social involvement.

Another effect of the mass media is embodied in the stereotypical couch potato, whose greatest physical and mental exercise is heading to the refrigerator during commercials. The Television Bureau of Canada estimates that the average Canadian watches almost 27 hours of television per week. The experience is primarily passive, and such **media-induced passivity** has been blamed, along with greater mobility and access to more leisure activities, for major changes in how people live their lives:

- **Worship services.** In 1955, Gallup found that 49 percent attended worship services weekly. Today, it is less than 40 percent.
- **Churches and lodges.** The role of church auxiliaries and lodges, once central in community social life with weekly activities, has diminished.
- **Neighbourhood taverns.** Taverns at busy neighbourhood corners and rural crossroads once were the centre of political discussion in many areas, but this is less true today.
- **Participatory sports.** Despite the fitness and wellness craze, more people than ever are overweight and out of shape, which can be attributed partly to physical passivity induced by television and media-based homebound activities.

Media People: Nancy Tellum

Entertainment in History

STUDY PREVIEW During their 550-year existence, the mass media have magnified the audience for entertainment. Technology has wrought many refinements, but the core categories of media entertainment remain storytelling and music.

Watch

ABC's Nightline: "Celebrity Worship"

Pre–Mass Media Roots

Entertainment predates the written history of the human species. Around the prehistoric campfire there was music. We know this from Neolithic animal-hide drums that archaeologists have unearthed. Certainly, the cave dwellers must have told stories. Who knows when the visual arts began? The record goes back to paintings on cave walls. Through the eons, entertainment became higher and higher art. Archaeologists know that the elites of ancient civilizations enjoyed lavish banquets that included performing entertainers: acrobats, musicians, and dancers. Sports and athletics became institutionalized entertainment by the time of ancient Greece with the Olympic Games and large stadiums. Then came ancient Rome with athletics and competition on an even larger scale. Circus Maximus in Rome could hold 170 000 spectators for chariot races and gladiator games.

Entertainment that has survived the ages includes music, literature, sports, and sex. Other breakdowns can be made, such as performing arts and visual arts. Some people distinguish entertainment from art, relegating entertainment to a somehow less worthy category. On close examination these distinctions blur, however. Art is in the eye of the beholder, a highly personal and subjective issue.

Learning Check

- What are categories into which entertainment can be sorted for analysis?

Technology-Driven Entertainment

What distinguished the Age of Mass Communication, which began with Gutenberg's movable type in the 1440s, was that messages, including entertainment, could be mass-produced to reach audiences of unprecedented size. The post-Gutenberg press gave literature wider and wider audiences. But even 200 years after Gutenberg, the audience for John Milton's *Paradise Lost*, to take one example, was remarkable for the time but minuscule compared to the audience for each book currently on *The New York Times* weekly bestseller list. As well, literature has taken on diverse forms, from academic tomes in the Milton tradition to pulp romances and westerns—and not all are in printed form.

As media technology leapfrogged into photographic and electronic forms, literature adapted to the new media. Movies extended the reach and the artistic form of books. So did radio and then television. Music, a rare treat in people's lives before audio recording was invented, is everywhere today. Indeed, the impact of the entertainment content of today's mass media is hard to measure, but it seems evident that people are being entertained more than ever before in history.

LEARNING CHECK

What is the role of media technology in entertainment?

Entertainment Genres

To make sense of the gigantic and growing landscape of entertainment in the mass media, people have devised **genres** that are, in effect, subdivisions of the major categories of storytelling and music.

genres Broad thematic categories of media content.

Storytelling Whether in the form of novels, short stories, television drama, or movies, literature can be divided into genres. Popular genres include suspense, romance, horror,

Perennial Cop Shows The police story is an enduring story genre that spikes periodically in popularity. The latest generation is led by the prime-time CBS/CTV series *CSI* and its spinoffs.

westerns, fantasy, history, and biography. Some genres are short-lived. In the early 1970s a movie genre dubbed *blaxploitation* emerged, for better or worse, with a black racist appeal to black audiences. The genre culminated in the *Shaft* series, which, although updated in 2003, had been eclipsed by the ongoing racial integration of society.

Music A lot of crossover makes for genre confusion in music. Wanting to define their tastes, aficionados keep reinventing thematic trends. The array of subgenres is dizzying. How is acid rock different from hard rock, from solid rock, from progressive rock, from alternative rock, from power rock, from metal rock? Don't ask. Categorizing is not a neat and clinical task.

Sports Genres are clearest in sports because the rules, although not set in granite, have been agreed on, as have the procedures for revising those rules. Nobody confuses baseball with hockey or lacrosse with NASCAR. Attempts at crossover genres, such as the wrestling-inspired XFL football experiment, don't do well.

LEARNING CHECK

- What are major genres of media-delivered entertainment?

Performance as Media Entertainment

STUDY PREVIEW The mass media's entertainment content is performance, but it's not pure performer-to-audience. The media change the performance. Authentic performance is live and eyeball-to-eyeball with the audience. Mediated performance is adapted to meet an unseen and distant audience.

Authentic Performance

When American liberal commentator Al Franken does a routine before a live audience, it's uproariously funny unless his bite hits a raw ideological nerve. That's why conservatives avoid his shows. But in 2004, when Franken took his humour to radio in a talk show on the new Air America network, his humour and bite didn't translate well. On radio, he was flat. As Canadian Marshall McLuhan would argue, "the medium was the message." There are many reasons for this.

authentic performance Live with on-site audience.

Audience At a play, whether at Prince Edward Island's Charlottetown Festival or in a rural high-school auditorium, the audience is assembled for one purpose. It's **authentic performance**, live with the audience on-site. Everyone is attentive to the performance and nuances are less likely to be missed.

Feedback Performers on stage are in tune with their audience's reactions. There can be reaction and interplay. For the same performance through a mass medium, performers guess—some better than others—at how they are coming across. The fact is, taking television as an example, what resonates in one living room does not resonate in another. Some performers are more gifted at maximizing their impact, but to reach the massive, scattered, heterogeneous mass audience requires pandering to some extent to common denominators. There is less edge.

Technology The equipment that makes mass communication possible is what sets it apart from interpersonal and group communication. Technology imposes its own requirements on performance. Media transform a performance. In ways large and small, it becomes a mediated performance.

Mediated Performance

mediated message Adjusted to be effective when carried by the mass media.

In ways we don't always realize, media technology affects and sometimes shapes the messages the media disseminate. The changes needed to make a **mediated message** work are a function of the technology that makes it possible to reach a mass audience.

Music Edison's mechanical recording technology, which captured acoustic waves in a huge horn, picked up no subtleties. Brass bands and loud voices recorded best. Scratchy background noise drowned out soft sounds. It's no wonder that the late 1800s and early 1900s were marked by popularity of martial music and marching bands. High-pitched voices came through best, which also shaped the popular music of the period.

When Joseph Maxwell's electrical technology was refined in the 1920s, subtle sounds that now could survive the recording and playback processes came into vogue. Rudy Vallee and Bing Crosby were in; John Philip Sousa was out. Improvements in fidelity beginning in the 1950s meant that music could be played louder and louder without unsettling dissonance—and many rockers took to louder renditions.

Movies Media technology profoundly affects art. When audio and film technology were merged to create talkies, moviemakers suddenly had all kinds of new creative options for their storytelling. Directors had more new possibilities when wide screens replaced squarish screens in movie houses. When technology changes the experience for the moviemaker, it also changes the experience for moviegoers.

Sports Technology has dazzled sports fans. Instant replays on television, tried first during an Army–Navy football game in the early 1960s, added a dimension that in-stadium fans could not see. Then came miniature cameras that allowed viewers to see what referees see on the field. Putting microphones on referees, coaches, and players let the mass audience eavesdrop on the sounds of the playing field that no one in the stands or sidelines could pick up.

Some digital cable channels allow viewers to select various static camera angles during a game. Viewers, in effect, can participate in creating the media coverage they see. This is a profound development. Watching television, once a largely passive activity, now can involve the viewer at least to some degree.

LEARNING CHECK

- What are the advantages of live performances over mediated performances?
- What are the advantages of mediated performances over live performances?

Storytelling as Media Entertainment

STUDY PREVIEW The media are powerful vehicles for exponentially extending the reach of literature. The most enduring include romances and mysteries, but variations and hybrids come and go in popularity.

Genres of Literature

Some of literature's storytelling genres have endured through the centuries. Shakespeare was neither the first nor the last to do romances and mysteries. Genres help us to make sense of literature, giving us a basis for comparison and contrast. Literature can be categorized in many ways, one as basic as fiction and nonfiction, another being prose and poetry. Bookstores use thematic genres to sort their inventory, including mysteries, romances, sports, biographies, and hobbies.

LEARNING CHECK

- What genres of media content can you identify besides those mentioned here?

Media-Defined Trends

Genres rise and fall in popularity. Early television was dominated by variety shows, which featured a range of comedy, song and dance, and other acts. Then came the wave

Genre du Jour Television series built around complex female characters—anti-heroines, they could be called—have been a recent genre rage. Kyra Sedgwick's character on *The Closer* and Julianne Margulies's character on *The Good Wife* fit squarely in this genre. Other edgy lead portrayals of flawed, nonstereotypical women include those by Mary-Louise Parker on *Weeds* and Holly Hunter on *Saving Grace*, both shown on Showcase in Canada.

of 1950s quiz shows, then westerns, then police shows. Early in the 21st century, the television programming fads were talk shows in the style pioneered by Phil Donahue and sustained by Oprah Winfrey, reality shows epitomized by the unending CBS/Global *Survivor* series, and yet another rush of "whodunit" police shows.

Genre trends are audience-driven. People flock to a particular book, song, film, or television show and then to the thematic sequels until they tire of it all. Although a lot of genre content is derivative rather than original art, new twists and refinements can reflect artistic fine tuning by authors, scriptwriters, and other creators. People may quibble about whether Francis Ford Coppola's *The Godfather* or *The Godfather, Part II*, was better, but almost everyone, including the critics, concur that both were filmic masterpieces. At the same time, nobody serious about creative media content is looking forward to Jason Voorhees returning anytime soon.

LEARNING CHECK

- What genres of media content have you seen come and go?

Music

Watch

Elvis Presley

Watch

The Beatles

STUDY PREVIEW Audio technology accelerated the effect of music as a social unifier. This is nowhere better illustrated than in the integration of traditional black music and white hillbilly music into rock 'n' roll, a precursor to the racial integration of society. The potency of music has been enhanced by its growing role in other media forms, including movies and television.

Rockabilly Revolution

Most music historians trace contemporary popular music to roots in two distinctive types of American folk music, both of which emerged in the South.

black music Folk genre from American black slave experience.

Black Music Africans who were brought to the American colonies as slaves used music to soothe their difficult lives. Much of the music reflected their oppression and hopeless poverty. Known as **black music**, it was distinctive in that it carried strains of slaves' African roots and at the same time reflected the black American experience. This music also included strong religious themes, expressing the slaves' indefatigable faith in a glorious afterlife. Flowing from the heart and the soul, this was folk music of the most authentic sort.

After the American Civil War, black musicians found a white audience on riverboats and in saloons and pleasure palaces of various sorts. That introduced a commercial component into black music and fuelled numerous variations, including jazz. Even with a growing white following, the creation of these latter-day forms of black music remained almost entirely with African-American musicians. White musicians who picked up on the growing popularity of black music drew heavily on black songwriters. Much of Benny Goodman's swing music, for example, came from black arranger Fletcher Henderson.

rhythm and blues Distinctive style of black music that took form in the 1930s.

In the 1930s and 1940s a distinctive new form of black music, **rhythm and blues**, emerged. The people who enjoyed this music lived all over the United States and included both blacks and whites. Mainstream American music had come to include a firm African-American presence.

Hillbilly Music Another authentic American folk music form, **hillbilly music**, flowed from the lives of Appalachian and Southern whites. Early hillbilly music had a strong colonial heritage in English ballads and ditties, but over time it evolved into a genre in its own right. Fiddle playing and twangy lyrics reflected the poverty and hopelessness of rural folk, "hillbillies" as they called themselves. Also like black music, hillbilly music reflected the joys, frustrations, and sorrows of love and family. However, hillbilly music failed to develop more than a regional following—that is, until the 1950s, when a great confluence of the black and hillbilly traditions occurred. This distinctive new form of American music, called **rockabilly** early on, became rock 'n' roll.

hillbilly music Folk genre from rural Appalachian and Southern white experience.

rockabilly Black-hillbilly hybrid that emerged in the 1950s.

LEARNING CHECK

- What distinctive American musical genres melded in rockabilly?

Early Rock 'n' Roll

Music aficionados quibble about who invented the term *rock 'n' roll.* There is no doubt, though, that Memphis disc jockey **Sam Phillips** was a key figure in the development of the genre. From his job at WREC, Phillips found an extra $75 a month to rent a 20-foot-by-35-foot storefront, the paint peeling from the ceiling, to go into business recording, as he put it, "anything, anywhere, anytime." His first jobs, in 1949, were weddings and bar mitzvahs, but in 1951 Phillips put out his first record, "Gotta Let You Go," by blues singer Joe Hill Louis, who played his own guitar, harmonica, and drums for accompaniment. In 1951, Phillips recorded B.B. King and then **Jackie Brenston**'s "Rocket 88," which many musicologists call the first rock 'n' roll record. Phillips sold his early recordings, all by black musicians mostly in the blues tradition, to other labels.

Sam Phillips Pioneered rockabilly and rock 'n' roll; discovered Elvis Presley.

Jackie Brenston Recorded "Rocket 88," first rock 'n' roll record, in 1951.

In 1952, Phillips began his own Sun Records label with a quest to broaden the appeal of the black music he loved to a wide audience. "If I could find a white man who had the Negro sound and the Negro feel, I could make a billion dollars," he said. In a group he recorded in 1954, the Starlight Wranglers, Sam Phillips found Elvis Presley.

Presley's first Sun recording, "That's All Right," with Scotty Moore and Bill Black, found only moderate success on country radio stations, but Sam Phillips knew that he was on to something. It wasn't quite country or quite blues, but it was a sound that could move both white country fans and black blues fans. Elvis moved on to RCA, a major label. By 1956 he had two of the nation's bestselling records, the flip-side hits "Don't Be Cruel" and "Hound Dog," plus three others among the year's top 16. Meanwhile, Sam Phillips was recording Carl Perkins, Roy Orbison, Johnny Cash, and Jerry Lee Lewis, adding to the distinctively American country-blues hybrid: wild, thrashing, sometimes reckless rock 'n' roll.

The new music found a following on radio stations that picked up on the music mix that Cleveland disc jockey Alan Freed had referred to as "rock 'n' roll" as early as 1951—occasional rhythm and blues amid the mainstream Frank Sinatra and Peggy Lee. By 1955 Freed was in New York and clearly on a roll. He helped to propel Bill Haley and the Comets's "Rock Around the Clock" to number one. Rock 'n' roll's future was cemented when "Rock Around the Clock" ran under the credits for the 1955 movie *Blackboard Jungle.* Young people flocked to the movie not only for its theme of teen disenchantment and rebellion but also for the music.

LEARNING CHECK

- How did Elvis Presley personify the music traditions that fused into rock 'n' roll?

Rock 'n' Roll in Canada

British Columbia's Red Robinson is credited with bringing rock 'n' roll to Canada. Robinson began playing rhythm and blues records on Vancouver's CJOR as early as 1953. He was also the first to play Elvis Presley on the radio in Canada. While rock 'n' roll is an American musical genre, many Canadians have been successful rock 'n' rollers. Paul Anka is the most obvious Canadian success story. His good looks, combined with his singing and songwriting abilities, brought him success—not only at home, but in the United States.

Anka wasn't alone in having success south of the border. As a member of the Guess Who, Randy Bachman reached the top of the charts in both countries with "These Eyes," "Undun," and, of course, "American Woman." Bachman's success in the United States continued when he left the Guess Who and formed Bachman Turner Overdrive, which reached number one with "You Ain't Seen Nothin' Yet." Throughout the 1960s, 1970s, 1980s, and 1990s, Canadians like Anne Murray, Gordon Lightfoot, Rush, Neil Young, Bryan Adams, Shania Twain, Céline Dion, and others became pop music stars in the United States. This trend continues in the 21st century with Avril Lavigne, Nelly Furtado, and Nickelback carrying the Cancon torch into America. Meanwhile, bands like the Tragically Hip, Sloan, Finger Eleven, and Sum 41 developed loyal followings in Canada but had limited success in the United States.

Rap

rap Dance music with intense bass and rhyming riffs, the lyrics often delivered with antiestablishment defiance.

As transforming as rock 'n' roll was, so too was **rap** 40 years later. Born in the impoverished Bronx section of New York, this new style of music had an intense bass for dancing with rhyming riffs, often delivered in a strong and rapid-fire attitude, overlaid on the music. Slowly, rap spread to other black urban areas. Indie-produced *Run-D.M.C.* and *King of Rock*, both by Run-D.M.C., were the first black rap albums to break into mainstream U.S. music. Major record companies soon were signing rap acts. Controversial groups Public Enemy and N.W.A., which had violence and racism as themes of their songs, made rap a public issue in the 1990s, which only fanned diehard enthusiasm.

Like with rock 'n' roll, major labels missed the significance of early rap, scrambling to catch up only after the catchy lyrics began siphoning sales from older pop genres. A maxim in media studies is that large enterprises become mired in tradition and have an aversion for risk taking.

LEARNING CHECK

- What was the role of independent labels in the rise of rap?
- Why was significant innovation, such as rock 'n' roll and rap, a business challenge for major media companies?

Music as Multimedia Content

Although music often is studied as the content issued by the recording industry, music is hardly a one-dimensional form of media message. Even in pre–mass media eras, going back to prehistoric times, music was integrated with dance and theatre. When movies were establishing themselves, music was an important component. Even before movie soundtracks were introduced with the "talkies," many movie houses hired a piano player who kept one eye on the screen and hammered out supportive music. D.W. Griffith's *The Birth of a Nation* of 1915 had an accompanying score for a 70-piece symphony. Some movies are little more than musical vehicles for popular performers, going back to Bing Crosby and continuing through Elvis Presley and the Beatles.

Early radio recognized the value of music. Jingles and ditties proved key to establishing many brand names. Today, many composers and lyricists derive significant income from their work being built into television, radio, and online advertisements. Jingle houses typically charge national advertisers $20 000 to $40 000, while undiscovered musicians earn a few hundred dollars for a few hours of work. The dynamics of jingles, however, are changing. With CD sales plummeting, established artists are cashing in on their names for radio and television ads. Sound Proof, a talent service that promotes top-name ad music, says that its cost to advertisers is less than the $10 million it can cost to license already-existing music. In some cases, top-name jingles have an afterlife as hit music.

LEARNING CHECK

- What is the difficulty in separating music from other forms of entertainment?

Sports as Media Entertainment

STUDY PREVIEW Early on, mass media people sensed the potential of sports to build their audiences, first through newspapers, then through magazines, radio, and television. The media feed what seems to be an insatiable demand for more sports. Why the huge public intrigue with sports? One expert suggests it's the mix of suspense, heroes, villains, pageantry, and ritual.

Mass Audiences for Sports

The brilliant newspaper publisher **James Gordon Bennett** sensed how a public interest in sports could build circulation for his *New York Herald* in the 1830s. Bennett assigned reporters to cover sports regularly. Fifty years later, with growing interest in horse racing, prize fighting, yacht racing, and baseball, **Joseph Pulitzer** organized the first separate sports department at his *New York World*. Sportswriters then began specializing in different sports.

James Gordon Bennett New York newspaper publisher in 1830s; first to assign reporters to sports regularly.

Joseph Pulitzer New York newspaper publisher in 1880s; organized the first newspaper sports department.

Audience appetite for sports was insatiable. Dozens of writers showed up for the 1897 Corbett–Fitzsimmons heavyweight title fight in remote Nevada. *The New York Times* introduced celebrity coverage in 1910 when it hired retired prizefighter John L. Sullivan to cover the Jeffries–Johnson title bout in Reno.

Sports historians call the 1920s the Golden Era of Sports, with newspapers glorifying athletes. Heroes, some with enduring fame, included Jack Dempsey in boxing, Knute Rockne and Jim Thorpe in football, and Babe Ruth in baseball. The 1920s also marked radio as a medium for sports. In 1921, **KDKA** of Pittsburgh carried the first play-by-play baseball game, the Davis Cup tennis matches, and the blow-by-blow of the Johnny Ray–Johnny Dundee fight. Sportswriter Grantland Rice, the pre-eminent sportswriter of the time, covered the entire World Series live from New York for KDKA, also in 1921. In 1923, *Hockey Night in Canada* began broadcasting on Canadian radio with the legendary **Foster Hewitt** as play-by-play announcer. Within a decade, Saturday night hockey games became a ritual for Canadian hockey fans. "The Hockey Theme," written by Dolores Claman in 1968 and now heard on TSN after being heard for decades on the CBC, is a staple in Canadian hockey households. Even those who aren't hockey fans recognize the song.

KDKA Pittsburgh radio station that pioneered sports broadcasting in 1920s.

Foster Hewitt First play-by-play announcer for *Hockey Night in Canada*.

Sports magazines have their roots in *American Turf Register*, which began a 15-year run in Baltimore in 1829. The *American Bicycling Journal* rode a bicycling craze from 1877 to 1879. Nothing has matched the breadth and scope of *Sports Illustrated*, founded in 1954 by magazine magnate **Henry Luce**. The magazine, launched with 350 000 charter subscribers, now boasts a circulation of 3.3 million a week.

Henry Luce Magazine publisher known for *Time*, *Life*, *Sports Illustrated*, and others.

Although television dabbled in sports from its early days, the introduction of *Wide World of Sports* in 1961 established that television was made for sports and, conversely, that sports was made for television. The show, the brainchild of ABC programming wizard **Roone Arledge**, covered an unpredictable diversity of sports, from ping-pong to skiing. In this period, professional athletic leagues agreed to modify their rules to accommodate commercial breaks and, eventually, to make games more exciting for television audiences.

Roone Arledge ABC television executive responsible for introducing *Wide World of Sports* in 1961.

Television commentator Les Brown explains that sports is the perfect program form for television: "At once topical and entertaining, performed live and suspensefully without a script, peopled with heroes and villains, full of action and human interest and laced with pageantry and ritual."

The launching of ESPN as an all-sports network for cable television systems prompted millions of households to subscribe to cable. By 1984, TSN began broadcasting in Canada. Since then, Sportsnet and The Score offer Canadians their daily dose of sports.

LEARNING CHECK

- What have been landmarks in the growth of media sports for amusement?

MEDIA PEOPLE Greg Oliver

Quebecor Media's Canoe is an excellent example of the recent emergence of online journalism. Canoe is a web portal for all kinds of online news, entertainment, and information. The "SLAM! Sports" link at **www.canoe.ca** will in turn take you to the place **Greg Oliver** has called home since 1996: the SLAM! Wrestling page.

Oliver's been writing about professional wrestling since 1985 when, as a high-school student, he created the *Canadian Wrestling Report*, a monthly newsletter that he published and marketed from his basement for five years. Then, after graduating from Toronto's Ryerson University, Oliver went to work for the *Toronto Sun*. He has also written several books for ECW Press: *The Pro Wrestling Hall of Fame: The Canadians, The Pro Wrestling Hall of Fame: The Tag Teams, The Pro Wrestling Hall of Fame: The Heels, SLAM! Wrestling: Shocking Stories from the Squared Circle,* and *Benoit: Wrestling with the Horror That Destroyed a Family and Crippled a Sport.*

Because wrestling is clearly entertainment, is this legitimate journalism? Greg Oliver thinks so: "SLAM! Wrestling is proof that pro wrestling journalism doesn't need to be an oxymoron. We're legitimate journalists. We just happen to write about wrestling. Wrestlers are fascinating people with fascinating tales. Isn't that what journalism is all about? Journalism is about telling stories. Sure, it's a worked sport, but how is it any different than an actor trying to get his or her break or the young baseball player trying to break into the majors? It's human interest in the end, and that's what any good story should be. We're not rumour mongers. Our strength is talking to people and telling their stories."

Oliver brings up the Chris Benoit double murder–suicide from June 2007 as an example of knowledge of pro wrestling being an asset and of the years of collecting sources being invaluable. "Benoit and I had met over the years, done a few interviews, and exchanged emails. After his best friend, fellow wrestler Eddie Guerrero, died I had sent him a condolence email and he sent back a few revealing looks into his own life and, in retrospect, fragile state of mind. The junk tabloids wanted what I had but, despite them offering twice the money, I sold my work to an Atlanta paper, with the rights to run it online staying with SLAM! Wrestling."

Greg Oliver (left)

Is SLAM! Wrestling true journalism? While many critics and mainstream journalists may not appreciate it, fans certainly do. SLAM! Wrestling gets approximately 50 000 page views a day.

WHAT DO YOU THINK?

1. What genre of storytelling does professional wrestling fall into?
2. What genre of entertainment does it fall into?
3. What makes professional wrestling so popular?

Greg Oliver Wrestling journalist.

Audience and Advertiser Confluence

The television networks and national advertisers found a happy confluence of interest in the huge audience for televised sports. This goes back at least to *Friday Night Fights*, sponsored by Gillette, and *Wednesday Night Fights*, sponsored by Pabst beer, in the 1950s. Today, sports and television are almost synonymous. Not only do the Stanley Cup finals pack fans into arenas, but hockey fans tune in to CBC to watch the games. The World Cup soccer tournament held every four years draws the largest worldwide television audiences.

In part to keep their names onscreen, some firms have bought the rights to put their names on sports stadiums. The value of brand-name exposure at places like the Air Canada Centre, the Bell Centre, or Rexall Place is impossible to measure.

LEARNING CHECK

- Why are advertisers attracted to sports?

Sex as Media Entertainment

STUDY PREVIEW Despite the risk of offending some people's sensitivities, the media have long trafficked in sexual content. Undeniably, there is a market. The media have fought for their right to carry sexually explicit content and for the right of adults to have access to it.

Adult Entertainment

Sexually oriented content has bedevilled the mass media for longer than anyone can remember. Clearly, there is a demand. Sales of banned books soared as soon as the courts overruled government restrictions, as was no better illustrated than by the Irish classic ***Ulysses*** by James Joyce in 1930. Firm data on the profitability of sexual content are hard to come by, partly because definitions are elusive. *Ulysses*, as an example, is hardly a sex book to most people, yet its sexual content once prompted a federal import ban. The difficulty surrounding definitions gives partisans the opportunity to issue exaggerated estimates of the scope of sexual media content.

Ulysses James Joyce novel banned in the United States until 1930 court decision.

It was not a sleazy outfit that first imported *Ulysses* but rather the venerable publisher Random House. Today, the major purveyors of adult content include Astral Media's TMN, which pipes late-night adult content to subscribers. Satellite providers Shaw and Bell TV also offer porn to their subscribers. Big-name hotel chains provide adult movies in their rooms, for a fee.

Pornography versus Obscenity in Canada

The Broadcasting Act states that Canadian broadcasters cannot broadcast anything "obscene," so why are sexually explicit movies available through all cable companies and satellite providers? The reason is simple: there is a difference between **pornography** and **obscenity** in Canada. This availability is due in large part to the 1992 **Butler ruling** by the Supreme Court of Canada. It has been the basis for the definition of obscenity in Canada. The Supreme Court ruled that any material that mixed sex with violence, included depictions of children having sex, or included any sex that is degrading or dehumanizing was obscene. Any other sexually explicit material would not seem to be considered obscene because, as the decision stated, under Canada's Charter of Rights and Freedoms, laws can't "inhibit the celebration of human sexuality."

pornography Sexually explicit depictions that are protected from government bans.

obscenity Sexually explicit media depictions that the government can ban.

Butler ruling Supreme Court ruling that defined legal differences between obscenity and pornography.

LEARNING CHECK

- Why is government regulation of sexual media content difficult?
- How are obscenity and pornography different?

Gaming as Media Content

STUDY PREVIEW Gaming has grown as a form of mass entertainment. Some games outdraw television. As is typical with new media content, gaming has become a whipping boy for society's ills with calls to restrict it. The courts have not found compelling reasons to impose restrictions.

Growing Entertainment Form

Nobody could doubt the significance of video games as a media form after 2001. Sales in the United States outpaced movies. In 2004, when Microsoft introduced Halo 2, it was a news event. Retailers nationwide opened at midnight on the release date to thousands of fans waiting in line, some for as long as 14 hours. Within 24 hours, sales surpassed $125 million—way ahead of the $70 million opening-weekend box office for that year's leading film, *The Incredibles*.

Watch

A Day in the Life: **"Inside the Video Game Industry (Activision)"**

The time that enthusiasts spend playing video games is catching up with the time spent watching television. Players of *Madden NFL 2004* each spent an estimated average of 100 hours a year on the game. With 4 million players, that is 400 million hours. By comparison, *The Sopranos*, at its heyday in 2004, claimed 143 million viewing hours across its full season. Do the math: *The Sopranos* averaged 11 million viewers for each of 13 episodes that year.

To catch consumers who spend less time with television and more time with video games, advertisers have shifted chunks of their budgets to gaming. The potential is incredible. The Entertainment Software Association of Canada says that almost half of Canadian households own a video game system. It's not just kids playing, either: the average age of a gamer in Canada is almost 36 years, plus women now make up 35 percent of the video game market in Canada.

LEARNING CHECK

- Why is gaming attractive as an advertising vehicle?

Impact of Gaming

Although gaming is distinctive as a form of media content, market-savvy executives have extended their franchise to other forms. The 2001 movie *Lara Croft: Tomb Raider*, adopted from a 1996 game and six sequels, generated $131 million in U.S. box office. *Resident Evil* grossed $90 million, while *Mortal Kombat* grossed $135 million. There is inverse cross-fertilization as well. Games have been based on movies, including *James Bond*, *Matrix*, *Shrek*, *Spider-Man*, and *Star Wars*. Gaming shows on television and gaming magazines have proliferated.

Music ranging from orchestral to hip-hop has replaced the blips and bleeps of early-generation games. For recorded music companies and artists, landing a spot in a game can provide wider exposure than MTV. For *Madden NFL 2005*, game manufacturer Electronic Arts auditioned 2500 songs submitted by recording companies. Twenty-one ended up in the game. Phoenix-based band Minibosses plays nothing but Nintendo music, note for note.

Not surprisingly, the integration of gaming into larger media conglomerates is under way. The Warner Brothers movie studio now has a gaming division. So does Disney's Buena Vista. Sumner Redstone, whose media empire includes CBS and MTV, has bought into the Midway gaming company. Hollywood and New York talent agencies have divisions that look for game roles for their client actors.

LEARNING CHECK

- Why is gaming shedding its status as a niche media?

Censorship and Gaming

Like other entertainment forms, gaming is a lightning rod of concern about the effects of explicit violence and sex on children. The industry devised a voluntary rating system ranging from EC for "early childhood" to AO for "adults only," but critics have called the system a joke among retailers. Three high-visibility American senators—Evan Bayh of Indiana, Hillary Clinton of New York, and Joe Lieberman of Connecticut—proposed a $5000 fine for every time a retailer violates the rating code for children under 17.

Madden NFL The sudden potency of gaming as a media content form was no better illustrated than with Electronic Arts' *Madden NFL 2004*, which earned $200 million within four months. *Chicago*, the Oscar-winning movie at that time, took nine months to earn $171 million. *Courtesy of Electronic Arts*

Similar attempts to codify ratings through law have not been viewed kindly in the courts. Since 2001, federal judges have found a lack of compelling evidence from opponents who claim that games like *Grand Theft Auto: San Andreas* cause harm. If anyone ever demonstrates that a game begets violent behaviour, the courts may change their stance. It would appear that Canada's Charter of Rights and Freedoms gives protection to game makers as freedom of expression and to game players as freedom to inquire and explore.

LEARNING CHECK

- How have gaming companies responded to calls to censor violence and sex?

Artistic Values

Watch

ABC's *Nightline:* "Blogebreties"

STUDY PREVIEW The mass media are inextricably linked with culture because it is through the media that creative people have their strongest sway. Although the media have the potential to disseminate the best creative work of the human mind and soul, some critics say that the media are obsessive about trendy, often silly subjects.

Media Content as Art

Mass media messages can be art of a high order, as was perhaps no better illustrated than by early filmmaker D.W. Griffith. In the 1910s, Griffith proved himself a filmmaking author whose contribution to the culture, for better or worse, was original in scale, content, and style. Griffith had something to say, and the new mass medium of film was the vehicle for his message.

In the 1950s, when French New Wave directors were offering distinctive stories and messages, film critic **André Bazin** devised the term **auteur** to denote their significant and original cinematic contributions. Bazin's auteurs included Jean-Luc Godard, who made *Breathless*, and François Truffaut, who made *The 400 Blows*. Their work was marked by distinctive cinematic techniques—freeze-frames, handheld cameras, and novel angles, many of them common in movies today. Perhaps the most famous of these highbrow filmmakers who developed a global following was the Swedish director Ingmar Bergman, who made *The Seventh Seal* and other dark, moody, and autobiographical works.

André Bazin French film critic who devised the term *auteur* for significant cutting-edge filmmakers.

auteur A filmmaker recognized for significant and original treatments.

American filmmakers have also contributed to the auteur movement. Among them was Stanley Kubrick, who directed *2001: A Space Odyssey.* Other notable contemporary American film auteurs include Martin Scorsese, whose films include *Taxi Driver*; David Lynch, who made *Blue Velvet*; and Spike Lee, who focuses on African-American life. In Canadian cinema, both David Cronenberg and Atom Egoyan are noted auteurs.

LEARNING CHECK

- Which media content easily ranks as worthy art?

Lesser Art

To be sure, not all media content is high art.

Production-Line Entertainment A television soap opera, whatever its entertainment value, lacks the creative genius of Leonard Cohen's novels, poetry, or music. Why can't all media content rank high on an artistic scale? Besides the obvious explanation that not everyone is born a Leonard Cohen, the modern mass media are commercial enterprises that must produce vast quantities of material. In the 1920s, for example, an insatiable public demand for movies led to the creation of the Hollywood **studio system**, in effect turning moviemaking into a factory process. Production quotas drove movie production. The studios, loaded with money, hired leading authors of the day, including F. Scott Fitzgerald and William Faulkner, for creative storylines and scripts, but relentless demands for material drained them. It has been said that Hollywood had some of the most gifted writers of the time doing their weakest work.

studio system A production-line movie production system devised by Hollywood in the 1920s.

The factory model, a product of the Industrial Age, extends throughout the media. The Canadian book publisher **Harlequin**, owned by Torstar, grinds out romance novels with their bodice-busting covers. Nobody confuses them with high art. Imagine, also, filling a television network's prime-time obligation: 42 half-hour slots a week. It can't all be great stuff, despite the promotional claims in pre-season ramp-ups. Besides, many in the mass audience don't want great art anyway.

Harlequin Canadian publisher known for romances with clichéd characters, settings, and themes; the term is applied generically to pulp romances.

Copycat Content

Significant amounts of media content are imitative. Copycat sounds abound in material from the recording industry. In network television, a sudden success, such as Fox's *American Idol*, spawns other talent-based reality shows, including *Canadian Idol.* Alas,

CASE STUDY

Has Hollywood Institutionalized Racism?

Following Hurricane Katrina, filmmaker Spike Lee was commissioned by HBO to create a two-hour documentary about the devastation. After a scouting trip to New Orleans, Lee told HBO he would need four hours and twice the budget. He got it.

That hasn't always been the case for the controversial, award-winning filmmaker. His breakout film, *She's Gotta Have It,* was made for $175 000 in 12 days at a single location and edited in Lee's apartment. It won an award for best new film at the 1986 Cannes Film Festival and eventually grossed more than $7 million.

However, even after he proved that black films about race relations could be profitable, finding financing has never been easy for Lee.

He spent years trying to raise money to make a movie about Jackie Robinson, who broke Major League Baseball's colour barrier in 1947. Robert Redford convinced Robinson's wife, now in her eighties, to take back the rights from Lee because Redford had the means to finance the movie. Redford himself plans to star as Branch Rickey, the Brooklyn Dodgers owner who signed Robinson. Commentator Gordon Jackson of *The Dallas Examiner* writes, "With white writers and producers, will Branch Rickey's character come out more of a hero than Robinson?"

Most Hollywood movies about African-Americans centre on "relatively insignificant white people," asserts writer Gabriella Beckles. She points to *Blood Diamond*, in which the black character was relegated to sidekick status.

While Lee acknowledges a rise in the number of African-American actors, such as Halle Berry, who can get $14 million for a movie, and Will Smith and Denzel Washington, who can command more than $20 million, he says that the television and film industries think they "just have to have black people on the screen, and don't care about the images."

For the characterizations of African-Americans on television and in films to change, Lee says, blacks need to achieve positions of power in those industries in order to have some control over the images that are produced.

Spike Lee

DEEPENING YOUR MEDIA LITERACY

Explore the Issue

Write down what you think makes a black film "black." Is it the story, the actors, or the director (or some combination of these)?

Dig Deeper

The 2000 U.S. census estimated that African-Americans comprise 13 percent of the American population, and black moviegoers are estimated to make up 25 to 30 percent of film audiences. Based on these figures, what percentage of films would you expect to be black films?

Get several copies of a publication with more than four ads for current movies. Does the percentage of ads for black films match the percentage of the black population?

What Do You Think?

Do you think Spike Lee's claim of racism in the entertainment industry is true?

even *American Idol* was hardly original. The concept was licensed from *Pop Idol*, a British show. In 2007, Global aired *Deal or No Deal Canada* as a way of cashing in on the success of the game show hosted by Howie Mandel in the United States.

Cross-Media Adaptations

The demand for content creates a vacuum that sucks up material from other media. Movie studios draw heavily on written literature, from bestselling novels to comic books to graphic novels. Conversely, fresh movies sometimes are adapted into book form.

Cross-media adaptations don't always work well. Movie versions of books often disappoint readers. Scenes change, as do characters. Inevitably, a lot is left out of the movie version. Some of the criticism is unfair because it fails to recognize that movies are a distinct medium. How, for example, could a screenwriter pack everything from a 100 000-word novel into a 100-minute script? These are different media. Remember McLuhan's idea that "the medium is the message." Passages that work brilliantly in a word-driven medium such as a short story can fall flat in a medium that has visual enhancements. Conversely, the nuances compactly portrayed by a master actor such as Meryl Streep or Jack Nicholson could take pages and pages to convey in a book and not work as well. Also, movie producers almost always need to appeal to the widest possible audience and so will alter plots, scenes, and characters and sometimes even change a storyline's climactic events.

Some cross-media adaptations are commercial disasters. Despite high expectations, the video game version of James Cameron's *Avatar* received mixed reviews in 2009. The explanation? Some critics cite the same difficulties that occur when transferring messages from books to movies. With video games, the audience member plays an active role by exercising some control over the storyline. Watching a movie, however, is relatively passive.

LEARNING CHECK

- What mass media dynamics work against consistent delivery of quality content?

Unpretentious Media Content

Although critics pan a lot of media content as unworthy, the fact is that lowbrow art and middlebrow art find audiences, sometimes large audiences, and have a firm place in the mix that the mass media offer. There is nothing artistically pretentious in **pulp fiction,** including Harlequin romances, or its soap-opera equivalents on television. However, this lack of pretension can have its own campy charm.

pulp fiction Quickly and inexpensively produced, easy-to-read short novels.

Elitist versus Populist Values

The mass media can enrich society by disseminating the best of human creativity, including great literature, music, and art. The media also carry a lot of lesser things that reflect the culture and, for better or worse, contribute to it. Over time, a continuum has been devised that covers this vast range of artistic production. At one extreme is artistic material that requires sophisticated and cultivated tastes to appreciate. This is called **high art.** At the other extreme is **low art,** which requires little sophistication to enjoy.

One strain of traditional media criticism has been that the media underplay great works and concentrate on low art. This **elitist** view argues that the mass media do society a disservice by pandering to low tastes. To describe low art, elitists sometimes use the German word **kitsch,** which translates roughly as "garish" or "trashy." The word captures their disdain. In contrast, the **populist** view is that there is nothing unbecoming in the mass media catering to mass tastes in a democratic, capitalistic society.

In a 1960 essay titled "Masscult and Midcult" that is still widely cited, social commentator **Dwight Macdonald** made a virulent case that all popular art is kitsch. The mass media, which depend on finding large audiences for their economic base, can hardly ever come out at the higher reaches of Macdonald's spectrum.

This kind of elitist analysis was given a larger framework in 1976 when sociologist **Herbert Gans** categorized cultural work along socioeconomic and intellectual lines. Gans said that classical music, as an example, appealed by and large to people of academic and professional accomplishments with higher incomes. These were **high-culture audiences,** which enjoyed complexities and subtleties in their art and entertainment. Next came **middle-culture audiences,** which were less abstract in their interests and liked Norman Rockwell and prime-time television. **Low-culture audiences** were factory and service workers whose interests were more basic; whose educational accomplishments, incomes, and social status were lower; and whose media tastes leaned toward kung fu movies, comic books, and supermarket tabloids.

Gans was applying his contemporary observations to flesh out the distinctions that had been taking form in art criticism for centuries—the distinctions between high art and low art.

high art Requires sophisticated taste to be appreciated.

low art Can be appreciated by almost everybody.

elitist Mass media should gear to sophisticated audiences.

kitsch Pejorative word for trendy, trashy low art.

populist Mass media should seek largest possible audiences.

Dwight Macdonald Said that all pop art is kitsch.

Herbert Gans Said that social, economic, and intellectual levels of audience coincide.

high-, middle-, and low-culture audiences Continuum identified by Herbert Gans.

Highbrow The high art favoured by elitists generally can be identified by its technical and thematic complexity and originality. High art is often highly individualistic because the creator, whether a novelist or a television producer, has explored issues in fresh ways, often with new and different methods. Even when it's a collaborative effort, a piece of high art is distinctive. High art requires a sophisticated audience to appreciate it fully. Often it has enduring value, surviving the test of time as to its significance and worth.

highbrow, middlebrow, and lowbrow Levels of media content sophistication that coincide with audience tastes.

The sophistication that permits an opera aficionado to appreciate the intricacies of a composer's score, the poetry of the lyricist, and the excellence of the performance sometimes is called **highbrow.** The label has grim origins in the idea that a person must have great intelligence to have refined tastes, and that a "high brow" is necessary to accommodate such a big brain. Generally, the term is used by people who disdain those who have not developed the sophistication to enjoy, for example, the abstractions of a Fellini film, a Matisse sculpture, or a Picasso painting. Highbrows generally are people who, as Gans noted, are interested in issues by which society is defining itself and look to literature and drama for stories on conflicts inherent in the human condition and between the individual and society.

Middlebrow **Middlebrow** tastes recognize some artistic merit but don't have a high level of sophistication. There is more interest in action than abstractions—in Captain Kirk aboard the Starship Enterprise, for example, than in the childhood struggles of Ingmar Bergman that shaped his films. In socioeconomic terms, middlebrow appeals to people who take comfort in media portrayals that support their status quo orientation and values.

Lowbrow Someone once made this often-repeated distinction: Highbrows talk about ideas, middlebrows talk about things, and **lowbrows** talk about people. Judging from the circulation success of the *National Enquirer, Hello!* and other celebrity tabloids, there must be a lot of lowbrows in contemporary North America. Hardly any sophistication is needed to recognize the machismo of Rambo, the villainy of Darth Vader, the heroism of Superman, or the sexiness of Lara Croft.

LEARNING CHECK

- What kinds of scales can be used to rank creative activity?

The Case against Pop Art

Pop art is of the moment, including things like body piercings and hip-hop garb and trendy media fare. Even elitists may have fun with pop, but they traditionally have drawn the line at anyone who mistakes it as having serious artistic merit. Pop art is low art that has immense although generally short-lived popularity.

popular art Art that tries to succeed in the marketplace.

Elitists see pop art as contrived and artificial. In their view, the people who create **popular art** are masters at identifying what will succeed in the marketplace and then providing it. According to this view, pop art succeeds by conning people into liking it. When capri pants were the fashion rage in 2006, it was not because they were superior in comfort, utility, or aesthetics but because promoters sensed that profits could be made by touting them through the mass media as new and cashing in on easily manipulated mass tastes. It was the same with pet rocks, Tickle-Me Elmo, and countless other products.

According to the critics, the mass media are obsessed with pop art. This is partly because the media are the carriers of the promotional campaigns that create popular followings but also because competition within the media creates pressure to be first, to be ahead, and to be on top of things. The result, say elitists, is that junk takes precedence over quality.

Much can said for this criticism of pop art. The success of Canada's *Trailer Park Boys,* as an example, created an eager audience that otherwise might have been reading something more critically "respectable." An elitist might chortle, even laugh, at the unbelievable antics and travails of Bubbles, Randy, and Mr. Lahey but might also be concerned all the while that low art is displacing high art in the marketplace and that society is the poorer for it.

LEARNING CHECK

- Why do elitists frown on pop art?

Pop Art Revisionism

Pop art has always had a few champions among intellectuals, although the voices of **pop art revisionism** often have been drowned out in the din of elitist pooh-poohing. In 1965, however, essayist **Susan Sontag** wrote an influential piece titled "On Culture and the New Sensibility" that prompted many elitists to take a fresh look at pop art.

pop art revisionism Pop art has inherent value.

Susan Sontag Saw cultural and social value in pop art.

Pop Art as Evocative Sontag made the case that pop art could raise serious issues, just as high art could. She wrote: "The feeling given off by a Rauschenberg painting might be like that of a song by the Supremes." Sontag soon was being called the High Priestess of Pop Intellectualism. More significantly, the Supremes were being taken more seriously, as were a great number of Sontag's avant-garde and obscure pop artist friends.

Pop Art as a Societal Unifier In effect, Sontag encouraged people not to look at art on the traditional divisive, class-conscious, elitist–populist continuum. Artistic value, she said, could be found almost anywhere. The word *camp* gained circulation among 1960s elitists who were influenced by Sontag. These highbrows began finding a perversely sophisticated appeal in pop art as diverse as Andy Warhol's banal soup cans and ABC's outrageous television show *Batman*.

High Art as Popular While kitsch may be prominent in media programming, it hardly elbows out all substantive content. In 1991, for example, Ken Burns's public television documentary *The Civil War* outdrew low-art prime-time programs on ABC, CBS, and NBC for five nights in a row. It was a glaring example that high art can appeal to people across almost the whole range of socioeconomic levels and is not necessarily driven out by low art. Burns's documentary was hardly a lone example. Another, also from 1991, was Franco Zeffirelli's movie *Hamlet*, starring pop movie star Mel Gibson, which was marketed to a mass audience yet could hardly be dismissed by elitists as kitsch.

LEARNING CHECK

- How do pop art revisionists defend pop art?

Chapter 3 Wrap-Up

Entertainment content of the mass media draws huge audiences and drives the economics of most media companies. The drama inherent in good storytelling is a major component that dates to prehistoric tribal gatherings around the campfire. The modern-day campfire is books, movies, and television. The emotive power of music, which also has prehistoric roots, is another major component of today's mass media entertainment content. So is sports, which has all of the fascination of compelling literature to keep people tuned in until the outcome reveals itself. Sometimes overlooked as a genre in media content is sex, probably best explained by the great mystery of sexuality and by irrepressible curiosity.

Mass media are not mere conduits for entertainment. The media themselves shape entertainment. Changes in media technology have thrust musical styles into popularity. The huge audiences that mass media can attract also shape entertainment content. The powerhouse media companies seek content that will attract national and even global audiences, which places a premium on entertainment that travels easily and widely.

Deepening Your Media Literacy: Entertainment

PEARSON mycanadiancommunicationlab

Visit **www.mycanadiancommunicationlab.ca** for access to a wealth of tools and resources that will enhance your learning experience. Features include the following:

- Personalized Study Plan
- Videos
- Activities
- Pearson eText–and much more!

Questions for Critical Thinking

1. Do you prefer live or mediated performance? Why? In which do you participate more often?
2. How do genres both clarify and cloud serious discussion of the quality of mass media content?
3. How do you explain the exponential growth of sports as a form of entertainment?
4. What is driving gaming into its new status as a mass media vehicle?
5. What are the legal obstacles facing people who oppose sexual content in mass media?
6. What works against the presence of significant art and creativity in mass media content?

Keeping Up to Date

Rolling Stone contains serious articles on music and movies.

Entertainment Weekly is one among an array of fan magazines, many of which are more gaga over celebrities than concerned with media issues.

Because the mass media are a major industry, you can find regular coverage of media entertainment issues in *The Globe and Mail*, the *National Post*, the *Toronto Star*, *Maclean's*, and other publications.

Print

4

LEARNING AHEAD

- Newspapers are the major source of news for most Canadians.
- Most newspapers are owned by chains, although chain ownership is in flux.
- Newspapers have gone online, but few have embraced their online potential fully.
- Most Canadian newspapers are local or metropolitan, with only two national dailies.
- Magazine innovations have included long-form journalism and visuals.
- Many magazine titles are unavailable on newsracks.
- Most magazines today are edited for segments of the mass audience.
- Magazines face challenges today from demassified sites and television.

Mary Junck The case of Mary Junck and the Lee Enterprises newspaper chain indicates that newspapers are not a dying medium, especially when it comes to local news.

MEDIA IN THEORY

Are Newspapers Dying?

Early in the 21st century, many felt that newspapers were a dying medium. There was certainly a lot of evidence to support this, as the *Rocky Mountain News* (Denver), the *Seattle Post-Intelligencer,* and *The Daily News* (Halifax) all closed down. Most newspapers were experiencing declining readership.

But don't tell Mary Junck that newspapers are past their prime as a mass medium. Since 1999, when she took over the Lee Enterprises newspaper chain, she has increased both circulation and profit at most of the company's 58 dailies.

Junck says that the secret to success for 21st-century newspapers includes a strong emphasis on local news. She earned a master's degree in journalism at the University of North Carolina and then rose to newspaper management through advertising. At Lee Enterprises, she created the position of vice-president for news to help local editors strengthen their coverage. This was at a time when many newspapers, facing declining advertising revenue in a sour economy, were cutting back on newsroom budgets.

If anyone asks Junck about Lee Enterprises's priorities, she whips out a business card featuring a five-point mission statement. There, prominently, is "Emphasize strong local news." Other Junck priorities are: "Grow revenue creatively and rapidly." "Improve readership and circulation." "Build our online future." "Exercise careful cost controls."

Mike Stobel, a columnist for the *Toronto Sun,* seems to agree with Junck. In his 2010 article titled "Don't Stop the Presses," he stated that "today's newspaper is the sum of its

MEDIA TIMELINE The Printed Word

1844 George Brown founded *The Globe and Mail.*

1905 *Busy Man's Magazine*, which would eventually be renamed *Maclean's*, was founded by John Baynes Maclean.

1955 Bohemian New York literati founded *The Village Voice.*

1956 O'Leary Commission looked at magazine publishing in Canada.

1967 Jim Michaels founded the Los Angeles–based *Advocate*, the first gay newspaper.

1970 Davey Committee examined Canadian newspapers.

1981 Kent Commission: more investigation of Canadian newspaper ownership.

1996 Magazines went online with Pathfinder and Time Warner. Others followed.

1998 Conrad Black launched the *National Post*.

2001 CanWest Global purchased the *National Post* from Conrad Black.

2001 Bell Globemedia, now known as CTVglobemedia, converged broadcasting and print.

2007 Amazon released Kindle, its handheld electronic e-book reader.

2008 *The Daily News* in Halifax ceased publication.

2009 CanWest Global filed for bankruptcy protection and put the *National Post* and other newspapers up for sale.

2009 Sony Reader, a handheld electronic e-book reader, introduced.

2010 Apple introduced the iPad, a tablet computer that can be used as an e-book reader.

2010 BCE sold *The Globe and Mail* to the Woodbridge Company, owned by Thomson.

printed and Internet parts, but it's still a newspaper. No Virginia, newspapers are not dying. Au contraire. And thank goodness. Think of how miserable life would be without them."

Life without newspapers? Not anytime soon, according to some people.

Importance of Newspapers

STUDY PREVIEW The newspaper industry is in crisis even though it's still large, profitable, and dominant in local coverage. Readers younger than 40 are hard to attract. Attempts to reach younger readers have included flashy big-city tabloids designed as quick reads.

Newspaper Industry Dimensions

The newspaper industry dwarfs other news media by almost every measure. More than half of all adult Canadians read a newspaper every day. The data are staggering:

- 98 daily newspapers put out 4.3 million copies a day in Canada. Including weekend editions, 30.6 million daily newspapers are sold in Canada each week. In the United States there are 1570 daily newspapers.
- 646 weekly newspapers in Canada publish 12.8 million copies each week; 74 percent of Canadians read their local weekly newspaper.

Sources: *The Canadian Newspaper Association's Scoop on Daily Newspapers in Canada (2008) and Canadian Community Newspapers Association's Snapshot 2007.*

Perhaps because television has stolen the glitz and romance that newspapers once had, the significance of newspapers is easy to miss. Although newspaper revenue is slipping, newspapers are a medium of choice for advertising. Canadian daily newspapers attracted $3.6 billion in revenues in 2008. Except for brief downturns in the overall economy and an occasional exceptional situation, daily newspapers were consistently profitable enterprises through the 20th century and into the early 21st century. Although it is facing difficult times, the newspaper is not to be underrated.

There is no foreign ownership of Canadian newspapers. According to the Income Tax Act, a newspaper is Canadian if the type is set in Canada, it is printed in Canada, and it is published by Canadians.

LEARNING CHECK

- Newspapers currently face challenges with regard to decline in readership but remain important. How so?

Content Diversity and Depth

In most communities, newspapers cover more news at greater depth than competing media. A metropolitan daily such as *The Province* (Vancouver) may carry hundreds of items—more than any British Columbia television or radio station and at greater length. Magazines, for example, offer more depth on selected stories, but the magazines are published relatively infrequently and run relatively few articles.

Cool Medium? The Canadian Newspaper Association's advertising campaign seems to be saying something about the value of reading a newspaper. Referring to the ideas of Marshall McLuhan discussed in Chapter 1, are newspapers a "hot" or "cool" medium?

Newspapers have a rich mix of content: news, advice, comics, opinion, puzzles, and data. It's all there to tap in to at will. Some people go right for the stock market tables, while others head to the sports section or a favourite columnist.

All of this does not mean that the newspaper industry is not facing problems from competing media, new technology, and ongoing lifestyle shifts. But to date, newspapers have reacted to change with surprising effectiveness. To offset the inroads made by television, newspapers have put new emphasis on being a visual medium and have shed their drab graphics for colour and aesthetics. To accommodate the work schedule transition in recent decades from factory jobs starting at 7 a.m. to service jobs starting at 9 a.m., newspapers have emphasized morning editions, now that more people have a little extra time in the morning, and phased out afternoon editions, because more people are at work later in the day. Knowing that the days of ink-on-paper technology are limited, the newspaper industry is examining electronic delivery methods for the 21st century. Some problems, such as the aversion many young people have to newspapers, are truly daunting. Also, chain ownership has raised fundamental questions about how well newspapers can do their work and still meet the profit expectations of shareholders.

LEARNING CHECK

- What are the implications of newspapers as essential lifestyle products for most people over age 40 but not for younger people?
- What explains this generational dividing line at age 40?

Explore

Deepening Your Media Literacy: Can a newspaper have a personality?

TABLE 4.1

Top Newspapers in Canada

Here are the top newspapers in Canada, ranked by weekly circulation, according to the Canadian Newspaper Association. Note the impact of conglomeration and convergence in terms of the ownership groups.

Newspaper	Weekly Circulation	Ownership Group
Toronto Star	2.2 million	Torstar
The Globe and Mail	1.9 million	Woodbridge
Le Journal de Montréal	1.5 million	Quebecor
La Presse (Montreal)	1.5 million	Power Corporation
The Gazette (Montreal)	1.1 million	Postmedia Network
The Vancouver Sun	1.1 million	Postmedia Network
Toronto Sun	1.0 million	Quebecor/Sun Media
The Province (Vancouver)	977 000	Postmedia Network
National Post	940 000	Postmedia Network
Ottawa Citizen	867 000	Postmedia Network

Source: *Canadian Newspaper Association, Canadian Daily Newspaper Circulation Data 2009. Reprinted with permission.*

Newspaper Products

Watch

ABC's Nightline: "The Most (Un)Reliable Name in News"

STUDY PREVIEW As ink-on-paper products, newspapers fall into numerous categories —broadsheet and tabloid among them. Newspapers have added web and mobile editions of their print editions, although some papers update their websites during the day.

Print Products

The first modern newspapers in the penny press period (see Chapter 10) were pint-sized. Ben Day's pioneering *New York Sun* of 1833 was the size of a handbill. Canada's first newspaper, *The Halifax Gazette*, founded in 1752, was about half the size of a sheet of foolscap paper. As large, steam-powered presses were introduced and as paper supplies became plentiful, page sizes grew into what came to be called broadsheets. Some were so wide that pages had nine two-inch columns per page, although 50-inch paper, folded into 25-inch wide pages, became standard until the 1980s.

To save costs, the newspaper industry settled on a trimmer new size, called **SAU**, short for **standard advertising unit**, in the 1980s. The SAU format made it easier for big advertisers to place ads in multiple papers, all with standardized dimensions. The introduction of SAU precipitated an almost universal change to a six-column format, in contrast with the formerly dominant eight-column format. The saving in newsprint cost was significant. A downside was that there was less room for news and other content.

standard advertising unit (SAU) A trimmer newspaper broadsheet format with standardized dimensions; introduced in the 1980s.

tabloid A newspaper format with pages half the size of a broadsheet; typically five columns wide and 14 to 18 inches long; not necessarily sensationalistic despite a connotation the term has acquired.

Mario Garcia Newspaper design expert who champions tabloid formats.

Tabloids

The word **tabloid** has a second-rate connotation from papers featuring eye-catching but tawdry headlines, but newspaper people use the word in a clinical sense for a half-size newspaper that is convenient to hold. Ironically, considering the association of the words *tabloid* and *sensationalism*, none of the papers in the sensationalistic yellow press period (which you will read about in Chapter 10) were tabloids—with the exception of a one-day experiment conducted by New York publisher Joseph Pulitzer on the first day of the 20th century to illustrate the newspaper of the future.

In recent years, with continuing readership declines, especially among young adults, newspaper executives have discovered through surveys that people prefer compact newspapers. The world's leading newspaper designer, **Mario Garcia**, traverses the globe for comprehensive redesigns. Garcia's team makes two to three broadsheet-to-tabloid conversions a month. Laura Gordon, in charge of a *Dallas Morning News* tabloid variation called *Quick*, makes the point that tabloids are portable in ways that broadsheets are not: "We call it the Taco Test, the idea that you can have a newspaper open and have a taco at Taco Bell without going into other people's space."

Still, the word *tabloid* carries a stigma. Garcia said in an interview with the trade journal *Editor & Publisher* that one of his newspaper clients wanted a tabloid prototype designed but couldn't handle the word *tabloid*: "He told me, 'You can do a tabloid—but don't call it a tabloid.'" Alternatives include *compact newspaper* and *laptop newspaper.*

The tabloid format is gaining popularity in Canada and many Canadian newspapers are changing formats. Tabloids account for about one-quarter of total newspaper circulation in Canada. This trend toward tabloids is expected to continue.

Downsizing The traditional broadsheet newspaper is giving way to the tabloid format, which tends to be more popular with both readers and advertisers. The downside to moving to a tabloid format is the negative connotation of the word *tabloid* to describe newspaper content.

RED EYE

Friday
September 21, 2007

An edition of the Chicago Tribune
redeyechicago.com

★ FREE ★

A protester joins thousands who attended a march Thursday in Jena, La.
(GETTY IMAGES PHOTO)

THE TRUE JESSICA ALBA
PAGE 48

Bears brace for T.O. and the 'Boys
PAGE 28

O.J. flies home— in coach
PAGE 7

metromix
It's Winefest in Chicago
PAGE 39

OUTRAGE & ACTION

Web-fueled protest over race and the justice system grows into civil rights surge PAGES 8-9

FREE THE JENA SIX

LEARNING CHECK

- Are the newspapers in your area broadsheets or tabloids?
- How did the word *tabloid* become corrupted to mean tawdry sensationalism?

Web Editions

The Albuquerque Tribune created the first newspaper website in 1992. It was "shovelware," meaning that it took items from the print edition and placed them on the web without much adaptation. However, this was a start. Other newspapers picked up on the idea, testing whether online readership would attract additional advertising. Early newspaper sites were not instant money-makers, but they gave newspapers a foothold in the new medium and didn't cost much.

When blogs became the rage during the 2004 election in the United States, *USA Today* put columnists and reporters online to interact with readers. The newspaper, in effect, hosted reader chat rooms on a wide range of subjects. Said editor Ken Paulson, "It's about responding to news." Other papers followed suit.

Newspaper-sponsored blogs are not without difficulties, among them the traditional North American journalistic premise that news must be presented in a detached, neutral tone. Joe Strupp, writing in the trade journal *Editor & Publisher*, put it this way: "Reporting can stray into the quicksand of opinion—leaving many writers wishing they had kept their mouths shut." At this point in the evolution of news blogging, the idea is for reporters to go beyond carefully crafting stories toward engaging in a spontaneous dialogue to add dimension, background, and interpretation—more than appears in their print coverage.

LEARNING CHECK

- How do you explain newspapers not being innovators in online news?
- Can reporters in online interactive conversations avoid what's been called "the quicksand of opinion"?

Free Distribution

Experiments with free mini-editions have been conducted in several European cities and then imitated in Canada and the United States. Designed as quick reads, the papers, issued weekdays, boil down content into snappy tidbits aimed at mass transit commuters. Much of the content is entertainment-oriented and of a "gee-whiz" variety, which editors perceive to be of interest to the elusive under-40 readers. The question, still up in the air, is whether these papers will attract sufficient long-term advertising for them to remain viable as giveaways. Examples of these publications include *Metro* and *24H*. They are available in Montreal, Toronto, Edmonton, Halifax, and other large Canadian cities.

LEARNING CHECK

- What is the typical content of giveaway dailies?
- Do free-distribution papers, with their superficial and entertainment-oriented thrust, insult young readers? Or is this what young adults want?

Newspaper Chain Ownership

STUDY PREVIEW High profits in the newspaper industry fuelled the growth of chains, which consolidated the ownership of newspapers into fewer and fewer major companies. This has created some issues in recent years.

Trend toward Chains

Reasoning that he could multiply profits by owning multiple newspapers, **William Randolph Hearst** put together a chain of big-city newspapers in the late 1880s. Although Hearst's chain was not the first, his empire became the model in the public's mind for much that was both good and bad about **newspaper chains**. Like other chains, Hearst's expanded into magazines, radio, and television. Chain ownership is also coming to dominate weeklies, which had long been a bastion of independent ownership, in both the United States and Canada.

William Randolph Hearst Chain owner who dictated the contents of all of his newspapers.

newspaper chain Company that owns several newspapers.

Is chain ownership good? The question raised in Hearst's time was whether diverse points of view were as likely to get into print if ownership were concentrated in fewer and fewer hands. While **local autonomy** is consistent with North American journalistic values, a corporate focus on profits raises a dark new question: Are chains so myopic about profits that they forget to practise good journalism? These are the types of questions that were the basis of two royal commissions in Canada: The Davey Committee in 1970 and the Kent Commission in 1981.

local autonomy Independence from chain headquarters.

In 1970, a special Senate committee on the status of the mass media in Canada, headed by Senator Keith Davey, released its report about the state of Canadian newspapers. In its report, the **Davey Committee** noted that "the media is passing into fewer and fewer hands, and that the experts agree that this trend is likely to continue."

Davey Committee 1970 Royal Commission into media ownership.

A little more than 10 years later, the situation had not improved. Ownership of Canada's newspapers, particularly in Quebec, had fallen into fewer and fewer hands. The 1981 **Kent Commission** on newspaper ownership in Canada, headed by Tom Kent, came about following an incident that was too convenient to be coincidental. On the same day in August 1980, the *Ottawa Journal*, which had been publishing for 94 years and was owned by the Thomson chain, and *The Winnipeg Tribune*, 90 years old and owned by the Southam chain, closed their doors and ceased publication, leaving Winnipeg and Ottawa as one-newspaper towns.

Kent Commission 1981 Royal Commission into newspaper ownership.

Why all the concern about **concentration of ownership** in Canada? While the players have changed in the last 30 years, both Davey and Kent leave us with the following points to consider when discussing the effects of concentration of ownership in a democracy:

concentration of ownership Conglomeration and convergence of media into fewer and fewer hands.

- News is a product that needs a variety of voices to be produced. Without this variety, newspapers "become more alike, less individual, less distinctive."
- As newspapers become part of a large corporation, the people who run them likely won't have a background in journalism but rather a background in business or management. Given this scenario, profits become more important than editorial content and the news-gathering and writing process.
- Too much power in too few hands contradicts the role of the press in a democracy. Concentration of press ownership in Canada may mean power without accountability.
- While it's true that newspapers face competition from radio and television, it's newspapers that have traditionally been used to record history.

LEARNING CHECK

- How did chains come to dominate the newspaper industry?
- Why is chain ownership an issue?

Daily Newspapers

STUDY PREVIEW Although a nation of mostly local newspapers, Canada has two established national dailies. Most daily newspapers in Canada are considered the voice of their hometown area, covering local news and carrying local advertising.

National Dailies

The Globe and Mail *The Globe* was founded in 1844 in Toronto by Scottish immigrant **George Brown**. Although labelled as politically conservative, Brown was also somewhat of a publishing innovator. He expanded the format of the paper and *The Globe* began publishing daily in 1853. He also published a weekly edition for readers living outside of Toronto. He was rewarded for his efforts; by 1872, circulation had almost tripled to 45 000. By the end of the 19th century, it had increased to 80 000. *The Globe* merged with the *Mail and Empire* in November 1936.

George Brown Founded *The Globe*.

As discussed in Chapter 1, *The Globe and Mail* was part of the multimedia platform owned by BCE. In 2010, it was sold to the Woodbridge Company. It's still a widely read and respected paper, with circulation of about 2 million weekly.

National Post For a relatively new newspaper, the *National Post* has quite a history. In 1998, **Conrad Black** sold his interest in *The Hamilton Spectator*, *The Record* (Kitchener-Waterloo), the *Guelph Mercury*, and the *Cambridge Reporter* to Sun Media for 80 percent of the *Financial Post* and $150 million. Then, on October 27, 1998, Black's Southam entered the national newspaper sweepstakes when it began publishing the *National Post*. In 2000, it was purchased by CanWest Global. However, in 2009, as part of a debt-reduction strategy, CanWest put the *National Post* (and other newspapers) up for sale. The *National Post* and 10 other Canadian newspapers were purchased by the Postmedia Network in 2010 for a reported $1.1 billion. It also owns the news agency Postmedia News.

NATIONAL POST

HER AND W.P.

LAST CHANCE

NATO JETS BOMB CITIES IN YUGOSLAVIA

POLICE PELTED WITH ROCKS AT TORONTO PROTEST

Clark fires his top advisor in wake of B.C. scandals

Quebec hotelier who met with PM paid to entertain Belgian tax officials

U.K. reconsiders Pinochet's extradition

Flasher spared public humiliation

U.S. firm buying 20% of Bell Canada

INDEX

B.C. museum tries to lose head

Innovation

National Post In 1998, Canada had its first "National" newspaper when Conrad Black launched the *National Post*. In 2001, he sold the paper outright to CanWest. In 2010, it was sold to PostMedia.

Metropolitan Dailies

In every region of the United States and Canada there is a newspaper whose name is a household word. These are metropolitan dailies with extensive regional circulation. Vancouver, Montreal, and Toronto feature strong metropolitan newspapers. The following is a snapshot of Canada's leading metropolitan daily, the *Toronto Star*.

Toronto Star The *Toronto Star* not only is a metropolitan daily, but also has the largest daily circulation of any newspaper in Canada: almost 300 000 copies. The *Star* was founded in 1892 as the Toronto Star and Publishing Company. Its founding fathers were 21 printers who were on strike (or locked out, depending on who you believe). They had worked for the *Toronto News* until a new typesetting process threatened their jobs. Within days of losing their jobs, they borrowed old printing presses and, with each printer assuming the roles of writer, reporter, ad salesperson, and proofreader, the first *Evening Star* was printed on November 3, 1892. The masthead proclaimed it "A paper for the people." This incident gave rise to the *Star* being identified as a "liberal" paper for many years.

The *Star*'s press centre produces more than 2.2 million newspapers per week, and the *Saturday Star* has a circulation of more than 318 000. The *Star* is owned by Torstar Corporation. The company also owns the Metroland Media Group, which includes 105 weekly newspapers and a handful of hometown dailies. It also publishes Harlequin Romances.

Hometown Dailies

Conrad Black Founded the *National Post.*

hometown daily Edited primarily for readers in a defined region.

With their aggressive reporting of national and regional issues, the metropolitan dailies receive more attention than smaller dailies, but most people read **hometown dailies**. By and large, these locally oriented newspapers, most of them chain-owned, have been incredibly profitable while making significant journalistic progress since World War II.

Fifty years ago, people in small towns generally bought both a metropolitan daily and a local newspaper. Hometown dailies were thin and coverage was hardly comprehensive. Editorial pages tended to offer only a single perspective. Readers had few alternative sources of information. Since then, these smaller dailies have hired better-prepared journalists, acquired new technology, and strengthened their local advertising base.

LEARNING CHECK

- What makes national dailies different from hometown dailies?
- How do newspapers fit in to your mix of sources for daily news?

Hometown Weeklies

Community weekly newspapers are making strong circulation gains, especially in suburban communities, and some have moved into publishing twice a week. In all, more than 600 weekly newspapers are published in Canada, the majority of them tabloids, with total weekly circulation approaching 12 million.

THE COMMUNITY NEWS LEADER SINCE 1929

The News Leader

SERVING SURREY AND NORTH DELTA

Wednesday, August 21, 1996

TOP STORY

COUNTERFEIT CASH SURFACES

Police warn business owners to be wary of cashing $10 bills • SEE A3

Golfing Gretsky

Consumer bankruptcies rise as job layoffs increase SEE: A12

Girl Guides are helping and seeing the world

Les Finnigan takes first prize in U.S. workshop

Community News Suburban weeklies are thriving. Readers appreciate the detailed local coverage and advertisers like the target market and the relatively low cost of ads.

To the discomfort of metro dailies, many advertisers are following their customers to the suburban weeklies. Advertisers have found that they can buy space in weeklies for less and reach their likeliest customers. Ralph Ingersoll, whose weeklies compete with the daily *Newsday* in New York, explained it this way in an interview with *Forbes*: "If you're an automobile dealer on Long Island, you can pay, say, $14 000 for a tabloid page in *Newsday*, most of which is wasted because the people that get it will never buy a car in your neck of the woods, or you can go into one of the weekender publications and pay a few hundred dollars and reach just the people likely to drive over to your shop."

Some weeklies, particularly those in upscale suburbs, offer sophisticated coverage of community issues. Others feature a homey mix of reports on social events such as who visited whom for Sunday dinner. The success of these weeklies sometimes is called **telephone book journalism** because of the emphasis on names, the somewhat overdrawn theory being that people buy papers to see their names in print. Weeklies have in common that they cover their communities with a detail that metro dailies have neither the staff nor the space to match. There is no alternative to keeping up with local news.

telephone book journalism Emphasizing readers' names in articles.

Rural Weeklies

Rural weeklies generally have fallen on rough times. Part of the problem is the diminishing significance of agriculture in the national economy and the continuing depopulation of rural North America. In communities that remain retail centres, rural weeklies can maintain a strong advertising base. However, the Main Street of many small towns has declined as improved roads and the construction of major retail stores such as Walmart draw customers from kilometres away. In earlier days, those customers patronized hometown retailers, which placed significant advertising in hometown weeklies. Today, many of these Main Street retailers, unable to compete with giant discount stores, are out of business.

Shoppers

shopper An advertising paper without news.

Free-distribution papers that carry only advertisements have become increasingly important as vehicles for classified advertising. In recent years, **shoppers** have attracted display advertising that earlier would have gone to regular newspapers. Almost all shoppers undercut daily newspapers on advertising rates.

By definition, shoppers are strictly advertising sheets, but beginning in the 1970s some shoppers added editorial content, usually material that came free over the transom, such as publicity items and occasional self-serving columns from legislators. Some shoppers have hired staff members to compile calendars and provide a modicum of news coverage. Most of these papers, however, remain ad sheets with little content that is journalistic. Their news-gathering efforts and expenses are minuscule compared with those of a daily newspaper.

LEARNING CHECK

- Describe the range of newspapers that are published weekly.
- How are most weeklies buffered from the competition faced by daily newspapers?

Gannett Initiative

STUDY PREVIEW Its readership in peril, American media giant Gannett has begun a chainwide project to reconceive news gathering and delivery. All 85 local Gannett dailies went into a 24/7 mode. Reporting for the web was made first priority. Planning the daily print edition comes later.

Information Centres

For years the newspaper industry was in denial. Wishful thinking had it that circulation declines somehow were an aberration that would self-correct. At the giant chain Gannett, which operates *USA Today* and 85 hometown dailies in the United States, planners understood the reality: Newspapers are losing their foothold in people's lives, especially among the under-40 set. But news is hardly out of style. The reality is that people are looking elsewhere, mostly on the web: Craigslist, Yahoo!, YouTube, and countless blogs. As Jennifer Carroll, a Gannett vice-president, put it: "Amazing disruptive events" are shaking the news business and leaving newspapers out.

In 2005, Gannett quietly began to lay out a blueprint to regain relevance. In tests at papers in Iowa, Florida, and South Dakota, Gannett replaced traditional newspaper newsrooms with what it called **information centres**. Reporters begin before dawn to update breaking stories on the web for morning readers, in contrast to stories in the print edition that were written the day before. The web edition is fresh. News alerts go out to mobile phones during the day as events warrant them. Web readers are invited to respond to stories and to each other online. In effect, stories become jumping-off points for reader interactivity. Massive databases of community information are posted: school statistics, municipal budgets, crime data. It is more than could ever fit in a print edition. Reporters are issued videocams to shoot footage for the web. Readers are invited to post photos and items, even notices about the bowling league and bridge club.

21st-Century News With a postcard theme, artist Lonnie Busch captures the essence of the Gannett newspaper chain's information centre 24/7 project. Every local Gannett daily has shifted its emphasis to web delivery with beefed-up local coverage.

information centres Gannett concept for newsrooms designed around web delivery of news and services.

mojos Roving reporters with cell phones, laptops, and videocams; short for mobile journalists.

LEARNING CHECK

- What are the "amazing disruptive events" that Gannett executive Jennifer Carroll cites as changing the landscape of news?
- In Gannett's new media initiative, why is "shovelware" out?

Mojos and Scoops

After test runs, the Gannett concept went live. Individual Gannett papers had their own take on the concept by 2008. The switch was hardly a budget buster. The corporation put only $3 million into the project for technology upgrades. That bought a lot of videocams. Of course, individual papers bore additional expenses.

Coverage of local breaking news is stronger with **mojos**. These mobile journalists, equipped with cell phones, laptops, and videocams, are on the scene quickly and can report live. A few mojos in the field can generate a lot of live reporting. While it may not be Pulitzer Prize–winning stuff, it acts as a live, exciting magnet for readers. The *Arizona Republic* has 15 college journalism students out early every morning, working part-time for $10 an hour to provide local coverage online.

LEARNING CHECK

- Is maintaining and updating huge databases a good use of a newspaper's resources in an era of shrinking newsroom staffs?

Gannett Lessons

The Gannett initiative implicitly acknowledges how lethargic newspapers had become in terms of local coverage. Without print competition, a function partly of the growth of chains like Gannett, the incentive to be on top of news in one-paper towns gradually had diminished. Local newspapers had a monopoly on news, and broadcasters were never much of a challenge.

Except for its technological bells and whistles, much of the Gannett concept is really old stuff. The New York *Daily News* pioneered the mojo concept in 1919, although nobody called it that back then. The *Daily News* had photographers roving the city in cars equipped with two-way radios to get to breaking events quickly and shoot exclusives. The idea of being on the scene and breaking news live also has roots in radio in the 1930s. Think of the *Hindenburg* disaster. In the 1980s, lightweight video equipment gave

MEDIA PEOPLE Bonnie Fuller

As a magazine editor, Fuller has always had a magic touch. In her six years as editor, she turned *Flare* into the largest fashion magazine in Canada. Then, in New York, she relaunched *YM*, a magazine geared toward women aged 15 to 24, more than doubling its circulation from 700 000 to over 1.7 million. In 1994, Fuller joined Hearst Magazines where she launched the French fashion, beauty, and lifestyle magazine *Marie Claire* for U.S. readers. Initial circulation of 250 000 rocketed past 500 000. Then Hearst put Fuller in charge of *Cosmopolitan*, which was still riding high on the sex-and-the-single-girl themes of Helen Gurley Brown after more than 30 years—quite an act to follow.

As the new *Cosmo* editor, Fuller used reader focus groups to guide her in making changes and additions. She included articles on AIDS and sexual harassment and, with no holds barred, any issue of concern and relevance to young women, at the same time maintaining the saucy, sexy tone established by Helen Gurley Brown. In Fuller's first year, *Cosmo* circulation flourished and drew more advertising. Fuller was named 1997 Editor of the Year by the trade journal *Advertising Age*. From 1998 to 2001, she served as editor of *Glamour*.

What next? Fuller took on the editorship of the celebrity magazine *Us Weekly*, which had floundered for years against Time Warner's *People*. Almost instantly, *Us* became a pop culture must-read.

In 2003, Fuller switched to tabloid publisher American Media. At American Media she not only was editing one magazine herself, but also was editor-in-chief for all of the company's magazines. It was a new level of responsibility. Said Fuller, "A chance to do this isn't going to necessarily come up in two years, in three years. It came up now." How could the era's most successful magazine editor stoop as low as American Media's *National Enquirer* and *Star*? Her stock answer in myriad interviews was the same: "Don't fool yourself. Every news outlet is doing tabloid stories." To reposition *Star*, Fuller had it printed on glossy paper. She shunned old *Star*-type scoops that, while tantalizing, often turned out to be untrue. A successful celebrity magazine, she said, needs credibility.

Fuller left American Media in 2008 and launched Bonnie Fuller Media, but the economic downturn took its toll on that venture. In 2009, she was hired by Jay Penske of Mail.com to revamp Hollywoodlife.com, an online celebrity gossip site. Given her past experiences in publishing, it's a beat that Fuller knows well. This type of journalism is about giving people what they want. In a *Globe and Mail* article by Sarah Hampson, Fuller claims that "people are born with the gossip gene. It's in our DNA. We are nosy. We are curious creatures." She also claims that our passion for celebrity news and gossip is beneficial: "Women see celebrities as mirrors of their own lives, so when they're looking at celebrities, in many cases, not all, they are evaluating the situation and relating it to something in their own lives or comparing it. It enhances your life."

Bonnie Fuller

WHAT DO YOU THINK?

1. What makes celebrity journalism so fascinating? Is Fuller right when she says that it's a natural curiosity?
2. Why does celebrity journalism need credibility to be successful?

local television stations a chance to go a mojo route, but stations never committed enough staff to do it well. Also, video transmission equipment was burdensome. Some lessons that Gannett is applying have been standard practices for more than a century with news agencies like the Associated Press that update stories continuously. News agency editors and reporters have always had some client somewhere on deadline every minute.

To be sure, there are downsides. By realigning newsroom staffs toward breaking on-scene news live, fewer resources are available for in-depth and investigative reporting. As well, stretching staff has added stress to newsroom jobs. It has increased workload pressure brought on by staff reductions and realignments not only at Gannett but also at other papers. Finally, the pressure to post news quickly online leads to errors, some merely typographical but others more serious.

LEARNING CHECK

- What is new in Gannett's information centre project? What's old?
- Is journalism from Gannett newsrooms going to be better with the shifts introduced by the information centre concept? Discuss.
- Are mojos a good idea? Discuss the pros and cons.

Influence of Magazines

STUDY PREVIEW Today, as through their whole history, the major magazines constitute a mass medium that targets a national audience. At their best, periodicals pack great literature and ideas into formats that, unlike books, almost anyone can afford.

A National Advertising Medium

Advertisers used magazines through the 19th century to build national markets for their products, which was an important factor in transforming North America from an agricultural economy to a modern one. This also contributed to a sense of nationhood. The other mass media could not do that as effectively. Few books carried advertisements, and newspapers, with few exceptions, delivered only local readership to advertisers. Today, advertising is still an important concern to Canadian magazine publishers. The majority of their total revenue is generated by advertisers.

Massive Magazine Audience

People have a tremendous appetite for magazines. There is a Canadian magazine for almost every city and region of the country and for almost any interest. While only 20 percent of magazines available on Canadian newsracks are actually homegrown, Canadians seem to prefer Canadian magazines over American ones because of the Canadian content. Canadian magazines are perceived by readers as being more relevant to the experiences of Canadian readers than are their U.S. counterparts. Here's a snapshot of the Canadian magazine industry from Magazines Canada, a non-profit organization that represents magazine publishers here in Canada:

- In 1960, there were only 660 magazines published in Canada. By 2010, that number had risen to close to 2300.
- Annual total circulation for all Canadian magazines is 770 million.
- Advertising revenue is close to $2 billion per year.

Protecting Canadian Magazines

June Callwood calls Canadian magazines "the only ones that will tell you how complex this country is, how interesting, how beautiful, where the troubled places are, they find our rascals and our heroes and they have become the fabric of our ordinary lives. We can look in a magazine and see ourselves." However, content and writing are not the only factors that make Canadian magazines successful. The Canadian government feels that "Canadians must have access to Canadian voices and Canadian stories" and that magazines play "a significant role in the cultural life of Canadians" by reflecting our own distinctive people, places, and lives.

For more than a hundred years, the government has helped to foster the growth and development of Canadian magazines through many different initiatives. This support is based on the idea that Canadian magazines are at a disadvantage when competing with larger American publications. In 2010, the **Canada Periodical Fund (CPF)** was introduced. Its mandate is to help Canadian magazine publishers and nondaily newspapers be innovative when creating and distributing content.

Canada Periodical Fund (CPF) Support for Canadian magazines through the Department of Canadian Heritage.

LEARNING CHECK

- How large is the Canadian magazine industry?
- What role do Canadian magazines play in developing Canadian culture?

Magazines as Media Innovators

STUDY PREVIEW Magazines have led other media with significant innovations in journalism, advertising, and circulation. These include investigative reporting, in-depth personality profiles, and photojournalism.

long-form journalism Lengthy treatments of subjects that go beyond spot news.

muckraking Early 20th-century term for investigative reporting.

Theodore Roosevelt Coined the term *muckraking*.

personality profile In-depth, balanced biographical article.

Harold Ross Pioneered the personality profile.

Hugh Hefner Adapted the personality profile to the Q-and-A.

Harper's Weekly Pioneered magazine visuals.

National Geographic Introduced photography in magazines.

Long-Form Journalism

Magazines became home to **long-form journalism** in the 1800s with fiction by major authors. The 1900s brought investigative reporting, with stories longer than the ones newspapers typically carried.

Investigative Reporting

Muckraking, usually called investigative reporting today, was honed by magazines as a journalistic approach in the first years of the 20th century. Magazines ran lengthy explorations of abusive institutions in society. It was U.S. President **Theodore Roosevelt** who coined the term *muckraking*. Roosevelt generally enjoyed investigative journalism, but one day in 1906, when the digging got too close to home, he likened it to the work of a character in a 17th-century novel who focused so much on raking muck that he missed the good news. The president meant the term derisively, but it came to be a badge of honour among journalists.

Personality Profiles

The in-depth **personality profile** was a magazine invention. In the 1920s, **Harold Ross** of *The New Yorker* began pushing writers to a thoroughness that was new in journalism. They used multiple interviews with a range of sources—talking not only with the subject of the profile but also with just about everyone and anyone who could comment on the subject, including the subject's friends and enemies. Such depth required weeks, sometimes months, of journalistic digging. It's not uncommon now in newspapers, broadcasting, or magazines, but before Harold Ross it didn't exist.

Under **Hugh Hefner**, *Playboy* took the interview in new directions in 1962 with in-depth profiles developed from a highly structured question-and-answer format. This format became widely imitated. *Rolling Stone* uses Q-and-A's regularly, often creating news. In 2003, presidential hopeful Wesley Clark, a retired general, told *Rolling Stone* that a three-star general in the Pentagon had told him that the Iraq invasion was planned only as the beginning of further U.S. invasions in the Middle East and elsewhere, and Clark named the additional target countries. It was a bombshell assertion that made news. Other magazines meanwhile are boiling down the Q-and-A into quick takes. *Time* introduced the "10 Questions" feature in 2002, tightly editing pointed questions and answers to fit on a single page.

National Geographic *National Geographic* has remained in the vanguard of magazines photographically. For its 100th anniversary in 1988, the cover was the first hologram, a three-dimensional photograph, ever published in a mass-audience magazine.

LEARNING CHECK

- Does the term *muckraking* capture what investigative reporting is about?
- What were the contributions of Harold Ross and Hugh Hefner to long-form journalism in their very different magazines?

Photojournalism

Magazines brought visuals to the mass media in a way books never had. ***Harper's Weekly*** sent artists to draw Civil War battles, leading the way to journalism that went beyond words.

The young editor of ***National Geographic,*** Gilbert Grosvenor, drew a map proposing a route to the South Pole for an 1899 issue,

Seeing the News Henry Luce's *Life* magazine pioneered photojournalism, beginning with Margaret Bourke-White's haunting shadows of the giant new Fort Peck Dam in Montana for the inaugural issue. When World War II came, *Life* dispatched Bourke-White and other photographers to capture the story, even the horrific details. With people eager for war news, circulation soared.

putting the publication on the road to being a visually oriented magazine. In subsequent issues, Grosvenor borrowed government plates to reproduce photos and encouraged travellers to submit their photographs to the magazine. This was at a time when most magazines scorned photographs. However, Grosvenor was undeterred as an advocate for documentary photography, and membership in the National Geographic Society, a prerequisite for receiving the magazine, swelled. Eventually, the magazine assembled its own staff of photographers and it gradually became a model for other publications that discovered they needed to play catch-up.

Explore

Margaret Bourke-White

Aided by technological advances involving smaller, more portable cameras and faster film capable of recording images under extreme conditions, photographers working for *National Geographic* opened a whole new world of documentary coverage to their readers.

Life magazine brought U.S. photojournalism to new importance in the 1930s. The oversized pages of the magazine gave new intensity to photographs, and the magazine, a weekly, demonstrated that newsworthy events could be covered consistently by camera.

LEARNING CHECK

- Although different in mission, *National Geographic* and *Life* both established magazines firmly as a visual medium. How so?

Consumer Magazines

STUDY PREVIEW The most visible category of magazines is general-interest magazines, which are available on newsracks and by subscription. Called **consumer magazines**, these include publications like *Reader's Digest* that try to offer something for everybody, but mostly they are magazines edited for narrower audiences. Outnumbering consumer magazines about 10 to 1, however, are sponsored magazines and trade journals.

consumer magazines Sold on newsracks.

Newsmagazines

Although it is often compared to *Time*, ***Maclean's***, "Canada's Weekly News Magazine," was founded in 1905 by John Bayne Maclean, almost 20 years before *Time* first appeared. However, the magazine we now know as *Maclean's* was called *Busy Man's*

Maclean's First Canadian newsmagazine.

Newsmagazines Canada's counterpart to *Time* magazine is *Maclean's*. It brings the Canadian journalism tradition of analysis to the newsstands.

Magazine until 1911. Originally, it was a large-format magazine, about the size of *Life*, but in 1969 it was reduced to a standard size. In content, *Maclean's* is similar to *Time*, with an emphasis on in-depth coverage of national and international stories. Columnists like Peter C. Newman (a former editor of *Maclean's*), Barbara Amiel, and Allan Fotheringham have offered their perspectives to Canadians in the pages of this magazine. *Maclean's* even issues a national edition written in Chinese.

Fresh out of Yale in 1923, classmates **Henry Luce** and Briton Hadden begged and borrowed $86 000 from friends and relatives and launched a new kind of magazine: ***Time***. The magazine provided summaries of news organized in categories such as national affairs, sports, and business. It took four years for *Time* to turn a profit, and some people doubted that the magazine would ever make money, noting that it merely rehashed what daily newspapers had already reported. Readers, however, came to like the handy compilation and the sprightly, often irreverent writing style that set *Time* apart.

Henry Luce Founder of *Time* and, later, *Life*.

Time First American newsmagazine.

While *Time*, *Newsweek*, and *U.S. News & World Report* cover a broad range of subjects, specialized newsmagazines focus on narrower subjects. The largest category is those magazines that feature celebrity news, including the gossipy sort. The supermarket tabloid ***National Enquirer*** focuses on the rich and famous, hyped-up medical research, and sensational oddball news and is an incredible commercial success, with a circulation of 2.1 million. Time Warner's *People* has a circulation of 3.6 million.

National Enquirer Magazine or newspaper?

Women's Magazines

The first U.S. magazine edited to interest only a portion of the mass audience, but otherwise to be of general interest, was *The Lady's Magazine*, which later became *Godey's Lady's Book*. **Sarah Josepha Hale** helped to start the magazine in 1828 to uplift and glorify womanhood. Its advice on fashions, morals, taste, sewing, and cooking developed a following, which peaked with a circulation of 150 000 in 1860.

Explore

Sarah Josepha Hale

Sarah Josepha Hale Founded first women's magazine.

The *Godey's* tradition is maintained today in the competing magazines *Better Homes and Gardens*, *Family Circle*, *Good Housekeeping*, *Ladies' Home Journal*, *Redbook*, *Woman's Day*, and the defunct *Rosie* (née *McCall's*). While each of these magazines can be distinguished from the others, there is a thematic connection: concern for home, family, and high-quality living from a traditional woman's perspective.

These traditional women's magazines are sometimes called the **Seven Sisters**. An eighth sister is *Cosmopolitan*, although it may more aptly be called a distant cousin. Under Helen Gurley Brown and later Canada's Bonnie Fuller, *Cosmopolitan* has geared itself to a subcategory of women readers: young, unmarried, and working. It's the most successful in a large group of women's magazines that seeks a narrow audience.

Seven Sisters Leading women's magazines.

Men's Magazines

Founded in 1933, ***Esquire*** was the first classy men's magazine. It was as famous for its pinups as for its literary content, which over the years has included articles by Ernest Hemingway, Hunter S. Thompson, and P.J. O'Rourke. Fashion has also been a cornerstone in *Esquire*'s content mix.

Esquire First classy men's magazine.

Hugh Hefner learned about magazines as an *Esquire* staff member, and he applied those lessons when he created ***Playboy*** in 1953. With its lustier tone, *Playboy* quickly overtook *Esquire* in circulation. At its peak, *Playboy* sold 7 million copies a month. By 2004, however, *Playboy* seemed tired. Circulation was down to 3.2 million. Meanwhile, upstarts like *Maxim* at 2.5 million, *FHM* at 1.1 million, and *Stuff* at 676 000 were ascending, despite critics who objected to their raciness. Responding to critics, some retail outlets, notably giant retailer Wal-mart, ceased stocking some men's titles as well as some women's magazines that had provocative covers.

Playboy Widely imitated girlie/lifestyle men's magazine.

Demassification Magazines were the first medium to demassify. *Chatelaine*, a magazine for Canadian homemakers, ranks as one of the bestselling magazines in Canada.

TABLE 4.2

Magazine Circulation Leaders: Canada

According to *Masthead Online*, here are the top Canadian magazines. Data were compiled by combining advertising revenue and circulation revenue.

Magazine	Total Estimated Revenue (Canadian dollars)
Chatelaine	51.4 million
Canadian Living	49.7 million
Reader's Digest	48.1 million
Maclean's	33.5 million
Canadian House and Home	21.1 million

Source: *The Top 50, June 2010, MastheadOnline.com. Reprinted by permission.*

Not all men's magazines dwell on sex, however. The outdoor life is exalted in *Field & Stream*, whose circulation tops 2 million. Fix-it magazines, led by *Popular Science* and *Popular Mechanics*, also have a steady following.

LEARNING CHECK

- What are the major genres of consumer magazines?

Non-Newsrack Magazines

STUDY PREVIEW Many organizations publish magazines for their members. Although these sponsored magazines, including *National Geographic*, resemble consumer magazines, they generally are not available at newsracks. In fact, consumer magazines are far outnumbered by sponsored magazines and by trade journals.

Sponsored Magazines

The founders of the National Geographic Society decided in 1888 to publish a magazine to promote the society and build membership. The idea was to entice people to join by bundling a subscription with membership and then to use the dues to finance the society's research and expeditions. Within a few years, *National Geographic* had become a phenomenal success both in generating membership and as a profit centre for the National Geographic Society. Today, more than 100 years old and with a U.S. circulation of 6.7 million, *NationalGeographic* is the most widely recognized **sponsored magazine** in the nation. Other sponsored magazines include *Zoomer Magazine*, published by the Canadian Association of Retired Persons for its members.

sponsored magazine Generally non-newsrack magazine, often member-supported.

Trade Journals

Every profession or trade has at least one magazine, or **trade journal**, for keeping abreast of what is happening in the field. In entertainment, *Billboard* provides solid journalistic coverage on a broad range of subjects in music: new releases, new acts, new technology, and new merger deals. *Billboard* is essential reading for people in the music industry. Trade journals covering the Canadian and American mass media include *Marketing* magazine for advertising and marketing, *The Publisher* for the newspaper industry, and *Broadcaster* and *Broadcast Dialogue* for the Canadian radio and television industries. About 4000 trade journals cover a mind-boggling range of businesses and trades. Consider the diversity in these titles: *Rock & Dirt*, *Progressive Grocer*, *Canadian Plastics*, *Hogs Today*, and *Hardware* Age.

trade journal Keeps members of a profession or trade informed.

Newsletters

Even more focused than trade journals are subscription newsletters, a billion-dollar industry. These newsletters are expensive, generally $600 to $1000 a year, with some as much as $5000. Why do people pay that much? Where else could Chamber of Commerce executives find the information that's in *Downtown Promotion Reporter*? And no other publication duplicates what's in *Food Chemical News*, *Beverage Digest,* and *Inside Mortgage Finance.* John Farley, vice-president of the largest newsletter company, Phillips Publishing, contends that newsletters are the purest form of journalism because they carry little or no advertising: "We're answerable to no one but our subscribers." Today, more than 5000 subscription newsletters are published in the United States and Canada. Some newsletters now have subscription websites.

LEARNING CHECK

- What are some of the audiences to which non-newsrack magazines are aimed? Give examples.
- Why are some trade journals less reputable and reliable for straight news than others?

Magazines as Niche Media

Deepening Your Media Literacy: Should magazines try for universal appeal?

STUDY PREVIEW Giant mass-audience magazines, led by *Life*, were major influences in their heyday, but television killed them off by offering larger audiences to advertisers. Today, the magazine industry thrives through demassification, the process of seeking audiences with narrow interests. Critics believe that demassification has changed the role of magazines in society for the worse.

Mass-Audience Magazines

Early magazines, edited for general audiences, were perfect advertising vehicles for nationally marketed products. Unlike network radio, the magazines were visual. People could see the products. There was no more efficient medium for advertisers to reach large audiences. These were magazines that epitomized the era. At its peak, *Life* claimed a circulation of 8.5 million, a real deal for advertisers. Then came television.

CPM Cost per thousand; a tool to determine the cost effectiveness of different media.

The villain for magazines was **CPM**, advertising jargon for cost per thousand readers (the *M* represents the Roman numeral meaning thousand). The television networks nibbled, and even gobbled, at the big magazines' CPMs. In 1970, a full-page advertisement in *Life* cost $65 000, representing a CPM of $7.75 at the time. In contrast, the networks' CPM was $3.60. It's not hard to see why advertisers shifted to television.

Doomsayers predicted the end of magazines. However, the prognosis wasn't so severe in reality. The Henry Luce model for magazine success simply needed to be rethought.

LEARNING CHECK

- What happened to the original business model for magazines, as epitomized by *Life*?
- What characteristics distinguish *Life* at its heyday from, say, the magazine *Snowboarding* today?

Demassification

Some categories of magazines, such as the weekly newsmagazines, survived the assault of television. Newsmagazines provided content that audiences could not find easily on television, which had not yet emerged as a competitive news medium. The quick-read *Reader's Digest*, portable and easy to pick up, was unshaken. Also surviving were special-interest magazines that focused on niche topics that the television networks ignored as they tried to build mass audiences.

Demassification Pursuit of narrow segments of the mass audience.

By and large, magazines needed to reinvent themselves. And they did just that through a process called **demassification**. The survivors delivered potential customers to narrowly focused advertisers. For manufacturers of sports equipment, *The Hockey News* made sense in terms of CPM. These demassified audiences were large and the magazines continued to be vehicles of mass communication; however, these were defined audiences—in contrast to the broader formula that sought to deliver something for everyone in every issue.

Magazine Demassification Advertisers favour magazines that are edited to specific audience interests that coincide with the advertisers' products. Fewer and fewer magazines geared to a general audience remain in business today.

Although a successful financial and survival tactic, demassification has its critics. These critics, of the elitist camp of social studies, say that the traditional role of magazines to help readers come to understandings of broad and important issues has been lost. As the critics see it, the social and cultural importance of magazines has largely been lost in a drive to amass narrow slices of readership that will attract a narrow range of advertisers. The result is a frothy mix of light, upbeat features with little that is thoughtful, hard-hitting, or broadly illuminating. Norman Cousins, once editor of the highbrow *Saturday Review*, put it this way: "The purpose of a magazine is not to tell you how to fix a faucet but to tell you what the world is about."

Scholar Dennis Holder put this "unholy alliance" of advertisers and readers this way: "The readers see themselves as members of small, and in some sense, elite groups—joggers, for example, or cat lovers—and they want to be told that they are terribly neat people for being in those groups. Advertisers, of course, want to reinforce the so-called positive self-image too, because joggers who feel good about themselves tend to buy those ridiculous suits and cat lovers who believe lavishing affection on their felines is a sign of warmth and sincerity are the ones who purchase cute little cat sweaters, or are they cat's pajamas." Magazine editors and writers, Holder said, are caught in the symbiotic advertiser–reader alliance and have no choice but to go along with it.

LEARNING CHECK

- **What magazines have survived demassification and still seek broad audiences?**
- **How do you respond to Norman Cousins's point that magazines have forfeited an important role in society?**
- **Would you categorize women's magazines as demassified?**

New Competition

STUDY PREVIEW **Television again is challenging magazines, this time with demassified programming on satellite and cable systems. The web also offers a wealth of information organized for tiny slivers of the mass audience that magazines earlier had carved out as their domain.**

Demassified Alternatives

The so-called 500-channel universe, with narrowly focused programming on satellite and cable television channels, is the latest challenge to magazines. This time, television has followed magazines' lead in demassification. CanWest's HGTV (Home and Garden

Television), for example, covers the same content as the home/lifestyle magazines. With personal video recorders (PVRs) and time-shifting, viewers can easily cue up whatever they want to watch whenever they want it.

Sensing that their exclusive turf is facing a challenge, some magazines have established a television presence, but generally only as a single program. These play among other programs on the 24/7 demassified channels.

Pathfinder An early Time Warner initiative to place magazines online.

Magazines have done better with the web. One of the first forays into digital delivery was by Time Warner, which in the mid-1990s created a massive website, called **Pathfinder**, for *Time, Sports Illustrated, Fortune,* and the company's other magazines. Pathfinder wasn't merely an online version of those magazines but a distinctive product. There were hopes that advertisers would flock to the site and make it profitable, but ad revenue only trickled in. In 1998, Pathfinder moved to a subscription service to supplement its meagre advertising revenue. All in all, the Pathfinder exercise was not a success, but lessons were learned.

Today, almost every magazine has a namesake website or an iPhone/iPod app that provides access to the content from the latest issue and usually bonus content that doesn't appear in print issues. Some web magazines charge subscription fees, but most do not. As well, advertisers have become comfortable with these sites as part of their mix for reaching potential customers.

LEARNING CHECK

- How is television challenging magazines today as a demassified medium?
- Can magazines meet the challenge of the new demassified competition?

Digital Delivery

Among advertisers, there is a lot of confusion about what their advertising budgets buy. Indeed, is $100 000 better spent on HGTV or on *Better Homes & Gardens*? It's the old CPM question, but the issue is more complex than simply dividing dollars by eyes.

Reader Usage Measure (RUM) A scale for measuring reader satisfaction.

A new way of measuring a magazine's value, the **Reader Usage Measure**, or **RUM**, was introduced in 2003 to ascertain positive and negative reader reactions. Thirty-nine statements are put to readers in carefully controlled surveys to ascertain positive and negative reactions. The statements are direct. Answering "yes" to the following statements contributes to a strong RUM score:

- I get value for my time and money.
- It makes me smarter.
- I often reflect on it.

Conversely, answering "yes" to the following statements lowers the RUM score:

- It disappoints me.
- I dislike some of the ads.
- It leaves me feeling bad.

Ellen Oppenheim, a marketing executive with Magazine Publishers of America, said that RUM data provide "a quantitative measure of qualitative information" that transcends circulation, ad pages, and ad revenue—all of which are advertising-rooted measures. RUM is a reader-rooted measure that points to a magazine's connectedness to its audience.

The first RUM study included 4347 readers of 100 leading magazines, which was a large enough sample to provide demographic breakdowns. Black readers, for example, wanted magazines about which they could say, "It touched me" and "It grabbed me visually." Generation Y women, who came of age in the 1990s, gravitate to magazines that help them to share experiences. Historically, the great magazines have been edited by people with an intuitive sense for their audiences. With RUM, there is concrete information to supplement instinctive knowledge about what attracts an audience.

LEARNING CHECK

- How does RUM differ from CPM? As an advertiser, would RUM merely add to your confusion? Or would it help you to make better decisions on where to place your ads?

CASE STUDY

Magazines and the Internet

Remember seeing *Teen People* on the magazine rack? Or *FHM, Jane, Cargo, Premiere, Elle Girl,* or *Celebrity Living*? All of these mainstream magazines and dozens of others folded in the past few years.

The competition is stiff among glossies. But Jane Pratt, founder of *Jane*, says it was another medium, the internet, that largely caused the downfall of her self-titled women's magazine. "With so many women going online, it's possible that there isn't much need for it." Pratt's point is clear: Readers don't need to wait for a monthly when the internet is always available with convenient, reliable content. Canadian new media expert Kaan Yigit says that "the market is so much more fragmented. The Internet is this vast sea of free content. What used to be the domain of magazines is already there."

So how can magazines survive in a volatile market where the World Wide Web always wins at getting information to consumers most quickly? If you can't beat 'em, join 'em. Many magazines have extended their presence to the web. For example, Claude Galipeau, Senior Vice-President of Canada's Rogers Digital Media, says, "It's difficult to find any magazine publisher across North America that would say their print product is the only thing that is really part of their stable. It's no longer just the glossy print product."

For several years Condé Nast, a major magazine publisher with numerous titles, has attempted to do this through general websites like www.epicurious.com. This site carries material from the company's food magazines. Similarly, Condé Nast's www.brides.com includes material from its bridal magazines. Although these sites are sponsored by the magazines, they are purposefully not named after any of the company's magazines. The goal for these sites is to reach readers who might not typically pick up an issue of *Modern Bride* or *Bon Appetit*.

Steven Newhouse, the Condé Nast executive who oversees the company's websites, believes in magazine companion sites: "You gain a broader audience and more loyalty from your subscribers if you extend the experience into the Web."

Then, there's the recent introduction of iPhone/iPod apps, which also allow readers to access online content. *GQ*, another Condé Nast publication, introduced an iPhone app in 2010. Given the male demographic of its readership, this made sense. Sarah Chubb, head of Condé Nast Digital, says, "It's a young male readership. They're very tech-comfortable, they're very aesthetically oriented."

Bye, Jane Battered by circulation shortfalls and advertiser defections, Jane Pratt's namesake magazine is among dozens of glossies that have said goodbye. Where have readers gone? In a word, to the web.

DEEPENING YOUR MEDIA LITERACY

Explore the Issue

Search the web and find a site that is either generally associated or specifically connected with a magazine that you read regularly.

Dig Deeper

Analyze the content of the website. Do you think it is aimed at subscribers or at readers who are unfamiliar with the magazine? As a reader of the magazine, do you think you can search the site more easily and/or understand the content better? Do you think a nonreader would be encouraged to pick up the magazine after searching this site?

What Do You Think?

Do magazines need to embrace the internet in order to survive in today's market? Are there any other ways for them to strengthen market share and increase readership?

Chapter 4 Wrap-Up

Can newspapers and magazines survive? Even if people were to stop buying newspapers and magazines tomorrow, newspaper organizations would survive because they have an asset that competing media lack: the largest, most skilled newsroom staffs in their communities. The printing presses and the ink-on-newsprint medium for carrying the message may not have a long future, but newspapers' news-gathering capability will endure.

The magazine industry once was defined by giant general-interest magazines that offered something for everybody. Advertisers soured on these oversized giants when television offered more potential customers per advertising dollar. Magazines then shifted to more specialized packages. This focused approach worked. Magazines found advertisers who were seeking readers with narrow interests. Now, as other media—particularly television—are becoming demassified, magazines stand to lose advertisers, which poses new challenges.

Questions for Critical Thinking

1. Describe the role of newspapers in the lives of many Canadians.
2. Explain the role of newspaper chains. Have they been good for readers?
3. Is Gannett on the right path in giving priority to web delivery of newspapers and news?
4. Explain how magazines have been content innovators over the years.
5. What forced the magazine industry into its current demassified state?

Keeping Up to Date

CARD (*Canadian Advertising Rates and Data*) is a listing of newspapers and magazines published in Canada. It includes circulation data and current ad rates.

Editor & Publisher is a weekly trade journal for the newspaper industry.

Folio is a trade journal on magazine management. Among major newspapers that track magazine issues in a fairly consistent way are *The New York Times*, *The Wall Street Journal*, and *USA Today*.

NewsInc. is a monthly trade journal on newspaper management.

Newspaper Research Journal is a quarterly publication that deals mostly with applied research.

The Publisher covers community newspapers across Canada.

Many general-interest magazines, such as *Maclean's*, cover print media issues on a regular basis.

5

Sound Recording

Individualism Reigns Download and playback devices, such as iPods, have cut into traditional retail outlets for recorded music. Been to a mom-and-pop music shop lately? Independent stores are hard to find these days, right? And why be a slave to a radio station's playlist when you can do your own programming and play what you want when you want?

LEARNING AHEAD

- Recorded music is everywhere in our lives.
- Four companies dominate the recording industry.
- File sharing threatens to upend the industry's economics.
- Apple's iPod and iTunes have eased file sharing losses.
- Technology has given performers new control of pop music.
- Censorship threats have been met by self-regulation.
- The recording and radio industries are symbiotic.

MEDIA IN THEORY

Power of Recorded Music

Music is more than the sum of its parts. The power of music transcends lyrics and notes. The semiotic school would argue that the notes and lyrics are simply the denotative aspect of a song. The true cultural power of song is in its connotation. It's at this second level that ideas are communicated. It's at this level that songs can be at their most powerful and even can be political, potently so. A folk revival was a centrepiece of the antiwar movement in the late 1960s and early 1970s. There were singers on the other side of the movement too, and they sold a lot of vinyl.

Watch

Rock the Vote

The power of recorded music is not a recent phenomenon. Even as far back as 1869, "The Anti-Confederation Song" expressed the feelings of Newfoundlanders about joining the Dominion of Canada. In World War I, "Over There" and other songs reflected an enthusiasm for involvement in the war. Composers who felt strongly about the Vietnam

Mixing Music and Politics The Dixie Chicks were no friend to the Iraq War, even before Bush-bashing became a national pastime in the waning months of his presidency. After Natalie Maines lashed out at the president in an aside at a London performance, Bush supporters pressured radio stations to stop playing their music. Sales of their music fell, but the group, unapologetic, didn't back down. Within months, their record sales rebounded. The saga demonstrated how the role of music and performers is perceived in public policy.

War wrote songs that put their views on vinyl. Sgt. Barry Sadler's "The Ballad of the Green Berets" cast U.S. soldiers in a heroic light and Merle Haggard's "Okie from Muskogee" glorified blind patriotism. And there were dozens of antiwar songs, such as Edwin Starr's "War."

An offhand remark, not their music, made the sassy Dixie Chicks the bad girls among George W. Bush loyalists. In 2003, at the height of enthusiasm for the Iraq War, lead singer Natalie Maines told a London audience that she was "ashamed" that the president was from Texas. Despite the popularity of their music, the Chicks were banned by many radio stations whose owners and managers were cowed by the volume of listener outrage. The Chicks had the last word, however. In 2006, with public sentiment shifted against the war, the group rebuffed the angry reaction with "Not Ready to Make Nice" on a CD that debuted at Number 28 on *Billboard*'s Hot 100.

The antiwar tradition continued in the 21st century with songs such as Green Day's "American Idiot" and Pearl Jam's "World Wide Suicide," which opened with a newspaper casualty report. Then came some dark lyrics: "Now you know both sides / Claiming killing in God's name / But God is nowhere to be found, conveniently." The anti–Iraq War sentiment was perhaps most strident in Neil Young's "Let's Impeach the President," in which he sings "flip" and "flop" amid George W. Bush quotes. Paul Simon, whose popularity, like Young's, dates to the Vietnam period, entered the antiwar revival in 2006 with the politically tinged album *Surprise*.

MEDIA TIMELINE Record Industry

1877 Thomas Edison introduced a recording-playback device, the Phonograph.

1887 Montreal's Emile Berliner introduced technology to record discs simultaneously.

1950s Rock 'n' roll, a new musical genre, shook up the record industry.

1960 Stereo recordings and playback equipment were introduced.

1971 Canadian Radio-television and Telecommunications Commission (CRTC) introduced Canadian content (Cancon) to radio.

1983 Digital recording on CDs introduced.

1998 Streaming technology made downloading from the web possible.

2001 Apple introduced the iPod, a handheld MP3-playing device, coupled with its online iTunes Music Store, a new model for music retailing.

2004 The Supreme Court of Canada ruled that music downloading is legal. The Canadian Recording Industry Association (CRIA) launched an immediate appeal of the ruling.

2004 PureTracks and Napster 2.0, legal music downloading services, introduced in Canada.

2004 Adam Curry invented the podcast.

2005 The recording industry won U.S. Supreme Court case against online file sharing facilitators, such as Grokster, slowing a drain on sales.

2009 ExploreMusic launched interactive site to promote music.

In short, music has tremendous effects on human beings, and the technology of sound recording amplifies these effects. Mothers still sing Brahms's Lullaby, but more babies are probably lulled to sleep by hearing Brahms on CD. When trying to create romance, lovers today rely more on recorded music than on their own vocal cords. The technology of sound recordings gives composers, lyricists, and performers far larger audiences than would ever be possible through live performances.

LEARNING CHECK

- What has historically been the role of protest music?

Recording Industry

STUDY PREVIEW Ever heard of Bertelsmann or EMI? Most people haven't. Most music fans know artists and perhaps their labels, but the industry is in fact dominated by four global companies that have corporate tentacles in other media enterprises.

Scope of the Recording Industry

When people in earlier eras wanted music, they arranged to attend a concert. Many middle-class people went to the parlour and sat at the piano. Rural folks had their music too: a fiddle on the front porch in the evenings, a harmonica around the campfire. Music was a special event, a social gathering that had to be arranged. To those people, life today would seem like one big party—music everywhere all the time. Yes, we arrange for concerts and major musical events, but we also wake up to music, shop to music, and drive to music. Many of us work to music and study to music. In fact, the recording industry has products in so many parts of our lives that many people take most of them for granted.

The recording industry that brings music, both the flashy stuff and everything else, to mass audiences is gigantic. Global sales in 2004 were estimated at $33.6 billion. In 2007, the **Canadian Recording Industry Association (CRIA)** reported that music sales were worth $439 million. Roughly $75 million of that represented (legal) digital downloads, meaning that $365 million represented the physical market (actual CDs) in Canada. These totals don't include symbiotic industries such as fan magazines, music television, and radio. They are worth billions more. Then there are concerts, performers' merchandise, sponsorships, and a miscellany of related enterprises.

Canadian Recording Industry Association (CRIA) Trade association of Canadian music recording companies and distributors.

Majors

The recording industry is concentrated in four major companies, known as the **Big Four,** which have 75 percent of the global market. Each of these companies, in turn, is part of a larger media conglomerate.

Big Four Major recording companies: Universal Music, Sony BMG, EMI, Warner Music.

The file sharing crisis in the early 21st century shook up the industry's corporate landscape. Sony and Bertelsmann merged their music units. Bertelsmann, the German company that is the world's fifth-largest media company, runs the combined Sony BMG. Alarmed at declining sales in the new file sharing era, Time Warner sold its Warner Music in 2004 to Edgar Bronfman Jr. and fellow investors. Bronfman, heir to the Seagram liquor fortune in Canada, previously had run the Universal movie and recording empire but sold it to the French media conglomerate Vivendi. Although Vivendi, financially overextended, sold off many holdings to solve its own crisis in 2003, it decided to stay the course with Universal Music. There were no buyers anyway. Times were tough in the industry, and prospects for a recovery were cloudy at best.

The following companies dominate the recording industry. Also listed are their major acts by label and their percentage of the global market.

- **Universal Music (French), 25.5 percent.** Guns N' Roses (Universal), Jay-Z (Def Jam), Nelly Furtado (Dreamworks), George Strait (MCA Nashville), Snoop Dogg (Geffen), Gwen Stefani (Interscope), The Killers (Island)
- **Sony BMG (German), 21.5 percent.** Bruce Springsteen (Columbia), Jennifer Lopez (Epic), Santana (Legacy), Travis Tritt (Sony Nashville), Sloan (Yep Roc)

- **EMI (Anglo-Dutch), 13.1 percent.** Beastie Boys (Capitol), Janet Jackson (Virgin), Tina Turner (Capitol)
- **Warner Music (American), 11.3 percent.** Doors (Elektra), Rush (Atlantic), Green Day (Reprise), Madonna (Maverick)

Adam Curry Pioneer in podcasting technology.

The Big Four may become three. Warner Music and EMI have been in a merger dance, trying to find a way to sidestep objections from the European Union about market

CASE STUDY

Podcasting Evolution

Bands used to send their singles on a 45-rpm record to radio stations across the country, hoping for airplay. Today, musicians who want to reach a global audience send their music in a digital file to podcasters. These are people who put together their own internet audio shows, typically in the form of an MP3 file that is delivered to a listener with an iPod or other audio player or a computer with an internet connection and speakers. Listeners can access the podcast at their convenience, and it's free.

As of 2010, there were almost 10 000 podcasts in the music category at Podcast Alley, a directory of podcasts featuring every type of music from jazz to metal. Chris McIntyre started Podcast Alley to index as many podcasts as he could find. Music is only part of what his site indexes. "I truly believe that podcasting is a powerful communication tool and will have a profound effect on the way we communicate in the future," says the Purdue University, Indiana, graduate.

While musicians are hoping for exposure from the new medium, PodShow Inc. founder **Adam Curry** is poised to make big bucks from it. "Podfather" Curry and software pioneer Dave Winer developed the computer programs that make podcasting possible. The same venture capital companies that invested in Yahoo! and Google invested $9 million in PodShow Inc. when it was founded in 2005.

The mainstream media "are so diluted, so packaged, so predictable. There's so very little that is new or interesting," Curry told Martin Miller of the *Los Angeles Times*. "We've lost a lot of social connectedness that used to come from that. And what we're building here is a social media network for human beings." Curry's critics claim that the former MTV VJ "promotes himself as a would-be revolutionary for the little guy, but he's actually as profit mad as the corporate giants."

Other companies are jumping on the podcast wagon. In 2006, Nokia announced that some of its new phones would include a podcasting client featuring PodShow's top 10, Podcast Alley picks, and podcasts from Digital Podcast.

"Thousands of bands are submitting their songs to the Podsafe Music Network. They're connecting with podcasters and listeners, and now they're figuring out that it makes sense to promote shows together and share their audience with each other," said Curry. "This is another way bands are benefiting from the DIY/digital revolution in music."

Adam Curry Curry invented podcasting, which he sees as a revolutionary vehicle that allows just about anybody to assemble radio-like programs for global listening. All you need is a computer, a modem, and easy-to-use podcast software.

DEEPENING YOUR MEDIA LITERACY

Explore the Issue

Canvass 10 people around you on whether podcasts have become a part of their media habit. Ask what they seek from podcasts. Video stories? News? Music? And which podcasts seem most popular?

Dig Deeper

Visit the most popular podcast sites. Rank them for ease of access. What are the access charges, if any?

What Do You Think?

Does music content available on podcasts represent a significant shift in the retail delivery of recorded music? Or is it a blip in the music retailing landscape?

domination. The European Union also continues to scrutinize the Sony–Bertelsmann arrangement.

Indies

For decades a secondary tier of independent recording companies—**indies**, as they were known in industry jargon—struggled against the majors and occasionally produced a hit. Some independent labels, including Sun and Motown, were responsible for transforming music. However, when an indie amassed enough successes, it invariably was bought out by a major. The Department of Canadian Heritage states that independent labels are responsible for roughly 90 percent of Cancon produced here at home. Most of the companies are based in Ontario, but Quebec and British Columbia are also responsible for much of our independent music. Major Canadian indies include Nettwerk, Aquarius, and Quebec's TACCA Musique.

indies Independently owned recording companies; not part of the Big Four.

LEARNING CHECK

- What are the largest recording companies and the country in which each is based?
- Historically, what becomes of successful independent recording companies?

Downloads

STUDY PREVIEW Napster and other file sharing technology that facilitates music swapping seriously eroded music sales and record industry viability until 2005, when the U.S. Supreme Court intervened. In Canada, the legal issue of downloading took longer to resolve.

Explore

Media People: Shawn Fanning

File Sharing

Shawn Fanning's Napster technology ushered in a frenzy of free **file sharing** on the internet in 2000. Suddenly, record stores found themselves unable to move inventory. Major music retailer Sam the Record Man and other stores closed their doors. The free fall continued. For the first time in its history, the record industry was not in control of new technology—unlike during earlier adjustments, such as the switch to high fidelity and stereo and the introduction of eight-tracks, cassettes, and CDs, when companies exploited developments to spur sales.

Shawn Fanning Inventor of Napster.

Napster First online file sharing software.

file sharing Sharing music, usually individual songs, over the internet.

The **Recording Industry Association of America (RIAA)**, which represents recording companies, went to court against Napster. A federal judge accepted the argument that Napster was participating in copyright infringement by facilitating illicit copying of protected intellectual property. Napster was toast. But other file sharing mechanisms remained, and some were harder to tackle. Kazaa, for example, kept moving its operations from one offshore site to another, where legal action was impossible.

Recording Industry Association of America (RIAA) Trade association of recording companies.

In a surreal initiative in 2003, the RIAA began legal action against individuals who downloaded music without paying. The association's goal was a few hundred highly publicized lawsuits, and perhaps some showcase trials, to discourage **downloading** piracy. In one respect, this strategy backfired, as it engendered hard feelings among people who were the industry's greatest consumers.

downloading Installing a file on a computer from an internet source.

In another legal manoeuvre, the industry challenged Grokster and other file sharing services. The argument was that Grokster was not passively involved in copyright infringement via those sharing files but rather had actively encouraged this infringement. In 2005, the U.S. Supreme Court agreed, in what was quickly hailed as a landmark gain for the recording industry. The decision did not end file sharing immediately but hobbled the file sharing services enough that the RIAA was confident it had largely stopped the drain on its revenues.

In Canada, the CRIA also went to court. In early 2004, the CRIA's hopes of having the law on its side were dealt a severe blow. The CRIA had hoped that the Supreme Court of Canada would force internet service providers (ISPs) to identify people who shared

peer-to-peer (P2P) file sharing File sharing software without a central server.

files using **peer-to-peer (P2P) file sharing** programs. The Supreme Court ruled that simply placing files in a shared P2P folder does not constitute copyright infringement.

There's no doubt that file sharing has affected music sales. Data from the Department of Canadian Heritage claim that one-third of Canadians download music for free. Not surprisingly, teenagers are the worst offenders, with 68 percent of them claiming that they prefer to download music for free. Proposed changes to Canada's Copyright Act in 2010 may have an effect on file sharing. Time will tell.

Jeff Rose-Martland, host of VOCM-Radio Labrador, claims that the decline in music sales has little to do with P2P file sharing. Rather, it is a result of the quality of music today. According to Rose-Martland, "CRIA suggests that sales of all albums are down. Not true. Sales of the currently hyped albums are down. Sales of good-quality standards are up, as downloaders discover *The White Album, Ziggy Stardust,* and *Nevermind.*" Some of that quality music is Canadian, as two of the RIAA's top 100 albums of all time are by Canadian artists: Shania Twain's *Come on Over* and Alanis Morissette's *Jagged Little Pill.*

LEARNING CHECK

- How did Shawn Fanning shake the recording industry out of its new technology blind spot?
- What do you believe is the main reason for file sharing: P2P technology or the quality of music today?

Pirate Dubbing (copy)

Until the recording industry's crisis with downloading, the biggest drain on sales had been criminal music dubbing. Pirate dubbing operations, well financed and organized, have been estimated by the industry to account for 20 to 30 percent of CD sales in the United States. There are no firm figures, but the RIAA estimates that the loss globally is $5 billion a year.

The dubbed CDs are from questionable sources, mostly in Asia but also in other countries, including Saudi Arabia. It is not uncommon for a back-alley Third World pirate operation to have a hundred "slave" copying machines working simultaneously 24 hours a day. These pirate operations have no artistic, royalty, or promotion expenses. They dub CDs produced by legitimate companies and sell them through black market channels. Their costs are low; their profits are high.

Music piracy is also an issue in Canada. *The Globe and Mail*'s Barrie McKenna writes that "Canada has earned a dubious distinction as a world hub for illegitimate file-sharing websites and a leader in Internet piracy." As of early 2010, Canadian websites were among the most popular sites in the world for P2P file sharing, mostly using BitTorrent. In 2007–2008, the CRIA, along with the authorities, confiscated 700 000 pirated CDs. The CRIA argues that piracy is an issue in Canada because of the lack of copyright legislation with teeth. Other countries, such as the United Kingdom, France, and Sweden, have imposed severe penalties for those who share files over the internet. Graham Henderson, president of the CRIA, says, "We need to set some rules of the road—so Canadians can know clearly the difference between legitimate and illegitimate on-line products and practices. We need to protect creators' livelihoods—the fruit of their creativity, hard work, and financial investment."

LEARNING CHECK

- How are profits made in the pirate dubbing of recorded music for the black market?
- Should Canada follow the lead set by other countries to try to offset this digital piracy?

Authorized Downloads

STUDY PREVIEW The recording industry has moved to get on top of downloading technology with new retailing models. These include the iPod/iTunes distribution structure introduced by Apple, as well as imitators. This shift in retailing has hurt bricks-and-mortar stores, whose sales have slipped. Some chains have gone out of business.

iTunes

The recording industry, comfortable and immensely profitable, was caught unaware by Napster-inspired online file sharing. When the industry finally woke up to the threat, a tremendous floundering occurred on how to tap in to the new technology. Numerous stabs at a new business model fell apart—until **Steve Jobs** of Apple Computer presented himself as a knight in shining armour with the online **iTunes** music store. On the iTunes site, people can sample songs with a single click and then download with another click for about $1 per song. Puretracks, Canada's first online music site, debuted in 2004.

Steve Jobs The driving force behind the Apple Computer revival, iPod, and iTunes.

iTunes Apple-owned online retail site for recorded music.

Unlike file sharing, iTunes isn't free. But it has advantages. For example, the sound quality is exceptional. Apple developed a new format that compresses music efficiently, downloads faster, and consumes less disk space. Also, it is a clean system, free of the annoying viruses that affected file sharing systems like Kazaa, Morpheus, and Grokster. Apple benefited, too, from the guilt trip that the RIAA and the CRIA were using on illegal downloaders.

The iPod started the mobile digital music revolution. Smart phones, such as Apple's iPhone, RIM's BlackBerry, and Google's Nexus One, added another vehicle for music portability.

LEARNING CHECK

- How does iTunes generate profits for both Apple and recording companies?
- Despite many products attempting to challenge iPod and iTunes, none have come close. Why?

Retailing

The iTunes concept drastically changed the retailing of recorded music. Record shops, once the core outlet for recording companies, were already under siege by big retailers. With iTunes, even the chains were in trouble. Canada's venerable Sam the Record Man closed its doors in 2007. The new retailing structure largely revolves around download services like iTunes, online retailers like Amazon.ca, and giant retailers like Walmart and Best Buy.

LEARNING CHECK

- Who have been the losers in the retailing change introduced by iTunes?
- Who are the survivors?

Do the Math Once considered an icon in the Canadian music industry, Sam the Record Man closed the doors on its flagship store in Toronto in 2007. Owners cited competition from music downloading as the primary reason.

Artistic Autonomy

STUDY PREVIEW Major labels once dominated the nation's music with expensive talent and recording operations that neither indies nor individual performers could match. Digital recording equipment in the 1980s loosened the majors' artistic control.

A&R Structure

AR (artist and repertoire) Units of recording company responsible for talent.

The heart of the recording industry once was the powerful **A&R (artist and repertoire)** units at major labels. In an arrogant tyranny over artists, A&R executives manufactured countless performers. They groomed artists for stardom, chose their music, ordered the arrangements, controlled recording sessions, and even chose their wardrobes for public performances.

ABC's *Nightline*: "Kanye West: Hip Hop's Creative Genius"

In his book *Solid Gold,* R. Serge Denisoff quotes a Capitol executive from the 1950s explaining how the A&R system worked: "The company would pick out 12 songs for Peggy Lee and tell her to be at the studio Wednesday at 8, and she'd show up and sing what you told her. And she'd leave three hours later and Capitol'd take her songs and do anything it wanted with them. That was a time when the artist was supposed to shut up and put up with anything the almighty recording company wanted."

Media People: 50 Cent

The muscle of the major recording companies, aiming for mass market sales, contributed to a homogenizing of culture. Coast to coast, everybody was humming the same new tunes from Peggy Lee and other pop singers, who served a robot-like role for A&R managers. The A&R structure was a top-down system for creating pop culture. A relatively small number of powerful A&R executives decided what would be recorded and marketed. It was the opposite of grassroots artistry.

LEARNING CHECK

- How do you think the Dixie Chicks would respond if A&R executives tried to dictate their repertoire, and even their style, as they did with Peggy Lee?
- Has our culture been enriched or damaged by the diminished A&R role today?

Performer Influences

garage bands Term coined for upstart performers without a studio contract.

In the 1980s, sophisticated low-cost recording and mixing equipment gave individual artists and **garage bands** a means to control their art. The million-dollar sound studio, controlled by major labels and their A&R people, became less important. As little as $15 000 could buy digital recorders and 24-channel mixing boards to accomplish what only a major studio could have a few years earlier. The upshot was creative liberation. Artists suddenly had an independence that big recording companies were forced to accommodate. Linda Ronstadt, for example, shifted her recording to a home studio in her basement. Some artists, such as LL Cool J, went so far as to create their own labels. The ability of artists to go out on their own gave them clout that was not possible in the A&R heyday.

LEARNING CHECK

- How has technology enabled artistic creativity?
- What is a cultural downside to the demassification that has come with greater artistic autonomy?

Social Issues and Music

Watch

ABC's *Nightline*: "Hip Hop and Violence"

STUDY PREVIEW The recording industry has been a scapegoat for social ills. To stay one step ahead of government censorship, the industry has taken a cue from other media groups and introduced self-regulation to head off crises.

Record Labelling

Parents Music Resource Center Crusaded for labels on "objectionable" music.

In the 1980s, complaints arose about lyrics regarding drugs and sexual promiscuity. In the United States, the **Parents Music Resource Center**, a group led by Tipper Gore and the wives of several other influential members of Congress, claimed that there were links between explicit rock music and teen suicide, teen pregnancy, abusive parents, broken homes, and other social ills. The group objected to lyrics such as those in Def Leppard's "High and Dry," which extols drug and alcohol use; Mötley Crüe's "Bastard," with its violent overtones; and Cyndi Lauper's "She Bop," which was a thinly veiled song about masturbation.

The Parents Music Resource Center argued that consumer protection laws should be invoked to require that records with offensive lyrics be labelled as dangerous, similar to cigarette warning labels or the movie industry's rating system. Record companies began labelling potentially offensive records with "Explicit Lyrics—Parental Advisory." In some cases, the companies printed lyrics on album covers as a warning. Online retailers, including iTunes, put a label of "explicit" on songs that might raise prudish eyebrows.

LEARNING CHECK

- Why did recording companies embrace the idea of labelling music with objectionable lyrics? Was this a good thing?
- What is the purpose of labelling objectionable music? Does labelling accomplish its purpose?

Dependence on Radio

STUDY PREVIEW The recording industry relies on radio for free advertising of its wares. Airplay has been essential for recordings to sell. This has led to legal issues, such as under-the-table payments to decision makers at influential stations in exchange for airtime.

Government Influence on Canadian Music

Historically, the radio and record industries have always been intimately connected. However, during the 1950s and 1960s, it was often difficult for Canadian musicians and songwriters to get their songs heard on the radio. During that period, it's estimated that Canadian music made up about 4 percent of all music heard on Canadian radio. In his autobiography, *Taking Care of Business,* Randy Bachman of The Guess Who and Bachman-Turner Overdrive said that quite often Canadian radio wouldn't play a Canadian song until it became a "hit" in the United States. That's why his group called itself The Guess Who: to eliminate any anti-Canadian bias from radio. It's hard to believe, but according to Nicholas Jennings in *Before the Goldrush,* when debate on the issue of Canadian content on radio began in the late 1960s, radio stations were against it. Jennings explains that the Canadian Association of Broadcasters claimed that imposing Canadian content regulations on radio would "lower the attractiveness of stations to the listener."

This was the main reason for instituting Canadian content regulations for radio in 1971. English-language stations must play 35 percent **Cancon,** while French-language stations need to play 65 percent Cancon. But what makes a song Canadian? In 1970, Stan Klees of *RPM* magazine developed the Cancon MAPL to help the industry define Canadian content. To be categorized as Cancon, a song must generally fulfill two of the following four conditions:

Cancon Short form for Canadian content.

- **M (music):** The music must be written by a Canadian (citizen or landed immigrant).
- **A (artist):** The music or lyrics must be principally performed by a Canadian artist.
- **P (produced/performed):** The recording must have been either produced in Canada or performed and broadcast live in Canada.
- **L (lyrics):** The lyrics must be written by a Canadian.

While the system seems to favour Canadian artists, it can also discriminate against Canadian singers. A controversy involving Bryan Adams is a good example of this discrimination. His song from *Robin Hood: Prince of Thieves,* "I Do It for You (Everything I Do)," and other songs on his album *WakingUp the Neighbours* originally were not considered Canadian content because he co-wrote them with a British songwriter. Due to the controversy that ensued, the CRTC amended the MAPL formula to allow for Canadian songwriters who collaborate with foreigners.

MEDIA PEOPLE Alan Cross

Since his days as a political science and history student, **Alan Cross** has had a passion for music and radio. His first show was on the University of Winnipeg's closed-circuit radio station, CKUW, in 1980. He turned that passion into a radio career that has seen him become somewhat of a music "guru" in Canada.

The radio program *The Ongoing History of New Music* has been a staple of the Canadian alternative music scene since its debut in February 1993. The show began as a way of educating listeners about the grunge revolution that was happening at the time. According to Cross, "It was obvious that there was a change happening in the world of rock and a new generation was about to take over and displace the hair metal bands that had been around since the 1980s. Our radio station jumped on the new music bandwagon. It was also decided that in order to put this new music into the appropriate context, it was necessary to have a documentary program that would help everybody understand where this music came from, why it's important, where it's going, and where its heritage was."

The music industry has undergone some seismic changes in the last 10 years. "Back in the 1960s, 1970s, and 1980s, bands were allowed to develop over time. REM really didn't have a hit until album number six. U2 had to wait until album number three until they had their breakthrough. The major record labels had patience for talent development. Those luxuries don't exist anymore. Although sales of digital downloads continue to climb, they have yet to offset the decline in the sales of physical CDs. Meanwhile, small, nimble independent record companies are able to pounce on trends more quickly—plus they're able to service niche music markets more effectively. In fact, most of the truly groundbreaking new music today is coming from the small independent labels—just like back in the 1950s and 1960s—and is once again becoming more and more prevalent. Small Canadian labels like Sonic Unyon, Arts&Crafts and Maple Music now wield considerable influence and power."

In regards to Canadian content, Cross also has an interesting point of view: "When the regulations were first introduced more than 35 years ago, Cancon was a necessary cultural and industrial strategy. The country was being completely overrun by international interests. Most record companies were simply branch offices of their American parents and they, naturally, were interested in marketing their American artists. Homegrown performers were squeezed out and not given a chance to develop in any way. It was a vicious circle. You couldn't get on the radio because you weren't good enough, and you couldn't get good enough because you couldn't get on the radio. It was tough, but the imposition of Cancon quotas has been a very successful strategy. It helped create an industry where we actually have vibrant, profitable, and relevant record labels, not to mention some world-class musicians. Canada probably exports more than its fair share of music, given our population."

That being said, Cross feels that since Cancon has made Canadian music successful, we have to ask ourselves, "At what point are the quotas no longer necessary? People will point to the cultural imperialism of the United States and say that the only way to maintain Canadian cultural sovereignty is to maintain or even raise these quotas. They feel the Cancon rules have accomplished their mission and now it's time for Canadian artists to stand on their own. After a few years, the question became 'Should Cancon quotas be raised, lowered or eliminated altogether?' During the CRTC's review of radio in 2006, some groups lobbied for Cancon to be increased from 35% to 40, 45 and even beyond 50% while others argued that with the increasingly popular and borderless world of the Internet, traditional broadcasters shouldn't be hobbled with additional regulation and quotas. When the dust cleared, though, the Commission left levels at 35%. Still, the subject of Cancon levels remains a very politically charged debate amongst broadcasters, record companies, artists, songwriters, music publishers, music collectives, the Heritage Ministry, and the CRTC."

Alan Cross

The issue isn't going to go away. With the infinite supply of music on the unregulated internet—and with the consumers' ability to get whatever song they want, wherever they happen to be on whatever device they choose—radio is no longer the primary cultural gatekeeper for music. Tough decisions will need to be made about Cancon in the very near future.

TABLE 5.1

Best Cancon Albums and Singles

Bob Mersereau, reporter for CBC-TV in New Brunswick, has written two books about Canadian music. In 2007, he wrote *The Top 100 Canadian Albums.* In 2010, his follow-up, *The Top 100 Canadian Singles,* was released. The lists were based on a cross-country survey of musicians, DJs, and music industry professionals. No list is definitive; as Mersereau points out in the introduction to the first book, "Let the arguments begin." In 2010, his follow-up, *The Top 100 Canadian Singles,* was released. The arguments continued.

Top Five Canadian Albums	Top Five Canadian Singles
1. *Harvest,* Neil Young	1. "American Woman," The Guess Who
2. *Blue,* Joni Mitchell	2. "Heart of Gold," Neil Young
3. *After the Gold Rush,* Neil Young	3. "The Weight," The Band
4. *Music from Big Pink,* The Band	4. "Summer of '69," Bryan Adams
5. *Fully Completely,* The Tragically Hip	5. "Hallelujah," Leonard Cohen

Source: Bob Mersereau, *The Top 100 Canadian Albums* (Goose Lane, 2008) and *The Top 100 Canadian Singles* (Goose Lane, 2010). Reprinted with permission.

What Is Canadian about Canadian Content?

Deepening Your Media Literacy: Does popular music reflect our personal identity?

From a semiotic perspective, if music and lyrics (as signs) signify something other than themselves, one might ask: What does the lyrical and musical content of Cancon say about Canadian culture?

A statistical analysis of all of the songs that reached number one on the CHUM chart for a 13-year period before and a 13-year period after the implementation of Cancon regulations might help to answer this question. CHUM was a Top 40 powerhouse in Toronto from May 1957 to 1986. The survey reveals that 13 Canadian songs reached number one between 1957 and 1969, while 19 Canadian songs reached number one between 1970 and 1982. On the surface, this seems to show that the regulations were successful in promoting Canadian talent and the music industry, as six more Canadian songs reached number one in an equivalent period. However, a closer analysis shows that these songs had few Canadian signifiers in their lyrics.

Alan Cross New music historian.

During the period before the regulations, 1957 to 1969, at least four of the Canadian songs that reached number one were written by Canadians but recorded by Americans. They included "It Doesn't Matter Anymore" by Buddy Holly, "Love Child" by the Supremes, "Aquarius/Let the Sun Shine In" by the Fifth Dimension, and "Sugar, Sugar" by the Archies. From an economic standpoint, these songs undoubtedly helped the Canadian music industry, but their lyrics say little, if anything, about Canada. In essence, they are American songs written for the American market. In addition, two of the number-one Canadian songs were included on American movie soundtracks. For example, "Born to Be Wild" by Steppenwolf was featured in the film *Easy Rider,* while "One Tin Soldier" by the Original Caste was used in the movie *Billy Jack*. The only Canadian song to reach number one that was explicitly about Canada was the novelty song "Clear the Track, Here Comes Shack" by Douglas Rankine & the Secrets. The song was a tribute to Eddie Shack, a hockey player with the Toronto Maple Leafs.

After the Canadian content regulations came into effect in 1971, the number of Canadian number-one singles on the CHUM charts in a 13-year period increased from 13 to 19. However, the same patterns that existed before the Cancon regulations were still evident: American artists continued to record songs written by Canadians. For example, "Puppy Love," recorded by Donny Osmond, and "She's a Lady," sung by Tom Jones, were both written by Paul Anka. "Woodstock," about the mythic American music festival, was written by Joni Mitchell and recorded by Crosby, Stills, Nash & Young. Perhaps only two number-one Canadian singles during this period were openly nationalistic. The first was "American Woman" (which also reached number one in the United States) by The Guess Who. The song's lyrics made clear distinctions between Canadian and American culture. The other uniquely Canadian number-one single was "Take Off" by Bob and Doug McKenzie (SCTV comics Rick Moranis and Dave Thomas). However, like "Clear the Track, Here Comes Shack," this brand of nationalism was humorous in nature and perhaps reached number one due to its novelty.

LEARNING CHECK

- How is Canadian content defined by the CRTC?
- Should Cancon levels be increased? Decreased?

Radio Partnership

airplay Radio time devoted to a particular recording.

payola Under-the-table payments made to plug a product in the mass media.

When radio shifted mostly to playing recorded music in the 1950s, **airplay** became essential for a new recording to succeed. Radio, in effect, became free advertising. To win airtime, record companies began bribing prominent disc jockeys to play their music. This gave rise to a **payola** scandal. One audit found that $230 000 in "consulting fees" had been paid to radio stations in 23 cities. The Federal Trade Commission in the United States issued charges of unfair competition.

Managers of American radio stations, worried that their licences would be rescinded by the Federal Communications Commission, began demanding signed statements from disc jockeys that they had not accepted payola. Dozens of disc jockeys in major markets quietly left town. The scandals demonstrated that the recording industry's partnership with radio had become a relationship of dependence.

LEARNING CHECK

- Radio needs music and the recording industry needs radio. Is this a mutual interdependence? Or is one party more dependent than the other?
- If payola is a crime, who is the victim?

Marketing through Radio

The relationship of dependence has created a series of payola issues over the years. In the 1980s, there were indictments for buying airtime under the table. In 1988, two independent promoters were charged with paying $270 000 to program directors at nine stations whose playlists were widely imitated by other stations. One station executive was charged with receiving $100 000 over two years. Some payola bribery involved drugs.

Although radio has declined in importance in terms of promoting records, because young people are opting for iPods and similar devices, nothing beats free advertising. Recording companies still supply stations with new music in hopes that it will find its way onto the air. In an imaginative move, country duo Montgomery Gentry recorded its single "*Lucky* Man" 81 times, each time with a different college or professional athletic team in the lyrics. The idea was to attract radio station directors in markets key to each version of the song and encourage airplay. At the very least, figured Montgomery Gentry's promoters, the local tie-in would prolong airplay more than normal.

LEARNING CHECK

- How has radio's importance in marketing new music changed over the years?

Measures of Success

gold record Award for sales of 1 million singles or 500 000 albums in the United States.

platinum record Award for sales of 2 million singles or 1 million albums in the United States.

gold seal Award for sales of 50 000 albums in Canada.

platinum seal Award for sales of 100 000 albums in Canada.

diamond seal Award for sales of 1 million albums in Canada.

It would be wrong to suggest that successful recordings can result only from manipulation. Once new music crosses the threshold to exposure, its commercial success rests with public acceptance. Exposure, however, is key. The publicity that comes with a Grammy award, for example, inevitably boosts sales, usually dramatically.

The most often-cited measure of success is sales. Once a single sells 1 million copies or an album sells 500 000 copies, the RIAA confers a **gold record** award. A **platinum record** is awarded for 2 million singles sold or 1 million albums. The CRIA awards a **gold seal** for sales of 50 000, a **platinum seal** for sales of 100 000, and a **diamond seal** for recordings that sell 1 million copies in Canada.

The Grammy Bounce In the two days after the 2005 Grammy Awards tribute to Ray Charles, sales of his *Genius Loves Company* album spiked 875 percent at the Tower Records chain. The Grammy bounce is a perennial phenomenon. In 2003, Norah Jones' *Come Away With Me* zoomed to number one within a week of the Grammys. Sales soon topped 9.2 million.

Two awards that honour the best in contemporary music are the Grammys and the Junos. The **Grammy** award has been the symbol of music success in the United States since 1957. Winners are determined by members of the National Academy of Recording Arts and Sciences (NARAS; also known as the Recording Academy). The **Junos** were named after Pierre Juneau, who was head of the CRTC when the Canadian content regulations were implemented. The idea of honouring the Canadian music industry came from Walt Grealis and Stan Klees, who published *RPM*, a music industry trade journal. Like the Grammy, the Juno is a peer award. Members of the Canadian Academy of Recording Arts and Sciences (CARAS) vote on nominees and winners.

Grammy Award for excellence in music in the United States.

Juno Award for excellence in music in Canada.

LEARNING CHECK

- What does it mean when a record goes gold in Canada? Platinum? Diamond?
- What is the Grammy bounce?
- What noneconomic measures can be used to evaluate a recording's success?

Watch

***A Day in the Life:* OM Records Marketing**

Chapter 5 Wrap-Up

The impact on the music industry of Shawn Fanning's Napster, which at one point threatened to force a fundamental restructuring of the industry, is a reminder that the mass media are technology driven. However, just as digital internet technology has bedevilled the recording industry, technology has also come to its rescue. The iTunes online store that coordinates downloading to personal computers and iPods has reshaped music retailing. The iPod also has allowed the recording industry to survive in its traditional form with a few dominant major companies.

PEARSON mycanadiancommunicationlab

Visit **www.mycanadiancommunicationlab.ca** for access to a wealth of tools and resources that will enhance your learning experience. Features include the following:

- Personalized Study Plan
- Videos
- Activities
- Pearson eText–and much more!

Questions for Critical Thinking

1. Why is music such a powerful force in our lives?
2. How has technology changed creativity in the music business?
3. What is the effect of file sharing on the music industry?
4. What has replaced radio as a marketing tool for music?
5. Should levels of Canadian content be increased on Canadian radio? Why or why not?

Keeping Up to Date

The weekly *Billboard* is the recording industry's leading trade journal.

Consumer magazines that track popular music and report on the recording industry include *Canadian Musician, Rolling Stone,* and *Spin.*

Entertainment Weekly and *Maclean's* both have regular sections on music, as do many daily papers, such as *The Globe and Mail* and the *National Post*

Radio

6

Howard Stern By taking shock jock Howard Stern's show to satellite radio, Sirius aimed to siphon more listeners from traditional stations. In a case study later in this chapter, you will have a chance to discuss the effect Stern has had on radio.

LEARNING AHEAD

- Radio is easily accessible, but the audience for traditional stations is slipping.
- Music, news, and talk are the primary radio content.
- Regulation relies on the idea of government and stations as trustees of the public airwaves.
- Chains have reshaped the radio industry.
- Public radio has filled a niche abandoned by commercial stations.
- Satellite radio has shaken the infrastructure of the radio industry.

MEDIA IN THEORY

What Makes Radio Different?

What makes radio different from other media? **Andrew Crisell**, a cultural theorist, refers to radio as a blind medium: You can't see it with your eyes, like you can television, a movie, or a newspaper. You can see the pictures only in your mind. Radio broadcasters use time, not space, as their canvas to communicate messages. Building on the ideas of Roland Barthes, radio uses four signs to create its imagery: words, sounds, music, and silence. As Canada's Radio Marketing Bureau puts it, radio lets you "imagine the possibilities." Even Marshall McLuhan referred to radio as a visual medium.

Andrew Crisell Uses the ideas of semiotician Roland Barthes to analyze how radio meaning is created.

As discussed earlier in this book, words can be symbolic in that they represent something other than themselves. The phrase *maple leaf* isn't a real maple leaf but simply a label that our culture attaches to the physical object of a maple leaf. This naming process is entirely arbitrary. However, words in radio differ from words in print because they are spoken. It's not so much what you say, but how you say it. The way in which an announcer or radio performer speaks also communicates meaning. Words end up working on two levels; not only do the words themselves stand for something else, but the way in which they are spoken signifies something as well. For example, an announcer can say "great!" and mean it in two different ways—one positive, one negative.

MEDIA TIMELINE Radio Technology and Regulation

1901 Guglielmo Marconi received a message from Cornwall, England, by radio in Signal Hill, Newfoundland.

1906 Reginald Fessenden broadcast to ships at sea on Christmas Eve.

1906 Lee de Forest created the audion tube that allowed voice transmission.

1912 David Sarnoff used radio to learn news of the *Titanic* disaster, putting radio in the public eye.

1920 XWA in Montreal began broadcasting in Canada.

1927 Canada's Diamond Jubilee was broadcast.

1929 Aird Commission released its report on radio broadcasting in Canada.

1936 CBC began broadcasting.

1939 Edwin Armstrong put the first FM station on air.

1998 CRTC relaxed regulations on radio ownership.

1999 Digital audio broadcasting (DAB) began in Canada.

2000s Ownership convergence of radio began.

2005 CRTC reviewed Canada's radio policy.

2005 Satellite radio arrived in Canada.

Sounds or sound effects are indexical signs. The sound of a creaking door is an index of a creaking door. To someone listening to Jerry Howarth broadcast a Blue Jays game, the loud crack of a bat and the cheering of a crowd signify that a home run has been hit. Sounds anchor the meaning or image created by radio; this is important due to the invisible nature of radio. Sounds let us know where we are and what's going on.

The third sign of radio, music, works on several levels. The music you hear on a radio station helps you to identify the station. When you hear Terri Clark or Emerson Drive, you know you're listening to a country station; if you hear Michael Bublé or Nickelback, you know the station is not country. Music can also act as a bridge between segments of a radio show, newsmagazine, or play, or it can be used to create a mood in a radio play.

An absence of any of these three signs signifies something in itself. As a sign, silence works to communicate meaning in two ways. First, it can be symbolic. A minute of silence on Remembrance Day symbolizes respect and honour for soldiers who died in war. But silence can also be an index that something's wrong with the broadcast; a power outage, a faulty microphone, or radio transmitter problems can all cause what is known as "dead air."

Influence of Radio

STUDY PREVIEW Radio has become a ubiquitous mass medium, available everywhere at any time. Within the industry, however, there are troubling signs. Radio's primary programming—music—has become available through other devices, many that have no advertising. A key radio audience, the segment aged 12 to 34, has fallen off in recent years.

Ubiquity

Radio is everywhere. The signals are carried on the electromagnetic spectrum to almost every nook and cranny. Hardly a place in the world is beyond the reach of radio. At no time in recent Canadian history was this more evident than during the massive east coast blackout in August 2003. At that time, people turned to their portable radios for the latest information. This is a wonderful example of radio doing what it does best. **Howard Christensen**, publisher of *Broadcast Dialogue*, says that the blackout illustrated "just how dependent we can be on local radio stations—and on our ownership of battery powered radios. On August 14 at 4:11 EST, more than 50 million people would have been left in a news dissemination void were it not for this century old, voices in the ether technology. It was radio's community involvement, its caring and, indeed, its sharing. The medium was—gadzooks—rediscovered."

Howard Christensen Publishes *Broadcast Dialogue* magazine.

But why would radio need to be rediscovered, given its ubiquity? Statistics abound about radio's importance. Consider the following data from the Canadian Radio-television and Telecommunications Commission's (CRTC) *2010 Monitoring Report*: Canada has 1221 radio stations and audio services.

Although radio is important, cracks are developing in the medium's reach. The audience is moving from traditional stations to iPods, direct-to-listener satellite services, and mobile devices. Millions still might tune in, but the audience is shifting. For example, the average Canadian listened to about 17.7 hours of radio each week in 2010, a decrease of 3.2 percent since 2009. Add to this the fact that Canadians aged 12 to 34 are listening to less radio than in the past. This presents serious challenges for radio's future.

Canada's **Radio Marketing Bureau (RMB)** sums up the power of radio in its annual Foundation Research Studies: "Radio is part of Canadian's daily routine, it reflects and adapts to their lifestyle. It's a perfect fit for modern life; it's effortless, easy to listen to during other activities; entertains and informs throughout the day; is compatible with other media and provides a soundtrack for life." Radio is also a nice complement to internet surfing. According to Gary Belgrave, president of the RMB, the organization's 2010 study suggests that "far from competing, the Internet gives radio a new dimension. Radio station brands translate well to the interactive world giving them a new platform to engage listeners."

Radio Marketing Bureau (RMB) Claims that radio is a perfect fit for modern life.

LEARNING CHECK

- What are some measures of radio's audience reach?
- Is the radio audience expanding or constricting?

Scope of the Radio Industry in Canada

Of the 1213 radio stations in Canada, more than 700 are commercial AM or FM stations. Most of these are owned by large corporations. Corus Entertainment, Rogers Communications, CTVglobemedia, and Astral Media are the largest Canadian radio companies. According to the CRTC, these companies combine for more than 70 percent of radio listening in Canada.

Canadian radio is significant as a $1.6-billion-a-year industry. The profits, however, are due not only to audience and advertising growth, which can be a challenge, but also to the chains' economies of scale and radical cost-cutting. This is an effect of media convergence.

LEARNING CHECK

- How has chain ownership made radio profitable?

Radio Content

STUDY PREVIEW Radio programming falls mostly into three categories: entertainment, mostly music; news; and talk.

Radio Entertainment

In 1918, the Montreal-based radio station XWA, owned by the Marconi Wireless Telegraph Company, was the first station to obtain a broadcasting licence from the federal government under the Radiotelegraph Act of 1913. Its first broadcast took place in May 1920, under Marconi's supervision. XWA was the first station to have regularly scheduled programs, the first of which was a musical program, a Dorothy Lutton concert to the Royal Society of Canada in Montreal. This was the beginning of people turning to their radios for entertainment.

Watch

A Day in the Life: **Radio DJ "Showbiz"**

During the 1920s, radios became an integral part of Canadians' living rooms. These were big radios, some as large as today's home entertainment units. People listened to the radio then in much the same way we watch television today: after supper, with or without the family. A radio was considered a status symbol, and much of the programming

MEDIA PEOPLE Gordon McLendon

A crisis hit American radio history in the 1950s. As comedies, dramas, and quiz shows moved to television, so did the huge audience that radio had cultivated. The radio networks, losing advertisers to television, scaled back what they offered to stations. As the number of listeners dropped, local stations switched to recorded music, which was far cheaper than producing programs.

To the rescue came Gordon McLendon, who perfected a new format, Top 40, that repeated the day's most popular new music in rotation. McLendon developed this format at KLIF in Dallas, Texas, by mixing the music with fast-paced newscasts, disc jockey chatter, lively commercials, and promotional jingles and hype. It was catchy, almost hypnotizing—and widely imitated.

With portable transistor radios coming onto the market and a growing number of automobiles outfitted with radios, Top 40 was right for the times. People could tune in and tune out while on the go. Most tunes lasted only three minutes or so. This was not programming designed for half-hour blocks. It reshaped radio as a medium that began a recovery in a new incarnation even as some observers were writing its epitaph.

McLendon was no one-hit wonder. He also designed so-called "beautiful music" as a format at KABL, San Francisco, in 1959; all-news at XTRA, Tijuana, Mexico, aimed at southern California, in 1961; and all–classified ads at KADS, Los Angeles, in 1967. In all of his innovations, McLendon was firm about maintaining a strict structure. In Top 40, for example, there were no deviations from music in rotation, news every 20 minutes, naming the station by call letters twice between songs, upbeat jingles, and no deadpan commercials. McLendon's classified-ad format bombed, but his other formats have survived. For better or worse, McLendon is the father of format radio.

Gordon McLendon

TABLE 6.1

Radio Tuning Shares, English-Language Station Formats

Radio was one of the first media to demassify, a trend that continues to this day. Here's a list of the most popular radio station formats in Canada, according to the CRTC:

Format	Share
Adult Contemporary	12.9%
Country	12.8%
News/talk	11.5%
CBC Radio One	9.4%
Mainstream Top 40	8.3%

Source: CRTC Communications Policy Monitoring Report, 2010. Reproduced with the permission of the Minister of Public Works and Government Services, 2010.

WHAT DO YOU THINK?

1. How would Gordon McLendon judge the advent of satellite radio?
2. What advice would Gordon McLendon offer commercial stations about losing audience to public radio?
3. What does Table 6.1, on popular radio station formats, say about who is listening to radio?

reflected this: broadcasts included concerts, political commentary, dramas, and comedies. Broadcasts of hockey games, sponsored by General Motors, were the most popular radio programs of the early days of the medium, beginning in 1923. Within 10 years, hockey broadcasts were heard on 20 Canadian radio stations from coast to coast. This sponsorship by General Motors also marked the beginning of "commercial" radio in Canada.

The comedies, dramas, variety shows, and quiz shows that dominated network-provided radio programming in the 1930s and 1940s moved to television in the 1950s. So did the huge audience that radio had cultivated. The radio networks, losing advertisers to television, scaled back what they offered to affiliates. As the number of listeners dropped, local stations switched to more recorded music, which was far cheaper than producing concerts, dramas, and comedies. Thus, radio reinvented itself, survived, and prospered.

The industry found itself shaken again in the 1970s when listeners flocked to new FM stations. Because FM technology offered superior sound fidelity, FM stations became the stations of choice for music. AM listenership seemed destined to tank until, in another reinvention, most AM stations converted to nonmusic formats. From its roots in 1961 with programming genius Gordon McLendon, who beamed the first 24/7 news into southern California from XTRA across the border in Tijuana, all-news radio took off as a format in major cities. So did listener call-in shows featuring colourful hosts.

LEARNING CHECK

- How did radio content change dramatically in the 1950s? Why did it change?

Radio News

Radio news preceded radio stations. In November 1916, Lee de Forest arranged with a New York newspaper, the *American*, to broadcast election returns. With home-built receivers, hundreds of people tuned in to hear an experimental transmission and heard de Forest proclaim: "Charles Evans Hughes will be the next president of the United States." It was an inauspicious beginning, as de Forest had it wrong. Actually, Woodrow Wilson was re-elected. In 1920, KDKA signed on as America's first licensed commercial station and began by reporting the Harding–Cox presidential race as returns were being counted at the Pittsburgh *Post*. This time, radio got the winner right.

Radio news today has diverse forms, some based on the notion of drawing listeners to reports on breaking events as they happen, some more focused on depth and understanding. Mostly, though, radio news is known for being on top of events as they happen. Prior to radio, Canadians relied on newspapers to report on events after they happened. Radio allowed them to experience news as it happened.

Explore

Media People: Edward R. Murrow

Breaking News In 1936, CBC news reporter J. Frank Willis kept Canadians on the edge of their seats reporting live from the scene of a mine disaster in Nova Scotia. Over two and a half days, Willis filed a two-minute report every 15 minutes. Willis described both the tragedy of the collapse of the mine and the thrill of the successful rescue of the trapped miners. According to the CBC Digital Archives, "It [was] North America's very first live 24-hour news event, changing forever the perception of what radio can do."

Radio news came into its own in World War II, when the networks sent correspondents abroad. Radio listeners, eager for news from Europe, developed a habit of listening to the likes of Edward R. Murrow and other giants of mid-20th-century journalism, including CBC reporter Matthew Halton. As a medium of instantaneous reporting, radio offered news on breakthrough events even before newspapers could issue special extra editions. The term *breaking news* emerged as something to which radio was uniquely suited.

Headline Service In the relatively tranquil period after World War II, with people less intent on news, the radio industry recognized that listeners tuned away from lengthy stories. News formats shifted to shorter stories, making radio a headline service. Details and depth were left to newspapers. Gordon McLendon's influential rock 'n' roll format in the 1960s epitomized the headline service, generally with three- to four-minute hourly newscasts.

All News As contradictory as it may seem, Gordon McLendon also invented all-news radio, also in the 1960s. For the Los Angeles market, McLendon set up a skeletal staff at XTRA across the border in Tijuana to read wire copy nonstop. When XTRA turned profitable, McLendon took over a Chicago station, renamed it WNUS, and converted it to all news. This was a dramatic departure from the idea of radio as a mass medium with each station trying for the largest possible audience. McLendon's WNUS and subsequent all-news stations sought niche audiences, finding early profitability in demassification—a narrow part of the larger mosaic of the whole radio market. Today, all-news stations are available in almost every Canadian market.

LEARNING CHECK

- What are the different formats for radio news?
- What stations and networks feature each of these formats in your hometown?

Talk Radio

Call-in formats were greeted enthusiastically at first because of their potential as forums for discussion of public issues, but there was a downside. Many stations with music-based formats used the advent of news and talk stations to reduce their news programming. In effect, many music stations were saying, "Let those guys do news and talk, and we'll do music." The rationale really was a profit-motivated guise to get out of news and public affairs, which are expensive to produce. By contrast, playing recorded music is cheap. The result was fewer stations offering serious news and public affairs programming. While some might lament the lack of news on all-music stations, in these days of demassification and diversification, people who tune in to a music station are tuning in for music; they don't want much in the way of news and information programming.

Talk radio may offer access to the "commoners," or so it would seem. Paul Rutherford, a communication professor at the University of Toronto, says that talk radio is "providing a voice for people who otherwise wouldn't have one." Today, many Canadians feel a sense of alienation; they believe that politicians simply aren't listening to them. To vent their frustrations, many turn to talk radio. This gives listeners a sense that they are finally being heard. Sometimes politicians listen; sometimes they don't.

Among many people, talk formats lead to a perception that there is more news and public affairs on radio than ever. The fact is that fewer stations offer news. Outside of major markets with all-news stations, stations that promote themselves as news-talk are really more talk than news, with much of the talk no more than thinly veiled entertainment that trivializes the format's potential.

LEARNING CHECK

- What technology was catalytic in creating talk radio as a major format?
- How is talk radio different from news radio?

Music Radio

Most radio today is based on music programming. Below are the terms used to distinguish radio's major music formats for private radio in Canada. Due to demassification, many formats have become fragmented.

Adult Contemporary (A/C) Many advertisers like the A/C format because so many people in the big-spending 25-to-40 age group listen to it. Variations of this format include "soft rock," such as the EZ-Rock brand across Canada.

Top 40 Top 40, also called CHR (short for Contemporary Hits Radio), emphasizes current rock but not as strictly as McLendon insisted on. These stations target teenagers. Some variations within this format include Rhythmic Top 40 and Adult Top 40.

Country Once called country and western, or CW for short, this format goes back to WSM's *Grand Ole Opry* program in Nashville. The music varies significantly from twangy western ballads to what's called "urban country." In Canada, "young country" and "new country" have become two popular music formats. By abandoning Loretta Lynn and George Jones in favour of Doc Walker and Crystal Shawanda, new country radio stations have been able to attract younger listeners.

Album-Oriented Rock (AOR) AOR formats offer songs from the 100 bestselling albums. A casual listener might confuse AOR with Top 40, but AOR stations go back a few years for wider variety. Audiences tend to be aged 18 to 24. This is one of the most diversified formats, with classic rock available on CIRK-FM (Edmonton), mainstream rock on The Goat (Lloydminster), and new music on CFNY (Toronto).

Oldies Oldies stations play music that the 45- to 64-year-old demographic grew up with, mostly music of the 1960s and 1970s. It's sometimes called "classic hits."

Ethnic More than 9 million Canadians belong to ethnic groups other than First Nations, French, or British. These people represent more than 70 different cultures. Given this fact and Canada's official status as a multicultural country, it's not surprising that full-time ethnic radio stations have taken root in many of Canada's urban centres, such as

CASE STUDY

Howard Stern and Satellite Radio

Howard Stern began his career at Boston University, where he volunteered at the college radio station. His show was cancelled after one broadcast. He had spoofed a game show with contestants confessing their worst sins. It was a precursor of Stern's unorthodoxy: a mix of phone chat, much of it inane; music, a lot of it offbeat; and crude, sophomoric shock-talk. His on-air antics earned him the label "shock jock," a new radio programming genre in the 1980s.

No matter how tasteless he was, Stern amassed a following. He soon had star status and big bucks—and critics who pushed for federal fines against his on-air vulgarities. At one point, the accumulated unpaid fines totalled $1.7 million. The corporate owner of Stern's flagship New York station had no problem paying the fines from the profits Stern was bringing in.

Howard Stern

People kept listening to Stern's bathroom-wall jokes and his topless female studio guests. He even arrived on Canadian airwaves in 1997. During his first Canadian broadcast, he thanked CHOM-FM for "opening up the sewer gate for me to pollute yet another country." During his first few shows broadcast in Canada, he referred to French Canadians as "peckerheads" and "jack-offs." To those Canadians who didn't like his approach to morning radio, Stern replied that the show was "just entertainment. Jokes, laughter and whatever's on our minds." By 1998, CHOM-FM had dropped Stern. Q107 dropped him in 2001.

The fines kept coming. A $495 000 fine in 2004 brought Stern's career total to $2.5 million. Analysts say that the giant Clear Channel chain, which acquired Stern's show in its purchase of radio stations, earned $25 million a year in advertising revenue from Stern's show, which played in 40 cities. That was after $70 million in production costs and Stern's $30 million salary. Clear Channel could afford the fines but, concerned that the U.S. government might revoke its stations' licences, the corporate executives became uneasy. In 2004, they tried to put a lid on Howard Stern.

Refusing to be bridled, Stern announced that he wouldn't renew with Clear Channel when his contract expired in 2006. Instead, he would leave so-called terrestrial radio and go to the unregulated airwaves of the fledgling Sirius satellite radio service. With Sirius, Stern's program would go directly to subscribers, bypassing the traditional delivery mechanism through federally licensed local stations that send their signals from land-based towers. His shows, *Howard 100* and *Howard 101*, are also available on satellite radio in Canada.

Typical of his egocentric confidence, Stern declared the death of terrestrial radio with stations licensed to broadcast to local audiences. The future, he said, was in national stations that transmitted directly to individuals and were not relayed through local stations. Howard Stern is not alone in seeing problems for the radio industry as everyone has come to know it since the 1920s. Radio has had to withstand the challenges of iPods, the internet, and satellite radio.

Depending on who you talk to, Howard Stern represents the best in radio, since he meets the interests and needs of a mass audience, or the worst in radio, since he panders to the lowest instincts in society and gets rich in the process.

DEEPENING YOUR MEDIA LITERACY

Explore the Issue

Identify a modern-day shock jock other than Howard Stern.

Dig Deeper

What makes this shock jock controversial?

What Do You Think?

Should satellite radio be allowed to continue to be a bastion of outlandish expression for shock jocks like Howard Stern?

Toronto, Vancouver, and Montreal. Many other radio stations feature ethnic programming on a part-time basis, during the evenings and on weekends. Community radio is also home to many ethnic radio programs.

Classical This format offers the basic repertoire of enduring music since the Baroque era, although some classical stations also play experimental symphonies, operas, and contemporary composers. Because highbrow music has a limited following, most classical stations are supported not by advertising but by listener donations, universities, and government funding. CBC Radio Two still broadcasts some classical music nationally.

Religious Inspirational music is the programming core of religious stations. The music is interspersed with sermons from evangelists who buy time for their programs, seeking both to proselytize and to raise funds to support ministries.

Other Formats The CRTC has recently issued licences for some new formats in Canada. These include "Proud-FM" in Toronto, "urban" in Vancouver, Calgary, and Toronto, and AVR (Aboriginal Voices Radio) across Canada.

LEARNING CHECK

- How are the ideas of Gordon McLendon reflected in the demassification of radio music formats?

Corporate Radio

STUDY PREVIEW A few corporations dominate the Canadian and American radio industries, using mostly programming geared to mass tastes. This approach, however, has earned the disapproving moniker "corporate radio" for its bland sameness. The chains have taken steps to win back listeners who have left for alternative sources of music, news, and information.

Chain Ownership

In a drive to cut costs in order to maximize profits, the big radio chains consolidated their new properties in the post-1996 era and centralized not only playlists but also disc jockeys. Through a system called voice tracking, a handful of announcers can be heard on several radio stations, owned by the same company, in different markets. This robo-programming was efficient. Canadian radio followed suit, with many stations voice tracking during evenings, overnights, and weekends.

Some stations that used robo-programming shifted gears in 2005 with Jack, a format developed by Rogers Media in Canada that featured a decidedly more eclectic mix of music. Jack playlists typically include 1200 songs. Unlike robo-programming, few songs are played even once a day in Jack's unlikely patterns, and there are no segues that slide one tune seamlessly into another. Eight U.S. stations licensed Jack from Rogers in 2005. Others are imitating it. At KSJK in Kansas City, which calls itself 105.1 Jack FM, program director Mike Reilly prides himself on "train wrecks," a collision of unlikely music in sequence: "If you hear MC Hammer go into the Steve Miller Band, I've done my job." It's the same kind of programming excitement that people can create on an iPod.

Jack, say critics, is less than it seems. The playlists don't venture beyond what is familiar to listeners. A Jack consultant, Mike Henry, put it this way in an interview in *The Wall Street Journal*: "You're only challenging them on a stylistic level. You're not challenging them on a familiar/unfamiliar level." Nirvana grunge may butt up against Village People disco, but both are proven pop hits.

Canadian media writer and director Doug Thompson argues that Jack, or any of its clones, such as Dave or Bob, isn't really radio but rather a jukebox: "That's not what radio was meant to be. I didn't grow up listening to radio for a bunch of songs played back to back. There is no substitute for a live person talking one on one with a listener." In short, corporate radio needs to develop new personalities for radio, not just new formats. Thompson adds that creative, personality radio DJs currently are an endangered species.

Campus Radio Campus and community radio stations in Canada allow members of the public access to the airwaves. There are currently almost 100 community radio stations in Canada, mostly in Quebec. There are an additional 53 campus stations across Canada. You probably have one on your campus.

A Public Alternative: CBC Radio

As Canada's public broadcaster, CBC Radio brought Canadian programming home to Canadians. Today, CBC Radio is known as Radio One, Radio Two, or Radio Three. Radio One features a mix of information, talk, and Canadian music while Radio Two's programming is an eclectic mix of music, including the classical, jazz, and blues it became known for over the years. The new CBC Radio Three targets a younger demographic with a format that highlights Canadian independent music. Radio Three is also available online and on Sirius satellite radio.

CBC Radio is commercial-free, funded through taxpayer money. Much of its programming, as mandated by the Broadcasting Act, is regional. More than 85 percent of CBC's English-language radio programming is produced at the local level, with much of that broadcast nationally. CBC Radio also spotlights Canadian talent. More than 60 hours of performance programming on Radio One and Radio Two focus on Canadian performers.

Other Alternatives: Campus and Community Radio

Campus and community radio stations in Canada, geared to neighbourhood service with low-power transmitters, have made possible a level of interactivity with their audiences not possible for traditional stations that seek large audiences to draw advertising and pay the bills. These low-power stations, many staffed by volunteers, are alternative voices in the radio universe. Under CRTC conditions of licence, programming on these stations must "differ in style and substance from the services provided by conventional broadcasters." These stations are usually funded through grants, student fees, and some advertising. They also support social causes. Every year since 2003, CKUT at McGill University in Montreal has been the host station for the Homelessness Marathon, which raises awareness of the growing problem of homelessness in Canada. Campus and community radio stations across the country simulcast the event, with each station contributing local reports and commentary.

There are other alternatives to corporate, playlisted radio. Some stations set themselves apart with local and distinctive content. These channels tend to be owned by small companies or corporations who are more likely to take a chance on something different. Radio Newfoundland features nothing but east coast artists. Country stations in the west continue to serve their largely agricultural listeners well, while CHWO in Oakville calls itself Prime Time Radio, with an emphasis on older listeners.

LEARNING CHECK

- What do you see as problems ahead for radio chains?
- What alternatives to corporate radio are available to listeners?

Whither Radio?

STUDY PREVIEW Radio and radio programming have become more populist, formulaic, and bland. Many stations are devoid of local identity. Plus, new technologies are both a challenge and a saviour.

Satellite Radio

satellite radio Delivery method of programming from a single source beamed to an orbiting satellite for transmission directly to individual end users.

Two **satellite radio** operations went on the air in Canada in 2005. Both Sirius and XM beamed multiple programs from multiple satellites, providing digital-quality sound, much of it commercial-free, for a monthly fee ranging between $10 and $15. Both Sirius and XM offered at least a hundred channels—pop, country, news, sports, and talk—but also specialized programming such as chamber music, Broadway hits, CBC Radio Three, NHL hockey, MLB baseball, audiobooks, and gardening tips.

Assault on Terrestrial Radio

terrestrial radio The industry based on audio transmission from land-based towers, as opposed to transmission via satellite.

IBOC (in-band, on-channel) A radio industry standard for digital transmission.

While XM and Sirius duke it out, a larger battle is shaping up between satellite radio and what's come to be called **terrestrial radio.** The term was devised to identify the traditional radio industry built around local stations that transmit from towers, in contrast to satellite transmission. Language purists object that *terrestrial radio* is a retronym like *print newspapers* and *broadcast television*. However, boosted derisively by Howard Stern while he hyped his 2006 move to Sirius, the term caught on.

Regardless of the semantics tiff, the reality is that traditional, commercial stations are under unprecedented competition for listeners. Other technologies also work against the traditional radio industry.

Snoop Dogg Satellite radio services have shared exclusive talent in their competition for listeners, including Snoop Dogg on XM and Howard Stern on Sirius. Satellite audiences are growing, but neither Sirius nor XM has found profitability and they are now in a merger dance.

iPod Handheld MP3 players, epitomized by the Apple iPod, are siphoning listeners from over-air local radio. With these devices and music downloaded from the internet or ripped from their own CDs, people are able to create their own playlists. There's no inane disc jockey patter, no commercials, no waiting through less-than-favourite tunes for the good stuff.

Podcasting Almost anybody who wants to create a show can prerecord a batch of favourite music, complete with narration, as an audio file on a personal computer. Then, by adding a hyperlink on a web server, that person can let the world download the show for playback on a computer or MP3 player. Whenever the listener links to the server again, a new show from the same source will be downloaded automatically. Podcasting has the potential to make everybody a disc jockey. This, too, has cut into the audience of traditional radio.

Digital Radio Radio in both Canada and the United States missed an opportunity to upgrade with digital transmission technology. The technology, which would have improved clarity, was deemed too costly. Joel Hollander, who began as chief executive at America's Infinity chain in 2005, is frank about this mistake: "If we had invested three to five years ago, people would be thinking differently about satellite."

In the United States, all of the largest chains have now committed to digital conversion. The system requires two transmitters, one for the traditional analog signal and one for the new digital signal, but a new industry-adopted standard, called **IBOC** (short for in-band, on-channel), allows old-style analog and new-style digital receivers to pick up either signal at the same spot on the dial. As of 2010, Canadian broadcasters were still debating this issue.

LEARNING CHECK

- Locally licensed terrestrial commercial radio is beleaguered. How has this happened?
- What are possibilities for technological innovation for terrestrial radio?

Reinventing Radio

Radio has had doomsayers before, as when network television stole the audience and advertisers in the 1950s. Radio reinvented itself then. Gordon McLendon, the low-budget niche programming innovator, led radio into a survival mode. Will a new knight in shining armour come along to reinvent terrestrial commercial radio once again?

Explore

Deepening Your Media Literacy: What Must Radio Do to Survive?

Local radio stations have assets to reposition themselves. As Canadian radio veteran Duff Roman, points out, "opportunities abound for radio to leverage its tremendous branding and heritage to become a true interactive, multi platform media that is technology agnostic. In the end, getting attractive content to the end user, regardless of the vehicle, is what radio should be all about."

One unfilled niche that radio should not neglect is local culture. Stations spend little airtime on local concerts, drama, poetry, and dialogue. When is the last time you heard a city council meeting broadcast live on radio? Or a poetry reading broadcast from a campus coffee shop? Or an intelligent interview with a local author? You're more likely to find a faraway baseball game than a local hockey game. Local content may not be riveting stuff for the large mass audiences that radio once garnered, but all signs point to those audiences continuing to dwindle. Radio's reinvention may be into niches even more demassified than those to which McLendon geared programs in the 1950s. Even so, there indeed are things that radio can do that competitors do not or cannot.

LEARNING CHECK

- What threatens the future of commercial terrestrial radio?
- How can commercial terrestrial radio survive?

Chapter 6 Wrap-Up

While radio will continue to be a presence in the life of Canadians for many years to come, the medium faces challenging times. Suddenly, at the dawn of the 21st century, new technologies have shaken the structure of the radio industry as listeners opt for cutting-edge alternatives including satellite direct-to-listener radio, iPods, podcasts and webcasts, and online music stations. How can a radio station compete with handheld devices that facilitate individual playlists? These devices put listeners in control. People no longer have to wait for the songs they want to hear. Nor do they have to listen to commercial breaks. Where can commercial radio go from here? Narrower, local-oriented niches are a possibility. Stronger local news and public affairs is another niche that commercial radio has largely forsaken. This alternative would require new business models. Local programming is costlier than playing recorded music.

PEARSON mycanadiancommunicationlab

Visit **www.mycanadiancommunicationlab.ca** for access to a wealth of tools and resources that will enhance your learning experience. Features include the following:

- Personalized Study Plan
- Videos
- Activities
- Pearson eText–and much more!

Questions for Critical Thinking

1. Explain why radio is a "blind" medium? How does radio communicate?
2. What is happening to the number of people who listen to traditional radio? What are the implications for radio's future?
3. How has the mix of entertainment and information changed through the course of radio's history?
4. How do you think radio can reinvent itself in the future?
5. Many radio stations have webcams set up in their studios. Given the fact that radio is a "blind" medium, is it still radio if you can see the participants? What would Marshall McLuhan think? Do webcams make radio "hotter" or "cooler"?

Keeping Up to Date

The trade journals *Broadcaster* and *Broadcast Dialogue* keep abreast of news and issues.

Other news coverage can be found in the *National Post, The Globe and Mail,* and other major daily newspapers.

Scholarly articles can be found in the *Canadian Journal of Communication, Journal of Broadcasting, Electronic Media, Journal of Communication,* and *Journalism Quarterly.*

Motion Pictures

7

The Sweet Hereafter Canadian directors such as Atom Egoyan have achieved critical success both here and abroad. *The Sweet Hereafter* is also an excellent example of what makes Canadian films different from American movies.

LEARNING AHEAD

- Canadian movies are different from American movies; not better or worse, just different.
- Movies are most powerful when viewed uninterrupted in a darkened auditorium.
- Besides feature films there are sub-genres, including animated and documentary films. Both of these sub-genres have strong Canadian roots.
- The movie industry is dominated by a handful of major studios.
- The exhibition component of the movie industry is in rapid transition.
- Blockbuster films can be spectacular but carry high risk.

MEDIA IN THEORY

American versus Canadian Movies: What's the Difference?

Why are Canadian movies different from American movies? Notice that the question doesn't imply that Canadian movies are "worse" than American movies, although among many Canadians that seems to be the common belief. For students of communication, the questions really should be "What makes Canadian movies different from American movies?" and "What do our films say about our culture?"

While funding, marketplace economics, and distribution have certainly all played a role in the development of the Canadian film industry and the "look" of Canadian films, particularly in the early days, there may be other differences as well. **Peter Harcourt**, in his 1976 essay "Introduction," argues that Canadian movie scripts symbolically reflect "our own social uncertainties—both our uncertainty of action as a nation and our own present lack of security in dealing with ethnic and cultural problems which, throughout our vast nation, we are trying to define ourselves."

Peter Harcourt Writes that Canadian movies reflect our own uncertainty.

This uncertainty is clearly evident in the films of one of Canada's best-known filmmakers, **Atom Egoyan.** Harcourt, in the journal *Film Quarterly*, described Egoyan's work as "expressing the classic Canadian dilemma as formulated by Northrop Frye . . . Egoyan devises films that register the personal uncertainties of people who are striving to find a place of rest within a culture not their own." **David Cronenberg**'s films also feature these themes, and don't always feature the happy endings typical of Hollywood cinema.

Atom Egoyan Directs movies about personal uncertainty.

David Cronenberg His films are the antithesis to Hollywood happy endings.

MEDIA TIMELINE Movies

1826 French scientist Joseph Niépce found chemicals to capture and preserve an image on a light-sensitive metal.

1888 William Dickson devised a camera to capture sequential motion.

1891 George Eastman devised flexible celluloid for film that could be run through projectors.

1895 Auguste and Louis Lumière opened a movie house in Paris.

1896 The Vitascope was demonstrated in Montreal.

1906 Canada's first movie theatre, the Ouimetoscope, opened in Montreal.

1922 Fox used sound in newsreels.

1927 Warner distributed the first talkie, *The Jazz Singer.*

1948 Canadian Nat Taylor opened the first multiplex theatre, The Elgin, in Ottawa.

1970s Multiscreen movie houses, many in the suburbs, became the norm.

1976 Toronto's Festival of Festivals, a precursor to the Toronto International Film Festival, began.

1999 George Lucas offered a version of *Star Wars: Episode I, The Phantom Menace* for digital projection.

2005 Movie studios agreed to finance a major part of converting theatres for digital movies.

2007 Cineplex Odeon began converting its Canadian cinemas to digital projection.

2009 *Avatar*, written and directed by Canada's James Cameron, became the highest-grossing movie of all time.

According to Cronenberg, both he and Egoyan "have a horror of the cheap emotional affect of Hollywood movies."

Meanwhile, French-Canadian cinema has developed a strong following in Quebec and around the world. French-Canadian directors such as **Denys Arcand** are among the best in the world. Arcand's works include *The Decline of the American Empire, Jesus of Montreal*, and *The Barbarian Invasions*. When asked if there are any similarities between French- and English-Canadian movies, Arcand said, "There might be something we share in our constant resistance to American genre film." Even the Canadian cult film *Ginger Snaps* encourages us to "forget the Hollywood rules."

Denys Arcand Award-winning French-Canadian film director.

In her history of Canadian film, *Weird Sex and Snowshoes*, **Katherine Monk** offers a "Canadian checklist" of themes in Canadian movies. These include the following variations of "uncertainty" that Harcourt introduced in 1976: identity issues, being an outsider, empty landscapes, internal demons, personal alienation, language barriers, being on a road to nowhere, questions of faith, survivor guilt, and ambiguous endings.

Katherine Monk Developed a Canadian movie checklist.

Perhaps our nation's preoccupation with developing a national identity is reflected in the uncertainties of Canadian movies. Many factors are at work here. First, since Canada is officially bilingual and multicultural, how can we have a truly "national cinema" as other countries do? Second, funding has always been an issue for Canadian filmmakers. We simply don't have the economic resources that Hollywood does. Finally, finding an audience for Canadian movies has always been a struggle. However, despite all of these factors, there have been success stories. Recently, the works of directors Bruce McDonald, Deepa Mehta, Don McKellar, and István Szabó have become successful here at home.

Significance of Movies

STUDY PREVIEW Movies can have a powerful and immediate effect, in part because theatres insulate moviegoers in a cocoon without distractions. By some measures, the powerful effect is short-lived. Nonetheless, movies can sensitize people to issues and have a long-term effect in shifting public attitudes on enduring issues.

Movie Power

As Dan Brown's thriller *The Da Vinci Code* picked up steam en route to becoming a mega-selling book, the debate intensified over his account of Catholic church history. It was a big deal, but nothing compared to the fury that occurred when Sony moved Ron

Suspension of Disbelief People are carrying their experiences and realities with them when they sit down for a movie. As a storyteller, a movie director needs to suck the audience into the plot quickly—to suspend disbelief, as novelists call it. Master directors, such as Canada's James Cameron, best known for *Avatar* and *Titanic*, strive to create this new reality in opening scenes to engross viewers in the story as it unfolds.

Howard's movie adaptation of the book toward release. The full crescendo came when the movie premiered. This unprecedented dialogue demonstrates the impact of movies as a storytelling and myth-making medium, which for mass audiences can far exceed the impact of other media for at least short windows of time.

LEARNING CHECK

- What impact, perhaps indelible, have the movies mentioned so far had on audiences?
- What recent movies would you add to the list? Why?

Cocoon Experience

Why the powerful and immediate effect of movies? There may be a clue in one of Thomas Edison's first shorts, which included ocean waves rolling toward a camera on a beach. Audiences covered their heads, such was their **suspension of disbelief**. Instinctively, they expected to be soaked by the waves. Natural human skepticism gets lost in the darkened cocoon of a movie-house auditorium, compounding the impact of what's onscreen.

suspension of disbelief Occurs when you surrender doubts about the reality of a story and become caught up in that story.

Although moviegoers are insulated in a dark auditorium, the experience is communal. You're not the only one sobbing or terrified or joyous. Among your fellow viewers is a reinforcement of emotions that other media can't match. Television, watched at home, often alone, is similarly disadvantaged, although television has most of the accoutrements of movies: visuals, motion, and sound. Remember what Canadian Marshall McLuhan had to say about the medium being the message? At their most potent, movies need to be seen in a theatre. A movie may be good on a DVD at home, as a computer download, or as pay-per-view on television, but nothing compares to the theatre phenomenon.

LEARNING CHECK

- In what situation are movies most likely to encourage suspension of disbelief?

Movies and Mores

As an especially powerful medium, movies have been targets of censors and the moral police from almost the beginning. In retrospect, some concern has been darkly comical—such as attempts in 1896 to ban *Dolorita in the Passion Dance*. Provocative or not, nobody has ever made the case that *Dolorita* corrupted anyone. Movies can be successful at moving emotions at the moment, but as for changing fundamentals in a person's lifestyle or triggering aberrant behaviour, the jury remains out.

More clear is that movies can sensitize people to issues through sympathetic portrayals. Such was the case in 2005 with *Brokeback Mountain*. A generation earlier, *Guess Who's Coming to Dinner* did the same. Conversely, terrorists have received deleterious portrayals in the ever-growing volume of action movies. Knowing the value of onscreen portrayals, special-interest groups have worked to eliminate negative stereotypes. It's wrong, say Italian-Americans, for characters involved in organized crime always to have Italian surnames. Feminists have gone after lopsided portrayals of women in homemaker and subordinate roles. Minority groups have levelled similar charges. The result, although hard to prove, has been a new **Hollywood** sensitivity to these issues that probably is playing out slowly in general attitudes in society.

Hollywood A Los Angeles enclave that was the early centre of American filmmaking; now, more of a metaphor for the industry.

LEARNING CHECK

- What is the difference in the immediate and long-term effects of a movie theatre experience?
- In fiction, what is the significance of suspension of disbelief?

Movie Products

Explore

Media People: Walt Disney

Explore

Media People: Steven Spielberg

STUDY PREVIEW To most people, the word *movie* conjures up the feature films that are Hollywood's specialty. Sub-genres include animated films and documentaries. Also, the historic distinction between Hollywood and television as rivals is disappearing.

Feature Films

Movies that tell stories, much in the tradition of stage plays, are **narrative films.** These are what most people think of as movies. They're promoted heavily, with their titles and actors on marquees. Most are in the 100-minute range.

narrative films Movies that tell a story.

A French magician and inventor, Georges Méliès, pioneered narrative films with fairy tales and science-fiction stories to show in his movie house in 1896. Méliès's *Little Red Riding Hood* and *Cinderella* ran less than 10 minutes—short stories, if you will. In 1902, Edwin Porter directed *Life of a Fireman*, the first coherent narrative film in the United States. Audiences accustomed to stage plays and to being a distance away from the actors were distressed, some even shocked, by Porter's close-ups, a new technique. They felt cheated at not seeing "the whole stage." Gradually, audiences learned what is called **film literacy,** the ability to appreciate moviemaking as an art form with unique-to-the-medium techniques that add impact or facilitate the telling of a story. Porter's next significant film, *The Great Train Robbery*, was shocking for cutting back and forth between robbers and a posse that was chasing them—something, like close-ups, that film can do and the stage cannot. Slowly, movies emerged as a distinctive art form.

film literacy Ability to appreciate artistic techniques used for telling a story through film.

From the earliest days of the medium, movies were also shot and produced in Canada. Douglas Fetherling says that the first film shot in Canada was made in Manitoba in 1897. Many other short films followed; however, the first Canadian feature film wasn't made until 1913. *Evangeline* was a five-reel film produced by the Canadian Bioscope Company of Halifax. Based on a poem by Longfellow about the flight of the Acadians, it was shot on location in the Annapolis Valley. It featured an American cast and turned a profit. The Canadian Bioscope Company was never able to match the success of *Evangeline*. The same was true of other early Canadian filmmakers. It's estimated that only about 70 Canadian feature films were produced during the first half of the 20th century.

Talkies At Thomas Edison's lab, the tinkerer William Dickson came up with a sound system for movies in 1889, but it didn't go anywhere. The first successful commercial application of sound was in Movietone newsreels in 1922. But it was four upstart moviemakers, the **Warner brothers**—Albert, Harry, Jack, and Sam Warner—who revolutionized **talkies,** or movies with sound. In 1927, the Warners released **The Jazz Singer,** starring Al Jolson. There was sound only for two segments, 354 words total, but audiences in movie houses that the Warners had equipped with loudspeakers were enthralled. **The Vikings**, released in 1930, was Canada's first talkie.

Warner brothers Introduced sound in movies.

talkies Movies with sound.

The Jazz Singer The first feature film with sound.

The Vikings Canada's first talkie.

Colour In 1939, a narrative movie with another technological breakthrough was released: *Gone with the Wind*, in colour. Although *Gone with the Wind* is often referred to as the first colour movie, the technology was devised in the 1920s, and **The Black Pirate** starring Douglas Fairbanks was released far earlier, in 1925. But *Gone with the Wind* was a far more significant film. It marked the start of Hollywood's quest for ever-more-spectacular stories and effects to attract audiences—in other words, the blockbuster.

The Black Pirate The first feature film in colour.

Computer-Generated Imagery You can imagine why early moviemaker Alfred Clark used a special effect for his 1895 movie *The Execution of Mary Queen of Scots.* "Illusion" is what special effects were called then. Although audiences were amazed, the effects were nothing like today's **CGI**, the acronym that movie people use for three-dimensional **computer-generated imagery.**

computer-generated imagery (CGI) The application of three-dimensional computer graphics for special effects, particularly in movies and television.

The first use of three-dimensional CGI in movies was *Futureworld* in 1976. University of Utah graduate students Edwin Catmull and Fred Parke created a computer-generated hand and face. There were CGI scenes in *Star Wars* in 1977, but the technology remained mostly an experimental novelty until 1989, when the pseudopod sea creature created by Industrial Light & Magic for *The Abyss* won an Academy Award.

Photorealistic CGI was firmly in place with the villain's liquid metal morphing effects in *Terminator 2*, also by Industrial Light & Magic and also recognized with a 1991 Academy Award for special effects.

CGI soon became the dominant form of special effects with technology opening up new possibilities. For stunts, CGI characters began replacing doubles that were nearly indistinguishable from the actors. Crowd scenes were easily created without hiring hundreds of extras. This raised the question of whether actors themselves might one day be replaced by pixels.

Then, in 2009, James Cameron's *Avatar* was nominated for nine Academy Awards. Although the motion capture technology used by Cameron didn't replace actors, it was a controversial move, one that may have cost Cameron an Oscar for best picture. Alex Ben Block of *The Hollywood Reporter* offers this explanation as to why Kathryn Bigelow's *The Hurt Locker* beat *Avatar* for best picture that year: "Cameron wanted to talk about [. . .] how frustrated he was that his actors, whose performances were captured by computer-generated technology, were not taken as seriously as live-action actors. While his righteousness was sincere, that didn't go over well with many real-life actors who feel threatened by the possibility that they might be replaced by synthetic performers. That backlash might have mattered, because actors are by far the largest bloc of voters in the Academy."

Movie commentator Neil Petkus worries that some filmmakers may overuse their CGI toys. "CGI effects can be abused and mishandled," Petkus says. "Directors sometimes allow the visual feasts that computers offer to undermine any real content a movie may have had." Petkus faults director George Lucas for going too far in later *Star Wars* movies: "Any interesting character developments that could have occurred in these movies were overwhelmed by constant CGI action sequences."

Movies that overdo CGI can lack the depth of character and nuance that human actors bring to the screen, says Petkus. "How can we relate to a character made up of pixels and mathematical algorithms and not flesh, blood and emotion? Sure, CGI movies are flashy, but they don't convey the sense of reality that we look for in a good cinematic story."

Another commentator, Matt Leonard, has made the point this way: "There are hundreds of Elvis impersonators in the world, some of which are very good, but none of them are good enough to fool us into thinking Elvis has returned. The closer we get to creating a completely digital character the more our senses seem to alert us to the fact that something is not completely right and therefore we dismiss it as a cheap trick or imitation."

So while CGI characters can make sense as stunt doubles or to perform humanly impossible, only-from-Hollywood contortions and feats, they probably don't spell doom for the Screen Actors Guild. About replacing actors, Dennis Muren of Industrial Light & Magic is clear: "Why bother! Why not focus on what doesn't exist as opposed to recreating something that is readily available."

Faster computers and massive data storage capacities have added efficiencies to computer-generated movie imagery, but offsetting these efficiencies is a pressure for greater detail and quality. CGI is labour-intensive. A single frame typically takes two to three hours to render. For a complex frame, count on 20 hours or more. The Warner Bros. budget for *Superman Returns*, a record $204 million, was eaten up largely by CGI effects.

LEARNING CHECK

- How would you define feature films?
- How has technology shaped feature films?

NFB Classic Richard Condie's Genie Award–winning *The Big Snit* (1985) is just one of many NFB animated shorts to receive plaudits worldwide. The NFB continues to trailblaze in the spirit of Norman McLaren.

Animated Films

The 1920s were pivotal in defining genres of narrative films. In his early twenties, **Walt Disney** arrived in Los Angeles from Missouri in 1923 with $40 in his pocket. Walt moved in with his brother Roy, and they rounded up $500 and went into the **animated film** business. In 1928, **Steamboat Willie** debuted as a short film to accompany feature films. The Willie character eventually morphed into Mickey Mouse. Disney took animation to full length with ***Snow White and the Seven Dwarfs*** in 1937, cementing animation as a sub-genre of narrative films.

Animated films were labour-intensive, requiring an illustrator to create 1000-plus sequential drawings for one minute of screen time. Computers changed all of that in the 1990s, first with digital effects for movies that otherwise had scenes and actors, notably the *Star Wars* series by George Lucas, then with animated features. Disney's *Toy Story* in 1995 was the first movie produced entirely by computers. The new technology, brought to a high level by Lucas's Industrial Light & Magic and Steve Jobs's Pixar, has led to a resurgence in animated films after a relatively dormant period.

Walt Disney Pioneer in animated films.

animated film Narrative films with drawn scenes and characters.

Steamboat Willie Animated cartoon character that became Mickey Mouse.

Snow White and the Seven Dwarfs First full-length animated film.

Norman McLaren Canadian pioneer in animation.

Canadian filmmakers went in a different direction with animation. The National Film Board's (NFB's) **Norman McLaren** had a love for animation. In 1949, McLaren, along with Evelyn Lambert, used a technique called drawn on film animation to bring to life the music of Oscar Peterson. McLaren's best-known work is the 1953 Oscar-winning short *Neighbours*. The eight-minute antiwar film is about two neighbours who fight over a flower. The dispute escalates into tribal warfare. The film used live actors, but they were animated with the same techniques used to animate puppets and drawings.

LEARNING CHECK

- What were pioneer successes in animated films?
- How can you explain the resurgence of animated films?

Documentaries

Nonfiction film explorations of historical or current events and natural and social phenomena go back to 1922 and **Robert Flaherty**'s look at Inuit life. Because of their informational thrust, early **documentaries** had great credibility.

Robert Flaherty First documentary filmmaker.

documentary A video examination of a historical or current event or a natural or social phenomenon.

Documentaries in Canada American movie mogul D.W. Griffith, whose narrative style was influential in the development of Hollywood movies, visited Toronto in 1925. During that visit, he told Canadian officials that Canada should make Hollywood-style movies to trade with the United States. Almost 15 years later, a British filmmaker disagreed with Griffith and the Canadian film industry went in another direction. That man was John Grierson, and the National Film Board of Canada was born.

NFB Canada's award-winning National Film Board.

John Grierson Founder of the NFB.

The **National Film Board (NFB)** was formed by an act of Parliament in 1939 to "interpret Canada to Canadians." The board's first commissioner was **John Grierson,** a British documentary filmmaker. Grierson advocated a strong national film industry. He wanted to make movies that celebrated Canada's geographic and social diversity. In a statement about government film policy, Grierson said that while Canada could never compete with the glamour of Hollywood, it should not abandon the idea of a national film industry. Grierson felt that making short, inexpensive films about Canadians and their experiences could complement more expensive Hollywood fare, while still giving Canadians a cinematic voice. Grierson also believed that films should tackle social issues and that filmmakers should try to produce films that make a difference.

During World War II, the NFB produced several propaganda films in support of the war effort. After the war, Grierson returned to England, but the NFB continued to make

CASE STUDY

In-Your-Face Documentaries

Not so long ago, moviegoers deemed documentaries to be dreary, dull, and dry. Today, some documentaries are the hottest money-makers in Hollywood. Michael Moore's in-your-face *Fahrenheit 9/11* grossed $100 million in its first month of release. With the release of each of his documentaries, including *Sicko* in 2007, Moore's critics say he's neither fair nor balanced. Moore stands by his accuracy but explains that his documentaries are his take on issues. He sees them as "balancing" the dominant interpretations offered in the mainstream media.

That contrarian thrust, says television writer Debi Enker, addresses a void in general media coverage of issues: "The current interest suggests people are seeking not just immediacy but also context and the kind of perspective that time, research, thoughtful analysis, and intelligent storytelling can bring." Dawn Dreyer of the Center for Documentary Studies at Duke University puts it this way: "It's narrative. It's storytelling. It's becoming engaged with people's lives."

Dreyer's characterization of documentaries also explains the success of former Vice-President Al Gore's *An Inconvenient Truth*, which grossed more than $41 million worldwide.

A documentary typically has a far lower budget than other movies, which can mean higher profits even if it gets only a limited theatrical release. *An Inconvenient Truth*, the first carbon-neutral documentary, started as a low-tech slide show. Filming took six months and a little more than $1 million—pocket change by Hollywood standards.

One of *An Inconvenient Truth*'s producers, Lawrence Bender, said: "Everything about this movie was a miracle." Not only did the film rake in cash, it earned two Oscars. Also, it made Al Gore a movie star. "When we took Gore to Sundance and Cannes, people just went crazy around him," said Bender. "It was really amazing. He doesn't sing or act, but he actually is kind of a rock star. He has this message that's drawing people to him, making him larger than life."

The British government purchased 3385 DVDs of *An Inconvenient Truth* to distribute to every secondary school. In the United States, 50 000 copies were given to teachers. The Documentary Organization of Canada launched a new green code of ethics for documentary filmmakers. Paramount Classics donated 5 percent of all box-office receipts to the Alliance for Climate Protection. The Alliance also received 100 percent of Gore's proceeds from the film.

Al Gore His documentary *An Inconvenient Truth* turned former Vice-President Al Gore into a movie star of sorts. Suddenly he had riveted public attention on climate issues that environmentalists as far back as Rachel Carson in the 1950s have been arguing threaten the habitat of the planet for both humans and other species.

DEEPENING YOUR MEDIA LITERACY

Explore the Issue

Pick an in-your-face muckraking documentary and a television news report on the same subject.

Dig Deeper

What makes the documentary different from the way a television news report might treat the same subject? Would the documentary resonate as well with the audience if the filmmaker did not feel passionately about the subject and the movie was completely fair and balanced?

What Do You Think?

Do you think these in-your-face documentaries fill a need? How have they contributed to the movie industry and to society?

successful documentary films. During this time, it became known for a style called **cinéma vérité**, which roughly translated means "truth in cinema." For the NFB, cinéma vérité has meant documentaries by Canadians about Canadians.

cinéma vérité Truth or realism in movies; the basis for the documentary tradition.

In 1950, Parliament passed the National Film Act, which changed the NFB's mandate to include producing, promoting, and distributing films in the national interest. In the NFB's early days, it would send projectionists from city to city and town to town to show its latest offerings in arenas, community centres, and even fields. These films were also shown in movie houses and eventually on television. Today, the NFB offers many of its films online, including three-dimensional (3-D) and high-definition (HD) content. As well, thanks to an app, viewers can also enjoy NFB films on their iPhones.

Television Network Documentaries In the 1950s, television journalists began producing documentaries using a just-the-facts mould. The television networks underwrote the budgets of these documentaries and their purpose was to build corporate prestige, not propagandize. Another factor in the neutral thrust of most of these documentaries was the U.S. Federal Communications Commission's (FCC's) licensing dictum for fairness in whatever was broadcast. Today, the CBC offers its Documentary Channel.

Docu-Ganda The FCC's **Fairness Doctrine** was withdrawn in 1987, setting in motion a new rationale for documentaries that, in many cases, seeks not so much to inform as to influence the audience. What emerged was a new genre that critics call **docu-ganda,** which plays not on the major television networks but in movie houses and niche outlets. Independent filmmaker Michael Moore has epitomized the new generation of documentary filmmakers, first with *Roger & Me*, a brutal attack on General Motors. Moore was no less savage in *Bowling for Columbine*, which takes aim at gun rights advocates, and *Fahrenheit 9/11*, released during the 2004 U.S. election campaign and aimed at President George W. Bush and his motivations for the Iraq War. *Fahrenheit 9/11* became the highest-grossing documentary in history, a demonstration of the economic viability of documentaries.

Fairness Doctrine A U.S. government requirement from 1949 to 1987 that broadcast presentations had to include both sides of competing public issues.

docu-ganda Documentaries that seek to influence viewers.

Relatively inexpensive digital filmmaking equipment has also driven the new wave of documentaries. For his *Super Size Me*, which explored the link between fast food and obesity, Morgan Spurlock never could have persuaded a major studio to cover the budget, several million dollars up front, for a documentary that attacked an American icon like McDonald's. But with a $3000 digital camera, $5000 in software, and an Apple computer, Spurlock created his personal statement on fast food. So compelling was *Super Size Me* that 200 theatres showed it and it grossed $7.5 million in one month. In all, Spurlock had spent only $65 000 to create the movie.

Single Point of View Critics fault many recent documentaries for usurping the detached, neutral tone of earlier documentaries and instead delivering only a single point of view. Guilty as charged, respond the new documentary filmmakers. David Zieger, who raised eyebrows with his *Sir! No Sir!* on the antiwar movement within the military during the Vietnam War, says: "If you make a film with both sides, you're going to make a boring film." Film is not journalism, Zieger says. Prolific documentary filmmaker Robert Greenwald says that he covers a subject as he sees it, albeit one-sided. Viewers, he says, need to accept responsibility for weighing his portrayal against what they can pick up elsewhere.

In other words, a docu-ganda requires viewers to have a higher level of media literacy than they had in the heyday of television network documentaries that laid out competing viewpoints within a single package. Canadian media executive Christopher Ian Bennett is less benign about the effect of point-of-view treatments. Bennett says that the contemporary documentaries that make the biggest splash are, in fact, dangerous because they can dupe viewers into accepting them as the whole truth.

LEARNING CHECK

- What are some historically important documentaries?
- Who are significant current documentary producers? What are their signature works?
- Some documentaries are journalistic explorations while others are highly opinionated. How can moviegoers recognize the difference?

MEDIA PEOPLE Robert Flaherty

Explorer Robert Flaherty, who attended Toronto's Upper Canada College, took a camera to the Arctic in 1921 to record the life of an Inuit family. The result was a new kind of movie: the documentary. While other movies of the time were theatrical productions with scripts, sets, and actors, Flaherty tried something different: recording reality.

His 57-minute *Nanook of the North* was compelling on its own merits when it started on the movie-house circuit in 1922, but the film received an unexpected macabre boost a few days later when Nanook, the father of the Inuit family, died of hunger on the ice. News stories of Nanook's death stirred public interest and also attendance at the movie houses, which helped to establish the documentary as an important new film genre.

Flaherty's innovative approach took a new twist in the 1930s when propagandists saw reality-based movies as a tool to promote their causes. In Germany, the Nazi government produced propaganda films, and other countries followed suit. Frank Capra directed the vigorous five-film series *Why We Fight* for the U.S. War Office in 1942.

After World War II, there was a revival of documentaries in Flaherty's style: a neutral recording of natural history. Walt Disney produced a variety of such documentaries, including the popular *Living Desert* in the 1950s.

Nanook of the North The documentary became a film genre with explorer Robert Flaherty's *Nanook of the North* in 1922. This film was an attempt to record reality; there were no actors and no props. The film was especially potent not only because it was a new approach and about a fascinating subject but also because, coincidentally, Nanook died of starvation on the ice around the time that the film was released.

Robert Flaherty

The CBS television network gained a reputation in the 1950s and 1960s for picking up on the documentary tradition with *Harvest of Shame,* about migrant workers, and *Hunger in America.* In the same period, the National Geographic Society established a documentary unit and French explorer Jacques Cousteau went into the television documentary business.

Full-length documentaries are now mostly relegated to airing on the CBC in Canada and on PBS in the United States. The CBC's Documentary Channel is also an excellent outlet for these types of films. The major networks, meanwhile, have shifted most documentaries away from full-length treatments. Typical is CBS's *60 Minutes*, a weekly one-hour program containing three short-form documentaries. These new network projects combine reality programming and entertainment in slick packages that attract larger audiences than do traditional documentaries.

Hollywood Studios

STUDY PREVIEW Hollywood is dominated by six movie studios, all of which engage in both producing and distributing movies. These studios, all parts of conglomerates, are enmeshed with the television industry through corporate connections.

Studio System

The structure of the U.S. movie industry is rooted historically in a few major companies that tightly controlled everything beginning in the 1920s. In this **studio system**, a handful of companies produced, distributed, and exhibited movies.

studio system A mass production, distribution, and exhibition process for movies.

Paramount

Hungarian immigrant Adolph Zukor started out poor in Hollywood, but through a series of innovations, none of them artistic, he invented the movie business as we know it today. Zukor's innovations are detailed below.

Star System When Zukor started in the movie business in 1912, moviemakers kept the names of their actors secret. Zukor saw things differently. He tracked fan letters for mentions of actors. Those mentioned most often were signed to exclusive contracts.

Production Efficiencies Zukor brought mass production to moviemaking. Paramount movies became factory-like products. By incorporating tight mass-production schedules and programmed progress, Paramount eventually was issuing a movie a week. So were competitors, in what came to be called the studio system.

block booking A rental agreement through which a movie house accepts a batch of movies.

Vertical Integration Studios like Paramount, which controlled the production, distribution, and exhibition of movies, squeezed out independent operators. **Block booking** was an example. Zukor booked his Paramount movies into Paramount-owned theatres. Paramount also provided movies to independent movie houses but only in packages that included overpriced clunkers. The profits were immense, funding the lifestyle and other excesses that gave Hollywood its gilded reputation.

vertical integration One company owning multiple stages of production, to the detriment of competition.

Paramount decision U.S. Supreme Court breakup of the movie industry oligarchy in 1948.

The major studios, which controlled the entire process from conception of a movie to the box office, had put the industry into what businesspeople call **vertical integration.** This control, including coercive practices such as block booking, in time attracted the antitrust division of the U.S. Justice Department. In a case decided by the U.S. Supreme Court in 1948, the studios were told to divest. As a result of the so-called **Paramount decision,** the lavish excesses of Hollywood's gilded age came to an end.

After Zukor The end of the studio system came when large conglomerates bought the studios and imposed new bottom-line expectations. Zukor continued, though, still chair of the board at Paramount until 1976, when he died at age 103. Today, Paramount is a unit of the U.S. media conglomerate Viacom, whose interests also include the CBS television network. Paramount prides itself as the only major studio still located in Hollywood.

LEARNING CHECK

- What were Adolph Zukor's enduring contributions to the American movie industry?
- How did the U.S. Supreme Court reshape Hollywood?

Disney

Classic Disney Although not realizing it, illustrator Walt Disney created the Disney franchise with a squeaky mouse in a synch-sound cartoon in 1928. Although the cartoon, *Steamboat Willie*, was only a short, intended to run with previews of coming attractions, audiences couldn't get enough. As revenue rolled in, Disney experimented with symphonies and cartoons, and in 1937 risked it all with a full-length animated film, *Snow White and the Seven Dwarfs*. Audiences wanted more and Disney responded with *Pinocchio*, *Dumbo*, *Bambi*, and *Fantasia*.

Disney Brand While other studios were fighting a losing battle with network television in the 1950s, Disney embraced the enemy. It struck a deal with the ABC network in 1954 to produce an original television series. In effect, it recycled its film content for television. The program *Disneyland*, a Sunday-night ritual for millions of television viewers, accounted for almost half of ABC's billing in the first year. For the next 20 years, the mandate at Disney was to cultivate the brand. Indeed, Disney had become a brand name for family-oriented entertainment.

Michael Eisner Post-Walt Disney executive who expanded Disney while protecting its wholesome cachet; engineered a merger with ABC.

Eisner Era To jump-start the company, in 1984 Disney shareholders brought in an energetic executive from Paramount, **Michael Eisner.** Over a 20-year period Eisner rejuvenated the company. He continued to recycle classic Disney products and expand the theme parks. Importantly, Eisner engineered a merger with ABC to create in-house outlets for Disney products. However, not all was perfect under Eisner. After *The Lion King*'s success in 1995, Disney had a series of animated feature flops. Profits slumped occasionally, which raised shareholder concerns. After a messy shareholder battle, Eisner was thrown out.

The post-Eisner leadership, concerned that Disney had lost its edge in animation, offered $7.4 billion to Steve Jobs, the genius behind Apple's resurgence, for his Pixar animation studio. It was Pixar that had stolen Disney's animation pre-eminence with blockbusters such as *Toy Story*, *Finding Nemo*, and *The Incredibles*. Within days, Apple's iTunes store added ABC and Disney video for downloading to iPods. Disney seemed well positioned for the new realities in media content delivery through traditional movie theatres, its ABC television access, and internet downloads.

Other Major Studios

The Big Six studios are Paramount, Disney, Columbia, 20th Century Fox, Universal, and Warner.

Columbia Columbia has moved through high-visibility ownership, including Coca-Cola and the Japanese electronics company Sony. Movies are produced and distributed under the brand names Columbia and TriStar and through frequent partnerships with Phoenix and Mandalay.

20th Century Fox This studio is part of the global media empire of Rupert Murdoch's News Corporation, whose roots are in Australia. Corporate siblings include Murdoch's Fox television network.

Universal The conglomerate General Electric bought Universal from the financially overextended French media giant Vivendi in 2002. Earlier, Universal was part of Canadian-based Seagram, known mostly as a distiller. The GE acquisition put the NBC television network and Universal under the same corporate umbrella. The goal was to create profitable synergies between these entities.

Warner Warner Bros. became part of the Time Inc. media empire in a 1989 acquisition, prompting the parent company to rename itself Time Warner. The company produces and distributes movies and television programs mostly through units carrying the Warner name but also the names Castle Rock, New Line, and Lorimar.

LEARNING CHECK

- **The movie industry once saw television as a rival, but no more. What happened?**
- **What is the extent of foreign ownership in the movie industry?**

Independents

Independent studios and producers come and go—often with a single breakthrough film, then not much else that attracts attention. The term *independent* is misleading in a sense because these indies frequently lean on the major studios for financing.

United Artists Unhappy with profit-obsessed studios limiting their creativity, friends Charlie Chaplin, Douglas Fairbanks, D.W. Griffith, and Mary Pickford created United Artists in 1919. With full creative control, they produced movies that scored well among critics and attracted huge audiences. Despite some box-office successes, United Artists has had its share of flops. After Michael Cimino's costly *Heaven's Gate* in 1980, United needed a white knight. The Transamerica insurance company bought the studio and then unloaded it on MGM. The new company, MGM/UA, produced one disaster after another.

Dreamworks In the spirit of United Artists, three Hollywood legends—David Geffen, Jeffrey Katzenberg, and Steven Spielberg—founded a new studio called Dreamworks in 1994. They were called the Hollywood dream team. Spielberg's *Saving Private Ryan* in 1998 established an early Dreamworks benchmark for film excellence. Then came *Gladiator*, named 2000's best picture at the Academy Awards. Like most upstarts, even the most successful ones, Dreamworks has disappeared. Geffen, Katzenberg, and Spielberg sold the enterprise in 2005 to Paramount for $1.6 billion.

Miramax Brothers Bob and Harvey Weinstein blew into Hollywood in 1979, introducing themselves as concert promoters from Buffalo, New York. They set up a movie distribution company, Miramax, with a simple premise: to find low-budget, independently produced movies, buy them cheap, and then promote them lavishly. After 10 years of struggling, the Weinsteins hit gold with the biopic *My Left Foot*, about Irish writer-painter Christy Brown. An Academy Award nomination as best picture stirred up box-office receipts, as did Daniel Day-Lewis's winning the Oscar for best actor.

Other hits followed, prompting Disney to buy in to Miramax in 1993. The deal left creative control with the hands-on Weinsteins, whose magic seemed to be a deft touch for cultural edginess that Disney lacked. More financial and critical successes followed, including *Pulp Fiction*, *Scary Movie 3*, and *Shakespeare in Love*; but then came *Cold Mountain* and *Gangs of New York*, neither of which earned back their $100 million production budgets.

Lions Gate Founded in 1997 by a Canadian investor, Lions Gate achieved early financial success by acquiring and producing tight-budget movies and then promoting them aggressively and imaginatively. Typical of this formula was *Crash*. Production cost $3.3 million but marketing cost $21 million. Global box office generated $254 million. *Crash* subsequently won the 2005 Academy Award for best picture, which generated a predictable bump in movie attendance and rentals.

Lions Gate releases fewer than 20 pictures in a typical year. In 2005 there were 18, of which 15 were profitable, an unusually high ratio in Hollywood. To see itself through slumps, Lions Gate invested in film libraries and gradually amassed an archive of 5500 titles that generate continuing revenue. Its catalogue includes *Basic Instinct*, *Total Recall*, *Dirty Dancing*, and the lucrative *Leprechaun* horror series.

LEARNING CHECK

- What is the role of independent studios in the movie industry?

Canadian Film Industry

STUDY PREVIEW While Hollywood's focus tends to be on blockbuster movies, the Canadian film industry pursued another direction. The National Film Board of Canada has won innumerable awards for its documentaries and animation. Feature films in Canada have also followed in the documentary tradition.

Canadian Movies

Jeannette Sloniowski, in *Canadian Communications: Issues in Contemporary Media and Culture*, sums up the plight of Canadian movies as follows: "Canadian Movies: Not Coming to a Cinema near You." Due to economic and distribution issues, Canadian movies account for less than 11 percent of all screen time at movie houses in Canada. Because of this, television is often the only outlet for Canadian films. Canadian channels, both conventional channels like the CBC and specialty channels, are the primary outlet for Canadian movies to be seen by Canadians. As a result of this exposure on television, the Canadian Film and Television Production Association (CFTPA) announced that more than 40 percent of revenue earned by Canadian movies comes from pay television.

Canadian movies have always lived in the shadow of American fare. As a result, they have had to struggle to mature and gain acceptance in this country. In his article titled "American Domination of the Motion Picture Industry," Garth Jowett points out that Canada has always been dependent on Hollywood for movies. Jowett writes, "From the outset, Canada because of its geographic situation was considered to be merely one of the many marketing areas designated by the American film industry." Jowett also claims that most Canadians have always preferred Hollywood movies to British or Canadian films. However, this does not mean that filmmaking traditions do not exist in this country.

Feature Films in Canada

Despite its success in the documentary and animated areas, Canada, with the exception of Quebec, has left the bulk of dramas and literary adaptations to the Americans. The feature film industry in Canada remained largely dormant until the 1960s. However, in 1964, two films marked the unofficial start of the feature film industry in Canada: Don Owen's *Nobody Waved Goodbye* and Gilles Groulx's *Le Chat dans le sac*. Both of these films were NFB productions, but they were feature films shot in the documentary tradition that highlighted regional themes without the glamour of Hollywood movies. The better-known Canadian films from this era include *Goin' down the Road* (1970), *Mon Oncle Antoine* (1971), *Paperback Hero* (1973), *Between Friends* (1973), and the classic *The Apprenticeship of Duddy Kravitz* (1974).

By the late 1970s, government incentives, such as those of the Canadian Film Development Corporation (now known as Telefilm) for producers investing in Canadian feature films, created a glut of product—some good, but mostly bad. It's this time period that gave Canadian movies a bad name. Many people invested money in movies simply as a tax break. The quality of the script, actors, and movie were not always important. *Why Shoot the Teacher?* (1978), *Atlantic City* (1980), *Scanners* (1981), and the largest-grossing Canadian movie of all time, the less-than-classy *Porky's* (1982), were all produced during this period.

Through the 1990s, Canadian films matured, particularly in English-language cinema with movies such as *Margaret's Museum* (1995), *Hard Core Logo* (1996), *The Hanging Garden* (1997), and *Last Night* (1999). This trend continued into the 21st century with such eclectic films as *Ginger Snaps* (2000), *My Big Fat Greek Wedding* (2002), *Away from Her* (2006), and *Passchendaele* (2008).

Issues of ethnicity and multiculturalism continue to be explored in more recent Canadian movies. Mina Shum's *Double Happiness* (1994), Davor Marjanovic's *My Father's Angel* (2000), Deepa Mehta's *Water* (2001), and Kevin Tierney's *Bon Cop, Bad Cop* (2006) are all excellent examples of Canadian films that explore these themes.

However, despite the increase in the quality of Canadian movies, English-speaking Canadians don't usually see these films at their local movie theatres. Instead, most watch their national cinema on television, particularly on specialty channels. Brian D. Johnson, the film critic for *Maclean's*, in his article titled "The Lost Picture Show," says, "Welcome to the Byzantine world of English Canadian film financing—a surreal maze of auteur dreams, bureaucratic nightmares and ritualized failure. It's a world where distributors routinely snap up publicly funded movies, flip the TV rights to broadcasters for an easy profit, then dump the films into a few theatres for a token release."

LEARNING CHECK

- Why have Canadian feature films lived in the shadow of American movies?

Exhibition Shift

STUDY PREVIEW The exhibition business has problems with the continuing erosion of box-office revenue. Attempts to address the declines include spiffier theatres, enforced audience conduct codes, and new technology: d-cinema.

Watch
Movie Palaces

Distribution

For moviegoers, the least visible part of the movie industry is distribution. The major studios are largely responsible for this task. They schedule the bookings for movie releases at the theatres, perform the marketing activities to promote the releases, and then supply the actual film to the movie houses. Big studios also provide distribution services.

The major film distributor in Canada is **Alliance Films**. It indirectly owns a majority interest in Motion Picture Distribution LP. In addition to distributing Canadian movies, such as *Trailer Park Boys: The Movie*, it distributes films and DVDs for New Line Cinema, Dimension Films, Miramax Films, The Weinstein Company, and others.

Alliance Films Canadian movie distributor.

How does Canada fit into Hollywood's distribution and exhibition plans? In effect, Canada is simply "America Junior." James Adams of *The Globe and Mail* says that "when the U.S. movie industry gathers statistics on how its films are faring at the box office, Canada isn't considered a sovereign nation: It's part of the American domestic market, right alongside Guam, Puerto Rico, the Virgin Islands and various other U.S. unincorporated territories."

Exhibition

exhibition What movie houses do.

The movie **exhibition** business has been boom and bust. The beginnings, early in the 1900s, were modest. Images were projected onto a white sheet spread across a wall in low-rent storefronts and onto whitewashed plywood hoisted upright in circus tents. In 1906, Canada's first movie house, the Ouimetoscope, opened in Montreal. By 1912, there was a new standard: the Strand in New York, an opulent 3300-seat theatre that rivalled the world's best opera houses. Nattily groomed and uniformed doormen and ushers made moviegoing an experience. So did expansive lobbies, lavish promenades, columns and colonnades, and plush velvet wall upholstery.

To capitalize on the popularity of movies, and to keep access affordable, less ostentatious movie houses were built in neighbourhoods and small towns. These were the core of the exhibition part of the movie industry at its peak. Although neither as large nor as lavish as the downtown palaces, the neighbourhood movie houses were the heart of moviegoing when attendance peaked in 1946. Movies were handy and affordable. For many people they were a habit two or three times a week. Attendance was so strong that Canada's Nat Taylor decided to split his Elgin Theatre in Ottawa into two, creating the first "multiplex" theatre.

The advent of network television in the 1950s cut into movie attendance. Families justified the purchase of their first television set, a major item in household budgets then, by saving quarters and half-dollars that otherwise would have gone toward movies. A lot of marquees went dark, some permanently, some at least a few nights a week.

The exhibition business adapted. Beginning in the 1970s, movie-house chains followed their customers to the suburbs and built a new form of movie house. Taking their cue from Nat Taylor, the multiscreen multiplex became popular. Attendance revived, although it fell far short of the 1946 peak and was also dependent on what movies were showing.

The multiplexes addressed the unevenness in attendance. With multiple auditoriums, each with a different seating capacity, movies could be switched among auditoriums to coincide with demand. Blockbuster films could be shown simultaneously in several auditoriums. With multiplexes, the new measure of a movie's success lay not in how many theatres it was booked into but onto how many screens it was projected.

Cineplex Entertainment LP Canada's largest movie theatre chain.

Cineplex Entertainment LP is the largest movie exhibitor in Canada, controlling 129 theatres and more than 1300 screens. Movie houses under its corporate umbrella include Cineplex Odeon, Galaxy, and Famous Players. Atlantic Canada's Empire Theatres is the second-largest movie exhibitor, with 50 theatres and more than 400 screens across Canada.

Exhibition Constriction

In the 1990s, sensing better days ahead, major movie-house chains in both Canada and the United States went on a spending spree to expand and upgrade theatres. Attendance was strong at multiplexes, some of which had as many as 30 screens. State-of-the-art sound systems were installed. Some auditoriums were outfitted with plush stadium seating.

Overexpansion The expansion and upgrades, however, overextended some chains financially. The situation worsened with continued box office slippage, down 7 percent in 2005, further reflecting competition from DVD sales and rentals for home viewing on television sets. Pay-per-view home satellite and cable options also hurt. So did video games, which particularly attracted young men who had been core movie-house patrons. The movie-house crisis is no better illustrated than through these 2005 figures:

- Box office revenue: $9.5 billion
- DVD revenue: $24.5 billion

Release Windows The exhibition segment of the movie business became increasingly uneasy over whether Hollywood was its friend. Ever since Hollywood had begun releasing movies to television in the 1950s, there had been a window of exclusivity for movie houses. Studio-owned distribution also maintained a protective window for movie houses as home videotapes became more popular, but distributors kept shrinking this window. What had been a window of six months in 1994 shrank to 4.5 months by 2004, with studios talking about possibly moving to simultaneous release. Clearly, Hollywood was coming to see that its best profit potential was not in staggering the release of new movies in different channels but in maximizing a single promotional burst with simultaneous theatrical and DVD releases.

With the expansion of home broadband access making an era of home downloading of feature-length movies possible, the future doesn't look good for exhibitors.

LEARNING CHECK

- Discuss how the interests of Hollywood and movie exhibition companies once coincided but now do so less.
- What is the effect of broadband access on movie attendance at theatres?

D-Cinema

Digital technology seems destined to replace film that is "pulled through the (chemical) soup" (described in Chapter 2). The pace of this transition is hard to forecast. Technical and financial impediments to big-screen digital projection remain, but the economic advantages of digital are driving a transition. Cameras and editing equipment are handier than massive celluloid filming equipment. Also, shipping the finished product on optical disks is far more efficient than using the back-breaking film canisters that now are carted from movie house to movie house on trucks. Even in the projection rooms, reels of film are awkward. Theoretically, the day will arrive when digital movies can be transmitted by satellite to movie-house projectors, even with central projection control.

Digital Transition George Lucas, producer of the *Star Wars* series, pioneered digital work through his Industrial Light & Magic production house. For his 1999 *Star Wars* instalment, *The Phantom Menace*, Lucas shot several scenes with digital equipment, which facilitated their integration into digitally created special effects scenes. For exhibition, there were two masters: one on film, which is what most moviegoers saw, and one in digital form, which was shown in a few theatres. Thus, *The Phantom Menace* became the first major motion picture to be seen in digital form, albeit only at the few theatres equipped with digital projectors.

Relatively few films have been released in digital form because the conversion of movie houses has been slow. Of 36 485 screens in 2005, only 92 had digital servers and projectors. From 1999 to 2004, a period that saw almost 3000 Hollywood releases, only 86 titles were digital.

Champions of **d-cinema**, as the new technology is called, expect a sudden upsurge in digital releases. Only one major director, Steven Spielberg, still edits on celluloid. As well, the studios are keen to cut the cost of making hundreds of celluloid prints that are shipped from theatre to theatre. Hollywood's distribution costs are roughly $630 million a year for the United States and Canada, and $1 billion worldwide. Distributing d-cinema via the internet or optical disks could cut costs by 90 percent.

d-cinema Movies that are filmed, edited, distributed, and exhibited digitally.

There are purists who prefer traditional technology over d-cinema technology, but their number is decreasing. Canada's James Cameron, best known for *Titanic* and *Avatar*, says that he will never shoot on film again.

Technical Standards The studios seem to be on the verge of making the plunge. In 2002, Disney, Fox, MGM, Paramount, Sony, Universal, and Warner combined forces to develop an industry-wide technical standard for d-cinema. The joint venture, Digital Cinema Initiatives, has narrowed the quest to two competing technologies, known as 2K and 4K.

One company, Texas Instruments, has devised a 2K-chip imaging device that displays 2048 pixels across. JVC and Sony are pushing 4K, which displays 4096 pixels on a wider canvas. The early d-cinema films used 4K with the Barco D-Cine DP100 projector, but critics say that 4K hogs bandwidth and offers a resolution far finer than the human eye can detect—so why bother? For practical purposes, say 2K advocates, the two images look equally sharp. As well, it's not just a pixel race. The rate at which images are updated is more important than the number of pixels to meet the upper limits of human persistence of vision. In 2007, Cineplex Odeon began converting some of their theatres to d-cinema using 2K projectors.

The remaining big issue is the financing of movie-house conversion. At a cost of $100 000 per theatre for new equipment, the big exhibition chains, always wary about increasing ticket prices, are hesitant to make this investment. In 2005, the studios proposed a $1000 incentive to theatres, called a virtual print fee, to offset the cost of the new equipment. The mathematics are promising. Studios will save about $1000 by not having to make and ship film prints. Assuming that each film runs for three weeks, theatres would average about $17 000 a year in new fees, which would pay for the new equipment in six years.

Movie-house chains are being cautious, noting that digital projection equipment has a notoriously short lifespan, about three years compared to decades for older equipment. But exhibitors may have no choice as people become enamoured of digital images on computer screens and the growing trend toward digital transmission in television.

LEARNING CHECK

- What is d-cinema?
- How likely is the conversion of movie houses to digital projection to draw audiences back?

The Next Platform

Hollywood distributors have been keen on DVD sales and rentals, which had buoyed their revenues as box-office revenue declined. But by 2007 the DVD market had plateaued. Concerned that the industry may have maxed out the potential of both theatrical and DVD releases, studios earnestly pondered what their next delivery platform might be. Computer downloads remain broadband hogs with little appeal. Downloads to handheld and other devices involve mostly short features, not full-length movies, and they compete for attention with all kinds of other internet content.

Confronted with the possibility that Hollywood may have reached the end of its cycle as a growth industry, major studios became cautious. Disney reduced its output in 2006 and laid off 650 employees. Studios cut back on deals with independent producers. The situation was put into startling financial terms by a Kagan Research study that found studios recouped only 84 percent of production and domestic marketing costs from domestic theatrical releases and home video sales in 2005. The shareholder-sensitive corporations that own the studios ordered more scrutiny on spending until bottom lines improve. The trade journal *Variety* put it this way: "In the eyes of Wall Street, studios are now seen as bloated entities."

Blockbuster Quest

STUDY PREVIEW Massive profits from a runaway movie success lure studio executives into big-budget epics and spectaculars, but some flop. The big stakes and also the risk are encouraged by conglomerate ownership, which pressures studios to outdo their profits season after season.

Escalation of Expectations

D.W. Griffith Early director known for innovations in *Birth of a Nation* and loose spending in *Intolerance.*

blockbuster A movie that is a great commercial success; also used to describe books.

Early directors, including **D.W. Griffith,** tested the storytelling potential of the new film medium. Growing public enthusiasm was the proof of what worked. Griffith's 1915 Civil War epic *Birth of a Nation* was cinematically innovative and a commercial success. By the standards of the time, it was a **blockbuster.** The movie fuelled Griffith to push the envelope further in a more complex project, *Intolerance*. In this movie, Griffith wanted to examine social justice through all of human history. He built huge sets and hired hundreds of actors. In all, he spent an unprecedented $2 million. In 1916, when *Intolerance* debuted, the critics were ecstatic at Griffith's audacity and artistry as a director. The movie bombed, however. Audiences were baffled by the movie's disparate settings, including ancient Babylon, Renaissance France, and the Holy Land at the time of Christ.

The *Intolerance* experience demonstrated a dynamic that continues to play out in Hollywood—the tension that erupts not infrequently between financiers and directors. A second lesson from *Intolerance* was another Hollywood reality—boom or bust. The quest for super-earning blockbusters has escalated, often with risky big budgets. There have been spectacular payoffs, such as *The Dark Knight* (2008) and *Avatar* (2009), the reigning box-office champ.

Risk Reduction

To balance the risk of blockbusters, studios look for safe bets. Profits can be made if production costs can be contained. The result is a preponderance of formulaic movies that offer little in terms of creative storytelling and fail to advance the art of moviemaking but that turn a profit. Called **B movies**, these include sequels, remakes, and franchises that, although hardly great movies, are almost sure to outearn their expenses.

B movie Low-budget movie, usually with little artistic aspiration.

Fast action, which doesn't require fine acting and is cheap to produce, has figured heavily in low-budget and mid-budget movies. So too have violence and sex. Dialogue is minimal in many of these movies, which makes them easy to adapt for distribution to non-English-speaking audiences abroad.

Studios also have hedged their bets by building product names into scripts for a fee. This is called **product placement.** Some New York and Los Angeles advertising agencies specialize in product placement, as do talent agencies such as Creative Artists. No, it was no accident that Tom Hanks's character in *Cast Away* worked for FedEx. Or that hulky Chrysler 300s appeared in so many 2005 movies or that Cadillacs appeared in MGM's *Be Cool*. In 2006, product placement even worked its way into movie titles: *How Starbucks Saved My Life* and *The Devil Wears Prada*. Universal changed *Flight 93* to *United 93*.

product placement Including a product in a script for a fee.

Studios also have found revenue in **merchandise tie-ins**, including trinkets sold at fast-food restaurants and entire lines of toys.

merchandise tie-in Products spun off from a movie, usually trinkets and toys.

Alternatives to Blockbusters

New structures have evolved that help moviemaking newcomers to interest the distribution units of major studios in their work.

Explore

Deepening Your Media Literacy: Are the most popular films the best films?

Film Festivals Every January in Park City, Utah, Hollywood dispatches teams to audition films by independent filmmakers at the Sundance Film Festival. These are low-budget projects that sometimes earn substantial returns on investment. *The Blair Witch Project*, made by a team of University of Central Florida grads, is a classic example. The movie cost just $35 000 to produce. The young filmmakers made a killing after scouts from Artisan Entertainment watched a Sundance screening of the movie in 1998 and paid $1.1 million for distribution rights. The movie went on to generate $141 million at the box office.

In Canada, for 10 days in September, the Toronto International Film Festival (TIFF) features films from around the world and from Canada. Many "little movies" debuted at the festival, including *Chariots of Fire*, *Slumdog Millionaire*, and *Hotel Rwanda*. The festival's Canada First!, Short Cuts Canada, and Canadian Open Vault programs showcase Canadian cinema. TIFF's Bell Lighthouse opened as part of the 2010 festival. It showcases movie history from a Canadian and international perspective.

TIFF isn't the only film festival in Canada. Vancouver is home to the Vancouver International Film Festival, the Vancouver Asian Film Festival, and the Vancouver Queer Film Festival. Meanwhile, the Atlantic Film Festival includes movies made by east coast filmmakers.

Exhibition Niches Movie theatres aren't just for movies anymore. For example, Front Row Centre Events features UFC and WWE events, the Metropolitan Opera, concerts, and live theatre broadcasts. Many 2010 Olympic events were broadcast to Cineplex and Empire theatres across Canada.

In 2010, Cineplex introduced the Great Digital Film Festival at Toronto's Scotiabank Theatre. It featured digitally remastered classic films such as *The Godfather*, *Goldfinger*, and *The Shawshank Redemption*, all shown on the big screen. In 2011, Cineplex held festivals across Canada, in Montreal, Ottawa, Edmonton, and Vancouver.

Foreign Movies Abroad, local-language movies are taking a large slice of home markets. The result is greater homegrown competition for Hollywood films in foreign countries. Hit hardest have been mid-range American movies that once had a sure market abroad. The growing number of homemade foreign movies has squeezed the availability of opening weekends and theatre screens.

The growth in foreign movies also means more competition for financing. Commercial investors that once financed only Hollywood productions now are recognizing the investment potential in other countries. The result is that more producers in more countries are vying for funding to produce movies.

While American movies are losing audience to local fare abroad, the U.S. movie industry is protecting itself financially. Several Hollywood studios are putting money into foreign endeavours. Sony has provided financing for foreign studios. In an unusual twist, one of these movies, *Crouching Tiger, Hidden Dragon*, became an import with a fairly strong U.S. box office. Twentieth Century Fox has invested in British and Russian projects, among them the smash trilogy *Night Watch*. Also, Fox owner Rupert Murdoch has put money into projects by emerging Middle East media giant Rotana, which is producing 20-plus movies a year and accounts for almost 50 percent of the Arab film market. Since 2005, Warner has been in joint production with Chinese studios, which gives the movies a favoured status for screens and opening dates that is not available to films made outside China.

***A Day in the Life:* Documentary Filmmaking**

LEARNING CHECK

- Why have little movies become a growing segment in Hollywood?

Chapter 7 Wrap-Up

For more than a century, movies have been an important element of North American culture. Movies can be great entertainers that also sensitize people to issues and have a long-term effect in shifting public attitudes on enduring issues. Although most people associate movies with heavily promoted Hollywood feature films, the medium lends itself to a wide range of content other than escapist fiction. Documentaries, a nonfiction genre, have a long tradition, as does the Canadian film industry. How people will view movies in the future is changing.

PEARSON mycanadiancommunicationlab

Visit **www.mycanadiancommunicationlab.ca** for access to a wealth of tools and resources that will enhance your learning experience. Features include the following:

- Personalized Study Plan
- Videos
- Activities
- Pearson eText–and much more!

Questions for Critical Thinking

1. What is required for movies to have a great impact on viewers?
2. Describe what makes American movies different from Canadian movies.
3. What is meant by the National Film Board's mandate to "explain Canada to Canadians"?
4. Would you invest your money in a movie exhibition chain? Explain.
5. Can you equate the quest for blockbusters with the goose that laid a golden egg? Explain.

Keeping Up to Date

People serious about movies as art will find *American Film* and *Film Comment* valuable sources of information.

Among consumer magazines with significant movie coverage are *Entertainment Weekly*, *Maclean's*, and *Rolling Stone.*

Trade journals include *Variety* and *Hollywood Reporter.*

Canadian newspapers that cover movies include the *Toronto Star*, the *National Post*, and *The Globe and Mai.*

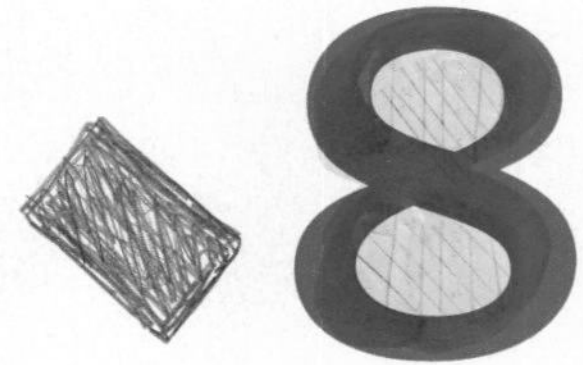

8 Television

LEARNING AHEAD

- The television industry is under siege from new technology.
- Television was built on the same two-tier system as radio.
- Cable television grew to challenge the affiliate–network monopoly.
- Satellite delivery has further fragmented the television delivery industry.
- New technology offers video-on-demand, which is reconfiguring the industry.
- Public television is an alternative to commercial television.
- Advertisers are eyeing alternatives created by time-shifting and portable devices.

Iconic TV To understand the cultural impact of television, one doesn't need to look any further than *Hockey Night in Canada*. The program, which began on radio, has become a Saturday night television ritual for many Canadians since its debut in 1952.

MEDIA IN THEORY

Cultural Impact of Television

There's no doubt that television is a big part of our lives. Many of us have two or more television sets and each of us watches about 28 hours of TV per week. We even watch TV on our iPods, laptops, and other portable devices. Scholars and broadcasters may have different views on the potency of television's effect on society, but they all agree that there is some degree of influence.

Fictional television characters can capture the imagination of the public. Perry Mason did wonders for the reputation of lawyers. Mary Tyler Moore's role as a television news writer showed that women could succeed in male-dominated industries. *The Cosby Show* changed the image of prime-time fatherhood in the 1980s. *Seinfeld* became a ritual on Thursday nights on NBC during the 1990s, while *Survivor* set the stage for reality TV in the 21st century.

Although television can be effective in creating short-term impressions, it also creates long-term effects. A whole generation of children grew up with *Teenage Mutant Ninja Turtles* as part of their generational identity. Later came *Pokémon* and *Beyblade*. The long-term effects exist at both a superficial level, as with *Teenage Mutant Ninja Turtles*, and a serious level. Social critic **Michael Novak** puts the effect of television in broad terms: "Television is a molder of the soul's geography. It builds up incrementally a psychic structure of expectations. It does so in much the same way that school lessons slowly, over the years, tutor the unformed mind and teach it how to think."

Michael Novak Believes that television is a broad shaper of issues.

MEDIA TIMELINE Television

1927 Philo Farnsworth devised a tube that picks up moving images for transmission.

1939 Television was demonstrated at the New York World's Fair and at the Canadian National Exhibition.

1952 Television arrived in Canada; CBFT (Montreal) and CBLT (Toronto) began broadcasting.

1958 Fowler Commission set first levels for Canadian content on television.

1961 CTV began broadcasting as a private network.

1975 Gerald Levin put HBO on satellite for cable systems.

1998 Networks began occasional digital transmissions.

2001 First wave of digital specialty channels was launched in Canada.

2005 Canadian channels began broadcasting in HDTV.

2005 Apple introduced the video iPod.

2009 All American television channels began broadcasting in digital.

2010 Online viewing surpassed traditional television viewing in Canada.

2011 Canadian television stations began broadcasting in digital.

What are the lessons to which Novak refers? Scholars **Linda and Robert Lichter and Stanley Rothman,** who have surveyed television's creative community, make a case that the creators of television programs are social reformers who build their political ideas in to their scripts. The Lichters and Rothman identify television's creative community as largely secular and politically liberal.

Linda and Robert Lichter and Stanley Rothman Scholars who claim that television is reformist.

Media scholar **George Comstock**, in his book *Television in America*, wrote, "Television has become an unavoidable and unremitting factor in shaping what we are and what we will become." But what about this American influence on English-Canadian culture? Canadian broadcaster **Moses Znaimer** claims that "as transmitter of information and entertainment, television is the acknowledged king. It's also very effective as a reflector of values and teacher of ideals, often in ways you don't notice." If Comstock, Novak, and Znaimer are correct, the need for Canadian television is obvious.

George Comstock Believes that television helps us to become who we are.

Moses Znaimer Believes that TV reflects values and ideals.

Influence of Television

STUDY PREVIEW Television's huge audiences have made it a medium with profound effects not only on people and culture but also on other media. Today, television is the dominant mass medium for entertainment and news.

Mass Media Shakeup

Since television's introduction in the early 1950s, its presence has reshaped the other media. Consider the following.

Books The discretionary time that people spend on television today is time that once went to other activities, including reading for entertainment and information. Today, a major consideration at publishing houses in evaluating fiction manuscripts is their potential as screenplays, and some publishers even consider how well an author will come across in television interviews once the book is published.

Newspapers Evening television newscasts and 24-hour news channels have been a major factor in the near disappearance of afternoon editions of newspapers. Most have either ceased publication or switched to morning editions. Also, hometown newspapers have lost almost all of their national advertisers, primarily to television. Most newspaper redesigns today attempt to be visually stimulating in ways that newspapers never were before television.

Explore

Deepening Your Media Literacy: Is television news on the decline?

Magazines Television took advertisers from the mass-circulation magazines such as *Life*, forcing publishers to shift to magazines that catered to smaller segments of the mass audience that television could not serve.

CASE STUDY

Television as Babysitter

ABC's *Good Morning America*: "Toddlers and TV"

The scene is typical. Dad plunks the kids in front of the television so he can do laundry. Mom does the same while cooking dinner. In school, children also find themselves being babysat by television. Teachers use it to give students a break from real learning or simply to settle them down. Now children can also watch TV on their cell phones.

A 2005 study by the Kaiser Family Foundation found that 83 percent of children under age 6 use what's called screen media (television, video, or computers) about two hours per day. And media use increases with age. Sixty-one percent of babies watch screen media in a typical day. Among 4- to 6-year-olds, it's 90 percent. Other studies have found that in lower-income homes, kids watch more television and are more likely to have a television set in their bedrooms, a practice discouraged by pediatricians.

A strong case can be made that too much television isn't good for kids. Why aren't they out exercising? And nobody would prescribe watching violence. At the same time, shows such as *Sesame Street*, *Arthur*, and *Dora the Explorer* can teach spelling, arithmetic, problem solving, and social skills. These shows employ experts with doctoral degrees to work with writers to set goals and review scripts. *Sesame Street* tests its shows in daycare centres. In the early 1970s, researcher and psychologist Daniel Anderson watched children watching *Sesame Street* and found that "television viewing is a much more intellectual activity for kids than anybody had previously supposed."

According to Joseph Blatt of the Harvard Graduate School of Education, *Dora the Explorer*, created by Nickelodeon's Brown Johnson, proved that it is possible to produce quality programming for children in a commercial environment. Now marketers spend a lot of money trying to convince parents that their shows will help children's brains to develop. This strategy has worked. The Kaiser study found that many parents are enthusiastic about the use of television. Two-thirds say that their children imitate positive behaviour, such as helping or sharing, as seen on television.

The phenomenon of using television as a babysitter has been debated since the first picture flickered on the small screen. "Like alcohol or guns, TV will be used sensibly in some homes and wreak havoc in others," writes Daniel McGinn in *Newsweek*. "Debating its net societal value will remain a never-ending pursuit."

Sesame Street At what price does a child's time spent watching television displace physical exercise? Has television been a factor in the new obesity epidemic?

DEEPENING YOUR MEDIA LITERACY

Explore the Issue

Check out the PBS Kids: Sesame Street, Parents & Teachers web page (www.pbs.org/parents/sesame/index.html) and the Playhouse Disney Guide for Grown-ups web page (http://tv.disney.go.com/playhouse/grown-ups/index.html).

Dig Deeper

What do you notice about these pages? What do you think their message is to parents?

What Do You Think?

Does the quality of children's shows matter in the debate about television as a babysitter? Are shows without commercials or merchandise marketing inherently better than commercialized shows?

Recordings The success of recorded music today hinges in many cases on the airplay that music videos receive on television on MuchMoreMusic and CMT Canada.

Movies Just as magazines demassified after television took away many of their advertisers, Hollywood demassified after television stole the bulk of its audience. Today, savvy moviemakers plan their projects both for the big screen and for television via the networks and home video rental.

Radio Radio demassified with the arrival of television. The television networks first took radio's most successful programs and moved them to the screen. After radio lost its traditional programming strengths, individual radio stations shifted almost entirely to recorded music and geared the music to narrower and narrower audience segments.

Television Industry in Crisis

Television transformed the mass media. In the 1950s, television, the new kid on the block, forced its media elders, notably movies, radio, and magazines, to reinvent themselves or perish. Year by year television entrenched itself in the latter half of the 20th century, first as a hot new medium and then as the dominant medium. Now the industries that developed around television technology are themselves in crisis. They have been overtaken by innovations in delivering video through other channels. Can the television industry reinvent itself? Can the industry get on top of the new technology? Or will television as an industry find itself subsumed, perhaps even replaced, by new competition? High drama is occurring even as you read this chapter.

LEARNING CHECK

- How did TV affect other media upon its arrival?
- How can TV now reinvent itself?

Over-the-Air Delivery

STUDY PREVIEW The original television industry was composed of local stations, generally with the most successful carrying network programming from NBC, CBS, and ABC. Canadian stations also carried American network programming.

The Early Days of Canadian TV

While there were several experimental television broadcasts in Canada through the 1930s and 1940s, Canadians were first exposed to American television signals. The first television broadcast signal was received in Canada in 1947. Engineers at General Electric in Windsor picked up the transmission of WWDT from Detroit. This set the trend for television viewing in the early years of television in Canada. If you lived close enough to the border and had access to a television, you probably watched some American programming.

Television officially arrived in Canada in 1952. As was the case with the first radio station 30 years earlier, the first television station was in Montreal. **CBFT**, a public station, began broadcasting on September 6, 1952, with **CBLT** Toronto broadcasting two days later. In 1953, stations began broadcasting in Vancouver, Sudbury, and Ottawa; by 1954, Winnipeg and Halifax had television stations. At first, programming was a mix of Canadian and American fare. Early Canadian programming also reflected its roots in radio. *Wayne and Shuster* was a staple of Canadian television during the 1960s and 1970s, while *Hockey Night in Canada*, which began on radio in the 1920s, continues to draw a huge audience for the CBC on Saturday nights. A microwave link between Buffalo and Toronto made it possible to carry American programs live. There was no doubt about it: television was a hit in Canada. One million television sets had been purchased in Canada by 1954. By 1958, the CBC network stretched from Victoria to Halifax. In 1961, CTV began as Canada's first private broadcaster.

CBFT First Canadian TV channel.

CBLT Second Canadian TV channel.

LEARNING CHECK

- Why was early programming on Canadian television a mix of Canadian and American shows?

Canadian Networks

At present, there are three national networks in Canada. Two of them are privately owned, while one, the CBC, is Canada's national public broadcaster.

CBC The CBC was created as a radio network by an act of Parliament in 1936. CBC television began in 1952. Today, despite cutbacks in funding, the CBC has developed a loyal following for its programming on several media platforms. CBC television programming outlets include CBC TV in English and French, CBC Newsworld, and Galaxie, a pay audio service available through digital cable and direct-to-home satellite. Over the last few years, some of CBC TV's best-known shows include *Hockey Night in Canada*, *The Rick Mercer Report*, *Dragon's Den*, *Battle of the Blades*, and *Little Mosque on the Prairie*.

In *Canada's Cultural Industries* (1983), Paul Audley sums up the history of television in Canada well. He writes, "The general pattern from the beginning of television in 1952 until the present has been one of a rapidly expanding private television broadcasting system and an underfinanced public system." Given the changes that occurred in the late 20th and early 21st centuries, this appears to be true. Writing in *Maclean's*, Peter C. Newman argues that Canadians need the CBC to become important again. Says Newman, "With our kids watching 900 hours or more of TV a year—and at least 80 percent of it spreading the gospel of the American way of life—we must maintain a vibrant indigenous alternative." Private broadcasters, such as Global and CTV, would disagree with Newman, claiming that the Canadian identity can be preserved by the private sector.

John Bassett Founded CFTO Toronto, CTV's flagship station.

Spence Caldwell Initiator of the CTV network.

CTV While the CBC is Canada's public network, CTV was Canada's first privately owned national network. In 1960, the Board of Broadcast Governors or BBG (the forerunner of today's CRTC) held hearings for privately owned television stations. One of the victors was **John Bassett**'s CFTO. His background in media included part ownership of both the *Sherbrooke Daily Record* and the *Toronto Telegram*; he founded Baton Broadcasting in 1960 and began broadcasting on CFTO, Channel 9, in Toronto. **Spence Caldwell** wasn't as lucky. His application for a TV channel was denied, but he didn't let that stop him from becoming a Canadian TV pioneer. He approached several of the new television channels, including Bassett's CFTO, with the idea of forming a network. He eventually was able to convince eight channels to form CTN in 1961, with CFTO as its flagship station. CTN changed its name to CTV in 1962. Today, CTV stations reach more than 99 percent of English Canada with their programming. In addition to airing American programming, CTV stations promote Canadian television through shows such as *Canada AM*, *Flashpoint*, *Hiccups*, and *W5*. In 2010, CTV was purchased by Bell Canada Enterprises (BCE).

Ken Soble and Al Bruner Dreamt of a Canadian superstation.

Izzy Asper Developed Global into Canada's third private TV network.

Global As far back as 1960, Ontario broadcasters **Ken Soble** and **Al Bruner** had an idea for a Canadian superstation. Although Soble passed away in 1966, Bruner formed Global Communications Limited in 1970. By 1974, CKGN-TV began broadcasting in Ontario. It wasn't a success and lost money from the outset. By 1975 it had been restructured and refinanced. One of its saviours was the late lawyer and journalist **Izzy Asper**. Through a series of buyouts and takeovers that began in the mid-1970s, CanWest Global became Canada's third national network and second private national network in 2000. Some notable Canadian productions aired by CanWest are *Blue Murder*, *Canada's Walk of Fame*, and *Deal or No Deal Canada*. Since 2010, Global has been owned by Shaw Media.

Canadian Programming and the CRTC

Getting Canadians to watch Canadian TV has been a struggle for English-language broadcasters. Although viewership has increased, the fact remains that Canadians watch American programming 52 percent of the time. It's worse for Canadian comedies and dramas; 77 percent of the time, we prefer American programming to homegrown shows. Meanwhile, in Quebec, 66 percent of all viewing is Canadian. The question for the industry and academics is how to get English Canadians to watch more Canadian programming.

According to Canadian writer, actor, and producer of Canadian television programs Steve Smith (known as Red Green to many), Canadian television has an important role as a vehicle for Canadian culture. Smith claims that with "Canadians being constantly exposed to and bombarded with American culture, there's a natural tendency to assimilate and, with Canadians, if all they're exposed to is American media, they will become more and more like Americans and less and less like Canadians. We'd be more like North

Dakota with more interesting currency. For some people, that doesn't bother them. For me I think that would be a terrible tragedy."

Smith feels very passionately about Canadian television. He says it's unfair to categorize all American TV shows as better than all Canadian shows. "There are some great Canadian shows. If you look at the ratings book, people would be surprised that a lot of Canadian shows outrate a lot of the American shows." Smith says that Canadian sports broadcasts are among the highest rated.

The real problem for English-Canadian television, says Smith, is "the philosophy behind some of the broadcast outlets in that they really aren't in the business of making Canadian television good or popular. They are really in the business of importing American shows. That bothers me. Canadian broadcasters should be judged on the Canadian shows that they offer to the public, not on how many American shows they run. If Canadian networks lived or died by the success of their Canadian programming, they would find a way to make them great." For many broadcasters in Canada, the production and scheduling of Canadian programming is an afterthought.

It's this last point about Canadian TV becoming an afterthought for Canadian networks that has many upset. As Paul Atallah and Leslie Shade argue in *Mediascapes*, the Cancon quota actually may be hurting English-Canadian television. "Content quotas set aside certain hours that *must* be filled with Canadian content. Since that content must be shown, it hardly matters whether it is very popular or very good. Indeed, it may be more rational to satisfy quota requirements as inexpensively as possible."

Over the years, Canada's broadcast regulator, the CRTC, has tried to address this issue. In 2010, it offered broadcasters additional flexibility in acquiring and scheduling Canadian programs, notably:

- Canadian stations need to schedule **55 percent Canadian content** overall, with at least 50 percent scheduled during prime time.
- The CRTC also offers a **drama credit** of up to 150 percent for new Canadian dramas. This means that a new one-hour Canadian drama would count as 90 minutes toward the channel's Cancon requirements for that week.

55 percent Canadian content Level of daily Canadian content required by the CRTC.

drama credit CRTC incentive for production sector and Canadian channels.

The goal for Canadian networks, according to **Michael McCabe**, former president of the Canadian Association of Broadcasters, is viewing. Says McCabe, "Viewing is what really counts. Not just how many hours we have or how many dollars we spend. These are just proxies for what should be the real goal—more Canadians watching, being informed by and, most importantly, enjoying Canadian television."

Michael McCabe Former head of Canadian Association of Broadcasters.

LEARNING CHECK

- **What role does the CRTC play in defining what we watch on Canadian TV?**
- **Why do you watch or not watch Canadian TV? What can be done to get more people to watch Canadian TV?**

American Networks

For most of American television's history, networks provided programming to local stations in prime time at night and during parts of the daytime, too. As with radio earlier, TV became a two-tier system featuring both local and national programming.

NBC The genius who built the NBC radio network within the RCA empire, David Sarnoff, moved into television as soon as the government resumed licensing local stations after World War II. For early programming, **NBC** raided its radio repertoire of shows and stars. Then came innovations. Pat Weaver, an advertising executive recruited by NBC as a vice-president in 1951, created a late-night comedy-variety talk show, a precursor to the venerable *Tonight Show*. Weaver also created a wake-up show, the still-viable *Today*. With those shows, NBC owned the early morning and late-night audience for years.

NBC National Broadcast Company; built from NBC radio network under David Sarnoff.

CBS Sarnoff's long-time rival in radio, **William Paley** of **CBS**, was not far behind in moving soap operas and other programs from radio to television. Soon CBS was fully competitive with its own innovations, which included the *Twilight Zone* science-fiction anthology. By 1953, *I Love Lucy*, which eventually included 140 episodes, was a major draw. Paley worked to create a cachet for CBS, which he relished calling the "Tiffany network" after the ritzy New York jewellery store.

William Paley Long-time CBS boss.

CBS Columbia Broadcasting System; built from CBS radio network under William Paley.

Making Fox *The Simpsons* was among a handful of programs that helped Fox, a Johnny-come-lately television network, to establish itself with a young audience. In Canada, the show has had a long run on Global.

CBS established a legacy in public affairs when **Edward R. Murrow**, famous for his World War II radio reporting from Europe, started *See It Now*. Three years later, in 1954, when Senator Joseph McCarthy was using the prestige of his office to smear people as communists even though they weren't, it was Murrow on *See It Now* who exposed the senator's dubious tactics. Many scholars credit Murrow not only for his courage but also for undoing McCarthy and easing so-called Red Scare phobias.

Edward R. Murrow Reporter who criticized Joseph McCarthy.

ABC American Broadcasting Company; built from ABC radio network.

Roone Arledge Created ABC's *Monday Night Football*.

Barry Diller Created early successful Fox programming.

Fox Network launched in 1986.

ABC **ABC** established its television network in 1948 but ran a poor third behind NBC and CBS. However, two programs gave ABC some distinction: *Disneyland* in 1954 and *The Mickey Mouse Club* in 1955. ABC picked up steam in 1961 with *Wide World of Sports*, a weekend anthology that appealed to more than just sports fans. **Roone Arledge**, the network's sports chief, created *Monday Night Football* in 1969. Network television was a three-way race once again. In 1976, ABC was leading by a hair.

Fox Rupert Murdoch, the Australian-born media magnate, made a strategic decision in 1986 to become a major media player in the United States. He bought seven non-network stations in major markets and also the movie studio 20th Century Fox. The stations gave Murdoch a nucleus for a fourth television network. With 20th Century Fox, Murdoch had production facilities and a huge movie library with which to fill airtime. He recruited **Barry Diller**, whose track record included a string of ABC hits, to head the new network, which Murdoch called **Fox**.

There were doubts that Fox would make it, but Diller kept costs low with low-budget shows like *Married . . . with Children*, which featured the crude and dysfunctional Bundy family. *The Simpsons* attracted young viewers, whom advertisers especially sought to reach. Fox outbid CBS to televise half of the Sunday National Football League games in 1994. Soon afterwards, some CBS affiliates defected to Fox. Murdoch's strategy worked. With almost 200 affiliates, Fox made network television into the Big Four.

CW network Network created in 2006 by merger of WB and UPN.

CW Two upstart networks fashioned in the Fox mould—Time Warner's WB and Viacom's UPN—went on the air in 1995, but neither caught on much with viewers or advertisers. In 2006, they merged into the **CW network** for another try. The *C* in CW comes from the Viacom corporate subsidiary CBS and the *W* comes from Warner.

LEARNING CHECK

- List the programming innovators who shaped each of the major networks. What were their contributions?

Educational TV

In addition to commercial broadcasting, North America is also home to many educational broadcasters. With U.S. federal funding in 1967, the Public Broadcasting Service began providing programs to noncommercial stations. While PBS has offered some popular programs, such as *Sesame Street*, the biography show *American Masters*, and the newsmagazine *Frontline*, commercial stations do not see it as much of a threat. In fact, with its emphasis on informational programming and high-quality drama and arts, PBS relieved public pressure on commercial stations for less profitable, highbrow programming. Like PBS in the United States, noncommercial broadcasting in Canada—including provincial broadcasters such as British Columbia's Knowledge Network, Saskatchewan's SCN, and Ontario's TVO—relies heavily on viewer contributions and provincial funding.

Cable and Satellite Delivery

STUDY PREVIEW The cable television industry has grown from independent small-town community antenna systems into a well-heeled, consolidated industry. Today, cable is a major threat to the traditional networks and their over-the-air affiliates. Television delivery fragmented further with satellite signals delivered directly to viewers.

Roots of Cable

In the early 1950s, television networks and their local affiliates reached only major cities. Television signals, like FM radio, do not follow the curvature of the earth, so communities 40 to 50 miles away were pretty much out of range. Rough terrain kept even nearer towns from receiving television. One by one, small-town entrepreneurs hoisted antennas on nearby hilltops to catch television signals from the nearest cities with over-the-air stations. These local cable television systems, called **CATV** (for community antenna television), ran cables into town and stretched wire on telephone poles to deliver pictures to houses from the hilltop antennas. Everybody was happy. Small towns got big-city television, local entrepreneurs made money, and the networks and their stations gained viewers they couldn't otherwise reach. With this larger, cable-enhanced audience, the networks and stations were able to hike advertising rates.

CATV Short for community antenna television; an early name for cable systems.

Interestingly, cable TV arrived in Canada before the first Canadian television station, perhaps reflecting our desire for American programming. An experiment with redistributing U.S. antenna signals in 1952 in London, Ontario, marked the start of cable TV in Canada. Later that year, cable companies were also established in Vancouver and Montreal. The CRTC refers to cable companies as broadcast distribution undertakings, or **BDUs**.

BDU Broadcast distribution undertakings; technical name for cable companies and satellite providers.

Although not a technological leap, the locally owned small-town cable systems were a new wrinkle in television delivery. The systems were a minor, relatively passive component in the U.S. television industry. Even into the 1970s nobody sensed what a sleeping giant they had become.

LEARNING CHECK

- Why was cable television only a small-town phenomenon for a quarter-century?

Gerald Levin and HBO

Television entered a new era in 1975 when **Gerald Levin** took over **HBO**, a Time Life subsidiary. HBO had been offering movies and special events, such as championship boxing, to local cable systems, which then sold the programs to subscribers willing to pay an extra fee. At that time, HBO was a **pay-per-view** service. However, Levin wanted to expand HBO to a pay-per-month service with 24-hour programming, mostly movies. If it worked, this would give local cable systems a premium channel from which to derive extra revenue.

Gerald Levin Offered exclusive HBO programming to cable systems.

HBO Short for Home Box Office; first cable programming via satellite.

pay-per-view Cable companies charge subscribers for each program they watch.

For an expanded HBO to succeed, Levin needed to cut the tremendous expense of relaying HBO transmission across the country from microwave tower to microwave tower. Then it occurred to him: Why not bypass microwave transmission and instead send the HBO signal to an orbiting satellite, which could then beam it back to earth in one relay to every local cable system in the country? Levin put up $7.5 million to use the Satcom 1 satellite. That allowed him to cut microwave costs while expanding programming and making HBO available to more of the United States.

LEARNING CHECK

- How did Gerald Levin transform cable?

Stanley Hubbard

The possibilities for satellite delivery were not lost on **Stanley Hubbard**, who owned television station KSTP in Minnesota. Like almost all network-affiliated stations, KSTP was incredibly profitable, but Hubbard believed it might become a dinosaur in the age of satellite communication. Why should people tune into local stations, which picked up

Stanley Hubbard Pioneer of direct-to-viewer satellite television.

network signals from satellite for retransmission to viewers, when the technology was available for viewers to pick up the signals directly from satellite? Skeptics scoffed, but in 1984 Hubbard joined General Motors, which was in a diversification mode, to offer a **direct broadcast satellite (DBS)** service. People could pick up signals from almost anyplace with home satellite dishes the size of a large pizza.

direct broadcast satellite (DBS) Transmission of television signals directly from orbiting satellites to viewers without a local station or cable system as intermediary.

LEARNING CHECK

- What television delivery innovation did Stanley Hubbard champion?

Satcoms

DirecTV Larger of two American satellite operators.

The cost of entry for DBS transmission has limited the number of American satcom operators to two. **DirecTV**, the larger operator, has 15.5 million subscribers. For several years, media mogul Rupert Murdoch controlled DirecTV with 34 percent ownership. He sold his interest in 2006 but continues to be involved with similar satellite services on other continents: Star TV in Asia, B-Sky-B in Britain, Sky Italia in Italy, and Foxtel in Australia. The Dish Network, the trade name for EchoStar, has 11 million subscribers. EchoStar has a fleet of nine satellites in orbit, while DirecTV has eight.

There are two satellite companies in Canada: BellTV, which as of 2010 had 1.9 million subscribers, and Shaw (formerly StarChoice) with 900 000 subscribers. Satellite companies are categorized as BDUs by the CRTC in Canada, just like cable companies.

LEARNING CHECK

- How big a factor are satcoms in the television industry? How big a factor are they globally?

Video-on-Demand

STUDY PREVIEW Time-shifting devices enable viewers to decide when they watch television. Portable devices let them decide where. These video-on-demand devices, as well as content designed for watching on the go, are undermining some of the long-term attraction of networks, stations, cable systems, and satcoms as advertising vehicles.

Time-Shifting

video-on-demand (VOD) Mechanisms that allow viewers to tune in to programs any time they choose.

TiVo Digital recording and playback device for television.

time-shifting Audience control of time for viewing a chosen program.

Devices that allow people to watch what they want when they want, **video-on-demand (VOD)**, date to Betamax videotape players introduced by Sony in 1976. Later devices, such as **TiVo** digital recorders, provide other options for what's called **time-shifting.** People don't have to schedule their activities around a television channel's schedule. It's possible to program a TiVo to record the news at 6 p.m. and then watch it whenever you want.

Time-shifting has dramatically reduced the tyranny that network and station programmers once had over people's lives. A troubling upshot of the technology for networks and stations is that they are losing their power to amass great numbers of people in front of the screen at the same time. That had been a selling point to advertisers. An advertiser for time-of-day products such as Subway sandwiches wants to reach viewers at mealtimes, not when viewers decide to watch a show. What good is an advertisement designed to stir up excitement for the weekend introduction of the new GM hybrid if viewers don't see the spot until a week later? Also, time-shifting devices allow viewers to skip commercials entirely.

LEARNING CHECK

- How did TiVo further empower viewers?

Portable Devices

video iPod A handheld Apple device for playing not only music but also video at the viewer's choice of time and place.

In 2005, a video-playing internet device introduced by Apple fully liberated viewers from planting themselves in front of large and stationary television sets. The Apple **video iPod** suddenly splintered television as an industry. By 2008, handheld iPods could store as many as 150 hours of video and display the images on a 2.5-inch (6-cm) colour screen.

Mobile Television Comic-strip detective Dick Tracy of the 1950s would love cell phone television. All Tracy had was a two-way wrist radio. Today, he could download content onto his new mobile device.

MEDIA PEOPLE Susan Zirinsky

As a television news producer, Susan Zirinsky has done it all. In college, she took a job answering phones in the CBS Washington bureau one day a week. By her senior year, she was typing scripts for the evening news. After graduation, she became a researcher and, at age 24, became an associate producer. In 1980, she took a producing assignment at journalism's premier beat of the era: the White House. She went on the road with Ronald Reagan and a CBS crew for the 1984 presidential campaign. More recently, she's been executive producer of the CBS newsmagazine *48 Hours*.

Webisodes CBS news producer Susan Zirinsky takes the proverbial busman's holiday. From the CBS drama *Jericho* she looks for possible news angles, arranges news interviews with subject-area experts, and weaves them into five-minute items for web delivery.

Most people would find themselves fully occupied by responsibilities like Zirinsky's at *48 Hours*, but in her spare time she is dabbling with a new form of television: webisodes. These are brief episodic stories for web delivery. Zirinsky, with her news-gathering skills honed covering Washington, will pick up a story line from the post-apocalyptic network drama *Jericho* and mix it with live interviews. A term hasn't been devised yet for these webisode hybrids with news angles. Zirinsky calls them webumentaries.

Are webisodes the future of television? Certainly, they are a departure from the prime-time bread and butter of television networks, which feature ongoing episodes mostly in 30-minute or 60-minute blocks. Those formats have worked for generations. But the industry has cause to be uneasy about whether the young audience, hooked on on-the-go media, will sit still for 30 minutes, let alone for 60. The new generation is going for web-style snippet drama and amusement.

Time will tell whether Zirinsky is on the ground floor of a reinvention of television programming.

WHAT DO YOU THINK?

1. Does the future of television lie in webisodes?

People could watch television shows on the road or wherever—and whenever—they wanted. It was true VOD, with people downloading programs from the internet to watch any time they wanted. Next, Apple came up with the iPhone, which had video-on-demand capabilities, followed by upgrades with greater capabilities. Then came the iPad. The BlackBerry and other mobile devices also have VOD capabilities.

Not to be left out, the major television networks scrambled to sell archived programming for iPods. The one-time monopoly of the big networks providing programming through over-the-air affiliates was further fractured.

Watch

ABC's *i-CAUGHT*: Viral Videos

LEARNING CHECK

- How has television viewing become untethered and more demassified?

Economics of Television

STUDY PREVIEW The backbone of television economics historically has been the 30-second spot. Even with audience numbers slipping in recent years, 30-second spots have remained popular enough with advertisers that the networks have continued to charge more. Some observers, however, see a softening in demand.

Network Advertising

The big television networks have become an enigma. While cable networks have nibbled steadily at the audience once devoted to the traditional networks, these major networks still have been able to continue to raise their advertising rates. Strange as it seems, advertisers are paying the networks more money than ever to reach fewer viewers. According to Statistics Canada, advertising on Canadian television was worth $3.1 billion in 2009.

30-Second Spot Even so, there are signs that advertiser demand for 30-second spots may be softening. Big networks are not filling slots as far in advance as they once did. Why? Cable channels, many of which have relatively low-cost programming, have eased the demand with cut-rate pricing while opening up many more slots, albeit for smaller slices of audience. Also, doubts have arisen among advertisers about whether pricey 30-second spots on the Big Four are as cost-effective as cable, the internet, and other emerging advertising platforms. In short, the 30-second spot as the economic engine of the television industry may be an endangered species.

Upfront Drama is intense every spring when the networks ask big advertisers to commit themselves upfront to spots for the future year's programming. The networks' lists show that they plan to continue some programs, as well as offer a sample of new programs, and announce their asking price per 30-second spot based on audience projections. Then begins the jockeying and bidding between the networks and the agencies that represent advertisers. The **upfront**, as the process is called, locks sponsors into specific shows three to five months ahead of the new season, although contracts generally have options that allow an advertiser to bail out.

upfront Advance advertiser commitments to buy network advertising time.

Eighty percent of a year's commercial time typically is spoken for in the upfront process. If a show misses the network's projected audience numbers, advertisers are given **make-goods**, the industry's term for additional spots intended to compensate advertisers. If a show turns into a smash hit and exceeds audience forecasts, the price per spot is raised or, in some cases, if there is no escalation clause, the advertisers end up with a real deal.

make-goods Additional time that networks offer advertisers when ratings fall short of projections.

Until recently, under CRTC regulations, Canadian TV stations could air only 12 minutes of advertising per hour. In 2008, that limit was increased to 15 minutes per hour to reflect a more American economic model. This was in response to the television industry's call for ways to make more revenue to help offset the cost of the transition to digital.

LEARNING CHECK

- What has happened to the traditional 30- or 60-second television commercial?
- What happens when a network doesn't deliver an audience to an advertiser as promised?

Cable Revenue Streams

Cable systems, going back to CATV, have a core revenue stream from subscribers, who are charged a monthly access fee. Cable networks tap in to that revenue stream by charging the local systems to carry their programming. This is referred to as **fee for carriage.** When cable networks emerged in the late 1970s, some sought national advertising in competition with the over-the-air networks. Also, local cable systems went head to head with local over-the-air stations for local advertising.

fee for carriage A fee paid by cable companies to TV companies for the right to broadcast channels.

Originally, since they were available "free" to anyone with an antenna, local broadcasters were not allowed to charge cable companies for their signal. In 2009, a battle between cable companies and the TV networks began over the networks' desire to begin charging for local TV signals. The debate surrounded fee for carriage, which has never been applied to local television. Both sides dug in their heels. The cable companies called it a "TV tax" that they would pass along to consumers. The local broadcasters argued that not paying for the signals was a threat to local television content. In 2010, the CRTC decided to let the battle continue in the hopes that both sides would negotiate a solution to the problem. One possible resolution, based on an American model, might lead to cable companies negotiating with individual local stations for a reasonable fee in order to carry that channel.

LEARNING CHECK

- How do cable networks and systems finance themselves?
- What is fee for carriage?

Whither Goes Television?

STUDY PREVIEW More than in other traditional mass media, the corporate and social structures that have been built around television are well suited to become the hub of tomorrow's mass communication.

Time Shifts

The television as a centrepiece in people's lives in the evening is already waning, as is the importance of prime time. With TiVo-like playback devices, people don't need to tune in at 8 p.m. for a favourite sitcom. To be sure, events like the Stanley Cup playoffs, elections, and the *American Idol* finale will still draw huge prime-time audiences. But the end may be in sight for prime-time scheduling for ongoing network series, the historic foundation of network programming.

A fundamental paradigm shift is occurring. Instead of people adapting their daily routines to television's scheduling, they are watching television when it suits them. This is a form of audience empowerment.

LEARNING CHECK

- More than ever, television networks are scouting for big events that will attract a real-time audience. Why?

Space Shifts

The portability of New Television, as it might be called, signals a transformation in programming. The old 30-minute blocks assumed an audience being in one place, seated for a whole program—hence the term *couch potato*. Thirty-minute blocks were also useful for affiliate breakaways and local patching of programming into network structures. On-the-move audiences with handheld screens are neither in place nor freed from other activities in neat 30-minute segments.

With space shifts, where people watch television programming is bound to change. Expect to see more mobisodes, short episodes for mobile viewers. For Verizon's V CAST service, which is geared for mobile devices, Fox created one-minute episodes of its program *24*, something to watch between checking for new email messages and playing a new online video game.

LEARNING CHECK

- Are couch potatoes an endangered species? Explain.

Advertising Shifts

Once the darling of almost every national brand for marketing, 30-second spots on network television are losing some of their lustre. This change reflects partly the declining audience for over-the-air stations served by the traditional networks and partly the continuing network push for higher rates. Also a factor is concern that time-shifting devices such as TiVo mean that more viewers are skipping ads.

Webisodes One brand-name advertiser that's shifted away from 30-second spots is American Express. In the mid-1990s, Amex put 80 percent of its advertising budget into network spots. By 2005, however, this amount was down to 35 percent. Where have Amex and other brand-name advertisers diverted their dollars? Some Amex dollars have stayed with the networks through product placement in scripts, which addresses TiVo leakage. But much has gone into web initiatives, concert sponsorships, and promotional experiments, such as stocking trendy health clubs with blue-labelled bottled water to hype Amex's blue card. There have been blue popcorn bags at movie houses and Amex-sponsored museum exhibits. Amex has been a leader in **webisodes**, those four-minute mini-movies on the web. Blue card logos were everywhere during an Amex-sponsored concert with Elvis Costello, Stevie Wonder, and Counting Crows at the House of Blues in Los Angeles, which was renamed the House of Blue for the event.

webisodes Mini-movies, generally four minutes long, on the web; usually sponsored and sometimes featuring the advertiser as part of the storyline.

Product Placement Mindful that advertisers are scouting for alternative media, television networks have moved to selling paid plugs for products and services in scripts. It's not unlike early radio and 1950s television, when hosts for sponsored programs touted products. For Arthur Godfrey, no tea was as good as Lipton—and viewers never knew when to expect a plug. This was left over from an era when radio advertisers produced their own programs. As the networks took over programs, selling commercial slots to the highest bidder, a purer distinction between creative control of programming content and advertising became a given.

In the 1980s, Hollywood began selling product mentions in movie scripts. The result was a continuing controversy. The controversy now is back in television, with networks—facing the drain from TiVo viewers who watch programs but skip the ads—weaving product names into scripts. CTV's *Corner Gas* was one of the first Canadian shows to include product placement, in its Christmas episode entitled "Merry Gasmas." The storyline included mentions of the Sears catalogue. Despite protests from some producers, the practice seems destined to stay. As of 2010, the CRTC had no plans to regulate the practice.

LEARNING CHECK

- What screen media alternatives to television are advertisers finding?
- What is the upside of product placement? What is the downside?

Chapter 8 Wrap-Up

Watch

A Day in the Life: Television Sports Reporter

Television transformed lifestyles and other mass media beginning in the 1950s. It's hard to imagine the Stanley Cup without television. Today, however, that huge audience is fragmenting. The fragmentation began with the arrival of cable networks in the 1970s and accelerated with direct broadcast satellite systems. Video-on-demand via the internet is the latest technology to beleaguer the traditional structure of television. Increasingly, advertisers are less enchanted with the major television networks that service local over-the-air stations—as well as with cable and satcom channels. The audience is dwindling, siphoned off by competing new media. Time-shift devices such as TiVo and portable video devices raise questions among advertisers about a new mushiness in network audiences. It's no surprise that more advertising dollars are going into these alternatives, at least experimentally. The traditional networks have responded with deals to work product placements into scripts, a controversial step. Over the objections of affiliates, the traditional networks are selling programs online to offset softening advertising revenue. In short, the television industry is in flux.

PEARSON
mycanadiancommunicationlab

Visit **www.mycanadiancommunicationlab.ca** for access to a wealth of tools and resources that will enhance your learning experience. Features include the following:

- Personalized Study Plan
- Videos
- Activities
- Pearson eText–and much more!

Questions for Critical Thinking

1. What did social critic Michael Novak mean when he described television as "a molder of the soul's geography?"
2. What new technological innovations are beleaguering the traditional television industry?
3. How are shifts in time and space affecting television viewing?
4. What role does the CRTC play in what consumers watch on Canadian television?
5. What makes Canadian television different from American television? What are some of your favourite Canadian television programs? Why?

Keeping Up to Date

Playback, *Broadcaster*, *Broadcast Dialogue*, and *Television/Radio* Age are broadcasting trade journals.

Journal of Broadcasting and Electronic Media and the *Canadian Journal of Communication* are quarterly scholarly journals published by the Broadcast Education Association.

Consumer magazines that deal extensively with television programming include *Entertainment Weekly* and *People*.

Newsmagazines that report on television issues more or less regularly include *Newsweek*, *Maclean's*, and *Time*.

Major newspapers with strong television coverage include the *National Post*, the *Toronto Star*, and *The Globe and Mail*.

9 The Internet

LEARNING AHEAD

- The internet emerged suddenly in the 1990s as a major mass medium.
- The internet resulted from a confluence of technological advancements.
- The World Wide Web links individual computers with the internet.
- Subscriptions and advertising are becoming the internet's foundation.
- The shape of the internet industry is still taking form.
- The internet is democratizing mass communication, albeit with side effects.
- Internet technology is blurring distinctions among traditional media.

Browser Genius At age 21, Marc Andreessen and a geek buddy created Mosaic, which facilitated web access. Then they trumped themselves by creating Netscape.

MEDIA IN THEORY

Push-Pull Model

push-pull model Some of the control in the communication process shifts to the receiver.

pull media Messages requested by the receiver.

push media Messages sent to the receiver with or without prior consent.

Web communication shifts much of the control of the communication through the mass media to the recipient, turning the traditional process of mass communication on its head. Receivers are no longer hobbled to sequential presentation of messages, as on a network television newscast. Receivers can switch almost instantly to dozens, hundreds even, of alternatives through a weblike network that, at least theoretically, can interconnect every recipient and sender on the planet. This is the basic idea behind the **push-pull model.**

The communication revolution requires a new model to understand new ways that the media are working. One new model classifies some media as passive. These are **pull media,** which you steer. Examples are the traditional media, such as radio and television, over which you have control to pull in a message. You can turn them on or off. You can pick up a book and put it down. You can go to a movie or not.

Push media, on the other hand, propel messages at you whether invited to or not. A simple, low-tech example is a recorded voice in a grocery store aisle that encourages you to buy a certain brand of cornflakes as you pass by the cereal display. Push media are taking sophisticated forms with the World Wide Web and new technologies that are making the media more pervasive than ever. They're always on.

Some push media you can program include:

- Signing up for an online newsletter on your favourite topic. Ipsos Reid claims that 8 out of 10 Canadians sign up for various internet newsletters.
- Your cell phone, which can update the score on a hockey game you can't watch while you're doing something else.

- News and travel updates from Egypt you ask for after booking airline tickets for a vacation to see the pyramids.

Other push media intrude gently or are in your face without your doing any programming:

- A heads-up automobile windshield display, such as OnStar, that flashes directions to nearby repair shops when sensors detect that your engine is overheating.
- Banners across your computer screen that advertise products that your past online purchases indicate you're likely to want.
- Wall screens that push items at you based on assumptions about your interests—for example, music video samplers for a performer who is popular on a radio station you listen to.

The editors of *Wired* magazine, describing push media, give this example: You are in your study, answering email from the office, when you notice something happening on the walls. Ordinarily, the large expanse in front of you features a montage generated by Sci-Viz (meaning *scientific visualization*), a global news feed of scientific discoveries plus classic movie scenes and 30-second comedy routines. You picked this service because it doesn't show you the usual disaster junk, yet the content is very lively, a sort of huge screen saver, which you usually ignore. But just now you noticed a scene from your hometown, something about an archaeological find. You ask for the full video. This is always-on, mildly in-your-face networked media.

No model is perfect, which means that push media and pull media are extremes that rarely exist in reality. Most media messages are push-pull hybrids. The "media wall" in the *Wired* magazine example intrudes without a specific invitation, but it also leaves it to you to choose what to pull in when you want more detail. Most emerging new media have such hybrid capabilities.

LEARNING CHECK

- What makes push media different from pull media?

Influence of the Internet

STUDY PREVIEW The internet has emerged as the eighth major mass medium with a range of content, especially through web coding, that exceeds that of traditional media in many ways.

New Mass Medium

From a dizzying array of new technologies, the internet emerged in the mid-1990s as a powerful new mass medium. The internet is a jury-rigged network of telephone and cable lines, satellite links, and wireless networks that connect computers and mobile devices

MEDIA TIMELINE Internet

1945 Vannevar Bush proposed a memex machine for associative links among all human knowledge.

1962 Ted Nelson introduced the term *hypertext*.

1969 U.S. military created ARPANET to link contractors and researchers.

1989 Tim Berners-Lee devised coding that made the web possible.

1993 Marc Andreessen created predecessor to the Netscape browser.

1997 Rob Malda, a college student, created Slashdot, "news for news," one of the first blogs.

1999 CRTC decided "not to govern the internet at this time."

2001 Dot-com bubble burst.

2003 Amazon.com demonstrated a new speed of search engines with "Search Inside a Book" feature.

2007 Apple introduced the iPhone.

2009 CRTC reaffirmed its decision not to regulate the internet.

such as cell phones and iPods. Almost anybody on the planet with a computer can tap into the network. A few clicks of a mouse button will bring in vast quantities of information and entertainment that originate all over the world.

Although in some ways the internet resembles a traditional mass medium that sends messages from a central transmission point, it is much more interactive and participatory. Message recipients are able to click almost instantly from one source to another—from downloading music from iTunes to tracking the latest celebrity gossip at TMZ.com to reading their local newspaper online. Users of the internet are also creators of content, on blogs, Wikipedia, and social networking sites such as Facebook, Twitter, and MySpace.

New Terminology

The terms *internet* and *web* are often tossed around loosely, leading to a lot of confusion. The fundamental network that carries messages is the internet. It dates to a military communication system created in 1969. The early internet carried mostly text.

The web is a structure of codes that permits the exchange not only of text but also of graphics, video, and audio. Web codes are elegantly simple for users, who don't need to know them to tap into the web's content. The underlying web codes are accepted universally, which makes it possible for anyone with a computer, a modem, and an internet connection to tap into anything introduced from anywhere on the global web. The term *web* comes from the spidery links among millions of computers that tap into the system—an ever-changing maze that not even a spider could visualize and that becomes more complex all the time.

William Gibson Sci-fi writer who coined the term *cyberspace*.

The term *cyberspace* was introduced by science-fiction novelist **William Gibson** in his book *Neuromancer.* At that point, in 1984, he saw a kind of integration of computers and human beings. Paraphrasing a bit, here is Gibson's definition of *cyberspace*: "A consensual hallucination experienced daily by billions of people in every nation. A graphic representation of data abstracted from the banks of every computer in the human system. Unthinkable complexity. Lines of light ranged in the nonspace of the mind. Clusters and constellations of data." Gibson got it right.

Internet technology led to many attempts at a name to set this new medium, its technological offspring, and its siblings apart from traditional media. In a 2001 book, Lev Manovich made a case for *new media*, which caught on. Even so, there was confusion over products that spanned older and newer technologies, such as digitally delivered newspapers. *New media* was further blurred when it became an advertising buzzword for anything more sophisticated than a flashing neon sign.

LEARNING CHECK

- How is the internet unique as a medium of mass communication?
- Why is the term *new media* problematic?

Internet Origins

STUDY PREVIEW As discussed in Chapter 2, the 1947 invention of the semiconductor led to digitization and compression that became building blocks for technology that made the internet possible. Web coding and the Netscape browser widened access.

Decentralized Network

The internet had its origins in a 1969 U.S. Department of Defense computer network called ARPANET, which stood for Advanced Research Projects Agency Network. The Pentagon built the network so that military contractors and universities doing military research could exchange information. In 1983, the National Science Foundation (NSF), whose mandate is to promote science, took it over.

This new NSF network attracted more and more institutional users, many of which had their own internal networks. For example, most universities that joined the NSF network had intracampus computer networks. The NSF network then became a connector for thousands of other networks. As a backbone system that interconnects networks, **internet** was a name that fit.

internet A network of computer networks.

Data Packets The key to the tremendous efficiency of the NSF system was the concept of **data packets**, which was drawn from earlier Bell Labs work for telephone communication. Data were broken into small packets to shoot into the decentralized network. The packets would each seek ways around jams and blockages and then reassemble at their destination, in less than the blink of an eye when all was working well.

data packets Clumps of digital data broken out of a larger package for transmission.

Transmission Protocols One of the obstacles to the internet becoming a universal vehicle for communication was that governments, universities, banks, and other institutions had local networks built on a polyglot of computer languages. It was a mishmash of incompatibility. In 1974, two University of California at Los Angeles researchers, **Vint Cerf** and **Bob Kahn**, introduced a common language called **Transmission Control Protocol (TCP)** that allowed the local networks to talk to each other.

For his contribution, Cerf has come to be called the father of the internet. The title also goes sometimes to Kahn. Both are uncomfortable with the appellation. Says Cerf, "None of this was happening in a vacuum."

Vint Cerf, Bob Kahn Coauthors of TCP; sometimes called the fathers of the internet.

Transmission Control Protocol (TCP) Universal system that connects individual computer systems to the internet.

Fibre Optics While AT&T was building on its off-on digital technology to improve telephone service in the 1960s, **Corning Glass** developed a cable that was capable of carrying light at incredible speeds—theoretically, at 186 000 miles per second. It was apparent immediately that this new **fibre optic cable** could carry far more digitized messages than could the copper wire used for telephones. The messages were encoded as light pulses rather than as the traditional electrical pulses used for transmission.

Corning Glass Company that developed fibre optic cable.

fibre optic cable Glass strands capable of carrying data as light.

By the 1980s, new equipment to convert data to light pulses for transmission was in place, and long-distance telephone companies were replacing their copper lines with fibre optics, as were local cable television systems. With fibre optic cable and other improvements, a single line could carry 60 000 telephone calls simultaneously.

Still, the internet, using the telephone system to carry messages, was limited mostly to text-only messages. Visuals were rare. Video? Forget it. The number of data packets for video was too much for the system to reassemble in a reasonable time.

But when the United States and Canada, and then the planet, were rewired with fibre optic cable in one of the greatest construction projects in history, the internet's capacity to scoot data packets from point to point grew dramatically. Messages that had massive amounts of coding, such as video, became commonplace. The process, called **streaming**, sometimes had reception that was jerky; this is still the case, but is becoming less so.

streaming Technology that allows playback of a message to begin before all of the components have arrived.

LEARNING CHECK

- What is meant by describing the internet as a decentralized network?

World Wide Web

The early internet created access to a lot of data at speeds that were unprecedented. But it was an uninviting place visually. Text and data were in black and white and image-free, something only a researcher could love. Even so, there were possibilities to take the new medium in commercial directions.

Internet Service Providers A new kind of company, **internet service providers (ISPs)**, went into business in the 1980s to give ordinary folks a portal to the internet and help in navigating the internet's inherent complexity and disorganization. Compuserv was the first to provide online service to consumers. ISPs charged subscription fees for a combination of services: internet access, email, and, most important, a mapping structure to help users get to where they wanted to go among the seemingly infinite number of places on the internet.

internet service provider (ISP) Company that charges a fee for online service.

Tim Berners-Lee A major breakthrough came from English engineer **Tim Berners-Lee**, who in 1991 devised an addressing system that could connect every computer in the world. The name that Berners-Lee came up with for his system, the **World Wide Web**, sounded audacious but it was accurate: a decentralized global network with the potential, theoretically, for everyone at a computer to communicate with everyone else at a computer anywhere on the planet.

Tim Berners-Lee Devised protocols and codes for the World Wide Web.

World Wide Web System that allows global linking of information modules in user-determined sequences.

Berners-Lee's invention was built on three components:

universal resource locator (URL) Address assigned to a page on the internet; now known as a uniform resource locator.

- **Universal resource locators (URL).** Now known as uniform resource locators, this addressing system was devised by Berners-Lee to give every computer a unique identifier, much like a postal address that enables mail to be delivered to the right place. The identifiers, URLs, allowed computers connected in a network to exchange messages. Being "universal," it was a comprehensive and standardized system that became the foundation for the World Wide Web.

hypertext transfer protocol (HTTP) Coding that allows computers to talk with each other to read web pages.

- **Hypertext transfer protocol (HTTP).** This is a protocol that allows computers to connect to read internet files.

hypertext markup language (HTML) Language that is used to code web pages.

- **Hypertext markup language (HTML).** This was a relatively simple computer language that permitted someone creating an internet message to insert so-called hot spots or links that, if clicked, would instantly switch the onscreen image to something else. For example, a research article could include visible indicators, usually the underlining of a term, that when clicked on with a mouse would cause the browser to move to another article on the subject.

hypertext System for nonsequential reading.

The term **hypertext** was devised by technologist Ted Nelson in his 1962 book *Literary Machines* for a system that would allow people to interrupt themselves while reading through material in the traditional linear way, from beginning to end, and transport themselves nonlinearly to related material. Nelson also called it *nonsequential writing,* but the term *hypertext* stuck.

A quarter-century later, Berners-Lee devised the HTML coding that made nonsequential reading possible.

LEARNING CHECK

- What sets URLs, HTTP, and HTML apart from Vint Cerf and Bob Kahn's TCP?

Web Browsers

Marc Andreessen Devised the Netscape browser.

Mosaic Predecessor browser to Netscape.

browser Software that allows access to websites.

Netscape Browser that made the web easily accessible and attractive to the average computer owner.

The importance of Berners-Lee's innovations in terms of scientists finding sites all around the internet was a landmark, but for the rest of us the content was geeky stuff. In 1993, the internet as we know it began to come to life. At the University of Illinois, grad student **Marc Andreessen** developed a software program, **Mosaic**, that improved the interconnections that permitted scientists to browse each other's research.

Enthusiasm for the potential of the **browser**, as it was called, quickly swelled. By tweaking Mosaic, Andreessen and a few colleagues created a new browser, **Netscape**, that could connect any of the three disparate computer operating systems that were becoming commonplace: Microsoft's Windows, Apple's Macintosh OS, and Unix. Netscape was a point-and-click system through which anyone with a computer could unlock more content than had ever been conceivable in human history. Competing browsers followed and eclipsed Netscape.

Commercialization of the internet, which had been gradual to that point, moved into high gear. A few retailers displayed their wares and took orders online, then shipped their products to customers. The old point-of-purchase concept, in which consumers are attracted at a store with displays and posters, took on a whole new meaning. In the new cyberworld, the point of purchase was not the merchant's shop but the consumer's computer screen. Sites for pitching products and services, some of them complete catalogues, sprouted by the thousands.

The Internet Industry

Explore

Media People: Marc Andreessen

STUDY PREVIEW A gold rush, the internet drew major investments when it became a vehicle for commercial traffic. The dot-com boom, however, turned into a major bust that derailed the economy. Although there is new stability now, the internet remains a nascent industry whose eventual shape is a matter of conjecture.

MEDIA PEOPLE Tim Berners-Lee

Tim Berners-Lee single-handedly invented the World Wide Web. Then he devoted his life to refining the web as a medium of communication open to everyone for free.

Berners-Lee, an Oxford engineer, came up with the web concept because he couldn't keep track of all of his notes on various computers in various places. It was 1989. Working at CERN, a physics lab in Switzerland, he proposed a system to facilitate scientific research by letting scientists' computers tap into each other. In a way, the software worked as the brain does. In fact, Berners-Lee said that the idea was to keep "track of all the random associations one comes across in real life and brains are supposed to be so good at remembering, but sometimes mine wouldn't."

The key was a relatively simple computer language known as HTML, short for hypertext markup language, which, although it has evolved over the years, remains the core of the web. Berners-Lee also developed the addressing system that allows computers to find each other. Every web-connected computer has a unique address, a universal (or uniform) resource locator (URL). For it all to work, Berners-Lee also created a protocol that actually links computers: HTTP, short for hypertext transfer protocol.

It's hard to overrate Berners-Lee's accomplishment. The internet is the information infrastructure that likely will eclipse other media, given time. Some liken Berners-Lee to Johannes Gutenberg, who 400 years earlier had launched the age of mass communication with the movable type that made mass production of the written word possible.

Tim Berners-Lee

WHAT DO YOU THINK?

1. Is Berners-Lee in the same league as Gutenberg, Edison, Fessenden or Farnsworth?

Emerging Companies

Early on, entrepreneurs saw the internet as a mountain of gold waiting to be mined. Investors poured millions into a wide range of ventures beginning in the early 1990s. Most didn't get it right. The financial landscape was littered with failed start-ups and bankruptcies by 1999, triggering a prolonged economic recession. The **dot-com** boom was a bust; the bubble had burst.

dot-com Informal general term for internet commercial sites, most of whose online addresses end with the suffix .com.

Google was first to figure out how to make massive profits from the internet. While everyone else focused on creating website content that attracted readers, Google trumped them all by indexing that content—all of it, everything that everyone else was posting. As a portal for finding content, Google captures millions of eyeballs daily. With every search, Google posts sponsored links onscreen, side by side with links to sites having some relevance to the search. Advertisers, eager for this exposure, pay Google for these sponsored links. By 2005, Google was the fastest-growing company in history, with annual revenue topping $6.7 billion. However, Google was not the first company to make money from the internet. On a lesser scale, the Lexis and Nexis databases had made money back in the 1970s.

Even today, with the internet reaching its second quarter-century as a medium for commercial traffic, the history of the shape of the industry is still to be written. Until the technology plateaus, the rough-and-tumble of energetic, hopeful new enterprises, followed by disappointments and setbacks amid successes, will mark the industry.

LEARNING CHECK

- What has risen from the ashes of the dot-com bust?
- What twist did Google add to the internet business?

Portals

The original model for internet fortunes was multi-purpose **portals**, which came to be epitomized by America Online (AOL) and its offering of email, access to the web, and a lot of

portal Entry point for further internet access.

exclusive content. Survivors of the dot-com bust include MSN and Yahoo!, but the failures were spectacular, including General Electric's GEnie and an elaborate AT&T venture.

Also, portals have found it harder to sell subscriptions, which was the original business model. Thanks to the Tim Berners-Lee protocols, people can go directly to a countless number of websites on their own. The problem facing traditional portals is no better illustrated than by AOL, which has shifted away from subscriptions to advertising to keep users. The media conglomerate Time Warner, which acquired AOL at its peak, has the unit up for sale—a far cry from when Time Warner even changed its name to Time Warner AOL. The company, now acknowledging a major acquisition error, has gone back to simply Time Warner.

LEARNING CHECK

- What eclipsed the success of the internet portal AOL?

Search Engines

With Google's success, search engine companies have become the darling of internet investors. Yahoo!, MSN, and others have all tried to rival Google.

Search engines dispatch automated crawlers through the internet to take snapshots of web pages. With millions of websites, it's a massive and time-consuming process, but slowly massive reference files have been amassed and then updated as the crawlers continue to make their rounds.

The original search engines, however, were not good at keeping up to date with blogs. With an estimated 17.1 million blogs, many updated several times a day, the task was too much. Then came blog searchers. Google's, for example, is built on an index of blogs, which sends a ping to Google with every update and then becomes part of a separate blog database for specialized searchers.

LEARNING CHECK

- How do search engines do what they do?

Gaming

Firmly established in the internet universe is video gaming. Gaming has grown from the simple games added to software packages that accompanied the first generation of home computers, before people had even heard of the internet. These games were hardly mass communication, any more than a Monopoly board is. Gradually, though, games began to appear on the internet, some with thousands of players.

With their huge and growing following, video games have become a natural target for advertising. It's an attractive audience. The Entertainment Software Association says that players average 6.5 hours a week playing their games. Players include a broad range of people. Thirty-eight percent are male and 39 percent earn $50 000 a year or more, an attractive group that advertisers have a hard time tapping into with other media.

Today, annual sales of gaming hardware, software, and accessories have topped $10 billion. The most popular games earn more money faster than the leading movies. The future looks bright, especially with interactive portable games. Game advertising revenue, which doubles annually, passed $4.3 million in 2005.

LEARNING CHECK

- How has gaming come to be seen by advertisers as a mass medium?

Reshaping the Internet

Explore

Media People: Gordon Moore

STUDY PREVIEW Wireless internet connections, called Wi-Fi, have added to the portability of the internet. Further untethering from the wired infrastructure is possible through ultrawideband and mesh network technology.

Wi-Fi

Another development in interactive media is wireless fidelity technology, better known as **Wi-Fi.** It untethers laptops and allows internet access anywhere through radio waves. The coffee chain Starbucks made a splash with Wi-Fi, encouraging their customers to linger. Hotels and airports were naturals for Wi-Fi. Many Canadian cities, from Chilliwack to St. John's, have free Wi-Fi "hot spots" in their downtown areas.

Wi-Fi Wireless fidelity technology.

One justification for municipal Wi-Fi is to bridge the **digital divide,** the socioeconomic distinction between people who can afford internet access and those who cannot.

digital divide The economic distinction between impoverished groups and societal groups with the means to maintain and improve their economic well-being through computer access.

LEARNING CHECK

- What is different about Wi-Fi?
- How is Wi-Fi changing internet usage?

Ultrawideband

Short-range Wi-Fi networks, which become sluggish as more people tap into them, may pick up capacity with **ultrawideband** (**UWB**) technology, unless its opponents prevail. UWB technology uses existing frequencies, including commercial broadcast channels, but with such low power that the primary signals seem to be unaffected. The aviation industry is concerned that frequencies used by on-board collision-avoidance systems could be compromised by crowding.

ultrawideband (UWB) Low-power Wi-Fi system that rides on existing frequencies licensed for other uses.

Mesh Networks

What comes after Wi-Fi? The most anticipated technology is **dynamic routing,** in which every wireless gadget also serves as a receiver and transmitter to every other wireless device within its range. Messages would just keep moving, skipping invisibly from device to device until each message reaches its intended destination. There is no formal network; messages go to whatever device has capacity at the moment—or, rather, at the nanosecond. Every wireless device outfitted for dynamic routing would be on call as a stepping stone for however many messages come its way. Engineers say that **mesh networking,** as it is called, using high-speed protocols, will be 15 times faster than currently touted DSL services.

dynamic routing Technology that makes every wireless device a vehicle for furthering a message along to its destination, rather than moving it within a structured network.

mesh networking The ad hoc network created for each single message to reach its destination; also called dynamic routing.

LEARNING CHECK

- What is the promise of UWB technology?
- Would it bother you to be part of a mesh network whenever you had your computer on?

Internet Issues

STUDY PREVIEW The ability of almost anyone to post content on the internet poses new public policy questions and issues. This new media world is illustrated by the free-wheeling nature of blogs. Media issues of privacy, decency, and access are posed in newly critical ways.

Watch

ABC's *Nightline*: "The Bloggers"

Blogs and Democracy

In an era when the price of entry to media ownership precludes most mortals, the internet, although young as a mass medium, is already democratizing mass communication. The rules are new. The most powerful member of the U.S. Senate, Trent Lott, never imagined that his political career would end under pressure created by a pipsqueak citizen in the hinterlands, but it happened.

People Power Joshua Marshall, who created his own website (www.talkingpointsmemo.com), picked up on a speech by Lott that, depending on your view, was either racist or racially insensitive. Lott uttered his comment at the 100th birthday party of Senator Strom Thurmond, who was once a strong segregationist.

blog An amateur website, generally personal in nature, often focused on a narrow subject such as politics; short for "web log."

Mainstream news media missed how Lott's comments could be interpreted, but Joshua Marshall did not. In his **blog**, he hammered away at Lott day after day. Other bloggers, also outraged, joined in. Three days later, the story hit NBC. Four days later, Lott apologized. Two weeks later, Lott's Senate colleagues voted him out as majority leader.

As a blogger who made a difference, Joshua Marshall is hardly alone. Best known is Matt Drudge, whose revelations propelled the dalliances between Bill Clinton and Monica Lewinsky in the Oval Office into a national scandal. Another blogger, college student Russ Kick, searched for information on government refusals to release photographs of the caskets of fallen American soldiers in Iraq and Afghanistan, which Kick regarded as documents to which the public, himself included, had legal access. He filed a request for the documents under the Freedom of Information Act and then posted the photographs of flag-draped coffins on his website (called The Memory Hole, now defunct), along with photos of the astronauts who died in the Space Shuttle *Columbia* disaster. The photos became front-page news. At one point, Kick's blog received 4 million hits a day, almost twice the circulation of *USA Today*.

Explore

Deepening Your Media Literacy: Can you trust what you read and see on the internet?

Accuracy, Truth Both the beauty and the bane of blogs is their free-for-all nature. On the upside, the web gives ordinary citizens access to mass audiences. It can be a loud and effective megaphone that operates outside of the traditional news media that have resulted from institutionalized practices and traditions.

Joshua Marshall's writing on Trent Lott is an example of outside-the-box news reporting. Most bloggers are amateurs at news reporting, and their lack of experience and unfamiliarity with journalistic traditions has a downside.

New Gatekeeping So-called mainstream media are introducing an element of old-fashioned, journalistically valued gatekeeping to blogging. *The New York Times*, for example, picks up news generated by bloggers when it meets the paper's standards for what's worth reporting. The imprimatur of being cited in the *Times*, which involves fact-checking and news judgment, lends credibility to a blogger. When mainstream media are silent on blog content, that silence speaks volumes.

Increasingly common are mainstream-media summaries of blog content as a barometer of what's on the minds of participants in this emerging forum. Several times daily, CNN, as an example, reports what's new from the blogs.

Newsrooms everywhere keep an eye on YouTube and other self-post sites. Oddities worth reporting are picked up every day. YouTube attained special status during the 2008 U.S. presidential campaign when people were invited to upload questions for candidates. Questions were then put to the candidates in CNN-hosted debates. Real questions asked by real people via video were undeniable as a new kind of vehicle by which voters could assess candidates. The videos cut through carefully manipulated campaign tactics that had come to mark American elections: staged photo ops, town hall meetings with only prescreened participants, and politically calibrated 30-second spots. Not all questions posted to YouTube made the debates, though. As a gatekeeper, CNN used journalistic standards to winnow the grain from the chaff.

LEARNING CHECK

- Has blogging added a common person's voice to the public dialogue on important issues?
- How is blogging being integrated into mainstream-media news reporting?

Privacy and the Internet

The genius of Tim Berners-Lee's original web concept was its openness. Information could be shared easily by anyone and everyone. Therein lies a problem. During the web's commercialization in the late 1990s, some companies tracked where people ventured on the internet. This tracking was going on silently, hidden in the background, as people moved their way around the internet. Companies that gathered information in this way were selling it to other companies. There was fear that insurance companies, health-care providers, lenders, and others had a new secret tool for profiling applicants.

CASE STUDY

How Do Bloggers Know What They Know?

Sean-Paul Kelley's fall from grace was anything but graceful.

The creator of the popular war blog Agonist was caught using as many as six unattributed verbatim reports a day from an Iraq War site operated by the intelligence firm Stratfor. Sometimes Kelley would attribute the Stratfor material to "a Turkish friend" or "a little birdie."

When Kelley was outed, Stratfor's chief analyst, Matthew Baker, said he was surprised at the volume of Stratfor material Kelley had used. Stratfor people were also offended by not getting credit. Stratfor's vice-president, Aaric Eisenstein, told *Wired* magazine that credit, and also profit, should accrue to the people actually doing the work. At the time, Stratfor had 150 000 subscribers, who paid between $50 and $600-plus a year for Stratfor's reports on the Iraq War.

Before Kelley's downfall, his site was racking up 120 000 page views a day. Kelley was becoming famous as a war expert. He was interviewed by *The New York Times*, NBC, *Newsweek*, and National Public Radio (NPR). On NPR, Kelley said that readers flocked to his site "based on my reporting and my integrity." After he was accused of plagiarism, Kelley said he lost 40 to 45 percent of his web traffic. He eventually agreed to use no more than two Stratfor items per day and always with attribution.

What did other bloggers think of Kelley?

University of Chicago political science professor and blogger Daniel W. Drezner was critical: "As a graduate student in international relations, Kelley knew (or should have known) he was in the wrong as he was lifting Stratfor's content." Also, Drezner said, Kelley was in the wrong when he initially tried to deny the plagiarism.

On his site Instapundit.com, Glenn Reynolds noted that he chose not to link to Kelley's site because most of his posts didn't have links to sources: "I'm generally skeptical of secondhand reports without clear sourcing."

Although Kelley's plagiarism drew critics, others see it as no big deal. Blogs, they say, aren't part of mainstream journalism anyway. Only 23 percent of the 10 230 respondents to a 2006 Globescan survey conducted in 10 countries said that they trusted blogs' current-affairs information.

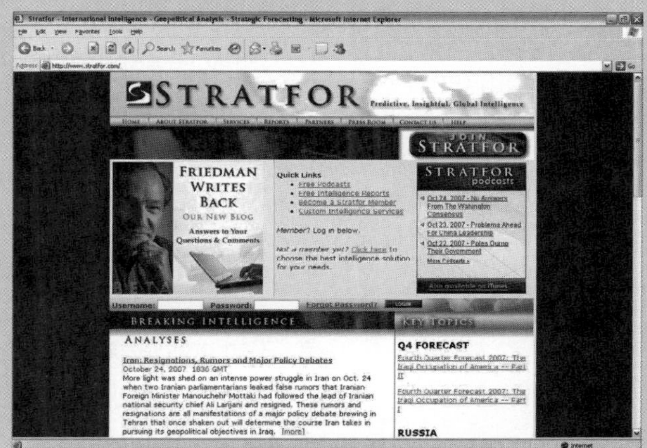

Trustworthy Sourcing The ease with which material can be picked up from one website and reused elsewhere has posed questions about plagiarism in a new framework. The people who run the Stratfor site on military intelligence grew tired of the leakage and outed a serial copier.

However, BBC's Paul Reynolds believes that asking people if they trust blogs is the wrong question. "Blogs do not really exist to provide people with 'news and information,'" Reynolds said. "More useful questions would be: 'Do you read them and how do you use the information?' Quite often, they just offer you a perspective you might not have thought about. You can use them to test your own judgment."

DEEPENING YOUR MEDIA LITERACY

Explore the Issue

Write out your definition of a blog.

Dig Deeper

Visit a blog. How does it compare to your definition of a blog? How would you evaluate a blog? Write down seven to nine questions you should ask yourself when you read a blog.

What Do You Think?

What are valid ways to use the information you gather by reading blogs? Can blogs be part of the mainstream media?

Government agencies began to hint at controls. Late in 1999, Berners-Lee and the web protocol-authoring consortium that he runs came up with a new architecture, **P3P** (short for Platform for Privacy Preferences Project), to address the problem. With P3P, people could choose the level of privacy they wanted for their web activities. Microsoft, Netscape, and other browser operators agreed to screen sites that were not P3P-compliant. In effect, P3P automatically bypassed websites that didn't meet a level of privacy expectations specified by individual web users.

P3P A web protocol that allows users to choose a level of privacy; short for Platform for Privacy Preferences Project.

In 2009, Facebook was found to be in violation of Canadian privacy laws. As a result, Facebook had to change how its user information was collected and used. Among the issues were:

- *Third-party applications.* Some applications could access personal information from Facebook users who used these applications.
- *Deactivation vs. deletion of accounts.* There was some confusion over the two terms. Facebook agreed to make it clear that only by deleting your account would your personal information also be deleted.

Canada's privacy commissioner, Jennifer Stoddart, said, "These changes mean that the privacy of 200 million Facebook users in Canada and around the world will be far better protected. This is extremely important. People will be able to enjoy the benefits of social networking without giving up control of their personal information."

LEARNING CHECK

- **How has the web concept introduced by Tim Berners-Lee led to privacy issues?**
- **Can problems of personal privacy on the internet be solved?**

Internet Future

STUDY PREVIEW **Traditional gatekeeping processes that filter media content for quality are less present on the internet. Users need to take special care in assessing the material they find.**

Media Convergence

Johannes Gutenberg brought mass production to books. The other primary print media, magazines and newspapers, followed. People never had a problem recognizing the differences among books, magazines, and newspapers. When sound recording and movies came along, they too were distinctive, and later so were radio and television. Today, the traditional primary media are in various stages of transition to digital form. Old distinctions are blurring.

technological convergence Melding of print, electronic, and photographic media into digitized form.

The cable television systems and the internet are consolidating with companies such as AT&T in the forefront. This **technological convergence** is fuelled by accelerated miniaturization of equipment and the ability to compress data into tiny digital bits for storage and transmission. All media companies, whether their products traditionally relied on print, electronic, or photographic technology, are involved in this convergence.

As *The Economist* noted, once-discrete media industries "are being whirled into an extraordinary whole." Writing in *Quill* magazine, *USA Today's* Kevin Manay put it this way: "All the devices people use for communicating and all the kinds of communication have started crashing together into one massive megamedia industry. The result is that telephone lines will soon carry TV shows. Cable TV will carry telephone calls. Desktop computers will be used to watch and edit movies. Cellular phone-computers the size of a notepad will dial into interactive magazines that combine text, sound and video to tell stories."

Unanticipated consequences of the new technology are no better illustrated than by Amazon.com. Amazon's site has a growing list of books that people can search internally for the frequency of key terms and phrases. In Scott Ritter's *Solving the Iraq Crises*, Amazon lists 52 pages that contain the term *weapons of mass destruction*. A person can call up each of these pages, as well as adjoining pages, to read the paragraphs around the use of the term *weapons of mass destruction*, usually amounting to several hundred words. In the business of selling books, Amazon won't allow people to view entire books, but the service, called **Search Inside**, demonstrates possibilities for the library of the future.

Search Inside Amazon.com's search engine that can find a term or phrase in any book whose copyright owners have agreed to have it scanned in to a database.

In 2005, Google began scanning the entire collections of five major libraries to post online. Although copyright-ownership issues in regard to many works created in the last 75 years remain unresolved, the Google project is under way at Harvard University,

New York Public Library, Oxford University, Stanford University, and the University of Michigan. When completed, the Google project will allow online access to just about everything ever put between book covers in the history of the English language: 15 million titles.

LEARNING CHECK

- Which mass media are furthest along in being subsumed into internet delivery?

Transition Ahead

Nobody expects the printed newspaper to disappear overnight or movie houses, video rental shops, and over-the-air broadcasters to go out of business all at once. But all of the big media companies have established stakes on the internet and, in time, digitized messages delivered over the internet will dominate.

Outside of the internet itself, major media companies also are trying to establish a future for themselves by reaching audiences in new digital ways. Companies that identify voids in their ability to capitalize on new technology have created joint ventures to ensure that they won't be left out. CTV, for example, provides news on Sympatico's MSN online service. Cable companies have moved into telephone-like two-way interactive communication systems that, for example, permit customers not only to receive messages but also to send them.

Some see a dark side to convergence, with a few major companies coming to dominate the internet and working against the democratization that others see as the fulfillment of the new technology's promise. Media mogul Barry Diller, who's consulted regularly for his vision on media directions, talks about the internet losing its diversity through ownership consolidation. Citing cable giant Comcast, he said in a *Newsweek* interview: "You can already see at Comcast and others the beginning of efforts to control the home pages that their consumers plug into. It's for one reason: To control a toll bridge or turnstile through which others must pay to go. The inevitable result will be eventual control by media giants of the Internet in terms of independence and strangulation. This is a situation where history is absolutely destined to repeat itself." Most internet users hope that Diller is wrong. He does, too.

LEARNING CHECK

- What effects has the internet had on each of the other major mass media?

CRTC and the Internet

The Canadian Radio-television and Telecommunications Commission (CRTC) was the first broadcast regulator in the world to address the issue of controlling the internet. In 2009, the CRTC reaffirmed its 1999 decision that it would not regulate the internet at that time, as the internet didn't fall under the authority of Canada's Broadcasting Act. It cited the following reasons for this conclusion:

- The internet is not, by definition, broadcasting. Its messages are largely communicated using alphanumeric text.
- The internet does not replace broadcasting; it simply complements it.
- Web material can be customized by the user; its messages are broadcast for a mass audience in the same way a radio or television broadcast is. The web is a "push" medium.
- There is already a large Canadian presence on the internet.
- The CRTC felt that the Criminal Code of Canada and the use of content-filtering software by users would be the best way to deal with offensive content on the internet.

LEARNING CHECK

- What industries are in a contest to control internet delivery systems?
- What law has shaped this contest?

Global Inequities

Canadian communication theorist Marshall McLuhan didn't invent the term global village, but he certainly cemented the notion in public dialogue. In numerous books and in the scholarly journal *Explorations*, which he founded in 1954, McLuhan talked about the world shrinking, at least metaphorically. In a wired world, he said, television could present live information from anywhere to everyone. The result, as he saw it, could change human existence profoundly, reversing a trend that started with Gutenberg's mass-produced printed word in the 1400s.

McLuhan argued that the print media had alienated human beings from their natural state. In pre–mass media times, McLuhan said, people acquired their awareness about their world through their own observation and experience and through their fellow human beings, whom they saw face to face and with whom they communicated orally.

retribalization Restoring humankind to a natural, tribal state.

global village Instantaneous connection of every human being.

McLuhan saw television bringing back tribalization. While books, magazines, and newspapers engaged the mind, television engaged the senses. In fact, the television screen could be so loaded with data that it could approximate the high level of sensual stimuli that people found in their environments back in the tribal period of human existence. **Retribalization**, he said, was at hand because of the new, intensely sensual communication that television could facilitate. Because television could far exceed the reach of any previous interpersonal communication, McLuhan called the new tribal village a **global village**.

The question for many now is: Has the internet fulfilled McLuhan's speculation that the world would become a global village? The internet has given us blogs, instant messaging, and access to information from anywhere in the world. The problem is that much of the world isn't plugged in. In 2009, Internet World Stats claimed that while almost 74 percent of North Americans and 52 percent of Europeans had access to the internet, only 7 percent of African countries and 19 percent of Asian countries had access.

In short, the internet may be creating new international inequities. North American village, maybe. Global village? Not yet.

LEARNING CHECK

- What effect has the internet had on the emergence of a global village?

Chapter 9 Wrap-Up

Watch

A Day in the Life: Social Networking

The internet is transforming mass communication. Traditional origin points for communication, such as a book publisher or a radio station, suddenly have been joined by millions of additional origin points, all of them interconnected. An individual with minimal equipment can be an originator of mass communication. The cost of entry is within almost everyone's means. Participation is impossible to measure. Have you tried counting the number of bloggers lately?

Questions for Critical Thinking

1. How is the internet being defined as a new and distinctive mass medium?
2. What technology breakthroughs made the internet possible?
3. Track the changes in successful business models for internet companies.
4. How well has the internet fulfilled its potential to democratize mass communication?
5. Are the earlier media of mass communication doomed by the internet? Explain.

Keeping Up to Date

Industry Standard is the main trade journal of e-commerce.

The magazines *Wired* and *Infoworld* offer coverage of cyberdevelopments, cyberissues, and people involved with the internet.

The trade journals *Editor & Publisher*, *Advertising Age*, *Playback*, *Broadcaster*, and *Broadcast Dialogue* have excellent ongoing coverage of their fields.

Widely available news media that explore cyberissues include *Time, Maclean's*, the *Toronto Star*, the *National Post*, and *The Globe and Mail.*

Don't overlook surfing the web for sites that track internet developments.

10 News

LEARNING AHEAD

- Many news media practices originated during periods of major change in history.
- The notion of objectivity in news is vexing.
- Journalists bring personal, social, and political values to their work.
- Variables affect what ends up being reported.
- Gatekeeping is both essential and hazardous to the news process.
- Journalistic trends include exploratory reporting, soft news, and 24/7 coverage.

Counter Science Scholars Jules and Maxwell Boykoff see journalists getting trapped in a desire for balance. The Boykoffs make the point that truth doesn't necessarily come from a tit-for-tat balance of opposing views.

MEDIA IN THEORY

When Balanced Reporting Isn't

In a massive study of news coverage on global warming, brothers Jules Boykoff, a political scientist, and Maxwell Boykoff, a geographer, reviewed four leading American newspapers—*The New York Times*, *The Wall Street Journal*, *The Washington Post*, and the *Los Angeles Times*—over a period of 14 years and identified 3542 news items, editorials, and other articles on global warming. Randomly, the Boykoffs chose 636 articles for analysis. Fifty-three percent, more than half, gave equal weight to opposing views. The easily inferred impression, the Boykoffs said, was that the scientific community was "embroiled in a rip-roaring debate on whether or not humans were contributing to global warming." The fact is that there was no such debate.

How could the news media, in their reporting of science, be so out of synch with scientists? It's a question at the heart of this chapter on news, which examines definitions of news and, importantly, how media-literate consumers can decide which reporting to trust.

The Boykoffs have a theory about what went wrong with the reporting on global warming: In a sense, as counterintuitive as it may seem, journalists try too hard to be fair.

"The professional canon of journalistic fairness requires reporters who write about a controversy to present competing points of view," the Boykoffs explained. "Presenting the most compelling arguments of both sides with equal weight is a fundamental check on biased reporting. But this canon causes problems when it is applied to issues of science. It seems to demand that journalists present competing points of view on a scientific question as if they had equal scientific weight, when actually they do not."

The fairness chink in journalistic armour has given special interests an opportunity to manipulate news by making misleading and even false information easily available to reporters who, dutifully if not mindlessly, apply the principle of fairness. A legion of

MEDIA TIMELINE News Practices

1690 Benjamin Harris published the first newspaper, *Publick Occurrences*, in Boston.

1735 Colonial jury exonerated John Peter Zenger of "seditious libel for publishing articles about the governor's incompetence."

1752 John Bushnell began publishing *The Halifax Gazette*, the first newspaper in Canada.

1833 Ben Day founded *The New York Sun*, the first penny newspaper.

1835 Joseph Howe was acquitted of publishing "seditious libel" in the *Novascotian*.

1880s Joseph Pulitzer and William Randolph Hearst's circulation war led to yellow press excesses.

1917 The Canadian Press was founded.

1980 CNN introduced 24-hour television news.

2001 CRTC warned conglomerates to keep newsroom management separate to ensure a diversity of voices in Canadian news.

2005 Government manipulation of news media intensified as people took issue with the information used to justify the war in Iraq.

2010 Al Jazeera arrived in Canada.

spokespersons, many funded by special interests, end up with roles in journalists' stories. The Boykoffs cite many examples, one being *The New York Times* quoting a global-warming skeptic stating that carbon dioxide emissions aren't a threat to the climate but "a wonderful and unexpected gift from the Industrial Revolution."

Who are these special interests? Former U.S. Vice-President Al Gore, himself a journalist early in his career, has been blunt: "A relatively small cadre of special interests including Exxon Mobil and a few other oil, coal and utilities companies." Why? "These companies want to prevent any new policies that would interfere with their current business plans that rely on the massive, unrestrained dumping of global-warming pollution of the Earth's atmosphere every hour of every day."

The Boykoffs put it this way: "Balanced reporting has allowed a small group of global warming skeptics to have their views amplified." Balanced coverage, according to the Boykoffs, has not translated into accurate coverage.

Are journalists dishonest? Jules Boykoff doesn't blame the journalists. He notes that giant media companies, intent on improving profits, have cut back on newsroom staffs and labour-intensive investigative reporting. The result is that more and more reporters are called upon to be generalists and are being denied time to build expertise on a complex subject such as climate change.

Journalism Traditions

STUDY PREVIEW American journalism has evolved through four distinctive eras: the colonial, partisan, penny press, and yellow periods. Each of these periods made distinctive contributions to contemporary news media practices in both the United States and Canada.

Media People: James Gordon Bennett

Colonial Period

In the American **colonial period, Benjamin Harris** published the first newspaper, ***Publick Occurrences***, in Boston in 1690. He was in hot water right away. Harris scandalized Puritan sensitivities by alleging that the king of France had dallied with his son's wife. In the colonies, just as in England, a newspaper needed royal consent. The governor had not consented, and Harris was put out of business after one issue.

colonial period From the founding of the colonies to the American Revolution.

Benjamin Harris Published *Publick Occurrences*.

Publick Occurrences First colonial newspaper, Boston, 1690.

Even so, Harris's daring was a precursor for emerging press defiance against authority. In 1733, **John Peter Zenger** started a paper in New York to compete with the existing Crown-supported newspaper. Zenger's paper was backed by merchants and lawyers who disliked the royal governor. From the beginning, the newspaper antagonized the governor with items challenging his competence. Finally, the governor arrested Zenger and the trial made history. Zenger's attorney, **Andrew Hamilton**, argued that there should be no punishment for printing articles that are true. This argument was a dramatic departure

John Peter Zenger Defied authorities in *New-York Weekly Journal*.

Andrew Hamilton Urged truth as a defence for charges of libel.

Zenger Trial Printer John Peter Zenger, in the dock, won his 1735 trial for criticizing New York's royal governor. The victory fed a colonial exuberance that culminated 46 years later in winning the revolution against British rule.

from the legal practice of the day, which allowed royal governors to prosecute for articles that might undermine their authority regardless of whether the information in the articles was true. Hamilton's argument prevailed, and Zenger, who had become a hero for standing up to the Crown, was freed.

These traditions from the colonial period remain today:

- The news media, both print and broadcast, relish their independence from government censorship and control.
- The news media, especially newspapers and magazines, actively try to mould government policy and mobilize public sentiment. Today this is done primarily on the editorial page.
- Journalists are committed to seeking truth, which was articulated as a social value in Zenger's "truth defence."
- In a capitalistic system the news media are economic entities that sometimes react in their own self-interest when their profit-making ability is threatened.

LEARNING CHECK

- **Both Harris and Zenger were slapped down by colonial governors for their early newspapers, but the cases were dramatically different. Which of these early printers would you regard as more heroic? Which was more important?**

Partisan Period

partisan period From the American Revolution at least to the 1830s.

After the American Revolution, newspapers divided along partisan lines. What is called the Federalist period in U.S. history is also referred to as the **partisan period** among newspaper historians. Intense partisanship characterized newspapers of the period, which spanned roughly 50 years to the 1830s.

Federalist Papers Essays with diverse views on the form the new nation should take.

Initially, the issue was over a constitution. Should the nation have a strong central government or remain a loose coalition of states? James Madison, Alexander Hamilton, Thomas Jefferson, John Jay, and other leading thinkers exchanged ideas through articles and essays in newspapers. The ***Federalist Papers***, a series of essays printed and reprinted in newspapers throughout the nation, were part of the debate.

John Adams Federalist president.

Alien and Sedition Acts Discouraged criticism of government.

David Brown Punished for criticizing the majority party.

Thomas Jefferson Anti-Federalist president.

After the Constitution was drafted, partisanship intensified, finally culminating lopsidedly when the Federalist party both controlled the Congress and had the party leader, **John Adams**, in the presidency. In firm control and bent on silencing their detractors, the Federalists pushed a series of laws through Congress in 1798. One of the things the **Alien and Sedition Acts** prohibited was "false, scandalous, malicious" statements about government. Using these laws, the Federalists made 25 indictments, which culminated in 10 convictions. Among those indicted was **David Brown**, a Revolutionary War veteran who felt strongly about free expression. He put up a sign in Dedham, Massachusetts, that read: "No stamp tax. No sedition. No alien bills. No land tax. Downfall to the tyrants of America. Peace and retirement to the president [the Federalist John Adams]. Long live the vice-president [the anti-Federalist **Thomas Jefferson**] and the minority [the anti-Federalists]. May moral virtues be the basis of civil government." If only criticisms of recent U.S. presidents were so mild! But the Federalists were not of a tolerant mind. Brown was fined $400 and sentenced to 18 months in prison.

Here are traditions from the partisan period that continue today:

- Government should keep its hands off the press.
- The news media are a forum for discussion and debate, as newspapers were in the *Federalist Papers* dialogue on what form the U.S. Constitution should take.
- The news media should comment vigorously on public issues.
- Government transgressions against the news media will ultimately be met by public rejection of those committing the excesses, which has happened periodically throughout history.

MEDIA PEOPLE Benjamin Day

Years later, reflecting on the instant success of his *New York Sun*, Benjamin Day shook his head in wonderment. He hadn't realized at the time that the *Sun* was such a milestone. Whether he was being falsely modest is something historians can debate. The fact is that the *Sun*, which Day founded in 1833, discovered mass audiences on a scale never before envisioned and ushered in the era of modern mass media. Day set up a shop in 1833, but business was slow. With time on his hands, he began a people-oriented handbill that contained brief news items and, most important, an advertisement for his printing business. He printed 1000 copies, which he sold for a penny apiece.

Mass Media Pioneer When Benjamin Day launched *The New York Sun* in 1833 and sold it for one cent a copy, he ushered in an era of cheap newspapers that common people could afford. Today, mass media have many of the Sun's pioneering characteristics. These include content of interest to a great many people, a financial base in advertising, and easy access.

Benjamin Day

Fifty years later, Day told an interviewer that the *Sun*'s success was "more by accident than by design." Even so, the *Sun* was the first newspaper that, at a penny a copy, was within the economic means of almost everyone. He filled the paper with local police court news, which is the stuff that arouses universal interest. True to its masthead motto, "It Shines for All," the *Sun* was a paper for the masses.

At only a penny a copy, Day knew he couldn't pay his bills, so he built the paper's economic foundation on advertising. This remains the financial basis of most mass media today: newspapers, magazines, television, and radio. Just as they do today, advertisers subsidized the *Sun* to make it affordable to great multitudes of people.

Today, it still is technology that makes the media possible. The *Sun* was a pioneer in using the technology of its time: engine-driven presses. The *Sun*'s messages—the articles—were crafted to interest large, diverse audiences, as are mass messages today. Also like today, advertising drove the enterprise financially. The story of Day's *Sun* also demonstrates a reality, as true then as it is now, that the mass media must be businesses first and purveyors of information and entertainment second.

WHAT DO YOU THINK?

1. What about *The New York Sun*'s content made it different at the time? How much of the *Sun*'s content formula remains part of news reporting today?
2. What parts of *The New York Sun*'s financial model have survived?

LEARNING CHECK

- What lesson can today's political leaders draw from public reaction to the Alien and Sedition Acts?

Penny Press Period

In 1833, when he was 22, the enterprising **Benjamin Day** started a newspaper that changed journalism: ***The New York Sun***. At a penny a copy, the *Sun* was within reach of just about everybody. Other papers were expensive, an annual subscription costing as much as a full week's wages. Unlike other papers, which were distributed mostly by mail, the *Sun* was hawked every day on the streets. The *Sun*'s content was different, too. It avoided the political and economic thrust of the traditional papers, concentrating instead on items of interest to common folk. The writing was simple, straightforward, and easy to follow. As a motto for the *Sun*, Day came up with "It Shines for All," the pun fully intended.

Benjamin Day Published *The New York Sun*.

The New York Sun First penny newspaper, 1833.

penny papers Affordable by almost everyone.

Merchants saw the unprecedented circulation of the **penny papers** as a way to reach great numbers of potential customers. Advertising revenue meant bigger papers, which attracted more readers, which attracted more advertisers. A snowballing momentum began that continues today with more and more advertising being carried by the mass media. A significant result was a shift in newspaper revenues from subscriptions to advertisers. Day, as a matter of fact, did not meet expenses by selling the *Sun* for a penny a copy. He counted on advertisers to pick up a good part of his production cost. In effect, advertisers subsidized readers, just as they do today.

Several social and economic factors, all resulting from the Industrial Revolution, made the penny press possible:

- **Industrialization.** With new steam-powered presses, hundreds of copies an hour could be printed. Earlier presses had been hand-operated.
- **Urbanization.** Workers flocked to the cities to work in new factories, creating a great pool of potential newspaper readers within delivery range. Until the urbanization of the 1820s and 1830s, the U.S. population had been almost wholly agricultural and scattered across the countryside. Even the most populous cities had been relatively small.
- **Immigration.** Waves of immigrants arrived from impoverished parts of Europe. Most were eager to learn English and found that penny papers, with their simple style, were good tutors.
- **Literacy.** As immigrants learned English, they hungered for reading material within their economic means. Also, literacy in general was increasing, which contributed to the rise of mass-circulation newspapers and magazines.

penny press period One-cent newspapers geared to mass audience and mass advertising.

Samuel Morse Invented the telegraph.

lightning news Delivered by telegraph.

inverted pyramid Most important information is presented first.

In 1844, late in the **penny press period**, **Samuel Morse** invented the telegraph. Within months, the nation was being wired. When the Civil War began in 1861, correspondents used the telegraph to get battle news to eager readers. It was called **lightning news**, delivered electrically and quickly. The Civil War also gave rise to a new convention in writing news, the **inverted pyramid**. Editors instructed their war correspondents to tell the most important information first in case telegraph lines failed—or were snipped by the enemy—as a story was being transmitted. That way, when a story was interrupted, editors would have at least a few usable sentences. The inverted pyramid, it turned out, was popular with readers because it allowed them to learn what was most important at a glance. They did not have to wade through a whole story if they were in a hurry. Also, the inverted pyramid helped editors to fit stories into the limited confines of a page; a story could be cut off at any paragraph and the most important parts remained intact. The inverted pyramid remains a standard expository form for telling event-based stories in newspapers, radio, and television.

Associated Press (AP) Co-operative for gathering and distributing news.

objective reporting Telling news without bias.

Several New York newspaper publishers, concerned about the escalating expense of sending reporters to gather faraway news, got together in 1848 to share stories. By sending only one reporter to represent all newspapers, publishers cut costs dramatically. They called their co-operative venture the **Associated Press (AP)**, a predecessor of today's giant global news service. The AP introduced a new tone in news reporting. So that AP stories could be used by member newspapers of different political persuasions, reporters were told to write from a nonpartisan point of view. The result was a fact-oriented kind of news writing often called **objective reporting**. It was widely imitated and is still the dominant reporting style for event-based news stories in the American news media.

There are traditions of today's news media, both print and electronic, that can be traced to the penny press period:

- Inverted pyramid story structures.
- Coverage and writing that appeal to a general audience, sometimes by trying to be entertaining or even sensationalistic.
- A strong orientation to covering events, including the aggressive ferreting out of news.
- A commitment to social improvement, which included a willingness to crusade against corruption.

- Being on top of unfolding events and providing information to readers quickly, something made possible by the telegraph but that also came to be valued in local reporting.
- A detached, neutral perspective in reporting events.

LEARNING CHECK

- News as we think of it today has roots in the penny press period. What are these roots?
- What was the connection between the telegraph and the inverted pyramid?

Yellow Period

The quest to sell more copies led to excesses that are illustrated by the Pulitzer-Hearst circulation war in New York in the 1890s, in what came to be known as the **yellow period.**

Joseph Pulitzer, a poor immigrant, made the *St. Louis Post-Dispatch* into a financial success. In 1883, Pulitzer decided to try a bigger city. He bought the *New York World* and applied his St. Louis formula to it. He emphasized human interest, crusaded for worthy causes, and ran a lot of promotional hoopla. Pulitzer's *World* also featured solid journalism. His star reporter, **Nellie Bly**, epitomized the two faces of the Pulitzer formula for journalistic success. For one story, Bly feigned mental illness, entered an insane asylum, and emerged with scandalous tales about how patients were treated. It was enterprising journalism of great significance and reforms resulted. Later, showing the less serious, show-biz side of Pulitzer's formula, Bly was sent out to circle the globe in 80 days, like Jules Verne's fictitious Phileas Fogg. Her journalism stunt took just 72 days.

yellow period Late 1800s; marked by sensationalism.

Joseph Pulitzer Emphasized human interest in newspapers; later sensationalized.

Nellie Bly Stunt reporter.

In San Francisco, Pulitzer had a young admirer, **William Randolph Hearst.** With his father's Nevada mining fortune and mimicking Pulitzer's *New York World* formula, Hearst made the *San Francisco Examiner* a great success. In 1895, Hearst decided to go to New York and take on the master. He bought the *New York Journal* and vowed to "out-Pulitzer" Pulitzer. The inevitable resulted. To outdo each other, Pulitzer and Hearst launched crazier and crazier stunts. Not even the comic pages escaped their competitive frenzy. Pulitzer ran the Yellow Kid, and then Hearst hired the cartoonist away. Pulitzer hired a new one and then both papers ran the yellow character and plastered the city with yellow promotional posters. The circulation war was nicknamed "yellow journalism," and the term came to be a derisive reference to sensational excesses in news coverage.

William Randolph Hearst Built circulation with sensationalism.

The yellow excesses reached a feverish peak as Hearst and Pulitzer covered the growing tensions between Spain and the United States. Fuelled by hyped stories of atrocities, the tensions between the two countries eventually exploded in war. One story, perhaps apocryphal, epitomizes the no-holds-barred competition between Pulitzer and Hearst. Although Spain had consented to all demands made by the United States, Hearst sent the artist **Frederic Remington** to Cuba to cover the situation. Remington cabled back: "Everything is quiet. There is no trouble here. There will be no war. Wish to return." Hearst replied: "Please remain. You furnish the pictures. I'll furnish the war."

Frederic Remington Illustrator sent by Hearst to find atrocities in Cuba.

jazz journalism 1920s; similar to yellow journalism.

Peter Desbarats Believes that Canadian journalism traditions are closely related to American traditions.

The yellow tradition lives on. The New York *Daily News*, founded in 1919 and almost an immediate hit, ushered in a period that some historians characterize as **jazz journalism.** It was Hearst and Pulitzer updated in tabloid form with an emphasis on photography. Today, newspapers like the commercially successful *National Enquirer* are in the yellow tradition. This tradition is obvious in tabloid television interview programs such as The *Jerry Springer Show*, which pander to public taste for the offbeat, tawdry, and sensational.

Joseph Pulitzer

LEARNING CHECK

- News that is sensationalized beyond what the facts warrant can be dangerous. Give an example from the yellow press period. Can you cite recent examples?

History of Journalism in Canada

In his *Guide to the Canadian News Media*, **Peter Desbarats** comments that journalism in Canada "has been closer to Main Street USA than to Fleet Street." By this he means that Canadian news traditions followed the American model and not the British model. A comparison of the press periods in Canada and the United States seems to indicate that

William Randolph Hearst

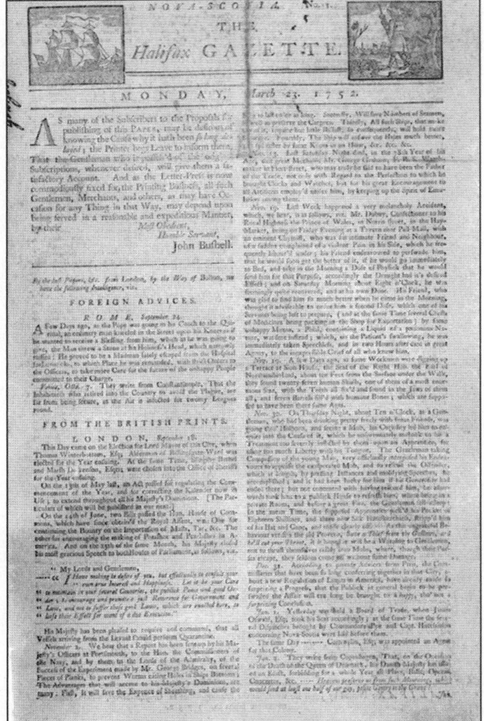

NOVA-SCOTIA. No. 1.

THE *Halifax* GAZETTE.

MONDAY, March 23. 1752.

AS many of the Subscribers to the Proposals for publishing of this PAPER, may be desirous of knowing the Cause why it hath been *so long delayed*; the Printer begs Leave to inform them, That the Gentleman who is possess'd of the original Subscriptions, whenever desired, will give them a satisfactory Account. And as the Letter-Press is now commodiously fixed for the Printing Business, all such Gentlemen, Merchants, and others, as may have Occasion for any Thing in that Way, may depend upon being served in a reasonable and expeditious Manner, by their

Most Obedient,
Humble Servant,
John Bushell.

FOREIGN ADVICES.

ROME, September 24.

FROM THE BRITISH PRINTS.

LONDON, September 18.

Early to Print A snapshot of the Monday, March 23, 1752, edition of *The Halifax Gazette*—Canada's first newspaper.

similar ideals developed, albeit at different times. **Wilfred Kesterton**'s research on the history and growth of journalism in Canada is regarded as the definitive work in this area. Kesterton observes that Canadian journalists were fuelled by ideals similar to those that characterized the partisan and colonial periods in American history. He breaks down journalism in Canada into four periods.

Wilfred Kesterton Canadian news historian.

The Transplant Period (1752–1807) Kesterton refers to this press period as the **transplant period** because Canada's first newspapers were literally British or American newspapers or publishers that transplanted, or resettled, in Canada. *The Halifax Gazette*, Canada's first newspaper, was published by John Bushnell, who moved to Halifax from Boston in 1752. The oldest Canadian newspaper in existence, the *Quebec* Gazette, was started by two printers from Philadelphia in 1764. *The Halifax Gazette* appeared every two weeks and had about 70 subscribers, while the *Quebec Gazette* had about 150 subscribers when it began publishing. As conditions improved and immigrants began to move down the St. Lawrence River and into Upper Canada, other newspapers began publishing.

transplant period First period in Canadian journalism, in which newspapers or publishers from Britain and the United States were "transplanted" to Canada.

As with their early American counterparts, most of the first papers in Canada were organs for the fledgling governments of British North America. Most of the content of these three- or four-page newsletter-type sheets was government information with a sprinkling of news from "back home." It was felt that for the settlements in the New World to be successful, the government needed this voice to inform and educate settlers. These newspapers were also a primitive advertising tool for early Canadian merchants. The first ads in Canadian newspapers appeared in 1752 when *The Halifax Gazette* printed three ads: for a lawyer, a clerical service, and butter. While some ads appeared in these publications, the main source of income for most early newspapers was printing government information. Therefore, the success of newspapers during this time was contingent on government support, both financial and ideological. As a result, most of these papers didn't "rock the boat." In 1766, *The Halifax Gazette* dared to question the government on the new stamp tax. As a result, the government suspended the publication.

The Growth Period (1807–1858) Following the War of 1812, immigration in Canada flourished, particularly in Upper Canada, where the population doubled by the mid-1820s. Combine this population surge with the effects of the Industrial Revolution and you will begin to understand the changing social climate in Canada. People stopped working at home or in the fields and began to work in factories. These factors contributed to the growth of newspapers, and thus to what Kesterton refers to as the **growth period** of Canadian journalism. At the end of the War of 1812, Canada had only a handful of newspapers; by the mid-1820s, that number had risen to almost 300. Canada's first daily newspaper arrived in 1833 with Montreal's *Daily Advertiser*.

growth period Second period in Canadian journalism; marked by expansion due to immigration following the War of 1812.

As during the penny press period in the United States, growth in immigration and urbanization created markets for Canadian newspapers. As a result, newspapers were less dependent on government revenue for their economic success. This, in turn, created a kind of "partisan" press period in Canada, as newspapers began to take sides along political lines.

The most significant event in this period in Canadian journalism history involved **Joseph Howe**. On New Year's Day, 1835, Howe published "the letter" signed by "the people" in his *Novascotian*. In the letter, he accused the local police and the lieutenant-governor of corruption. In his defence, he asked the jury "to leave an unshackled press as a legacy to your children." Despite the fact that Howe was charged with seditious libel under the criminal code of the day, and that the presiding judge instructed the jurors to bring back a verdict of guilty, the jury acquitted him of libel in only 10 minutes. The jury felt that publishing something that is true shouldn't be illegal. As with the earlier American example of Zenger's *New York Journal*, the message to Canadian journalists was clear: Freedom of the press and intellectual freedom were important principles.

Joseph Howe Advocate of an unshackled press.

Third Canadian Press Period: Westward Growth (1858–1900) During the latter half of the 1800s, immigration and migration became two important factors in the growth of Canadian newspapers. As the Canadian population increased, it moved west and north and newspapers soon followed. Kesterton calls this the **westward growth** period of Canadian journalism. The gold rushes in the west made Victoria, British Columbia, a centre for commerce and transportation. In 1858, *The Victoria Gazette and Anglo-American* began publishing. New papers also began publishing in central and eastern Canada: the *Montreal Star* in 1869, the *Toronto Telegram* in 1876, and the *Ottawa Journal* in 1885. By the turn of the century, more than 1200 newspapers served Canada's population, which at that time stood at close to 5.5 million.

westward growth Third period in Canadian journalism; as Canadians moved west, so did the press.

This period was also a sort of "partisan period" for Canadian journalism. The debate over Confederation, the Riel rebellion, and the completion of the Canadian National Railway were the subjects of many an article. Thomas D'Arcy McGee, George Brown, and Joseph Howe were among the country's most opinionated journalists.

Fourth Canadian Press Period: The 20th Century Onward In the 1900s, journalism came of age in Canada. Although immigration levels and migration patterns were inconsistent due to the world wars and the Great Depression during the first half of the 20th century, improvements in technology helped the newspaper grow to new heights. This technology included better printing presses and better-quality newsprint, which helped to improve the form of the newspaper. Improvements in communication and transportation helped distribution. As a result of these changes and the continuing growth of cities, the large metropolitan daily as a business enterprise became the norm for many newspapers.

News agencies arrived in Canada during this period. The Canadian Press (**CP**) was founded in 1917. A statute of Parliament officially made the Canadian Press a corporation in 1923. Today, more than 250 journalists write stories for CP, which supplies news for print and broadcast outlets.

CP The Canadian Press

Canadian Television News The arrival of television added an element to Canadian journalism. In *A Guide to Canadian News Media*, Peter Desbarats reports that by the late 1950s, Canadian news programs were becoming in-depth and analytical. René Lévesque's *Point de mire* and Pierre Berton's *Close-Up* were popular newsmagazine-style shows. Probably the best-known newsmagazine in the 1960s was *This Hour Has Seven* Days, hosted by Laurier LaPierre and Patrick Watson. It debuted in the fall of 1964. The program became known for its controversial style and was taken off the air in 1966 after only 50 episodes. *W5* began broadcasting in 1966 on CTV and is now the longest-running newsmagazine in North America. CBC's *The Fifth Estate* is also known for hard-hitting, take-no-prisoners journalism. CBC's *The Hour* with George Stroumboulopoulos continues this tradition with a millennial attitude.

CTV aired its first nightly newscast in 1961 with Harvey Kirck as the anchor. Today, people tune in to the trustworthy images of Lisa LaFlamme on the *CTV National News*, Dawna Friesen on *Global National*, or Peter Mansbridge on CBC's *The National*.

LEARNING CHECK

- Historically, how has the growth of news in Canada paralleled the traditions in the United States? How has it differed?
- How are Canadian news traditions different from American traditions? How are they similar?

Concepts of News

STUDY PREVIEW The contemporary notion that news media content should be objective is relatively recent. Also, it is a notion not shared in all modern democracies. The word *objectivity* is overused and not very useful. It's better to think of journalism as the process of pursuing truth to tell truth.

Watch

ABC's *Nightline:* "Differences in Press Coverage in Great Britain and the U.S."

Definition of News

Brian Green Canadian journalism professor who defines news as "the significant, the unusual, that which affects us."

news A report on change.

Ask anybody: "What's news?" Everyone thinks they know, but press them and you'll hear a lot of fumbling. In *Canadian Broadcast News: The Basics*, journalism professor **Brian Green** says that news is "the significant, the unusual, that which affects us."

A useful definition of news involves two concepts: news and newsworthiness. In short, **news** is a report on change. This is no more apparent than in traditional newspaper headlines that contain a verb, the vehicle in a language used to denote change:

> **Obama *wins* Democratic Iowa caucus**
> **Roadside IEDs *kill* four Canadian soldiers**
> **Paris Hilton *leaves* jail a "new person"**

newsworthiness A ranking of news that helps to decide what makes it into news packages.

Not all change can fit into the limited time allotted in a newscast or the limited space allotted in a newspaper. Nor does all change warrant audience time online. So what change makes the news? Journalists apply the concept of **newsworthiness** to rank change. When U.S. President Barack Obama sniffles, it's change—and the whole world cares. A lot is at stake. For most of us, when we sniffle, only Mom cares. Applying a newsworthiness test to a series of events that might be reported requires judgment. No two people will assign all priorities in the same way.

LEARNING CHECK

- News is a report on change, but clearly more change is occurring than is possible to report. What principles do journalists apply to identify change that most merits reporting?
- Why is it unavoidable that journalists disagree among themselves on what merits being reported on a given day?

Objectivity

objectivity A concept in journalism that news should be gathered and told value-free.

Despite the high quotient of judgment in deciding what changes to report, a lot of people use the term **objectivity** to describe news. By this they mean a value-free process in making choices about what to tell and how to tell it. It's a self-contradictory concept: Choice, by definition, is never value-free. So how did we end up with this idea that news should be objective when it cannot be? History has the answer.

Explore

Deepening Your Media Literacy: Is objectivity a duty?

Penny Press Part of the answer goes back to the era of Benjamin Day and his *New York Sun*, the first of the penny papers with a mass audience. Day looked for stories with mass appeal. Suddenly, what made the paper was not the opinionated ramblings of the preceding partisan press but stories chosen to appeal to the largest possible audience. Opinion was out; storytelling was in. The writer became subordinate to the tale, even to the point of near invisibility. There were no more first-person accounts. Facts carried the story.

Associated Press In 1848, several cost-conscious New York newspaper publishers agreed to a joint venture to cover distant news. The Associated Press (AP), as they called the venture, saved a lot of money. It also transformed journalism in a way that was never anticipated. Inherent in the AP concept was that its stories needed to be nonpartisan to be usable by all of its member newspapers, whose political persuasions ran the spectrum. The result was an emphasis—some say fetish—on fact-driven journalism devoid of even a hint of partisanship.

Newspaper Economics Another fundamental shift cemented the detached, neutral AP tone, often characterized as objective. News became profitable—highly so. The fortune that Benjamin Day made with *The New York Sun* in the mid-1830s was puny compared with that of the news empires of Pulitzer, Hearst, and other that followed within 50 years. These super-publishers saw their newspapers as money machines as much as political tools. The bottom line gradually and inevitably gained more weight. The safest route to continue building their mass audiences and enhancing revenue was to avoid antagonizing readers and advertisers. There was money to be made in presenting news in as neutral a tone as possible. Picking up a lesson from the AP, but with a different motivation—to make money rather than save money—profit-driven publishers came to favour information-driven news.

By the early 20th century, when news practices became institutionalized in the first journalism textbooks and in the formation of professional organizations, the notion of a detached, neutral presentation was firmly ensconced. Ethics codes, new at the time, dismissed other approaches as unacceptable and unethical, even though they had been dominant only three generations earlier. The word *objectivity* became a newsroom mantra.

To be sure, there are exceptions to the detached, neutral presentation, but traditionalists are quick to criticize these departures. The goal is to keep the reporter, and even the reporter's inherently necessary judgment, as invisible as possible in the presentation of news.

LEARNING CHECK

- How did so many people come to the conclusion that news should be objective?

Journalists' Personal Values and Biases

STUDY PREVIEW As gatekeepers, journalists make important decisions on which events, phenomena, and issues are reported and which are not. The personal values that journalists bring to their work and that therefore determine which stories are told—and also how they are told—generally coincide with mainstream values.

Explore

Media People: Seymour Hersh

The journalistic ideal, an unbiased seeking of truth and an unvarnished telling of it, dictates that the work be done without partisanship. Yet, as human beings, journalists have personal values that influence all that they do, including their work. Because the news judgment decisions that journalists make are so important to an informed citizenry, we need to know what makes these people tick.

When asked whether biases exist in journalism, **David Rooney**, author of *Reporting and Writing for Canadian Journalists* and a teacher at Calgary's Mount Royal College, says, "Of course they do. No one gets through life without acquiring political attitudes and prejudices and journalists are no different in that regard. But, for the most part, conscientious reporters keep their biases out of their copy. They leave it to fellow journalists—the columnists and editorial writers—to openly advocate particular policies or ideologies."

David Rooney Believes that bias in journalism is inevitable.

As a sociologist who studied stories in the American news media for 20 years, **Herbert Gans** concluded that journalists have a typical North American value system. Gans identified primary values, all in the North American mainstream, that journalists use in making news judgments:

Herbert Gans Concluded that journalists have mainstream values.

- *Ethnocentrism.* **Ethnocentrism** means that journalists see things through their culture's eyes, which affects news coverage.
- *Commitment to democracy and capitalism.* Coverage of other governmental forms dwells on corruption, conflict, protest, and bureaucratic malfunction. Gans also found that when they report corruption and misbehaviour in business, journalists treat these events as aberrations.
- *Small-town pastoralism.* Like most of their fellow citizens, journalists romanticize rural life. Given similar stories from metropolitan Vancouver and tiny Estevan, Saskatchewan, editors usually opt for the small town. This helps to explain the success of Wayne Rostad's long-running *On the Road Again* series on CBC.
- *Individualism tempered by moderation.* Gans found that journalists love stories about rugged individuals who overcome adversity and defeat powerful forces. This is a value that contributes to a negative coverage of technology as something to be feared because it can stifle individuality.
- *Social order.* Journalists cover disorder: earthquakes, catastrophes, protest marches, the disintegrating nuclear family, and transgressions of laws and mores. This coverage, noted Gans, is concerned not with glamorizing disorder but with finding ways to restore it.

ethnocentrism Seeing things on the basis of personal experience and values.

In the final analysis, news is the result of journalists scanning their environment and making decisions, first on whether to cover certain events and then on how to cover them. The decisions are made against a backdrop of countless variables, many of them changing during the reporting, writing, and editing processes.

LEARNING CHECK

- Which of the values that Herbert Gans attributed to North American journalists do you share?
- What additional values do you hold?

Variables Affecting News

STUDY PREVIEW The variables that determine what is reported include things beyond a journalist's control, such as how much space or time is available to tell a story. Also, a story that might receive top billing on a slow news day might not even appear on a day when an overwhelming number of major stories are breaking.

News Hole

news hole Space for news in a newspaper after ads are inserted; also time in a newscast for news after ads.

A variable affecting what ends up being reported as news is called the **news hole.** In newspapers, the news hole is the space left after the advertising department has placed in the paper all of the ads it has sold. The volume of advertising determines the number of total pages; generally, the bigger the issue, the more room for news. Newspaper editors can squeeze more stories into a fat Wednesday issue than a thin Monday issue.

In broadcasting, the news hole tends to be more consistent. A 30-minute television newscast may have room for only 22 minutes of news, but the format doesn't vary. When the advertising department doesn't sell all seven minutes available for advertising, public-service announcements, promotional messages, and program notes—not news—pick up the slack.

LEARNING CHECK

- Why does the news hole frustrate journalists?

News Flow and News Staffing

flow Variation from day to day in significance of events worth covering.

Besides the news hole, the **flow** varies from day to day. A story that might be played prominently on a slow news day can be passed over entirely in the competition for space on a heavy news day.

On one of the heaviest news days of all time—June 4, 1989—death claimed Iran's Ayatollah Khomeini, a central figure in the Middle East; Chinese young people and the government were locked in a showdown in Tiananmen Square; the Polish people were voting to reject their one-party communist political system; and a revolt was under way in the Soviet republic of Uzbekistan. That was a heavy news day, and the flow of major nation-rattling events pre-empted many stories that otherwise would have been considered news, such as the grand opening that weekend of SkyDome (now Rogers Centre) in Toronto.

staffing Available staff resources to cover news.

Staffing—for example, whether reporters are in the right place at the right time—affects news coverage. A newsworthy event in Nigeria will receive short shrift on television if the network correspondents for Africa are occupied with a natural disaster in next-door Cameroon. A radio station's city government coverage will slip when the city hall reporter is on vacation or if the station can't afford a regular reporter at city hall.

LEARNING CHECK

- Look at your local newspaper over the past week. Which was the heaviest news day? Which was the slowest news day? Explain.
- Which is cheaper for a newspaper or television station to report: a session of the city council or a session of the British Parliament? Explain.

Perceptions about Audience

How a news organization perceives its audience affects news coverage. The *National Enquirer* lavishes attention on unproven cancer cures that *The Globe and Mail* treats briefly, if at all. Canada's BNN (Business News Network) sees its purpose as providing news for viewers who have a special interest in finance, the economy, and business.

The perception that a news organization has of its audience is evident in a comparison of stories on different networks' newscasts. CTV News Channel may lead off its newscasts with a coup d'état in another country, while BNN will lead off with a new government economic forecast and MTV Canada will lead off with the announcement of a teen sensation's upcoming tour.

LEARNING CHECK

- How do your expectations differ regarding the news coverage on *The Daily Show* and the CBC?

Competition

One trigger of adrenaline for journalists is landing a scoop or, conversely, being scooped. Journalism is a competitive business, and the drive to outdo other news organizations keeps news publications and newscasts fresh with new material.

Competition has an unglamorous side. Journalists constantly monitor each other to identify events that they missed and that they need to catch up on to be competitive. This catch-up aspect of the news business contributes to similarities in coverage, which scholar Leon Sigal calls the **consensible nature of news.** It also is called "pack" or "herd" journalism.

consensible nature of news News organization second-guessing competition in deciding on coverage.

In the final analysis, news is the result of journalists scanning their environment and making decisions, first on whether to cover certain events and then on how to cover them. The decisions are made against a backdrop of countless variables, many of which change during the reporting, writing, and editing processes.

LEARNING CHECK

- How can similar content in competing news media be explained?

Gatekeeping

Although individual reporters have a lot of independence in determining what to report and how, news work is a team effort. News dispatches and photographs are subject to change at many points in the communication chain. At these points, called gates, **gatekeepers** delete, trim, embellish, and otherwise try to improve messages.

gatekeeper Person who decides whether to shorten, drop, or change a story en route to the mass audience.

Just as a reporter exercises judgment in deciding what to report and how to report it, judgment also is at the heart of the gatekeeping process. Hardly any message, except live reporting, reaches its audience in its original form. Along the path from its originator to the eventual audience, a message is subject to all kinds of deletions, additions, and changes of emphasis. With large news organizations, this process may involve dozens of editors and other persons.

The gatekeeping process affects all news. A public relations practitioner who doesn't tell the whole story is a gatekeeper. A reporter who emphasizes one aspect of an event and neglects others is a gatekeeper. Even live, on-the-scene television coverage involves gatekeeping because a gatekeeper decides where to point the camera, and that decision affects the type of information that reaches viewers. The Cable Public Affairs Channel's (CPAC) live, unedited coverage of Parliament, for example, never shows members of Parliament sleeping or reading newspapers during debate, even though such things happen.

Gatekeeping can be a creative force. Trimming a news story can add potency. A news producer can enhance a reporter's field report with file footage. An editor can call a public relations person for additional detail to illuminate a point in a reporter's story. A newsmagazine's editor can consolidate related stories and add context that makes an important interpretive point.

Most gatekeepers are invisible to the news audience, working behind the scenes and making crucial decisions in near anonymity on how the world will be portrayed in the evening newscast and the next morning's newspaper.

CASE STUDY

Cultivating Readers

Newspapers are worried that young people don't read them. Long before television, Yahoo!, iPods, Facebook, Twitter, and blogs, newspapers were the dominant media. They were the one source everyone turned to for information about the world. That's not so anymore.

After slipping for several years, newspaper circulation dipped precipitously in 2005. Research firm Veronis Suhler Stevenson reported that the number of hours spent annually with a daily newspaper was down to 169 per American adult and would fall almost another 1 percent in 2008. The greatest loss was projected for young adults, an audience that many advertisers covet.

Anxious to change those statistics, newspapers stepped up their industry's long-standing Newspapers in Education (NIE) program aimed at elementary school readers. The goal is to excite a new generation about current affairs, which the industry hopes will stem circulation losses. For years, many papers have carried the boilerplate NIE features that incorporate newspapers into the classroom. In the 1990s, NIE's Barbara Goldman created It's News to Me, a board game available in many toy stores. Now she's devised flash cards that newspapers can buy emblazoned with their brand names and sell to schools. The cards have questions that can be answered by reading the local paper.

But what about teens and young adults? Why don't they read newspapers? One theory is that mass audiences are hardly static. Today's youth are a fickle bunch. A prime-time television hit one year can flicker out the next. YouTube grew from an idea to a billion-dollar reality in less than two years. Another theory is that "old media" don't employ enough young people.

The Associated Press (AP), the giant news agency that reaches more than 1 billion people daily and is known for its to-the-point reporting, created Asap, a special service aimed at young people 25 to 34 years old. Asap boasts "bold and innovative coverage" that embraces diverse interactive media elements, including video, blogs, diaries, and photos. A team of writers, mostly in their twenties and thirties, draws from the work of 2000 AP reporters worldwide with a fresh, if not sometimes flip, tone. About 200 American newspapers have subscribed, posting Asap content on their websites or in their papers.

Youth Outlook, a project of the nonprofit alternative Pacific News, employs only young writers and does not count on sources from "old media," such as the AP. Pacific says that the writers and editorial staff of its youth media are all in their twenties or younger. "Young people can tell if the stories are coming from peers or just being reported by others," says Kevin Weston, age 37, the director of Youth Outlook.

It's News to Me! The newspaper industry's Newspapers in Education project is trying to excite a new generation of readers about current affairs. One initiative was Barbara Goldman's It's News to Me, a board game. Now her flash cards pose questions that can be answered by checking the local paper.

Will these innovations bring back young readers? Have today's newspapers figured out why young people don't need newspapers as much as newspapers need them?

DEEPENING YOUR MEDIA LITERACY

Where are newspaper readers going? Can a mass medium that's in its maturity, like newspapers, stall the shift of its audience to newer medium forms?

Explore the Issue

What is your dominant local newspaper? Also identify a metropolitan daily in a different major city.

Dig Deeper

Check into the circulation patterns of both newspapers going back 5 or 10 years. You can do this with data provided quarterly by each newspaper to the Audit Bureau of Circulations (ABC). If you have difficulty finding ABC data at your library or online, the circulation directors at the newspapers you are studying will be pleased to provide it. You can also find online information about Canadian newspapers from the Canadian Newspaper Association (www.cna-acj.ca). Check also on the census data for these two newspapers' home cities for the time frame you are studying, either 5 or 10 years.

What Do You Think?

Do the circulations of the two newspapers reflect population changes? What is your theory on why this is so or why it is not so? Is there a reason to conclude that the national slippage in young readers applies to these newspapers? If one or both newspapers are an exception, why?

LEARNING CHECK

- Why is gatekeeping unavoidable in the process of reporting news?
- Explain how gatekeeping worked for any recent story from far away that was reported in your local news media. How about a local story?

Journalism Trends

Watch

ABC's *i-CAUGHT*: News Bloopers

STUDY PREVIEW The explosion of 24/7 news on television and the internet is transforming news gathering and redefining news practices and audience expectations. Traditional avenues for news, sometimes called mainstream media, were shaken during the 2004 U.S. political campaign by individuals, mostly without journalistic training and generally operating alone, who created hundreds of blog sites. Bloggers offer an interconnected web of fascinating reading. Sometimes they even score scoops.

Newsrooms in Transition

Two dynamics are reshaping newsrooms. One is the transition to internet delivery of news, which is pushing editors to find ways to stretch their staffs to produce their traditional products plus offer competitive websites. The other dynamic is financial, primarily at newspapers, where recent years have seen drastic reductions in staff. Newspaper industry reporter Joe Strupp, writing in the trade journal *Editor & Publisher*, put it this way: "So with newsrooms shrinking and corporate demands growing, the question inevitably may be asked: 'What gives?'" Most television newsrooms face the same issue. How can the extra duty of a 24/7 website or perhaps multiple websites, some of them interactive, be absorbed by existing staff?

Among the new realities are the following.

Less Comprehensive Coverage Newsrooms once put a lot of energy into catching up on their competitors' scoops and taking the coverage further. This happens less so now. Ken Paulson, editor of *USA Today*, said he now applauds *The New York Times* and *The Washington* Post when they break an exclusive story. He applauds—and then forgets about it. Said Paulson: "We have to make judgment calls on what our priorities are."

The new *USA Today* practice, common in strapped newsrooms, doesn't speak well for the kind of excellence that competition has generated historically in journalism. The coverage of historically significant stories, such as the Pentagon Papers and Watergate in the 1970s, was marked by intense competition. Independent coverage by competing newsrooms led to revelations that no one news organization could have managed single-handedly. Every breakthrough from competing newsrooms in Watergate, for example, further peeled away at the truth and became a stepping stone for new rounds of pursuit.

Less Enterprise With smaller, stretched staffs, newsrooms are opting for easier stories. This has meant a greater quotient of stories that chronicle events and fewer stories that require labour-intensive digging. This further means fewer reporters being freed for what David Boardman, executive editor at *The Seattle Times*, calls "two- and three-day stories." There was a time in the lore of *The Wall Street Journal* that editors would work up a promising story possibility with a veteran reporter, give the reporter a credit card, and tell the reporter to come back with a story in six months. Although the *Journal* still features exhaustive journalistic examinations, these are becoming less common in American journalism.

Fewer Beats Reporters assigned to cover specialized topics or geographic areas are being given broader beats. Some police beat reporters, for example, now also cover the courts. To cover some beats, editors in some newsrooms have shuffled reporters from general assignment duties to beats, which means there are fewer resources for day-to-day coverage of breaking news that doesn't fall in the bailiwick of one of the surviving beats.

Less Independent Reporting Newsrooms are sharing stories among corporate siblings, which fills space cheaply but reduces the traditional value of competitive reporting yielding better coverage overall. Many newspapers and newscasts fill up with a growing percentage of faraway content from the Canadian Press (CP), which is much less costly per story than staff-generated local coverage. One upshot is less diversity in content when CP stories, appearing word for word in news packages province-wide, or even nation-wide, displace local coverage.

Efficient? Yes. That repackaging is better than fresh content, however, is hard to argue.

LEARNING CHECK

- The Watergate coverage by Carl Bernstein and Bob Woodward of *The Washington Post* began with a brief, routine account of a break-in at the Democratic Party's national headquarters. Discuss whether Bernstein and Woodward would have had the time to pursue the story in a newsroom today. How would history have been different if their news coverage had stopped with a burglary item?
- How much duplicate reporting—competing reporters all doing the same stories—do you see in your local news media?

Nonstop Coverage

Reporters for news agencies were a breed apart through most of the 20th century. In contrast to most newspaper reporters, who had one deadline a day, agency reporters sent dispatches to hundreds of news organizations, each with its own deadline. Agency reporters literally had a deadline every minute.

The advent of all-news radio and then the demassified 24/7 news channels expanded nonstop coverage beyond the news agencies. Nowhere is this better illustrated than on Parliament Hill, where reporters race from an event or interview to a camera for a live stand-up report, often ad libbing from notes scribbled on the run. Then, adrenaline surging, they run back to their sources for a new angle or event. This is event-based reporting, which emphasizes timely reports but has a downside. Going on the air a dozen times a day, perhaps more often when the news flow is heavy or especially significant, stand-up reporters have scant time to think through implications and context. Their job entails a race to cover events more than to provide understanding. This, too, was a classic criticism of the news agencies.

In short, nonstop coverage, whatever its advantage in terms of keeping people on top of breaking events, has shortcomings. The pressure for new angles tends to elevate the trivial. As well, context and understanding are sacrificed.

LEARNING CHECK

- What industries are in a contest to control internet delivery systems?
- Do these changes have a downside?

Live News

Over the past 150 years, the news media have evolved standard and accepted practices. These practices, taught in journalism schools and institutionalized in codes of ethics, guide reporters and editors in preparing their summaries and wrap-ups. In general, the traditional practices worked well when newspapers were the dominant news medium, and they worked well in broadcasting too—until the advent of highly portable, lightweight equipment that enabled broadcasters to carry news events live, bypassing the traditional editing process.

With television cameras focused on the towers of the World Trade Center as they turned into infernos in the 2001 terrorist attack, trapped people began to jump from windows hundreds of feet above ground. The plunges were desperate and fatal, of course, and audiences viewing the scene live were shocked and horrified. Neither the video nor still photographs were included in some later newscasts or newspapers.

LEARNING CHECK

- How has the role of gatekeeping been changed by live broadcast coverage?

Unedited Blogs

When the *Columbia Journalism Review* created a website for commentary on reporting of the 2004 U.S. presidential campaign, the magazine went out of its way to distance the new site from the thousands of web log sites, called **blogs**, on which amateurs post whatever is on their minds. Its website would be held to the highest journalistic standards. Its concern was that a lot of irresponsible content is posted on the web by people who lack any journalistic training or sense of journalistic standards. The web has made it possible for anyone to create a blog that is as easily accessible as are sites from news organizations that consciously seek to go about journalism in the right way.

blog An amateur website, generally personal in nature, often focused on a narrow subject, such as politics; short for web log.

The Globe and Mail's Roy MacGregor is worried about this new approach to journalism. He says "it's no longer so much about the five W's—who, what, where, when and why—but increasingly this nervous, uncertain business is about the five thousand, five hundred thousand, five million H's." As in "hits." In other words, it's about the "eyeballs" reading blogs and other online journalism. The key to getting the "hits" is simple: celebrities and gossip. It's a variation of "if it bleeds, it leads." In this online world, the latest sex or drug scandal involving a celebrity will attract interest. According to MacGregor, "the end result should be obvious: lazy journalism. Why search out something new when the old tried and true work best?"

Richard Gruneau of Simon Fraser University agrees with MacGregor, but adds that being an abrasive blogger often increases the number of hits: "When journalism becomes nothing more than digital hits, the more provocative you are—often, the more obnoxious you are—the higher the hit count. In that sense, the system pressures you to become a dick. Who cares if what you say is good, let alone whether there is any truth in it or not? When everything becomes opinion, the most opinionated, most strident and least comprising journalists are the ones who rattle enough cages, or inspire enough like minded devotees, to build the hit count. And if you can somehow get the people you piss off arguing with your devotees, then your hit count will really soar."

No gnashing of teeth will make blogs go away, however—and their impact is substantial. Blog rumours, gossip, and speculation, even when untrue, gain such currency that the mainstream media cannot ignore them. It's become a cliché, drawn from the tail-wags-dog metaphor, that blogs can wag the media.

LEARNING CHECK

- What do you think of *Columbia Journalism Review*'s distinction between good blogs and bad blogs?
- Do you agree with Roy MacGregor and Richard Gruneau about the state of online journalism/blogs?

Exploratory Reporting

Although in-depth reporting has deep roots, the thrust of American journalism until the 1960s was a chronicling of events: meetings, speeches, crimes, deaths, and catastrophes. That changed dramatically in 1972. Two persistent *Washington Post* reporters, **Carl Bernstein** and **Bob Woodward**, not only covered a break-in at the Democratic Party's national headquarters, at a building called the Watergate, but also linked the crime to the White House of Republican President Richard Nixon. The morality questions inherent in the reporting forced Nixon to resign. Twenty-five aides went to jail. The **Watergate** scandal created an enthusiasm for **investigative reporting** and in-depth approaches to news that went far beyond mere chronicling, which is relatively easy to do and, alas, relatively superficial.

Carl Bernstein *Washington Post* reporter who dug up Watergate.

Bob Woodward Bernstein's colleague in the Watergate revelations.

Watergate Reporting of the Nixon administration scandal.

investigative reporting Enterprise reporting that reveals new information, often startling; most often these are stories that official sources would rather not have told.

LEARNING CHECK

- All reporting results from inquiry. What sets investigative reporting apart?
- List five examples of investigative reporting that have affected history.

Soft News

In contrast to hard investigative reporting came a simultaneous trend toward **soft news**. This included consumer-help stories, lifestyle tips, entertainment news, and offbeat "gee-whiz" items often of a sensational sort. The celebrity-oriented *National Enquirer*,

soft news Geared to satisfying an audience's information wants, not needs.

whose circulation skyrocketed in the 1960s, was the progenitor of this trend. *Time Life* launched *People* magazine. The staid *New York Times* created *Us*. Newspaper research found that readers liked soft stuff. Soon, many dailies added "People" columns. The television show *Entertainment Tonight Canada* focuses on glamour and glitz, usually as a follow-up to the evening news on many Global stations.

LEARNING CHECK

- In what divergent directions is news moving today?

War Zones: Combat Reporting

Explore

Media People: Kimberly Dozier

STUDY PREVIEW The need in a democracy for people to be informed doesn't square easily with military necessity in time of war. The United States has tried a wide range of policies for war coverage. The latest—embedded reporters in the Iraq War—generally worked well from the military, media, and public perspectives. All historic media–government arrangements for war coverage, however, raise the looming question of how global media serving international audiences can be faithful both to truth and to competing national causes.

Watch

ABC's *Nightline*: "Editorial Decisions Regarding Violent Images"

War is a danger zone for journalists. The Committee to Protect Journalists, which tracks reporters in peril, tallied 54 reporters killed doing their work in 2004—23 in Iraq alone—compared to 13 in 2003. In addition, 22 journalists were kidnapped in Iraq.

Early Lessons

The struggle to find ways for journalists to report from the battlefield without getting in the way or jeopardizing operations is not recent.

In World War II, correspondents wore uniforms with the rank of captain and usually had a driver and a Jeep. The reporters generated a lot of field coverage, but the reporting, reflecting the highly patriotic spirit of the times, as evidenced by the reporters' actually wearing military uniforms, was hardly dispassionate and sometimes propagandist.

Vietnam Reporting

rice-roots reporting Uncensored field reporting from the Vietnam War.

Reporters had great freedom in reporting the Vietnam War in the 1960s and 1970s. Almost at will, reporters could link up with South Vietnamese or American units and go on patrols. The result, dubbed **rice-roots reporting**, included many negative stories on what was, in fact, an unsuccessful military campaign that was unpopular among many troops and a growing majority at home. For the first time, the reporting was filmed for television, with gruesome footage being pumped by the networks into living rooms across the United States on the evening news, deepening opposition to the war.

Commanders didn't like negative reports, which some blamed for losing the public's support for the war. In the end, demoralized, the United States withdrew in defeat—the first war it had lost in its history. For the next wars, which were relatively quick incursions, the Pentagon had new rules. In 1983, when the United States took over the Caribbean nation of Grenada, a naval blockade kept reporters out. The war, planned in secret, surprised the news media. Scrambling to get on top of the story but barred from the action, enterprising reporters hired small boats to run the blockade but were intercepted.

Pool System

pool system Reporters chosen on a rotating basis to cover an event to which access is limited.

Major newspapers, the networks, and news agencies protested loudly at being excluded. Acknowledging that the policy had ridden roughshod over the democratic principles on which the nation was founded, with an informed electorate essential for the system to work, the Pentagon agreed to sit down with news media leaders to devise new ground rules. The result was a **pool system**, in which a corps of reporters would be on call on a rotating basis to be shuttled to combat areas on short notice for the next quick war.

In 1989, when U.S. forces invaded Panama to capture dictator Manuel Noriega on drug charges, the Pentagon activated the pool system and took reporters along. Top military commanders, however, still smarting from their Vietnam experience and blaming the news media, carefully controlled the reporters and their access to information. Army drivers took reporters only to secure areas. For a while reporters were locked in a windowless building and received only the information that the U.S. Army fed them. When the military had accomplished its mission, news organizations again protested. Plainly, the Pentagon had failed to find a system that met both military necessity and democratic principles.

LEARNING CHECK

- **Would news audiences today have problems with a policy to put journalists in military uniforms?**
- **What are the advantages and disadvantages of reporter pools?**

Embedded Reporters

The Iraq War was covered by journalists like no other. The U.S. government, after flip-flopping on rules for war correspondents for 50 years, seemed to recognize the futility of trying to manipulate information in the digital age. Months before the invasion of Iraq, the Pentagon chief for media relations, Victoria Clarke, invited news organizations to send reporters to special combat mini-courses to get up to speed—and also into physical shape—to go to war with combat units. These reporters would be embedded in the units to cover combat for the duration of the hostilities. The reporters, called **embeds**, would need to supply their own equipment, including vehicles, but would be free to tell the story of the war as they saw it. Commanders were told to let the cameras roll whenever the journalists wanted.

embeds An Iraq War term for reporters who accompany, or are embedded with, U.S. military combat units.

The ground rules were few. Among them was not to disclose unit positions, lest the enemy be tipped off to locations. Also, the Pentagon warned that it might need to black out reports for "operational security, success of the mission, and the safety of the people involved."

News organizations sent hundreds of reporters to Pentagon boot camps. Time Warner set aside $30 million to cover the war and dispatched Eason Jordan, CNN's chief news executive, to the Middle East to buy a fleet of Humvees to haul crews and their equipment, including satellite uplink dishes, into combat.

How well did the embedded reporter system work?

The Pentagon was pleased. Yes, the embeds showed the ugliness of war, as well as gaffes. But the invasion went well for the United States and its allies, and the Pentagon concluded that the coverage, perceived by the public as honest and independent, contributed to public enthusiasm for the war during the initial combat phase. The news media were pleased, too, remembering that only 10 years earlier, during the Gulf War, reporters were kept away from combat and had access only to the information fed to them at headquarters briefings.

Critics said that the embeds were too limited in their perspective and lacked an overview, and that, losing their objectivity, they picked up the gung-ho spirit of the units to which they were assigned. However, this criticism missed the fact that reporters were in regular contact with editors and producers in their home newsrooms, as well as in field newsrooms, who fed them information from other sources. Also, reports from the embeds were integrated into newscasts and stories that presented a broad picture.

Could the embedded system work better? The late Walter Cronkite, whose war reporting experience went back to World War II, noted that embeds, almost all embedded with frontline units, missed details in the haste of moving forward. He suggested that reporters be assigned to follow up, verify information, and ask questions that frontline embeds didn't have time to pursue.

Another challenge faces embedded journalists: surviving. Sadly, sometimes journalists become casualties of war. Michelle Lang, a reporter for the *Calgary Herald*, was killed while reporting from the Middle East in late 2009. She was Canada's first journalist killed in Afghanistan. Lang and four Canadian soldiers were killed by an improvised explosive device (IED). She was posthumously awarded the Canadian World Press Freedom Award. David Gollob, president of the Canadian Committee for World Press Freedom, said, "Michelle Lang paid the ultimate price for her craft. One of the greatest risks a Canadian journalist faces is not reporting or investigating news in this country, but stepping into harm's way to send the story back home."

Whatever the critics say, embedded journalism in times of war is likely here to stay. While CBC News did not allow its journalists to embed, Tony Burman, editor-in-chief of CBC News, said, "The introduction of technology, the video phone, the satellite phone, the incredible ease to satellite feeds, pictures, sound reports and obviously the whole embedding experience, the whole notion that you can, in fact, get live pictures from the front, is quite unprecedented." The president of CTV News, Robert G. Hurst, says that in the future we may see battles live on TV and journalists embedded on both sides of a conflict. Bill Schiller, formerly the foreign editor for the *Toronto Star*, says that would not be in the best interests of journalism. He says that embedded journalists do no more than serve the interests of the status quo; in the case of the Iraq War, that would be the Pentagon. Says Schiller, "Editorial independence is everything. It's fundamental to what we do, no matter how good the pictures are."

LEARNING CHECK

- Have embedded reporters given you a clearer feel for what's happening in the Iraq War?
- Does embedding as a policy resolve the vexing issue of how an independent news media can cover combat without jeopardizing military tactics?
- As a reporter in a Baghdad news bureau, would you volunteer for embed missions? Explain.

Chapter 10 Wrap-Up

Watch

***A Day in the Life:* Newsvine**

Journalism is an art, not a science. Judgments, rather than formulas, determine which events and issues are reported and how—and no two journalists approach any story in exactly the same way. This leaves the whole process of gathering and telling news subject to second-guessing and criticism. Journalists ask themselves all the time whether there are ways to do a better job. All journalists can do is try to find truth and to relate it accurately. Even then, the complexity of modern news gathering—which involves many people, each with an opportunity to change or even kill a story—includes dozens of points at which inaccuracy and imprecision can creep into a story that started out well.

PEARSON mycanadiancommunicationlab

Visit **www.mycanadiancommunicationlab.ca** for access to a wealth of tools and resources that will enhance your learning experience. Features include the following:

- Personalized Study Plan
- Videos
- Activities
- Pearson eText–and much more!

Questions for Critical Thinking

1. What contemporary news practices are rooted in the major periods in U.S. and Canadian journalism history?
2. What variables about news gathering and news packaging are beyond the control of reporters and even editors but nonetheless affect what people read, hear, and see?
3. What pressures from outside the media affect news reporting?
4. What are good arguments for and against news reporters becoming embeds?
5. Trends in news reporting are going in divergent directions. Why? Evaluate these trends and their long-term prospects.

Keeping Up to Date

Among publications that keep current on journalistic issues are *Columbia Journalism Review*, *Quill*, *American Journalism Review*, and *Editor & Publisher*.

Bridging the gap between scholarly and professional work is *Newspaper Research Journal*.

11 Public Relations

LEARNING AHEAD

- Public relations grew out of public disfavour with big business.
- Public relations is an important management tool.
- Public relations includes promotion, publicity, lobbying, fundraising, and crisis management.
- Advertising and public relations are distinctive undertakings.
- Public relations usually involves a candid, proactive relationship with mass media.
- Public relations organizations are working to improve the image of their craft.

Michael J. Fox Special-interest groups can personify their messages and broaden their appeals through celebrity support for the cause. Canada's Michael J. Fox not only drew support for funding of stem cell research, but also drew more people in to the debate.

MEDIA IN THEORY

Dialogic Public Relations

dialogic theory Dialogue-based approach to negotiating relationships.

Among scholars, enthusiasm has developed for applying **dialogic theory** for a kinder, gentler practice of public relations. Advocates draw on the concept of genuine dialogue, which is deeply rooted in philosophy, psychology, rhetoric, and relational communication. Rather than focusing on communication to publics, as in the traditional public relations model, dialogic theory insists on genuine listening in a true exchange. The theoretical shift is from managing communication to using communication as a tool for negotiating relationships without any manipulative or Machiavellian tricks.

Scholars Michael Kent and Maureen Taylor have summarized five major features of dialogic theory in operation.

- **Mutuality.** A corporation or other institution engaged in public relations must recognize a responsibility to engage in communication on an even playing field. This means not taking advantage of financial might to talk down or push ideas without also listening.
- **Propinquity.** For communication to be genuine, interaction with publics must be spontaneous.
- **Empathy.** The institution must have a sincere sympathy in supporting and confirming public goals and interests.
- **Risk.** Dialogic theory can work only if there is a willingness to interact with individuals and publics on their own terms.
- **Commitment.** An institution must be willing to work at understanding its interactions with publics. This means that significant resources must be allocated not only to the dialogue but also to interpretation and understanding.

Dialogic theory offers a framework for a highly ethical form of public relations, but it is not without difficulties. As Kent and Taylor have noted, institutions have many publics, which makes dialogue a complex process. Participants in dialogic public relations put themselves in jeopardy. When publics engage in dialogue with organizations, they run the risk that their disclosures will be used to exploit or manipulate them.

Even so, discussion about dialogic theory is sensitizing many people in public relations to honesty and openness as ideals in the democratic tradition of giving voice to all. The theory is based on principles of honesty, trust, and positive regard for the other rather than simply a conception of the public as a means to an end.

Importance of Public Relations

STUDY PREVIEW Public relations is a persuasive communication tool that people can use to motivate other people and institutions to help them achieve their goals.

Defining Public Relations

Edward Bernays, the public relations pioneer, lamented how loosely the term *public relations* is used. To illustrate his concern, Bernays told about a young woman who approached him for career advice. He asked her what she did for a living. "I'm in public relations," she said. He pressed her for details and she explained that she handed out circulars in Harvard Square. Bernays was dismayed at how casually people regard the work of public relations. In reality, public relations is multi-layered. Terence Flynn, Fran Gregory, and Jean Valin of the Canadian Public Relations Society (CPRS) say that public relations is "the strategic management of relationships between an organization and its diverse publics, through the use of communication, to achieve mutual understanding, realize organizational goals, and serve the public interest."

Four steps are necessary for public relations to accomplish its goals.

Identify Existing Relationships In modern society, institutions have many relationships. A college, for example, has relationships with its students, its faculty, its staff, its alumni, its benefactors, the neighbourhood, the community, the legislature, other colleges, accreditors of its programs, and perhaps unions. The list could go on and on. Each of these constituencies is called a public—hence the term *public relations.*

MEDIA TIMELINE Public Relations

1859 Charles Darwin advanced survival-of-the-fittest theory, which led to social Darwinism.

1880s Public became dissatisfied with unconscionable business practices justified by social Darwinism.

1906 Ivy Lee began the first public relations agency.

1917 George Creel headed a federal agency that generated support for World War I.

1927 Arthur W. Page became the first corporate public relations vice-president.

1930s Paul Garrett created the term *enlightened self-interest* at General Motors.

1942 Elmer Davis headed a federal agency that generated support for World War II.

1947 Public Relations Society of America (PRSA) was formed.

1951 PRSA adopted Professional Standards for the Practice of Public Relations, a forerunner to the current Code of Ethics.

1953 The Canadian Public Relations Society (CPRS) was formed.

1965 PRSA created an accreditation system.

1969 CPRS introduced a voluntary accreditation program.

1970s Herb Schmertz pioneered adversarial public relations at Mobil Oil.

2000 PRSA revised its Code of Ethics.

2002 Some advertising and public relations agencies merged to broaden client services.

2006 Dialogic theory emerged in public relations.

2007 CPRS developed social media guidelines for social media use and public relations.

Evaluate the Relationships Through research, the public relations practitioner studies these relationships to determine how well they are working. This evaluation is an ongoing process. A college may have excellent relations with the legislature one year and win major appropriations, but after a scandal related to the president's budget the next year, legislators may be downright unfriendly.

Paul Garrett Devised the notion of enlightened self-interest.

Design Policies to Improve the Relationships The job of public relations people is to recommend policies to top management to make these relationships work better, not only for the organization but also for the partners in each relationship. **Paul Garrett**, a pioneer in corporate relations, found that General Motors (GM) was seen in unfriendly terms during the Great Depression, which put the giant automaker at risk with many publics, including its own employees. GM, Garrett advised, needed new policies to seem neighbourly rather than like a far-removed, impersonal, monolithic industrial giant.

enlightened self-interest Mutually beneficial public relations.

Implement the Policies Garrett used the term **enlightened self-interest** for his series of policies intended to downsize GM in the eyes of many of the company's publics. Garrett set up municipal programs in towns with GM plants and grants for schools and scholarships for employees' children. GM benefited from a revised image and, in the spirit of enlightened self-interest, so did GM employees, their children, and their communities.

LEARNING CHECK

- What does it mean to describe public relations as a management function?
- What did Paul Garrett mean by the term *enlightened self-interest?*

Explore

Deepening Your Media Literacy: Do press releases serve the public?

The Value of Public Relations

Misconceptions about public relations include the idea that it is a one-way street for institutions and individuals to communicate to the public. Actually, the good practice of public relations seeks two-way communication between and among all people and institutions concerned with an issue.

Terry Flynn, past president of the CPRS and professor and director of the Master of Communication Management degree program at the DeGroote School of Business at McMaster University, says that public relations is not just a process, but a product. This product has value. According to Flynn, this value "can be economic, social or relational. It can be measured in currency, reputation or loyalty. It can be converted into goodwill, repeated purchases, and increased visibility and emotional appeal. For organizational leaders, value is realized when the organization achieves its stated goals and objectives."

LEARNING CHECK

- Draw on your knowledge and experience for examples of public relations having value in a society.

Explore

Media People: Paul Garrett

Origins of Public Relations

STUDY PREVIEW Many big companies found themselves in disfavour in the late 1800s for ignoring the public good to make profits. Feeling misunderstood, some moguls of industry turned to Ivy Lee, the founder of modern public relations, for counsel on gaining public support.

Moguls in Trouble

William Henry Vanderbilt Embodied the bad corporate images of the 1880s and 1890s with "The public be damned."

Nobody would be tempted to think of **William Henry Vanderbilt** as being very good at public relations. In 1882 it was Vanderbilt, president of the New York Central Railroad, who said, "The public be damned," when asked about the effect of changing train schedules. Vanderbilt's utterance so infuriated people that it became a banner in the populist crusade against robber barons and tycoons in the late 1800s. Under populist pressure, state governments set up agencies to regulate railroads. Then the federal government established the Interstate Commerce Commission to control freight and passenger rates.

Government began insisting on safety standards. Labour unions formed in the industries with the worst working conditions, safety records, and pay. Journalists added pressure with muckraking exposés on excesses in the railroad, coal, and oil trusts; on meat-packing industry frauds; and on patent medicines.

The leaders of industry were slow to recognize the effect of populist objections on their practices. They were comfortable with **social Darwinism**, an adaptation of **Charles Darwin's** survival-of-the-fittest theory. In fact, they thought themselves forward-thinking in applying Darwin's theory to business and social issues. It had been only a few decades earlier, in 1859, that Darwin laid out his biological theory in *On the Origin of Species by Means of Natural Selection*. To cushion the harshness of social Darwinism, many tycoons espoused paternalism toward those whose "fitness" had not brought them fortune and power. No matter how carefully put, paternalism seemed arrogant to the "less fit."

social Darwinism Application of Darwin's survival-of-the-fittest theory to society.

Charles Darwin Devised survival-of-the-fittest theory.

George Baer, a railroad president, epitomized both social Darwinism and paternalism in commenting on a labour strike: "The rights and interests of the laboring man will be protected and cared for not by labor agitators but by the Christian men to whom God in His infinite wisdom has given the control of the property interests of the country." Baer was quoted widely, further fuelling sentiment against big business. Baer may have been sincere, but his position was read as a cover for excessive business practices by barons who assumed superiority over everyone else.

George Baer Epitomized offensive corporate paternalism in the 1890s.

Meanwhile, social Darwinism came under attack as circuitous reasoning: Economic success accomplished by abusive practices could be used to justify further abusive practices, which would lead to further success. Social Darwinism was a dog-eat-dog outlook that hardly jibed with democratic ideals, especially not as described in the preamble to the U.S. Constitution, which sought to "promote the general welfare, and secure the blessings of liberty" for everyone—not for only the chosen "fittest." Into these tensions at the turn of the century came public relations pioneer Ivy Lee.

LEARNING CHECK

- **How was social Darwinism appealing to religious people who found themselves with massive wealth while others suffered at their expense?**

The Ideas of Ivy Lee

Coal mine operators, like railroad magnates, were held in the public's contempt at the start of the 20th century. Obsessed with profits and caring little about public sentiment or even the well-being of their employees, mine operators were vulnerable in the new populist wave. Mine workers organized and 150 000 in Pennsylvania went out on strike in 1902, shutting down the anthracite industry and disrupting coal-dependent industries, including the railroads. The mine operators snubbed reporters, which probably contributed to a pro-union slant in many news stories and worsened the operators' public image. Not until six months into the strike, when President Theodore Roosevelt threatened to take over the mines with U.S. Army troops, did the operators settle.

Shaken finally by Roosevelt's threat and recognizing the president's responsiveness to public opinion, the mine operators began to reconsider how they went about their business. In 1906, with another strike looming, one operator heard about **Ivy Lee**, a young publicist in New York who had new ideas about winning public support. He was hired. In a turnabout in press relations, Lee issued a news release that announced: "The anthracite coal operators, realizing the general public interest in conditions in the mining regions, have arranged to supply the press with all possible information." Then followed a series of releases with information attributed to the mine operators by name—the same people who earlier had preferred anonymity and refused all interview requests. There were no more secret strike-strategy meetings. When operators planned a meeting, reporters covering the impending strike were informed. Although reporters were not admitted into the meetings, summaries of the proceedings were given to them immediately afterward. This relative openness eased long-standing hostility toward the operators, and a strike was averted.

Ivy Lee Laid out fundamentals of public relations.

Lee's success with the mine operators began a career that rewrote the rules on how corporations deal with their various publics. The following are among his accomplishments.

Ludlow Massacre Colorado militiamen, called in to augment company guards, opened fire during a 1914 mine labour dispute and killed women and children. Overnight, John D. Rockefeller Jr. became the object of public hatred. A Rockefeller company owned the mine and, even in New York, where Rockefeller lived, there were rallies demanding his head. Public relations pioneer Ivy Lee advised Rockefeller to tour the Ludlow area as soon as tempers cooled to show his sincere concern and to begin work on a labour contract to meet the concerns of miners. Rockefeller ended up a popular character in the Colorado mining camps.

Ivy Lee

Institutional Openness Railroads had notoriously secretive policies, not only about their business practices but also about accidents. When the Pennsylvania Railroad sought Ivy Lee's counsel, he advised against suppressing news, especially on things that inevitably would leak out anyway. When a train jumped the rails near Gap, Pennsylvania, Lee arranged for a special car to take reporters to the scene and even take pictures. The Pennsylvania line was applauded in the press for the openness, and coverage of the railroad, which had been negative for years, began to change. A "bad press" continued to plague other railroads that persisted in their secretive tradition.

Finding Upbeat Angles When the U.S. Senate proposed investigating International Harvester for monopolistic practices, Lee advised the giant farm implement manufacturer against reflexive obstructionism and silence. A statement went out announcing that the company, confident in its business practices, not only welcomed but also would facilitate an investigation. Then began a campaign that pointed out International Harvester's beneficence toward its employees. The campaign also emphasized other upbeat information about the company.

John D. Rockefeller Jr. Ivy Lee client who had been the target of public hatred.

Giving Organizations a Face In 1914, when workers at a Colorado mine went on strike, company guards fired machine guns and killed several men. More battling followed, during which 2 women and 11 children were killed. It was called the Ludlow Massacre, and **John D. Rockefeller Jr.**, the chief mine owner, was pilloried for what had happened. Rockefeller was an easy target. Like his father, widely despised for the earlier Standard Oil monopolistic practices, John Jr. tried to keep himself out of the spotlight, but suddenly mobs were protesting at his mansion in New York and calling out, "Shoot him down like a dog." Rockefeller asked Ivy Lee what he should do. Lee began whipping up articles about Rockefeller's human side, his family, and his generosity. Then, on Lee's advice, Rockefeller announced that he would visit Colorado to see the conditions there himself. He spent two weeks talking with miners both at work and in their homes and meeting their families. It was a news story that reporters could not resist, and it unveiled Rockefeller as a human being, not a far-removed, callous captain of industry. A myth-shattering episode occurred one evening when Rockefeller, after a brief address to miners and their wives, suggested that the floor be cleared for a dance. Before it was all over, John D. Rockefeller Jr. had danced with almost every miner's wife, and the news stories about the evening did a great deal to mitigate antagonism and distrust toward him.

P.T. Barnum Known for exaggerated promotion.

puffery Inflated claims.

Straight Talk Ivy Lee came on the scene at a time when many organizations were making extravagant claims about themselves and their products. Circus promoter **P.T. Barnum** made this kind of **puffery** a fine art in the late 1800s, and he had many imitators. It was an age of puffed-up advertising claims and fluffy rhetoric. Lee noted, however, that people soon saw through hyperbolic boasts and lost faith in those who made them. In launching his public relations agency in 1906, Lee vowed to be accurate in everything he said and to provide whatever verification anyone requested. This became part of the creed of good practice in public relations, and it remains so today.

LEARNING CHECK

- How did public relations pioneer Ivy Lee help to revolutionize the way that business conducted itself in the early 1900s?
- What are the enduring pillars of Ivy Lee's concept of good business practice?

Public Relations Services

STUDY PREVIEW Public relations deals with publicity and promotion, but it also involves less visible activities. These include lobbying, fundraising, and crisis management. Public relations is distinct from advertising.

Explore

Media People: Leslie Unger

How Public Relations Is Organized

No two institutions are organized in precisely the same way. At GM, 200 people work in public relations. In smaller organizations, public relations may be one of several hats worn by a single person. Except in the smallest operations, the public relations department usually has three functional areas of responsibility:

External Relations **External public relations** involves communication with groups and people outside the organization, including customers, dealers, suppliers, and community leaders.

external public relations Gearing messages to outside organizations, constituencies, and individuals.

Internal Relations **Internal public relations** involves developing optimal relations with employees, managers, unions, shareholders, and other internal groups. In-house newsletters, magazines, and brochures are important media for communicating with organizations' internal audiences.

internal public relations Gearing messages to inside groups, constituencies, and individuals.

Media Relations Communication with large groups of people outside an organization is practicable only through the mass media. An organization's coordinator of **media relations** responds to news media queries, arranges news conferences, and issues news releases. These coordinators coach executives for news interviews and sometimes serve as their organization's spokesperson.

media relations Using mass media to convey messages.

LEARNING CHECK

- Would you classify media relations more as an external or an internal public relations function?

Public Relations Agencies

Even though many organizations have their own public relations staff, they may go to **public relations agencies** for help on specific projects or problems. Hundreds of companies specialize in public relations counsel and related services.

public relations agencies Companies that provide public relations services.

The biggest agencies offer a full range of services on a global scale. Hill & Knowlton has offices in Cleveland (its original home), Dallas, Frankfurt, Geneva, London, Los Angeles, New York (now its headquarters), Paris, Rome, Seattle, Toronto, and Washington, DC. It will take on projects anywhere in the world, either on its own or by working with local agencies.

Some agencies bill clients only for services rendered. Others charge clients just to be on call. Agency expenses for specific projects are billed in addition. Staff time usually is charged at an hourly rate that covers the agency's overhead and allows a profit margin. Other expenses are usually billed with a 15 to 17 percent markup.

LEARNING CHECK

- When does an organization with its own public relations operation also need to hire an outside public relations agency?

Publicity and Promotion

publicity Brings public attention to something.

promotion Promoting a cause or idea.

Full-service public relations agencies provide a wide range of services built on two of the cornerstones of the business: **publicity** and **promotion.** These agencies are ready to conduct media campaigns to rally support for a cause, create an image, or turn a problem into an asset. Publicity and promotion, however, are only the most visible services offered by public relations agencies. Others include the following.

lobbyists Influence public policy, usually legislation or regulations.

Lobbying Every province in Canada has hundreds of public relations practitioners whose specialty is representing their clients to legislative bodies and government agencies. In one sense, **lobbyists** are expediters. They know local traditions and customs and they know who is in a position to affect policy. Lobbyists advise their clients, which include trade associations, corporations, public interest groups, and regulated utilities and industries, on how to achieve their goals by working with legislators and government regulators. Many lobbyists call themselves "government relations specialists."

LEARNING CHECK

- Why does lobbying have a bad name? Is it deserved or undeserved?

political communication Advising candidates and groups on public policy issues, usually during elections.

Political Communication Every provincial capital has political consultants whose work is mostly advising candidates for public office in **political communication.** Services include campaign management, survey research, publicity, media relations, and image consulting. Political consultants also work on elections, referendums, recalls, and other public policy issues.

LEARNING CHECK

- Is it naive to think that a candidate for office can succeed without political consultants?

image consulting Coaching individuals for media contacts.

Image Consulting **Image consulting** has been a growing specialized branch of public relations since the 1970s. Jacqueline Thompson, author of *Directory of Personal Image Consultants*, listed 53 entries in 1981 and has been adding up to 157 new entries a year since then. About these consultants, Thompson says: "They will lower the pitch of your voice, remove your accent, correct your 'body language,' modify your unacceptable behavior, eliminate your negative self-perception, select your wardrobe, restyle your hair, and teach you how to speak off the cuff or read a speech without putting your audience to sleep."

LEARNING CHECK

- What would Ivy Lee think of image consulting for top executives?

Financial Public Relations Financial public relations dates to the 1920s and 1930s, when the U.S. Securities and Exchange Commission cracked down on abuses in the financial industry. Regulations on promoting sales of securities are complex. It is the job of people in financial public relations to know not only the principles of public relations but also the complex regulations governing the promotion of securities in corporate mergers, acquisitions, new issues, and stock splits.

Fundraising Some public relations people specialize in fundraising and membership drives. Many colleges and universities, for example, have their own staffs to perform these functions. Others look to fundraising firms to manage capital drives. Such an agency employs a variety of techniques, from mass mailings to telephone soliciting, and charges a percentage of the amount raised.

contingency planning Developing programs in advance of an unscheduled but anticipated event.

crisis management Helping a client through an emergency.

Contingency Planning Many organizations rely on public relations people to design programs to address problems that can be expected to occur, known as **contingency planning.** Airlines, for example, need detailed plans for handling inevitable plane crashes—situations that require quick and appropriate responses under tremendous pressure. When a crisis occurs, an organization can turn to public relations people for advice on dealing with it. Some agencies specialize in **crisis management**, which involves picking up the pieces either when a contingency plan fails or when there was no plan to deal with a crisis.

LEARNING CHECK

- If you were hired by an airline to design a contingency plan for an eventual inevitability of an accident, what would you lay out?

Polling Public-opinion sampling is essential in many public relations projects. Full-service agencies can either conduct surveys themselves or contract with companies that specialize in surveying.

Events Coordination Many public relations people are involved in coordinating a broad range of events, including product announcements, news conferences, and convention planning. Some in-house public relations departments and agencies have their own artistic and audiovisual production talent to produce brochures and other promotional materials. Other agencies contract for these services.

Public Relations and Advertising

STUDY PREVIEW Although public relations and advertising both involve crafting media messages for mass audiences, public relations is involved in creating policy. Advertising is not. Even so, there has been a recent blending of the functions, some under the umbrella concept of integrated marketing.

Different Functions

Both public relations and advertising involve persuasion through the mass media, but most of the similarities end there.

Management Function Public relations people help to shape an organization's policy. This is a management activity, ideally with the organization's chief public relations person offering counsel to other key policymakers at the vice-presidential level. Advertising, in contrast, is not a management function. The work of advertising is much narrower. It focuses on developing persuasive messages, mostly to sell products or services, after all management decisions have been made.

Measuring Success Public relations "sells" points of view and images. These are intangibles and therefore are hard to measure. In advertising, success is measurable with tangibles, such as sales, that can be calculated from the bottom line.

Control of Messages When an organization decides that it needs a persuasive campaign, there is a choice between public relations and advertising. One advantage of advertising is that the organization controls the message. By buying space or time in the mass media, an organization has the final say on the content of its advertising messages. In public relations, by contrast, an organization tries to influence the media to tell its story a certain way, but the message that actually goes out is up to the media. For example, a news reporter may lean heavily on a public relations person for information about an organization, but the reporter also may gather information from other sources. In the end, it is the reporter who writes the story. The upside of this is that the message, coming from a journalist, has a credibility with the mass audience that advertisements do not. Advertisements are patently self-serving. The downside of leaving it to the media to create the messages that reach the audience is surrendering control over the messages that go to the public.

LEARNING CHECK

- What are the similarities and differences of advertising and public relations?

Integrated Marketing

For many persuasive campaigns, organizations use both public relations and advertising. Increasingly, public relations and advertising people find themselves working together. This is especially true in corporations that have adopted **integrated marketing communication** (IMC), which attempts to coordinate advertising as a marketing tool

integrated marketing communication (IMC) Comprehensive program that links public relations and advertising.

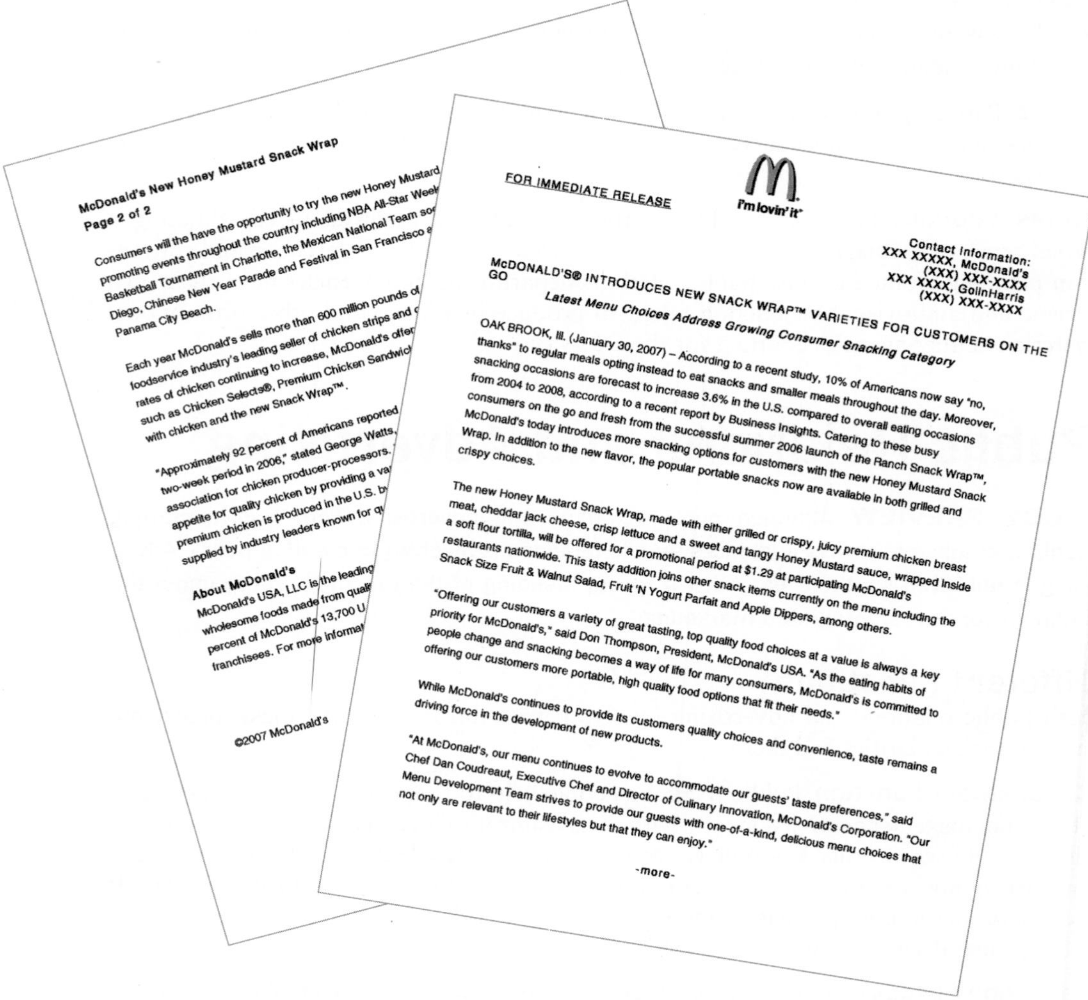

McDonald's New Honey Mustard Snack Wrap
Page 2 of 2

Consumers will the have the opportunity to try the new Honey Mustard
promoting events throughout the country including NBA All-Star Week
Basketball Tournament in Charlotte, the Mexican National Team so
Diego, Chinese New Year Parade and Festival in San Francisco a
Panama City Beach.

Each year McDonald's sells more than 600 million pounds of
foodservice industry's leading seller of chicken strips and c
rates of chicken continuing to increase, McDonald's offer
such as Chicken Selects®, Premium Chicken Sandwic
with chicken and the new Snack Wrap™.

"Approximately 92 percent of Americans reported
two-week period in 2006," stated George Watts,
association for chicken producer-processors.
appetite for quality chicken by providing a va
premium chicken is produced in the U.S. b
supplied by industry leaders known for q

About McDonald's
McDonald's USA, LLC is the leading
wholesome foods made from qual
percent of McDonald's 13,700 U
franchisees. For more informat

©2007 McDonald's

FOR IMMEDIATE RELEASE

i'm lovin' it

Contact Information:
XXX XXXXX, McDonald's
(XXX) XXX-XXXX
XXX XXXX, GolinHarris
(XXX) XXX-XXXX

McDONALD'S® INTRODUCES NEW SNACK WRAP™ VARIETIES FOR CUSTOMERS ON THE GO

Latest Menu Choices Address Growing Consumer Snacking Category

OAK BROOK, Ill. (January 30, 2007) – According to a recent study, 10% of Americans now say "no, thanks" to regular meals opting instead to eat snacks and smaller meals throughout the day. Moreover, snacking occasions are forecast to increase 3.6% in the U.S. compared to overall eating occasions from 2004 to 2008, according to a recent report by Business Insights. Catering to these busy consumers on the go and fresh from the successful summer 2006 launch of the Ranch Snack Wrap™, McDonald's today introduces more snacking options for customers with the new Honey Mustard Snack Wrap. In addition to the new flavor, the popular portable snacks now are available in both grilled and crispy choices.

The new Honey Mustard Snack Wrap, made with either grilled or crispy, juicy premium chicken breast meat, cheddar jack cheese, crisp lettuce and a sweet and tangy Honey Mustard sauce, wrapped inside a soft flour tortilla, will be offered for a promotional period at $1.29 at participating McDonald's restaurants nationwide. This tasty addition joins other snack items currently on the menu including the Snack Size Fruit & Walnut Salad, Fruit 'N Yogurt Parfait and Apple Dippers, among others.

"Offering our customers a variety of great tasting, top quality food choices at a value is always a key priority for McDonald's," said Don Thompson, President, McDonald's USA. "As the eating habits of people change and snacking becomes a way of life for many consumers, McDonald's is committed to offering our customers more portable, high quality food options that fit their needs."

While McDonald's continues to provide its customers quality choices and convenience, taste remains a driving force in the development of new products.

"At McDonald's, our menu continues to evolve to accommodate our guests' taste preferences," said Chef Dan Coudreaut, Executive Chef and Director of Culinary Innovation, McDonald's Corporation. "Our Menu Development Team strives to provide our guests with one-of-a-kind, delicious menu choices that not only are relevant to their lifestyles but that they can enjoy."

-more-

News Release The workhorse of media relations is the news release. Studies have found that as many as 90 percent of news stories rely to some extent on information in news releases. Some releases even are reported verbatim, particularly in small-market, low-budget newsrooms.

with promotion and publicity of the sort that public relations experts can provide. Several major advertising agencies, aware of their clients' shift to integrated marketing, have acquired or established public relations subsidiaries to provide a wider range of services under their roof.

This overlap has prompted some advertising agencies to move more into public relations. The WWP Group of London, a global advertising agency, has acquired both Hill & Knowlton, the third-largest public relations company in the United States, and Ogilvy PR Worldwide, the ninth largest. The Young & Rubicam advertising agency has three public relations subsidiaries: Burson-Marsteller, the largest; Cohn & Wolf, the thirteenth largest; and Creswell, Munsell, Fultz & Zirbel, the fiftieth largest. These are giant enterprises that reflect the conglomeration and globalization of both advertising and public relations.

To describe IMC, media critic James Ledbetter suggests thinking of the old Charlie the Tuna ads, in which a cartoon fish made you chuckle and identify with the product—and established a brand name. That's not good enough for IMC. "By contrast," Ledbetter says, "IMC encourages tuna buyers to think about all aspects of the product. If polls find that consumers are worried about dolphins caught in tuna nets, then you might stick a big 'Dolphin Safe' label on the tins and set up a website featuring interviews with tuna fishermen." The new wave of IMC, according to one of its primary texts, is "respectful, not patronizing; dialogue-seeking, not monologuic; responsive, not formula-driven. It speaks to the highest point of common interest—not the lowest common denominator."

Public relations and advertising crossovers are hardly new. One area of traditional overlap is **institutional advertising**, which involves producing ads to promote an image rather than a product. The fuzzy, feel-good ads of agricultural conglomerate Archer Daniels Midland, which pepper Sunday morning U.S. network television, are typical.

institutional advertising Paid space and time to promote an institution's image and position.

LEARNING CHECK

- **Interagency competition among advertising agencies has blurred some distinctions between public relations and advertising. How so, and why?**

Media Relations

STUDY PREVIEW Public relations people generally favour candour in working with the news media. Even so, some organizations opt to stonewall journalistic inquiries. An emerging school of thought in public relations is to challenge negative news coverage aggressively and publicly.

Open Media Relations

The common wisdom among public relations people today is to be open and candid with the mass media. It is a principle that dates back to Ivy Lee, and case studies abound to confirm its effectiveness. A classic case study on this point is the Tylenol crisis.

Johnson & Johnson had spent many years and millions of dollars to inspire public confidence in its painkiller Tylenol. By 1982, the product was the leader in a crowded field of headache remedies, with 36 percent of the market. Then disaster struck. Seven people in Chicago died after taking Tylenol capsules laced with cyanide. James Burke, president of Johnson & Johnson, and Lawrence Foster, vice-president for public relations, moved quickly. Within hours, Johnson & Johnson had accomplished the following:

- Halted the manufacture and distribution of Tylenol.
- Removed Tylenol products from retailers' shelves.
- Launched a massive advertising campaign requesting people to exchange Tylenol capsules for a safe replacement.
- Summoned 50 public relations employees from Johnson & Johnson and its subsidiary companies to staff a press centre to answer media and consumer questions forthrightly.
- Ordered an internal company investigation of the Tylenol manufacturing and distribution process.
- Promised full co-operation with government investigators.
- Ordered the development of tamper-proof packaging for the reintroduction of Tylenol products after the contamination problem was resolved.

Investigators determined within days that an urban terrorist had poisoned the capsules. Although the news media exonerated Johnson & Johnson of negligence, the company nonetheless had a tremendous problem: how to restore public confidence in Tylenol. Many former Tylenol users were reluctant to take a chance, and the Tylenol share of the analgesic market dropped to 6 percent.

To address the problem, Johnson & Johnson called in the Burson-Marsteller public relations agency. Burson-Marsteller recommended a media campaign to capitalize on the high marks the news media had given the company for openness during the crisis. Mailgrams went out inviting journalists to a 30-city video teleconference to hear James Burke announce the reintroduction of the product. Six hundred reporters turned out, and Johnson & Johnson officials took their questions live.

Sarah Evans of the CPRS says that "this is the classic example in public relations annals of how to deal with a situation. You take immediate action, you worry about people

James Burke

Product-Tampering Crisis When cyanide-laced Tylenol capsules killed seven people in Chicago, the manufacturer, Johnson & Johnson, responded quickly. Company president James Burke immediately pulled the product off retailers' shelves and ordered company publicists to set up a press centre to answer news media inquiries as fully as possible. Burke's actions and candour helped to restore the public's shaken confidence in Tylenol.

first, you provide as much information as you can as fast as you've got it. Did Johnson & Johnson stock suffer? No. Did Tylenol suffer? No."

Proactive Media Relations

For successful crisis management, public relations people need strong, ongoing relationships with their organization's top management. Otherwise, when crisis strikes, public relations people will face delays in rounding up the kind of breaking information they need to deal effectively with the news media.

Crisis Response Although public relations campaigns cannot control what the media say, public relations people can help to shape how news media report issues by taking the initiative. Perhaps using lessons learned by Tylenol in 1982, Maple Leaf Foods' (MLF) handling of the 2008 listeriosis outbreak is an excellent example of **proactive media relations.**

proactive media relations Taking initiative to release information.

During the summer of 2008, 20 Canadians died after eating meat tainted with *Listeria monocytogenes* bacteria. MLF reacted quickly and decisively and took control of disseminating information, which, coupled with full disclosure, headed off false rumours that could have caused further damage to the company. At the time, many Canadians said they would never buy MLF products again.

A principle in crisis management is to seize leadership on the story. This involves anticipating what journalists will want to know and providing it to them before they have time to formulate their questions. Ivy Lee did this time and again, Johnson & Johnson did it in 1982, and **Michael McCain,** CEO of Maple Leaf Foods, did it in 2008. Not only did McCain make himself available to the media, but he accepted responsibility for the outbreak of listeriosis. The message was clear and was communicated using both traditional media and YouTube. McCain became the face not only of MLF but of the company's concern for its customers.

Michael McCain CEO of Maple Leaf Foods.

Sylvain Charlebois, from the Kenneth Levine Graduate School of Business at the University of Regina, says that McCain and MLF "demonstrated that corporate leadership can prevail in trying times. McCain speedily accepted full responsibility on behalf of his company for the listeriosis outbreak. As CEO, McCain exuded presence, compassion, authenticity and refused to hide behind professionally-groomed spokespersons. There was no doubt regarding his personal integrity during the crisis." Because of how he responded to the crisis, Canadian Press named him CEO of the year in 2008.

CASE STUDY

Crisis Management at *Time*

When *Time*'s cutting-edge journalism brings heat on the magazine, the Time Inc. senior vice-president for corporate communications finds herself trying to set the facts straight from the company's perspective. In her job of handling media relations for the company, Dawn Bridges finds herself frequently put to the test.

In 2005, when *Time*'s editor decided to comply with a federal prosecutor's demand for reporter Matt Cooper's notes in the Valerie Plame spy-outing scandal, everyone clamoured for an explanation. Cooper's notes revealed his confidential source, and people wanted to know how *Time* could break the journalism standard of shielding confidential sources. Reporters were pounding at Dawn Bridges's door for answers.

The crisis was a career challenge for Bridges. Many supporters of the Iraq War shuddered at the possibility that Matt Cooper's notes would place the leak close to President George W. Bush himself. The journalism community was outraged at the notes being handed over. At the same time, many people in the judicial system were pleased, as there was court pressure for the notes.

In addition, there was the drama of *New York Times* reporter Judith Miller gaining heroic martyrdom for refusing to give up notes for her stories on Valerie Plame. Miller had gone to jail in the name of good journalism, so how could *Time* have sold out?

To news reporters, Bridges made her points on behalf of *Time:*

- **Unfair Comparison.** Bridges explained to reporters that critics were taking shortcuts with the facts in equating the Judith Miller and Matt Cooper subpoenas. *The New York Times* was never asked for Judith Miller's notes. Miller's decision to go to jail was hers alone, not that of the newspaper as her employer. In the Cooper case, *Time* magazine was subpoenaed. Although this distinction did not go to the heart of the criticism of *Time,* Bridges called the Miller and Cooper situations apples and oranges. To lionize *The New York Times* and to pillory *Time*, she said, was misleading.
- **Unique Situation.** The journalistic standard to shield whistle-blowers, Bridges argued, was less the issue than dirty politics. The allegation under federal investigation was that a political partisan had leaked Plame's name to discredit revelations made by her husband. He had criticized the rationale for the U.S. war against Iraq and angered the White House. "This," said Bridges, "was allegedly a case of a political partisan breaking a law about national security in a time of war for political gain." Bridges said that the case was far from one involving a typical whistle-blowing confidential source.

Dawn Bridges Public relations challenges include explaining decisions that may not be popular with everyone.

DEEPENING YOUR MEDIA LITERACY

Crisis management is one of the greatest challenges for public relations. By definition, crises are unexpected. Each has twists that could not have been anticipated and requires sharp analytical and communication skills to address the crisis.

Explore the Issue

Go to your library or go online to brief yourself on the facts of this case.

Dig Deeper

Tap into the wealth of commentary on both sides of the issue. Online search terms include *Valerie Plane, Judith Miller*, and *Matt Cooper.*

What Do You Think?

If you were a journalist with grave doubts about *Time*'s decision to surrender Matt Cooper's notes, what questions would you put to Dawn Bridges in an interview to expand on the points she made in her statement? If you were in Bridges' position, how would you respond to these questions? And what further questions would those answers prompt?

LEARNING CHECK

- Why is being proactive an important communications tool in public relations?

Ongoing Media Relationships Good media relations cannot be forged in the fire of a crisis. Organizations that survive a crisis generally have a history of solid media relations. Their public relations staff know reporters, editors, and news directors on a first-name basis. They avoid hyping news releases on routine matters and they work hard at earning the trust of journalists. Many public relations people, in fact, are seasoned journalists themselves, and they understand how journalists go about their work. It is their journalistic background that made them attractive candidates for their public relations jobs.

LEARNING CHECK

- Why are so many public relations jobs filled by people with journalism degrees and backgrounds?

Sound Operating Principles An underlying strength that helped to see Johnson & Johnson through the Tylenol crisis was the company's credo. The credo was a written vow that Johnson & Johnson's first responsibility was to "those who use our products and services." Meanwhile, MLF follows this vision statement: "Create customer value through our people, brands, food safety capabilities and our national sales, production and distribution network."

With such sound operating principles, both MLF's and Johnson & Johnson's crisis responses were, in some respects, almost reflexive. Going silent, for example, would have run counter to the principles that both companies had accepted as part of their corporate culture for years.

Ambivalence in Media Relations

Despite the advantage of open media relations, not all companies embrace this approach. As an example, giant retailer Walmart long resisted putting resources into public relations. Founder Sam Walton saw public relations as a frill. It didn't fit into his keep-costs-minimal concept. In 2005, even though Walton was dead, his philosophy remained in place. The company had only a 17-member public relations staff—minuscule in today's business. How minuscule? Walmart sales exceeded $285 billion, yet the company had only one public relations staffer per $16 billion in earnings. Put another way, the company had one public relations person per 76 000 employees.

Walmart's spectacular growth, with a new store opening every day in 2005, masked problems. The company was generating legions of critics, whose mantra was epitomized in Anthony Bianco's title for his Walmart-bashing book in 2006: *The Bully of Bentonville*. In Irvine, California, voters killed a planned store. Public opposition undid plans in the Queens section of New York City for another store. Reflecting growing employee discontent, there were rumblings to unionize—anathema in the Walmart culture. There was a scandal about illegal immigrants doing overnight cleanup work. A class-action suit alleging gender discrimination was filed by some female employees.

Walmart to the Rescue While the U.S. federal emergency response agency was spinning its bureaucratic wheels in hopeless confusion and disarray, Walmart dispatched 2400 truckloads of relief supplies to victims of Hurricane Katrina. Walmart scored mightily with the public, although the rescue caravans were more a demonstration of the company's adroit delivery system than a sound public relations strategy.

Walmart's attempts at damage control were clumsy. Occasional spectacular public relations successes flowed more from a corporate conscience in crisis than a methodical public relations strategy. In 2005, for example, Walmart upstaged federal agencies in moving relief supplies to the Gulf Coast after Hurricane Katrina. More than 2400 truckloads of merchandise were dispatched to stricken communities, the first 100 loads of donated merchandise arriving before the fumbling federal mobilization. Walmart drivers also transported water and other essentials.

Occasional image successes, however, weren't doing the job. With a vague sense that something methodical in the public relations spirit was needed, Walmart created an executive position in 2006 with the curious title of Senior Director Stakeholder Engagement. The job description had some earmarks of public relations, albeit not quite at the vice-presidential level. Strangely, perhaps in homage to Sam Walton, the words *public relations* appeared nowhere in the job description's 3000 words. You could, however, read a lot into wording such as "an innovative out-of-the-box thinker" and "fundamental changes in how the company does business" and "social responsibility."

LEARNING CHECK

- Some companies have a notorious history of weak media relations and often snub reporters' queries. Would you defend this practice? Why or why not?

Adversarial Public Relations

Public relations sometimes takes on aggressive, even feisty, tactics. A pioneer in **adversarial public relations** as a vice-president at Mobil Oil in the 1970s, **Herb Schmertz** launched an assault on the ABC television network for a documentary critical of the U.S. oil industry. Schmertz bought full-page newspaper and magazine space for **advertorials**, a contrived word that combined *advertising* and *editorial*, to provide word-heavy, point-by-point rebuttals. Schmertz gave six Mobil executives a crash course on becoming spiffy interviewees and sent them on the talk-show circuit. They appeared on 365 television and 211 radio shows and talked with 85 newspaper reporters, not only tackling the ABC show but spinning Mobil practices in a positive light.

adversarial public relations Attacking critics openly.

Herb Schmertz Pioneered advertorials.

advertorials Paid advertisements that state an editorial position.

Another adversarial approach is the corporate pout. Upset with *The Wall Street Journal*, automaker GM at one point launched an **information boycott** of the newspaper. Contact with *Journal* reporters was cut off. So was GM advertising in the *Journal*. GM eventually came to its senses after learning that information boycotts carry great risks:

information boycott A policy to ignore news coverage and reporters' queries.

- By going silent, an organization loses avenues for conveying messages to mass audiences.
- Yanking advertising is perceived by the public as coercive wielding of economic might.
- Because advertising is designed to boost sales, discontinuing ads is counterproductive.

Thirty years later, the jury is still out on Schmertz's adversarial public relations. Certainly, though, it has not been widely adopted, perhaps because more sophisticated tools have emerged for getting institutional messages across in society's ever-richer media mix. Glossy magazines are rife with paid content deliberately intended to blend with articles. Spokespersons are more practiced in avoiding a bite as they counter detractors in media forums.

LEARNING CHECK

- If you were president of a major corporation, would you hire Herb Schmertz as your public relations vice-president? Why or why not?

Directions for Public Relations

STUDY PREVIEW Public relations has a tarnished image that stems from short-sighted promotion and whitewashing techniques of the late 1800s. Although some dubious practices continue, public relations leaders are working to improve standards.

A Tarnished Image

whitewashing Covering up.

Joyce Nelson Says public relations has two sides: the shadow and the persona.

Unsavoury elements in the heritage of public relations remain a heavy burden. P.T. Barnum, whose name became synonymous with hype, attracted crowds to his stunts and shows in the late 1800s with extravagant promises. Sad to say, some promoters still use Barnum's tactics. The claims for snake oils and elixirs from Barnum's era live on in commercials for pain relievers and cold remedies. The early response of tycoons to muckraking attacks, before Ivy Lee came along, was **whitewashing**—covering up the abuses but not correcting them. It is no wonder that the term *public relations* is sometimes used derisively. To say that something is "all public relations" means that it lacks substance. Of people whose apparent positive qualities are a mere façade, it may be said that they have "good public relations."

Public relations operates in the realm of what Canadian **Joyce Nelson** calls the "legitimacy gap" in her book *The Sultans of Sleaze: Public Relations and the Media.* The term *legitimacy gap* was coined by business professor Prakash Sethi to describe the difference between a corporate image and the corporate reality. Nelson applies Jungian psychology to the term in her analysis of public relations. She argues that a corporation has two sides: a persona and a shadow. The persona is its corporate image, the positive image that is promoted via advertising; the shadow is its dark side, which is not usually seen in the news media and certainly not in advertising. According to Nelson, the shadow may include "the ways in which [the corporation's] activities infringe upon our health and safety, our environment, [and contribute] to our oppression or to that of others, despite what all their persona-related activity would like us to believe." When something happens that threatens the persona and reveals the shadow of a corporation, public relations professionals are called to fix the problem.

LEARNING CHECK

- **Will contemporary public relations people ever live down the legacy of P.T. Barnum?**
- **Is public relations "sleazy," as Joyce Nelson suggests?**

Standards and Certification

Canadian Public Relations Society (CPRS) Professional public relations association.

In 1948, two public relations groups, one in Montreal and the other in Toronto, merged. In 1953, they became the **Canadian Public Relations Society (CPRS)**. In 1957, they were recognized as a national society. Today, CPRS has 16 member societies in major cities across Canada. The association adopted the following code of professional standards. Although CPRS is a Canadian association, its codes clearly reflect lessons learned in both the United States and Canada.

Canadian Public Relations Society Code of Professional Standards

Members of the Canadian Public Relations Society feel strongly about standards within the profession and abide by the following codes of ethics:

- A member shall practice public relations according to the highest professional standards.
- A member shall deal fairly and honestly with the communications media and the public.
- A member shall practice the highest standards of honesty, accuracy, integrity and truth, and shall not knowingly disseminate false or misleading information.
- A member shall deal fairly with past or present employers/clients, with fellow practitioners, and with members of other professions.
- A member shall be prepared to disclose the name of their employer or client for whom public communications are made and refrain from associating themselves with anyone that would not respect such policy.
- A member shall protect the confidences of present, former and prospective employers/clients.
- A member shall not represent conflicting or competing interests without the express consent of those concerned, given after a full disclosure of the facts.
- A member shall not guarantee specified results beyond the member's capacity to achieve.

MEDIA PEOPLE Edward Bernays

After graduating from college in 1912, Edward Bernays tried press agentry. He was good at it, landing free publicity for whoever would hire him. Soon his bosses included famous tenor Enrico Caruso and actor Otis Skinner. However, Bernays felt that his success was tainted by the disdain in which press agents were held in general. He also saw far greater potential for affecting public opinion than his fellow press agents did. From Bernays's discomfort and vision was born the concept of modern public relations. His 1923 book *Crystallizing Public Opinion* outlined a new craft that he called public relations.

Bernays viewed good public relations as counsel to clients. He called the public relations practitioner a "special pleader." The concept was modelled partly on the long-established lawyer–client relationship in which the lawyer, or counsellor, suggests courses of action. Because of his seminal role in defining public relations, Bernays sometimes is called the Father of Public Relations, although some people say the honour should be shared with Ivy Lee.

Regardless, there is no question of Bernays's ongoing contributions to public relations. He taught the first course in public relations in 1923 at New York University. He encouraged firm methodology in public relations, a notion that was captured in the title of a book he edited in 1955: *The Engineering of Consent.* He long advocated the professionalization of the field, which laid the groundwork for the sort of accreditation that the PRSA has developed and the CPRS advocates.

Throughout his career, Bernays stressed that public relations people need a strong sense of responsibility. In one reflective essay, he wrote, "Public relations practiced as a profession is an art applied to a science in which the public interest and not pecuniary motivation is the primary consideration. The engineering of consent in this sense assumes a constructive social role. Regrettably, public relations, like other professions, can be abused and used for antisocial purposes. I have tried to make the profession socially responsible as well as economically viable."

Bernays became the Grand Old Man of public relations, still attending PRSA and other professional meetings past his 100th birthday. He died in 1993 at age 102.

Edward Bernays

WHAT DO YOU THINK?

1. Edward Bernays liked to call himself the Father of Public Relations. Who deserves the accolade more, Bernays or Ivy Lee? Explain your choice.
2. Bernays likened the relationship of public relations practitioners and their clients to lawyer–client relationships. Is it a fair comparison?

- Members shall personally accept no fees, commissions, gifts or any other considerations for professional services from anyone except employers or clients for whom the services were specifically performed.

  (*Reprinted by permission of the CPRS.*)

In a further step toward professionalization, the CPRS established a certification process. Those who meet the criteria and pass exams are allowed to place **APR**, which stands for accredited public relations professional, after their names. Canadian public relations professionals can apply for accreditation only after they've worked in the business for at least five years. Exams are held once a year.

APR Indicates CPRS accreditation.

Technology and Public Relations

The workhorse of public relations, the news media, made an easy transition to the internet in the 1990s, but pretty much only the medium changed. A standard release that was once mailed out was now mass-delivered through email. In 2006, a Boston public relations agency, Shift Communications, reinvented the news release for the digital age. Shift's Todd Defren, who devised the new release, called it one-stop shopping for journalists to whom releases are targeted. The release includes tech-rich features, such as links to blogs that relate to the subject, links to related news releases and sites, downloadable company logos, and videos.

social media news release Internet-based news release with links to related material and interactive opportunities for news reporters.

Defren calls it the **social media news release** because it encourages interactive and ongoing communication. With a Shift release posted to the Digg consumer-generated news site, journalists, bloggers, and anyone else can click to sites that add to the dialogue. "This gives journalists everything they need in one place," Defren said.

The basis of Defren's invention is the Web 2.0 bevy of internet services that facilitate the creation of content and exchange of information online. Within months of the Shift creation, which was downloadable free as a template, larger public relations agencies were onto the concept. The giant public relations firm Edelman unveiled its variation by the end of the year.

Chapter 11 Wrap-Up

Watch

A Day in the Life: Manning, Selvage, and Lee

When Ivy Lee hung up a shingle in New York for a new publicity agency in 1906, he wanted to distance himself from the huckstering that marked most publicity at the time. To do that, Lee promised to deal only in legitimate news about the agency's clients and no fluff. He invited journalists to pursue more information about the agency's clients. He also vowed to be honest and accurate. Those principles remain the main beliefs of good public relations practice today.

PEARSON mycanadiancommunicationlab

Visit **www.mycanadiancommunicationlab.ca** for access to a wealth of tools and resources that will enhance your learning experience. Features include the following:

- Personalized Study Plan
- Videos
- Activities
- Pearson eText–and much more!

Questions for Critical Review

1. What is public relations? How is public relations connected to the mass media?
2. Why did big business become interested in the techniques and principles of public relations beginning in the late 1800s?
3. How is public relations a management tool?
4. What is the range of activities in which public relations people are involved?
5. What is the difference between public relations and advertising? What are the similarities?
6. What kind of relationship do most public relations people strive to have with the mass media?
7. Why does public relations have a bad image? What are public relations professionals doing about it?

Keeping Up to Date

PRWeek is the industry trade journal.

The trade journal *O'Dwyer's PR Services* tracks the industry on a monthly basis.

Other sources of ongoing information are *Public Relations Journal*, Public Relations Quarterly, and *Public Relations Review*.

Advertising

12

A Society of Choices By presenting choices to consumers, advertising mirrors the democratic ideal of individuals choosing intelligently among alternatives. The emphasis is on individuals making up their own minds: Liberal, Conservative, or NDP? Nike or Reebok? Coke or Pepsi?

LEARNING AHEAD

- Advertising is key in consumer economies, democracy, and the mass media.
- Most advertising messages are carried through the mass media.
- Advertising agencies create and place ads for advertisers.
- Advertisements are placed with care in media outlets.
- Advertisers are experimenting with new platforms.
- Brand names as an advertising strategy are in transition.
- Advertising tactics include lowest common denominators, redundancy, and testimonials.
- New advertising tactics include encouraging social media and consumer-generated content.
- Challenges ahead for advertisers include ad clutter and creative excesses.

MEDIA IN THEORY

Advertising and Prosperity

Advertising's phenomenal continuing growth has been a product of a plentiful society. In a poor society with a shortage of goods, people line up for necessities like food and clothing. Advertising has no role and serves no purpose when survival is the question. With prosperity, however, people have not only discretionary income but also a choice of ways to spend it. Advertising is the vehicle that provides information and rationales to help them decide how to enjoy their prosperity.

Besides being a product of economic prosperity, advertising contributes to prosperity. By dangling desirable commodities and services before mass audiences, advertising can inspire people to greater individual productivity so that they can have more income to buy the things that are advertised.

Advertising also can introduce efficiency into the economy by allowing comparison shopping without in-person inspections of all of the alternatives. Efficiencies also can result when advertising alerts consumers to superior and less costly products and services, which displace outdated, outmoded, and inefficient offerings.

On the other hand, Canadian economist **John Kenneth Galbraith**, in his classic book *The Affluent Society*, argued that advertising does more than just satisfy our *needs*. It actually creates *wants*. By creating wants, those in power can sell products that make people live beyond their means and buy more than they need. Andrew Potter, writing in *Maclean's*, refutes Galbraith's ideas. Potter claims that each of us has free will (or at least self-restraint) and isn't easily duped by every ad campaign we see: "That is not to say that advertising isn't harmless, but that it's more like seduction than brainwashing. Just as you can't seduce someone who is not interested in sex, you can't sell teeth whitener to someone who is not concerned about their appearance."

John Kenneth Galbraith Argued that advertising isn't about needs, it's about wants.

Explore

Deepening Your Media Literacy: How does advertising affect the consumer?

MEDIA TIMELINE Development of Advertising

1468 William Caxton promoted a book with the first printed advertisement.

1704 Joseph Campbell included advertisements in *The Boston News-Letter.*

1833 Benjamin Day created *The New York Sun* as a combination news and advertising vehicle.

1869 F. Wayland Ayer opened the first advertising agency, in Philadelphia.

1889 Anson McKim opened the first Canadian advertising agency.

1890s Brand names emerged as an advertising technique.

1950s David Ogilvy devised brand imaging technique.

1960s Rosser Reeves devised unique selling proposition technique.

1963 Canadian Code of Advertising Standards was established.

1980s Conglomeration hit the advertising world through mergers and acquisitions.

2003 Store brands emerged as a major challenge to brand names.

2004 Thirty-second spot during the Super Bowl cost US$2.5 million.

2008 Bride and her "wig out" debuted on YouTube.

2009 iPod apps were introduced, adding another platform for advertisers.

Importance of Advertising

STUDY PREVIEW **Advertising is vital in a consumer economy. Without it, people would have a hard time even knowing what products and services were available. Advertising also is the financial basis of important contemporary mass media.**

Consumer Economies

The essential role of advertising in a modern consumer economy is obvious if you think about how people decide what to buy. If a shoe manufacturer were unable to tout the virtues of its footwear by advertising in the mass media, people would have a hard time learning about the product, let alone knowing whether it is what they want.

In *Canadian Advertising in Action*, Keith Tuckwell estimates that Canadian companies spend more than $12 billion a year on advertising. When production of goods and services is up, so is advertising spending. When production falters, as it did during the 2009 recession, many manufacturers, distributors, and retailers reduce their advertising expenditures.

LEARNING CHECK

- **Could a consumer economy work without advertising? Explain.**
- **What is the link between advertising and prosperity?**

Advertising and Democracy

Advertising first took off as a modern phenomenon in the United States and Canada more than elsewhere, which has given rise to a theory that advertising and democracy are connected. This theory notes that North Americans, early in their history as a democracy, were required by their political system to hold individual opinions. They looked for information so that they could evaluate their leaders and vote on public policy. This emphasis on individuality and reason paved the way for advertising: Just as North Americans looked to the mass media for information on political matters, they also came to look to the media for information on buying decisions.

Advertising has another important role in democratic societies in generating most of the operating revenue for newspapers, magazines, television, and radio. Without advertising, many of the media on which people rely for information, for entertainment, and for the exchange of ideas on public issues would not exist as we know them.

LEARNING CHECK

- **How does advertising dovetail with the democratic ideal of individual decision making?**

Persuasion versus Coercion

Advertising has critics who point out that almost all ads are one-sided. Ads don't lay out options, which violates the principle of honesty that is essential in persuasive communication. Persuasiveness requires a full presentation of available options and then argumentation based on all evidence and premises. Ads don't do that. The argument in advertisements—sometimes screaming, often emotional—is direct: "Buy me." What an ad doesn't say speaks volumes. Critics say this makes advertising a type of coercive communication—far short of honest persuasion.

Whatever the criticism, advertising is a major element in mass communication. The financial base of newspapers, magazines, radio, television, and—more and more—the internet and mobile devices depends on advertising. The role of advertising both in the media as we know them today and in our consumer economy cannot be denied.

LEARNING CHECK

- What is the difference between coercive and persuasive communication?
- Can you find any ads that meet the criteria of being persuasive rather than coercive?

Origins of Advertising

STUDY PREVIEW Advertising is the product of great forces that have shaped modern society, beginning with Gutenberg's movable type, which made mass-produced messages possible.

Stepchild of Technology

Advertising is not a mass medium, but it relies on media to carry its messages. **Johannes Gutenberg**'s movable type, which permitted mass production of the printed word, made mass-produced advertising possible. First came flyers. Then advertisements in newspapers and magazines were introduced. In the 1800s, when technology created high-speed presses that could produce enough copies for larger audiences, advertisers used them to expand markets. With the introduction of radio, advertisers learned how to use electronic communication. Then came television and the internet.

Johannes Gutenberg Inventor of printing press which, in turn, made mass media and advertising possible.

Flyers were the first form of printed advertising. The British printer **William Caxton** issued the first printed advertisement in 1468 to promote one of his books. In the United States, publisher **John Campbell** of *The Boston News-Letter* ran the first advertisement in 1704, a notice from somebody wanting to sell an estate on Long Island. Colonial newspapers listed cargo arriving from Europe and invited readers to come, look, and buy.

William Caxton Printed the first advertisement.

John Campbell Published the first ad in the British colonies.

LEARNING CHECK

- How is advertising dependent on media technology?
- How is advertising efficient for selling products and services?

Industrial Revolution

The genius of **Benjamin Day**'s *New York Sun*, in 1833 the first penny newspaper (see Chapter 10), was that it recognized and exploited so many changes spawned by the Industrial Revolution. Steam-powered presses made large press runs possible. Factories drew great numbers of people to jobs within geographically small areas to which newspapers could be distributed quickly. The jobs also drew immigrants who were eager to learn—from newspapers as well as other sources—about their adopted country. Industrialization, coupled with the labour union movement, created unprecedented wealth, with labourers gaining a share of the new prosperity. A consumer economy was emerging, although it was primitive by today's standards.

Benjamin Day His penny newspaper brought advertising to a new level.

A key to the success of Day's *Sun* was that, at a penny a copy, it was affordable for almost everyone. Of course, Day's production expenses exceeded a penny a copy. Just as the commercial media do today, Day looked to advertisers to pick up the slack. As Day wrote in his first issue, "The object of this paper is to lay before the public, at a price within the means of everyone, all the news of the day, and at the same time afford an advantageous medium for advertising." Day and imitator penny press publishers sought larger and larger circulations, knowing that merchants would see the value in buying space to reach so much purchasing power.

National advertising took root in the United States in the 1840s as railroads, another creation of the Industrial Revolution, spawned new networks for mass distribution of manufactured goods. National brands developed, and their producers looked to magazines, also delivered by rail, to promote sales. By 1869, the U.S. rail network linked the Atlantic and Pacific coasts. By 1886, Canada had a railroad that joined the east and west coasts.

LEARNING CHECK

- What was the genius of Benjamin Day?

Advertising Agencies

STUDY PREVIEW Central to modern advertising are the agencies that create and place ads on behalf of their clients. These agencies are generally funded by the media in which they place ads. In effect, this makes agency services free to advertisers. Other compensation systems are also emerging.

Pioneer Agencies

F. Wayland Ayer Founded the first ad agency in the United States.

By 1869, most merchants recognized the value of advertising but they grumbled about the time it took away from their other work. In that grumbling, a young Philadelphia man sensed opportunity. **F. Wayland Ayer**, aged 20, speculated that merchants, and even national manufacturers, would welcome a service company to help them create advertisements and place them in publications. Ayer feared, however, that his idea might not be taken seriously by potential clients because of his youth and inexperience. So when Ayer opened a shop, he borrowed his father's name, N.W. Ayer, for the shingle. The Ayer agency not only created ads but also offered the array of services that agencies still offer clients today:

- Counsel on selling products and services.
- Design services, that is, actually creating advertisements and campaigns.
- Expertise on placing advertisements in advantageous media.

Anson McKim Founded the first ad agency in Canada.

In 1872, Toronto newspapers began selling advertising space to clients outside its geographic area when the *Toronto Mail* sent a young man to Montreal to sell advertising space. **Anson McKim** saw this as a great opportunity and he began to act as a broker for other publications in south-central Ontario. In 1889, McKim opened Canada's first ad agency in Montreal, A. McKim and Company. McKim also published the first directory of media in Canada, *The Canadian Newspaper Directory*, in 1892.

Agency Structure

Full-service advertising agencies conduct market research for their clients, design and produce advertisements, and choose the media in which the advertisement will run. The 500 leading American agencies employ 120 000 people worldwide. The responsibilities of people who work at advertising agencies fall into these broad categories:

creative director Key person in ad campaigns.

Creativity This category includes copywriters, graphics experts, and layout people. These creative people generally report to **creative directors**, art directors, and copy supervisors.

account executives Agency reps to clients.

Liaison Most of these people are **account executives** who work with clients. Account executives are responsible for understanding clients' needs, communicating those needs to the creative staff, and going back to clients with the creative staff's ideas.

media buyers Decide where to place ads.

Buying Agency employees called **media buyers** determine the most effective media in which to place ads, and then place them.

Research Agency research staffs generate information on target consumer groups, data that can guide the creative and media staffs.

Many agencies also employ technicians and producers who turn ideas into camera-ready proofs, colour plates, videotape, audio clips, digital files, and web-based ads, although a lot of production work is contracted to specialty companies. Besides full-service agencies there are creative boutiques, which specialize in preparing messages; media buying houses, which recommend strategy on placing ads; and other narrowly focused agencies.

LEARNING CHECK

- What services of a modern advertising agency can be traced to F. Wayland Ayer and Anson McKim?

Agency Compensation

Advertising agencies once earned their money in a standard way: 15 percent of the client advertiser's total outlay for space or time. On huge accounts, such as Procter & Gamble (P&G), agencies made killings.

Commissions The 15 percent **commission contract** system broke down in the 1990s when businesses scrambled to cut costs to become more competitive. Today, according to a guesstimate by the trade journal *Advertising Age*, only 10 to 12 percent of agency contracts use a standard percentage. Agency compensation generally is negotiated. Big advertisers, such as P&G, are thought to be paying 13 percent on average, but different agencies handle the company's brands, each in a separate contract. For competitive reasons, all parties tend to be secretive about actual terms.

commission contract An advertising agency earns an agreed-upon percentage of what the advertising client spends for time and space, traditionally 15 percent.

Performance Commission contracts have been replaced largely with **performance contracts**. The advertiser pays an agency's costs plus a negotiated profit. In addition, if a campaign works spectacularly, agencies land bonuses.

performance contract An advertising agency earns expenses and an agreed-upon markup for the advertising client, plus bonuses for exceeding minimal expectations.

Equity In the 1990s dot-com boom, a performance contract variation was to pay agencies with shares in the company. **Equity contracts** are risky for agencies because an advertiser's success hinges on many variables, not just on the advertising, but the return for an agency with a soaring client can be stratospheric.

equity contract An advertising agency is compensated with shares of stock in an advertising client.

Advertiser's Role in Advertising

Although they hire agencies for advertising services, most companies have their own advertising expertise among the in-house people who develop marketing strategies. These companies look to ad agencies to develop the advertising campaigns that will help them to meet their marketing goals. For some companies, the **advertising director** is the liaison between the company's marketing strategists and the ad agency's tacticians. Large companies with many products have in-house **brand managers** for this liaison. Although it is not the usual pattern, some companies have in-house advertising departments and rely on agencies hardly at all.

advertising director Coordinates marketing and advertising.

brand manager Coordinates marketing and advertising for a specific brand.

LEARNING CHECK

- How does the commission system in advertising work?
- What has forced changes in the commission system? What are these changes?

Placing Advertisements

STUDY PREVIEW The placement of advertisements is a sophisticated business. Not only do different media have inherent advantages and disadvantages in reaching potential customers, but so do individual publications and broadcast outlets.

Media Plans

Agencies create **media plans** to ensure that advertisements reach the right target audience. Developing a media plan is no small task. Consider the number of media outlets available: daily or weekly newspapers, magazines, radio stations, and television stations. Other

media plan Lays out where ads are placed.

Global Marketing Knowing the following that Houston Rockets star Yao Ming has in his China homeland, the distributor for the Chinese beer Yanjing paid $6 million for Chinese-language billboards at the Rockets' arena.

possibilities include direct mail, banners on websites, billboards, blimps, skywriting, and even printing the company's name on T-shirts.

Media buyers use formulas, some very complex, to decide which media are best for reaching potential customers. Most of these formulas begin with a factor called **CPM**, short for cost per thousand readers, listeners, or viewers. If airtime for a radio advertisement costs 7.2 cents per thousand listeners, it's probably a better deal than a magazine with a 7.3-cent CPM, assuming that both reach the same audience. CPM by itself is just a starting point in choosing media. Other variables that media buyers consider include whether a message will work in a particular medium. For example, radio wouldn't work for a product that lends itself to a visual pitch and sight gags.

CPM Cost per thousand; a tool to determine the cost effectiveness of different media.

Media buyers have numerous sources of data to help them decide where advertisements can be placed for the best results. The **Audit Bureau of Circulations**, created by the newspaper industry in 1914, provides reliable information based on independent audits of the circulation of most newspapers. Survey organizations such as Nielsen Media Research and BBM conduct surveys on television and radio audiences. *Canadian Advertising Rates and Data* (*CARD*) and the Canadian Media Directors Council publish volumes of information on media audiences, circulations, and advertising rates.

Audit Bureau of Circulations Verifies circulation claims.

LEARNING CHECK

- Why are media plans necessary in advertising?
- Why is CPM an essential advertising tool?
- How do advertisers know they are getting the audience to which they buy access?

Traditional Media Choices

Below are the pluses and minuses of major media as advertising vehicles. All data are from TVB Canada's *2009 Canadian Net Advertising Revenue by Medium*.

Newspapers The hot relationship that media theorist Marshall McLuhan described between newspapers and their readers attracts advertisers. Newspaper readers are predisposed to consider information in advertisements seriously. Studies show that people, when ready to buy, look more to newspapers than to other media. Because newspapers are tangible, readers can refer back to advertisements just by picking up the paper a second time, which is not possible with ephemeral media such as television and radio. Coupons are possible in newspapers. Newspaper readers tend to be older, better educated, and higher earning than television and radio audiences. Space for newspaper ads usually can be reserved as late as 48 hours ahead, and eleventh-hour changes are possible. In 2008, daily newspapers accounted for 24.5 percent ($2.5 billion) of all advertising revenue in Canada.

However, newspapers are becoming less valuable for reaching young adults. To the consternation of newspaper publishers, there has been an alarming drop in readership among these people in recent years, and it appears that, unlike their parents did, young adults are not picking up the newspaper habit as they mature.

Another drawback to newspapers is printing on newsprint, a relatively cheap paper that absorbs ink like a slow blotter. The result is that ads in newspapers do not look as good as they do in slick magazines. Slick, stand-alone inserts offset the newsprint drawback somewhat, but many readers pull out and discard the inserts as soon as they open the paper.

Magazines As another print medium, magazines have many of the advantages of newspapers plus a longer **shelf life**, an advertising term for the amount of time that an advertisement remains available to readers. Magazines remain in the home for weeks, and sometimes months, which offers greater exposure to advertisements. People share magazines, which gives them high **pass-along circulation**. Magazines are more prestigious, with their slick paper and splashier graphics. With precise colour separations and enamelled papers, magazine advertisements can be beautiful in ways that newspaper advertisements cannot. Magazines, specializing as they do, offer more narrowly defined audiences

shelf life How long a periodical remains in use.

pass-along circulation All of the people who see a periodical.

than do newspapers. In 2008, 8 percent ($692 million) of all advertising revenue was spent on magazines.

On the downside, magazines require reservations for advertising space up to three months in advance. Opportunities for last-minute changes are limited and often impossible.

Radio Radio stations with narrow formats offer easily identified target audiences. Time can be bought on short notice, with changes possible almost until airtime. Comparatively inexpensive, radio lends itself to repeated play of advertisements to drive home a message introduced in more expensive media like television. Radio also lends itself to jingles that can contribute to a lasting image.

However, radio offers no opportunity for a visual display, although the images that listeners create in their minds from audio suggestions can be more potent than those set out visually on television. Radio is a mobile medium that people carry with them. The extensive availability of radio is offset, however, by the fact that people tune in and out. Another negative is that many listeners are inattentive. Also, there is no shelf life. Still, radio accounted for 15 percent ($1.6 billion) of all Canadian advertising revenue in 2008.

Television As a moving and visual medium, television can offer unmatched impact, and the rapid growth of both network and local television advertising, far outpacing other media, indicates its effectiveness in reaching a diverse mass audience. It's the king of all media. In 2008, television was still king, responsible for a full third ($3.4 billion) of all advertising revenue spent in Canada.

Drawbacks include the fact that production costs can be high. So are rates. The expense of television time has forced advertisers to move to shorter and shorter advertisements. A result is **ad clutter**, a phenomenon in which advertisements compete against each other and reduce the impact of all of them. Placing advertisements on television is a problem because demand outstrips the supply of slots, especially during prime hours. Slots for some hours are locked up months, or even whole seasons, in advance. Because of the audience's diversity and size, targeting potential customers with any precision is difficult with television, with the exception of emerging narrowly focused cable services.

ad clutter So many competing ads that all of them lose impact.

Pre-Movie Advertising

Although it's been around for a long time, advertising as a lead-in for movies is taking off. Why? Because it works. The research company Arbitron surveyed moviegoers as they left theatres and found that 80 percent remembered ads shown at the beginning of the movie. Other media aren't close to that in terms of recall, recently spurring a 37 percent increase in movie ad revenue to $356 million in one year. Also, according to Arbitron, the notion that most people resent ads is mythical. Among viewers aged 12 to 24, 70 percent weren't bothered by the ads.

LEARNING CHECK

- **What are the advantages and disadvantages of each of the advertising-funded mass media?**

New Advertising Platforms

STUDY PREVIEW **The internet is proving to be an effective and frustrating platform for advertisers. Internet search engines are a growing advertising vehicle not only because of their high traffic but also because they organize the audience into subject categories. Game sites attract advertisers because of their young, male audience, which has always been hard to reach.**

Online

Hesitation about using the internet for advertising has yielded to its advantages. Literally thousands of sites serve niche audiences, enhancing the likelihood of reaching people with an inherent interest in specific products. For advertisers that choose the right sites, there is less waste than with traditional mass media, such as the television networks that seek massive heterogeneous audiences. TVB Canada estimates indicate that, in 2008, **online advertising** was worth $1.6 billion in Canada. That number will rise in the next decade.

online advertising Provides messages to computers.

Mail-order products can be ordered over the internet right from the ad. With older media, ads only whet the consumer's appetite. A phone call or a visit to a showroom is necessary—and many otherwise likely customers frequently don't take that next step.

Another advantage of internet advertising is cost. Except for high-demand sites, space is relatively inexpensive.

Search Engines

The internet search engine Google, capitalizing on its super-fast search technology, has elbowed into the traditional placement service provided by advertising agencies. Google arranges for advertising space on thousands of websites, many of them narrowly focused, like blogs, and places ads for its clients on those sites. Every blog visitor who clicks a **sponsored link** placed by Google will go to a fuller advertisement. Google charges the advertiser a **click-through fee**. Google pays the site for every click-through. Google matches sites and advertisers, so that a search for new Cadillacs doesn't display ads for muffler shops.

sponsored link Onscreen hot spot to move to an online advertisement.

click-through fee A charge to advertisers when an online link to their ads is activated; also a fee paid to websites that host the links.

Google also places what it calls "advertiser links" on search screens. *The New York Times*, for example, has a licence to use Google technology when readers enter search terms on the *Times* site. The licence allows Google to display ads of likely interest whenever a *Times* site reader conducts an internal site search. A search for *Times* coverage of Jamaica news, for example, will also produce links to *Times* stories on Jamaica, as well as to advertisements for Caribbean travel elsewhere on the internet. If a *Times* reader clicks on an ad, Google pays the *Times* a click-through fee—from the revenue the advertiser paid to Google to place its ads.

Google has quickly become a major player in web advertising. Of the estimated $10 billion spent by advertisers for online messages in 2004, Google had $1.9 billion. No other site earned more advertising revenue from the internet. According to comScore qsearch, Google represents a 79 percent share of the search engine market in Canada.

LEARNING CHECK

- Why are search engines a hot new medium for advertising?

Gaming

To catch consumers who spend less time with television and more time with video games, advertisers have shifted chunks of their budgets to gaming. The potential is incredible. Half of Americans age 6 and older play video games, and men 18 and older, that elusive target for advertisers, make up 26 percent of gamers.

For an onscreen plug, advertisers typically pay $20 000 to $100 000 for a message integrated into the game. In gaming's early days, game makers and product markets worked directly with each other, but now many ad agencies have gaming divisions that act as brokers.

Game ads have advantages, particularly for online games. Messages can be changed instantly: a background billboard showing a Pepsi ad can become a Chevy Cobalt ad or a movie trailer. One company, Massive, uses unseen interactive coding to identify gamers and adjust plug-ins that, for example, list stores near specific players and make geographic and other ad content adjustments. Nielsen, known primarily for television ratings, and game publisher Activision have an interactive system for tracking how many players see advertiser impressions—that is, how many gamers see an ad and even how many recall an ad.

Although online gaming has advantages for advertisers, there are downsides. Online gaming ads, although generally cost-effective, are problematic. Games can take months to develop, requiring far more lead time than advertisers usually have for rolling out a comprehensive multimedia campaign. For simple billboard messages, however, games have the advantage of being instantly changeable.

Game Platform Jeep has found video games as a new advertising platform. Background billboards on Tony Hawk's *Pro Skater 2* can be updated with new products either as new DVD editions are issued or with downloads for internet-connected games.

Established brands have created their own games, which appear on their websites. In an early **advergame**, as these ads are called, the shoe manufacturer Nike created a soccer game at Nikefootball.com. Kraft Foods had an advergaming race at Candyland.com. However, because advergames are accessible only through a brand's site, they don't make sense for emerging brands.

advergame A sponsored online game, usually for an established brand at its own site.

LEARNING CHECK

- What are the attractions of the internet and internet-based games for advertisers?

Brand Strategies

STUDY PREVIEW Branding is a time-proven advertising strategy for establishing a distinctive name among consumers to set a product apart from competitors. The recent history of branding has moved beyond products into arrays of unrelated products. Special K is no longer just a breakfast cereal. Now it's an extensive line of diet products. Branding now includes building lines of products around celebrity images.

Brand Names

A challenge for advertising people is the modern-day reality that mass-produced products intended for large markets are essentially alike: toothpaste is toothpaste is toothpaste. When a product is virtually identical to the competition, how can one toothpaste maker move more tubes?

Brand Names Through trial and error, tactics were devised in the late 1800s to set similar products apart. One tactic, promoting a product as a **brand** name, aims to make a product a household word. When it is successful, a brand name becomes almost the generic identifier, such as Coke for cola and Kleenex for facial tissue.

brand A nongeneric product name designed to set the product apart from the competition.

Techniques of successful brand-name advertising came together in the 1890s for an English product, Pears' soap. A key element in the campaign was multimedia saturation. Advertisements for Pears' soap were everywhere: in newspapers and magazines and on posters, vacant walls, fences, buses, and lampposts. Redundancy hammered home the brand name. "Good morning. Have you used Pears' today?" became a good-natured greeting among Britons that was still being repeated 50 years later. Each repetition reinforced the brand name.

LEARNING CHECK

- What brand names would you list as household words?
- How effective are brand names with you personally?
- Do you resent the manipulation that is part of brand-name advertising?

David Ogilvy Championed brand imaging.

brand image Spin put on a brand name.

Brand Images **David Ogilvy**, who headed the Ogilvy & Mather agency, developed the **brand image** in the 1950s. Ogilvy's advice: "Give your product a first-class ticket through life."

Explaining the importance of image, Ogilvy once said: "Take whisky. Why do some people choose Jack Daniel's, while others choose Grand Dad or Taylor? Have they tried all three and compared the taste? Don't make me laugh. The reality is that these three brands have different images which appeal to different kinds of people. It isn't the whisky they choose, it's the image. The brand image is 90 percent of what the distiller has to sell. Give people a taste of Old Crow, and tell them it's Old Crow. Then give them another taste of Old Crow, but tell them it's Jack Daniel's. Ask them which they prefer. They'll think the two drinks are quite different. They are tasting images."

Using Ogilvy's assumptions, do Canadians taste coffee or image? Consider this: Many Canadians don't go for coffee anymore. For some, the brand Tim Hortons has become synonymous with coffee. They "go to Hortons" or "go to Timmy's" rather than "go for coffee." It's no wonder that Tim Hortons was among the top brands in Interbrand's list of the Best Canadian Brands of 2008. Why is Tim Hortons successful? Interbrand claims that Canadians view Tim Hortons as their "fourth place, after home, work and the hockey/curling rink." Meanwhile, John Gray, writing in *Canadian Business*, says, "The brand has become a part of Canadian culture. That happened by design and not by accident. The company measures just about everything it does against its list of brand characteristics: unpretentious, friendly, dependable, caring—characteristics you might use to describe an ideal Canadian." Other successful Canadian brands include TD Canada Trust, Rogers, Shoppers Drug Mart, Sobeys, and Husky Energy.

Some Canadian brands are going global. BlackBerry topped Interbrand's list of Best Canadian Brands of 2008. According to Interbrand, "This smartphone has set a new standard for the efficiency of mobile communications and is helping drive the pace of our modern world. Investing heavily in its local community, BlackBerry is a hometown hero. And it's now a global champion that has broken ground establishing a new precedent in Canada for the development of a global brand."

LEARNING CHECK

- What twist did David Ogilvy put on brand names?
- What makes some of the Canadian brands listed memorable?

Store Brands

store brands Products sold with a store brand, often manufactured by the retailer. Also called *house brands* and *private labels*.

Retailers are pushing **store brands**, on which they typically score 10 percent higher profits. Every time somebody buys the President's Choice or Our Compliments store brand at the grocery store, brand-name manufacturers lose a sale. The store-brand assault has struck at a whole range of venerable brand names: Kellogg's, Kraft, P&G, and Unilever. Forrester Research, which tracks consumer trends, said in a 2002 report: "Walmart will become the new P&G."

Some brands, such as automobile lines, remain strong but many manufacturers of consumer goods, whose advertising has been a financial mainstay of network television and magazines as well as newspapers and radio, have had to cut back on ad spending. P&G spent $13.9 million advertising its Era detergent in 2001, but only $5.4 million in 2002. Some manufacturers have dropped out of the brand-name business. Unilever has only 200 brands left, compared to 1600 in the mid-1990s.

Retail chains, led by Walmart, have the gigantic marketing channels necessary to sell great quantities of products without advertising expenses. Some retailers even own the factories. The Kroger supermarket chain in the United States owns 41 factories that produce 4300 store-brand products for its grocery shelves.

Dave Nichol Canadian who was a store-brand pioneer.

Before the mega-retailers, brand names gave products an edge, with network television and national magazines carrying the messages. In those days, the major television

MEDIA PEOPLE Dave Nichol

Dave Nichol didn't invent store brands, but he was the wizard of the phenomenon that is rewriting the rules of consumer marketing. When he was an executive at the Canadian grocery chain Loblaws, he introduced knock-off products under the brand No Name in 1978. Nichol's emphasis was quality on par with that of brand names at a lower cost. After all, he had no advertising expenses, which can add 25 cents to the cost of a tube of toothpaste.

Nichol then created a coffee blend, President's Choice, modelled on the coffee sold in a top Toronto restaurant. Then came Decadent chocolate chip cookies with 39 percent chocolate chips, compared to 19 percent in Chips Ahoy. While Kellogg's proclaimed two scoops of raisins in its bran flakes, Nichol's Loblaws brand included four scoops.

Nichol, who has a law degree from Harvard, regards himself as a food connoisseur and has his own vineyard.

His contribution to marketing consumer products has been to package higher quality into store products than is in brand-name products and sell them for less. He also expanded the Loblaws store brands by selling them to American grocery chains. President's Choice coffee picked up a quick following—without advertising—in 15 chains in 36 American states.

In 1990, Walmart founder Sam Walton hired Nichol to devise a store-brand plan for Walmart. A year later, Sam's Choice, modelled on Loblaws' President's Choice, was on Walmart shelves. Next came a value brand of Walmart coffee, called Great Value. Then came vitamins, batteries, toilet paper, and even tuna. By 2000, 40 percent of Walmart's sales were store brands, and that share continues to grow.

Dave Nichol

WHAT DO YOU THINK?

1. What makes store brands appealing to consumers? Is it just price?
2. What impact have store brands had on name brands?

networks delivered messages to millions of consumers with greater effect than could small retailers. Not only are small retailers disappearing, but the networks also can't deliver what they used to. Television systems with 500 channels and the highly diverse web have divided and subdivided the audience into fragments. In a 2003 newsletter to clients, the ad agency Doremus noted, despairingly, that "it's almost impossible to get your name in enough channels to build substantial awareness." Willard Bishop Consulting came to a similar conclusion in a study of network television, noting that airing only three commercials could reach 80 percent of one target audience, 18- to 49-year-old women, in 1995. That same penetration level required the airing of 97 ads in 2000.

In an analysis of the phenomenon, *Fortune* magazine writer Michael Boyle said that the big superstores are displacing brand-name advertising as the new direct connection to consumers. The new mass channel, he said, is the superstore.

branding Enhancing a product image with a celebrity or already-established brand name, regardless of any intrinsic connection between the product and the image.

LEARNING CHECK

- Is there evidence that brand names are losing their lustre? Explain.

Branding

Brand names have taken on a new dimension. Today, the concept includes lending a recognized name to an array of unrelated products: a Paris Hilton handbag, a Paris Hilton wristwatch, a Paris Hilton whatever. It's called **branding**. Originally, brand names were for products from a particular company, but the

Celebrity Branding Hybrid branding, such as for Paris Hilton productions, integrates implied testimonials and celebrity names. Hilton showed off her namesake hair extensions at a hyped launch.

concept now includes products whose only connection is a name. Celebrities willing to objectify their image lend their names to an array of products, giving the products a marketing cachet.

LEARNING CHECK

- How has branding drifted from the original brand-name concept?

Advertising Tactics

STUDY PREVIEW When the age of mass production and mass markets arrived, common wisdom in advertising favoured aiming at the largest possible audience of potential customers. These are called lowest-common-denominator approaches and such advertisements tend to be heavy-handed so that no one can possibly miss the point. Narrower pitches, aimed at segments of the mass audience, permit more deftness, subtlety, and imagination.

Lowest Common Denominator

lowest common denominator (LCD) Messages for the broadest audience possible.

Early brand-name campaigns were geared to the largest possible audience, sometimes called an LCD, or **lowest-common-denominator**, approach. The term *LCD* is adapted from mathematics. To reach an audience that includes members with IQs of 100, the pitch cannot exceed their level of understanding, even if some people in the audience have IQs of 150. The opportunity for deft touches and even cleverness is limited by the fact that they might be lost on some potential customers.

unique selling proposition (USP) Emphasizing a single feature.

Rosser Reeves Devised the term *unique selling proposition*.

LCD advertising is best epitomized in contemporary advertising by USP, short for **unique selling proposition**, a term coined by **Rosser Reeves** of the giant Ted Bates agency in the 1960s. Reeves's prescription was simple: Create a benefit of the product, even if from thin air, and then tout that benefit authoritatively and repeatedly as if the competition doesn't have it. One early USP campaign boasted that Schlitz beer bottles were "washed with live steam." The claim sounded good, because who would want to drink from dirty bottles? However, the fact was that every brewery used steam to clean reusable bottles before filling them again. Furthermore, what is "live steam"? Although the implication of a competitive edge was hollow, it was done dramatically and pounded home with emphasis, and it sold beer. Just as hollow as a competitive advantage was the USP claim for Colgate toothpaste: "Cleans Your Breath While It Cleans Your Teeth."

Leo Burnett Argued that unique selling proposition doesn't need to be insulting.

Perhaps to compensate for a lack of substance, many USP ads are heavy-handed. A unique selling proposition need be neither hollow nor insulting, however. **Leo Burnett**, founder of the agency bearing his name, refined the USP concept by insisting that the unique point be real. For Maytag, Burnett took the company's slight advantage in reliability and dramatized it with the lonely Maytag repairman.

LEARNING CHECK

- What is lowest-common-denominator advertising?
- What is a unique selling proposition in advertising? Give examples from your own experience.

Redundancy Techniques

redundancy Repetition of media messages.

barrages Intensive repetition of ads.

flights Intensive repetition of ads.

waves Intensive repetition of ads.

bunching Short-term ad campaign.

Advertising people learned the importance of **redundancy** early on. To be effective, an advertising message must be repeated, perhaps thousands of times. Redundancy is expensive, however. To increase effectiveness at less cost, advertisers use several techniques:

- **Barrages**. Scheduling advertisements in intensive bursts called **flights** or **waves.**
- **Bunching**. Promoting a product in a limited period, such as running advertisements for school supplies in late August and September.

- **Trailing.** Running condensed versions of advertisements after the original has been introduced, as automakers do when they introduce new models with multipage magazine spreads followed by single-page placements.
- Multimedia trailing. Using less expensive media to reinforce expensive advertisements. Relatively cheap drive-time radio in major markets is a favourite follow-through to expensive television advertisements created for major events like the Super Bowl.

trailing Running shorter, smaller ads after a campaign is introduced.

Marshall McLuhan, the media theorist prominent in the 1960s, is still quoted as saying that advertising is important after the sale to confirm for purchasers that they made a wise choice. McLuhan's observation has not been lost on advertisers that seek repeat customers.

LEARNING CHECK

- If repeating an advertisement annoys people, why do advertisers do it?

Explore

Media People: Dave Balter

New Advertising Techniques

STUDY PREVIEW What goes around comes around. The original pre-media advertising, word of mouth, has new currency in techniques that go by the name *buzz communication*. The goal is to create buzz about a product. Many buzz campaigns are started on the internet with the hope that they'll spread like a computer virus. The term *viral advertising* has come into fashion.

Watch

ABC's *i-CAUGHT*: The Art of Viral Ads

Word-of-Mouth Advertising

Watch

Advertising on Facebook

A problem in advertising is credibility. Consumers are not sponges who absorb any line laid on them through the mass media. Far more credible for most are stories from friends and acquaintances who have had a favourable experience with a product or service.

Buzz Advertising Word-of-mouth testimonials, friends talking to friends, is strong advertising. But how does word-of-mouth advertising get the buzz going? And how can the buzz be sustained? In the advertising industry's desperation in recent years to find new avenues for making pitches, buzzing has turned into an art. Several agencies specialize in identifying individuals with a large circle of contacts and introducing them to a product. These agents sample the product and are generally able to keep the samples for their help in talking the product up with family, co-workers, and anyone else within earshot. The agents file occasional reports, with the incentive of being eligible for prizes.

A simple way to get buzz going is through the use of social media such as Facebook and Twitter, which have become tools for both advertisers and consumers. While social media may seem like a new trend, it's actually a throwback to the days prior to the Industrial Revolution. Prior to mass media and mass production of goods, people talked to each other and looked to each other for advice. After the development of mass media, people turned to the media for information about products and services. With social media, consumers can now tap into each other's experiences and opinions.

Canadian advertising professor Keith Tuckwell claims that there are three kinds of social network sites. Broad-reach sites are the ones with the most users. These would include YouTube, Facebook, Twitter, and MySpace. Second, there are demographically focused sites. For example, www.carp.ca is a community that deals with the issues of aging. Finally, specific topic sites are social media that centre on one type of topic of discussion. For example, www.exploremusic.com is a community of music fans.

How do buzz and social media stack up against traditional advertising media? Nobody knows, but it's cheap enough that advertisers have seen it as worth trying.

Viral Advertising Another word-of-mouth tactic is **viral advertising**, so called because, when successful, it spreads virus-like through the population via email and social media. Advertisers create clever clips that they hope will prompt viewers to pass the message on

viral advertising Media consumers pass on the message, like a contagious disease, usually on the internet.

Viral Advertising Automakers have experimented with what's called "viral advertising," producing compelling action stories on the web that viewers will want to pass on, virus-like, to friends.

to friends. People open messages from friends, which tangentially increases an ad's reach at low cost. On the downside, however, advertisers can't cancel viral ads, which have a life of their own and can float around the internet for months, or even years.

The video "Bride Has Massive Wig Out" is an excellent example of how advertisers are using viral ads. Posted on YouTube in early 2007, the video appears to show a bride to be cutting her own hair because she's not happy with it. Her "wig out" was an instant hit. Many thought it was real; others questioned its validity. In the final analysis, the ad was commissioned by Toronto advertising agency Capital C to help promote Sunsilk. In the CBC documentary *The Selling Game*, Tony Chapman, the man behind the "wig out" video says it was a really cost-effective way to get the buzz out on Sunsilk: "If you can get it on the digital world, you can go from zero to 3 million downloads, and be the topic of conversation in pop culture media, consumed by it for 3 weeks, for a $3000 investment. That's pretty good marketing." Good marketing, indeed. According to CRTC data, the "Wig Out" video was viewed 2.8 million times in just two weeks after it was posted.

Some advertisers have experimented with consumer-created content on sponsored blog sites. An advantage of these post-your-own-clip sites is the consumer interest created by the bizarre stuff that people post. The sites have a high level of credibility because of their free-for-all nature. But there is also great risk. GM, for example, invited homemade clips about its Chevrolet Tahoe, a large sport utility vehicle. The site ended up hosting TV spot–like messages about the Tahoe contributing to global warming. An advertiser that edits or shuts off negative input runs the risk of losing credibility.

Heavy consumer traffic on social networking sites such as MySpace, YouTube, and Facebook attracts advertising. However, these sites also carry risk because people can post pretty much whatever they want on their pages, including negative information on a product that works against the effectiveness of the paid-for sponsored ads.

LEARNING CHECK

- Who in your group of friends would make a good buzz agent? Why? How about you?
- What are some examples of viral advertising?

Under-the-Radar Advertising

Inundated with advertisements, 6000 per week on network television, double the amount shown in 1983, many people tune out. Some do this literally, with their remotes. Ad people are concerned that traditional modes are losing effectiveness. People are overwhelmed. Consider, for example, that a major grocery store carries 30 000 items, each with packaging that screams "buy me." More commercial messages are put there than a human being can handle. The problem is ad clutter. Advertisers are trying to address the clutter in numerous ways, including stealth ads, new-site ads, and alternative media. Although not hidden or subliminal, stealth ads are subtle, even covert. You might not know you're being pitched unless you're really attentive.

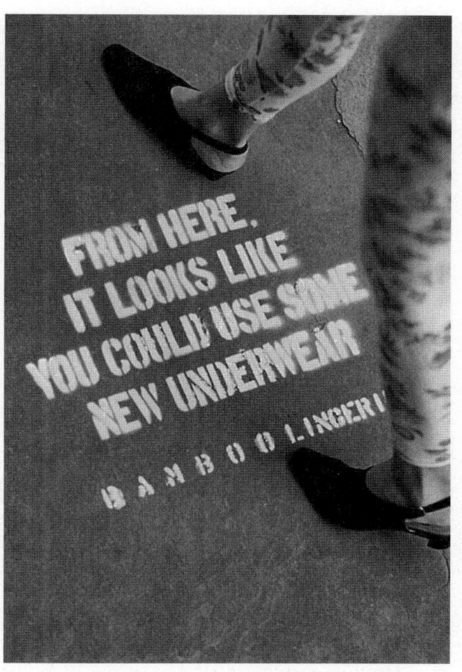

Omnipresent Ads Bamboo Lingerie's stencilled sidewalk messages may have been unsettling to some folks, but they sold underwear. Like many advertisers worried that their messages are lost in ad-crammed traditional media, Bamboo has tried nontraditional territory to be noticed. Regina Kelley, director of strategic planning for the Saatchi & Saatchi agency in New York, said: "Any space you can take in visually, anything you can hear, in the future will be branded."

Stealth Ads So neatly can **stealth ads** fit into the landscape that people may not recognize that they're being pitched. Consider the Bamboo lingerie company, which stencilled messages on a Manhattan sidewalk: "From here it looks like you could use some new underwear." Sports arenas such as Rexall Place in Edmonton work their way into sportscasts and everyday dialogue, subtly reinforcing product identity. In 2007, movie theatres began being sponsored when the Paramount Theatre in Toronto was renamed the Scotiabank Theatre.

stealth ads Advertisements, often subtle, in nontraditional, unexpected places.

Product Placement In the 1980s, advertisers began wriggling brand-name products into movie scripts, creating an additional although minor revenue stream for moviemakers. The practice, called **product placement**, stirred criticism about artistic integrity but gained momentum. Fees zoomed upward. For the 2005 release of *The Green Hornet*, Miramax was seeking an automaker willing to pay at least $35 million for its products to be written into the script, topping the $15 million that Ford paid for its 2003 Thunderbird, Jaguar, and Aston Martin lines to be in the James Bond movie *Die Another Day*.

product placement Writing a brand-name product into a television or movie script.

Later, placing products into television scenes gained importance with the advent of **TiVo** and DVRs that allow people to record shows and replay them commercial-free at their convenience. Their growing popularity worried the television industry, whose business model was dependent on revenue from advertisers to which it guaranteed an audience for ads. With TiVo and DVRs, audiences no longer were trapped into watching commercials. Was the 30-second commercial doomed? The television and advertising industries struck product placement deals that went beyond anything seen before. For a fee, products are being built into scripts not only as props but also for both implicit and explicit endorsement.

TiVo A television recording and playback device that allows viewers to edit out commercials; also called a digital video recorder (DVR) or personal video recorder (PVR).

Infomercials Less subtle is the **infomercial**, a program-length television commercial dolled up to look like either a newscast, a live-audience participation show, or a chatty talk show. With the proliferation of 24-hour television service and of cable channels, airtime is so cheap at certain hours of the day that advertisers of even offbeat products can afford it.

infomercial Program-length broadcast commercial.

'Zine A print media variation is the **'zine**, a magazine published by a manufacturer to plug a single line of products with varying degrees of subtlety. 'Zine publishers, including such stalwarts as IBM and Sony, have even been so brazen as to sell these wall-to-wall advertising vehicles at newsstands. In 1996, if you bought a splashy new magazine called *Colors*, you paid $4.50 for it. Once inside, you probably would realize it was a thinly veiled ad for Benetton casual clothes. *Guess Journal* may look like a magazine, but guess who puts it out as a 'zine? It's the makers of the Guess fashion brand.

'zine Magazine whose entire content—articles and ads—pitches a single product or product line.

An under-the-radar advertisement tries "to morph into the very entertainment it sponsors," wrote Mary Kuntz, Joseph Weber, and Heidi Dawley in *Business Week*. The goal, they said, is "to create messages so entertaining, so compelling—and maybe so disguised—that rapt audiences will swallow them whole, oblivious to the sales component."

Air Canada Centre New site ads, like corporate sponsorship of sports arenas such as the Air Canada Centre in Toronto, offer a new revenue stream for owners but may add to the problem of "ad clutter."

LEARNING CHECK

- How do advertisers try to avoid being lost in ad clutter?

Problems and Issues

Watch

ABC's *Nightline*: "Gas Guzzlers"

STUDY PREVIEW People are exposed to such a blur of ads that advertisers worry that their messages are being lost in the clutter. Some advertising people see more creativity as the answer so that people will want to see and read ads, but there is evidence that creativity can work against an ad's effectiveness.

Advertising Clutter

Leo Bogart of the Newspaper Advertising Bureau noted that the number of advertising messages doubled through the 1960s and 1970s and, except for during the recession at the start of the 1990s, the trend continues. This proliferation of advertising creates a problem: too many ads. The problem has been exacerbated by the shortening of ads from 60 seconds in the early days of television to today's widely used 15-second format. At one time the CRTC limited the amount of TV commercials a station could air to 12 minutes per hour. In 2008, that limit was raised to 15 minutes per hour. While this may make it easier for TV stations to make money, it will only contribute to ad clutter.

Ad clutter is less of an issue in the print media. Many people buy magazines and newspapers to look at ads as part of their comparative shopping process. Even so, some advertisers, concerned that their ads are overlooked in massive editions, such as a 3-kilogram metro Sunday newspaper or a 700-page bridal magazine, are looking to alternative means to reach potential customers in a less cluttered environment.

The clutter that marks much of commercial television and radio today may be alleviated as the media fragment further. Not only will demassification create more specialized outlets, such as narrowly focused cable television services, but there will be new media. The result will be advertising aimed at narrower audiences.

LEARNING CHECK

- Why is ad clutter more of a problem in broadcast media than in print media?
- How might demassification ease the ad clutter problem?

Harry McMahan Dubious about the effectiveness of ad creativity.

Clio Award Award for advertising creativity.

Creative Excess

Advertisers are reviewing whether creativity is as effective an approach as a hard sell. **Harry McMahan** studied **Clio Awards** for creativity in advertising and discovered that

CASE STUDY

Countering Cultural Imperialism

Cultural imperialism occurs when indigenous cultures are displaced, lost forever, by cultural icons and values from more powerful countries and societies. Movies, television shows, and newspapers carry the messages of cultural imperialism. So does advertising. The concept was articulated well in a 1971 book titled *Para leer al pato Donald*, which translates as *How to Read Donald Duck*. Authors Armand Mattelart, a professor of mass communication and ideology at the University of Chile, and Ariel Dorfman, a literary critic and novelist, saw a cultural threat in a growing Walt Disney global popularity that "forces us Latin Americans to see ourselves as they see us." The book went through more than 15 editions and was translated into several languages.

Pure cultural exportation, the Disney model to which Mattelart and Dorfman objected, doesn't work quite the same anymore. U.S.-based MTV customizes its content regionally for 14 different 24-hour feeds around the world. Still, all of these feeds have a commonality. Tellingly, MTV calls the feeds "all different and all similar."

Complicating thing further, some home-country media are accelerating the loss of their own distinctive cultures. In India, the news media have been so influenced by Western media content that European fashion design and American-style beauty queens receive a lot of coverage. Outside influences also are affecting Bollywood, India's domestic film industry. In other places, too, the spread of Western culture has lessened enthusiasm for homegrown works.

This insidious imperialism has become a target of pirate or tactical media that try to undermine the imported influence, sometimes through ridicule. Patricia Aufderheide, professor of communication at American University, defines tactical media as "projects that people do opportunistically—seizing temporarily available or unclaimed resources—to claim or reclaim some communicative channels or some expressive space." One example is billboard "pirating" by Adbusters, a global network of artists, activists, writers, pranksters, students, educators, and entrepreneurs. Its publication, *Adbusters Magazine*, is based in Vancouver.

Autolabs teaches cheap, do-it-yourself media tactics to young people in poor districts and slums in São Paulo, using free software and open-source operational systems. In workshops, the students, ages 17 to 21, recycle discarded computers, learn how to use them, and produce their own media: websites, movies, music, radio programs, and a storytelling archive.

After a year of workshops, the network of interlinked community media centres totalled about 200 countrywide. The plan was to create as many as 1000 centres.

Tactical Media One response in other countries to imported cultural values and icons has been called tactical media. Organizations such as Adbusters and Autolabs turn loose their creative talent to ridicule slick intrusions.

DEEPENING YOUR MEDIA LITERACY

Explore the Issue

The television shows *CSI* and *The Price Is Right* and American soap operas are popular around the world. Watch one of these shows.

Dig Deeper

Make a list of the American values featured and the messages that the show subtly or overtly promotes. Look for unstated and underlying messages. What kind of lifestyle is being presented? Is it glamorized? How? What values are expressed? Is the promotion of these values a product of commercialism? Is there any benefit for local cultures?

What Do You Think?

Do you think projects like Adbusters can be effective?

36 agencies that produced 81 winners of the prestigious awards for advertisements had either lost the winning account or gone out of business.

Advertising commentator E.B. Weiss predicted: "Extravagant license for creative people will be curtailed." The future may hold more heavy-handed pitches, perhaps with over-the-counter regimens not only promising fast-fast-fast relief but also spelling it out in all caps and boldface with exclamation marks: **F-A-S-T! F-A-S-T!! F-A-S-T!!!**

LEARNING CHECK

- Does creativity in advertising translate into sales successes? Explain.

Chapter 12 Wrap-Up

The role of advertising in North American mass media cannot be overstated. In one sense, advertisers subsidize readers, viewers, and listeners, who pay only a fraction of the cost of producing publications and broadcasts. The bulk of the cost is paid by advertisers, who are willing to do so to make their pitches to potential customers who, coincidentally, are media consumers. Besides underwriting the mass media, advertising is vital for a prosperous, growing consumer economy.

The original pre-media advertising, word-of-mouth, is back. This time it's called buzz communication. The goal is to get people talking about a product. Many buzz campaigns originate on the internet with the hope of spreading virus-like. The term *viral advertising* has come into favour.

PEARSON mycanadiancommunicationlab

Visit **www.mycanadiancommunicationlab.ca** for access to a wealth of tools and resources that will enhance your learning experience. Features include the following:

- Personalized Study Plan
- Videos
- Activities
- Pearson eText–and much more!

Questions for Critical Thinking

1. What is advertising's role in a capitalistic society, in a democracy, and in the mass media?
2. Trace the development of advertising since Johannes Gutenberg.
3. What new platforms and tactics are advertisers trying? What are the long-term prospects for each?
4. How is brand-name advertising morphing?
5. What unanswered issues face the advertising industry? What answers do you see?

Keeping Up to Date

Weekly trade journals include *Marketing* magazine, *Advertising Age*, and *AdWeek*.

Scholarly publications include the *Journal of Marketing Research* and the *Journal of Advertising*. *The Globe and Mail* regularly reports on the industry.

The *Journal of Consumer Psychology* includes analysis, reviews, reports, and other scholarship on the role of advertising in consumer psychology.

Media Research

13

Billboard Meter To measure the number of people who pass electronically tagged billboards, Nielsen Media Research issues palm-size devices that tell when participants pass an electronically coded billboard. Data are uploaded from the device to a satellite, then down to Nielsen data keepers who keep score.

LEARNING AHEAD

- Surveys of mass audiences factor into media content.
- Mass audience size is measured by press runs, sales, and surveys.
- Audience measuring companies have gone electronic to track media habits.
- Reactions of mass audiences are part of media content decision making.
- Audience analysis includes demographics, geodemographics, and psychographics.

MEDIA IN THEORY

Applied and Theoretical Research

Media-Sponsored Research

Studies sponsored by mass media companies seek information that can be put to use. This is called **applied research.** When broadcasters pay someone to conduct research on media consumption, they do it because the information will help them to make programming decisions. It's called *applied research* because the audience measures and analysis are used to enhance profits.

applied research Usefulness, usually economic, is apparent.

Mass media research ranges from developing new technology to seeking historical lessons from previous practices. Here are some fields of applied media research:

Technological Research Mass media companies and their suppliers finance **technological research** to take economic advantage of new opportunities. Early radio in Canada, for example, was spearheaded by the Canadian National Railway, which saw it as a business opportunity.

technological research To improve technology and find new technology.

Policy Analysis The media have intense interests in how changes in public policy will affect their business. The importance of good **policy analysis** was illustrated by the decision of the government 30 years ago to allow people to install backyard satellite dishes to pick

policy analysis Seeks implications of public policy and future effects.

up television signals. Analysts had anticipated correctly that the television networks would go to satellites to send programs to their affiliates.

opinion surveys Seek audience reactions and views.

Opinion Surveys When anchor Dan Rather began wearing a sweater on the *CBS Evening News*, ratings improved. The network learned about the "sweater factor" from audience **opinion surveys.** Survey research also helps media executives to make content decisions: whether to expand sports coverage, to hire a disc jockey away from the competition, or to axe a dubious sitcom. Advertisers and public relations practitioners also look to public-opinion surveys.

Mass Communication Scholarship

theoretical research Goal is to advance knowledge.

In contrast to applied research, **theoretical research** looks for truths regardless of practical application. Scholars consider most theoretical research to be on a higher level than applied research, partly because the force that drives it is the seeking of truths for their own sake rather than for any economic goal. Here are some of the kinds of studies and analyses that are the subject of theoretical research:

Effects Studies The greatest ferment in mass communication scholarship has involved questions about effects. In the 1920s, as mass communication theory took form, scholars began exploring the effects of mass communication and of the mass media themselves on society and individuals. Conversely, scholars are also interested in how ongoing changes and adjustments in society influence the mass media and their content. The research is known as **effects studies.**

effects studies Impact of media on society and of society on media.

Process Studies A continuing interest among scholars is the mystery of how the process of mass communication works. Just as human beings have developed theories to explain other great mysteries, such as whether thunder is caused by unhappy gods thrashing about in the heavens, mass communication scholars have developed, in **process studies,** a great many explanations to help us understand mass communication.

process studies To understand the mass communication process.

Uses and Gratifications Studies Beginning in the 1940s, studies about how and why individuals use the mass media attracted scholarly interest. Today, these are called **uses and gratifications studies** (see also the discussion in Chapter 15).

uses and gratifications studies Theory that people choose media that meet their needs and interests.

content analysis Measuring media content to establish a database for analysis.

Content Analysis George Gerbner, a scholar of media violence, studied the 8 P.M. hour of network television over a period of 19 years and found an average of 168 violent acts a week. Gerbner arrived at his disturbing statistic through **content analysis,** a research method involving the systematic counting of media content. Gerbner's tallying became a basic reference point for important further studies that correlated media-depicted violence with changes in incidence of violence in society at large.

It is also content analysis when a researcher tallies the column inches of sports in a newspaper to determine what percentage of available space goes to sports. While interesting for its own sake, such information can become a significant indicator of the changing role of sports in contemporary life.

LEARNING CHECK

- What's the difference between applied and theoretical research?

MEDIA TIMELINE Media Research

1914	Advertisers and publications created the Audit Bureau of Circulations to verify circulation claims.
1929	Archibald Crossley conducted the first listenership survey.
1932	George Gallup used quota sampling in an Iowa election.
1936	Gallup used quota sampling in a presidential election.
1940s	A.C. Nielsen conducted a demographic listenership survey.
1948	Gallup used probability sampling in a presidential election.
1970s	SRI introduced VALS psychographics.
1979	Jonathan Robbin introduced PRIZM geodemographics.
2004	Nielsen began using larger sample sizes for TV ratings.
2006	Nielsen added measures of internet, iPod, and mobile devices.
2009	Portable People Meters were introduced to track media consumption.

Public-Opinion Sampling

STUDY PREVIEW The effectiveness of mass media messages is measured through research techniques that are widely recognized in the social sciences and in business.

Survey Industry

Public-opinion surveying is a multi-billion-dollar-a-year business whose clients include major corporations, political candidates, and the mass media. Hundreds of companies are in the survey business in the United States and Canada, most of them performing advertising- and product-related opinion research for private clients. During election campaigns, political candidates become major clients. There are dozens of other survey companies that do confidential research for and about the media. Their findings are important because they determine what kind of advertising will run and where, what programs will be developed and broadcast, and which ones will be cancelled. The major companies in North America include:

Explore

Media People: George Gallup

- **BBM.** This company has been providing data for Canadian radio stations since 1944. It also supplies data on Canadian television viewing.
- **Nielsen.** Nielsen Media Research, owned by Dutch publisher VNU, is known mostly for its network television ratings, although it also does local television ratings in major markets and other sampling.
- **Arbitron.** Arbitron measures mostly radio audiences in local markets.
- **Gallup.** The Gallup Organization studies human nature and behaviour and specializes in management, economics, psychology, and sociology.
- **Pew.** The Pew Research Center is an independent opinion research group that studies attitudes toward the press, politics, and public policy issues.
- **Harris.** Market research firm Harris Interactive Inc. is perhaps best known for the Harris Poll and for pioneering and engineering internet-based research methods.

LEARNING CHECK

- Name as many major public opinion sampling companies as you can.
- To whom do polling companies sell their information?

Probability Sampling

Although polling has become a high-profile business, many people do not understand how questions asked of a few hundred individuals can tell the mood of 350 million North Americans. In the **probability sampling** method pioneered by **George Gallup** in the 1940s, four factors figure into accurate surveying.

probability sampling Everyone in population being surveyed has an equal chance of being sampled.

George Gallup Introduced probability sampling.

Sample Size To learn how students from a certain college or university feel about abortion on demand, you must start by asking one student. Because you can hardly generalize from one student to the whole student body of 10 000, you must ask a second student. If both agree, you start to develop a tentative sense of how students feel, but because you cannot have much confidence in such a tiny sample, you must ask a third student and a fourth and a fifth. At some point between interviewing just one and all 10 000 students, you can draw a reasonable conclusion.

How do you choose a **sample size**? Statisticians have found that **384** is a magic number for many surveys. Put simply, no matter how large the **population** being sampled, if every member has an equal opportunity to be polled, you need ask only 384 people to be 95 percent confident that you are within 5 percentage points of a precise reading. For a lot of surveys, that is close enough.

sample size Number of people surveyed.

384 Number of people in a properly selected sample for results to provide 95 percent confidence that results have less than 5 percent margin of error.

population Group of people being studied.

Here is a breakdown, from Philip Meyer's *Precision Journalism*, a book for journalists on surveying, on necessary sample sizes for 95 percent confidence and being within 5 percentage points:

Population Size	Sample Size
Infinity	384
500 000	384
100 000	383
50 000	381
10 000	370
5 000	357
3 000	341
2 000	322
1 000	278

At a college or university with a total enrolment of 10 000, the sample size would need to be 370 students.

sample selection Process for drawing individuals to be interviewed.

Sample Selection The process of choosing whom to interview is known as **sample selection.** Essential in probability sampling is giving every member of the population being sampled an equal chance to be interviewed. If, for example, you want to know how people in Winnipeg intend to vote, you cannot merely go to the corner of Portage and Main and survey the first 384 people who pass by. You would need to check a list of the province's registered voters (450 000) and then divide by the magic number, 384.

$$\frac{450\,000}{384} = 1172$$

You would need to talk with every 1172nd person on the list.

Besides the right sample size and proper interval selection, two other significant variables affect survey accuracy: margin of error and confidence level.

margin of error Percentage that a survey may be off the mark.

Margin of Error For absolute precision, every person in the population must be interviewed, but such precision is hardly ever needed, and the process would be prohibitively expensive and impracticable. Pollsters must therefore decide what an acceptable **margin of error** is for every survey they conduct. This is a complex matter, but in simple terms you can have a fairly high level of confidence that a properly designed survey with 384 respondents can yield results within 5 percentage points, either way, of being correct. If the survey finds that two candidates for provincial office are running 51 to 49 percent, for example, the race is too close to call with a sample of 384. If the survey says that the candidates are running 56 to 44 percent, however, you can be reasonably confident who is ahead in the race because, even if the survey is 5 points off on the high side for the leader, the candidate at the very least has 51 percent support (56 percent minus a maximum

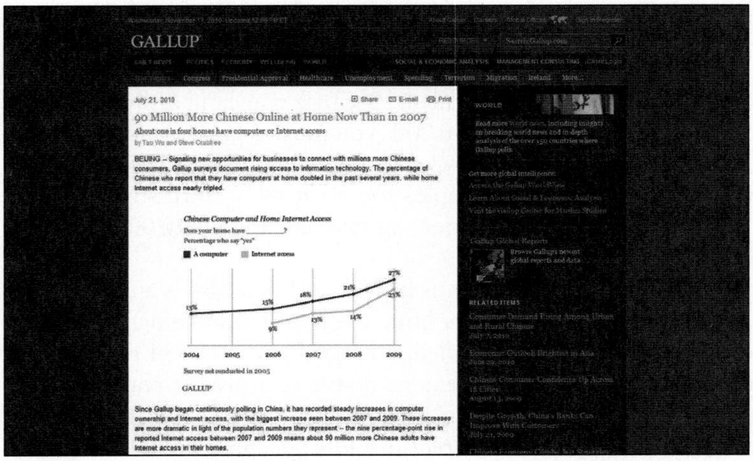

Probability Sampling Data collection has become more sophisticated since George Gallup began polling in the 1930s. Polls today track changes in public attitudes over the several decades that data have been accumulated.

5 percentage points for possible error). At best, the trailing candidate has 49 percent (44 percent plus a maximum 5 percentage points for possible error).

statistical extrapolation Drawing conclusions from a segment of the whole.

Increasing the sample size will reduce the margin of error. Meyer gives this breakdown:

Population Size	Sample Size	Margin of Error
Infinity	384	5 percentage points
Infinity	600	4 percentage points
Infinity	1067	3 percentage points
Infinity	2401	2 percentage points
Infinity	9605	1 percentage points

MEDIA PEOPLE George Gallup

George Gallup

George Gallup was excited. His mother-in-law, Ola Babcock Miller, had decided to run for secretary of state. If elected, she would become not only Iowa's first Democrat but also the first woman to hold the statewide office. Gallup's excitement, however, went beyond the novelty of his mother-in-law's candidacy. The campaign gave him an opportunity to pull together his three primary intellectual interests: survey research, public opinion, and politics. In that 1932 campaign, George Gallup conducted the first serious poll in history for a political candidate. Gallup's surveying provided important barometers of public sentiment that helped Miller to gear her campaign to the issues that were most on voters' minds. She won and was re-elected twice by large margins.

Four years after that first 1932 election campaign, Gallup used his polling techniques during the presidential race and correctly predicted that Franklin Roosevelt would beat Alf Landon. Having called Roosevelt's victory accurately, his Gallup Poll organization soon had clients knocking at his door.

Gallup devoted himself to accuracy. Even though he predicted Roosevelt's 1936 victory, he was bothered that his reliability was not better. His method, quota sampling, could not call a two-way race within four percentage points. With quota sampling, a representative percentage of women and men was surveyed, as was a representative percentage of Democrats and Republicans, Westerners and Easterners, Christians and Jews, and other constituencies.

In 1948, Gallup correctly concluded that Thomas Dewey was not a shoo-in for president. Nonetheless, his pre-election poll was 5.3 percentage points off. So he decided to switch to a tighter method, probability sampling, which theoretically gave everyone in the population being sampled an equal chance to be surveyed. With probability sampling, there was no need for quotas because, as Gallup explained in his folksy Midwestern way, it was like a cook making soup: "When a housewife wants to test the quality of the soup she is making, she tastes only a teaspoonful or two. She knows that if the soup is thoroughly stirred, one teaspoonful is enough to tell her whether she has the right mixture of ingredients." With the new method, Gallup's **statistical extrapolation** narrowed his error rate to less than 2 percentage points.

Even with improvements pioneered by Gallup, public-opinion surveying has detractors. Some critics say that polls influence undecided voters toward the front-runner and create a bandwagon effect. Other critics say that polls make elected officials too responsive to the momentary whims of the electorate and discourage courageous leadership. George Gallup, who died in 1984, tirelessly defended polling, arguing that good surveys give voice to the "inarticulate minority" that legislators otherwise might not hear. Gallup was convinced that public-opinion surveys help to make democracy work.

WHAT DO YOU THINK?

1. What variables determine how close is close enough in probability sampling?
2. Explain George Gallup's metaphor of polling as making soup.
3. Do you trust election polls? What do you need to know to have confidence in a poll?

Professional polling organizations that sample American voters typically use sample sizes between 1500 and 3000 to increase accuracy. Also, measuring subgroups within the population being sampled requires that each subgroup, such as men and women, Catholics and non-Catholics, or Northerners and Southerners, be represented by 384 properly selected people.

confidence level Degree of certainty that a survey is accurate.

Confidence Level With a sample of 384, pollsters can claim a relatively high 95 percent **confidence level**; that is, that they are within 5 percentage points of being on the mark. For many surveys, this is sufficient statistical validity. If the confidence level needs to be higher, or if the margin of error needs to be decreased, the number of people surveyed will need to be increased. In short, the level of confidence and margin of error are inversely related. A larger sample can improve confidence, just as it also can reduce the margin of error.

LEARNING CHECK

- How does probability sampling work?
- Does probability sampling necessarily yield accurate results with samples of 384?
- What is margin of error?

Quota Sampling

quota sampling Demographics of the sample coincide with those of the whole population.

Besides probability sampling, pollsters survey cross-sections of the whole population. With **quota sampling**, a pollster checking an election campaign interviews a sample of people that includes a quota of men and women that corresponds to the number of male and female registered voters. The sample might also include an appropriate quota of Liberals, Conservatives, and New Democrats; of poor, middle-income, and wealthy people; of Catholics, Jews, and Protestants; of the employed and unemployed; and other breakdowns significant to the pollster.

Both quota sampling and probability sampling are valid if done correctly, but Gallup abandoned quota sampling because he could not pinpoint public opinion more closely than four percentage points on average. With probability sampling, he regularly came within two percentage points.

LEARNING CHECK

- How does quota sampling differ from probability sampling?
- What attracted George Gallup to probability sampling?

Evaluating Surveys

Deepening Your Media Literacy: How reliable are person in the street interviews?

Sidewalk interviews cannot be expected to reflect the views of the population. The people who respond to such polls are self-selected by virtue of being at a given place at a given time. Just as unreliable are phone-in polls with 1-800 or 1-900 telephone numbers. These polls test the views only of people who are aware of the poll and who have sufficiently strong opinions to go to the trouble of calling in.

Journalists run the risk of being duped when special-interest groups suggest that news stories be written based on their privately conducted surveys. Some organizations selectively release self-serving conclusions.

To guard against being duped, the Canadian Press (CP) insists on knowing methodology details before running poll stories. In *The Canadian Press Stylebook*, CP tells reporters to ask:

- **How many people were interviewed and how were they selected?** Any survey of fewer than 384 people selected randomly from the population group has a greater margin for error than is usually tolerated.
- **When was the poll taken?** Reporters should make note of the date on which the survey was taken. Opinions shift over time. During election campaigns, shifts can be quick, even overnight.
- **Who paid for the poll?** A sponsored poll may be biased; therefore, reporters should be skeptical, asking whether the results being released constitute everything learned in the survey. It is not uncommon for the timing of the release of political polls to be politically advantageous.

- **How was the sample selected?** Reporters should ensure that respondents were selected via random selection. Margins of error exist in all surveys unless everyone in the sample had an equal chance of being surveyed.
- **How was the poll conducted?** Whether a survey was conducted over the telephone or face to face in homes is important. Polls conducted on street corners or in shopping malls are not worth much statistically. Mail surveys are flawed unless surveyors follow up on people who do not answer the original questionnaires.
- **How were questions worded and in what order were they asked?** Drafting questions is an art. Sloppily worded questions yield sloppy conclusions. Leading questions and loaded questions can skew results. So can question sequencing.

It is with great risk that a polling company's client misrepresents survey results. Most polling companies, concerned about protecting their reputations, include a clause in their contracts with clients that gives the pollster the right to approve the release of findings. The clause usually reads: "When misinterpretation appears, we shall publicly disclose what is required to correct it, notwithstanding our obligation for client confidentiality in all other respects."

LEARNING CHECK

- What information do you need to assess what a survey purports to have found?
- How can survey outcomes be manipulated?

Latter-Day Straw Polls

Many media outlets dabble, some say irresponsibly, with phone-in polling on public issues. The vehicle is the **1-900 telephone number**, which listeners dial at 50 cents a call to register yea or nay on a question. These **straw polls** are conducted on the internet too. While they can be fun, statistically they are meaningless.

1-900 telephone numbers Used for phone-in surveys; respondents select themselves to participate and they pay for the call.

straw poll Respondents select themselves to be polled; unreliable indicator of public opinion.

Just as dubious are the candid camera features, popular in weekly newspapers, in which a question is put to people on the street. The photos of half a dozen individuals and their comments are then published, often on the editorial page. These features are circulation builders for small publications whose financial success depends on how many local names and mug shots can be crammed into an issue, but it is only coincidental when the views expressed are representative of the population as a whole.

These **roving photographer** features are at their worst when people are not given time to formulate an intelligent response. The result too often is a contribution to the public babble, not public understanding. The result is irresponsible pseudo-journalism.

roving photographer Statistically unsound way to tap public opinion.

LEARNING CHECK

- Why are listener call-in polls statistically suspect?

Measuring Audience Size

STUDY PREVIEW To attract advertisers, the mass media need to know the number and kinds of people they reach. This is done for the print media by audits and for the broadcast media by surveys. Some approaches are more reliable than others.

Explore

Media People: Andy Kohut

Newspaper and Magazine Audits

The number of copies a newspaper or magazine puts out, called **circulation**, is fairly easy to calculate. It is simple arithmetic involving data such as press runs, subscription sales, and unsold copies returned from newsracks. Many publishers follow strict procedures, which are checked by independent audit organizations, such as the **Audit Bureau of Circulations** (**ABC**), to assure advertisers that the system is honest and that circulation claims are comparable.

circulation Number of readers of a publication.

Audit Bureau of Circulations (ABC) Checks newspaper circulation claims.

The ABC was formed in 1914 to remove the temptation for publishers to inflate their claims to attract advertisers and hike ad rates. Inflated claims, contagious in some cities, were working to the disadvantage of honest publishers. Today, most newspapers and magazines belong to ABC, which means that they follow the bureau's standards for reporting circulation and are subject to the bureau's audits.

Print Measurement Bureau (PMB) Checks magazine circulation claims.

The **Print Measurement Bureau (PMB)** tracks magazine sales in Canada. In 2001, it introduced a new method to measure readership in Canada. The "recent reading" method doesn't measure how many magazines have been sold, but rather how many have been read. A survey asks respondents when they last read an issue of *Maclean's* or *Reader's Digest*. PMB feels that this helps to paint a truer picture of how successful Canadian magazines are. This method is also used worldwide to measure magazine readership.

LEARNING CHECK

- How do advertisers know how much circulation they are buying in print media?

Broadcast Ratings

Radio and television audiences are difficult to measure, but advertisers still need counts to help them decide where to place ads and what is a fair price. To keep track of broadcast audiences, a whole **ratings** industry, now with about 200 companies worldwide, has developed. Today in Canada, the Bureau of Measurement (BBM) and Nielsen Media Research both provide useful data for Canadian advertisers by measuring radio, television, and web audiences. In 2006, the two companies entered into a joint venture and formed **BBM Nielsen Media Research.**

ratings Measurements of broadcast audience size.

BBM Nielsen Media Research Surveys TV and radio in Canada.

Radio ratings began in 1929 when advertisers asked pollster Archibald Crossley to determine how many people were listening to network programs. Crossley checked a small sample of households and then extrapolated the data into national ratings, the same process that radio and television audience tracking companies still use, though there have been refinements.

In the 1940s, Nielsen began telling advertisers which radio programs were especially popular among men, women, and children. Nielsen also divided listenership into age brackets: 18 to 34, 35 to 49, and 50-plus. These were called **demographic** breakdowns. When Nielsen moved into television monitoring in 1950, it expanded audience data into more breakdowns. Today, breakdowns include income, education, religion, occupation, neighbourhood, and even which products the viewers of certain programs use frequently.

demographics Characteristics of groups within a population being sampled, including age, gender, and affiliations.

LEARNING CHECK

- Why are advertisers interested in broadcast audience ratings?
- How do television networks and radio stations use ratings?

Audience Measurement Techniques

The primary techniques, sometimes used in combination, for measuring broadcast audiences are interview, diaries, and meters.

Interviews In his pioneer 1929 listenership polling, Archibald Crossley placed telephone calls to randomly selected households. Although many polling companies use telephone **interviews** exclusively, they're not used much in broadcasting anymore. Also rare in broadcasting are face-to-face interviews. Although eyeball-to-eyeball interviewing can elicit fuller information, it is labour-intensive and relatively expensive.

interviews Face-to-face, mail, or telephone survey technique.

Diaries Nielsen began using **diaries** in the 1950s. Instead of interviews, Nielsen mailed forms to selected families in major markets to list program titles, times, channels, and who was watching. This was done in major sweep periods: February, May, July, and November. Although diaries were cost-efficient, viewers would forget their duty and then try to remember days later what they had watched. The resulting data were better than no data but were rather muddy.

diaries Sampling technique in which respondents keep their own records.

Meters Meters were introduced in the 1970s as a supplement to diaries to improve accuracy. Some Nielsen families had their sets wired to track what channel was on. Some were issued meters that household members could click so that Nielsen could determine for whom programs have their appeal: men, women, or children.

People Meters In 1987, Nielsen introduced **people meters**. These were two-function units, one on the television set to scan the channels being watched every 2.7 seconds and a handheld remote that monitored who was watching. With data flowing in nightly to Nielsen's central computers, the company generates next-day reports, called **overnights**, for the networks and advertisers.

people meters Devices that track individual viewers.

overnights Next-morning reports on network viewership.

Portable Meters In 2001, Nielsen and **Arbitron**, which focuses on radio audiences, jointly tested portable meters for people to carry around. The pager-size meters, weighing about 70 grams, were set to pick up inaudible signals transmitted with programs. The goal: to track away-from-home audiences at sports bars, offices, and airports and, in the case of radio, cars. Tracking those "lost listeners" could affect ratings. The Portable People Meters, or PPMs as they are called, also track commuter radio habits for the first time. In 2009, BBM began using these in major Canadian markets.

Arbitron International media and marketing research company.

LEARNING CHECK

- What methods do ratings companies use to measure broadcast audiences?

Internet Audience Measures

The leading internet audience measuring company, **Media Metrix**, uses a two-track system to determine how many people view websites. Media Metrix gathers data from 40 000 individual computers whose owners have agreed to be monitored. Some of these computers are programmed to track internet usage and report data back by email. In addition, Media Metrix has lined up other computer users to mail in a tracking disk periodically. In 1998, the Nielsen television ratings company set up a similar methodology. Other companies also are in the internet ratings business.

Media Metrix A service measuring internet audience size.

How accurate are internet ratings? Some major content providers, including CNN, ESPN, and Time Warner, claim that the ratings undercount their users. Such claims go beyond self-serving comments because, in fact, different rating companies come up with widely divergent ratings. The question is: Why can't the ratings companies get it right? The answer, in part, is that divergent data flow from divergent methodologies. Data need to be viewed in terms of the methodology that was used. Also, the infant internet ratings business undoubtedly is hobbled by methodology flaws that have yet to be identified and corrected.

LEARNING CHECK

- How accurate are ratings of commercial internet sites?

Multimedia Measures

Recognizing that television viewers were increasingly mobile and less set-bound, Nielsen began remaking its ratings system in 2006 to measure the use of personal computers, video game players, iPods, cell phones, and other mobile devices. Nielsen said that the program, called **Anytime Anywhere Media Measurement**, or **A2/M2** for short, represented a commitment to "follow the video" with an "all-electronic measurement system that will deliver integrated ratings for television viewing regardless of the platform." Nielsen's chief researcher, Paul Donato, put it this way: "The plan is to try to capture it all."

Anytime Anywhere Media Measurement (A2/M2) Nielsen plan to integrate audience measurements on a wide range of video platforms.

An initial step was creating a panel of 400 video iPod users to track the programs they download and watch. Nielson also began fusing data from its television-tracking unit and its Nielsen/Net Ratings unit to measure the relation between conventional television viewing and web surfing with meters on both televisions and personal computers.

LEARNING CHECK

- What is A2/M2? Why is it important?

Mobile Audience Measures

Over-the-air networks tried to address the audience leakage to DVD and TiVo-like devices when the Nielsen ratings service introduced its Live Plus Seven measure in 2006. The new measure tracked live viewing plus any viewing within seven days. The networks built the extended period into their audience guarantees with advertisers. The network argument was that DVD and TiVo viewers are more affluent as a group and therefore worth more to advertisers. Advertisers balked, arguing that ads viewed after the fact have diminished value. Also, the new Nielsen gizmo for recording viewers didn't record ads that were skipped, which TiVo facilitates. Advertisers were more comfortable with Nielsen's live-plus-same-day counts, which included DVD viewing before the next morning.

Despite the issue over the counting period being spread out, Nielsen continued to install the new measuring devices. By 2007, about 18 percent of measured American households were included.

LEARNING CHECK

- How do devices like TiVos and PVRs complicate the data gathering process?

Criticism of Ratings

However sophisticated the ratings services have become, they have critics. Many fans question the accuracy of ratings when their favourite television program is cancelled because the network finds the ratings to be inadequate. Something is wrong, they say, when the viewing preferences of a few thousand households determine network programming for the entire nation. Ratings have problems, some of which are inherent in differing methodologies and some of which are attributable to human error and fudging.

Discrepancies When different ratings services come up with widely divergent findings in the same market, advertisers become suspicious. Minor discrepancies can be explained by different sampling methods, but significant discrepancies point to flawed methodology or execution.

Slanted Results Sales reps of some local stations, eager to demonstrate to advertisers that their stations have large audiences, extract only the favourable data from survey results. It takes a sophisticated local advertiser to reconcile slanted and fudged claims.

Sample Selection Some ratings services select their samples meticulously, giving every household in a market a statistically equal opportunity to be sampled. Some sample selections are seriously flawed. How reliable, for example, are the listenership claims of a rock 'n' roll station that puts a disc jockey's face on billboards all over town and then sends the disc jockey to a high school to ask about listening preferences?

sweeps Period when broadcast ratings are conducted.

hyping Intensive promotion to attract an audience during ratings periods.

Hyping Ratings-hungry stations have learned how to build audiences during **sweeps** weeks in February, May, and November when major local television ratings are done. Consider these examples of **hyping:**

- Radio giveaways often coincide with ratings periods.
- Many news departments promote sensationalistic series for the sweeps period and then retreat to routine coverage when the ratings period is over. Just ahead of a Minneapolis sweeps, one station mailed out thousands of questionnaires, asking people to watch its programs and mail back the form. Accused of trickery to look good in the ratings, the station responded with a straight face that it merely was trying a new technique to strengthen viewership. The timing, it argued, was a coincidence.
- Besides sweeps weeks, there are **black weeks** when no ratings are conducted. In these periods some stations run all kinds of odd and dull serve-the-public programs that they would never consider airing during a sweeps period.

black weeks Periods when ratings are not conducted.

Respondent Accuracy Respondents don't always answer truthfully. People may tell interviewers or diaries that they watched *Masterpiece Theatre* on PBS when they really watched a rerun of *Trailer Park Boys* on Showcase. For the same reason, shock radio and trash television may have a larger audience than the ratings show.

Zipping, Zapping, and Flushing Ratings services measure audiences for programs and for different times of day, but they do not measure whether commercials are watched. Advertisers are interested, of course, in whether the programs in which their ads are sandwiched are popular, but more important to them is whether people are watching the ads.

CASE STUDY

New Tracking Technology

As Ron Kolessar was developing the Portable People Meter (PPM), he knew it could shape the future of media and advertising. Kolessar, the chief engineer at Arbitron, began work on the PPM in early 1992 when his bosses asked him to find a less expensive way to monitor television and radio audiences at the same time.

At first, research companies collected data by asking people to keep a diary. Then Nielsen began using its electronic People Meter, which automatically recorded what channel a television set was tuned to. But Kolessar realized that to get the complete story, research companies needed to "monitor the person." His PPM records what the wearer is hearing at all times, not just at home but also at the sports bar, at work, in the supermarket, and in hotel rooms. After 13 years and $80 million in development, tests were run in Philadelphia and Houston in which people wore the pager-size device all day, docking it at night so it could send information back to its mother computer.

The device works through a process known as psychoacoustic masking. Arbitron has asked radio and television stations around the country to run their broadcasts through an encoding device that embeds a signal that is inaudible to humans but that can be picked up by the PPM.

The object is to track audience fragmentation, the emerging phenomenon in which members of a family no longer sit on the couch together to watch a television program. Today's family views different television, radio, and internet fare at the same time. As time becomes more precious, people seek content in whatever way works best for them: broadband, digital satellite, or terrestrial. As the audience fragments, the economic model for advertisers changes and bigger samples are needed. BBM Nielsen Media Research began using PPMs in 2002 on a trial basis in Quebec markets. The rest of Canada soon followed. By 2009, PPMs were in use in major Canadian markets.

Once feared by advertisers, audience fragmentation now is seen as a great opportunity. Advertisers will be able to target small niche audiences. David Bray of Canada's Hennesey-Bray Communications has this to say about PPMs and collecting radio data: "We can now see tuning behaviour in tremendous detail. Reporting is reliable. Tuning is broken down into one minute increments which are much more precise. We can watch as a listener moves through his pre-sets or walks from store to store with different stations playing over the sound system. Diary generally reports that people listen to three stations. PPM says six to seven stations. Certain types of stations seem to suffer with PPM. Heritage stations such as CBC can experience a bit of 'halo' tuning in diary reporting (which relies on the listener's memory) which disappears with the passive recording of PPM. Conversely 'office' stations thrive under the passive reporting format. Younger rock stations, which had trouble getting young adult males to fill out diaries, seem to come back strong with PPM."

Outside-the-Home Television Measuring television audiences has become a greater challenge with the proliferation of sets in airports, bars, and even gyms. Companies are working on devices that will allow researchers to check exposure to various media. The "walking meters" pick up codes embedded in the audio of television, radio, and streamed programs, as well as signals sent out by billboards as volunteers pass by.

As the technology of the mass media continues to progress, audience measurement companies must find ways to keep up. That could mean dramatic changes in the way that viewership figures are tallied. And it could result in major shifts in the way that advertising dollars are spent and received. Stay tuned.

DEEPENING YOUR MEDIA LITERACY

Explore the Issue

Find someone who has been asked to participate in a public opinion poll. Does that person know why he or she was chosen?

Dig Deeper

Ask about the reliability of the information given to the polling company. Were answers based on recollection? Ask the person how completely he or she collected the information. Was it merely from memory or recollection?

What Do You Think?

Will consumers benefit as much as advertisers from the newest audience tracking technology?

flush factor Viewers leave during commercials to go to the refrigerator, bathroom, etc.

This vacuum in audience measurements was documented in the 1960s when somebody with a sense of humour correlated a major drop in Chicago water pressure with the Super Bowl halftime, in what became known as the **flush factor**. Football fans were getting off the couch by the thousands at halftime to go to the bathroom. Advertisers were missing many people because although viewers were watching the program, many were not watching the ads.

zipping Viewers change television channels to avoid commercials.

zapping Viewers record programs and eliminate commercial breaks.

This problem has been exacerbated with the advent of handheld television remote controls and DVR systems. Viewers can **zip** from station to station to avoid commercials, and when they record programs for later viewing they can **zap** out the commercials.

LEARNING CHECK

- Why are broadcast ratings susceptible to criticism?

Measuring Audience Reaction

Explore

Media People: Richard Schwartz

STUDY PREVIEW The television ratings business has moved beyond measuring audience size to measuring audience reaction. Researchers measure audience reaction through numerous methods, including focus groups, galvanic skin checks, and prototypes.

Focus Groups

focus groups Small groups interviewed in loosely structured ways for opinions and reactions.

Television consulting companies measure audience reaction through **focus groups**. Typically, an interview crew goes to a shopping centre, chooses a dozen individuals by gender and age, and offers them cookies, soft drinks, and $25 each to sit down and watch a taped local newscast. A moderator then asks for their reactions, sometimes with loaded and leading questions to open them up. It is a tricky research method that depends highly on the skill of the moderator. In one court case, an anchor who had lost her job as a result of responses to a focus group complained that the moderator had contaminated the process with prejudicial assertions and questions, such as:

- "This is your chance to get rid of the things you don't like to see on the news."
- "Come on, unload on those sons of bitches who make $100 000 a year."
- "This is your chance to do more than just yell at the TV. You can speak up and say I really hate that guy or I really like that broad."
- "Let's spend 30 seconds destroying this anchor. Is she a mutt? Be honest about this."

Even when conducted skilfully, focus groups have the disadvantage of reflecting the opinion of the loudest respondent.

LEARNING CHECK

- What is the role of analysis in focus group research?
- What is the role of a focus group moderator?

Galvanic Skin Checks

galvanic skin checks Monitor pulse and skin responses to stimuli.

Consulting companies hired by television stations run a great variety of studies to determine audience reaction. Local stations, which originate news programs and not much else, look to these consultants for advice on news sets, story selection, and even which anchors and reporters are most popular. Besides surveys, these consultants sometimes use **galvanic skin checks**. Wires are attached to individuals in a sample group of viewers to measure pulse and skin reactions, such as perspiration. Advocates of these tests claim

If It Bleeds, It Leads Audience researchers have found that newscast ratings go up for stations that consistently deliver graphic video. This has prompted many stations to favour stories about fires, for example, if graphic video is available—even if the fire wasn't consequential. The ratings quest also prompts these stations to favour crimes and accidents over more substantive stories, such as government budgets, that don't lend themselves to gripping graphics.

that they reveal how much interest a newscast evokes and whether that interest is positive or negative.

These tests were first used to check audience reaction to advertisements, but today some stations look to them in deciding whether to remodel a studio. A dubious use, from a journalistic perspective, is using galvanic skin checks to determine what kinds of stories to cover and whether to find new anchors and reporters. The skin checks reward short, photogenic stories such as fires and accidents rather than significant stories, which tend to be longer and don't lend themselves to flashy video. The checks also favour good-looking, smooth anchors and reporters, regardless of their journalistic competence. One wag was literally correct when he called this "a heartthrob approach to journalism."

LEARNING CHECK

- How would you as a television program executive use physiological indicators from galvanic skin checks?

Prototype Research

Before making major investments, media executives need to obtain as much information as they can to determine how to enhance a project's chances for success or whether it has a chance at all. This is known as **prototype research.**

prototype research Checks response to product still in development.

Movie Screenings Movie studios have previewed movies since the days of silent film. Today the leading screening contractors are units of Nielsen and OTX. Typically about 300 people, selected carefully to fit a demographic, watch the movie and fill out comment cards. Were they confused at any point? Did they like the ending? What were their favourite scenes? Would they recommend the movie to a friend? The audience usually is filmed watching the movie, and producers and studio executives later look for reactions on a split screen with the movie running. Usually 20 or so testers are kept after a screening as a sit-down focus group with the studio people listening in.

Screenings make a difference. How a movie is promoted can be shaped by the test audience's reactions. Some endings have been changed. Astute moviegoers noticed that Vince Vaughn seemed thinner toward the end of *The Break-Up*. The fact is that Universal executives had decided for a happier ending and ordered Vaughn and a crew back to Chicago to reshoot. He had lost weight in the meantime. More widely known is that Paramount took the advice of a Nielsen screener and had Glenn Close's character in *Fatal Attraction* be murdered rather than commit suicide.

Many directors don't like their creative control contravened by test screenings. Some directors, indeed, have the clout to refuse screenings. Steven Spielberg famously forsakes them. The usual objection from directors is that they don't want to surrender creative control. Put another way, some directors see screenings as a way for studio executives to cover their backsides by claiming to their supervisors, if a movie flops, that they did all they could to ensure its success.

In recent years, screenings have been squeezed out of tighter and tighter production schedules, especially when computer-generated imaging plays a big role in a movie. For *The Da Vinci Code*, *Superman Returns*, and *Pirates of the Caribbean: Dead Man's Chest*, all big 2006 summer releases, there were no screen tests. There was no time to line up preview audiences, let alone make any changes that might have bubbled up through the process.

Some studio execs also have cooled to screenings because of negative leaks that can derail promotion plans. In 2006, a blogger posted a review of Oliver Stone's *World Trade Center* within hours of a screening in Minneapolis. One site, Ain't It Cool News, works at infiltrating screenings. Drew McSweeney, a site editor, defends the crashing of screenings as a way to stunt executive interference in movies and return power to directors.

Publication Protoypes When Gannett decided to establish a new newspaper, *USA Today*, it created prototypes, each designed differently, to test readers' reactions. Many new magazines are preceded by at least one trial issue to sample marketplace reaction and to show to potential advertisers.

Advertising agencies, too, often screen campaigns before launch to fine-tune them.

pilot A prototype television show that is given an on-air trial.

Television Pilots In network television, a prototype can even make it on the air in the form of a **pilot**. One or a few episodes are tested, usually in prime time with a lot of promotion, to see whether the audience goes for the program's concept. Some made-for-television movies actually are test runs to determine whether a series might be spun off from the movie.

LEARNING CHECK

- Why do strong-willed screenwriters and directors bristle at prototype research to adjust storylines?
- What role should an audience have in determining mass media content?

Audience Analysis

STUDY PREVIEW Traditional demographic polling methods divided people by gender, age, and other easily identifiable population characteristics. Today, media people use sophisticated lifestyle breakdowns such as geodemographics and psychographics to match the content of their publications, broadcast programs, and advertising to the audiences they seek.

Demographics

Early in the development of public-opinion surveying, pollsters learned that broad breakdowns had limited usefulness. Archibald Crossley's pioneering radio surveys, for example, revealed the number of people who were listening to network programs, which was valuable to the networks and their advertisers, but Crossley's figures did not tell how many listeners were men or women, urban or rural, old or young. Such breakdowns of overall survey data, called demographics, were developed in the 1930s as Crossley, Gallup, and other early pollsters refined their work.

Today, if demographic data indicate that a prime ministerial candidate is weak in the Maritimes, campaign strategists can gear the candidate's message to Maritime concerns. Through demographics, advertisers keen on reaching young women can identify magazines that will carry their ads to that audience. If advertisers seek an older audience, they can use demographic data to determine where to place their television ads.

While demographics remains valuable today, newer methods can break the population into categories that have even greater usefulness. These newer methods, which include cohort analysis, geodemography, and psychographics, provide lifestyle breakdowns.

LEARNING CHECK

- What are common demographic breakdowns in survey research?

Cohort Analysis

Marketing people have developed **cohort analysis**, a specialized form of demographics, to identify generations and then design and produce products with generational appeal. Advertising people then gear media messages with the images, music, humour, and other generational variables that appeal to the target cohort. The major cohorts are dubbed

cohort analysis Demographic tool to identify marketing targets by common characteristics.

- **Millennials**, who came of age in the 1990s and early 21st century.
- **Generation X**, who came of age in the 1980s.
- **Baby Boomers**, who came of age in the late 1960s and 1970s.
- **Postwar Generation**, who came of age in the 1950s
- **World War II Veterans**, who came of age in the 1940s.
- **Depression Survivors**, who came of age during the economic depression of the 1930s.

Millennials Today's twentysomething generation; sometimes referred to as Generation Y.

Generation X Today's fortysomething generation.

Baby Boomers Today's fiftysomething and sixtysomething generations.

Postwar Generation Today's seventysomething generation.

World War II Veterans Today's eightysomething generation.

Depression Survivors Today's ninetysomething (and older) generations.

Cohort analysis has jarred traditional thinking that people simply adopt their parents' values as they get older. The new 50-plus generation, for example, grew up on Coke and Pepsi and, to the dismay of coffee growers, may prefer to start the day with cola and not the coffee that their parents drank.

The Chrysler automobile company was early to recognize that Baby Boomers aren't interested in buying Cadillac-type luxury cars even when they have amassed the money to afford them. In 1996, Chrysler scrapped plans for a new luxury car to compete with Cadillac and instead introduced the $35 000 open-top 1997 Plymouth Prowler that gave Baby Boomers a nostalgic feel for the hot rods of their youth. Chrysler also determined that greying Baby Boomers prefer upscale Jeeps to the luxo-barge cars that appealed to the Postwar Generation.

Advertising people who use cohort analysis know that Baby Boomers, although now in their fifties, are still turned on by pizzas and the Rolling Stones. In short, the habits of youth stick with a generation as it gets older. And what appealed to the thirtysomethings a decade ago won't necessarily sail with today's thirtysomethings. David Bostwick, Chrysler's marketing research director, puts it this way: "Nobody wants to become their parents."

LEARNING CHECK

- How can cohort analysis help mass communicators to craft their messages?
- What kind of cohort would be useful for analysis by an advertiser for toothpaste? An automobile? A laptop?
- Do you like being pigeonholed as a target for advertising and other media messages?

Geodemographics

While demographics, including cohort analysis, remains valuable today, new methods can break the population into categories that have even greater usefulness. These newer methods, which include geodemography, provide lifestyle breakdowns.

Computer whiz **Jonathan Robbin** provided the basis for more sophisticated breakdowns in 1974 when he began developing his **PRIZM** system for **geodemography**. From U.S. census data, Robbin grouped every zip code by ethnicity, family life cycle, housing style, mobility, and social rank. Then he identified 34 factors that statistically distinguished neighbourhoods from each other. All of this information was cranked through a computer programmed by Robbin to plug every zip code into 1 of 40 clusters. Here are the most frequent clusters created through PRIZM, which stands for Potential Rating Index for Zip Markets, with the labels Robbin put on them:

Jonathan Robbin Devised PRIZM geodemography system.

PRIZM Identifies population characteristics by zip code.

geodemography Demographic characteristics by geographic area.

- **Blue-Chip Blues.** These are the wealthiest blue-collar suburbs. These Blue-Chip Blues, as Robbin calls them, make up about 6 percent of households. About 13 percent of these people are college graduates.

- **Young Suburbia.** Child-rearing outlying suburbs, 5.3 percent of population; 24 percent are college grads.
- **Golden Ponds.** Rustic mountain, seashore, or lakeside cottage communities, 5.2 percent of population; 13 percent are college grads.
- **Blue-Blood Estates.** Wealthiest neighbourhoods; 51 percent are college grads.
- **Money and Brains.** Posh big-city enclaves of townhouses, condos, and apartments; 46 percent are college grads.

Geodemographic breakdowns are used not only for magazine advertising but also for editorial content. At Time Warner magazines, geodemographic analysis permits issues to be edited for special audiences. *Time*, for example, has a 600 000 circulation edition for company owners, directors, board chairs, presidents, other titled officers, and department heads. Among others are editions for physicians and students.

LEARNING CHECK

- How is geodemographics different from demographics?
- Geodemographics cubbyholes people. In what cubbyholes do you fit, more or less?

Psychographics

psychographics Breaking down a population by lifestyle characteristics.

VALS Psychographic analysis by values, lifestyle, and life stage.

A refined lifestyle breakdown introduced in the late 1970s, **psychographics,** divides the population into lifestyle segments. One leading psychographics approach, the Values and Life-Styles program, known as **VALS** for short, uses an 85-page survey to identify broad categories of people:

- **Belongers.** Comprising about 38 percent of the U.S. population, these people are conformists who are satisfied with mainstream values and are reluctant to change brands once they're satisfied. Belongers are not very venturesome and fit the stereotype of Middle America. They tend to be churchgoers and television watchers.
- **Achievers.** Comprising about 20 percent of the population, these are prosperous people who fit into a broader category of inner-directed consumers. Achievers pride themselves on making their own decisions. They're an upscale audience to which a lot of advertising is directed. As a group, achievers aren't heavy television watchers.
- **Societally Conscious.** Comprising 11 percent of the population, these people are aware of social issues and tend to be politically active. The societally conscious also are upscale and inner-directed, and they tend to prefer reading to watching television.
- **Emulators.** Comprising 10 percent of the population, these people aspire to a better life but, not quite understanding how to do it, go for the trappings of prosperity. Emulators are status seekers, prone to suggestions on what makes the good life.
- **Experientials.** Comprising 5 percent of the population, these people are venturesome, willing to try new things in an attempt to experience life fully. They are a promising upscale audience for many advertisers.
- **I-Am-Me's.** Comprising 3 percent of the population, these people work hard to set themselves apart and are susceptible to advertising pitches that offer ways to differentiate themselves, which gives them a kind of subculture conformity. SRI International, which developed the VALS technique, characterized I-Am-Me's as "a guitar-playing punk rocker who goes around in shades and sports an earring." Rebellious youth, angry and maladjusted, fit this category.
- **Survivors.** This is a small downscale category that includes pensioners who worry about making ends meet.
- **Sustainers.** These people live from paycheque to paycheque. Although they indulge in an occasional extravagance, they have slight hope for improving their lot in life. Sustainers are a downscale category and aren't frequent advertising targets.
- **Integrateds.** Comprising only 2 percent of the population, integrateds are both creative and prosperous. They are willing to try different products and different ways of doing things and they have the wherewithal to do it.

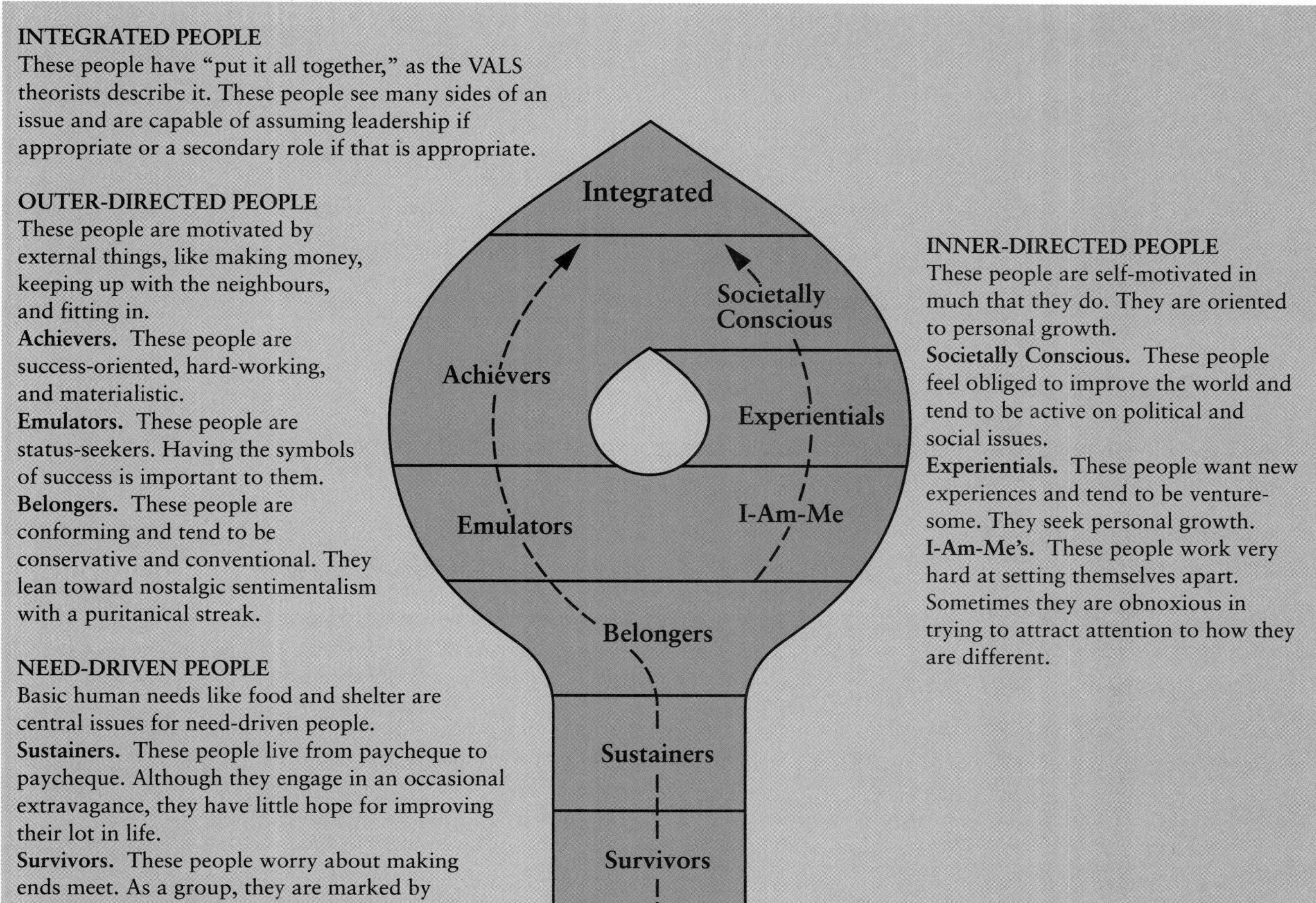

Figure 13.1 VALS Hierarchy Developmental psychologists have long told us that people change their values as they mature. Today, to identify potential consumers and to design effective messages, many advertisers rely on the Values and Life-Styles model, VALS for short, which was derived from developmental psychology. Relatively few advertising messages are aimed at survivors and sustainers, who have little discretionary income. However, belongers and people on the divergent outer-directed or inner-directed paths are lucrative advertising targets for many products and services.

Applying psychographics is not without hazard. The categories are in flux as society and lifestyles change. SRI researchers who chart growth in the percentage of I-Am-Me's, experientials, and the societally conscious project that they total one-third of the population. Belongers are declining.

Another complication is that no person fits absolutely the mould of any one category. Even for individuals who fit one category better than another, there is no single mass medium to reach them. VALS research may show that achievers constitute the biggest market for antihistamines, but belongers also head to the medicine cabinet when they're congested.

LEARNING CHECK

- Think about a person who is the same age as your grandparents and plug them into the VALS category that fits them best today. Discuss how you came to your conclusion.
- Into what category did this same individual best fit 40 years ago?
- Compare where you are on the VALS system with where you expect to be in 20 years.

Chapter 13 Wrap-Up

Theoretical research, which mostly takes place in the academic realm, and applied research, which the media eagerly fund, use many of the same tools. A unifying tool of these disparate research approaches is public-opinion sampling. It is used to track public opinion, which is essential in public relations work; to learn which television programs are the most watched, which is essential in programming and advertising decisions; and to determine the effects of media and how people use the media, which are scholarly endeavours.

PEARSON mycanadiancommunicationlab

Visit **www.mycanadiancommunicationlab.ca** for access to a wealth of tools and resources that will enhance your learning experience. Features include the following:

- Personalized Study Plan
- Videos
- Activities
- Pearson eText–and much more!

Questions for Critical Thinking

1. What variables determine whether surveys based on probability sampling can be trusted?
2. How is the size of newspaper, radio, and television audiences measured?
3. What lifestyle and media changes have prompted media survey companies to update their techniques? What are these new techniques?
4. How are audience reactions to mass media content measured? What results from these measurements?
5. What are techniques of audience analysis? How are data from these analyses used?

Keeping Up to Date

Public Opinion Quarterly is a scholarly publication. *American Demographics* and *Public Opinion* have a lot of general-interest content for media observers.

Online, BBM Canada publishes *In Sync* on a quarterly basis. It highlights trends in audience measurement.

Mass Media Law and Ethics

Jim DeFede Reflexively, *Miami Herald* columnist Jim DeFede did what seemed right when a suicidal friend called him. He taped the call but, in Florida, taping a call without permission is against the law. Does being illegal make something immoral?

LEARNING AHEAD

- The heart of Canadian mass media law is the Charter of Rights and Freedoms.
- The CRTC governs broadcasters in Canada, including by setting rules on Canadian content.
- Anyone falsely slandered by the mass media may sue for defamation.
- Copyright law protects intellectual property, with a lot of twists wrought by emerging technology.
- Mass media ethics codes cannot anticipate all moral questions.
- Mass media people draw on numerous moral principles, some of which are inconsistent with each other.
- Some mass media people prefer process-based ethics systems, while others prefer outcome-based systems.
- The Potter Box is a useful tool to sort through ethics issues.
- Some mass media people confuse ethics, law, prudence, and accepted practices.

MEDIA IN THEORY

Does Illegal Equal Immoral?

Jim DeFede, a hard-hitting investigative reporter for *The Miami Herald*, was home late in the afternoon when his phone rang. It was an old friend, former city and county commissioner Arthur Teele Jr. Teele was distraught that another newspaper had outed him for trysts with a transvestite prostitute. "What did I do to piss off this town?" Teele asked DeFede. The transvestite allegation had followed 26 charges of fraud and money laundering. Teele said that he was being smeared by prosecutors. He was afraid that the transvestite story would hurt him with "the ministers and the church."

Worried about his friend's anguish, DeFede turned on his telephone recorder to record Teele's pain. He also asked if Teele wanted to go public about the prosecutors using the media to smear him. Teele said no, but the discussion meandered to a potentially explosive story for which Teele claimed he had documents. A couple of hours later, Teele called back and said that he was leaving the documents for DeFede. Then he hung up, put a pistol to his head, and killed himself.

DeFede briefed his editor, Judy Miller, who told him to write a story for Page 1. In the meantime, higher executives at *The Miami Herald* realized that DeFede had violated a law that forbids taping a telephone conversation without permission. Over Miller's objections, publisher Jesus Diaz Jr., corporate attorney Robert Beatty, and two other

MEDIA TIMELINE Landmarks in Canadian Media Law and Ethics

1919 Upton Sinclair exposed newsroom abuses in his book *The Brass Check.*

1923 First code of ethics was adopted as the Canons of Journalism of the American Society of Newspaper Editors.

1926 Canadian Association of Broadcasters (CAB) was formed.

1928 Canada's first royal commission into broadcasting began looking at the role that radio plays in the daily lives of Canadians.

1932 Canadian Radio Broadcasting Act was passed.

1957 Fowler Report was released, and the Board of Broadcast Governors (BBG) was formed to regulate broadcasters in Canada. It also introduced the idea of Canadian content for television.

1982 Canadian Charter of Rights and Freedoms was passed into law, guaranteeing media freedom.

1990s CRTC began the slow process of deregulating radio and television.

1990 SOCAN was formed in Canada.

1990 Canadian Broadcast Standards Council (CBSC) was formed by the Canadian Association of Broadcasters.

1994 Dagenais ruling set the foundation for publication bans in Canada.

2003 Jayson Blair was fired from *The New York Times* for plagiarism.

2004 For the first time in history, the CRTC revoked the licence of a radio station: CHOI in Quebec.

2009 Responsible communication added as a defence for defamation in Canada.

2010 CAB ceased operations; CBSC remained Canada's broadcast self-regulator.

2010 Canadian Copyright Act was updated.

corporate executives decided to fire DeFede—even though *The Miami Herald* had once fought this Florida law, even though anyone who calls a reporter is implicitly consenting to being quoted, even though tape recording is just a more detailed form of note taking, and even though *Herald* executives decided to draw on DeFede's notes from the taped conversation for the Page 1 story on the suicide.

If DeFede acted unethically, how do we interpret the fact that *The Miami Herald* drew on his information from the phone call? In a twist that makes the issue even murkier, the state's attorney cleared DeFede of violating the anti-recording statute. Further, only 12 states, including Florida, have such a law. If what DeFede did was unethical in Florida, is it less so in the 38 states that don't have such restrictions?

Clearly, the law and ethics don't always coincide, which is a major issue in the media. In this chapter, you will learn tools that have been developed across centuries to sort through complexities posed by dilemmas of right and wrong, and by what is legal and what is ethical, when choosing a course that has downsides as well as upsides.

The Canadian Charter of Rights and Freedoms

Watch

ABC's *i-CAUGHT*: How to Be Bad

STUDY PREVIEW Since 1982, the Canadian Charter of Rights and Freedoms has barred the government from limiting freedom of expression, including expression in the mass media, or so it seems. There are limits to freedoms.

Canadian Charter of Rights and Freedoms Basis for all laws, including media laws, in Canada.

The **Canadian Charter of Rights and Freedoms** is the basis for both media law and ethics codes. Interestingly, in the United States, "freedom of the press" has been a First Amendment right since 1791. While the phrase *freedom of the press* was included in Canada's Bill of Rights in 1961, it only covered federal statutes and still wasn't a protected constitutional right. Officially, the media in Canada have held these press freedoms only since Queen Elizabeth II signed the Constitution Act on April 17, 1982. In his *Pocket Guide to Media Law*, Stuart Robertson states that three specific parts of the Charter affect the Canadian media.

- *Section 1.* The Charter "guarantees the rights and freedoms set out in it subject only to such reasonable limits prescribed by law as can be demonstrably justified in a free and democratic society."

- *Section 2.* All Canadians have "freedom of thought, belief, opinion and expression, including freedom of the press and other media of communication."
- *Section 52(1).* "The Constitution of Canada is the supreme law of Canada, and any law that is inconsistent with the provisions of the Constitution is, to the extent of the inconsistency, of no force or effect."

Robertson goes on to argue that the Charter has affected the media in at least two ways. First, it has granted all Canadians the same basic rights and freedoms. Second, it protects everyone, including those who work in the media, from unfair limitations on expression.

However, although freedom of the media is listed in the Charter, it isn't guaranteed. That is made explicit in Section 1 of the Charter. The rights in the Charter are guaranteed only "to such reasonable limits prescribed by law as can be demonstrably justified in a free and democratic society." In simpler terms, this means that while there is media freedom, the media must also take responsibility for their actions and there may be times when the media's right to free speech may be limited.

LEARNING CHECK

- **Describe the importance of the Charter of Rights and Freedoms in determining freedom of thought, belief, and expression for both individuals and the media.**

Publication Bans

For many years, the courts tended to put an individual's right to a fair trial above the rights of the media. Although the media are granted freedom of speech under the Charter, **publication bans** limiting what could be reported by the media were often issued. That changed in 1994 when the Supreme Court of Canada issued its **Dagenais ruling.** It all began when the CBC scheduled the National Film Board's movie *The Boys of St. Vincent* about atrocities at a Maritime orphanage. The movie was based on actual events at the Mount Cashel orphanage in Newfoundland and it was set to air nationally during the real-life trial. Lawyers for the defence argued that the movie might affect the defendants' right to a fair trial. The judge agreed and, based on legal precedent, ordered the CBC not to air the movie. The CBC appealed the ban and, in a landmark ruling, the Supreme Court of Canada quashed the publication ban. Dean Jobb, writing in *Media Law for Canadian Journalists,* explains Chief Justice Lamer's rationale for the outcome: "the Charter entrenches the right of accused persons to a fair trial . . . the publication ban imposed on *The Boys of St. Vincent* however had a profound impact on the right of the film director to express himself, the CBC's interest in broadcasting the film, the public's interest in viewing it and society's interest in having an important issue—child abuse—publicly exposed and debated." Since the Dagenais ruling, judges need to weigh the individual's right to a fair trial against the media's freedom of speech before deciding to issue a publication ban.

publication bans Limitations on media freedom of speech.

Dagenais ruling Rights need to be balanced.

Deepening Your Media Literacy: How important is freedom of press to you?

There are times when the judge has no choice but to issue a publication ban. For example, under Canada's **Youth Criminal Justice Act** it is illegal to print or broadcast the name of anyone under 18 who has been charged with or convicted of a crime, unless that person received an adult sentence. It also prohibits the naming of parents or siblings of those who have been charged, underage witnesses, or victims of crimes unless parental consent is given.

Youth Criminal Justice Act Prohibits reporting on trials involving minors.

LEARNING CHECK

- **How useful is the Dagenais ruling in balancing the rights of the individual and the rights of the media?**

Defamation

STUDY PREVIEW **When the mass media carry disparaging descriptions and comments, they risk being sued for defamation, which is a serious matter. Not only are reputations at stake when defamation occurs, but losing a suit can be so costly that it can put a publication or broadcast organization out of business.**

The Concept of Defamation

A civil limitation on the media's freedom of speech is the issue of defamation. If someone punched you in the face for no good reason, knocking out several teeth, breaking your nose, and causing permanent disfigurement, most courts would rule that your attacker should pay your medical bills. If your disfigurement or psychological upset causes you to lose your job, to be ridiculed or shunned by friends and family, or perhaps to retreat from social interaction, the court would probably order your attacker to pay you additional amounts. Like fists, words can cause damage. Freedom of speech and of the press is not a licence to say absolutely anything about anybody.

defamation False comments that harm a reputation.

libel A written defamation.

slander A spoken defamation.

Defamation is sometimes referred to as **libel** or **slander**. Traditionally, slander referred to spoken defamation, while libel was defamation in print. Canadian lawyer Michael G. Crawford, who has worked for both CBC and CTV, defines defamation in *The Journalist's Legal Guide* as the publication or broadcast of a statement that harms someone's reputation. If someone can prove the following three things, that person may be able to sue for defamation under Canadian law.

- The words or pictures were defamatory.
- The words or pictures were published or broadcast.
- The words or pictures refer to a specific, living person.

If a defamatory statement is false, the utterer may be liable for millions of dollars in damages. When *Toronto Life* published an article about the Reichmann family, the Reichmanns sued for $102 million. After four years in the courts, the case was settled out of court. *Toronto Life* issued a statement that it made "serious mistakes" in the research and writing of the story. In 1999, the *Red Deer Advocate* published a letter from Stockwell Day, who was then a member of the Alberta legislature. In the letter, Day made defamatory remarks that compared a lawyer who was representing a client charged with possession of child pornography to a pedophile. Day tried to use the fair comment defence but lost. The letter cost Day $792 000 in damages and legal costs.

These types of awards and cases are the foundation of what has become known as "libel chill." Many journalists, editors, and others in the media are deciding to play it safe and not publish controversial material that may result in a lawsuit. While this may make economic sense, one needs to question the role that libel chill plays in a democratic country that relies on information to educate its people.

LEARNING CHECK

- **What is the rationale for defamation law?**
- **Why isn't defamation protected as free speech?**

Defences for Defamation

defences for defamation Consent, truth, privilege, fair comment, responsible communication.

It is up to the media to prove any of the following as **defences for defamation** to avoid conviction:

- The person mentioned in the story or picture consented to its broadcast or publication.
- The words or pictures are true.
- The words or pictures were published under privilege. This means reporting and commenting fairly and accurately any comments made on public record. For example, quoting something that was said during a town council meeting or in a courtroom, or contained in a media release would constitute privilege.
- The words or pictures were fair comments.
- The words and pictures were responsible communication.

Cherry Sisters Complainants in a case that barred performers from suing critics.

What is fair comment? For the answer to this question, we look to the **Cherry Sisters**. People flocked to see the Cherry Sisters' act. Effie, Addie, Jessie, Lizzie, and Ella toured the United States with a song-and-dance act that drew big crowds. They were just awful. They could neither sing nor dance, but people came to see them because the sisters were so funny. Sad to say, the Cherry Sisters took themselves seriously. In 1901, desperate for respect, they decided to sue the next newspaper reviewer who gave them a bad notice. That reviewer, it turned out, was Billy Hamilton, who included a lot of equine metaphors in his piece for the *Des Moines Leader*: "Effie is an old jade of 50 summers, Jessie a frisky filly of 40, and Addie, the flower of the family, a capering monstrosity of 35. Their long skinny arms, equipped with talons at the extremities, swung mechanically, and anon waved frantically at the suffering audience. The mouths of their rancid features opened like caverns, and sounds like the wailings of damned souls issued there from. They pranced around the stage with a motion that suggested a cross between the *danse du ventre* and the fox trot—strange creatures with painted faces and hideous mien. Effie is spavined, Addie is stringhalt, and Jessie, the only one who showed her stockings, has legs with calves as classic in their outlines as the curves of a broom handle."

Fair Comment and Criticism Upset with what an Iowa reviewer had written about their show, the Cherry Sisters sued. The important 1901 court decision that resulted said that journalists, critics, and anybody else can say whatever they want about a public performance. The rationale was that someone who puts on a performance for public acceptance also has to take a risk of public rejection.

The outcome of the lawsuit was another setback for the Cherry Sisters. They lost in a case that established that actors or others who perform for the public must be willing to accept both positive and negative comments about their performances. This right of fair comment and criticism, however, does not make it open season on performers in aspects of their lives that do not relate to public performance. The *National Enquirer* could not defend itself when entertainer Carol Burnett sued for a story that described her as obnoxiously drunk at a restaurant. Not only was the description false (Carol Burnett abstains from alcohol), but Burnett was in no public or performing role at the restaurant. This distinction between an individual's public and private lives also has been recognized in cases involving public officials and candidates.

The new defence of responsible communication, which has been available to the media since 2009, focuses less on the reputation of the individual and more on the role of the media to inform on matters of public interest. It's a broadly based defence that not only requires the media to prove that the publication or broadcast is a matter of public interest, but also requires the media to show that, while the story may be defamatory, they practiced due diligence in ensuring that the story was fair and balanced, that sources were reliable, and that it was a matter of significance to the general public.

LEARNING CHECK

- Disparaging comments made about an individual in the mass media are acceptable in some situations but not others. Consider a major celebrity. What's off limits? What's not off limits? What could be considered "fair comment"?

Defamation and the Internet

Although this is new territory for the law, with no case law to look to for precedents, it appears that defamation laws will extend to the internet. On several occasions, Canadian bloggers have found themselves guilty of defamation. University of Ottawa law professor Michael Geist says that defamation laws "apply online as well as offline. Just because bloggers have the ability to write whatever they want doesn't give them the licence to defame anyone." Geist also says that we're likely to see more defamation lawsuits aimed at bloggers in the future, as "people are increasingly realizing that blogs have an impact and that more people are reading them." This means that defamation laws extend beyond the traditional media to bloggers, citizen journalists, or anyone who posts anything on the internet.

Many websites insert a "gatekeeper" to ensure that any content being posted is legal. Kenny Yun, an editor with globeandmail.com, says, "We review thousands of them every month. We have clear guidelines and every reader is asked to register with us before they are allowed to comment." The CBC allows anonymous postings on cbc.ca, but postings are scanned for anything that might be legally inappropriate. Other websites rely on their readers to flag stories that are unacceptable. Reviewing postings is a huge undertaking, but ultimately part of the responsibility that comes with free speech. As Canadian law professor Dean Jobb says in *The New Journalist*, good journalism is the best defence against defamation: "If journalists simply passed along rumours or allegations without separating fact from fiction, the news media would have no credibility." It would appear that quote applies to online journalism as well.

LEARNING CHECK

- What are the special challenges of online defamation?

The CRTC and Broadcast Regulation in Canada

STUDY PREVIEW The Canadian Radio-television and Telecommunications Commission (CRTC) has regulated broadcasting in Canada since the early days of radio in the 1930s. With the advent of television and the internet, regulations have been updated.

You're "on the Aird": Canada's First Royal Commission on Broadcasting

Aird Commission First royal commission into Canadian broadcasting.

The idea that radio could help to build a country was one of the factors behind the first Royal Commission on Broadcasting. The fact that Canadians were listening to more American than Canadian programming worried Ottawa, especially since there were 400 000 radios in Canada. For the first time (and certainly not the last time) in Canadian media history, politicians began to worry about the domination of Canada by American mass media. To solve this problem, they set up the first of many royal commissions on broadcasting in Canada. The **Aird Commission** (named after Sir John Aird) was created to examine the danger that American programming posed to Canadian culture. The verdict it reached in 1929 wasn't surprising: American networks were a threat to our airwaves and our culture.

The commission recommended that Canada set up and fund a public broadcasting network similar to the BBC in England. This network would produce and broadcast Canadian programs for and by Canadians. This recommendation caused quite a conflict between the owners of private radio stations, who were making a tidy profit, and those who preferred the public system. By 1932, Prime Minister R.B. Bennett laid out the government's official position on radio broadcasting in Canada: Canada would have both public and private radio stations. The government's proposal regarding public broadcasting revolved around three issues, which still form the basis of CRTC policy today:

- National sovereignty was to be preserved.
- Broadcasting services were to be made available to anyone in Canada, no matter where they lived.
- Broadcasting was not to be exploited by private interests.

Canadian Radio Broadcasting Act First statute governing broadcasting in Canada.

In 1932, the **Canadian Radio Broadcasting Act** was passed, resulting in the creation of the Canadian Radio Broadcasting Commission (CRBC), which began broadcasting in 1933. The CRBC was a direct product of the Aird Commission. Initially, it broadcast for only one hour a day. By the time it was replaced by the newly formed CBC in 1936, it was reaching just less than half of the Canadian population. In addition to being a national radio network, CBC was responsible for granting licences to private radio broadcasters, even though the government did not officially recognize private broadcasting—an ideal position for the government to be in.

The Evolution of Canada's Broadcasting Act

The evolution of television in Canada paralleled the growth of radio, a system with both public and private broadcasting. Initially, private television broadcasters had to apply to the CBC for broadcast licences. Private television broadcasters were not happy, as they felt that a conflict of interest existed. During this time, even private broadcasters had to carry 10 hours of CBC programming each week. How could the CBC, a broadcaster itself, also be responsible for overseeing private broadcasting?

In 1955, a royal commission into broadcasting was formed. The **Fowler Commission**, headed by Robert Fowler, analyzed Canadian broadcasting from the points of view of culture and regulations. Its report, tabled in 1957, formed the basis of the Broadcasting Act of 1958, which made the following changes.

Fowler Commission Royal commission into television broadcasting in Canada.

- The forming of the **Board of Broadcast Governors (BBG)**, which would oversee the granting of broadcasting licences.
- Official government recognition of private broadcasters in Canada. This allowed stations to affiliate themselves with a body other than the CBC and would lead to the formation of Canada's first private television network, CTV.
- Programming on radio and TV that was as Canadian in "content and character" as possible.

Board of Broadcast Governors (BBG) Forerunner of the current CRTC.

The 1968 Broadcasting Act

In March 1968, another broadcasting act further defined the broadcast system and the function it should serve in Canada. This act resulted in the formation of the Canadian Radio-television Commission (CRTC), the precursor to the Canadian Radio-television and Telecommunications Commission. The changes to television were as follows:

- The CRTC replaced the BBG and had the power to regulate broadcasting in Canada.
- The CBC was given its mandate to provide a national broadcasting service in both official languages and to provide Canadian programming that helped to develop national unity and allowed for Canadian cultural expression.
- Canadian broadcasting should be owned and operated by Canadians.

The 1991 Broadcasting Act

In 1975, the CRTC became the Canadian Radio-television and Telecommunications Commission when it assumed responsibility for regulating the telephone industry. In 1991, a new broadcasting act was issued to help further define broadcasting and cultural issues in Canada. The new act

- Stressed the importance of radio and television programming that was Canadian in content and character.
- Redefined the CBC's role as the national broadcaster, which was to help create a "Canadian consciousness." However, no attempt to define the term *Canadian consciousness* was made, nor was the issue of funding addressed.

The CRTC and the Broadcasting Act

The **CRTC** is the federal regulator in charge of regulating and supervising the broadcast media in Canada. It's an independent authority whose mandate is "to maintain a delicate balance, in the public interest, between the cultural, social and economic goals of the legislation on broadcasting and telecommunications." Its roots and traditions echo the findings of the Aird Commission in 1929. The CRTC is the law-making authority for all television, radio, and direct-to-home (DTH) systems in Canada. The CRTC reports to the prime minister through the Minister of Canadian Heritage.

CRTC Canadian broadcast regulator.

The CRTC is the political apparatus through which the spirit of the **Broadcasting Act** is made manifest. According to the CRTC, the main objective of the Broadcasting Act is "to ensure that all Canadians have access to a wide variety of high-quality Canadian programming." Specifics regarding the Broadcasting Act and its effect on radio and television content were discussed earlier in the text. The main thrust of the act today is as follows:

Broadcasting Act Governs the CRTC and all broadcasters in Canada.

- Canadian radio and television stations should be "effectively owned and operated by Canadians."
- The Canadian system has two parts: a public system and a private system.
- Canadian broadcasters should "safeguard, enrich and strengthen" life in Canada. This is the reason for Canadian content regulations on radio and television.

- Anyone who is involved in broadcasting in Canada is responsible for what he or she broadcasts.
- Adding another limitation to "freedom of the press" in Canada, the Broadcasting Act specifically states that broadcasts should not include anything "in contravention of the law," nor should they contain obscenities, profanities, or false news.

CASE STUDY

CHOI-FM

The Canadian Charter of Rights and Freedoms gives everyone in Canada, including those that work in the media, "freedom of thought, belief and expression." In short, we are given the right to think, believe, and say what we want. However, as this chapter has outlined, there are limitations to "freedom of speech."

The CRTC strives to work with Canadian radio and television stations to ensure that they operate within a profitable environment. However, in 2004, the CRTC showed how far-reaching its powers were when it did not renew the licence of radio station CHOI-FM, owned by Genex, in Quebec City. Some saw this as censorship. Genex felt that CHOI-FM was only exercising its right to free speech and that certain comments were not considered in context. The CRTC saw the matter as a radio station consistently not adhering to the objectives of the Broadcasting Act and flaunting its right to freedom of speech. The decision not to renew the licence was not a knee-jerk reaction by the CRTC. It had been a long time coming, as CHOI-FM had a history of questionable content:

- Allegedly making defamatory comments about former Quebec Premier Daniel Johnson.
- Referring to a rival talk show host on another radio station as a "conceited asshole," a "worthless piece of trash," a "piece of vomit," a "shit disturber," and a "tree with rotten roots."
- Calling anyone who worked for Radio Énergie, a competitor in the Quebec City market, "a bunch of faggots."
- Suggesting that there be an "Indian hunting season" and that severely mentally disturbed patients at a local psychiatric hospital be gassed just like during the Holocaust.

In its decision, the CRTC noted that these complaints "did not reflect isolated incidents, but appeared to be part of a pattern of behaviour by the licensee that continued and even grew worse, over the course of two consecutive licence terms, despite clear unequivocal warnings from the Commission." The CRTC cited the following section of the Canadian Radio Broadcasting Act as the basis for its decision: "A licensee shall not broadcast any abusive comment that, when taken in context, tends to or is likely to expose an individual or a group or class of individuals to hatred or contempt on the basis of race, national or ethnic origin, colour, religion, sex, sexual orientation, age or mental or physical disability."

Freedom of Speech or Censorship? CHOI-FM tested the boundaries of free speech . . . and lost.

As a result of this history, the CRTC decided not to renew CHOI-FM's licence in August 2004. It also immediately issued a call for applications to take over the licence for Quebec City.

CHOI-FM immediately appealed the ruling and was able to continue broadcasting during the appeal process. However, in 2005, the Supreme Court of Canada agreed with the CRTC. In its decision, it stated that "freedom of expression, freedom of opinion and freedom of speech do not mean freedom of defamation, freedom of oppression and freedom of opprobrium." Again, CHOI-FM appealed the ruling. On June 14, 2007, the Supreme Court said that it would not hear the appeal. Genex, owners of CHOI-FM, sold the station to Radio Nord, which runs it today as a rock station.

DEEPENING YOUR MEDIA LITERACY

Explore the Issue

Review the CRTC's decision on CHOI-FM at www.crtc.gc.ca/eng/archive/2004/db2004-271.htm.

Dig Deeper

What role did the CRTC play? What role did the Charter of Rights and Freedoms play?

Could any of the comments made by some of CHOI-FM's announcers be protected as "fair comment"? Why or why not?

What Do You Think?

Was the case of CHOI-FM a simple matter of freedom of speech or censorship?

Advertising Regulation

STUDY PREVIEW The "buyer beware" underpinning of much of 19th-century advertising has given way to "seller beware." Today, Canadian advertising is governed by the Competition Act.

Watch

ABC's *20/20*: "Deception in Advertisments"

A Tarnished History

A dramatic reversal in thinking about advertising has occurred in the 20th century. The earlier **caveat emptor** ("let the buyer beware") mindset tolerated extravagant claims. Anyone who believed that the same elixir could cure dandruff, halitosis, and cancer deserved to be conned, or so went the thinking. Over the years, owing partly to the growing consumer movement, the thinking changed to **caveat venditor** ("let the seller beware"), placing the onus on the advertiser to avoid misleading claims and to demonstrate the truth of claims.

Caveat emptor Let the buyer beware.

Caveat venditor Let the seller beware.

In advertising's early days, newspapers and magazines skirted the ethics question posed by false advertisements by saying that their pages were open to all advertisers. Under growing pressure, publications sometimes criticized dubious advertisements editorially, but most did not ban them. Edward Bok, who made *Ladies' Home Journal* a runaway success in the 1890s, crusaded against dishonest advertising. In one exposé on Lydia E. Pinkham's remedies for "female maladies," Bok reported that Lydia, to whom women readers were invited to write for advice, had been dead for 22 years. Yet the advertisements continued.

Canada's Competition Act

The advertising industry in Canada must adhere to a variety of laws and regulations, most notably the **Competition Act**. While each province has its own set of rules and regulations that advertisers and marketers must follow, the Competition Act is the federal statute that covers advertising in Canada. According to the Act, any representation (flyer, brochure, in-store display, newspaper ad, or material on the internet, radio, or television) that offers a product or service for sale must adhere to specific guidelines. Some specific aspects covered by the act include false and misleading advertising, bait-and-switch advertising, selling at a price higher than advertised, and testimonials.

Competition Act Federal regulator of advertising in Canada.

The key element of the Competition Act is that it is illegal to make a "representation to the public that is false or misleading in a material respect." It's the phrase **material respect** that gives the Competition Act its power. Advertisements in Canada are scrutinized not only if they mislead the consumer, but also if they have the potential to mislead the public.

material respect An advertisement's potential impact on a consumer.

Material respect is determined by subjecting the ad in question to the **general impression test**. This means that both the literal meaning of the ad (what it says) and the implied meaning of the ad (what it suggests) are examined for anything that might be false and

general impression test Combination of an ad's literal and implied meaning.

misleading. Fines levied under the Competition Act can be steep; repeat offenders may be fined up to $15 million.

LEARNING CHECK

- Explain the scope of the Competition Act.
- How are ads scrutinized by the Competition Act?

Copyright

STUDY PREVIEW Mass media people are vulnerable to thievery. Because it is so easy for someone to copy someone else's creative work, copyright laws prohibit the unauthorized re-creation of intellectual property, including books, music, movies, and other creative production.

Copyright in Canada

Copyright law is meant to encourage creativity. With creative work classified as property, creative people have a legal right to derive income from their works by charging for their use. For example, an author can charge a book publisher a fee for publishing the book. Actually, it's a little more complicated, but that's the general idea. The goal is to guarantee a financial incentive for creative people to continue creating. The rationale is that a society is richer for literature, music, and other creative works. Inventions, which are covered by patents, are a separate area of **intellectual property** law.

intellectual property Creative works.

Copyright law allows creators to control their creations. They can sell them, lease them, give them away, or just sit on them. The law is the vehicle through which creative people earn a livelihood just as carpenters earn money from carpentry and landlords earn money by renting out real estate. Creators of intellectual property grant **permissions** for the use of their work, usually for a fee. Freelance photographers charge magazines that want to use their photographs. Composers charge music publishers that want to issue their music. Songwriters use performing rights organizations to ensure that broadcasters pay for the right to play their songs.

permissions Grant of rights for a second party to use copyright-protected work.

Canada has had a copyright law on the books since 1924. It was most recently updated in 2010. The Copyright Act of Canada, governed by Canadian Heritage and Industry Canada, covers all forms of communication: books, pamphlets, newspapers, magazines, maps, sheet music, movies, videos, and music. The Act defines **copyright** as "the sole right to produce or reproduce the work of any substantial part thereof in any material form whatever or to perform the work or any substantial portion thereof in public." Basically, all original works in Canada are protected by copyright for the life of the creator plus 50 years. In the United States, copyright laws protect a creative work for the lifetime of the author plus 70 years. After this time, either in Canada or the United States, the work enters what is called the **public domain** and anyone may use it without permission. The creator of the "act" of communication has the sole right to copy it or have it performed in public. That right may be granted to others.

copyright Protects intellectual property from theft.

public domain Intellectual property that may be used without the permission of the creator or owner.

In 2010, Industry Minister Tony Clement introduced legislation, Bill C-32, that updated Canada's Copyright Act. If passed into law, it will be legal to shift formats (transferring a song from a CD to an MP3 player), to record media content (TV, podcasts) for personal use, and to create audio or video "mash ups." It would be illegal to break digital locks on CDs and DVDs; to have more than one backup copy of a movie, CD, or software; and to upload or download copyrighted material over the internet. These changes were subject to debate and had not been passed as of fall of 2010.

The works of Canadians are also protected internationally under the copyright protection of the Berne Convention and the Universal Copyright Convention. These also protect the works of international artists in Canada. Several Canadian organizations exist to ensure that creators of communication content are compensated for their efforts and that copyright laws are not broken.

LEARNING CHECK

- Define copyright.
- What does the Copyright Act of Canada cover?

Music Licensing in Canada

SOCAN, the Society of Composers, Authors and Music Publishers of Canada, licenses the public performance of music. It was formed in 1990, when two other performing rights organizations, PROCAN (Performing Rights Organization of Canada) and CAPAC (Composers, Authors and Publishers Association of Canada), combined to form a new, nonprofit organization. Its jurisdiction includes the playing of music not only on radio and television, but also in restaurants, by mobile disc jockeys, in parades, at sporting events, and at the movies. Almost anywhere you hear music, SOCAN is there to ensure that the songwriters get paid.

SOCAN Society of Composers, Authors and Music Publishers of Canada; music licensing organization.

SOCAN collects tariffs from anyone who uses music and passes them along to the songwriters. No one, other than the songwriter, has the right in Canada to use a song's material in any way, shape, or form without permission. SOCAN recognizes several types of rights held by the songwriters pertaining to music:

- *Performance rights.* These cover songwriters when their material is performed publicly. This can include a song on the radio, on television, or performed by a band at the local bar. These tariffs are collected by SOCAN.
- *Reproduction rights.* There are two types of reproduction rights. Mechanical rights are the rights to copy the music to a tape or CD, while synchronization rights refer to using the music in a film or video.
- *Moral rights.* A creator can claim violation of moral rights if, after selling performance and/or reproduction rights, he or she feels that the original vision is altered. For example, members of Canadian pop group the Parachute Club claimed that their moral rights were violated first when their 1983 hit "Rise Up" was used in a commercial for frozen pizza and then when the song was used to promote a political event in 1999. They felt that their song, with its spiritual and self-empowering message, was morally diminished when it began to be associated with pizza and politicians.

SOCAN collects several tariffs as a performing rights organization. For example, Canadian radio stations pay SOCAN 3.2 percent on the first $1.25 million of their advertising revenue and an additional 4.4 percent on anything above that. Noncommercial radio stations, such as campus and community stations, pay 1.9 percent of their operating costs. Meanwhile, TV stations pay 1.9 percent of their advertising revenue.

Three other organizations license the use of music in Canada. AVLA (the Audio-Visual Licensing Agency) overlooks the exhibition of music videos, while SODRAC (the Society for Reproduction Rights of Authors, Composers and Publishers in Canada Incorporated) and CMRRA (the Canadian Musical Reproduction Rights Agency Limited) authorize the reproduction of music (onto tapes and CDs) and the use of music in videos and film.

There are other large performance rights organizations worldwide. They are known in the trade by their abbreviations: **ASCAP** (The American Society of Composers, Authors and Publishers) and **BMI** (Broadcast Music, Inc.).

ASCAP Music licensing organization.

BMI Music licensing organization.

LEARNING CHECK

- What role does SOCAN play in protecting copyright holders?

The Difficulty of Ethics

STUDY PREVIEW Mass media organizations have put together codes of ethics that prescribe how practitioners should go about their work. Although useful in many ways, these codes neither sort through the bedevilling problems that result from conflicting prescriptions nor help much when the only available options are negative.

Explore

Media People: Charlie Gay

Differentiating Ethics and Law

Ethics is an individual matter that relates closely to conscience. Because conscience is unique to each individual, no two people have exactly the same moral framework. There are, however, issues about which there is consensus. No right-minded person condones murder, for example. When there is a universal feeling, ethics becomes codified in law, but laws do not address all moral questions. The issues of right and wrong that do not have a consensus are what make ethics difficult.

Ethics and law are related but separate. The ethics decisions of an individual mass media practitioner usually are more limiting than the law. There are times, though, when a journalist may choose to break the law on the grounds of ethics. Applying John Stuart Mill's principle of "the greatest good," a radio reporter might choose to break the speed limit to reach a chemical plant where an accident is threatening to send a deadly cloud toward where her listeners live. Breaking a speed limit might seem petty as an example, but it demonstrates that obeying the law and obeying one's conscience do not always coincide.

Accepted Practices

accepted practices What media do as a matter of routine, sometimes without considering ethics implications.

Just as there is no reliable correlation between law and ethics, neither is there one between accepted media practices and ethics. What is acceptable at one advertising agency to make a product look good in photographs might be unacceptable at another. Even universally accepted practices should not go unexamined, for unless **accepted practices** are examined and reconsidered on a continuing basis, media practitioners can come to rely more on habit than on principles in their work.

Prudence and Ethics

prudence Applying wisdom, not principles, to an ethics situation.

Prudence is the application of wisdom in a practical situation. It can be a levelling factor in moral questions. Consider the case of Irvin Lieberman, who had built his *Main Line Chronicle* and several other weeklies in the Philadelphia suburbs into aggressive, journalistically excellent newspapers. After being hit with nine libel suits, all of which were costly to defend, Lieberman softened the thrust of his newspapers. "I decided not to do any investigative work," he said. "It was a matter of either feeding my family or spending my whole life in court." Out of prudence, Lieberman decided to abandon his commitment to hard-hitting, effective journalism.

Courageous pursuit of morally lofty ends can, as a practical matter, be foolish. Whether Lieberman was exhibiting a moral weakness by bending to the chilling factor of libel lawsuits, which are costly to fight, or being prudent is an issue that could be debated forever. The point, however, is that prudence cannot be ignored as a factor in moral decisions.

LEARNING CHECK

- Can breaking the law ever be justified?

Prescriptive Ethics Codes

Canons of Journalism of the American Society of Newspaper Editors First media code, 1923.

prescriptive ethics Follow the rules and your decision will be the correct one.

The mass media abound with codes of ethics. The earliest, the **Canons of Journalism of the American Society of Newspaper Editors**, was adopted in 1923. Many newcomers to the mass media make an erroneous assumption that the answers to all of the moral choices in their work exist in the prescriptions of these codes, a stance known as **prescriptive ethics**. While the codes can be helpful, ethics is not so easy. Attitudes toward codes of ethics vary, but most Canadian media organizations have a code, as do public relations and advertising associations. These codes go far beyond the question of "freebies" and at least try to address issues of social equality, controversy, offensive content, and fairness in handling complex stories.

Many media critics feel that ethics are not taken as seriously as they might be. According to journalism professor Brian Green, one news director's perspective on ethics was as follows: "It's hard to remember you're here to drain the swamp when you're up to your ass in alligators." Peter Desbarats argues that many media critics feel that while the media may talk a good line when it comes to ethics, it's more talk than walk. Other critics feel that codes of ethics are merely public relations tools that the media use to perpetuate the myth that they are holier than thou. This may or may not be true. But the fact remains that most Canadian media organizations have a **code of ethics** that, if nothing else, serves as a guideline to follow should an alligator creep up on them. The same applies to the public relations and advertising industries. These codes are based in Canadian law but, because they are codes, violation of them may not necessarily result in legal problems.

code of ethics Statement that defines acceptable and unacceptable behaviour.

The study of ethics manifests itself in the world of media in the form of codes of conduct. Among the many media organizations that have codes of conduct for their members are the Canadian Broadcast Standards Council, the Canadian Newspaper Association, the Radio-Television News Directors Association of Canada, and Advertising Standards Canada.

The Canadian Broadcast Standards Council Formed in 1990 by the now defunct Canadian Association of Broadcasters (CAB), the **CBSC** (Canadian Broadcast Standards Council) is a self-regulating council funded for and by private broadcasters in Canada. Its mandate is to promote high standards in radio and television broadcasting through self-regulation. If a viewer or listener has a complaint about programming in Canada, he or she writes to the CBSC. It administers several ethics codes, including the CAB Code of Ethics, the CAB Violence Code, and the CAB Sex-Role Portrayal Code. All of its decisions are available online in more than 30 languages (www.cbsc.ca).

CBSC Canadian Broadcast Standards Council; self-regulatory body for Canadian radio and television broadcasters.

Canadian Newspaper Association In 1919, the Canadian Daily Newspaper Association (CDNA) was formed. In 1996, it was renamed the Canadian Newspaper Association (CNA). The CNA represents 101 English-language and French-language daily newspapers, 99 percent of all newspapers sold in Canada on a daily basis. The CNA's statement of principles, which was originally adopted by the CDNA in 1977, was revised in 1995. This statement can be found at the CNA website (www.cna-acj.ca). Some of the issues dealt with in the statement are freedom of the press, loyalty to the public good, accuracy, fairness, and community responsibility.

Radio-Television News Directors Association of Canada The **Radio-Television News Directors Association (RTNDA)** was founded more than 50 years ago. It's an international organization with affiliations in Canada. Recognizing the importance to a democracy of an informed public, the members of the RTNDA of Canada believe that the broadcasting of factual, accurately reported, and timely news and public affairs is vital. To this end, RTNDA members in Canada pledge to observe a code of ethics, which can be found at the RTNDA website (www.rtndacanada.com).

Radio-Television News Directors Association (RTNDA) Organization that believes that the broadcasting of factual, accurately reported, and timely news and public affairs is vital.

Advertising Standards Canada Advertising Standards Canada (**ASC**) is the self-regulatory body that oversees advertising in Canada. The Canadian Code of Advertising Standards, which has been in place since 1963 but was updated most recently in 2005, includes 14 clauses with an emphasis on accuracy, clarity, and honesty. ASC administers many other industry codes, such as guidelines on gender portrayal, children's advertising, and alcohol advertising.

ASC Advertising Standards Canada; the self-regulatory body for advertising.

LEARNING CHECK

- How can codes of ethics help media people to make the right decisions? Do codes always work? Why or why not?

Conflict in Duties

Media ethics codes are well-intended, usually helpful guides, but they are simplistic when it comes to knotty moral questions. When media ethicists Clifford Christians, Mark Fackler, and Kim Rotzoll compiled a list of five duties of mass media practitioners in their book *Media Ethics*, some of these inherent problems became obvious.

Duty to Self Self-preservation is a basic human instinct, but is a photojournalist shirking a duty to subscribers by avoiding a dangerous combat zone?

Self-aggrandizement can be an issue too. Many newspaper editors are invited, all expenses paid, to Hollywood movie premieres. The duty-to-self principle favours going, since the trip would be fun. In addition, it is a good story opportunity and would not cost the newspaper anything. However, what of an editor's responsibility to readers? Readers have a right to expect writers to provide honest accounts that are not coloured by favouritism. Can a reporter write fairly after being wined and dined and flown across the continent by movie producers who want a gung-ho story?

Duty to Audience Television programs that re-enact real cases of violence are popular with audiences, but do they do a disservice because they frighten many viewers into thinking that the streets are more dangerous than they really are?

Writing about real situations with humour also may do the audience a disservice. Tom Wicker of *The New York Times* tells a story about his early days as a reporter in Aberdeen, North Carolina. He was covering a divorce case involving one spouse chasing the other with an axe. Nobody was hurt physically and everyone who heard the story in the courtroom, except for the divorcing couple, had a good laugh. "It was human comedy at its most ribald, and the courtroom rocked with laughter," Wicker recalled years later. In writing his story, Wicker captured the darkly comedic details so skilfully that his editor put the story on Page 1. Wicker was proud of the piece until the next day, when the woman in the case called on him. Worn out, haggard, hurt, and angry, she asked, "Mr. Wicker, why did you think you had a right to make fun of me in your paper?" The lesson stayed with Wicker for the rest of his career. He had unthinkingly hurt a fellow human being for no better reason than to evoke a chuckle, or perhaps a belly laugh, from his readers. The duty-to-audience principle would never again transcend his moral duty to protect the dignity of the subjects of his stories.

Duty to Employer Does loyalty to an employer transcend the ideal of pursuing and telling the truth when a news reporter discovers dubious business deals involving the parent corporation? This is a growing issue as the mass media become consolidated into fewer gigantic companies owned by conglomerates. In 1989, for example, investigative reporter Peter Karl of Chicago television station WMAQ broke a story that General Electric had manufactured jet engines with untested and sometimes defective bolts. Although WMAQ is owned by NBC, which in turn is owned by General Electric, Karl's exclusive, documented, and accurate story aired. However, when the story was passed on to the network itself, Marty Ryan, executive producer of the *Today* show, ordered that the references to General Electric be edited out.

Duty to the Profession At what point does an ethically motivated advertising agency employee blow the whistle on misleading claims by other advertising people?

Duty to Society Does duty to society ever transcend the duty to self, to audience, to employer, or to the profession? Does ideology affect a media worker's sense of duty to society? Consider how Joseph Stalin, Adolf Hitler, and Franklin Roosevelt would be covered by highly motivated communist, fascist, and libertarian journalists.

LEARNING CHECK

- If you were the editor of a college or university newspaper and were offered an all-expenses-paid trip to a Hollywood movie premiere, would you accept? In explaining your decision, keep in mind that avoiding controversy may be an attractive response but a weak ethical choice.

Media Ethics

STUDY PREVIEW Media ethics is complicated by the different performance standards that mass media operations establish for themselves. This is further complicated by the range of expectations in the mass audience. One size does not fit all.

Media Commitment

A single ethics standard is impossible to apply to the mass media. Nobody holds a supermarket tabloid like *News of the World*, which specializes in stories about celebrities being visited by aliens, to the same standard as *The New York Times*. Why the difference?

Media ethics, in part, is a function of what a media operation promises to deliver to its audience and what the audience expects. *News of the World* is committed to fun and games in a tongue-in-cheek news context. *The New York Times* considers itself a "newspaper of record." There is a big difference.

CNN touts accuracy in its promotional tagline: "News You Can Trust." Explicitly, the network promises to deliver truthful accounts of the day's events. CNN establishes its own standards. A lapse, such as a misleading story, especially if intentional or the result of sloppiness, represents a broken promise and an ethics problem.

Audience Expectation

The audience brings a range of ethics expectations to media relations, which further thwarts any attempt at one-size-fits-all media ethics. Readers have far different expectations of a fantasy and science fiction book imprint than they do of *CBC News*, which, except for plainly labelled opinion, is expected to deliver unmitigated nonfiction.

A range in the type of messages purveyed by the mass media also leads to a variety of ethics expectations. Rarely is falsity excusable, but even the courts allow puffery in advertising. The news releases that public relations people produce are expected, by their nature, to be from a client's perspective, which doesn't always coincide with the perspective expected of a news reporter.

Ethics as an Intellectual Process

A set of rules, easily memorized and mindlessly employed, would be too easy. Ethics doesn't work that way. Rather, ethics needs to be an intellectual process of sorting through media commitments, audience expectations, and broad principles. However, even on broad principles there is more to be said, as discussed in the next section.

LEARNING CHECK

- **Why do ethics expectations differ among media organizations?**

Moral Principles

STUDY PREVIEW **Concern about doing the right thing is part of human nature, and leading thinkers have developed a great number of enduring moral principles over the centuries.**

Aristotle Advocate of the golden mean.

golden mean Moderation is the best course.

The Golden Mean

The Greek philosopher **Aristotle,** writing almost 2400 years ago, devised the **golden mean** as a basis for moral decision making. The golden mean sounds simple and straightforward: Avoid extremes and seek moderation. Modern journalistic balance and fairness are founded on this principle.

Golden Mean The Greek thinker Aristotle told his students almost 2400 years ago that right courses of action avoid extremes. His recommendation was moderation.

The golden mean's dictate, however, is not as simple as it sounds. As with all moral principles, application of the golden mean can present difficulties. Consider the CRTC requirement that over-the-air broadcasters give equal opportunity to candidates at election time. On the surface, this application of the golden mean, embodied in federal law, might seem to be reasonable, fair, and morally right, but the issue is far more complex. The equality requirement, for example, gives an advantage to candidates who hold simplistic positions that can be expressed compactly. Good and able candidates whose positions require more time to explain are disadvantaged, and the society is damaged when inferior candidates are elected to public office.

Although minute-for-minute equality in broadcasting can be a flawed application of the golden mean, Aristotle's principle is valuable to media people when making moral decisions, as long as they do not abdicate their power of reason to embrace formulaic tit-for-tat measurable equality. It takes the human mind, not a formula, to determine fairness. And therein lies the complexity of the golden mean. No two human beings think exactly alike, which means that applying the golden mean involves individuals making judgment calls that are not necessarily the same. This element of judgment in moral decisions can make ethics intellectually exciting. It takes a sharp mind to sort through issues of balance and fairness.

Universal Law Immanuel Kant, an 18th-century German philosopher, urged people to find principles that they would be comfortable having applied in all situations. He called these principles categorical imperatives.

"Do unto Others"

The Judeo-Christian principle of "**Do unto others** as you would have them do unto you" appeals to most Canadians. Not even this prescription is without problems, however. Consider the photojournalist who sees virtue in serving a mass audience with a truthful account of the human condition. This might manifest itself in portrayals of great emotions, such as grief. However, would the photojournalist appreciate being photographed herself in a grieving moment after learning that her own infant had died in an accident? If not, her pursuit of truth through photography for a mass audience would be contrary to the "do-unto-others" dictum.

Categorical Imperatives

About 200 years ago, German philosopher **Immanuel Kant** wrote that moral decisions should flow from thoroughly considered principles. As he put it, "Act on the maxim that you would want to become universal law." He called his maxim the categorical imperative. A **categorical imperative,** well thought out, is a principle that the individual who devised it would be willing to apply in all moral questions of a similar sort.

Kant's categorical imperative does not dictate specifically what actions are morally right or wrong. Moral choices, says Kant, go deeper than the context of the immediate issue. He encourages a philosophical approach to moral questions, with people using their intellect to identify principles that they, as individuals, would find acceptable if applied universally.

Kant does not encourage the kind of standardized approach to ethics represented by professional codes. His emphasis, rather, is on hard thinking. Says philosopher Patricia Smith, writing in the *Journal of Mass Media Ethics*, "A philosophical approach to ethics embodies a commitment to consistency, clarity, the principled evaluation of arguments and unrelenting persistence to get to the bottom of things."

Utilitarianism American journalists tend to like 19th-century British thinker John Stuart Mill's utilitarianism, which favours actions that result in the greatest good for the greatest number of people. This approach to ethics dovetails well with majority rule and modern democracy.

Utilitarian Ethics

In the mid-1800s, British thinker **John Stuart Mill** declared that morally right decisions are those that result in "happiness for the greatest number." Mill called his idea the **principle of utility**. It sounds good to many of us because it parallels the democratic principle of majority rule, with its emphasis on the greatest good for the greatest number of people.

By and large, journalists embrace Mill's utilitarianism today, as evinced in notions such as the *people's right to know*, a concept originally meant to support journalistic pursuit of information about government, putting the public's interests ahead of government's interests, but which has come to be almost reflexively invoked to defend pursuing very personal information about individuals, no matter what the human toll.

Pragmatic Ethics

John Dewey, an American thinker who wrote in the late 1800s and early 1900s, argued that the virtue of moral decisions had to be judged by their results. Dewey's **pragmatic ethics**, like other ethics systems, has problems. One is that people do not have crystal balls to tell them whether their moral actions will have good consequences.

John Dewey He saw decisions as ethical if the ascertainable outcomes were good.

Egalitarian Ethics

In the 20th century, philosopher **John Rawls** introduced the **veil of ignorance** as an element in ethics decisions. Choosing a right course of action, said Rawls, requires blindness to social position or other discriminating factors. This is known as **egalitarianism**. An ethical decision requires that all people be given an equal hearing and the same fair consideration.

According to Rawls, a brutal slaying in an upscale suburb deserves the same journalistic attention as a similarly brutal slaying in a poor urban neighbourhood. All other things being equal, a $20 000 bank burglary is no more newsworthy than a $20 000 embezzlement.

LEARNING CHECK

- Can you identify the ethics principle or system most associated with Aristotle? Immanuel Kant? John Stuart Mill? John Dewey? John Rawls?

Process versus Outcome

STUDY PREVIEW The various approaches to ethics fall into two broad categories: deontological ethics and teleological ethics. Deontologists say that people need to follow good rules. Teleologists judge morality not by the rules but by the consequences of decisions.

Deontological Ethics

The Greek word *deon*, which means "duty," is at the heart of **deontological ethics**, which holds that people act morally when they follow good rules. Deontologists feel that people are duty bound to identify these rules.

Deontologists include people who believe that Scripture holds all of the answers for right living. Their equivalent among media practitioners are those who rely entirely on codes of ethics drafted by organizations they trust. Following rules is a prescriptive form of ethics. At first consideration, ethics might seem as easy as following the rules, but not all questions are clear-cut. In complicated situations, the rules sometimes contradict each other. Some cases are dilemmas with no right option but only a choice among less-than-desirable options.

Deontological ethics becomes complicated, and also more intellectually interesting, when individuals, unsatisfied with other people's rules, try to work out their own universally applicable moral principles.

Here are some major deontological approaches:

- **Theory of divine command.** This theory holds that proper moral decisions come from obeying the commands of God, with blind trust that the consequences will be good.
- **Theory of divine right of kings.** This theory sees virtue in allegiance to a divinely anointed monarch.
- **Theory of secular command.** This theory is a nonreligious variation that stresses allegiance to a dictator or other political leader from whom the people take cues when making moral decisions.
- **Libertarian theory.** This theory stresses a laissez-faire approach to ethics. If you give free rein to the human ability to think through problems, people almost always will make morally right decisions.
- **Categorical imperative theory.** This theory holds that virtue results when people identify and apply universal principles.

Teleological Ethics

Unlike deontological ethics, which is concerned with the right actions, teleological ethics is concerned with the consequences of actions. The word **teleology** comes from the Greek word *teleos*, which means "result" or "consequence."

Teleologists see flaws in the formal, legalistic duty to rules among deontologists, noting that great harm sometimes flows from blind allegiance to rules.

Here are some major teleological approaches:

- **Pragmatic theory.** This theory encourages people to look at human experience to determine the probable consequences of an action and then decide on its desirability.
- **Utilitarian theory.** This theory favours ethics actions that benefit more people than they damage—the greatest good for the greatest number.

Situational Ethics

Firm deontologists see two primary flaws in teleological ethics:

- Imperfect foresight.
- Lack of guiding principles.

John Rawls He favoured turning a blind eye to all issues except rightness and wrongness.

"Do unto others" Judeo-Christian principle for ethical behaviour.

Immanuel Kant Advocated the categorical imperative.

categorical imperative Follow principles as if they had universal application.

John Stuart Mill Advocated utilitarianism.

principle of utility Best course bestows the most good on the most people.

John Dewey Advocate of pragmatism.

pragmatic ethics Judge acts by their results.

John Rawls Advocated egalitarianism.

veil of ignorance Making decisions with a blind eye to extraneous factors that could affect the decision.

egalitarianism Treat everyone the same.

deontological ethics Good actions flow from good processes.

theory of divine command Proper decisions follow God's will.

theory of divine right of kings Monarchs derive authority from God, not from their subjects.

theory of secular command Holds that authorities legitimately hold supreme authority, although not necessarily a divine authority.

libertarian theory Given good information and time, people ultimately make right decisions.

teleology Good decisions are those with good consequences.

situational ethics Make ethics decisions on the basis of situation at hand.

Despite these flaws, many media practitioners apply teleological approaches, sometimes labelled **situational ethics**, to arrive at moral decisions. They gather as much information as they can about a situation and then decide, not on the basis of principle but on the facts of the situation. Critics of situational ethics worry about decisions governed by situations. Much better, they argue, would be decisions flowing from principles of enduring value. With situational ethics the same person might do one thing one day and on another day go another direction in a similar situation.

Consider a case at the *Rocky Mountain News* in Denver. Editors learned that the president of a major suburban newspaper chain had killed his parents and sister in another state when he was 18. After seven years in a mental hospital the man completed college, moved to Colorado, lived a model life, and became a successful newspaper executive. The *Rocky Mountain News* decided not to run a story on it. Said a *News* official, "The only reason for dredging up [his] past would be to titillate morbid curiosity or to shoot down, maliciously, a successful citizen."

However, when another newspaper revealed the man's past, the *Rocky Mountain News* reversed itself and published a lengthy piece of its own. Why? The newspaper that broke the story had suggested that *News* editors knew about the man's past and had decided to protect him as a fellow member of the journalistic fraternity. *News* editors denied that their motivation was to protect the man. To prove it, they reconsidered their decision and published a story on him. The *News* explained its change of mind by saying that the situation had changed. *News* editors, concerned that their newspaper's credibility had been challenged, thought that printing a story would set that straight. Of less concern, suddenly, was that the story would titillate morbid curiosity or contribute to the destruction of a successful citizen. It was a classic case of situational ethics.

Flip-flops on moral issues, such as what happened at the *Rocky Mountain News*, bother critics of situational ethics. The critics say that decisions should be based on deeply rooted moral principles and not on immediate, transient facts or changing peripheral contexts.

LEARNING CHECK

- As someone who reads newspapers and watches newscasts, do you favour deontological or teleological ethics? Which system do you think most journalists favour, and why?
- What is the attraction of situational ethics for sorting out dilemmas? What is the problem with situational ethics?

The Potter Box

Explore

Media People: Arthur Ashe

STUDY PREVIEW Moral problems in the mass media can be so complex that it may seem that there is no solution. While ideal answers without any negative results may be impossible, a process exists for identifying a course of action that integrates an individual's personal values with moral principles and then tests conclusions against loyalties.

Four Quadrants

Ralph Potter Ethicist who devised the Potter Box.

Potter Box Tool for sorting through the pros and cons of ethics questions.

A Harvard Divinity School professor, **Ralph Potter**, devised a four-quadrant model for sorting through ethics problems. The quadrants of the square-like model, called the **Potter Box**, each pose a category of questions. Working through these categories helps to clarify the issues and leads to a morally justifiable position. These are the quadrants of the Potter Box:

Situation In Quadrant 1, the facts of the issue are decided. Consider a newsroom in which a series of articles on rape is being developed and the question arises whether to identify rape victims by name. Here is how the situation could be defined: The newspaper has access to a young mother who has been abducted and raped and who is willing to describe the assault in graphic detail and to discuss her experience as a witness at the assailant's trial. Also, the woman is willing to be identified in the story.

Ralph Potter

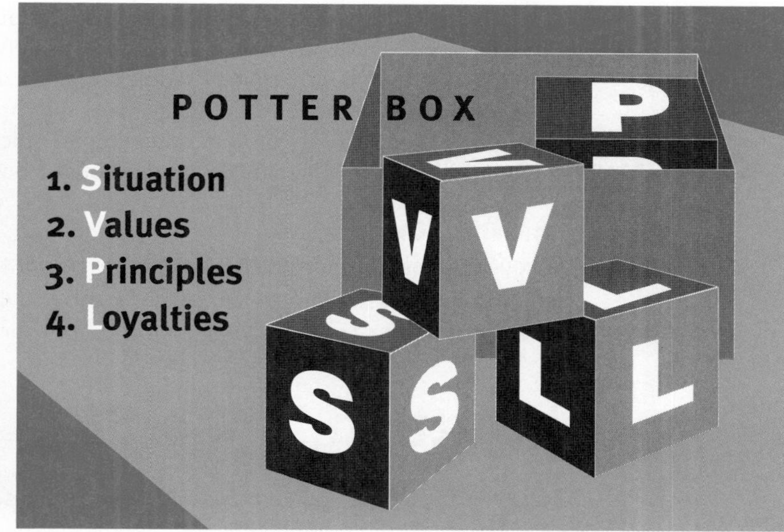

Figure 14.1 **Clarifying Process** The Potter Box offers four categories of questions to help develop morally justifiable positions.

Values Moving to Quadrant 2 of the Potter Box, editors and reporters identify the values that underlie all of the available choices. This process involves listing the positive and negative values that flow from conscience. One editor might argue that full and frank discussion of social issues is necessary to deal with them. Another might say that identifying the rape victim by name might discourage others from even reporting similar crimes. Other positions are: Publishing the name is in poor taste. The newspaper has an obligation to protect the victim from her own possibly bad decision to allow her name to be used. The purpose of the rape series can be accomplished without using the victim's name. Readers have a right to all relevant information that the newspaper can gather. An editor who is torn between such contrary thoughts is making progress toward a decision by at least identifying all of the values that can be posited.

Principles In Quadrant 3, decision makers search for moral principles that uphold the values they identified in Quadrant 2. John Stuart Mill's principle of utility, which favours the majority over individuals, would support using the victim's name because it could add poignancy to the story, enhance the chances of improved public sensitivity, and perhaps even lead to improved public policy, all of which, Mill would say, outweigh the harm that might come to an individual. On the other hand, people who have used Immanuel Kant's ideas to develop inviolable operating principles—categorical imperatives—look to their rule book: We never publish information that might offend readers. One value of Potter's Quadrant 3 is that it gives people confidence in the values that emerged in their debates over Quadrant 2.

Loyalties In Quadrant 4, the decision maker folds in an additional layer of complexity that must be sorted through: loyalties. The challenge is to establish a hierarchy of loyalties. Is the first loyalty to a code of ethics and, if so, to which code? To readers and, if so, to which ones? To society? To employer? To self? Out of duty to self, some reporters and editors might want to make the rape series as potent as possible, with as much detail as possible, to win awards and bring honour to themselves and perhaps earn a raise, a promotion, or a better job with another newspaper. Others might be motivated by their duty to their employer: The more detail in the story, the more newspapers it will sell. For others their duty to society may be paramount: The newspaper has a social obligation to present issues in as powerful a way as possible to spur reforms in general attitudes and perhaps public policy.

Limitations of the Potter Box

The Potter Box does not provide answers. Rather, it offers a process through which the key elements in ethics questions can be sorted out.

Also, the Potter Box focuses on moral aspects of a problem, leaving it to the decision maker to examine practical considerations separately, such as whether prudence supports making the morally best decision. Moral decisions should not be made in a vacuum. For example, would it be wise to go ahead with the rape victim's name if 90 percent of the newspaper's subscribers would become so offended that they would quit buying the paper and, as a result, the paper would go out of business?

LEARNING CHECK

- You are a news reporter. A candidate for mayor tells you that the incumbent mayor is in cahoots with organized crime. It's a bombshell story! Use the Potter Box to decide whether to rush to your microphone with the story.

Unsettled, Unsettling Questions

Watch

ABC's *Nightline*: "Rathergate"

STUDY PREVIEW When mass media people discuss ethics, they talk about right and wrong behaviour, but creating policies on ethics issues is not easy.

Plagiarism

Perhaps the most fiercely loyal media fans are those who read romance novels and swear by a favourite author. In an internet chatroom in 1997, romance writer Janet Dailey found herself boxed into an admission that she had plagiarized from rival writer Nora Roberts. There is no scorn like that of creative people for those who steal their work, and Roberts was "very, very upset." HarperCollins recalled *Notorious*, Dailey's book that contained the plagiarism, and Roberts's fans, many of them long-time Dailey detractors, began a hunt for other purloined passages.

plagiarism Using someone else's work without permission or credit.

What is **plagiarism**? Generally, it's considered passing off someone else's creative work as your own, without permission. It's still plagiarism if it's changed a bit, as was Dailey's loose paraphrasing.

The fact that Dailey's 93 books over 20 years had sold an average of more than 2 million each made the scandal all the juicier. In the end, Roberts proposed a financial settlement, and the proceeds went to promote literacy.

Everyone agrees that plagiarism, a form of thievery, is unethical, but the issue is not simple. The fact is that, in many media, people draw heavily on other people's ideas and work. Think about sitcom storylines that mimic each other or the bandwagon of movies that follow an unexpected hit with an oddball theme that suddenly becomes mainstream. Journalists, most of whom consider themselves especially pristine compared to their media brethren, have standard practices that encourage a lot of "borrowing." Among factors that make journalists uncomfortable when pressed hard on questions of plagiarism are:

Swapping Stories Some creative work, such as scholarship, requires that information and ideas be attributed to their sources. Journalists are not so strict, as shown by story swapping through the Canadian Press (CP). CP picks up stories from its members and distributes them to other members, generally without any reference to the source. Some publications and broadcasters do not even acknowledge CP as the intermediary.

JANET DAILEY
New York Times bestselling author of Illusions
Notorious

Copycat Romance Widespread internet access is facilitating plagiarism, much of it among people who don't know better. But it remains a taboo in media work. Janet Dailey's *Notorious* was withdrawn and shredded by publisher HarperCollins after rival romance writer Nora Roberts spotted passages that Dailey had lifted.

News Releases In many newsrooms, the plagiarism question is clouded further by the practice of using news releases from public relations people word for word without citing the source. Even in newsrooms that rewrite releases to avoid the embarrassment of running a story that is exactly the same as the competition's, it is standard practice not to cite the source. Public relations people, who are paid for writing favourable stories on their clients, have no objections to being plagiarized, and news organizations find it an easy and inexpensive way to fill space. Despite the mutual convenience, the arrangement raises serious questions of ethics to which many in the media have not responded. Marie Dunn White, in the *Journal of Mass Media Ethics*, wrote: "In order for the reader to evaluate the information he or she is receiving correctly and completely, he or she must know which information came from a press release and, therefore, may be biased."

Monitoring the Competition Competitive pressure also contributes to fuzziness on the plagiarism issue. To avoid being skunked on stories, reporters monitor each other closely to pick up tips and ideas. Generally, reporters are not particular about where they pick up information as long as they are confident that it is accurate. For background, reporters tap newsroom libraries, databases, journals, books, and other sources, and in the interest of not cluttering their stories, they do not use footnotes.

Subliminal Memory Covering breaking events has its own pressure that puts journalists at special risk. Almost every journalist who writes under the pressure of a deadline has had the experience of writing a story and later discovering that phrases that came easily at the keyboard were actually somebody else's. In their voracious pursuit of information, reporters store phrases and perhaps whole passages subliminally in their memories. It's this concept of innocent recall that concerned Canadian columnist Don McGillivray, who argued that plagiarism is often a simple case of unintentionally borrowing from others. Journalists are like any other group of professionals: They like to "talk shop" when in the presence of other journalists. They discuss stories they've written and articles they've read. Later, while writing a story, a journalist may subconsciously remember a certain phrase from a conversation with a colleague and use it in a story. Is this plagiarism? McGillivray doesn't think so. It's simply the outcome of a psychological process.

The final word on plagiarism in journalism goes to Nick Russell, who, in *Morals and the Media*, writes, "Genuine plagiarism is theft and is indefensible; serious incidents of plagiarism happen rarely and there is a difference between plagiarism and lack of attribution . . . . Some media critics seem to think it's growing, but it may be more of a matter of perception. Partly because readers have a growing sense of empowerment and ownership so are now much more likely to blow the whistle and newsroom colleagues who might have tolerated such activities as hijinks in the past now see them as undermining everybody's credibility."

Misrepresentation

Janet Cooke Classic case of representing fiction as truth.

Janet Cooke's meteoric rise at *The Washington Post* unravelled quickly the day after she received a Pulitzer Prize. Her editors had been so impressed with her story "Jimmy's World," about a child who was addicted to heroin, that they nominated it for a Pulitzer. The gripping tale began: "Jimmy is 8 years old and a third-generation heroin addict, a precocious little boy with sandy hair, velvety brown eyes and needle marks freckling the baby-smooth skin of his thin brown arms." Cooke claimed that she had won the confidence of Jimmy's mother and her live-in male friend, a drug dealer, to do the story. Cooke said she had promised not to reveal their identities as a condition for her access to Jimmy.

The story, which played on the front page, so shocked Washington that people demanded that Jimmy be taken away from his mother and placed in a foster home. *The Post* declined to help authorities, citing Cooke's promise of confidentiality to her sources. The mayor ordered the police to find Jimmy with or without the newspaper's help, and millions of dollars in police resources were spent on a door-to-door search. After 17 days, the police stopped knocking on doors for tips on Jimmy. Some doubts emerged at *The Post* about the story, but the newspaper stood behind its reporter.

Janet Cooke, age 25 when she was hired by *The Post*, had extraordinary credentials. Her résumé showed a baccalaureate degree, magna cum laude, from Vassar; study at the Sorbonne in Paris; a master's degree from the University of Toledo; abilities in several languages; and two years of journalistic experience with the Toledo *Blade*. Said Ben Bradlee, editor of *The Post*: "She had it all. She was bright. She was well spoken. She was pretty. She wrote well." She was black, which made her especially attractive to *The Post,* which was working to bring the percentage of black staff reporters nearer to the percentage of blacks in its circulation area.

"Jimmy's World" was published in September 1980. Six months later, the Pulitzer committee announced its decision and issued a biographical sheet on Cooke. The

MEDIA PEOPLE Jayson Blair

Jayson Blair

On one level, Jayson Blair's stories in *The New York Times* marked him as a rising star. Assigned in late 2002 to the team covering the Beltway Sniper story around Washington, D.C., Blair produced scoop after scoop that indicated a knack for ferreting out knowledgeable sources and charming information from them. Blair, age 27, exuded self-confidence. He even floated a prospectus for a book on the sniper case.

Then, what to many had seemed a promising if not skyrocketing career imploded. Blair, it turned out, had fabricated sources, played fast and loose with the facts, concocted details that weren't true, and purported to have conducted interviews that never took place. These transcended the kinds of forgivable errors that news reporters, being human, make from time to time. Blair was a serial liar. Time and again, he had sallied into fiction while pretending to be reporting the news of the day accurately. Confronted with his lies in May 2003, his career suddenly in shambles, Blair resigned.

His ethics transgressions shook *The New York Times*, the most prestigious newspaper in the United States, with more Pulitzer Prizes than any other paper—seven in 2002 alone. Said publisher Arthur Sulzberger Jr., "It's a huge black eye."

In an act of self-flagellation, the paper's editors assigned an eight-reporter team to investigate how Blair, who had worked at the paper for six years, had attained the kind of trust that news organizations place in their reporters. *The Times* had a long reputation for truth-seeking and often aggressive reporting—and also for the confidence to back up its reporters when critics came down on them.

So what went wrong? For whatever reason, *Times* editors had fast-tracked Blair without putting his work through the rigours that other newsroom newcomers experienced. Factual errors in his work, an incredible 50 to 60 errors by some counts, had been gently excused. Although editors generally are leery about unnamed sources in stories, the anonymous sources who peppered Blair's stories went unchallenged. Surprisingly, none of the sources whom Blair did name in his stories complained about fabricated quotes and details.

It all began to unravel after Blair wrote a story containing details from interrogators of a Beltway Sniper suspect. The information, not true, rattled the investigators who were conducting the interrogation. Statements attributed to the suspect in Blair's front-page story had never been made. People at *The Times* began to watch Blair. They suddenly realized that he was turning out stories from faraway places without ever leaving town. Then the editor at the *San Antonio Express-News* called to complain that details in a Blair story purported to have been written in Texas had been lifted from his newspaper. Blair hadn't even been to Texas.

Associated Press, while trying to flesh out the biographical information, spotted discrepancies right away. Cooke, it turned out, had attended Vassar for one year but had not graduated with the honours she claimed. As well, the University of Toledo had no record of awarding her a master's degree. Suddenly, doubts that had surfaced in the days immediately after "Jimmy's World" was published took on a new intensity. *The Post*'s editors sat Cooke down and grilled her on the claims on which she was hired. No, she admitted, she was not multilingual. The Sorbonne claim was fuzzy. More important, the editors pressed her on whether there was really a Jimmy. The interrogation continued into the night, and finally Janet Cooke confessed all: There were no confidential sources and there was no Jimmy. She had fabricated the story. She resigned, and *The Post,* terribly embarrassed, returned the Pulitzer.

In cases of outright fabrication, as in "Jimmy's World," it is easy to identify the lapses in ethics. When Cooke emerged briefly from seclusion to explain herself, she said that she was responding to pressures in *The Post* newsroom to produce flashy, sensational copy. Most people found this explanation unsatisfying, considering the pattern of deception that went back to her falsified résumé.

Some **misrepresentations**, however, are not as clearly unacceptable. Much debated are the following.

misrepresentation Deception in gathering or telling information.

Re-Creations Some television **reality programs** feature **re-enactments** that are not always labelled as such. Philip Weiss, writing in *Columbia Journalism Review*, offered this litany: shadows on the wall of a woman taking a hammer to her husband, a faceless actor grabbing a tin of kerosene to blow up his son, a corpse in a wheelbarrow with a hand dangling, a detective opening the trunk of a car and reeling from the smell of a decomposing body. Although mixing re-creations with strictly news footage rankles many critics, others argue that it helps people to understand the situation. The same question arises with docudramas, which mix actual events and dramatic re-creations.

reality programs Broadcast shows with a nonfiction basis.

re-enactments Re-creating real events.

Selective Editing The editing process, by its nature, requires journalists to make decisions on what is most worth emphasizing and what is least worth including. In this sense, all editing is selective, but the term **selective editing** refers to making decisions with the goal of distorting. Selective editing can occur in drama too, when writers, editors, and other media people take literary licence too far and intentionally misrepresent.

selective editing Misrepresentation through omission and juxtaposition.

Fictional Methods In the late 1960s, many experiments in media portrayals of people and issues came to be called the **new journalism**. The term was hard to define because it included so many approaches. Among the most controversial were applications of fiction-writing methods to topical issues, an approach widely accepted in book publishing but suddenly controversial when it appeared in the news media. Character development became more important than before, including presumed insights into the thinking of people being covered. The view of the writer became an essential element in much of this reporting. The defence for these approaches was that traditional, facts-only reporting could not approach complex truths that merited journalistic explorations. The profound ethics questions that these approaches posed were usually mitigated by clear statements about what the writer was attempting. Nonetheless, it was a controversial approach to the issues of the day. There was no defence when the fictional approach was complete fabrication passing itself off as reality, as in "Jimmy's World."

new journalism Mixing fiction techniques with nonfiction.

LEARNING CHECK

- How have mass media practices muddied plagiarism as an issue?
- If plagiarism is so bad, why do more and more people do it? Are there any ethics principles or systems that would condone plagiarism?

Gifts, Junkets, and Meals

In his 1919 book ***The Brass Check***, a pioneer examination of newsroom ethics, **Upton Sinclair** told how news people took bribes to put stories in the paper. Today, all media ethics codes condemn gifts and certainly condemn bribes. Even so, there are still people who curry favour with the mass media through gifts, such as a college sports publicist who gives a fifth of whisky at Christmas to a sportswriter as a gesture of goodwill. Favours can take many forms: media-appreciation lunches; free trips abroad, known as **junkets**, especially for travel writers; season passes to cover the opera; discounts at certain stores.

The Brass Check 1919 book that exposed newsroom corruption.

Upton Sinclair Author of *The Brass Check*.

junket Trip with expenses paid by someone who may expect favours in return.

Despite the consistent exhortation of the ethics codes against gifts, favours, free travel, and special treatment and privileges, there is nothing inherently wrong in accepting them if they do not influence coverage and if the journalist's benefactor understands that. The problem with favours is more a practical one than one of ethics. Accepting a favour may or may not be bad, but it *looks* bad. Many ethics codes do not make this important distinction. One code of ethics that does is that of the Canadian Association of Journalists (CAJ). Its Statement of Principles and Ethical Guidelines states: "We should not accept or solicit gifts, passes or favours for personal use. We must pay our own way to ensure independence. If another organization pays our expenses to an event that we are writing about we should say so, so that the reader, viewer or listener can take this into account. (We will make sure exceptions are understood. For example, it is common practice to accept reviewers' tickets for film previews and theatrical performances.)"

The CAJ's admonitions at least recognize the distinction between the inherent wrongness of impropriety, which is an ethics question, and the perception that something may be wrong, which is a perception that is unwise to encourage, even if the action being examined is not necessarily unethical.

LEARNING CHECK

- As a news editor, why is it important to act independently to avoid both impropriety and the appearance of impropriety? Is there a difference between the two?

Chapter 14 Wrap-Up

The mass media enjoy great freedom under the Canadian Charter of Rights and Freedoms, which forbids the government from impinging on expression. Even so, this freedom has limits. Major restrictions on the mass media involve publication bans, censorship, and defamation. Plus, there is government regulation of the mass media through the CRTC, the Copyright Act of Canada, and the Competition Act.

Media people have no shortage of ethics codes. Every professional organization has one. This multitude of ethics codes makes it easy for people to infer that ethical behaviour is a simple matter of learning and obeying the rules. However, they are missing the complexity of moral issues. No matter how well intentioned the ethics codes, they have limited usefulness. Merely following prescribed rules with unique, sometimes nuanced subtleties makes for a particular dilemma. No prescriptive code, cast in broad terms as they must be, can replace a good mind and the application of broad, universal principles.

Questions for Critical Thinking

1. The Canadian Charter of Rights and Freedoms grants everyone in Canada, including the media, freedom of speech. Can this freedom of speech ever be absolute?
2. What is the rationale underlying copyright law?
3. What is defamation? What are the five legal defences for the media?
4. What is the role of the CRTC and the Broadcasting Act?
5. Why can't ethics codes anticipate all moral questions? And does this limit the value of codes for mass media people?

Keeping Up to Date

Censorship News is published by the National Coalition Against Censorship.

Media Law Bulletin tracks developments in media law.

News Media and the Law is published by the Reporters Committee for Freedom of the Press.

Media Law Reporter is an annual collection of major court cases.

Student Press Law Reports, from the Student Press Law Center in the United States, follows events in the high-school and college press and broadcast media.

The *National Post*, the *Toronto Star* and *The Globe and Mail* often have sections and articles on media law and ethics.

Ethicists sort through moral dilemmas involving mass communication in the scholarly *Journal of Mass Media*.

Many trade and professional journals also deal with media ethics, including the *Columbia Journalism Review*, *The Canadian Journal of Communication*, *Broadcast Dialogue*, and *Broadcaster* magazine.

15 Media Effects

LEARNING AHEAD

- Scholars today believe that the effects of mass communication generally are cumulative over time.
- Mass messages are significant in helping children to learn society's expectations.
- Most of the effects of mass communication are difficult to measure and predict.
- Mass communication binds large audiences culturally but also can reinforce cultural fragmentation.
- Some notions about the effects of mass messages, including subliminal messages, have been overstated.
- Scholars differ on whether media-depicted violence triggers aggressive behaviour.

Orson Welles Young Orson Welles scared the living daylights out of several million radio listeners with the 1938 radio drama *The War of the Worlds*. Most of the fright was short-lived, though. All but the most naive listeners quickly realized that Martians, marching toward the Hudson River to destroy Manhattan, really had not devastated the New Jersey militia.

MEDIA IN THEORY

Orson Welles

Explore

Media People: Orson Welles

Orson Welles His radio drama cast doubt on powerful effects theory.

The War of the Worlds Novel that inspired a radio drama that became the test bed of the media's ability to instill panic.

The boy genius **Orson Welles** was on a roll. By 1938, at age 23, Welles's dramatic flair had landed him a network radio show, *Mercury Theater on the Air*, during prime time on CBS on Sunday nights. The program featured adaptations of well-known literature. For their October 30 program, Welles and his colleagues decided on a scary 1898 British novel, H.G. Wells's ***The War of the Worlds***.

Orson Welles opened with the voice of a wizened chronicler from some future time, intoning an unsettling monologue. That was followed by an innocuous weather forecast, then hotel dance music. Then the music was interrupted by a news bulletin. An astronomer reported several explosions on Mars, propelling something at enormous velocity toward Earth. The bulletin over, listeners were transported back to the hotel orchestra. After some applause the orchestra started up again, only to be interrupted by a special announcement: Seismologists had picked up an earthquake-like shock in New Jersey. Then it was one bulletin after another.

MEDIA TIMELINE Mass Media Effects

1922 Walter Lippmann attributed powerful effects to the mass media.

1938 Hadley Cantril concluded that *The War of the Worlds* panic was drastically overstated.

1940s Mass communication scholars shifted from studying effects to uses and gratification.

1948 Paul Lazarsfeld challenged powerful effects theory in voter studies.

1967 George Gerbner launched his television violence index.

1970s Mass communication scholars shifted to cumulative effects theory.

1972 Maxwell McCombs and Donald Shaw concluded that media create public agendas, not opinion.

1992 Virginie Larivière presented Prime Minister Brian Mulroney with a petition urging the government to do something about violence on TV.

1993 A new violence code was introduced by Canada's AGVOT.

Giant Martians were moving across the countryside spewing fatal gas. One at a time, reporters at remote sites vanished off the air. The Martians had decimated the U.S. Army and were wading across the Hudson River. Amid sirens and other sounds of emergency, a reporter on a Manhattan rooftop described the monsters advancing through the streets. From his vantage point, he described the Martians felling people by the thousands and moving in on him, the gas crossing Sixth Avenue, then Fifth Avenue, then 100 yards away, then 50 feet. Then silence.

To the surprise of Orson Welles and his crew, the drama triggered widespread mayhem. Neighbours gathered in streets all over the country, wet towels held to their faces to slow the gas. In Newark, New Jersey, people—many undressed—fled their apartments. Said a New York woman, "I never hugged my radio so closely. . . . I held a crucifix in my hand and prayed while looking out my open window to get a faint whiff of gas so that I would know when to close my window and hermetically seal my room with waterproof cement or anything else I could get a hold of. My plan was to stay in the room and hope that I would not suffocate before the gas blew away."

Researchers estimate that one out of six people who heard the program, more than 1 million in all, suspended disbelief and braced for the worst.

The effects were especially amazing considering that:

- An announcer identified the program as fiction at four points.
- Almost 10 times as many people were tuned to a popular comedy show on another network.
- The program ran only one hour, an impossibly short time for the sequence of events that began with the blastoffs on Mars, included a major military battle in New Jersey, and ended with New York's destruction.

Unwittingly, Orson Welles and his Mercury Theater crew had created an evening of infamy and raised questions about media effects to a new level. Theoretically, how could this happen? In this chapter, you will learn what scholars have found out about the effects of the mass media on individuals.

Effects Theories

STUDY PREVIEW Early mass communication scholars assumed that the mass media were so powerful that ideas and even ballot-box instructions could be inserted as if by hypodermic needle into the body politic. Doubts arose in the 1940s about whether the media were really that powerful, and scholars began to shape their research questions and ask about long-term, cumulative media effects.

ABC's *Good Morning America*: "Video Game Addiction"

Magic Bullet Theory

The first generation of mass communication scholars thought that the mass media had a profound, direct effect on people. Their idea, called **powerful effects theory**, drew heavily

powerful effects theory Theory that media have immediate, direct influence.

Walter Lippmann His book *Public Opinion* assumed powerful media effects in 1920s.

Harold Lasswell His mass communication model assumed powerful effects.

on social commentator **Walter Lippmann**'s influential 1922 book, *Public Opinion*. Lippmann argued that we see the world not as it really is but as "pictures in our heads." The "pictures" of things we have not experienced personally, he said, are shaped by the mass media. The powerful impact that Lippmann ascribed to the media was a precursor of the powerful effects theory that evolved among scholars over the next few years.

Yale psychologist **Harold Lasswell**, who studied World War II propaganda, embodied the effects theory in his famous model of mass communication: *who, says what, in which channel, to whom, with what effect*. At their extreme, devotees of powerful effects theory assumed that the media could inject information, ideas, and even propaganda into the public. The theory was explained in terms of a hypodermic needle model or a bullet model. Early powerful effects scholars would agree that newspaper coverage and endorsements of political candidates decided elections.

The early scholars did not see that the hypodermic metaphor was hopelessly simplistic. They assumed wrongly that individuals are passive and absorb uncritically and unconditionally whatever the media spew forth. The fact is that individuals read, hear, and see the same things differently. Even if they did not, people are exposed to many, many media and hardly to a single, monolithic voice. Also, there is skepticism among media consumers that is manifested at its extreme in the saying "You can't believe a thing you read in the paper." People are not mindless, uncritical blotters.

third-person effect One person overestimating the effect of media messages on other people.

W.P. Davison Scholar who devised third-person effect theory.

A remnant of now-discredited perceptions that the media have powerful and immediate influence is called **third-person effect**. In short, the theory holds that people overestimate the impact of media messages on other people. Scholar **W.P. Davison**, who came up with the concept in 1983, told a story about a community film board that censored some movies because they might harm people who watch them—even though the board members denied that they themselves were harmed by watching them. The theory can be reduced to this notion: "It's the other guy who can't handle it, not me." Davison's pioneering scholarship spawned many studies. Most of the conclusions can be boiled down to these:

- Fears about negative impact are often unwarranted.
- Blocking negative messages is often unwarranted.

LEARNING CHECK

- Explain the ink blotter metaphor for mass audiences in the early thinking about mass communication effects.
- What evidence supports the conclusion that the magic bullet theory simplistically overstates the effects of mass communication?

Minimalist Effects Theory

Paul Lazarsfeld Found voters more influenced by other people than by mass media.

minimalist effects theory Theory that media effects are mostly indirect.

Scholarly enthusiasm for the hypodermic needle model dwindled after two massive studies of voter behaviour, one in Erie County, Ohio, in 1940 and the other in Elmira, New York, in 1948. The studies, led by sociologist **Paul Lazarsfeld** of Columbia University, were the first rigorous tests of media effects on an election. Lazarsfeld's researchers went back to 600 people several times to discover how they developed their campaign opinions. Rather than citing particular newspapers, magazines, or radio stations, as had been expected, these people generally mentioned friends and acquaintances. The media had hardly any direct effect. Clearly, the hypodermic needle model was off base and the powerful effects theory needed rethinking. From that rethinking emerged the **minimalist effects theory**, which included:

two-step flow Media effects on individuals come through opinion leaders.

opinion leaders Influence friends and acquaintances.

Two-Step Flow Model Minimalist scholars devised the **two-step flow** model to show that voters are motivated less by the mass media than by people they know personally and respect. These people, called **opinion leaders**, include many clergy, teachers, and neighbourhood merchants, although it is impossible to list categorically all those who are opinion leaders. Not all clergy, for example, are influential, and opinion leaders are not necessarily in an authority role. The minimalist scholars' point is that personal contact is more important than media contact. The two-step flow model, which replaced the hypodermic needle model, showed that whatever effect the media have on the majority of the population is through opinion leaders. Later, as mass communication research became more sophisticated, the two-step model was expanded into a **multistep flow** model to capture the complex web of social relationships that affects individuals.

multistep flow Media effects on individuals come through complex interpersonal connections.

Status Conferral Minimalist scholars acknowledge that the media create prominence for issues and people by giving them coverage. Conversely, neglect relegates issues and personalities to obscurity. Related to this **status conferral** phenomenon is **agenda setting** (see further discussion in the section titled Agenda Setting and Status Conferral, later in this chapter). Professors **Maxwell McCombs and Donald Shaw**, describing the agenda-setting phenomenon in 1972, said that the media do not tell people *what* to think but rather tell them *what to think about*. This is a profound distinction. In covering a political campaign, explain McCombs and Shaw, the media choose which issues or topics to emphasize, thereby helping to set the campaign's agenda. "This ability to affect cognitive change among individuals," say McCombs and Shaw, "is one of the most important aspects of the power of mass communication."

status conferral Media attention enhances attention to people, subjects, and issues.

agenda setting Media tell people what to think about, not what to think.

Maxwell McCombs and Donald Shaw Articulated agenda-setting theory.

Narcoticizing Dysfunction Some minimalists claim that the media rarely energize people into action, such as getting them to go out to vote for a candidate. Rather, they say, the media lull people into passivity. This effect, called **narcoticizing dysfunction**, is supported by studies that find that many people are so overwhelmed by the volume of news and information available to them that they tend to withdraw from involvement in public issues. Narcoticizing dysfunction occurs also when people pick up a great deal of information from the media on a particular subject—poverty, for example—and believe that they are doing something about a problem when they are really only smugly well informed. Intellectual involvement becomes a substitute for active involvement.

narcoticizing dysfunction People deceive themselves into believing they're involved when actually they're only well informed.

LEARNING CHECK

- What layers of complexity did Paul Lazarsfeld add to our understanding of the effects of mass communication?

Cumulative Effects Theory

In recent years, some mass communication scholars have parted from the minimalists and resurrected the powerful effects theory, although with a twist that avoids the simplistic hypodermic needle model. German scholar **Elisabeth Noelle-Neumann**, a leader of this school, concedes that the media do not have powerful immediate effects but argues that effects over time are profound. Her **cumulative effects theory** notes that nobody can escape either the media, which are ubiquitous, or the media's messages, which are driven home with redundancy. To support her point, Noelle-Neumann cites multimedia advertising campaigns that hammer away with the same message over and over. There's no missing the point. Even in news reports there is a redundancy, with the media all focusing on the same events.

Elisabeth Noelle-Neumann Leading cumulative effects theorist.

cumulative effects theory Theory that media influence is gradual over time.

Noelle-Neumann's cumulative effects theory has troubling implications. She says that the media, despite surface appearances, work against diverse, robust public consideration of issues. Noelle-Neumann bases her observation on human psychology, which she says encourages people who feel that they hold majority viewpoints to speak out confidently. Those views gain credibility in their claim to be dominant when they are carried by the media, whether they are actually dominant or not. Meanwhile, says Noelle-Neumann, people who perceive that they are in a minority are inclined to speak out less, perhaps not at all. The result is that dominant views can snowball through the media and become consensus views without being sufficiently challenged.

To demonstrate her intriguing theory, Noelle-Neumann has devised the ominously labelled **spiral of silence** model, in which minority views are intimidated into silence and obscurity. Noelle-Neumann's model raises doubts about the libertarian concept that the media provide a marketplace in which conflicting ideas fight it out fairly, all receiving a full hearing.

spiral of silence Vocal majority intimidates others into silence.

LEARNING CHECK

- Explain the way that Elisabeth Noelle-Neumann and most contemporary scholars see mass communication as having an effect on people.
- Do you have an example of the spiral of silence model from your own life experience? Explain.

Lifestyle Effects

STUDY PREVIEW Mass media have a large role in initiating children into society. The socialization process is essential in perpetuating cultural values. For better or worse, mass media have accelerated socialization by giving youngsters access to information that adults kept to themselves in earlier generations. While the mass media affect lifestyles, they also reflect lifestyle changes that come about for reasons altogether unrelated to the mass media.

Media's Initiating Role

Nobody is born knowing how to fit into society. This is learned through a process that begins at home. Children imitate their parents and siblings. From listening and observing, children learn values. Some behaviour is applauded; some is scolded. Gradually this culturization and **socialization** process expands to include friends, neighbours, school, and at some point the mass media.

socialization Learning to fit into society.

In earlier times, the role of the mass media came late because books, magazines, and newspapers required reading skills that were learned in school. The media were only a modest part of early childhood socialization. Today, however, television is omnipresent from the cradle. A young person turning 18 will have spent more time watching television than doing any other activity except sleeping. Television, which requires no special skills to use, has displaced much of the socializing influence that once came from parents. *Sesame Street* imparts more information on the value of nutrition than does Mom's admonition to eat spinach.

By definition, socialization is **pro-social** rather than anti-social in that it teaches behaviour that will benefit others or society. Children learn that buddies frown on tattling, that honesty is virtuous, and that hard work is rewarded. The stability of a society is ensured through the transmission of such values to the next generation.

pro-social Socialization perpetuates positive values.

LEARNING CHECK

- Why is mass communication a growing issue in child development?

Living Patterns

The mass media both reflect lifestyles and shape them. The advent of television in the mid-1950s, for example, kept people at home in their living rooms in the evening. Lodge memberships tumbled. Wednesday-night vespers became an anachronism of earlier times. Television supplanted crossroads taverns in rural areas as a means of socializing and keeping up to date.

Media and lifestyle are intertwined. To find and keep audiences, media companies adjust their products according to the changes caused by other changes. Department stores, a phenomenon in the 1880s, put shopping into the daily routine of housewives, giving rise to evening newspapers that carried store ads so women could plan their next day's shopping expeditions. Newspapers previously were almost all in morning publication.

A century later, with the growing influx of women into full-time, outside-the-home jobs, newspapers dropped their evening editions. Today, almost all newspapers have only morning publication. Other societal changes also contributed to the demise of evening newspapers. In the old industrial economy, most job shifts were 7 A.M. to 3 P.M., which allowed discretionary evening time to spend with a newspaper. With the emergence of a service economy, and with 9 A.M. to 5 P.M. job shifts coming into dominance, the market for evening newspapers withered. As an alternative evening activity, television also squeezed into the time available for people to read an evening paper.

LEARNING CHECK

- Can you offer examples from your own life experience of mass media reflecting lifestyles?
- How about examples of lifestyles reflecting mass media?

Intergenerational Eavesdropping

The mass media, especially television, have eroded the boundaries between the generations, genders, and other social institutions that people once respected. Once, adults whispered when they wanted to discuss certain subjects, such as sex, when children were around. Today, children "eavesdrop" on all kinds of adult topics by seeing them depicted on television. Though meant as a joke, these lines ring true today to many squirming parents:

Father to a friend: My son and I had that father-and-son talk about the birds and the bees yesterday.

Friend: Did you learn anything?

Joshua Meyrowitz, a communication scholar at the University of New Hampshire, brought the new socialization effects of intergenerational eavesdropping to wide attention with his 1985 book, *No Sense of Place*. In effect, the old socially recognized institution of childhood, which long had been protected from "grown-up issues" such as money, divorce, and sex, is disappearing. From television sitcoms, children today learn that adults fight and goof up and sometimes are just plain silly. These are things that children may always have been aware of in a vague sense, but now they have front-row seats.

Joshua Meyrowitz Noted that media have reduced generational and gender barriers.

Television also cracked other protected societal institutions, such as the "man's world." Through television, many women enter the man's world of the locker room, the fishing trip, and the workplace beyond the home. Older mass media, including books, had dealt with a diversity of topics and allowed people in on the "secrets" of other groups, but the ubiquity of television and the ease of access to it accelerated the breakdown of traditional institutional barriers.

LEARNING CHECK

- Has modern media content eroded the innocence of childhood? Explain.

Attitude Effects

STUDY PREVIEW When media messages rivet people's focus, public opinion can take new forms almost instantly. These quick cause-and-effect transformations are easily measured. More difficult to track are the effects of media messages on opinions and attitudes that shift over time, such as customs and social conventions. Studies on role models and stereotype shifts seek to address these more elusive effects and how media messages can be manipulated to influence opinions and attitudes.

Influencing Opinion

How malleable are opinions? People, in fact, change their minds. In politics, the dominance of political parties shifts. Going into the 2008 U.S. election, polls found a growing disaffection with the Democratic and Republican parties. More people were calling themselves independents. Enthusiasm for products can spiral to success overnight and collapse just as fast. We know that people adjust their opinions, sometimes gradually, sometimes suddenly. Also, we know that media messages are important in these processes.

Some cause and effect is tracked easily. A horrendous event, such as the unexpected Japanese attack on U.S. Navy facilities at Pearl Harbor in 1941, instantly transformed American public opinion. Before the attack, sentiment had been against armed resistance to Japanese and German expansionism. In an instant, a massive majority decided to go to war. In 2005, public confidence in the U.S. government bottomed out with the failure to deal with the hurricane devastation in New Orleans and the Gulf Coast. This was repeated in 2010 during the BP oil crisis in the Gulf. These sudden shifts result from information carried by mass media, including statements from opinion leaders.

Causal explanations for gradual opinion shifts are elusive, although mass messages are a factor. What puts a company atop lists of most-admired brands? What makes the rest of the country view Toronto as it does? Many institutions, including state tourism agencies, budget millions of dollars to promote an image that they hope will be absorbed over time. One concentration of corporate image messages airs weekly on Sunday-morning television talk shows.

Scholars have puzzled for decades over how to measure the effects of media content on opinion. Except for major events that trigger sudden turnarounds, media effects on opinion are gradual.

LEARNING CHECK

- Give an example of sudden and drastic changes in public opinion based on media information and other content.
- How frequently do mass media trigger turnarounds in public opinion?

Role Models

The extent of media influence on individuals may never be sorted out with any precision, in part because every individual is a distinct person and because media exposure varies from person to person. Even so, some media influence is undeniable. Consider the effect of entertainment idols as they come across through the media. Many individuals, especially young people seeking identities of their own, groom themselves to conform with the latest heartthrob. Consider Mickey Mantle butch haircuts and then Elvis Presley ducktails in the 1950s, Beatles mopheads in the 1960s, and punk spikes in the 1980s. Then there were the Spice Girls look-alikes some years ago. This imitation, called **role modelling**, even includes speech mannerisms and phrases from whoever is hip at the moment: "Show me the money," "Hasta la vista, baby," and "I'm the king of the world." And let's not forget "yadda-yadda-yadda" from *Seinfeld*.

role modelling Basis for imitative behaviour.

No matter how quirky they are, fashion fads are not terribly consequential, but serious questions can be raised about whether role modelling extends to behaviour. Many people who produce media messages recognize their responsibility for role modelling. Whenever Batman and Robin leaped into their Batmobile in the campy 1960s television series, the camera always managed to show them fastening their seat belts. Many newspapers have a policy of mentioning in accident stories whether seat belts were in use. In the 1980s, as concern about AIDS mounted, moviemakers went out of their way to show

Asics Revival When Uma Thurman slashed her way through Quentin Tarantino's movie *Kill Bill*, the 1949 vintage Asics sneakers she wore, the Onitsuka Tiger model, were suddenly a hit again. In the first quarter after the movie, Asics's net profits outperformed expectations ($1.8 billion) by $800 million. The question was whether Thurman would wear Asics in the sequel in 2004 and whether interest in the Tiger model could be sustained.

condoms as a precaution in sexual situations. For example, in the movie *Broadcast News* a character slips a condom into her purse before leaving the house on the night of an awards dinner.

If role modelling can work for good purposes, such as promoting safety consciousness and disease prevention, it would seem that it could also have a negative effect. Some people linked the Columbine High School massacre in Littleton, Colorado, to a scene in the Leonardo DiCaprio movie *The Basketball Diaries*. In one scene, a student in a black trench coat executes fellow classmates. An outbreak of shootings followed other 1990s films that glorified thug life, including *New Jack City*, *Juice*, and *Boyz N the Hood*.

LEARNING CHECK

- **From your experience, cite examples of role modelling on issues more consequential than fashion and fads.**

Stereotypes

Close your eyes. Think of a "professor." What image forms in your mind? Before 1973, most people would have envisioned a harmless, absent-minded eccentric. Today, *The Nutty Professor* movie remake is a more likely image. Both the absent-minded and nutty professor images are known as stereotypes. Both flow from the mass media. Although neither is an accurate generalization about professors, both have long-term impact.

Stereotyping is a kind of shorthand that can facilitate communication. Putting a cowboy in a black hat allows a movie director to sidestep complex character exploration and move quickly into a storyline because moviegoers hold a generalization (a stereotype) about cowboys in black hats: They are the bad guys.

stereotyping Using broad strokes to facilitate storytelling.

Newspaper editors pack a lot of information into headlines by drawing on stereotypes held by readers. Consider the extra meanings implicit in headlines that refer to the "right wing," a "separatist," or a "terrorist." Stereotypes paint broad strokes that help to create impact in media messages, but they are also a problem. A generalization, no matter how useful, is inaccurate. Not all Scots are tight-fisted, nor are all Wall Street brokers crooked, nor are all college jocks dumb.

By using stereotypes, the mass media perpetuate them. With benign stereotypes there is no problem, but the media can perpetuate social injustice with stereotypes. In the late 1970s, the U.S. Commission on Civil Rights found that blacks on network television were portrayed disproportionately in immature, demeaning, or comic roles. By using a stereotype, television was not only perpetuating false generalizations but also being racist. Worse, network thoughtlessness was robbing black people of strong role models.

Feminists have levelled objections that women are both underrepresented and misrepresented in the media. One study by sociologist Eve Simson found that most female television parts are decorative, played by pretty California women in their twenties. Worse are the occupations represented by women, said Simson. Most frequent are prostitutes, at 16 percent. Traditional female occupations—secretaries, nurses, flight attendants, and receptionists—represent 17 percent. Career women tend to be man-haters or domestic failures. Said Simson, "With nearly every family, regardless of socioeconomic class, having at least one TV set and the average set being turned on seven hours per day, TV has emerged as an important source for promulgating attitudes, values and customs. For some viewers it is the only major contact with outside 'reality,' including how to relate to women. Thus, not only is TV's sexism insulting, but it is also detrimental to the status of women."

Media critics like Simson call for the media to become activists to revise demeaning stereotypes. Although often right-minded, such calls can interfere with accurate portrayals. Italian Americans, for example, have lobbied successfully against Mafia characters being identified as Italian. Exceptions such as HBO's Soprano family remained irritants, however. In general, activists against stereotyping have succeeded. Simson would be pleased with the female, black, and Latino characters in nonstereotypical roles in popular shows such as *Law & Order* and *CSI*.

CASE STUDY

Media Agenda-Setting

A few years ago hardly anyone cared about it, but pick up any newspaper today and you'll find a story about immigration. Many claim that the immigration debate parallels the debate about black civil rights. Even in Canada, hearings into Canada's refugee system in 2010 became a hot-button issue filled with emotion, conflict, and drama.

Just as the news media keeps the immigration story in the forefront of our consciousness, today's media advocacy mirrors the role of the media in the civil rights movement 50 years ago.

In California in 2006, a few advocacy groups wanted to organize a protest to a bill in U.S. Congress that would criminalize millions of unauthorized workers and punish those who helped them, including social and religious groups. It also called for the construction of a wall along the U.S.–Mexico border.

About 10 groups wanted to organize a protest in Los Angeles, said Noé Hernández, an immigrant rights activist: "Then they invited members of the Spanish press, and everything changed." Spanish-language DJs spread the word. So did television stations, with information on how to participate.

The stunned mainstream news media stepped up their coverage. An estimated 500 000 people took to the streets of Los Angeles. Another 300 000 participated in Chicago. Similar protests were held in other cities across the United States. In Atlanta, 80 000 Latinos did not show up for work for one day as part of a citywide boycott.

The media were criticized, mostly by those who leaned to the political right. They charged that the news coverage of the issue was advocacy. Critics on the left objected to the words used in the media to frame the debate. Saurav Sarkar of Fairness & Accuracy in Reporting said, "The mainstream media helped to set the terms of the debate by endlessly repeating catchphrases and buzzwords like *porous borders* and *comprehensive immigration reform.*"

The words most often criticized were *illegal* and *alien*. The National Association of Hispanic Journalists said that the use of these words dehumanized people and stereotyped them as having committed a crime. An estimated 40 percent of the group referred to as *illegal immigrants* initially had valid visas but did not return to their native countries when those visas expired. Some former students fell into this category. However it was worded, the news media set the agenda to debate the immigration question.

Immigration Demonstration An estimated 500 000 people took to the streets in Los Angeles to protest a proposal in U.S. Congress to criminalize millions of unauthorized workers in the United States from other countries. Critics faulted the news media for picking up the protesters' arguments in the coverage. What all sides agreed on was that news coverage kept the issue on the public agenda.

DEEPENING YOUR MEDIA LITERACY

Explore the Issue

Check a major news site such as CNN, CBC, *The Globe and Mail,* or the *National Post* for a recent story on illegal immigration or on refugee policy in which a special-interest group is a source for information or opinion.

Dig Deeper

What can you find out about this group and its leadership, financing, positions, activism, and lobbying?

What Do You Think?

Does media coverage of the group help to set the agenda for national debate on immigration policy? Should media coverage be setting the agenda? If the media should not be setting the agenda, who should?

LEARNING CHECK

- Why are stereotypes an essential element in mass communication?
- What media-perpetuated stereotypes do you see that are false, misleading, and damaging?

Agenda Setting and Status Conferral

Media attention lends a legitimacy to events, individuals, and issues that does not extend to things that go uncovered. This conferring of status occurs through the media's role as agenda-setters. It puts everybody on the same wavelength, or at least on a similar one, which contributes to social cohesion by focusing our collective attention on issues we can address together. Otherwise, each of us could be going in separate directions, which would make collective action difficult if not impossible.

Examples of how media attention spotlights certain issues abound. An especially poignant case occurred in 1998 when a gay University of Wyoming student, Matthew Shepard, was savagely beaten, tied to a fence outside of town, and left to die. It was tragic gay-bashing and coverage of the event moved gay rights higher on the national agenda. Coverage of the gruesome death was an example of the media agenda-setting and of status conferral.

LEARNING CHECK

- How does mass communication wield power through status conferral on some issues and neglect others?

Cultural Effects

STUDY PREVIEW Mass media messages to large audiences can be culturally unifying, but media demassification, with messages aimed at narrower audiences, has had a role also in the fragmentation of society. On a global scale, media have imposed American and Western values on the traditional values of other cultures. Even in countries with emerging media systems, the indigenous media continue to be influenced by media content from dominant cultures.

Values

Historical Transmission Human beings have a compulsion to pass on the wisdom they have accumulated to future generations. There is a compulsion, too, to learn from the past. In olden times, people gathered around fires and in temples to hear storytellers. It was a ritual through which people learned the values that governed their community. This is a form of **historical transmission**.

historical transmission Communication of cultural values to later generations.

Five thousand years ago, the oral tradition was augmented when Middle Eastern traders devised an alphabet to keep track of inventories, transactions, and rates of exchange. When paper was invented, clay tablets gave way to scrolls and eventually to books, which became the primary vehicle for storytelling. Religious values were passed on in holy books. Military chronicles laid out the lessons of war. Literature provided lessons by exploring the nooks and crannies of the human condition.

Books remain the primary repository of our culture. For several centuries it has been between hard covers, in black ink on paper, that the experiences, lessons, and wisdom of our forebears have been recorded for posterity. Other mass media today share in the preservation and transmission of our culture over time. Consider these archives:

- Museum of Television and Radio in New York, with 1200 hours of television documentaries; great performances, productions, debuts, and series; and a sample of top-rated shows.
- Rock and Roll Hall of Fame in Cleveland, Ohio, explores the music and musicians that have helped music to become a social and political force since the emergence of rock 'n' roll in the 1950s.

- TIFF Bell Lightbox in Toronto is the permanent home of the Toronto International Film Festival. The collection includes both Canadian and international film artifacts and exhibits, including an exhibit of the 100 Essential Movies of all time.
- MZTV, also in Toronto, not only showcases the history of the television set, but also explores the cultural impact of the medium.

contemporary transmission Communication of cultural values to different cultures.

diffusion of innovations Process through which news, ideas, values, and information spread.

Contemporary Transmission The mass media also transmit values among contemporary communities and societies, sometimes causing changes that otherwise would not occur. This is known as **contemporary transmission**. Anthropologists have documented that mass communication can change society. When Edmund Carpenter introduced movies to an isolated New Guinea village, the men adjusted their clothing toward the Western style and even remodelled their houses. This phenomenon, which scholars call **diffusion of innovations**, occurs when ideas move through the mass media. Consider the following:

- **Music, fashion, and pop culture**. In modern-day pop culture, the cues come through the media, mostly from New York, Hollywood, and Nashville.
- **Third World innovation**. The United Nations creates instructional films and radio programs to promote agricultural reform in less developed parts of the world. Overpopulated areas have been targets of birth control campaigns.
- **Democracy in China**. As China opened itself to Western tourists, commerce, and mass media in the 1980s, the people glimpsed Western democracy and prosperity, which precipitated pressure on the Communist government to westernize and resulted in the 1989 Tiananmen Square confrontation. A similar phenomenon was a factor in the glasnost relaxations in the Soviet Union in the late 1980s.
- **Demise of Main Street**. Small-town businesses are boarding up throughout the country as rural people see advertisements from regional shopping malls, which are farther away but offer greater variety and lower prices than on Main Street.

Explore
Deepening Your Media Literacy: Reality shows: more than just entertainment?

Scholars note that the mass media can be given too much credit for the diffusion of innovations. Diffusion almost always needs reinforcement through interpersonal communication. Also, the diffusion is hardly ever a one-shot hypodermic injection but a process that requires redundancy in messages over an extended period. The 1989 outburst for democracy in China did not happen because one Chinese person read Thomas Paine one afternoon, nor do rural people suddenly abandon their local Main Street for a Walmart 65 kilometres away. The diffusion of innovations typically involves three initial steps in which the mass media can be pivotal:

- **Awareness**. Individuals and groups learn about alternatives, new options, and possibilities.
- **Interest**. Once aware, people need to have their interest further whetted.
- **Evaluation**. By considering the experience of other people, as relayed by the mass media, individuals evaluate whether they wish to adopt an innovation.

The adoption process has two additional steps in which the media play a small role: the trial stage, in which an innovation is given a try, and the final stage, in which the innovation is either adopted or rejected.

LEARNING CHECK

- What is the role of mass communication in connecting us to the past?
- How does mass communication resolve diverse values in contemporary society?

Cultural Imperialism

cultural imperialism One culture's dominance over another.

Nobody could provoke debate quite like Herbert Schiller, whether among his students or in general society. He amassed evidence for a pivotal 1969 book, *Mass Communications and American Empire*. His argument was that American media companies were coming to dominate cultural life abroad. He called this **cultural imperialism**.

Schiller sensitized readers to the implications of exporting movies and other American media products. He also put leading media companies on notice that Mickey Mouse in Borneo, no matter how endearing, had untoward implications for the indigenous culture. American corporate greed, he said, was undermining native cultures in developing countries. He described the process as insidious. People in developing countries found American media products to be so slickly produced and packaged that, candy-like, they were irresistible no matter the destruction they were causing to the local traditions and values that were fading fast into oblivion.

Plenty of evidence supported Schiller's theory. In South Africa, robbers have taken to shouting, "Freeze!" a word that has no root in Afrikaans or other indigenous languages. The robbers had been watching too much American television. A teen fashion statement in India became dressing like *Baywatch* characters, a fashion hardly in the subcontinent's tradition. In India, too, television talk shows began to feature American-like probing into private lives. Said media observer Shailaja Bajpai, "American television has loosened tongues, to say nothing of our morals."

Schiller's observations were a global recasting of populist–elitist arguments. Populists, whose mantra is "Let the people choose," called Schiller hysterical. These populists noted that Hollywood and other Western media products weren't being forced on anyone. People wanted the products. Some elitists countered that traditional values, many of which go back centuries, were like endangered species and needed protection against Western capitalistic instincts that were smothering them. Elitists noted, too, that the Western media content that was most attractive abroad was hardly the best stuff. *Rambo* was a case in point at the time that Schiller was becoming a bestselling author with his ideas.

U.S. Media Imperialism Herbert Schiller is one of many media theorists concerned about the influence of American culture on smaller nations.

Post-Schiller Revisionism Schiller's ideas took firmer hold in the 1990s as major American and European media companies extended their reach. MTV and ESPN turned themselves into global brands. Rupert Murdoch's empire was flying high as his SkyTV satellite serviced virtually all of Asia; plus, he had similar ventures in Europe and Latin America. Hollywood was firmly in place as a reigning international icon. The largest American newspaper, *USA Today,* launched editions in Europe and Asia.

LEARNING CHECK

- Why was Herbert Schiller alarmed by what he called cultural imperialism?
- Was Schiller's concern about cultural imperialism warranted?

The Canadian Experience with Cultural Intrusion

The notion of latter-day imperialism is one of the reasons why the Canadian Radio-television and Telecommunications Commission (CRTC) and the Canadian government have always had some form of content regulations for most Canadian-owned broadcast media. However, this fear is not unique to Canada; other countries feel the same way. In fact, many countries look to the CRTC for guidance in how to deal with cultural intrusion. In 1998, the World Trade Organization adopted the so-called "Canadian model of regulation." What this means, according to the CRTC, is that other countries want to "understand how Canada meets public interest goals while encouraging the growth of the public sector."

Devi In an attempt to stop Bala, a fallen god, the other gods each place a part of themselves into a warrior woman to create Devi. The manga comic book is part of an exploding mix of transcultural media content from East to West and every other direction on the globe.

Media-Depicted Violence

Watch

ABC's *i-CAUGHT:* "Dangerous Stunt Videos"

STUDY PREVIEW Some individuals mimic aggressive behaviour they see in the media, but such incidents are exceptions. Some experts argue, in fact, that media-depicted violence actually reduces real-life aggressive behaviour.

Learning about Violence

Violence and its effect on children has been an important political issue for Canadians for many years. In 1990, a group of school-age children presented a petition with more than 150 000 names to the federal Minister of Communications, urging the government to "enact rules to eliminate violent and war programming for children on television." The issue became more meaningful in 1992, when Virginie Larivière presented Prime Minister Brian Mulroney with a petition containing 1.3 million names, asking him to initiate legislation that would require broadcasters to reduce the level of violent programming on television and asking Canadians to boycott violent TV shows. Larivière's sister, Marie-Eve, had been robbed, sexually assaulted, and murdered. Larivière believed that violence on television was a factor that had influenced her sister's murderer.

observational learning Theory that people learn behaviour by seeing it in real life and in depictions.

The mass media help to bring young people into society's mainstream by demonstrating dominant behaviours and norms. This pro-social process, called **observational learning,** turns dark, however, when children learn deviant behaviours from the media. In Manteca, California, two teenagers, one only 13, lay in wait for a friend's father in his own house and attacked him. They beat him with a fireplace poker, kicked him and stabbed him, and choked him to death with a dog chain. Then they poured salt in his wounds. Why the final act of violence: the salt in the wounds? The 13-year-old explained that he had seen it on television. While there is no question that people can learn about violent behaviour from the media, a major issue of our time is whether the mass media are the cause of aberrant behaviour.

Individuals on trial for criminal acts occasionally plead that "the media made me do it." That was the defence in a 1974 California case in which two young girls playing on a beach were raped with a beer bottle by four teenagers. The rapists told police that they had picked up the idea from a television movie they had seen four days earlier. In the movie a young woman was raped with a broom handle, and in court the youths' attorneys blamed the movie. Although the courts have never accepted transfer of responsibility as a legal defence, it is clear that violent behaviour can be imitated from the media. Some experts, however, say that the negative effect of media-depicted violence is too often overstated and that media violence actually has a positive side.

LEARNING CHECK

- Why do the courts refuse to excuse violent criminals who blame their behaviour on media-depicted violence?

Media Violence as Positive

cathartic effect People release violent inclinations by seeing them portrayed.

Aristotle Defended portrayals of violence.

People who downplay the negative effect of media portrayals of blood, guts, and violence often refer to a **cathartic effect**. This theory, which dates to ancient Greece and the philosopher **Aristotle**, suggests that watching violence allows individuals vicariously to release pent-up everyday frustration that might otherwise explode dangerously. By seeing violence, so goes the theory, people let off steam. Most advocates of the cathartic effect claim that individuals who see violent activity are stimulated to fantasy violence, which drains off latent tendencies toward real-life violence.

Seymour Feshbach Found evidence for media violence as a release.

In more recent times, scholar **Seymour Feshbach** has conducted studies that lend support to the cathartic effect theory. In one study, Feshbach lined up 625 junior high-school boys at seven California boarding schools and showed half of them a steady diet of violent television programs for six weeks. The other half were shown nonviolent fare. Every day during the study, teachers and supervisors reported on each boy's behaviour in and out of class. Feshbach found no difference in aggressive behaviour between the two groups. Further, there was a decline in aggression among boys who were determined by personality tests to be more inclined toward aggressive behaviour.

Opponents of the cathartic effect theory, who include both respected researchers and reflexive media bashers, were quick to point out flaws in Feshbach's research methods. Nonetheless, his conclusions carried a lot of influence because of the study's unprecedented massiveness: 625 individuals. Also, the study was conducted in a real-life environment rather than in a laboratory, and there was a consistency in the findings.

LEARNING CHECK

- How did Aristotle defend violence as a spectator activity?
- How is the cathartic effect theory controversial?

Prodding Socially Positive Action

Besides the cathartic effect theory, an argument for portraying violence is that it prompts people to socially positive action. This happened after NBC aired *The Burning Bed*, a television movie about an abused woman who could not take any more abuse and set fire to her sleeping husband. On the night the movie aired, battered-spouse centres were overwhelmed by calls from women who had been putting off doing anything to extricate themselves from relationships with abusive mates. On the negative side, one man set his estranged wife on fire and explained that he had been inspired by *The Burning Bed*. Another man who beat his wife senseless gave the same explanation.

LEARNING CHECK

- Offer an example from your life experience of media-depicted violence having a positive effect on an individual.

Media Violence as Negative

The preponderance of evidence is that media-depicted violence has the potential to cue real-life violence. However, the **aggressive stimulation** theory is often overstated. The fact is that few people act out media violence in their lives. For example, do you know anybody who saw a murder in a movie and went out afterwards and murdered somebody? Yet you know many people who see murders in movies and *don't* kill anyone.

aggressive stimulation Theory that people are inspired to violence from media depictions.

We need to be careful in talking about aggressive stimulation. Note how scholar Wayne Danielson, who participated in the 1995–1997 National Television Violence Study, carefully qualified one of the study's conclusions: "Viewing violence on TV *tends* to increase violent behavior in viewers, more *in some situations* and less in others. For whatever reason, *when the circumstances are right*, we *tend* to imitate what we see others doing. Our inner resistance to engage in violent behavior *weakens*."

The study concluded that children may be more susceptible than adults to media violence, but that was also far, far short of a universal causal statement.

Why, then, do many people believe that media violence begets real-life violence? Some early studies pointed to a causal link. These included the 1960 **Bobo doll studies** of **Albert Bandura**, who showed children a violent movie and then encouraged them to play with oversize, inflated dolls. Bandura concluded that children who saw the film were more inclined to beat up the dolls than were other children. Critics have challenged Bandura's methodology and said that he mistook childish playfulness for aggression. In short, Bandura and other aggressive stimulation scholars have failed to prove their theory to the full satisfaction of other scholars.

Bobo doll studies Children seemed more violent after seeing violence in movies.

Albert Bandura Found media violence stimulated aggression in children.

When pressed, people who support the aggressive stimulation theory point to particular incidents they know about. A favourite is the claim by serial killer Ted Bundy that *Playboy* magazine led him to stalk and kill women. Was Bundy telling the truth? We will never know. He offered the scapegoat explanation on his way to the execution chamber, which suggests that there may have been other motives. The Bundy case is anecdotal, and anecdotes cannot be extrapolated into general validity.

LEARNING CHECK

- What evidence supports the theory that media-depicted violence leads to real-life violence?
- How are catalytic effects of media-depicted violence different from causal effects?

Catalytic Theory

catalytic theory Media violence is among factors that sometimes contribute to real-life violence.

An alternative to aggressive stimulation theory is a theory that people whose feelings and general view of the world tend toward aggressiveness and violence are attracted to violence in movies, television, and other media. This alternative theory holds that people who are violent are predisposed to violence, which is far short of saying that the media made them act violently. This leads us to the **catalytic theory**, which sees media-depicted violence as having a contributing role in violent behaviour, not as triggering it.

Simplistic readings of both cathartic effect and aggressive stimulation research can yield extreme conclusions. A careful reading, however, points more to the media having a role in real-life violence but not necessarily triggering it and doing so only infrequently—and only if several nonmedia factors are also present. For example, evidence suggests that television and movie violence, even in cartoons, is arousing and can excite some children to violence, especially hyperactive and easily excitable children. These children, like unstable adults, become wrapped up psychologically with the portrayals and are stirred to the point of acting out. However, this happens only when a combination of other influences is also present. Among these other influences are:

- **Whether violence portrayed in the media is rewarded.** In 1984, David Phillips of the University of California at San Diego found that the murder rate increases after publicized prizefights, in which the victor is rewarded, and decreases after publicized murder trials and executions, in which, of course, violence is punished.
- **Whether media exposure is heavy**. Researcher Monroe Lefkowitz studied grade 3 students in upstate New York who watched a lot of media-depicted violence. Ten years later, Lefkowitz found that these individuals were rated by their peers as violent. This suggests cumulative, long-term media effects.
- **Whether a violent person fits other profiles**. Studies have found correlations between aggressive behaviour and many variables besides violence viewing. These include income, education, intelligence, and parental child-rearing practices. This is not to say that any of these variables cause violent behaviour. The suggestion, rather, is that violence is far too complex to be explained by a single factor.

Most researchers note, too, that screen-triggered violence is increased if the aggression

- Is realistic and exciting, such as in a chase or suspense sequence that sends adrenaline levels surging.
- Succeeds in righting a wrong, such as helping an abused or ridiculed character to get even.
- Includes situations or characters similar to those in the viewer's own experience.

Wilbur Schramm Concluded that television has minimal effects on children.

All of these things would prompt a scientist to call media violence a catalyst. Just as the presence of a certain element will allow other elements to react explosively but not be part of the explosion itself, the presence of media violence can be a factor in real-life violence but not a cause by itself. This catalytic theory was articulated by scholars **Wilbur Schramm**, Jack Lyle, and Edwin Parker, who investigated the effects of television on children and came up with the following statement in their 1961 book *Television in the Lives of Our Children*, which has become a classic on the effects of media-depicted violence on individuals: "For *some* children under *some* conditions, *some* television is harmful. For *other* children under the same conditions, or for the same children under *other* conditions, it *may* be beneficial. For *most* children, under *most* conditions, *most* television is *probably* neither particularly harmful nor particularly beneficial."

LEARNING CHECK

- Why is it difficult to demonstrate that media-depicted violence directly causes real-life violence?
- What variables may contribute to a person's proneness for violence after an experience with media-depicted violence?

Societally Debilitating Effects

Media-depicted violence scares far more people than it inspires to violence, and this, according to **George Gerbner**, a leading researcher on screen violence, leads some people to believe the world is more dangerous than it really is. Gerbner calculates that 1 in 10 television characters is involved in violence in any given week. In real life, the chances are only about 1 in 100 per *year*. People who watch a lot of television, Gerbner found, see their own chances of being involved in violence as nearer the distorted television level than their local crime statistics or even their own experience would suggest. It seems that television violence leads people to think they are in far greater real-life jeopardy than they really are.

George Gerbner Speculated that democracy is endangered by media violence.

The implications of Gerbner's findings go to the heart of a free and democratic society. With exaggerated fears about their safety, Gerbner says, people will demand greater police protection. They are also likelier to submit to established authority and even to accept police violence as a trade-off for their own security.

LEARNING CHECK

- Does media-depicted violence misrepresent the extent of real-life violence in society?
- Does media-depicted violence lead people to have unwarranted concern for their personal safety?

Tolerance of Violence

An especially serious concern about media-depicted violence is that it has a numbing, callousing effect on people. This **desensitizing theory**, which is widely held, says not only that individuals are becoming hardened by media violence but also that society's tolerance for such anti-social behaviour is increasing.

desensitizing theory Tolerance of real-life violence grows because of media-depicted violence.

Media critics say that the media are responsible for this desensitization, but many media people, particularly movie and television directors, respond that desensitization has forced them to make the violence in their shows even more graphic. They explain that they have run out of alternatives to get the point across when the storyline requires that the audience be repulsed.

Desensitization is apparent in news as well. In 2004, *The New York Times*, traditionally cautious about gore, showed a photo of corpses hanging from a bridge in Fallujah, Iraq. Only a few years earlier, there was an almost universal ban on showing the bodies of crime, accident, and war victims in newspapers and on television newscasts. Photos of U.S. troops torturing Iraqi prisoners, integral in telling a horrible but important story, pushed back those earlier limits. No mainstream media showed the entire execution of Saddam Hussein in 2006, but millions of people found longer versions of the gruesome sequence online. This desensitizing did not come suddenly with the 2003 Iraq War and its aftermath, but coverage of that war clearly established new ground rules.

It's undeniable that violence has had a growing presence in the mass media, which makes it even more poignant that we know far less about media violence than we need to. What *do* we know? Various theories explain some phenomena, but the theories themselves do not dovetail. The desensitizing theory, for example, explains audience acceptance of more violence, but it hardly explains research findings that people who watch a lot of television actually have heightened anxiety about their personal safety. People fretting about their own safety are hardly desensitized.

LEARNING CHECK

- Does media-depicted violence desensitize us individually to be more tolerant of real-life violence?
- Is society more tolerant of real-life violence because of exposure to media depictions?

Violence Studies

The mass media, especially television and movies that deal in fiction, depict a lot of violence. Studies have found as many as six violent acts per hour on prime-time network television. In and of itself, that may seem a lot, but a study at the University of California, Los Angeles (UCLA), operating on the premise that the issue should not be how much violence is depicted but the context in which it occurs, came to a less startling conclusion: Slapstick comedic violence shouldn't be lumped in with graphic homicide in counting depictions of violence. Nor should a violent storm.

Television Violence Monitoring Project Conducted contextual nonviolence studies and found less serious media depictions than earlier thought.

The UCLA research, called the **Television Violence Monitoring Project**, concluded in its first year that distressing human violence was much less prevalent than earlier studies had counted. Of 121 prime-time episodes, only 10 had frequent violence and only 8 had occasional violence. This was after comedic violence and nonhuman violence, such as hurricanes, were excluded. The next year, 1996, found violence in only five prime-time shows—half the number of the year before. Also, most of those shows didn't survive the season. In 1998, the number was down to two series.

William McQuire Found most media violence research flawed.

The UCLA study added sophistication to counting acts of media-depicted violence but still didn't assess whether the violence affected people. In 1986, scholar **William McQuire** reviewed the literature on mediated violence and found that hardly any of the studies' evidence was statistically reliable. The exception was controlled laboratory studies, for which the statistics were more meaningful but didn't indicate much causality.

MEDIA PEOPLE George Gerbner

George Gerbner worried a lot about media violence. And when he died in 2005, he had been doing that longer than just about anybody else. In 1967, Gerbner and colleagues at the University of Pennsylvania created a television violence index and began counting acts of violence. Today, more than four decades later, the numbers are startling. Gerbner calculated that the typical American 18-year-old has seen 32 000 murders and 40 000 attempted murders at home on television.

In a dubious sense, there may be good news for those who fear the effects of media violence. Gerbner's index found no significant change in the volume of violence since the mid-1970s. Maybe it maxed out.

Gerbner theorized that media violence has negative effects on society. It's what he called "the mean-world syndrome." As he saw it, people exposed to so much violence come to perceive the world as a far more dangerous place than it really is. One of his concerns is that people become overly concerned for their own safety and, in time, may become willing to accept a police state to ensure their personal security. That, he said, has dire consequences for the free and open society that has been a valued hallmark of the American lifestyle.

Are there answers? Gerbner pointed out that the global conglomeration of mass media companies works against any kind of media self-policing. These companies are seeking worldwide outlets for their products, whether movies, television programs, or music, and violence doesn't require any kind of costly translations. "Violence travels well," he said. Also, violence has low production costs.

Gerbner noted that violence is an easy fill for weak spots in a television storyline. Also, in television, violence serves as an effective cliff-hanger before a commercial break.

While Gerbner's statistics are unsettling, they have critics who say that his numbers make the situation seem worse than it really is. The Gerbner index scores acts of violence without considering their context. That means that when Bugs Bunny is bopped on the head, it counts the same as Rambo doing the same thing to a villain in a skull-crushing, blood-spurting scene. A poke in the eye on *The Three Stooges* also scores as a violent act.

Despite his critics, Gerbner provided a baseline for measuring changes in the quantity of television violence. Virtually every scholar cites him in the ongoing struggle to determine whether media violence is something that should worry us all.

George Gerbner

WHAT DO YOU THINK?

1. Why do scholars need to measure the incidence of media violence?
2. Kung fu blood and guts or Bugs Bunny being bopped on the head: how do you classify the media depiction of violence?
3. What do you make of Gerbner's observation that violence travels well?

LEARNING CHECK

- What difficulty do researchers have in measuring violent media content?

Violence in the Canadian Media

Canadian broadcasters have had a violence code since 1987. However, with the social and political developments brought about by the Larivière petition in 1992, the Canadian Association of Broadcasters (CAB) and the CRTC took a hard look at the issue. In 1993, Larivière's petition was the subject of a Standing Committee on Communications and Culture. This, in combination with two conferences on the effects of media violence on children, led to the creation of the Action Group on Violence on Television (**AGVOT**). Members included the CAB, the CBC, the Canadian Cable Television Association, the Association of Canadian Advertisers, and the Canadian Film and Television Production Association.

AGVOT Action Group on Violence on Television; helped develop programming codes for Canadian television.

A new violence code was introduced by AGVOT in late 1993. Some of the main elements of the code's rules for programming aimed at children less than 12 years of age involve the following criteria:

- Only violence essential to the plot is allowed.
- Violence cannot be the central theme in cartoons.
- Violence cannot be seen as the only way to resolve conflict.
- Realistic scenes of violence that downgrade the effects of violent behaviour are not allowed.
- Programming cannot invite imitation of violent or perilous acts.

For children over 12 years of age, 9 p.m. has become what AGVOT refers to as the "watershed" hour. In addition, a viewer advisory must accompany any program containing violence, nudity, or strong language.

However, should just the media be criticized for children's having access to violent imagery? What about parents? That was the one of the themes that emerged during a 2007 debate about the level of violence in the Canadian media, including music and video games. *Toronto Star* columnist Antonia Zerbisias says that "in the 1990s, the industry and the federal broadcast regulator spent millions on studies to raise awareness and to formulate codes of ethics. Still the problem exists. Which means the solution lies in one place alone. The power switch. You (parents) have the power. Use it."

LEARNING CHECK

- How much responsibility should broadcasters take when it comes to airing violent content?

Chapter 15 Wrap-Up

The mass media influence us, but scholars are divided about how much. There is agreement that the media help to initiate children into society by portraying social and cultural values. This is a serious responsibility because portrayals of aberrant behaviour such as violence have effects, although we are not sure about their extent. This is not to say that individuals are unwitting pawns of the mass media. People choose what they read and what they tune in to, and they generally filter the information and images to conform with their preconceived notions and personal values.

In short, the media have effects on individuals and on society, but it is a two-way street. Society is a shaper of media content, but individuals make the ultimate decisions about subscribing, listening, and watching. The influence issue is a complex one that merits further research and thought.

mycanadiancommunicationlab

Visit **www.mycanadiancommunicationlab.ca** for access to a wealth of tools and resources that will enhance your learning experience. Features include the following:

- Personalized Study Plan
- Videos
- Activities
- Pearson eText–and much more!

Questions for Critical Thinking

1. Why has the magic bullet theory of mass communication effects lost support? What has replaced the magic bullet theory?
2. How is the role of mass messages in childhood development changing?
3. What are examples of the influence of mass communication on attitudes and opinions?
4. What continues to fuel magic bullet theory beliefs about immediate, powerful effects of mass messages, including subliminal messages?
5. Identify and discuss different ideas about the effects of media-depicted violence.

Keeping Up to Date

The interdisciplinary scholarly journal *Media Psychology,* a quarterly, focuses on theory-based research on media uses, processes, and effects.

Global Mass Media

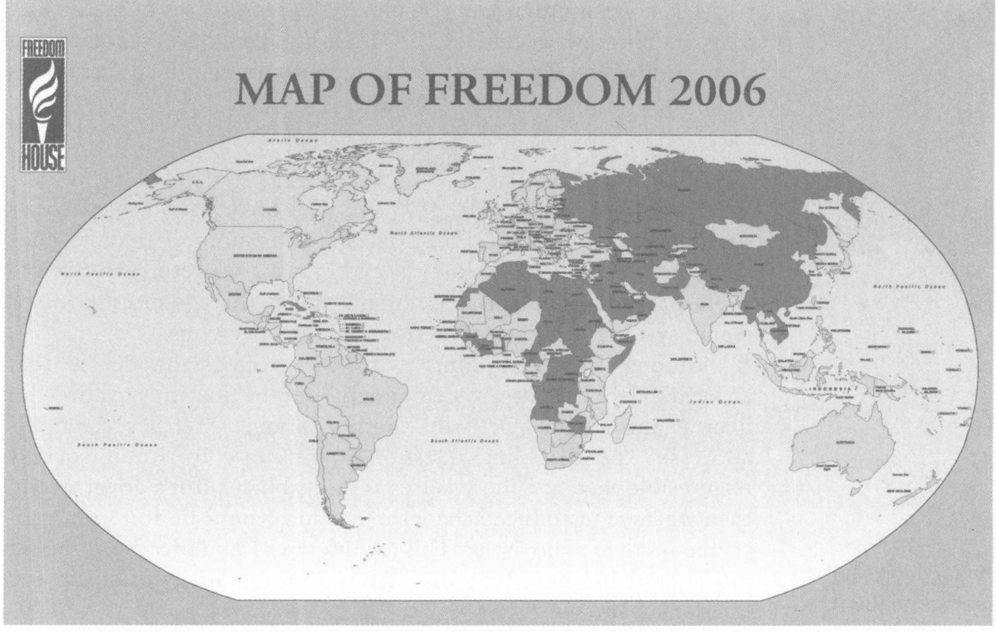

Coding Freedom Freedom House, which tracks the freedom of the new media worldwide, reports relatively few countries where news and information flow freely within and across their borders. Countries shaded dark are not considered "free."

LEARNING AHEAD

- Mass media reflect a nation's political system.
- War can force compromises in media freedom.
- Market forces are transforming some Arab media.
- Terrorists have adapted digital media as a propaganda tool.
- Media are central in a Cold War–style battle for reforms in Iran.
- China has the broadest censorship apparatus in history.

MEDIA IN THEORY

Global Media Models

Models help us to visualize different media systems. Models have different levels of sophistication, such as going from a bipolar model for political systems to a more complex continuum model to an even more complex compass model. Besides political systems, models can demonstrate media cultural environments, developmental states, and other characterizing criteria.

Bipolar Model

To compare media systems, some scholars use a **bipolar model** with two extremes: authoritarianism at one end and libertarianism at the other. The model demonstrates opposites in an extreme way. Just as east is opposite from west, so is freedom opposite from control. Bipolar models are useful beginning points to separate political systems.

bipolar model Portrays extremes as opposites, such as libertarian and authoritarian political systems.

Continuum Model

More sophisticated than a simple bipolar model is a variation called the **continuum model**. The basics of the continuum political system model are bipolar, with the

continuum model A scale with authoritarianism at one end, libertarianism at the other, and media systems at varying points in between.

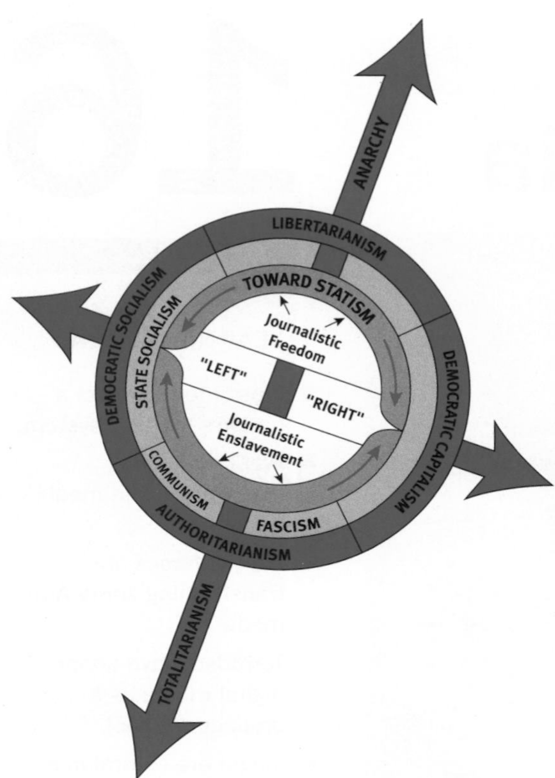

Figure 16.1 Compass Model Scholar John Merrill rethought the libertarian–authoritarian continuum to develop this compass model. The result was a graphic representation showing that a responsible press, if responsibility is by government mandate, is frighteningly close to traditional authoritarianism.

extremes being authoritarianism and libertarianism, but there is an added element of sophistication. The media system of each country is placed not at an extreme but at points along the line. Canada and the United States would be near the libertarian end, although not quite at the extreme because, indeed, North American media operate within limitations, such as laws of treason, libel, and intellectual property and also broadcast regulations.

The continuum model recognizes the uniqueness of media systems in different countries. By assessing variables, scholars can plant individual countries on the continuum, which facilitates grouping countries for comparison.

Compass Model

In his book *The Imperative of Freedom*, scholar **John Merrill** loops the libertarian–authoritarian continuum around so that its ends meet themselves. On the loop, Merrill marks the four major philosophical underpinnings as compass points that define the major media systems and their underlying political systems.

Among Merrill's points with the **compass model** is that a social responsibility system might not be just a variation on libertarianism but actually authoritarian. Merrill's compass addresses the troubling question about how to attain socially responsible media: Who ensures responsibility? If it's government, then we have introduced shades of authoritarianism. If it's not government, then who is it? This chapter will explore the different media systems and offer a discussion of both authoritarianism and libertarianism.

John Merrill Introduced the compass model, which showed that social responsibility and authoritarianism could be bedmates.

compass model A looped model that juxtaposes traditional authoritarian and social responsibility models.

Explore

Media People: Orhan Pamuk

Mass Media and Nation-States

STUDY PREVIEW The world's nations and media systems fall into competing, philosophically irreconcilable systems. Authoritarianism places confidence in political and sometimes theocratic leadership for governance. In contrast, libertarianism emphasizes the ability of human beings to reason their own way to right conclusions and therefore believes that humans are capable of their own governance. Democracy and a free mass media are in the libertarian tradition.

MEDIA TIMELINE Global Mass Media Milestones

1598 James VI of Scotland (later James I of England) claimed kings had the "divine right" to rule.

1644 John Milton's *Areopagitica* argued against censorship.

1974 John Merrill wrote *The Imperative of Freedom.*

1996 Qatar sheik created Al Jazeera news channel.

1998 The World Trade Organization adopted the Canadian model of media regulation.

2001 China installed filters on incoming internet communication.

2003 Dubai launched media enterprise for multinational audiences.

2009 Iran clamped down on social media, such as Twitter, due to election protests.

2010 Al Jazeera arrived in Canada.

Global Communication

After the 2005 terrorist subway and bus bombings in London, the British news media flooded the streets and airwaves with stories about the suspects. Understandably, coverage was emotional. When the first arrests were made, the front page of the tabloid *Sun* blared: "Got the Bastards." Then the media went silent. British law forbids news coverage once a criminal charge has been filed. The rationale is to not prejudice potential jurors.

Hungry for news about the terrorism investigation and the people arrested, Britons needed to look no further than the internet. The internet's most-used coding structure is called the World Wide Web for a reason. As well, just down the street, newsstands stocked foreign newspapers and magazines full of ongoing revelations about the suspects. Legally, the imported publications, as well as internet coverage, could have been banned under the 1981 Contempt of Court Act. But how? The logistics would have been overwhelming.

Throughout the world, not only in Britain, the power that governments once wielded over mass communication has eroded. The challenge for governments, especially in countries with repressive regimes, is how to impede unwanted outside messages from getting in. On a global scale, the struggle is between two intellectual traditions: long-dominant **authoritarianism** and historically more recent freedom-favouring **libertarianism**.

authoritarianism Top-down governance, such as a monarchy or dictatorship.

libertarianism Given time and access to good information, people ultimately make the right decisions; basis of democratic governance.

LEARNING CHECK

- What are the two philosophical traditions that define different media systems around the globe?

Authoritarianism

Throughout mass media history, authoritarian political systems have been the most common. The powerful monarchies were authoritarian. So were Nazi Germany and Spain under Francisco Franco in the 1900s. The Soviets had their own twist on authoritarianism. Today, dictatorships and theocracies continue the tradition. A premise of authoritarian systems is that the government is infallible, which places its policies beyond questioning. The media's role in an authoritarian society is subservience to government.

Authoritarian Premises

Authoritarian media systems make sense to anyone who accepts the premise that the government, whether embodied by a monarch or a dictator, is right in all that it says and does. Such a premise is anathema to most Canadians, but merely 400 years ago it was mainstream Western thought. **King James VI** of Scotland, who later became James I of England, made an eloquent argument for the **divine right of kings** in 1598. He claimed that legitimate monarchs were anointed by an Almighty and therefore were better able to

King James VI & I Articulated the divine right of kings theory.

divine right of kings Proper decisions follow the monarch's will, which is linked to an Almighty.

Authoritarian Execution Authoritarian governments prevent mass media criticism of their policies with numerous methods, including execution. In authoritarian England, the Crown made spectacles of executions.

express righteousness and truth than anyone else. By definition, anybody who differed with the monarch was embracing falsity and probably heresy.

The authoritarian line of reasoning justifies suppression of ideas and information on numerous grounds:

- Truth is a monopoly of the regime. Commoners can come to know truth only through the ruler, who in King James's thinking had an exclusive pipeline to an Almighty. Advocates of authoritarianism hold little confidence in individuals.
- Challenges to government are based on falsity. It could not be otherwise, considering the premise that government is infallible.
- Without strong government, the stability necessary for society to function may be disrupted. Because challenges to government tend to undermine stability and because challenges are presumed to be false to begin with, they must be suppressed.

Explore

Deepening Your Media Literacy: What is the cultural message of the Marlboro Man?

To the authoritarian mind, media people who support the government are purveying truth and should be rewarded. The unfaithful, those who criticize, are spreading falsity and should be banished. An inherent contradiction in authoritarianism is the premise that the ruler is uniquely equipped to know truth. Experience over the centuries makes it clear that monarchs and dictators come in many stripes. Regimes have been known to change their definitions of truth in midstream.

LEARNING CHECK

- What is the notion of truth that is at the heart of authoritarianism?

Libertarianism

Libertarian thinkers, in contrast to authoritarians, have faith in the ability of individual human beings to come to know great truths by applying reason. This distinction is the fundamental difference between libertarian and authoritarian perspectives.

Physicists love to tell young students the story of an English lad, Isaac Newton. Sitting in an orchard one late summer day, Isaac was struck on the head by a falling apple. At that moment, the law of gravity was instantly clear to him. It's a good story, although probably not true. Deriving the law of gravity was a much more sophisticated matter for Newton, the leading 17th-century physicist. Nevertheless, the orchard story lives on. It's also told to pupils in world history classes to illustrate a period in intellectual history called the **Enlightenment**. In that version of the story, young Newton not only discovered gravity at the very instant that he was bumped on the head, but also realized that he could come to know great truths like the law of gravity by using his own mind. He did not need to rely on a priest or a monarch or on anyone else who claimed a special relationship with an Almighty. Instead, he could do it on his own. This revelation, say the history teachers, was a profound challenge to authoritarian premises and ushered in the era of rational thinking that sets the modern age apart. Individually and together, people are capable of learning the great truths, called natural law, unassisted by authorities. The insight was that human beings are rational beings. It was a realization that began quantum leaps in the sciences. The insight also contributed to the development of libertarianism, which held the intellectual roots of modern democracy.

Enlightenment Period of rationalist thought; beginning foreshadowed by early libertarians.

Marketplace of Ideas An English writer, **John Milton**, was the pioneer libertarian. In his 1644 pamphlet *Areopagitica*, Milton made a case for free expression based on the idea that individual human beings are capable of discovering truth if given the opportunity. Milton argued for a free and open exchange of information and ideas: a **marketplace of ideas**. Just as people at a farmers' market can pinch and inspect many vegetables until they find the best, so can people find the best ideas if they have a vast array from which to choose. Milton's marketplace is not a place but a concept. It exists whenever people exchange ideas, whether in conversation or in letters or the printed word.

John Milton Early libertarian thinker.

marketplace of ideas An unbridled forum for free inquiry and free expression.

Milton was eloquent in his call for free expression. He saw no reason to fear any idea, no matter how subversive, because human beings inevitably will choose the best ideas and values. He put it this way: "Let Truth and Falsehood grapple: whoever knew Truth put to the worse in a free and open encounter." Milton reasoned that people would gain confidence in their ideas and values if they tested them continually against alternative views.

CASE STUDY

Twitter Revolution

It was an online showdown.

It started when the Iranian government tried to block media coverage of events following the disputed 2009 presidential election. Supporters of an opposition candidate, Hossein Mousavi, claimed that the election was rigged and took to the streets. Demonstrations became violent when the government of Mahmoud Ahmadinejad cracked down. There was blood in the streets. The government banned both local and foreign media on the protests and rallies. When news continued to leak out of the country, journalists were confined to their bureaus.

At that point, the "Twitter Revolution" happened. Everyone became a reporter. Ordinary Iranians sent real-time updates to Twitter about the protest marches. They shot video from their windows of government agents beating protesters. As people walked through the streets, they used their cell phones to shoot images of people shouting from the rooftops. These images were uploaded using social media such as YouTube, Flickr, and Facebook. One of the videos showed a young woman named Neda as she died after being shot. The video sent shockwaves around the world. Without any alternatives, mainstream media used the reports on Twitter and other social media as their sources.

The government's actions against the protestors were swift, brutal, and naive. Somehow they forgot that Iranians had been using social media for years. Sixty percent of Iranians are under age 30. Most own cell phones. This is a population accustomed to blogging and text messaging. Indeed, Iran ranks near the top of the worldwide list of bloggers per capita. It should have been no surprise that Iranian citizens would put their social media skills to use.

The government did fight back. Agents posed online as opposition activists or foreign journalists to catch dissidents. The government also tried to shut down internet access but then found that it needed the internet as much as the dissidents did.

All of this was online warfare—and also a challenge for the mainstream media. How to verify these reports from untrained and sometimes partisan observers? Various

Twitter Revolution Social media proved to be a new adversary to governments hoping to control the media message.

blogs claimed that anywhere from 30 to 3000 people were killed. Some photos posted by the Iranian government appeared to be doctored. Most reports in the mainstream media were qualified with the phrase *unable to verify*. But the mainstream media had to keep up and they used these citizen reports because there was no other way to provide up-to-date coverage.

DEEPENING YOUR MEDIA LITERACY

Explore the Issue

How would authoritarian regimes view social media? Libertarians?

Dig Deeper

How can tweeting and blogging democratize mass communication?

What Do You Think?

Is the social media revolution truly a revolution? Are we at last embracing new media and using them to their full potential?

It was an argument against censorship. People need to have the fullest possible choice in the marketplace if they are going to go home with the best product, whether vegetables or ideas. Also, bad ideas should be present in the marketplace because, no matter how objectionable, they might contain a grain of truth.

Milton and his libertarian successors acknowledged that people sometimes err in sorting out alternatives, but these mistakes are corrected as people continually reassess their values against competing values in the marketplace. Libertarians see this truth-seeking as

self-righting process Although people make occasional errors in truth-seeking, they eventually discover and correct them.

a never-ending, lifelong human pursuit. Over time, people will shed flawed ideas for better ones. This is called the **self-righting process.**

Global Libertarianism On its scale of *Free* and *Not Free*, the Freedom House organization, which tracks freedom globally, says that democracy and freedom are the dominant trends in Canada, Western and east-central Europe, the Americas, and increasingly the Asia-Pacific region. In the former Soviet Union, Freedom House says that the picture remains mixed. In Africa, free societies and electoral democracies are a minority despite recent progress. The Middle East has experienced gains for freedom, although the region as a whole overwhelmingly consists of countries that Freedom House rates as *Partly Free* or *Not Free.*

LEARNING CHECK

- Explain how libertarianism is optimistic about human reason and how authoritarianism is pessimistic.
- How does the Enlightenment relate to libertarianism?

Arab Media Systems

STUDY PREVIEW Media in Islamic regions do not fit a single mould. They operate in diverse political systems, some driven by theologies that themselves are inconsistent. Others are pragmatically oriented to create pan-Arabic mass audiences. Among the most successful is Al Jazeera, which debuted in Canada in 2010.

Diverse Media Structures

Media systems of the nations comprising Islam-dominated regions are as diverse as the nations themselves. These nations span from northern Africa to Southeast Asia. Many resemble classic authoritarian systems and some are among the planet's last theocracies, with clerics dominating public policy. Variations, however, are significant. Islamic dogma ranges widely among sects vying for dominance. The civil war into which Iraq fell during the U.S. occupation, for example, was due to a clash of different traditions and strains of Islam going back centuries. In contrast, in the sheikdom of Dubai, whose governance resembles a monarchy, economic growth has trumped divisive issues with overt pan-Arabic attempts to accommodate diverse traditions.

Media systems in some Arabic areas reflect values from periods of overbearing European dominance, mixed with resurgent indigenous traditions and values. Some of this Western influence continued long after this dominance had ended. In the 1990s, for example, the British Broadcasting Corporation (BBC), which has a history of international broadcasting in the region, spent two years setting up an Arab-language service. Obstacles led the BBC to abandon the project in 1996. Then, seeing a vacuum, the government of the tiny Gulf state of Qatar, already committed to making itself a regional media centre, created a 24/7 television news service modelled on CNN. Sheikh **Hamad bin Khalifa** put up the money. Thus, **Al Jazeera,** which today is ranked the world's fifth-best-known brand, was born.

Hamad bin Khalifa Founder of Al Jazeera television news network.

Al Jazeera Qatar-based satellite news channel for Arab audiences; now global.

LEARNING CHECK

- Describe the diversity in political systems and their media components in Arabic and Islamic regions.

Al Jazeera

Based in Qatar, Al Jazeera picked up its journalistic tradition largely through Britons who had been working on the now-abandoned BBC project. For the Middle East, the approach was fresh: live coverage of breaking news told dispassionately and as thoroughly as possible, no holds barred. Viewers flocked to the channel. Call-in shows were

Control Room The Al Jazeera control room in Qatar is staffed by a mix of former BBC employees and Arabian journalists. Al Jazeera's Canadian correspondent, Imtiaz Tyab, was once a reporter for the CBC in Vancouver. Al Jazeera's Canadian bureau is located in Toronto.

uncensored. Arabs suddenly had an avenue to unload on their governments, many of which were unevenly responsive to public needs.

Al Jazeera was applauded in the West as a voice for democracy and reform. However, things changed after Arab terrorists killed thousands of people in New York City and Washington in 2001. As the Bush administration in the United States moved toward war in Iraq, the Arab perspective inherent in Al Jazeera included independent reporting that sometimes was at odds with American portrayals. Commentary was from all sides, including insurgents whom the U.S. government wanted to deny a voice.

Meanwhile, Al Jazeera's reporting continued in the BBC tradition, seeking multiple perspectives to get at the facts and truth. The reporting carried a high price to intolerant factions that claimed their own monopolies on truth. Twice, Al Jazeera bureaus were bombed, including a 2001 U.S. aerial attack on the Al Jazeera bureau in Baghdad. Several Arab governments banned Al Jazeera, although with little effect. The network's audience, already 50 million in 2000, has continued to grow.

Al Jazeera's influence has grown as well. In 2003, the network entered into a news-sharing agreement with BBC. CNN added Al Jazeera to its sources of video feeds. Al Jazeera launched an English-language network in 2006 to extend its global reach. The English-language anchors have familiar faces; some were formerly with CNN, Sky News, and the BBC. Al Jazeera began broadcasting in Canada in 2010. The managing editor of Al Jazeera Canada, Tony Burman, is a former CBC editor-in-chief.

LEARNING CHECK

- What challenges do Al Jazeera and its competitors face in reaching Arab audiences?
- When agents of Osama bin Laden supplied video of his anti-Western political messages to Al Jazeera, the network aired them as news. Was this the right thing to do?

Transnational Arabic Competition

The Arabic television field is becoming increasingly crowded. Saudi **satcaster** MBC has set up an all-news channel. Dubai TV's One TV has added an English-language entertainment network. Lebanon has become a powerhouse of pan-Arab television programming, including reality shows and talent contests. The BBC, meanwhile, has decided to try an Arab-language news network again. The global reach of Arab media has extended to Latin America, where Telsur has gone into multinational satellite newscasts.

satcaster A television station that transmits to an orbiting satellite, which beams signals back down directly to individual receivers.

In Arab countries, the proliferation of satellite channels is expected to peak at some point soon. The survivors will be operations with very deep pockets. The business development manager at MBC in Saudi Arabia, Michel Constandi, estimates the combined operating budgets of the region's free satellite channels at $3 billion a year. The estimated ad market is only $30 million.

The significance of these multinational Arab media services is that, to attract large enough audiences to survive financially, they need to address audiences that subscribe to variations in Islamic readings of the Quran as well as to divergent traditions, many of which have evolved confusingly and become intertwined with religious values.

LEARNING CHECK

- How can media companies seeking pan-Arab audiences be successful in such a fractured part of the world?

Dubai Media Incorporated

As a nation, Dubai might seem a mere speck of sand on the Persian Gulf; it contains 674 000 people, only 265 700 in its main city. From under that sand, though, has come oil that has brought spectacular wealth to the tiny emirate. But what will happen when the wells run dry? Resources extracted from the earth inevitably run out.

The government has set a deliberate course to create a post-oil financial infrastructure. The plan includes lavish hotels to transform Dubai into a tourism magnet. Beaches line the Gulf for miles, and are easily only a day's flight from major population centres in Europe, south Asia, and, of course, the rest of the Arab world.

Dubai has so much sunshine. Could it also become the Arabian Hollywood? It was California sunshine, after all, that drew the infant American filmmaking industry from the east coast to Hollywood early in the 1900s. The more sunshine there is, the more days there are for outdoor shooting. With moviemaking could come a host of related media industries, particularly television.

Dubai Media Incorporated Quasi-government agency building Dubai into a Mideast entertainment production centre.

The brainstorming that began with a tourist-oriented Dubailand complex mushroomed. In 2003, the government converted its Ministry of Information into **Dubai Media Incorporated** (DMI) to run the nation's television system. DMI is a quasi-government agency but is set up to operate like a private company. Already, $97 billion has gone into construction. More than 1000 television and film companies have taken up residence, availing themselves of both the sunshine and the government's tax-free incentives.

DMI, with audience goals far beyond the emirate's borders, operates four television channels. These include an Arab-language general entertainment channel, which became the second-most-watched pan-Arabian satellite station, second only to the older, Saudi-owned, London-based MBC. The Dubai Sports Channel, the only 24-hour Arab sports channel, has exclusive rights to the World Cup of horse racing. Arab soccer also is exclusive. An English-language service carries mostly movies and imported programs. In addition, a local channel aims at audiences within the United Arab Emirates, of which Dubai is part.

In the culturally and religiously fractured Arab region, Dubai TV and its competitors are on a tightrope in choosing content. Hussein Ali Lootah, chief executive, sees Dubai TV's greatest achievement in introducing Gulf-oriented programming that does not alienated Arabs on the Mediterranean. Creativity is within the bounds of local sensitivities, he says. For news, Dubai TV avoids the hard-hitting journalism of Al Jazeera by taking a deliberately friendly, informal approach. On magazine and talk shows there is more analysis, less polemics.

On the English-language One TV, programs and movies are chosen because they are "relevant and sensitive to our culture," says manager Naila Al-awadhi. Shows are subtitled and promoted in Arabic.

Dubai TV claims a 50 percent market penetration, which means a reach of 100 million Arabs across the region. Dubai's pre-2004 predecessor earned less than $4 million, but 2006 grosses were $40 million. DMI claims that English-language One TV can reach 70 million Arab households.

LEARNING CHECK

- How is the emirate of Dubai seeking to become a global entertainment industry player?
- What obstacles does the Dubai enterprise face?

Media and Terrorism

STUDY PREVIEW Mass media are a new battleground in civilization's great struggles. Saudi Arabians have tackled terrorism with pan-Arab television drama. But old-style media may have maxed out their effectiveness. In Iraq, despite the high production quality and big spending, American messages have failed to offset insurgents' YouTube-style video calls for violent resistance.

Saudi Anti-Terrorism

Until November 2003, some members of the royal family that controls Saudi Arabia were channelling their oil wealth into al-Qaeda terrorism and to militant Islam imams who believed that their holy book, the Quran, justified terrorism. Then came a 2003 terrorist bombing in Saudi Arabia itself. Eighteen people, all Arabs, were killed. It was a pivotal moment. Soon after came a wave of miniseries and dramas, some produced in Saudi Arabia, challenging the notion that Islam somehow justifies terrorism. These programs play on Arab channels throughout the Middle East. Some, like *The Beautiful Virgins*, lead the ratings with an anti-terrorism theme woven into a trans-Arab storyline with characters of Egyptian, Jordanian, Lebanese, Moroccan, Palestinian, and Syrian descent.

The Beautiful Virgins, written by a former al-Qaeda member, is narrated by a Syrian girl who was burned in the 2003 attack. Amid all kinds of problems, including marital infidelity, drug addiction, and wife beating, the core issue of the program is the loving side versus the dark side of Islam as told through the conflict within a young Saudi man torn between militant and moderate readings of the Quran. Which way does he go to find the virgins who the Quran, at least metaphorically, says await good Islamic men in paradise?

Militant imams deride *The Beautiful Virgins* as sacrilege, which points out that Islamic Arabs are hardly of one mind. The show was panned on militant websites. Station executives have received death threats. Even so, the show has led viewership not only in Saudi Arabia but also in other Islamic countries. At the Saudi-owned Middle East Broadcasting Corporation, based in Dubai, production manager Abe al Masry has described *The Beautiful Virgins* as an integral part of the new Arab battle against terrorism.

It wasn't always so. The producer of a 2001 show, *The Road to Kabul*, which portrayed the Afghan Taliban negatively, caved to death threats after eight instalments. But that was before the 2003 attack in Saudi Arabia. Today, *The Rocky Road's* storyline hints at hypocrisy and Afghan corruption. Another show, *What Will Be, Will Be*, portrays conservative village sheiks as bumbling bumpkins, not unlike the sheriff in *The Dukes of Hazzard*, albeit with political edginess.

LEARNING CHECK

- Why has anti-terrorism become fashionable in Saudi Arabian media?

Media as Terrorism Tool

Radicals have adapted low-cost digital media to their needs. During the American presence in Iraq, insurgents have learned to plan multi-camera, high-resolution video shots of large-scale attacks on U.S. forces. The videos are quickly edited into hyped narratives and spliced with stock clips of snipers felling American soldiers, and play against a background of religious music or martial chants. The videos are meant to inspire triumphal passions. The videos sell in Baghdad markets as fundraisers for the cause. More potently, they make the video cell phone rounds incredibly quickly. Within minutes after an attack, video is in virtually unlimited circulation on handheld devices.

The adroit use of technology—all it takes is a laptop—figures into internecine tensions. A ghoulish sectarian video of a Sunni militiaman sawing off the head of a Shiite prisoner with a 12-centimetre knife stirred Sunni emotion. The Shiites, of course, have no monopoly on these new tools of the information and propaganda war. When secretly shot video of the hanging of Iraqi leader Saddam Hussein leaked to the internet, incensed Shiites rioted in the Anbar province of Iraq.

New media can give underdogs an identity against forces that are superior by traditional measures. In Fallujah, Iraq, an insurgent stronghold northwest of Baghdad, the United States created a multimillion-dollar campaign with traditional public relations and propaganda tools to win over the people. The other side, however, carried the day. The people renamed a major thoroughfare the Street of the Martyr Saddam Hussein.

LEARNING CHECK

- How have underground forces used inexpensive new media forms to mobilize many Iraqis to their cause?
- How can the United States deal with grassroots media tactics in Iraq that use new digital media?

Battle for Iran

STUDY PREVIEW Geopolitically strategic, Iran has emerged in the crosshairs of the East–West confrontation that has been shaped by global terrorism. In Los Angeles, where many Iranian expatriates live, satellite television stations aim at homeland reforms. The U.S. State Department, meanwhile, has implemented soft diplomacy with its own media messages. In reaction, Iran's government is trying to block transborder communication.

Tehrangeles

Tehrangeles Nickname for Los Angeles as home to more Iranians than any city other than Tehran.

Outside of Iran itself, no city is home to more Iranians than Los Angeles. The nickname **Tehrangeles**, however, didn't catch on much until Zia Atabay realized that he could lease time on an orbiting satellite to send television programs from Los Angeles to anybody with a dish receiver in Iran. Atabay's goal was to encourage political reform and democracy in an Islamic society that's divided between old ways and new. In 2000, the National Iranian TeleVision (NITV) network was born, in Los Angeles.

Atabay poured $6 million into NITV, hoping it would become financially self-sustaining through advertising. It didn't. In 2006, the operation went dark. By then, however, 20 other satellite stations, funded by Iranians living in the United States, were beaming signals to Iran. Although most are talk shows, the programming at surviving Tehrangeles operations is all over the map. Think Iranian MTV. Or Iranian ESPN.

How effective has Tehrangeles television been as an alternative to state-controlled television and radio in Iran, all of which are heavily censored? Measures are hard to come by. There's no doubt, though, that the Los Angeles stations have audiences overseas, judging by talk show call-ins from Iran. Although satellite television is illegal in Iran, about half of the population, roughly 20 million people, has dishes. But is it effective? The 2005 election of conservative Islamic Mahmoud Ahmadinejad as president has been called a backlash against the often-virulent anti-regime polemics from Los Angeles. Some observers say, however, that the music clips and sports on other satellite stations may be doing more to encourage social and other fundamental reforms by broadening the cultural exposure of Iranian young people.

LEARNING CHECK

- Is it wrong for Iranian expatriates to try to influence public policy in Iran with appeals made directly to the Iranian people?
- Can such projects succeed?

U.S.-Sponsored Media

Radio Farda U.S. government-funded Farsi-language service aimed at Iran.

Voice of America U.S. government-funded broadcast service sent into nations with state-controlled media to articulate American policies directly to the people.

For years, the U.S. government has funded **Radio Farda**, a 24-hour service in the Farsi language. Farda transmits from facilities in the Czech Republic. There also is a **Voice of America** satellite television service that the U.S. State Department beams into Iran. Unlike the fiery commercial stations broadcast from Los Angeles, the State Department hopes to sway Iranians with "soft diplomacy." This includes news programs that, although from an American perspective, are not propagandistic.

Web Censorship China and Iran are the most aggressive nations in blocking political content from other countries, but they are not alone. The Open Net Initiative—a consortium of Harvard, Cambridge, Oxford, and Toronto universities—says that at least 25 nations restrict citizen access to certain websites, some for political reasons, some for cultural reasons, and some for both.

The U.S. State Department has decades-long experience in broadcasting directly to people in repressed areas. Radio Free Europe and Voice of America were created after World War II, initially under the guise of being citizen-generated projects. The goal ostensibly was to present information on American positions on issues that were being distorted or unreported in Eastern Europe and the Soviet Union. It was soft-sell propaganda but it also exposed people behind the so-called Iron Curtain to Western pop culture and music and dangled lures of advanced Western countries before repressed and impoverished people.

Old-style Voice of America and similar American projects, including Radio Martí and television aimed at Cuba, also carried an antagonistic message to regimes in target countries. The projects have since added digital components. Attempts by the government to connect directly with Iranians, for example, include a Farda website. The main Iranian target is young adults, who tend to be well educated and technically savvy and more inclined as a group to political reform.

LEARNING CHECK

- What do you know about the role of Voice of America in facilitating the collapse of the Soviet Union and ending the Cold War?
- What are the prospects for the U.S. State Department's Radio Farda?

Iran Blockages

Typical of authoritarian regimes, the Iranian government tries to block signals from sources it considers to be unfavourable. The militia-like Revolutionary Guard jams signals. The BBC's Farsi service is a frequent target. The state's Administration for Culture and Islamic Guidance assumed control of blogs in 2006, with robot and human censors and blocking. In addition, the agency hired hundreds of agents to create blogs carrying the government's message.

Blogging has worked against the government in specific cases. In 2006, word came from a prison that dissident journalist Akbar Ganji, who had been locked up five years earlier, was engaging in a hunger strike and could die. After bloggers spread the word about Ganji's prison treatment, reigniting public interest in his case, the government freed him.

LEARNING CHECK

- Eastern European regimes jammed Voice of America and similar programs during the Cold War, but with limited success. Voice of America changed frequencies often. Would you expect Iran to be more successful in its blocking attempts?

China Media

STUDY PREVIEW The struggle between freedom and tyranny plays and replays itself out, with the mass media offering case studies on broader issues. Among major nations, China has suppressed challenges to government authority with the most labour-intensive censorship initiative in history.

Chinese Policy

Chinese authorities were less than amused at the freewheeling satire of someone on the internet going by the name Stainless Steel Mouse. The Mouse was tapping out stinging quips about ideological hypocrisy among the country's communist leaders. When government agents tracked the commentaries to **Liu Di**, a psychology major at a Beijing university, they jailed her for a year without charges. Finally, figuring that the publicity about the arrest would be enough to chill other freethinkers into silence, the authorities let Liu Di go—on the condition that she not return to her old ways.

Liu Di Under the pseudonym Stainless Steel Mouse, she satirized the Chinese government until arrested and silenced.

The government's rationale has been articulated at the highest levels. In a speech, President Jiang Zemin put the necessity of absolute government control this way: "We must be vigilant against infiltration, subversive activities, and separatist activities of international and domestic hostile forces. Only by sticking to and perfecting China's socialist political system can we achieve the country's unification, national unity, social stability, and economic development. The Western mode of political systems must never be copied."

LEARNING CHECK

- How does China justify its tight controls on media content?

Chinese News Control

The rise of a market economy in China has loosened the financial dependence of newspapers on the ruling Communist Party. Competing for readers in this emerging marketplace, the predictable and dull propagandist thrust of many newspapers has begun to dim. More reporting is appearing, for example, on disasters and other previously off-limits spot news.

In 2005, after 121 Guangdong miners died in a mine flood, *China Business Times* launched a journalistic examination that concluded that mine authorities had known of safety violations and had taken bribes to look the other way. After this revelation, the government had no choice but to prosecute. Eighteen men, including a high-ranking government official, were hauled into court. In the past, misdeeds within the power structure had been ignored or dealt with quietly. That is no longer so easily done, now that a journalistic dragon is stirring.

Most accidents, even disasters, still go unreported. Of the 3300 mine accidents in China in 2005, few garnered much coverage. But some newspapers have started to pursue these kinds of stories. When a Jilin factory explosion dumped 100 tonnes of toxic chemicals into the Songhua River, the government naively assumed that it could keep a lid on the situation. Wrong. Chinese newspapers told the story, albeit in bits and pieces. The government was embarrassed when Russians living downstream learned that the river was dangerous. It was an international incident that the government blamed on the newspapers.

The extent to which the Chinese go to keep negative information out of circulation was demonstrated in 2007 when a contaminated ingredient imported from China began killing pets in North America. When international inspectors arrived at the facilities of origin, the equipment was nowhere to be found. It was as if the place had never existed. The Chinese explained that they had completed their own inspection and corrected any problems. No plant, no story.

Emergency Response Law Chinese limits on news reporting of disasters, ostensibly to ensure social stability.

To rein in journalism, the influential State Council has proposed an **Emergency Response Law** to "manage news" about emergencies. Is this censorship? The proposal's language is iffy. Permission would be required for reporting that "causes serious consequences," but what does that mean? The State Council says that "normal" reporting, whatever that means, would be okay under its law.

The government's justification for the restrictions on coverage is to encourage stability. News about government corruption, as in the Guangdong mine flood, or about government incompetence, as in disaster relief, does not inspire public confidence in the government. The nation's leadership is aware of an estimated 87 000 demonstrations in 2005 alone, many directed against public policies and government action and inaction.

The Emergency Response Law would apply to 812 500 news outlets. Some newspapers, feeling a new sense of journalistic self-empowerment, have taken strident positions against the proposed law. Editors have scoffed in print at the law's provision for local governments to be the sole source of disaster and accident information and to report such information in "a timely manner." The problem, the editors argue, is government cover-ups. Besides, who defines what is "timely"? Who decides how much information is released?

LEARNING CHECK

- How would China's proposed Emergency Response Law affect reporting about disasters?
- Do you accept the Chinese government's argument that restrictions on journalists are needed to prevent inaccuracies in reporting that could work against social and political stability?

Chinese Firewall

The Chinese government has expended major resources to limit internet communication, particularly from abroad. To exclude unwanted messages, the Chinese government has undertaken numerous initiatives. One of them has been likened to a 21st-century version of the Great Wall of China, a 2400-kilometre fortress barrier built in ancient times along the Mongolian frontier to keep out invaders.

The Chinese didn't invent their **firewall.** It came from the network design company Cisco, which devised filters in the early 1990s that corporate clients could use to filter employee access to the internet. The goal of these firewalls was productivity, to keep employees who are equipped with desktop computers from whiling away company minutes, hours even, on sites featuring entertainment and diversions. When Cisco courted the

firewall A block on unauthorized access to a computer system while permitting outward communication.

MEDIA PEOPLE Bill Xia

Chinese web surfers who crave uncensored news have friends at a handful of American companies that penetrate the Chinese government's firewall that's designed to block outside information. Bill Xia, a Chinese expatriate in the United States, operates one such company, Dynamic Internet Technology (DIT). Xia sets up websites with pass-through links to Voice of America and other outside sites that the Chinese government bans.

It works this way:

- The sponsor of a censored site, such as Voice of America, Human Rights in China, or Radio Free Asia, hires DIT to create a proxy site at a new internet address.
- DIT sends mass emails to Chinese web surfers with the address of the new site.
- Chinese web users can then download software that hides their visits to the DIT site.
- When Chinese web police identify the proxy sites and shut them down, often within 24 hours and never more than 72, DIT creates a new proxy site at a new address. And the process begins again.

It's a cat-and-mouse game and also a hassle, but DIT, always one step ahead of the censors, claims as many as 160 000 users. A few other companies, including UltraReach, provide similar proxy services.

Xia sees traffic spikes after the occurrence of major events on which the Chinese government has placed a lid. This happened when authorities tried to conceal news of an epidemic of the infectious SARS virus in 2003. It happened again in 2005 when police shot protesters in a village in southern China.

Traffic also increased in 2006 when Google yielded to Chinese pressure to co-operate with the government's censorship in order to be allowed to build its business in China. Microsoft and Yahoo! had previously made the same business decision.

DIT and other proxy companies reflect a zealous aversion to censorship. In some cases, they reflect insurgent politics. DIT's Bill Xia, for example, is a member of the revolutionary Falun Gong movement, which Chinese leaders particularly fear. Concerned that his family in China might be persecuted, Xia declines to be photographed or even to identify his home region or divulge his birthday. He won't even talk about DIT's location except to say that it's somewhere in North Carolina.

WHAT DO YOU THINK?

1. Who will win the cat-and-mouse game between Chinese web censorship and companies like DIT? Could it go on forever?

Chinese as customers, the filters seemed like a perfect method for China to block unwanted material from outside the country. Cisco filters soon were installed at the gateways for internet messages into China. Here's how it works: The filters subtly "lose" messages from banned sites abroad. If a Chinese user seeks access to a forbidden foreign site, an error message or a message saying "site not found" appears on the screen. Whether it's censorship or a technical glitch, the user never knows.

There is dark humour among critics of the Chinese firewall. Noting the role of Cisco, they say: "The modern Great Wall of China was built with American bricks."

LEARNING CHECK

- How does the Chinese firewall work?

Internal Chinese Controls

Golden Shield Chinese system to control internal internet communication within the country.

Next Carrying Network (CN2) Fast Chinese internet protocols built on new technical standards; incompatible with other protocols.

To control communication within the country, the Chinese Ministry of Public Security bans internet service providers from carrying anything that might jeopardize national security or social stability, or even to spread false news, superstition, or obscenity. As a condition of doing business in China, Yahoo! agreed to these terms in 2002. So have Microsoft and other service providers. The system is called the **Golden Shield**. The shield complements the work of the firewall against unwanted foreign messages by controlling communication inside the country.

Even tighter control is expected through a huge intranet that the Chinese government is building within the country: the **Next Carrying Network (CN2)**. CN2 was designed from scratch, unencumbered by the older technical standards that have been cobbled together for the system that serves the rest of the planet. CN2's technical advantages include exceptional capacity and speed. Also, because CN2 uses its own technical standards that are not easily compatible with the global internet, the system fits neatly with the government's policy to limit contact with the outside. Communication from abroad can be received on CN2 only after code translations stall delivery and, importantly, make them subject to more scrutiny.

LEARNING CHECK

- How will China's CN2 strengthen the Golden Shield?
- How could CN2 work against Chinese integration into the global community? Could this work against China's commercial goals?

Chinese Censorship Apparatus

prior censorship Government review of content before it is disseminated.

Because **prior censorship**, reviewing messages before they reach an audience, is very labour-intensive, seldom in human history has it been practised on a large scale. Past authoritarian regimes have relied almost entirely on post-publication sanctions with severe penalties against wayward printers and broadcasters to keep others in line. The Chinese, however, are engaging in prepublication censorship on an unprecedented scale.

Chinese censorship is partly automated. Internet postings are machine-scanned for words and terms such as *human rights*, *Taiwan independence*, and *Falun Gong* (a forbidden religious movement) and dropped from further routing. The system also catches other terms that signal forbidden subjects, such as *oral sex* and *pornography*.

No one outside the government has numbers on the extent of human involvement in censorship, but there appears to be significant human monitoring at work. Western organizations, including Reporters Without Borders, occasionally test the Chinese system by posting controversial messages, some with terms that machines can spot easily but others with trickier language. Postings with easy-to-catch terms such as *Falun Gong* never make it. Postings with harder-to-spot language but nonetheless objectionable content last a bit longer, although seldom more than an hour, which suggests an additional review by human eyes.

Who are these censors and how many are there? The consensus among experts outside the country is that China, whose internet users exceed 100 million, must be a massive censorship bureaucracy. A rare peek inside the system appeared in a 2005 interview in

Nanfang Weekend with a censor in Siquan, Ma Zhichun, whose background is in journalism. Ma discusses his job as an "*internet* coordinator" in the municipal External Propaganda Office, where, without identifying himself online as a government agent, he guides discussions in the government's favour. Ma is part of elaborate mechanisms to keep online dialogue on the right track, particularly in chat rooms, but like thousands of other propaganda officers throughout the country, he is in a position to spot banned postings and report them.

LEARNING CHECK

- If you were a Chinese censor, what terms would you use to intercept internet content that should be checked?

Overt Chinese Controls

Although much Chinese government control of internet postings is invisible, some is overt. Because users are required to use a government-issued personal identification number to log on, citizens know that they're subject to being monitored. Operators of blog sites, which number 4 million, need to register with the government. Cybercafes, which have been woven into the lifestyles of many Chinese, must be licensed. At cybercafes, cameras look over users' shoulders to see what's onscreen. Police also spend a lot of time in cafes looking over shoulders.

The government's seriousness about regulating the internet was unmistakable when thousands of illegal cafes were shut down in a series of sweeps in the early 2000s.

Arrests are publicized, which has a chilling effect. One especially notable case involved Wang Youcai, who, during President Bill Clinton's historic 1998 visit to China, proposed an opposition political party in the American tradition. Wang filed papers to register the China Democratic Party. Within a day, government officials knocked on his door, interrogated him for three hours, and hauled him away. He was sent to prison for 11 years and ordered into political abstinence for an additional 3 years for "fomenting opposition against the government."

The subsequent case of the imprisonment of Liu Di, a.k.a. Stainless Steel Mouse, for satirizing the government was a similarly chilling warning to those who want to engage in full and open dialogue.

LEARNING CHECK

- Chinese punishments for bloggers who engage in frowned-upon content have a chilling effect. What is that chilling effect?
- As a traveller in China, would you be comfortable in a cybercafe engaging in the kinds of everyday internet communication that you do at home?

Chinese Broadcasting

Although political issues are the major focus of Chinese censorship, the government discourages what it sees as a creeping intrusion of Western values and sexuality. In a clampdown on racy radio talk and, lo and behold, orange-tinted hair on television, the State Administration for Radio, Film and Television issued an edict: Enough. To television hosts, the order was no vulgarity, which included "overall appearance." Specifically forbidden were "multicolor dyed hair" and "overly revealing clothing." There also are new bans on sexual content. Violence, murder, and horrors are out until 11 P.M. So, too, are "fights, spitting, littering and base language."

The restrictions, which are periodically issued as the media stray, are consistent with the communist notion that government and media are inseparably linked in moving the society and culture to a better future. As the Chinese put it, the media are the *houshe*, the throat and tongue, of the ruling Communist Party.

Chinese nationalism takes unexpected turns. Broadcasters, for example, periodically are instructed to use only Mandarin. Foreign words, including Westernisms such as *okay* and *yadda-yadda*, are not allowed. Not allowed either are dialects from separatist Taiwan. Also, a strict cap was put on imported soap operas and martial arts programs for television. Imports cannot constitute more than 25 percent of the total of such programs.

Even in Hong Kong, the British colony that was returned to China in 1997 and which was to be governed by different rules that honoured its tradition of free expression, Beijing-approved governors were appointed to comport with official policies. Political cartoonists also have been reined in.

Is government pressure effective? In Fujian Province, the hosts of the program *Entertainment Overturning the Skies* gave up their blond dye jobs after one crackdown. Some television programs imported from Taiwan, the United States, and elsewhere have suddenly and quietly disappeared. Hong Kong radio is tamer. However, clampdowns come and go. Kenny Bloom of the Beijing-based AsiaVision production house told a *Wall Street Journal* interviewer: "Commentators will follow the rules for a couple months, and then their clothes will get tighter and their hair will get wilder."

Even so, legal scholars Jack Goldsmith of Harvard and Tim Wu of Columbia, who have studied government controls on media content globally, say that controls do not have to be absolute to be effective. Goldsmith and Wu offer copyright law as an example. Infringements of copyright in, say, illegal music downloads are inevitable, but the threat of civil or criminal sanctions keeps violations at a rate that copyright owners are willing to live with. Such, they note, is the situation with the censorious Chinese government. Nobody is so unrealistic to claim that all dissidence can be suppressed. The goal, rather, is to keep dissidence from breaking beyond an easily manageable level.

LEARNING CHECK

- Why are Chinese media discouraged from using Westernisms, such as *yadda-yadda* and *okay*, in scripts?

Effectiveness of Chinese Controls

An *Idol*-like mania swept China when an upstart television station in remote Hunan Province put its show *Supergirl* on satellite. Despite admonitions against lyrics in English and gyrating hips, contestants pushed the envelope of government acceptability in front of huge audiences. That viewers could vote their preferences by mobile phones raised a spectre of nascent democracy in a country where people can't vote for their leaders. Most analysts, however, have concluded that the phenomenon was an anomaly in the tightly controlled society. Even so, winners, who are called Mongolian Cow Sour Yogurt Supergirls, because of the dairy that sponsored the show, have gone on to singing and modelling careers.

LEARNING CHECK

- Could *Idol*-like television shows that encourage viewers to vote be a precursor to democracy in China?

Yogurt Girl A touch of democracy swept China when people were asked to vote for their favourite talent in an *Idol*-style television show sponsored by the Mongolian Cow Sour Yogurt brand. Authorities didn't much like the idea. Whether societal reforms will be inspired by the show seems dubious, although Mongolian Cow Sour Yogurt Supergirl winners have catapulted their acts into entertainment careers.

Distinctive Media Systems

STUDY PREVIEW Nations organize their media systems differently. Even largely similar systems like those in Britain and Canada have distinctive methods for funding. Some countries like India have unique features. Some countries have unique developmental needs.

Britain

Almost everybody has heard of the BBC, Britain's venerable public-service radio and television system. Parliament created the British Broadcasting Corporation in 1927 as a government-funded entity that, despite government support, would have as much programming autonomy as possible. The idea was to avoid private ownership and to give the enterprise the prestige of being associated with the Crown. The government appoints a 12-member board of governors to run the BBC. Although the government has the authority to remove members of the board, it never has. The BBC has developed largely independently of the politics of the moment, which has given it a credibility and stature that are recognized worldwide.

The Beeb, as the BBC is affectionately known, is financed through an annual licensing fee of about $230 on television receivers.

The BBC is known for its global news coverage. It has 250 full-time correspondents, compared to CNN's 113. The Beeb's reputation for first-rate dramatic and entertainment programs is known among English-speaking people everywhere. The 1960s brought such enduring comedies as David Frost's *That Was the Week That Was* and later *Monty Python's Flying Circus*. Sir Kenneth Clark's *Civilisation* debuted in 1969. Then came dramatic classics like *The Six Wives of Henry VIII*, *War and Peace*, and *I, Claudius*.

Much like the debate over Canada's CBC, the great issue today is whether the BBC should leave the government fold. Advocates of privatization argue that the BBC could exploit its powerful brand name better if it were privatized. The privatization advocates also say that the BBC's government ties keep it from aggressively pursuing partnerships that could make it a global competitor with companies like Time Warner and Rupert Murdoch's News Corporation. Continuing to do business as always, they say, will leave the Beeb in everybody else's dust.

LEARNING CHECK

- What sets the BBC apart from other international broadcast organizations?
- Is the BBC a government mouthpiece? Explain.

India

The world's largest democracy, India, has a highly developed movie industry that took root by providing affordable entertainment to mass audiences when the country was largely impoverished. The industry, called **Bollywood**, a contrivance of its historic roots in Bombay and the American movie capital Hollywood, is adapting as India moves rapidly out of its Third World past. Today India is becoming a model for new media applications, such as Wi-Fi, as the country brings itself into modern times.

Bollywood Nickname for India's movie industry.

Bollywood At 85 cents a seat, people jam Indian movie houses in such numbers that some exhibitors schedule five showings a day starting at 9 a.m. Better seats sell out days in advance in some cities. There is no question that movies are the country's strongest mass medium. Even though per capita income is only $1360 a year, Indians find enough rupees to support an industry that cranks out as many as 1200 movies each year, twice as many as American moviemakers produce. Most are B-grade formula melodramas and action stories. Screen credits often include a Director of Fights. Despite their flaws, Indian movies are so popular that it is not unusual for a movie house in a Hindi-speaking area to be packed for a film in another Indian language that nobody in the audience understands. Movies are produced in 16 Indian languages.

Watch
Bollywood

Bollywood The Indian movie industry, centred in Bombay and sometimes called Bollywood, pumps out an incredible 1200 movies a year. Although India has some internationally recognized moviemakers, most Bollywood productions are formulaic action movies that critics derisively label "curry westerns."

The movie mania centres on stars. Incredible as it may seem, M.G. Ramachandran, who played folk warriors, and M.R. Radha, who played villains, got into a real-life gun duel one day. Both survived their wounds, but Ramachandran exploited the incident in a bid for public office. He campaigned with posters that showed him bound in head bandages and was elected chief minister of his state. While in office, Ramachandran continued to make B-grade movies, always starring as the hero.

Billboards, fan clubs, and scurrilous magazines fuel the obsession with stars. Scholars Erik Barnouw and Subrahmanyam Krishna, in their book *Indian Film*, characterize the portrayals of stars as "mythological demigods who live on a highly physical and erotic plane, indulging in amours." In some magazines, compromising photos are a specialty.

Wi-Fi India has taken a lead in linking remote villages with the rest of the world through wireless technology. Villagers and farmers who once had to walk several kilometres to pay their power bills now go to a "knowledge centre"—several rooms equipped with desktop computers, connected by **Wi-Fi** to the internet—and pay online. Such "knowledge centres" are being installed in 600 000 villages in a government-entrepreneurial program launched in 2005. Eventually, all 237 000 villages in India large enough to have a governing unit will be equipped.

Wi-Fi Wireless fidelity technology, which offers limited-range downloading.

The Indian experience serves as a model for extending mass media links into isolated, poverty-ridden areas in Africa and Eastern Europe. Farmers can learn market corn prices to decide when it's best to sell. Faraway doctors can diagnose illnesses through digital electrocardiography. In India, a company named n-Logue has designed Wi-Fi kiosks for rural villages at $1200 a unit, complete with a computer, software, a digital camera, paper, and a backup power supply. Kiosks can have ATM banking too.

A remaining obstacle is the diversity of languages in many underdeveloped parts of the world. Google doesn't translate universally.

LEARNING CHECK

- How do you explain the powerful influence of the Indian movie industry?
- Is Wi-Fi the way to bring remote parts of India into the country's mainstream economic expansion? How so?

Colombia

High drama is popular on Colombian radio stations, but it is hardly theatrical. In Colombia, thousands of people, both wealthy and ordinary, are kidnapped captives. Families go on the air to express their love and support in the hope that their kidnapped kin are listening. It makes for powerful radio. Tragically, it's real.

Drug lords and petty criminals alike have found kidnapping to be lucrative in a country where anarchy is practically an everyday reality. The mass media are hardly immune. In the 1990s, according to the U.S.-based Committee to Protect Journalists, 31 journalists were killed because of their work in Columbia. Sixteen others have died in incidents that may or may not have been related to their work. In a typical year, 6 to 10 journalists are kidnapped.

A political satirist, Jamie Garzón, was shot to death in 1999 after a television show. *El Espectador*, a leading newspaper, has armed guards at every entrance and around its perimeter, as do most media operations. Many reporters are assigned bodyguards, usually two, both armed. Two *El Espectador* reporters have fled the country under threat. The editor of another daily, *El Tiempo*, fled in 2000 after supporting a peace movement.

Beset with corruption fuelled by the powerful cocaine industry, the government has no handle on assaults against the media. Although hypersensitive to negative coverage, the drug industry is not the only threat to the Colombian media. The Committee to Protect Journalists, Human Rights Watch, Amnesty International, and other watchdogs blame renegade paramilitary units and guerrillas, some of whom are ideologically inspired. Also, the Colombian military itself and some government agencies have been implicated.

LEARNING CHECK

- What steps can be taken in a country like Colombia to create an environment in which news people can perform their highest service?

MEDIA PEOPLE Jineth Bedoya Lima

After Jineth Bedoya Lima wrote about executions during a Bogotá prison riot, she got word that a paramilitary leader inside the prison wanted to give her his side. "Come alone," she was told. Like all Colombian journalists, Bedoya, age 25 at the time, was aware of the dangers of reporting news, especially on subjects sensitive to warring factions. Her editor and a photographer went with her.

As they waited outside the prison, the photographer left to buy sodas and then the editor followed him. When they came back, Bedoya was gone. Guards at the prison gate said they had seen nothing.

Many hours later, a taxi driver found Bedoya at a roadside garbage dump. She said that two men had grabbed her and forced a drugged cloth over her face. She regained consciousness in a nearby house, where her captors taped her mouth, blindfolded her, and bound her hands and feet. They then drove her three hours to another city. They said they were going to kill her, as well as several other journalists they named. Then they beat and raped her and threw her out at the dump.

Her story, typical of violence against media people in Colombia, was disseminated widely by the Committee to Protect Journalists. It's a cautionary tale. Bedoya, who believed that she was still being trailed months later, was assigned two government bodyguards. Even so, she feels at risk. Why does she continue to be a journalist? Frank Smyth of the Committee to Protect Journalists, writing in *Quill* magazine, quoted her: "I love my work, and I want to keep doing it. The worst thing that could happen has already happened."

In Pursuit of a Story Jineth Bedoya Lima was kidnapped and raped while pursuing a story.

WHAT DO YOU THINK?

1. Consider a world where journalists refuse to take risks. How would society be different?

Chapter 16 Wrap-Up

The world's nations and media systems can be measured on a scale of media freedom. At one extreme are nations in a libertarian tradition, which accords high levels of autonomy and independence to the mass media. Libertarianism emphasizes the ability of human beings to reason their own way to correct conclusions and therefore believes that humans are capable of their own governance. Democracy and a free mass media are in the libertarian tradition. At the other extreme are authoritarian nations with top-down leadership in control, sometimes overtly and onerously, sometimes less so. Libertarianism and authoritarianism are philosophically irreconcilable systems, a fact that explains many divisions in the world.

Questions for Critical Thinking

1. List countries that fit the definition of libertarianism. List also those that fit the definition of authoritarianism. Justify your choices.
2. How well have various wartime efforts to accommodate free news reporting worked throughout history?
3. What generalizations can be made about government and media systems in Islam-dominated regions? How do these generalizations miss many realities?
4. What are the echoes of the Cold War in the battle over information and ideas in Iran? What are the differences?
5. How effective have China's efforts at controlling mass media been? What do you see as the future of these efforts?

Keeping Up to Date

Index on Censorship is published in London and provides monthly country-by-country status reports.

Professional journals that carry articles on foreign media systems and on media responsibility include *Columbia Journalism Review*, *Quill*, and *American Journalism Review*.

Mass Media and Governance

Deep Throat Thirty-plus years after helping in the Watergate scandal revelations published in *The Washington Post*, the retired number-two man at the FBI, Mark Felt, identified himself as the knowledgeable insider source. The revelation renewed the ongoing debate on anonymous sources in the news but also emphasized the symbiotic relationship between the news media and the government.

LEARNING AHEAD

- The news media are a watchdog of government on the people's behalf.
- The mass media are major shapers of the public's agenda of issues.
- Government has many tools for manipulating media coverage.
- Watchdog performance is uneven, with voids in some government coverage.

MEDIA IN THEORY

Does the News Media "Manufacture Consent?"

In their classic work, *Manufacturing Consent: The Political Economy of the Mass Media*, **Noam Chomsky** and **Edward Herman** argue that through gatekeeping, various filters create an environment whereby news is used as propaganda to keep the elite in power. In many ways, it echoes the work of Ben Bagdikian, whose theories on the effects of conglomeration were introduced in Chapter 1. According to Chomsky and Herman, the "propaganda model" limits diversity of opinion and thought in the news media, thereby "**manufacturing consent**" among media consumers by limiting debate on important social and political issues. It does so in the following ways:

Noam Chomsky Believes that the news media is an ideological apparatus for the elite in society.

Edward Herman Co-wrote *Manufacturing Consent* with Noam Chomsky.

manufacturing consent A system limiting debate on political and social issues.

- In these days of conglomeration, the members of the upper class of North America are also the primary owners of the North American mass media. More and more media are owned by fewer and fewer people. As a result, their point of view will be largely conservative. That, in turn, sets up a conservative agenda for news reporting.

- Most experts used by the media tend to be members of the elite themselves. According to Chomsky and Herman, this is because "government and corporate sources also have the great merit of being recognizable and credible by their status and prestige." This limits diversity of voices and opinion in the news media, which is not beneficial in a democracy.

Antonio Gramsci Italian theorist who expanded on Marxism to include ideas, not just economics.

hegemony Coercion through consent.

Another variation of the effects of the news media comes from Italian cultural theory. **Antonio Gramsci** argued that the elite rule through a process called **hegemony**. Gramsci, a Marxist, maintained that class struggle isn't a conflict based only on economics; ideas are also involved. In 1995, Dominic Strinati offered this definition of hegemony: "Dominant groups in society, including fundamentally but not exclusively the ruling class, maintain their dominance by securing the 'spontaneous consent' of subordinate groups, including the working class, through the negotiated construction of a political and ideological consensus which incorporates both dominant and dominated groups." In other words, it isn't just that the ruling class dominates the lower classes, but that the ruling class gets the lower classes to consent to be dominated. One of the ways that the elite influence the lower classes is through manipulation of the *ideas* communicated by the news media.

Jürgen Habermas German sociologist who believed that political ideas need to be debated.

public sphere Where political ideas need to be debated.

Another critique of the government's control of the news media comes from German sociologist **Jürgen Habermas**, who felt that true knowledge can be acquired only through the exchange of ideas. He argued that in the early days of mass media (the 1800s) people used to gather to read newspapers in coffee houses and discuss important political and social issues. He called this the **public sphere**. Only when issues are debated in public can anyone become truly informed. That doesn't happen anymore with the rise of mass media conglomerates. Media has now become a commodity—something to be bought and sold, rather than a tool for political information and debate. There is no more public sphere for real discourse.

There is a symbiotic relationship between the media and the government. It is through the news media that we learn about issues that face Canada and the world. The media are key in helping people sort through issues as part of the political process. Some argue that the media act as a watchdog on behalf of informed citizens in a democracy and help to set the agenda for political debate. Others, like Chomsky, Gramsci, and Habermas, see it as a tool for the ruling class to stay in power by controlling the messages about political matters.

Media Role in Governance

Media People: Donna Brazile

STUDY PREVIEW The news media are sometimes called the fourth estate or the fourth branch of government. These terms identify the independent role of the media in reporting on the government. The media act as a kind of watchdog on behalf of the citizens.

Fourth Estate

fourth estate The press as a player in medieval power structures, in addition to the clerical, noble, and common estates.

Edmund Burke British member of Parliament who is sometimes credited with coining the term *fourth estate*.

Medieval English and French societies were highly structured into classes of people called *estates*. The first estate was the clergy. The second estate was the nobility. The third estate was the common people. After Gutenberg, the mass-produced written word began to emerge as a player in the power structure, but it couldn't be pigeonholed as part of one or another of the three estates. In time, the press came to be called the **fourth estate**. Where the term came from isn't clear, but **Edmund Burke**, a British member of Parliament, used it in the mid-1700s. Pointing to the reporters' gallery, Burke said, "There sat a Fourth Estate more important by far than them all." The term remains to refer to all journalistic activity today. The news media report on the other estates, ideally with roots in none and a commitment only to truth.

The media haven't always had the role of the "fourth estate." In the days after Confederation, newspapers in Canada were largely gazettes of business and government information. Some papers took political sides on issues, but they tended not to be too critical of the government of the day because of the consequences. Canadian media historian Wilfred Kesterton writes that "editors who refused to toe the official line risked prosecution, heavy fines, imprisonment, or worse—pro government thugs sometimes ransacked print shops and assaulted editors as authorities turned a blind eye."

That changed on January 1, 1835, when **Joseph Howe** published "the letter" signed by "the people" in the *Novascotian*. In the letter, he accused the local police and the lieutenant-governor of corruption: "It is known that from the pockets of the poor and distressed, at least 1000 pounds are drawn yearly and pocketed by men whose services the country might very well spare." Howe was charged with seditious libel under the criminal code of the day for "wickedly, maliciously and seditiously desiring and intending to stir up and excite discontent among His Majesty's Subjects." During his six-hour defence, Howe invited the jurors to "leave an **unshackled press** as a legacy to your children." A jury acquitted him in only 10 minutes. The message to Canadian journalists was clear: Freedom of the press and intellectual freedom were important values in journalism. Canada's Fourth Estate was now an unshackled fourth estate that could not be controlled.

Joseph Howe Advocate of an "unshackled press."

unshackled press The idea that the press should be able to print the truth.

How good a job is our news media doing as a watchdog or "fourth estate" that keeps tabs on our politicians? News coverage of politics has been the subject of disappointment among many, even among media people. Canadian Anne McGrath claims that "the public sees media portrayals of government on television that reinforce the impression that politicians are negative, self-interested and arrogant." Her colleague at the University of Calgary, David Taras, writes that the news is "dominated by blood and gore crime stories, celebrity news, sports hype and the latest tidbits from the world of entertainment, while reports about political and social policies rarely grab the spotlight unless they feature high-octane confrontation or pathetic victims."

LEARNING CHECK

- What is meant when the news media are called watchdogs?
- What did Edmund Burke mean by his term *fourth estate*?

Media Effects on Governance

STUDY PREVIEW Media coverage shapes what we think about as well as how to think about it. This means that the media are a powerful linkage between the government and how people view their government. A negative aspect is the trend of the media to pander to transitory public interest in less substantive subjects, such as scandals, gaffes, and negative events.

Watch

ABC's *Nightline:* "Impact of New Media on Politics"

Agenda Setting

A lot of people think that the news media are powerful, affecting the course of events in godlike ways. It's true that the media are powerful, but scholars, going back to sociologist **Paul Lazarsfeld** in the 1940s and even Robert Park in the 1920s, have concluded that they're not powerful in a direct, tell-the-people-how-to-vote-and-they-will kind of way. Media scholars Maxwell McCombs and Donald Shaw cast media effects succinctly when they said that the media don't tell people *what to think* but rather *what to think about.* This is a profound distinction. In covering a political campaign, explain McCombs and Shaw, the media choose which issues or topics to emphasize, thereby setting the campaign's agenda. "This ability to affect cognitive change among individuals," say McCombs and Shaw, "is one of the most important aspects of the power of mass communication." As discussed in Chapter 15 and 16, this has come to be called **agenda setting.**

Paul Lazarsfeld Sociologist who concluded that media influence on voters generally is indirect.

agenda setting Media tell people what to think about, not what to think.

Watergate Continuing coverage lends importance to an issue. A single story on a bribed senator might soon be forgotten, but day-after-day follow-ups can fuel ethics reforms. Conversely, if gatekeepers are diverted to other stories, a hot issue can cool overnight; out of sight, out of mind. Luckily, this did not happen in 1973. Had *The Washington Post* not doggedly followed up on a break-in at the Democratic Party's national headquarters in 1972, the public would never have learned that people around the Republican president, Richard Nixon, were behind it. *The Post* set the national agenda.

Sex Scandals People trust the news media to sort through the events of the day and make order of them. Lead stories on a newscast or articles on Page 1 are expected to be the most significant. Not only does how a story is played affect people's agendas, but so do the time and space afforded it. For example, nobody would have spent much time pondering whether U.S. President Bill Clinton engaged in sexual indiscretions if David Brock, writing in *The American Spectator* in 1993, had not reported allegations by Paula Jones. Nor would the issue have reached a feverish level of public attention without Matt Drudge's 1997 report in his online *Drudge Report* about Monica Lewinsky. Lavish graphics can propel an item even higher.

Child Pornography Only if individuals are aware of an issue can they be concerned about it. Concern about the effects of child pornography became a major issue with media coverage of the Holly Jones case in Toronto. In 2004, Michael Brière pleaded guilty to the abduction, rape, and murder of 10-year-old Holly Jones. He blamed his addiction to child pornography as the reason he abducted and raped Jones. As a result, child pornography became a federal election issue. Shortly after Brière's conviction, police began to crack down on child pornography.

LEARNING CHECK

- How is news coverage catalytic in public decision making?
- What is media agenda-setting?

CNN Effect

Television is especially potent as an agenda setter. For years, nobody outside Ethiopia cared much about a devastating famine there. Not even after four articles in *The New York Times* was there much response. *The Washington Post* ran three articles and the Associated Press distributed 228 stories, but there was still hardly any response. The next year, however, disturbing videos aired by the CBC's Brian Stewart captured public attention and triggered a massive relief effort. In recent years, many scholars who study the agenda-setting effect of television have focused on CNN and its extensive coverage. As a result, the power of television to put faraway issues in the minds of domestic audiences has been labelled the **CNN effect**.

CNN effect The ability of television, through emotion-raising video, to elevate faraway issues on the domestic public agenda.

LEARNING CHECK

- What examples of the CNN effect have you seen in your campus news media and in other local news media?

A Failure of Government
CNN deployed hundreds of staff to the Gulf Coast when Hurricane Katrina struck, documenting not only the disaster but also the failure of the U.S. government to respond adequately. Similar coverage and criticism occurred after the BP oil spill in the Gulf in 2010.

Framing

Related to agenda setting and the CNN effect is a process called **framing**, in which media coverage shapes how people see issues. Because the Pentagon allowed news reporters to accompany combat units during the 2003 Iraq War, there was concern that the war coverage might be decontextualized (see also Chapter 10, section titled War Zones: Combat Reporting). Critics anticipated coverage that focused on tactical encounters of the combat units and missed the larger strategic stories. In other words, highly dramatic and photogenic stories from combat units might frame the telling of the war story in terms of the minutiae of the conflict. As well, Pentagon war planners were aware that reporters living with combat units would, not unnaturally, see the story from the soldiers' perspective. The Pentagon, in fact, had carefully studied the 1982 war between Britain and Argentina, in which embedded British journalists were entirely reliant on the military not only for access to the battle zone but also for such basics as food. The resulting camaraderie gave an understandable favourable twist to coverage. As it turned out, scholars who analyzed the coverage of the Iraq War concluded that the framing from combat zones was largely, though not wholly, as the Pentagon had intended. The tone was favourable to

framing Selecting aspects of a perceived reality for emphasis in a mass media message, thereby shaping how the audience sees the reality.

MEDIA PEOPLE Donna Brazile

A political activist at age 9, Donna Brazile went on to become the first African-American woman to lead a major presidential campaign. The talented field operative and grassroots organizer grew up in poverty in a small town near New Orleans and began her political activism by campaigning for a city council candidate who promised a playground in her neighbourhood. The third of nine children, she was encouraged by her grandmother to follow her dreams.

On the road to being named Al Gore's campaign manager, Brazile worked on campaigns for Democratic candidates Jimmy Carter and Walter Mondale in 1976 and 1980, the Reverend Jesse Jackson's historic bid for the presidency in 1984, Walter Mondale and Geraldine Ferraro in 1984, Dick Gephardt in 1988, Michael Dukakis and Lloyd Bentsen in 1988, and Bill Clinton and Al Gore in 1992 and 1996. Gore's 2000 loss to George W. Bush was the most heartbreaking for Brazile. Many political observers praised Brazile for her strategic planning and her effort to get out the vote, which resulted in Gore winning the popular vote even though he lost in the electoral college.

Since the 2000 campaign, Brazile has served as a fellow at Harvard's Institute of Politics, where she has taught students how a multimillion-dollar presidential campaign is structured, managed, and organized. The Gore campaign lost, she says, "because we failed to educate voters, failed to remove structural barriers, failed to have every ballot counted."

In her autobiography, *Cooking with Grease: Stirring the Pots in American Politics*, Brazile named each chapter for a favourite dish to reflect her lifelong habit of stirring the pot for social change. Now she wants to focus on the themes that have resonated through her life: voter participation, voter education, trying to make the system better, and letting people vote without harassment. She is the founder and managing director of Brazile and Associates, a political consulting and grassroots advocacy firm based in Washington, D.C.

Brazile is a contributor and political commentator on CNN's *Inside Politics*, MSNBC's *Hardball*, and Fox's *Hannity and Colmes*. She is chair of the Democratic National Committee's Voting Rights Institute, which was established in 2001 to help protect and promote the rights of all Americans to participate in the political process. She told the *Detroit Free Press:* "I talk to the hip-hop generation 24/7, every day of my life. I want to be part of what they see as their vision of this country."

Political Strategist Although she failed in masterminding Al Gore's presidential campaign in 2000, Donna Brazile has emerged as a respected voice of reason, albeit from a partisan perspective.

WHAT DO YOU THINK?

1. What qualifies Brazile as a frequent talk-show guest on campaign politics?
2. Is Brazile's partisan perspective an asset or a liability when she offers campaign analysis?

the military and to individual combat units. However, the reports from embedded reporters were packaged in larger-perspective accounts that included material from war protesters, mostly in Europe, and the fractured diplomatic front.

In Canada, framing is a common activity in politics. For years, Stephen Harper was framed by his opposition and the media as having a "hidden right-wing agenda." Liberals have also been framed by their political adversaries. Michael Ignatieff has been defined as arrogant, while his predecessor, Stéphane Dion, was often referred to as not being leadership material.

Partisan framing is the easiest to spot. But news, though usually cast in a dispassionate tone, is also subject to framing. Framing cannot be avoided. Not everything about an event or issue can be compacted into a 30-second television item or even into a 3000-word magazine article. Reporters must choose what to include and what to exclude. Whatever a reporter's choices, the result is a framing of how the audience will see the reality.

LEARNING CHECK

- Why is it impossible for the news media to be complete and comprehensive?

Media Obsessions

Although critics argue that the media are politically biased, studies don't support this. Reporters perceive themselves as being middle-of-the-road politically, and by and large they work to suppress personal biases. Even so, reporters gravitate toward certain kinds of stories to the neglect of others, and this flavours coverage.

Scandals Journalists know that their audiences like scandal stories, a fact that trivializes political coverage. Talking about the coverage of Bill Clinton early in his presidency, political scientists Morris Fiorina and Paul Peterson said, "The public was bombarded with stories about Whitewater, Vince Foster's suicide, $200 haircuts, parties with Sharon Stone, the White House travel office, Hillary Clinton's investments, and numerous other matters that readers will not remember. The reason you do not remember is that, however important these matters were to the individuals involved, they were not important for the overall operation of government. Hence, they have been forgotten."

Canadian politics has also had its share of political scandals that were driven by media coverage. "Shawinigate" referred to the discovery that then Prime Minister Jean Chrétien might have used his influence not only as the member of Parliament for the riding of Shawinigan, but also as prime minister to help the owners of the hotel Auberge Grand-Mère get a loan from the Business Development Bank of Canada. Although the federal ethics commissioner found no evidence of wrongdoing, the story was front-page news for many months. Then, in 1999, came the federal sponsorship scandal that became known as "AdScam" or "Sponsorgate." Many politicians and bureaucrats were implicated in the scandal. Between 1996 and 2004, the federal government spent money on advertising campaigns to help promote Canadian unity in Quebec. In 2004, federal auditor Sheila Fraser found that much of the money had been misspent and was unaccounted for. This led to the Gomery Commission in 2004. In 2010, media coverage of the exploits of and rumours about Helena Guergis and her husband, Rahim Jaffer, led to a discussion of how the government handled the situation. Many felt that Prime Minister Stephen Harper acted too quickly on too little evidence when Guergis was thrown out of caucus.

No matter how transitory their news value, scandal and gaffe stories build audiences, which explains the increased coverage they receive. Robert Lichter and Daniel Amundson, analysts who monitor Washington news coverage, found that policy stories outnumbered scandal stories 13 to 1 in 1972 but only 3 to 1 in 1992. During that period, news media became more savvy at catering to audience interests and less interested in covering issues of significance. This also has led to more negative news being covered. Lichter and Amundson found that negative stories from U.S. Congress outnumbered positive stories 3 to 1 in 1972 but 9 to 1 in 1992.

Politics News reporters and editors have long recognized that people like stories about people, so any time an issue can be personified, so much the better. In Washington coverage, this has meant focusing on the president as a vehicle for treating issues. A study of the *CBS Evening News* found that 60 percent of the opening stories featured the president. Even in nonelection years, the media have a near-myopic fix on the White House. This displaces coverage of other important government institutions, such as Congress, the courts, and state and local governments.

Conflict Journalists learn two things about conflict early in their careers. First, their audiences like conflict. Second, conflict often illustrates the great issues by which society defines and redefines its values. Take, for example, the ongoing debates on capital punishment, abortion, and same-sex marriage. People get excited about these issues because of the fundamental values involved. This also makes them the subject of political discussion through the Canadian media.

Part of journalists' predilection for conflict is that conflict involves change: whether to do something differently. All news involves change, and conflict almost always is a signal to the kind of change that's most worth reporting. Conflict is generally a useful indicator of newsworthiness.

Horse Races In reporting political campaigns, the news media obsess on reporting the polls. Critics say that this treatment of campaigns as horse races results in substantive issues being underplayed. Even when issues are the focus, as when a candidate announces a major policy position, reporters connect the issue to its potential impact in the polls.

Brevity People who design media packages, such as a newspaper or a newscast, have devised presentation formats that favour shorter stories. This trend has been driven in part by broadcasting's severe time constraints. Network anchors have complained for years that they have to condense the world's news into 45 minutes in their evening newscasts. The result is short, often superficial treatments. The shorter-story format shifted to many newspapers and magazines, beginning with the launch of *USA Today* in 1982. *USA Today* obtained extremely high story counts, covering a great many events by running short stories, many of them only a half-dozen sentences. The effect on political coverage has been profound.

The **sound bites** used in campaign stories—that is, the actual voice of a candidate used in a broadcast news story—dropped from 47 seconds in 1968 to 10 seconds in 1988 and have remained short. Issues that require lengthy explorations, say critics, get passed over. Candidates, eager for airtime, have learned to offer quippy, catchy, clever capsules that are likely to be broadcast rather than to articulate thoughtful persuasive statements.

sound bite The actual voice of someone in the news, sandwiched into a correspondent's report.

Some people defend brevity, saying that it's the only way to reach people whose increasingly busy lives don't leave them much time to track politics and government. In one generalization, brevity's defenders note that the short attention span of the MTV generation can't handle much more than 10-second sound bites. Sanford Ungar, previously the communication dean at American University and now the president of Goucher College in Baltimore, Maryland, applauds the news media for devising writing and reporting styles that boil down complex issues so they can be readily understood by great masses of people. Says Ungar, "If *USA Today* encourages people not to think deeply, or not to go into more detail about what's happening, then it will be a disservice. But if *USA Today* teaches people how to be concise and get the main points across sometimes, they're doing nothing worse than what television is doing, and doing it at least as well."

LEARNING CHECK

- What is the problem with political news that fits predictable models?
- How are people short-changed by sound bites and other media tools that are used for brevity?

Government Manipulation of Media

STUDY PREVIEW Many political leaders are preoccupied with media coverage because they know the power it can have. Over the years, they have developed mechanisms to influence coverage to their advantage.

Watch

Prelude to War

Influencing Coverage

Many political leaders stay up nights figuring out ways to influence media coverage. James Fallows, in his book *Breaking the News*, quoted a Clinton White House official as saying, "When I was there, absolutely nothing was more important than figuring out what the news was going to be. . . . There is no such thing as a substantive discussion that is not shaped or dominated by how it is going to play in the press."

The game of trying to outsmart the news media to help those in power to set the agenda is nothing new. Theodore Roosevelt, at the turn of the 20th century, chose Sundays to issue many announcements. Roosevelt recognized that editors producing Monday newspapers usually had a dearth of news because weekends, with government and business shut down, didn't generate much worth telling. Roosevelt's Sunday announcements, therefore, received more prominent play in Monday editions. With typical bullishness, Roosevelt claimed that he had "discovered Mondays." Compared to how sophisticated government leaders have become at manipulating press coverage today, Roosevelt's approach was simple but effective.

Even Canada's first prime minister, Sir John A. Macdonald, was known to influence the media. In the book *Scrum Wars*, Allan Levine tells the story of a certain Lord Dufferin, who was a speaker at McGill University's convocation in 1873. His speech was entirely in Greek. Despite the fact that none of the journalists in attendance understood Greek, the news media reported that Lord Dufferin's speech was "the purest ancient Greek without mispronouncing a word." When asked how the media knew that the speech was perfect, Macdonald replied that *he* had told them. While it was true that Macdonald didn't speak a word of Greek, he did know a little bit about politics.

Government influence on news media has also occurred in recent Canadian politics. For example, in 1997, during a demonstration at the Asia-Pacific Economic Cooperation (APEC) summit held in Vancouver, the RCMP used pepper spray on protestors, even though it appeared to be a simple, peaceful protest. The media began to question whether the prime minister's office was involved in the decision to use force. The CBC's Terry Milewski had arranged an interview with one of the protestors. In an email between the two, Milewski used the term *forces of darkness* to describe the government. Ottawa, looking to divert attention from the incident itself, began to focus attention on Milewski instead. Pressure from the government resulted in Milewski being removed from the story. The government had succeeded in turning attention away from questions about the prime minister's involvement with the RCMP toward questions about "biased" journalism.

Scrums

scrum Members of the Parliamentary Press Gallery meet with politicians after Question Period.

Scrums have been a staple of Canadian politics since the 1950s. Reporters, microphones, and television cameras surround politicians in the hallway outside the House of Commons to ask questions about the issues raised during Question Period. Shortly after taking power in 2006, Prime Minister Stephen Harper introduced a new way of dealing with the news media. Instead of holding scrums on a regular basis, Harper's government tried to control the message as much as possible. Shanda Deziel, columnist for *Maclean's*, writes that "not in 30 years have the photographers had so little to work with. Trudeau, Mulroney, Chrétien and Martin all mugged in some way, but not Harper." The prime minister's office also wanted journalists to sign an "attendance sheet" in order to be able to ask questions during media conferences. Journalists balked at the idea; some even boycotted Harper's next few media conferences in protest.

LEARNING CHECK

- How do political leaders use the calendar and news flow to their advantage?
- What is a scrum?

Trial Balloons and Leaks

trial balloon A deliberate leak of a potential policy, usually from a diversionary source, to test public response.

To check weather conditions, meteorologists send up balloons. To get an advance peek at public reaction, political leaders also float **trial balloons**. Nick Russell, in *Morals and the Media*, writes that during the 1960s, Prime Minister John Diefenbaker would often have tea with Peter Dempson, the Ottawa Bureau Chief for the now defunct *Toronto Telegram*.

At those meetings, the prime minister would "offer snippets of information, provided they were not directly attributed to him. If public reaction was adverse, Diefenbaker would simply dismiss it as press speculation."

Trial balloons are not the only way in which the media can be used. Partisans and dissidents use **leaks** to bring attention to their opponents and people they don't much like. In leaking, someone passes information to reporters on the condition that he or she not be identified as the source. While reporters are leery of many leakers, some information is so significant and from such reliable sources that it's hard to pass up.

leak A deliberate and anonymous disclosure of confidential or classified information by someone who wants to advance the public interest, embarrass a bureaucratic rival or supervisor, or disclose incompetence or skullduggery.

It's essential that reporters understand how their sources intend information to be used. It is also important for sources to have some control over what they tell reporters. Even so, reporter–source relationships lend themselves to abuse by manipulative government officials. Worse, the structures of these relationships allow officials to control what the people hear. As political scientists Karen O'Connor and Larry Sabato said, "Every public official knows that journalists are pledged to protect the confidentiality of sources, and therefore the rules can be used to an official's own benefit—like, say, giving reporters derogatory information to print about a source without having to be identified with the source." In his work *The Newsmakers*, University of Calgary political science professor and media commentator David Taras refers to this practice as a "backchannel game, a tango between politicians and officials and reporters" that is likely inescapable. This game has been played for many years. Paul Wells, writing in *Maclean's*, says that "Trudeau's cabinet leaked so badly the *Ottawa Citizen* ran a cartoon showing a reporter with a fake moustache sitting at the cabinet table." This manipulation is a regrettable, though unavoidable, part of the news-gathering process.

LEARNING CHECK

- **How do reporter relationships with sources affect news positively and negatively?**
- **Should reporter–source relationships be transparent to news audiences? How?**

Stonewalling

When U.S. President Richard Nixon was under fire for ordering a cover-up of the Watergate break-in, he went months without holding a news conference. His aides plotted his movements to avoid even informal, shouted questions from reporters. He hunkered down in the White House in a classic example of **stonewalling.** Experts in the branch of public relations called political communication generally advise against stonewalling because people infer guilt or something to hide. Nonetheless, it is one way to deal with difficult media questions.

stonewall To refuse to answer questions, and sometimes refuse even to meet with reporters.

A variation on stonewalling is the **news blackout**. When American troops invaded Grenada, the Pentagon barred the press. Reporters who hired runabout boats to get to the island were intercepted by an American naval blockade. While heavy-handed, such limitations on media coverage do, for a limited time, give the government the opportunity to report what's happening from its self-serving perspective.

news blackout When a person or institution decides to issue no statements despite public interest and also declines news media questions.

LEARNING CHECK

- **Do "no comment" answers from political leaders serve democracy well?**
- **What about ducking questions or giving evasive answers?**

Overwhelming Information

During the Persian Gulf buildup in 1990 and then the war itself, the Pentagon tried a new approach in media relations. Pete Williams, the Pentagon's chief spokesperson, provided so much information, including video, sound bites, and data, that reporters were overwhelmed. The result was that reporters spent so much time sorting through Pentagon-provided material, all of it worthy, that they didn't have time to compose difficult questions or pursue fresh story angles of their own. As a result, coverage of the war was almost entirely favourable to President George H.W. Bush's administration.

LEARNING CHECK

- **How can news people deal with information overloads that work against sorting out significant news from lesser stuff?**

Political Campaigns

Watch

Entertainment and Politics

STUDY PREVIEW Elections are a key point in democratic governance, which explains the scrutiny that news media coverage receives. Also, the partisanship inherent in a campaign helps to ensure that media missteps are identified quickly. Some criticism of media is of news; other criticism is of the advertisements that media are paid to carry.

Campaign Coverage

Critics fault the news media for falling short in covering political campaigns. The following are frequent criticisms:

- **Issues.** Reporters need to push for details on positions and ask tough questions on major issues, and not accept generalities. They need to bounce one candidate's position off those of other candidates, creating a forum of intelligent discussion from which voters can make informed choices.
- **Agenda.** Reporters need to assume some role in setting a campaign agenda. When reporters allow candidates to control the agenda of coverage, they become mere conduits for self-serving news releases and images from candidates. **Pseudo-events** with candidates, such as visits to photogenic flag factories, lack substance. So do staged **photo ops.** Reporters need to guard against letting such easy-to-cover events squeeze out substantive coverage.
- **Interpretation.** Campaigns are drawn out and complicated, and reporters need to keep trying to pull together what's happened for the audience. Day-to-day spot news isn't enough. There also need to be explanations, interpretations, and analyses to help voters see the big picture.
- **Inside coverage.** Reporters need to cover the machinery of the campaigns: who's running things and how. This is especially important with the growing role of campaign consultants. Who are these people? What history do they bring to a campaign? What is their agenda?
- **Polling.** Poll results are easy to report but tricky and inconsistent because of variations in methodology and even questions. News operations should report on competing polls, not just on their own polls. In tracking polls, asking the same questions over time for consistency is essential.
- **Instant feedback.** Television newsrooms have supplemented their coverage and commentary with email instant feedback from viewers. Select messages are flashed onscreen within minutes. In some programs a reporter is assigned to analyze incoming messages and identify trends. While all this makes for "good television," the comments are statistically dubious as indicators of overall public opinion. Too much can be read into them.
- **Depth.** With candidates going directly to voters in debates and talk-show appearances, reporters need to offer something more than what voters can see and hear for themselves. Analysis and depth add a fresh dimension that is not redundant in terms of what the audience already knows.

pseudo-event A staged event to attract media attention, usually lacking substance.

photo op Short for photo opportunity; a staged event, usually photogenic, to attract media attention.

LEARNING CHECK

- Rank the list of common criticisms of campaign news coverage. How do you justify your ranking?

Lessons from Recent Campaigns

Just as historians see the first television political commercials in 1952 as swaying the election for Dwight Eisenhower, so may the campaign documentary, which made its appearance in 2004, be seen as a new essential in political campaigns.

Campaign Movies Propagandist movie documentaries emerged as a potential campaign tool with **Michael Moore**'s George W. Bush–bashing ***Fahrenheit 9/11*** in 2004. With slanted juxtapositioning of news and interview clips and scripting that frequently implied more than was said, *Fahrenheit 9/11* hit like a bombshell early in the presidential

Michael Moore Documentary producer whose *Fahrenheit 9/11* demonstrated the genre's potential in political campaigns.

Fahrenheit 9/11 Propagandist documentary that helped to shape issues in the 2004 presidential campaign.

CASE STUDY

Is the Internet Changing the Government–Media Landscape?

Watch

ABC's *Nightline:* "Campaign 2.0"

Politicians are learning to adjust to the realities of social media, some better than others. The CNN-YouTube candidate debates in 2007 attempted to employ the immense new popularity of video sharing on the internet, a sudden staple of youth culture, in the public policy dialogue during the U.S. presidential campaign. In the initial CNN-YouTube debate for Democratic candidates, voters submitted questions using creative videos, some of which put candidates on the spot. In other words, the traditional gatekeepers weren't in control.

One candidate, Mitt Romney, at first declined to participate in the debates. He said that he preferred questions from professional journalists and characterized YouTube questions as "disrespectful." Referring to a cartoon video about global warming, Romney said that he didn't want to take questions from a snowman. In the end, Romney decided to participate.

Since 2007, politicians have used new media to interact with voters. President Barack Obama used YouTube to deliver a State of the Union address in 2009, while Prime Minister Stephen Harper used YouTube to respond to questions about the 2010 Speech from the Throne. In what is referred to as a variation of the "crowd-sourced interview," more than 5000 people submitted almost 2000 questions prior to the online event. While the videos were pre-recorded, there wasn't any editing of content. Google, who hosted the online event, did provide Harper with a list of questions, but there was little message control. Even contentious questions on Afghan detainees and the legalization of marijuana were addressed. Harper answered questions based on their popularity. According to Google's Wendy Rozeluk, "The questions were based on votes, to be representative of the hot topics of interest as voted by Canadians and of course representative of English and French Canadians." Some 35 000 people logged on to the internet to watch Harper's video.

Other social media also offer a chance for the public to voice their concerns. In 2010, 200 000 people joined the Facebook group "Canadians Against Proroguing Parliament." In a study of those Facebook group members, called *Facebook and Prorogation*, the Rideau Institute found that 88 percent of those who joined the group were "politically engaged." That wasn't surprising. However, what *was* surprising was the age of the group members. Almost half were over age 45 and 34 percent were between the ages of 31 and 44. Of those surveyed, 95 percent had voted in the previous federal election.

Not MyTube Presidential hopeful Mitt Romney turned down an initial invitation to the CNN-YouTube debates because he didn't want to encourage "disrespectful" questions.

What does this tell us about the role of social media in the political process? The Rideau Institute claims that some may feel that Facebook (and other social media) may "be the dumbest way to advocate for a political cause, while others have urged decision makers to heed this new form of political engagement." Ivor Tossell, writing in *The Globe and Mail*, says that this type of interaction with voters is neither the future of social media nor the future of politics. According to Tossell, "Mr. Harper's not going viral, he's just got a new communications strategy." He adds, "Real interaction on the Web requires honesty, an unfiltered voice—and a personality to go along with the policy."

DEEPENING YOUR MEDIA LITERACY

Explore the Issue

Log on to your favourite social media site. What types of political discussions are taking place there?

Dig Deeper

List some of the advantages and disadvantages of using social media to explain a political issue. Is it the future of democracy or is it simply a new strategy employed by the government?

What Do You Think?

Are social media the new "fourth estate"?

campaign. The film opened on 900 screens five months before the election and grossed $23.9 million on the first weekend, a record for a documentary. It played the movie-house circuit for weeks. One month before the election, *Fahrenheit 9/11* was issued on DVD. The questions that Moore framed dogged Bush for the rest of the campaign.

Explore

Deepening Your Media Literacy: Is the internet changing the government-media landscape?

Bloggers and Social Media Political junkies created dozens of websites in 2004, many offering news, often slanted, but mostly featuring commentary. Importantly, the sites had links to like-minded sites. These sites, called blogs as a shortened form of "web logs" because they are a kind of a personal journal or log, grew in importance as sources of information and ideas. The blogs, maintained by individuals, not media organizations, represented a kind of democratization in news coverage outside the structure of established news organizations. Although mostly amateurish, often one-person sideline operations, blogs scooped the major news media on occasion and led the way on some coverage.

negative ads Political campaign advertising, usually on television, in which a candidate criticizes the opponent rather than emphasizing his or her platform.

attack ads A subspecies of negative ads, especially savage in criticizing an opponent; many play loose with context and facts.

Attack Ads The 2004 U.S. presidential campaign spawned **negative ads** and **attack ads** in unprecedented quantity. With little regard for facts or truth, Republicans loosely connected to the Bush campaign, under the banner of Swift Boat Veterans for Truth, challenged the war-hero record of Democratic candidate John Kerry. Then there was the entry in a campaign advertising contest that likened George W. Bush to Adolf Hitler, which an anti-Bush group, Moveon.org, let sit on its website for days. In Canada, Stephen Harper's Conservatives wasted little time in launching a series of negative ads in 2007 aimed at Liberal leader Stéphane Dion that framed him as wishy-washy. When Michael Ignatieff became Liberal leader in 2008, his patriotism was attacked.

Campaign Advertising

Herbert Alexander His studies have concluded that media advertising is only one of many variables in political campaigns.

Can candidates buy their way into office with advertising? While a candidate who vastly outspends another would seem to have an advantage, well-heeled campaigns can fail. For example, in U.S. presidential campaigns, no correlation has been established between winning and media spending. **Herbert Alexander**, a University of Southern California political scientist who tracks campaign spending, noted that George H.W. Bush outspent Bill Clinton $43 million to $32 million in 1992 and lost. Ross Perot also outspent Clinton, buying almost $40 million in media time and space. In 1988, however, Bush outspent Michael Dukakis $32 million to $24 million and won. The data point to campaign advertising as being only one of many variables in elections.

The fact remains, however, that a political campaign has a cost of admission. Candidates need media exposure, and a campaign without advertising would almost certainly be doomed.

Thomas Patterson and Robert McClure Effect of political advertising on voters is critical only in close campaigns.

It would be a mistake to conclude that political advertising has no effect. A major 1976 study by **Thomas Patterson** and **Robert McClure** concluded that 7 percent of the people in a 2700-person sample were influenced by ads on whether to vote for Richard Nixon or George McGovern for president. While that was a small percentage, many campaigns are decided by even slimmer margins. The lesson from the Patterson-McClure study is that political advertising can make a critical difference.

In Canada, broadcast election advertising is governed by the Canadian Radio-television and Telecommunications Commission (CRTC). According to the CRTC, broadcasters "shall allocate time for the broadcasting of programs, advertisements or announcements of a partisan political character on an equitable basis to all accredited political parties and rival candidates represented in the election or referendum." On the surface, this would seem to be a fair practice. However, "equitable" doesn't mean "equal." But, generally, all candidates and parties are entitled to some coverage that will give them the opportunity to expose their ideas to the public.

LEARNING CHECK

- Negative political advertising is easy to criticize, but what can be done about it?
- Have you used social media to become politically active? Why or why not?

Chapter 17 Wrap-Up

The democratic system relies on the mass media as an outside check to keep government accountable to the people. The concept has many labels, including the press as a fourth branch of government. The similar label *fourth estate* comes from feudal European times. A more modern variation characterizes the press as a watchdog on government. The concept has given rise to the informally put goal of "keeping them honest." The impact of new social media is just beginning.

PEARSON mycanadiancommunicationlab

Visit **www.mycanadiancommunicationlab.ca** for access to a wealth of tools and resources that will enhance your learning experience. Features include the following:

- Personalized Study Plan
- Videos
- Activities
- Pearson eText–and much more!

Questions for Critical Thinking

1. By what authority are news media the people's watchdog for government accountability?
2. How do mass media influence public policy?
3. What are major government tools for manipulating news coverage?
4. Why is news coverage of political issues often formulaic and superficial?
5. What role will social media play in the political process?

Keeping Up to Date

Professional journals that carry articles on media coverage of political issues and governance include *Columbia Journalism Review*, *Quill*, and *American Journalism Review*.

Online, BBM Canada publishes *In Sync* on a quarterly basis. It highlights trends in audience measurement.

Ongoing discussion of media responsibility also appears in the *Journal of Mass Media Ethics*.

Glossary

1-900 telephone numbers Used for phone-in surveys; respondents select themselves to participate and they pay for the call.
384 Number of people in a properly selected sample for results to provide 95 percent confidence that results have less than 5 percent margin of error.
55 percent Canadian content Level of daily Canadian content required by the CRTC.
ABC American Broadcasting Company; built from ABC radio network.
accepted practices What media do as a matter of routine, sometimes without considering ethics implications.
account executives Agency reps to clients.
ad clutter So many competing ads that all of them lose impact.
Adam Curry Pioneer in podcasting technology.
advergame A sponsored online game, usually for an established brand at its own site.
adversarial public relations Attacking critics openly.
advertising director Coordinates marketing and advertising.
advertorials Paid advertisements that state an editorial position.
agenda setting Media tell people what to think about, not what to think.
aggressive stimulation Theory that people are inspired to violence from media depictions.
AGVOT Action Group on Violence on Television; helped develop programming codes for Canadian television.
Aird Commission First royal commission into Canadian broadcasting.
airplay Radio time devoted to a particular recording.
Al Jazeera Qatar-based satellite news channel for Arab audiences; now global.
Alan Cross New music historian
Albert Bandura Found media violence stimulated aggression in children.
Alien and Sedition Acts Discouraged criticism of government.
Alliance Films Canadian movie distributor.
amplification Giving a message to a larger audience.
André Bazin French film critic who devised the term *auteur* for significant cutting-edge filmmakers.
Andrew Crisell Uses the ideas of semiotician Roland Barthes to analyze how radio meaning is created.
Andrew Hamilton Urged truth as a defence for charges of libel.
animated film Narrative films with drawn scenes and characters.
Anson McKim Founded the first ad agency in Canada.
Antonio Gramsci Italian theorist who expanded on Marxism to include ideas, not just economics.
Anytime Anywhere Media Measurement (A2/M2) Nielsen plan to integrate audience measurements on a wide range of video platforms.
applied research Usefulness, usually economic, is apparent.
APR Indicates CPRS accreditation.
AR (artist and repertoire) Units of recording company responsible for talent.
Arbitron International media and marketing research company.
Aristotle Advocate of the golden mean; defended portrayals of violence.
Arthur C. Clarke Devised the concept of satellites in geosynchronous orbits for communication.
ASC Advertising Standards Canada; the self-regulatory body for advertising.
ASCAP Music licensing organization.
Associated Press (AP) Co-operative for gathering and distributing news.
Atom Egoyan Directs movies about personal uncertainty.
attack ads A subspecies of negative ads, especially savage in criticizing an opponent; many play loose with context and facts.
Audit Bureau of Circulations (ABC) Checks newspaper circulation claims.
auteur A filmmaker recognized for significant and original treatments.
authentic performance Live with on-site audience.
authoritarianism Top-down governance, such as a monarchy or dictatorship.
B movie Low-budget movie, usually with little artistic aspiration.
Baby Boomers Today's fiftysomething and sixtysomething generations.
barrages Intensive repetition of ads.
Barry Diller Created early successful Fox programming.
BBM Nielsen Media Research Surveys TV and radio in Canada.
BDU Broadcast distribution undertakings; technical name for cable companies and satellite providers.
Ben Bagdikian A critic of media consolidation.
Benjamin Day Published *The New York Sun*; his penny newspaper brought advertising to a new level.
Benjamin Harris Published *Publick Occurrences*.
bias in communication Theory that media can have a bias for time and space.
Big Four Major recording companies: Universal Music, Sony BMG, EMI, Warner Music.
bipolar model Portrays extremes as opposites, such as libertarian and authoritarian political systems.
black music Folk genre from American black slave experience.
black weeks Periods when ratings are not conducted.
block booking A rental agreement through which a movie house accepts a batch of movies.

pulp fiction Quickly and inexpensively produced, easy-to-read short novels.

push media Messages sent to the receiver with or without prior consent.

push-pull model Some of the control in the communication process shifts to the receiver.

quota sampling Demographics of the sample coincide with those of the whole population.

Radio Farda U.S. government–funded Farsi-language service aimed at Iran.

Radio Marketing Bureau (RMB) Claims that radio is a perfect fit for modern life.

Radio-Television News Directors Association (RTNDA) Organization that believes that the broadcasting of factual, accurately reported, and timely news and public affairs is vital.

Ralph Potter Ethicist who devised the Potter Box.

rap Dance music with intense bass and rhyming riffs, the lyrics often delivered with antiestablishment defiance.

ratings Measurements of broadcast audience size.

Reader Usage Measure (RUM) A scale for measuring reader satisfaction.

reality programs Broadcast shows with a nonfiction basis.

Recording Industry Association of America (RIAA) Trade association of recording companies.

redundancy Repetition of media messages.

re-enactments Re-creating real events.

regulators Nonmedia people who influence messages.

retribalization Restoring humankind to a natural, tribal state.

rhythm and blues Distinctive style of black music that took form in the 1930s.

rice-roots reporting Uncensored field reporting from the Vietnam War.

Robert Flaherty First documentary filmmaker.

rockabilly Black–hillbilly hybrid that emerged in the 1950s.

role modelling Basis for imitative behaviour.

Roone Arledge ABC television executive responsible for introducing *Wide World of Sports* in 1961; also created ABC's *Monday Night Football.*

Rosser Reeves Devised the term *unique selling proposition.*

roving photographer Statistically unsound way to tap public opinion.

Sam Phillips Pioneered rockabilly and rock 'n' roll; discovered Elvis Presley.

sample selection Process for drawing individuals to be interviewed.

sample size Number of people surveyed.

Samuel Morse Inventor of the telegraph in 1844.

Sarah Josepha Hale Founded first women's magazine.

satcaster A television station that transmits to an orbiting satellite, which beams signals back down directly to individual receivers.

satellite radio Delivery method of programming from a single source beamed to an orbiting satellite for transmission directly to individual end users.

scrum Members of the Parliamentary Press Gallery meet with politicians after Question Period.

Search Inside Amazon.com's search engine that can find a term or phrase in any book whose copyright owners have agreed to have it scanned in to a database.

selective editing Misrepresentation through omission and juxtaposition.

self-righting process Although people make occasional errors in truth-seeking, they eventually discover and correct them.

semantic noise Sloppy message crafting.

semiconductor Silicon chip that is used in digitization.

Seven Sisters Leading women's magazines.

Seymour Feshbach Found evidence for media violence as a release.

Shawn Fanning Inventor of Napster.

shelf life How long a periodical remains in use.

shopper An advertising paper without news.

situational ethics Make ethics decisions on the basis of situation at hand.

slander A spoken defamation.

Snow White and the Seven Dwarfs First full-length animated film.

SOCAN Society of Composers, Authors and Music Publishers of Canada; music licensing organization.

social Darwinism Application of Darwin's survival-of-the-fittest theory to society.

social media news release Internet-based news release with links to related material and interactive opportunities for news reporters.

socialization Learning to fit into society.

soft news Geared to satisfying an audience's information wants, not needs.

sound bite The actual voice of someone in the news, sandwiched into a correspondent's report.

Spence Caldwell Initiator of the CTV network.

spiral of silence Vocal majority intimidates others into silence.

sponsored link Onscreen hot spot to move to an online advertisement.

sponsored magazine Generally non-newsrack magazine, often member-supported.

staffing Available staff resources to cover news.

standard advertising unit (SAU) A trimmer newspaper broadsheet format with standardized dimensions; introduced in the 1980s.

Stanley Hubbard Pioneer of direct-to-viewer satellite television.

statistical extrapolation Drawing conclusions from a segment of the whole.

status conferral Media attention enhances attention to people, subjects, and issues.

stealth ads Advertisements, often subtle, in nontraditional, unexpected places.

Steamboat Willie Animated cartoon character that became Mickey Mouse.

stereotyping Using broad strokes to facilitate storytelling.

Steve Horgan Adapted halftone technology for high-speed newspaper presses.

Steve Jobs The driving force behind the Apple Computer revival, iPod, and iTunes.

stonewall To refuse to answer questions, and sometimes refuse even to meet with reporters.

store brands Products sold with a store brand, often manufactured by the retailer; also called house brands and private labels.

straw poll Respondents select themselves to be polled; unreliable indicator of public opinion.

streaming Technology that allows playback of a message to begin before all of the components have arrived.

studio system A mass production, distribution, and exhibition process for movies devised by Hollywood in the 1920s.

Susan Sontag Saw cultural and social value in pop art.

suspension of disbelief Occurs when you surrender doubts about the reality of a story and become caught up in that story.

sweeps Period when broadcast ratings are conducted.

symbol A sign that has an arbitrary connection to what it signifies.

tabloid A newspaper format with pages half the size of a broadsheet; typically five columns wide and 14 to 18 inches long; not necessarily sensationalistic despite a connotation the term has acquired.

talkies Movies with sound.

technological convergence Melding of print, electronic, and photographic media into digitized form.

technological research To improve technology and find new technology.

Tehrangeles Nickname for Los Angeles as home to more Iranians than any city other than Tehran.

telegraph Electricity-enabled long-distance communication, used mostly from Point A to Point B.

teleology Good decisions are those with good consequences.

telephone book journalism Emphasizing readers' names in articles.

Television Violence Monitoring Project Conducted contextual nonviolence studies and found less serious media depictions than earlier thought.

Telstar First communication satellite.

terrestrial radio The industry based on audio transmission from land-based towers, as opposed to transmission via satellite.

The Black Pirate The first feature film in colour.

The Brass Check 1919 book that exposed newsroom corruption.

The Jazz Singer The first feature film with sound.

The New York Sun First penny newspaper, 1833.

The Vikings Canada's first talkie.

The War of the Worlds Novel that inspired a radio drama that became the test bed of the media's ability to instill panic.

Theodore Roosevelt Coined the term *muckraking*.

theoretical research Goal is to advance knowledge.

theory of divine command Proper decisions follow God's will.

theory of divine right of kings Monarchs derive authority from God, not from their subjects.

theory of secular command Holds that authorities legitimately hold supreme authority, although not necessarily a divine authority.

third-person effect One person overestimating the effect of media messages on other people.

Thomas Jefferson Anti-Federalist president.

Thomas Patterson and Robert McClure Effect of political advertising on voters is critical only in close campaigns.

Tim Berners-Lee Devised protocols and codes for the World Wide Web.

Time First American newsmagazine.

time-shifting Audience control of time for viewing a chosen program.

TiVo A television recording and playback device that allows viewers to edit out commercials; also called a digital video recorder (DVR) or personal video recorder (PVR).

trade journal Keeps members of a profession or trade informed.

trailing Running shorter, smaller ads after a campaign is introduced.

Transmission Control Protocol (TCP) Universal system that connects individual computer systems to the internet.

transplant period First period in Canadian journalism, in which newspapers or publishers from Britain and the United States were "transplanted" to Canada.

trial balloon A deliberate leak of a potential policy, usually from a diversionary source, to test public response.

two-step flow Media effects on individuals come through opinion leaders.

ultrawideband (UWB) Low-power Wi-Fi system that rides on existing frequencies licensed for other uses.

Ulysses James Joyce novel banned in the United States until 1930 court decision.

unique selling proposition (USP) Emphasizing a single feature.

universal resource locator (URL) Address assigned to a page on the internet; now known as a uniform resource locator.

unshackled press The idea that the press should be able to print the truth.

upfront Advance advertiser commitments to buy network advertising time.

uplink A ground station that beams a signal to an orbiting communication satellite.

Upton Sinclair Author of *The Brass Check*.

uses and gratifications studies Theory that people choose media that meet their needs and interests.

VALS Psychographic analysis by values, lifestyle, and life stage.

veil of ignorance Making decisions with a blind eye to extraneous factors that could affect the decision.

vertical integration One company owning multiple stages of production, to the detriment of competition.

video iPod A handheld Apple device for playing not only music but also video at the viewer's choice of time and place.

video-on-demand (VOD) Mechanisms that allow viewers to tune in to programs any time they choose.

Vint Cerf, Bob Kahn Coauthors of TCP; sometimes called the fathers of the internet.

viral advertising Media consumers pass on the message, like a contagious disease, usually on the internet.

Voice of America U.S. government–funded broadcast service sent into nations with state-controlled media to articulate American policies directly to the people.

Walt Disney Pioneer in animated films.

Walter Lippmann His book *Public Opinion* assumed powerful media effects in 1920s.

Warner brothers Introduced sound in movies.

Watergate Reporting of the Nixon administration scandal.

waves Intensive repetition of ads.

webisodes Mini-movies, generally four minutes long, on the web; usually sponsored and sometimes featuring the advertiser as part of the storyline.

westward growth Third period in Canadian journalism; as Canadians moved west, so did the press.

whitewashing Covering up.

Wi-Fi Wireless fidelity technology, which offers limited-range downloading.

Wilbur Schramm Concluded that television has minimal effects on children.

Wilfred Kesterton Canadian news historian.

William Caxton Printed the first advertisement.

William Dickson Developed the first motion picture camera.

William Gibson Sci-fi writer who coined the term *cyberspace*.

William Randolph Hearst Chain owner who dictated the contents of all of his newspapers; built circulation with sensationalism.

William McQuire Found most media violence research flawed.

William Paley Long-time CBS boss.

William Henry Vanderbilt Embodied the bad corporate images of the 1880s and 1890s with "The public be damned."

World War II Veterans Today's eightysomething generation.

World Wide Web System that allows global linking of information modules in user-determined sequences.

W.P. Davison Scholar who devised third-person effect theory.

yellow period Late 1800s; marked by sensationalism.

Youth Criminal Justice Act Prohibits reporting on trials involving minors.

zapping Viewers record programs and eliminate commercial breaks.

'zine Magazine whose entire content—articles and ads—pitches a single product or product line.

zipping Viewers change television channels to avoid commercials.

For Further Learning

Chapter 1

Ken Auletta. *Three Blind Mice: How the TV Networks Lost Their Way* (Random House, 1991).

Ben H. Bagdikian. *The Media Monopoly*, Fifth edition (Beacon, 1997).

Ben H. Bagdikian. "Special Issue: The Lords of the Global Village." *The Nation* 248 (June 12, 1989): 23, 805–20.

Erik Barnouw and others. *Conglomerates and the Media* (The New Press, 1998).

Paul Benedetti and Nancy DeHart. *On McLuhan: Forward Through the Rear View Mirror* (Prentice Hall, 1996).

Arthur Asa Berger. *Media USA: Process and Effect* (Longman, 1988).

Andrew Cardozo. "Big Applications and the CRTC." *Broadcast Dialogue* (October 2006): 6.

Benjamin M. Compaine and Douglas Gomery. *Who Owns the Media? Competition and Concentration in the Mass Media Industry*, Third edition (Erlbaum, 2000).

CRTC. *Communications Monitoring Report 2009.*

Matthew Fraser. "How Much Con in Convergence?" *National Post* (July 30, 2001).

Matthew Fraser. "Iron Law Brought Us Convergence, Heaven's Gate." *National Post* (June 11, 2001).

Thomas Friedman. *The World Is Flat: A Brief History of the 21st Century* (Farrar, Straus & Giroux, 2005).

Laurel Hyatt. "Letting the Genie out of the Bottle." *Broadcaster Magazine* (March 2001).

Harold Innis. *Empire and Communications* (Oxford University Press, 1950).

Daphne Lavers. "deKerckhove." *Broadcast Dialogue* (September 1999).

Robert Lichter, Linda S. Richter and Stanley Rothman. *Watching America: What Television Tells Us about Our Lives* (Prentice Hall, 1991).

Stephen W. Littlejohn. *Theories of Human Communication*, Third edition (Wadsworth, 1989).

Michelle Martin. *Mainstream Models in Mass Communication Research from Communication and Mass Media: Culture, Domination and Opposition* (Prentice Hall Canada, 1997).

Eric McLuhan and Frank Zingrone. *Essential McLuhan* (Anansi, 1995).

Marshall McLuhan. *The Gutenberg Galaxy: The Making of Typographical Man* (University of Toronto Press, 1967).

Marshall McLuhan. *Understanding Media* (Signet, 1964).

Mark Crispin Miller. "Can Viacom's Reporters Cover Viacom's Interests?" *Columbia Journalism Review* (November–December 1999): 48–50.

Mark Crispin Miller. "Free the Media." *Nation* (June 3, 1996): 9–28.

Glen O'Farrell. "What's to Become of Canadian Media?" *Broadcast Dialogue* (November 2006): 6.

Tara Perkins and Rick Westhead. "CanWest Buying Alliance." *Toronto Star* (January 11, 2007).

Sumner Redstone with Peter Knobler. *A Passion to Win* (Simon & Schuster, 2001).

Anthony Smith. *The Age of the Behemoths: The Globalization of Mass Media Firms* (Priority Press, 1991).

Susan Sontag. "One Culture and New Sensibility." *Against Interpretation* (Farrar, Straus & Giroux, 1966).

Kara Swisher. *There Must Be a Pony in Here Somewhere* (Crown, 2003).

Bohdan Szuchewycz and Jeannette Sloniowski, editors. *Canadian Communications*, Second edition (Prentice Hall Canada, 2001).

Alexis S. Tan. *Mass Communication Theories and Research* (Macmillan, 1986).

James R. Taylor. "The Office of the Future: Weber and Innis Revisited." In *Communications in Canadian Society*, edited by Benjamin Singer (Addison-Wesley, 1983).

Kevin G. Wilson. "The Rise and Fall of Teleglobe." Montreal *Gazette* (May 18, 2002).

Samuel P. Winch. *Mapping the Cultural Space of Journalism: How Journalists Distinguish News from Entertainment* (Praeger, 1998).

Tony Wong. "Redrawing the Media Map." *Toronto Star* (July 13, 2006).

Antonia Zerbisias. "Ready or Not, CRTC Takes on Media Convergence." *Toronto Star* (April 14, 2001).

Chapter 2

Paul Benedetti and Nancy DeHart. *On McLuhan: Forward Through the Rear View Mirror* (Prentice Hall, 1996).

Arthur Asa Berger. *Media USA: Process and Effect* (Longman, 1988).

Thomas Friedman. *The World Is Flat: A Brief History of the 21st Century* (Farrar, Straus & Giroux, 2005).

Daphne Lavers. "deKerckhove." *Broadcast Dialogue* (September 1999).

Stephen W. Littlejohn. *Theories of Human Communication*, Eighth edition (Wadsworth, 2004).

Michelle Martin. *Mainstream Models in Mass Communication Research from Communication and Mass Media: Culture, Domination and Opposition* (Prentice Hall Canada, 1997).

Eric McLuhan and Marshall McLuhan. *Laws of Media: The New Science* (University of Toronto Press, 1988).

Eric McLuhan and Frank Zingrone. *Essential McLuhan* (Anansi, 1995).

Marshall McLuhan. *The Gutenberg Galaxy: The Making of Typographical Man* (University of Toronto Press, 1967).

Marshall McLuhan. *Understanding Media* (Signet, 1964).

Denis McQuail and Sven Windahl. *Communication Models for the Study of Mass Communication*, Second edition (Longman, 1993).

Mark Crispin Miller. "Can Viacom's Reporters Cover Viacom's Interests?" *Columbia Journalism Review* (November–December 1999): 48–50.

Mark Crispin Miller. "Free the Media." *Nation* (June 3, 1996): 9–28.

Linda Simon. *Dark Light: Electricity and Anxiety from the Telegraph to the X-Ray* (Harcourt, 2004).

Alexis S. Tan. *Mass Communication Theories and Research* (Macmillan, 1986).

Chapter 3

Glenn C. Altschuler. *All Shook Up: How Rock 'n' Roll Changed America* (Oxford University Press, 2004).

Barry Diller. "Don't Repackage, Redefine!" *Wired* (February 1995): 82–85.

Entertainment Software Association of Canada (ESAC). *2009 Essential Facts from ESAC.* Available online at http://www.theesa.ca/documents/EssentialFacts2009EN.pdf.

Stuart Evey. *ESPN: Creating an Empire* (Triumph, 2004).

Elliot Gorn and Warren Goldstein. *A Brief History of American Sports* (Hill and Wang, 1993).

Robert L. Hilliard and Michael C. Keith. *Dirty Discourse: Sex and Indecency in American Radio* (Iowa State Press, 2003).

Steven Johnson. *Everything Bad Is Good for You* (Riverhead, 2005).

Steven L. Kent. *The Ultimate History of Video Games: From Pong to Pokemon—The Story Behind the Craze That Touched Our Lives and Changed the World* (Random House, 2001).

Kathleen Krull. *The Book of Rock Stars: 24 Musical Icons That Shine Through History* (Hyperion, 2004).

James A. Michener. *Sports in America* (Random House, 1976).

Guthrie P. Ramsey Jr. *Race Music: Black Culture from Bebop to Hip-Hop* (University of California Press, 2003).

Eric Schlosser. "Empire of the Obscene." *The New Yorker* (March 10, 2003): 60–71.

Ronald A. Smith. *Radio, Television, and Big-Time College Sport* (Johns Hopkins University Press, 2001).

Larry Starr, Christopher Waterman and Jay Hodgson. *Rock: A Canadian Perspective* (Oxford University Press, 2009).

Richard Saul Wurman. *Information Anxiety* (Bantam, 1990).

Dolf Zillmann and Peter Voderer. *Media Entertainment: The Psychology of Its Appeal* (Erlbaum, 2000).

Chapter 4

James Adams. "A Good News, Bad News Issue." *The Globe and Mail* (July 25, 2006).

J. Antonio Alpalhao and Victor Da Rosa. *A Minority in a Changing Society: The Portuguese Communities of Quebec* (University of Ottawa Press, 1980).

Roland Barthes. "The Photographic Message." In *Image-Music-Text* (Fontana, 1973).

James L. Baughman. *Henry R. Luce and the Rise of the American News Media* (Tawyne, 1987).

Bill Bishop. "A Warning from Smithville: Owning Your Own Weekly." *Washington Journalism Review* (May 10, 1988): 4, 25–32.

Myrna Blyth. *Spin Sisters* (St. Martin's Press, 2005).

Leo Bogart. *Preserving the Press: How Daily Newspapers Mobilized to Keep Their Readers* (Columbia University Press, 1991).

Reginald Bragonier Jr. and David J. Fisher. *The Mechanics of a Magazine* (Hearst, 1984).

Walter M. Brasch. *Forerunners of Revolution: Muckrakers and the American Social Conscience* (University of America Press, 1990).

Robert Brehl. "Conrad Black Takes on Toronto." *The Globe and Mail* (June 13, 1998).

Iain Calder. *The Untold Story: My 20 Years Running the* National Enquirer (Miramax, 2004).

Canada. Royal Commission on Newspapers, 1981.

Canada. Senate Special Committee on the Mass Media, *Report.* 3 vols., 1970.

J. William Click and Russell N. Baird. *Magazine Editing and Production*, Fifth edition (Wm. C. Brown, 1990).

Ellis Cose. *The Press* (Morrow, 1989).

Jonathan Curiel. "Gay Newspapers." *Editor & Publisher* 224 (August 3, 1991): 32, 14–19.

Gregory Curtis. "The End of the Trail." *Brill's Content* (November 2000): 76–80.

Keith Damsell. "Magazine Numbers Unravelled." *The Globe and Mail* (July 6, 2001).

Francis X. Dealy. *The Power and the Money: Inside* The Wall Street Journal (Birch Lane Press, 1993).

Peter Desbarats. *Guide to the Canadian News Media* (Harcourt, Brace, Jovanovich, 1990).

Edwin Diamond. *Behind the Times: Inside* The New York Times (Villard Books, 1994).

Robert Draper. *Rolling Stone Magazine: The Uncensored History* (Doubleday, 1990).

Elizabeth L. Eisenstein. *The Printing Press as an Agent of Change: Communications and Cultural Transformation in Early-Modern Europe*, 2 vols. (Cambridge University Press, 1980).

Bob Ferguson. "Critics Crank Up Pressure over Black's Newspaper Play." *Toronto Star* (May 23, 1998).

Douglas Fetherling. *The Rise of the Canadian Newspaper* (Oxford University Press, 1990).

Otto Friedrich. *Decline and Fall* (Harper & Row, 1969).

John Geddes. "The Izzy and Leonard Show." *Maclean's* (August 14, 2000).

Douglas H. George. *The Smart Magazines: 50 Years of Literary Revelry and High Jinks at* Vanity Fair, The New Yorker, Life, Esquire *and* The Smart Set (Archon Books, 1991).

The Globe and Mail: 150 Years in Canada (1994).

Sarah Hampson. "Bonnie Fuller: Click to the Tabloid Queen's New Domain." *The Globe and Mail* (December 20, 2009).

Dennis Holder, Robert Love, Bill Meyers and Roger Piantadosi, contributors. "Magazines in the 1980s." *Washington Journalism Review* 3 (November 1981): 3, 28–41.

Ernest C. Hynds. *American Newspapers in the 1980s* (Hastings House, 1980).

M. Thomas Inge, editor. *Handbook of American Popular Culture*, Second edition (Greenwood, 1989).

Amy Janello and Brennon Jones. *The American Magazine* (Harry N. Abrams, 1991).

Sammye Johnson and Patricia Projatel. *Magazine Publishing* (NTC, 2000).

Lauren Kessler. *Against the Grain: The Dissident Press in America* (Sage, 1984).

Wilfred Kesterton. "The Growth of the Newspaper in Canada, 1981." In *Communications in Canadian Society*, edited by Benjamin Singer (Addison-Wesley, 1983).

Wilfred Kesterton. *A History of Journalism in Canada* (McClelland & Stewart, 1967).

Michael Leapman. *Arrogant Aussie: The Rupert Murdoch Story* (Lyle Stuart, 1985).

Kent MacDougall. *The Press: A Critical Look from the Inside* (Dow Jones Books, 1972).

Magazines Canada. *Fast Facts 2006.*

Ted Magder. "Franchising the Candy Store." *Canadian American Public Policy Centre* (April 1998).

Casey Mahood. "Black Daily Marks Sector's Boom." *The Globe and Mail* (April 9, 1998).

Barbara Matusow. "Allen H. Neuharth Today." *Washington Journalism Review* 8 (August 1986): 8, 18–24.

Richmond M. McClure. *To the End of Time: The Seduction and Conquest of a Media Empire* (Simon & Schuster, 1992).

Marshall McLuhan. *The Gutenberg Galaxy* (University of Toronto Press, 1962).

Minister of Supply and Services Canada. *A Question of Balance: Report of the Task Force on the Canadian Magazine Industry* (1994).

Al Neuharth. *Confessions of an S.O.B.* (Doubleday, 1989).

Alan and Barbara Nourie. *American Mass-Market Magazines* (Greenwood, 1990).

D.M. Osborne. "Paying Respects." *Brill's Content* (October 1998): 93–95.

Andrew M. Osler. "From Vincent Massey to Thomas Kent: The Evolution of National Press Policy in Canada, 1981." In *Communications in Canadian Society*, edited by Benjamin Singer (Addison-Wesley, 1983).

Theodore Peterson. *Magazines in the Twentieth Century* (University of Illinois Press, 1964).

Sam G. Riley, editor. *Corporate Magazines in the United States* (Greenwood Press, 1992).

Sam G. Riley and Gary W. Selnow, editors. *Regional Interest Magazines of the United States* (Greenwood Press, 1991).

Gene Roberts and Thomas Kunkel, editors. *Breach of Faith: A Crisis of Coverage in the Age of Corporate Newspapering* (University of Arkansas Press, 2002).

Katherine Rosman. "The Secret of Her Success." *Brill's Content* (November 1998): 102–111.

Edward E. Scharfe. *Worldly Power: The Making of* The Wall Street Journal (Beaufort, 1986).

William Shawcross. *Murdoch* (Simon & Schuster, 1993).

Ted Curtis Smythe. "Special Interest Magazines: Wave of the Future or Undertow." In *Readings in Mass Communication*, Sixth edition, edited by Michael Emery and Ted Curtis Smythe (Wm. C. Brown, 1986).

James D. Squires. *Read All About It! The Corporate Takeover of America's Newspapers* (Times Books, 1993).

Jim Strader. "Black on Black." *Washington Journalism Review* 14 (March 1992): 2, 33–36.

W.A. Swanberg. *Luce and His Empire* (Scribners, 1972).

William H. Taft. *American Magazines for the 1980s* (Hastings House, 1982).

John Tebbel. *A History of Book Publishing in the United States*, Vols. 1–3 (R.R. Bowker, 1972–1977).

John Tebbel and Mary Ellen Zuckerman. *The Magazine in America, 1741–1990* (Oxford University Press, 1991).

Hunter S. Thompson. *Fear and Loathing in America: The Brutal Odyssey of an Outlaw Journalism 1968–1976* (Simon & Schuster, 2000).

Times Mirror Center for the People and the Press. *The Age of Indifference* (Times Mirror Company, 1990).

Eric Utne. "Tina's New Yorker." *Columbia Journalism Review* 31 (March/April 1993): 6, 31–37.

Jeannette Walls. *Dish: The Inside Story of World Gossip* (Avon/Spike, 2000).

Jennifer Wells. "Assessing Black's Toronto Plan." *Maclean's* (October 13, 1997).

Anthony Wilson-Smith. "The Scoop on Black." *Maclean's* (March 30, 1998).

Mary Ellen Zuckerman. *History of Popular Women's Magazines in the United States, 1792–1995* (Greenwood, 1999).

Chapter 5

Jason Scott Alexander. "Record Labels Got Hip to the Download Culture: Now It's Radio's Turn." *Broadcast Dialogue Magazine* (March 2004).

Paul Audley. *Canada's Cultural Industries* (Lorimer and Company, 1983).

Randy Bachman and John Einarson. *Taking Care of Business* (McArthur and Company, 2000).

Karen Bliss. "25 Years of Canadian Artists." *Canadian Musician* (March/April 2004).

Robert Brehl. "CRTC Causes Static among Radio Bosses." *The Globe and Mail* (June 9, 1998).

Ethan Brown. *Queens Reigns Supreme* (Anchor, 2005).

Iain Chambers. *Urban Rhythms: Pop Music and Popular Culture* (St. Martin's Press, 1985).

Steve Chapple and Reebee Garofalo. *Rock 'n' Roll Is Here to Pay: The History and Politics of the Music Industry* (Nelson-Hall, 1977).

Stan Cornyn, with Paul Scanlon. *Exploding: The Highs, Hits, Hype, Heroes and Hustler of the Warner Music Group* (Harper, 2002).

R. Serge Denisoff, with William Schurk. *Tarnished Gold: The Record Industry Revisited* (Transaction Books, 1986).

Colin Escort, with Martin Hawkins. *Good Rockin' Tonight: Sun Records and the Birth of Rock 'n' Roll* (St. Martin's Press, 1991).

Peter Fornatale and Joshua E. Mills. *Radio in the Television Age* (Overlook Press, 1980).

Roland Gelatt. *The Fabulous Phonograph: From Tin Foil to High Fidelity* (J.B. Lippincott, 1955).

Peter Goddard and Phillip Kamin, editors. *Shakin' All Over: The Rock and Roll Years in Canada* (McGraw-Hill Ryerson, 1989).

Hugh Graham. "Rule Changes May See Rebirth of Top 40 Radio." *The Globe and Mail* (July 19, 1997).

Steven Hagar. *Hip Hop: The Illustrated History of Break Dancing, Rap Music, and Graffiti* (St. Martin's Press, 1984).

Ron Hall. *The CHUM Chart Book* (Stardust Publications, 1984).

Dick Hebdige. *Cut 'N' Mix: Culture, Identity and Caribbean Music* (Methuen, 1987).

David N. Howard. *Sonic Alchemy: Visionary Music Producers and Their Maverick Recordings* (Hal Leonard, 2004).

Laurel Hyatt. "Back in the Black." *Broadcaster* (February 1998).

Nicholas Jennings. *Before the Gold Rush: Flashbacks to the Dawn of the Canadian Sound* (Viking, 1997).

Nicholas Jennings. "Canadian Rock Explodes." *Maclean's* (March 27, 1995).

Jill Jonnes. *Empires of Light: Edison, Tesla, Westinghouse, and the Race to Electrify the World* (Random House, 2003).

Ted Kennedy. *Oh! Canada Cuts* (Canadian Chart Research, 1989).

Nancy Lathier. "The CanCon Ghetto." *Music Scene* (May/June 1989).

Daphne Lavers. "Canadian Music Week: 2006: That Was Then, This Is Now." *Broadcast Dialogue* (May 2006).

Daphne Lavers. "Canadian Music Week: 2004." *Broadcast Dialogue* (April 2004).

Daphne Lavers. "The Canadian Music Industry." *Broadcast Dialogue* (April 2000).

Elianna Lev. "Music Mogul Wants to Change How Music Is Sold." *Canadian Press* (November 30, 2006).

Nanda Lwin. *Canada's Top Hits of the Year, 1975–1996* (Music Data Canada, 1998).

Katherine Macklem. "Turn Up the Music." *Maclean's* (July 30, 2001).

Greil Marcus. *Mystery Train: Images of America in Rock 'n' Roll Music* (Penguin Usapaper Plume, 1997).

Michael McCabe. "CANCON Not the Only Measure of Radio's Contribution." *Broadcaster* (February 1998).

Darryl McDaniels with Bruce Haring. *King of Rock: Respect, Responsibility and My Life with Run-DMC* (St. Martin's Press, 2001).

Steve McLean. "HMV Analysis Reveals 23% Canadian Sales." *The Record* (May 25, 1998).

Martin Melhuish. *Heart of Gold: 30 Years of Canadian Pop Music* (CBC Enterprises, 1983).

James Miller. *Flowers in the Dustbin: The Rise of Rock 'n' Roll, 1947–1977* (Simon & Schuster, 1999).

Angela Pacienza. "Court Rejects Music Copyright Suit." *Toronto Star* (March 31, 2004).

Mike Roberts. "Finger on the Pulse: MuchMusic Still Strong after 10 Years." Montreal *Gazette* (January 22, 1995).

Jeff Rose-Martland. "Takin' Care of Business: Is Suing Your Clientele a Sound Idea?" *Broadcast Dialogue* (May 2004).

Heather Schoffield and Robert Brehl. "Radio Stations Told to Turn Up the Volume" and "CRTC Opens Radio Markets." *The Globe and Mail* (May 1, 1998).

Barry L. Sherman and Joseph R. Dominick. "Violence and Sex in Music Videos: TV and Rock 'n' Roll." *Journal of Communication* 36 (Winter 1986): 1, 79–93.

Stephen Singular. *The Rise and Rise of David Geffen* (Birch Lane, 1997).

Justin Smallbridge. "Think Global: Act Local." *Canadian Business* (June 1996).

Nancy Smith. "Morality in the Media." *Broadcast Dialogue* (May 2006).

Larry Starr, Christopher Waterman and Jay Hodgson. *Rock: A Canadian Perspective* (Oxford University Press, 2009)

Barry Truax. *Acoustic Communication*, Second edition (Greenwood, 2001).

Dick Weissman. *The Music Business: Career Opportunities and Self-Defense* (Crown Publishers, 1979).

Chapter 6

Jason Scott Alexander. "Newcap's Latest Arrival is Bringing iPod Listeners Back to Ottawa Radio." *Broadcast Dialogue* (April 2006).

Len Arminio. "Broadcasting's Overlooked Genius." *Broadcast Dialogue* (October 2006).

Erik Barnouw. *The Image Empire: A History of Broadcasting in the United States, 1953–On* (Oxford University Press, 1970).

Erik Barnouw. *The Golden Web: A History of Broadcasting in the United States, 1933–1953* (Oxford University Press, 1968).

Erik Barnouw. *A Tower in Babel: A History of Broadcasting in the United States to 1933* (Oxford University Press, 1966).

Gary Belgrave. "Study Demonstrates Radio's Effectiveness." *Broadcast Dialogue* (March 2010).

John R. Bittner. *Broadcast Law and Regulation* (Prentice Hall, 1982).

Robert Brehl. "CRTC Causes Static among Radio Bosses." *The Globe and Mail* (June 9, 1998).

John Bugailiskis. "Stern's Show Slim on Canadian Content." *Broadcaster* (September 1997).

"CAB Fires Back at Music Industry Radio Content Claims." *Broadcaster Industry News* (April 1996).

Canadian Association of Broadcasters. *A Broadcaster's Guide to Canada's Cultural Mosaic, 1988.*

Gerald Carson. *The Roguish World of Dr. Brinkley* (Holt, Rinehart & Winston, 1960).

CBC Enterprises. *Fifty Years of Radio: A Celebration of CBC Radio 1936–1986.*

Howard Christensen. "Blackout: Radio to the Rescue." *Broadcast Dialogue* (October 2003).

Ray Conlogue. "Radio Shock Jock Strikes a Nerve." *The Globe and Mail* (September 3, 1997).

Andrew Coyne. "Cracking Down on Howard." *St. Catharines Standard* (September 20, 1997).

Andrew Crisell. *Understanding Radio* (Methuen, 1990).

CRTC. *Broadcast Policy Monitoring Report 2007.*

Guy Dixon. "Out of Tune?" *The Globe and Mail* (March 14, 2006).

Thomas Doherty. "Return with Us Now to Those Thrilling Days of Yesteryear: Radio Studies Rise Again." *Chronicle of Higher Education* (May 21, 2004): B12–B13.

Gerald Eskenazi. *I Hid It Under the Sheets: Growing Up with Radio* (University of Missouri Press, 2006).

Philip Fine. "Radio Stations Ponder Fate of Stern's Show." *The Globe and Mail* (November 22, 1997).

Marc Fisher. "Resurgent Radio." *American Journalism Review* (December 2000): 32–37.

James C. Foust. *Big Voices of the Air: The Battle over Clear Channel Radio* (Iowa State University Press, 2000).

"The Fowler Years: A Chairman Who Marches to His Own Drummer." *Broadcasting* 112 (March 23, 1987): 12, 51–54.

Peter Goddard. "It's Talk, Talk, Talk All over the Radio." *Toronto Star* (October 29, 1995).

Lynne Schafer Gross. *Telecommunications: An Introduction to Radio, Television and Other Electronic Media*, Second edition (Wm. C. Brown, 1986).

John Harding. "Radio—The Momentum Continues." *Broadcast Dialogue* (January 2001).

Susanne Hiller. "That You Bas? After 40 Years on Air, Bas Jamieson's Not Allowed to Retire." *Newfoundlanders Abroad, 2002.*

Robert L. Hilliard and Michael C. Keith. *Dirty Discourse: Sex and Indecency in American Radio* (Iowa State Press, 2003).

Laurel Hyatt. "Back in the Black." *Broadcaster* (February 1998).

Laurel Hyatt. "Radio's Recipe for Success." *Broadcaster* (April 1996): 12–15.

Donald Jack. *Sinc, Betty and the Morning Man* (Macmillan, 1977).

Daphne Lavers. "DAB Launch." *Broadcast Dialogue* (August 1999).

Murray B. Levin. *Talk Radio and the American Dream* (D.C. Heath, 1987).

Kirk Makin. "Brrrrring . . . brrrrring: You're on the Air." *The Globe and Mail* (July 16, 1994).

Michael McCabe. "CANCON Not the Only Measure of Radio's Contribution." *Broadcaster* (February 1998).

Doug Saunders. "AM Listeners Tuning Out." *The Globe and Mail* (October 20, 1997).

Heather Schoffield and Robert Brehl. "Radio Stations Told to Turn Up the Volume" and "CRTC Opens Radio Markets." *The Globe and Mail* (May 1, 1998).

Philip M. Seib. *Going Live: Getting the News Right in a Real-Time, Online World* (Rowman & Littlefield, 2000).

Sandy Stewart. *A Pictorial History of Radio in Canada* (Gage, 1975).

Doug Thompson. "Ode to the Disc Jockey." *Broadcast Dialogue* (May 2006).

Kevin G. Wilson. *Deregulating Telecommunications: U.S. and Canadian Telecommunications, 1840–1997* (Rowman & Littlefield, 2000).

Erik Zorn. "The Specialized Signals of Radio News." *Washington Journalism Review* 8 (June 1986): 6, 31–33.

Chapter 7

James Adams. "Our Box Office Not So Boffo." *The Globe and Mail* (February 3, 2007).

Sid Adilman. "Nat Taylor, 98: Canada's First Movie Mogul." *Toronto Star* (March 2, 2004).

Peter Biskind. *Down and Dirty Pictures: Miramax, Sundance and the Rise of Independent Film* (Simon & Schuster, 2004).

Paul Buhle and Dave Wagner. *A Very Dangerous Citizen: Abraham Lincoln Polonsky and the Hollywood Left* (University of California Press, 2001).

Steven DeRosa. *Writing with Hitchcock: The Collaboration of Alfred Hitchcock and John Michael Hayes* (Faber & Faber, 2001).

Bernard F. Dick. *Engulfed: Paramount Pictures and the Birth of Corporate Hollywood* (University Press of Kentucky, 2001).

Harvey Enchin. "Film Industry Has Its Critics." *The Globe and Mail* (September 8, 1997).

Gary Evans. "Canadian Film." In *Mediascapes: New Patterns in Canadian Communication* (Thomson, 2002).

Seth Feldman and Joyce Nelson. *Canadian Film Reader* (Peter Martin and Associates, 1977).

Douglas Fetherling. *Documents in Canadian Film* (Broadview Press, 1988).

Richard E. Foglesong. *Married to the House: Walt Disney World and Orlando* (Yale University Press, 2001).

Louis Giannetti and Jim Leach. *Understanding Movies*, Third Canadian edition (Prentice Hall, 2005).

Dade Hayes and Jonathan Bing. *Open Wide: How Hollywood Box Office Became a National Obsession* (Miramax, 2004).

Nicholas Jarecki. *Breaking In: How 20 Film Directors Got Their Start* (Broadway, 2002).

Brian D. Johnson. "The Lost Picture Show." *Maclean's* (April 17, 2006).

Garth Jowett. "American Domination of the Motion Picture Industry." In *Movies as Mass Communication*, edited by Garth Jowett and James M. Linton (Sage, 1980).

Jim Leach. *Film in Canada* (Oxford University Press, 2006).

Spike Lee, as told to Kaleem Aftab. *Spike Lee: That's My Story and I'm Sticking to It* (Norton, 2005).

Peter Lefcourt and Laura J. Shapiro, editors. *The First Time I Got Paid for It: Writers' Tales from the Hollywood Trenches* (Public Affairs, 2000).

Emmanuel Levy. *Oscar Fever: The History and Politics of the Academy Awards* (Continuum, 2001).

Jon Lewis. *Hollywood v. Hardcore: How the Struggle over Censorship Created the Modern Film Industry* (New York University Press, 2001).

Gayle Macdonald. "The Vast Picture Show." *The Globe and Mail* (January 17, 1998).

Colin McGinn. *The Power of Movies* (Pantheon, 2006).

Katherine Monk. *Weird Sex and Snowshoes and Other Canadian Film Phenomena* (Raincoast Books, 2001).

David L. Robb. *Operation Hollywood: How the Pentagon Shapes and Censors Movies* (Prometheus, 2004).

Kazi Stastna. "The Golden Age of the Silver Screen." Montreal *Gazette* (January 13, 2006).

Bohdan Szuchewycz and Jeannette Sloniowski. *Canadian Communications: Issues in Contemporary Media and Culture* (Prentice Hall, 2001).

Chapter 8

Paul Atallah and Leslie Regan Shade. *Mediascapes: New Patterns in Canadian Communication* (Thomson Nelson, 2002).

Paul Audley. *Canada's Cultural Industries* (Lorimer and Company, 1983).

Patricia Bailey. "Why Canuck TV Sucks—And Quebec Shows Thrive." *Winnipeg Free Press* (July 6, 2003).

Erik Barnouw. *Tube of Plenty: The Evolution of American Television* (Oxford University Press, 1975).

Warren Bennis and Ian Mitroff. *The Unreality Industry* (Carol Publishing, 1989).

Roger Bird. *Documents in Canadian Broadcasting* (Carleton University Press, 1988).

Donald Bogle. *Primetime Blues: African Americans on Network Television* (Straus & Giroux, 2001).

Robert Brehl. "Specialty Channels Change TV Patterns." *The Globe and Mail* (March 21, 1998).

Jennings Bryant and J. Alison Bryant, editors. *Television and the American Family*, Second edition (Erlbaum, 2001).

John Bugailiskis. "TV Finally Gets Interactive." *Broadcaster* (April 2000).

CanWest Global Communications. *2006 Annual Report.*

Mary Lu Carnevale. "Untangling the Debate over Cable Television." *Wall Street Journal* (March 19, 1990): 107, B1, B5, B6.

Bill Carter. *Desperate Networks* (Doubleday, 2006).

CBC. *2005–2006 Annual Report.*

Mark Christensen and Cameron Stauth. *The Sweeps* (Morrow, 1984).

CRTC. *Broadcasting Policy Monitoring Report 2009.*

CRTC. "Dramatic Choices: A Report on English Language Drama." (2003).

CRTC. "The New Policy on Canadian Television: More Flexibility, Diversity and Programming Choice." (1999).

CTV. *2006 Annual Report.*

Peter Desbarats. *Guide to the Canadian News Media* (Harcourt Brace, 1990).

Ian Edwards. "Specs Enjoy Stellar Growth." *Playback* (March 2004).

John Greenwood. "Shaw Bid a Bet on Content." *National Post* (May 4, 2010).

Danylo Hawaleshka. "Converging on Your Living Room." *Maclean's* (August 6, 2001).

Helen Holmes and David Tara. *Seeing Ourselves: Media Power and Policy in Canada* (Harcourt Brace, 1996).

Laurel Hyatt. "Canadian Content Key to New Television Policy." *Broadcaster* (July 1999).

Ed Joyce. *Prime Times, Bad Times* (Doubleday, 1988).

J.D. Lasica. *Darknet: Hollywood's War against the Digital Generation* (Wiley, 2005).

John McGrath. "The Smart Road to HDTV in Canada." *Broadcaster* (July 2000).

Joshua Meyrowitz. *No Sense of Place: The Impact of the Electronic Media on Social Behavior* (Oxford University Press, 1985).

Peter C. Newman. "Save the Country by Salvaging the CBC." *Maclean's* (February 19, 1996).

Peter B. Orlik. *Electronic Media Criticism: Applied Perspectives*, Second Edition (Erlbaum, 2000).

Lucas A. Powe Jr. *American Broadcasting and the First Amendment* (University of California Press, 1987).

John P. Robinson and Mark R. Levy. *The Main Source* (Sage, 1986).

Reese Schonfeld. *Me and Ted Against the World: The Unauthorized Story of the Founding of CNN* (HarperCollins, 2001).

Roger P. Smith. *The Other Face of Public Television: Censoring the American Dream* (Algora, 2002).

Statistics Canada. "Television Broadcasting." *The Daily* (July 12, 2010).

Duncan Stewart. "Video on Demand." *National Post* (September 29, 2003).

Bohdan Szuchewycz and Jeannette Sloniowski. *Canadian Communications: Issues in Contemporary Media and Culture* (Prentice Hall, 2001).

Mary Vipond. *The Mass Media in Canada* (James Lorimer and Company, 1992).

Jennifer Wells. "Izzy's Dream." *Maclean's* (February 19, 1996).

Hank Whittemore. *CNN: The Inside Story* (Little, Brown, 1990).

Chapter 9

Alan B. Albarran and David H. Goff, editors. *Understanding the Web: Social, Political and Economic Dimensions of the Internet* (Iowa State University Press, 2000).

Ken Auletta. *World War 3.0* (Random House, 2001).

Tim Berners-Lee, with Mark Fischetti. *Weaving the Web: The Original Design and the Ultimate Destiny of the World Wide Web by Its Inventor* (Harper San Francisco, 1999).

David Bondanis. *Electric Universe* (Crown, 2005).

Robert Brehl. "Brave New World." *Toronto Star* (March 30, 1996).

Vannevar Bush. "As We May Think." *Atlantic Monthly* (July 1945).

Bruce Cheadle. "Beware: There's Bad News Behind Internet Headlines." *Hamilton Spectator* (January 15, 2007).

Adam Cohen. "A Wired Village." *Time Digital* (December 2000): 58–62.

"Crime in Cyberspace." *Maclean's* (May 22, 1995): 50–58.

CRTC. *Broadcast Policy Monitoring Report 2006.*

CRTC. "CRTC Won't Regulate the Internet." (May 19, 1999).

Ben Elgin, with Steve Hamm. "The Last Days of Net Mania." *Business Week* (April 16, 2001): 110–118.

Martha FitzSimons, editor. *Media, Democracy and the Information Highway* (Freedom Forum Media Studies Center, 1993).

Urs E. Gattiker. *The Internet as a Diverse Community: Cultural, Organizational and Political Issues* (Erlbaum, 2001).

George Gilder. *Telecosm: How Infinite Bandwidth Will Revolutionize Our World* (Free Press, 2000).

Jack Goldsmith and Tim Wu. *Who Controls the Internet? Illusions of a Borderless World* (Oxford University Press, 2006).

J. Storrs Hall. *Nanofuture* (Prometheus, 2005).

John Heilemann. *Pride Before the Fall: The Trials of Bill Gates and the End of the Microsoft Era* (HarperCollins, 2001).

Industry Canada. "An Anti Spam Plan for Canada" (May 2004).

Ipsos Reid Canada. "Digital Divide Remains Wide: Only 6 in 10 Canadians Aged 55+ Have Access to the Internet" (February 15, 2007).

Ipsos Reid Canada. "The Canadian Inter@ctive Reid Report: Fact Guide." (April 2006).

Robert Lucky. *Silicon Dreams* (St. Martin's Press, 1989).

Steve Maich. "Pornography, Gambling, Lies, Theft, and Terrorism: The Internet Sucks." *Maclean's* (October 30, 2006): 44–49.

Kevin Maney. "Will the Techno Tsunami Wash Us Out?" *Quill* (March 1994): 16–18.

Gordon Moore. "Solid State Physicist: William Shockley." *Time* (March 29, 1999): 193–195.

JoAnn Napier. "Online Advertising Rise 96% in a Year." *Ottawa Citizen* (March 20, 2000).

John V. Pavlik. *New Media Technology: Cultural and Commercial Perspectives* (Allyn & Bacon, 1995).

Mark Slouka. *War of the Worlds* (Basic Books, 1996).

Statistics Canada. "Internet Service Providers." *The Daily* (December 18, 2006).

Statistics Canada. "Canadian Internet Use Survey." *The Daily* (August 15, 2006).

Neal Stephenson. "Mother Earth, Motherboard." *Wired* (December 1996): 97–160.

Robert Wright. "The Man Who Invented the Web." *Time* (May 19, 1997): 160–164.

Chapter 10

Angus Reid Group. *Canadians and the News Media* (Canadian Corporate News, 1998).

Jim Bawden. "Taking Care of Business." *Starweek Magazine* (May 17, 1997).

L. Brent Bozell III and Brent H. Baker, editors. *And That's the Way It Isn't: A Reference Guide to Media Bias* (Media Research Center, 1990).

Ben Bradlee. *A Good Life: Newspapering and Other Stories* (Simon & Schuster, 1996).

"Brits vs. Yanks: Who Does Journalism Right?" *Columbia Journalism Review* (May/June 2004): 44–49.

Canada. *Kent Commission on Newspapers: Canadian News Services*, Volume 6 (Supply and Services, 1981).

Canada. *Kent Commission on Newspapers: The Journalists*, Volume 2 (Supply and Services, 1981).

Canadian Media Research Consortium. *Report Card on Canadian News Media.* (2004). Available online at http://www.cmrcccrm.ca/english/reportcard2004/01.html.

Robert Cribb. "Iraqi War Reshaped Reporting." *Toronto Star* (April 16, 2003).

James L. Crouthamel. *Bennett's New York Herald and the Rise of the Popular Press* (Syracuse University Press, 1989).

Daniel J. Czitrom. *Media and the American Mind: From Morse to McLuhan* (University of North Carolina Press, 1982).

Peter Desbarats. *Guide to the Canadian News Media* (Harcourt Brace, 1990).

Hazel Dicken-Garcia. *Journalistic Standards in the Nineteenth Century* (University of Wisconsin Press, 1989).

Rosie DiManno. "Too Many Critics Shooting the Messenger in Iraq." *Toronto Star* (March 26, 2004).

Edwin Emery and Michael Emery. *The Press and America*, Fourth edition (Prentice Hall, 1984).

Kathleen L. Endress. "Help-Wanted Finale: *Editor & Publisher* Frames Civil Rights Issue." *Journalism and Mass Communication Quarterly* (Spring 2004): 7–21.

Mark Fishman. *Manufacturing the News* (University of Texas Press, 1980).

Thomas L. Friedman. *From Beirut to Jerusalem* (Farrar, Straus & Giroux, 1989).

Herbert J. Gans. *Deciding What's News: A Study of* CBS Evening News, NBC Nightly News, Newsweek *and* Time (Pantheon, 1979).

Brian Green. *Canadian Broadcast News: The Basics* (Harcourt Canada, 2001).

Jane T. Harrigan. *Read All About It! A Day in the Life of a Metropolitan Newspaper* (Globe Pequot Press, 1987).

Michael Higgins. "Vigilant, Honest Media Imperative in a War." *The Record* (March 25, 2003).

Norman E. Isaacs. *Untended Gates: The Mismanaged Press* (Columbia University Press, 1986).

Ryszard Kapuscinski. *The Soccer War* (Alfred A. Knopf, 1991).

H.G. Kariel and L.A. Rosenvall. *Places in the News: A Study of News Flows* (Carleton University Press, 1995).

Wilfred Kesterton. *A History of Journalism in Canada* (McClelland & Stewart, 1967).

Anne Kingston. "Pamela Wallin's Wild Kingdom." *Saturday Night* (June 1997).

Brooke Kroeger. *Nellie Bly: Daredevil, Reporter, Feminist* (Random House, 1994).

Roy MacGregor. "When Journalism is About the Hits, The Craft Goes Amiss." *The Globe and Mail* (March 14, 2010).

Molly Moore. *A Woman at War: Storming Kuwait with the U.S. Marines* (Scribner's, 1993).

Michael Parenti. *Inventing Reality: The Politics of the Mass Media* (St. Martin's Press, 1988).

Nancy Roberts. *The Press and America: An Interpretive History of the Mass Media*, Eighth edition (Allyn & Bacon, 1997).

David F. Rooney. *Reporting and Writing for Canadian Journalists* (Prentice Hall, 2001).

Karenna Gore Schiff. *Lighting the Way: Nine Women Who Changed Modern America* (Miramax, 2006).

Michael Schudson. *Discovering the News: A Social History of American Newspapers* (Basic Books, 1978).

Pamela J. Shoemaker, with Elizabeth Kay Mayfield. *Building a Theory of News Content: A Synthesis of Current Approaches.* Journalism Monographs, No. 103 (June 1987).

William David Sloan, editor. *The Media in America*, Sixth edition (Vision Press, 2005).

Joe Strupp. "What Gives?" *Editor & Publisher* (May 2007).

Deborah Tetley. "Calgary Herald Reporter Michelle Lang Given Press Award." Regina *Leader-Post* (May 3, 2010).

David Walkis, editor. *Killed: Great Journalism Too Hot to Print* (Nation, 2004).

David H. Weaver and G. Cleveland Wilhoit. *The American Journalist: A Portrait of U.S. News People and Their Work*, Second edition (Indiana University Press, 1991).

Anthony Wilson-Smith. "Wall to Wall News." *Maclean's* (March 2, 1998).

Bob Woodward and Carl Bernstein. *All the President's Men* (Simon & Schuster, 1974).

Antonia Zerbisias. "The News about TV News." *Toronto Star* (July 20, 1997).

Chapter 11

Scott M. Cutlip, Allen H. Center and Glen M. Broom. *Effective Public Relations*, Sixth edition (Prentice Hall, 1985).

Stewart Ewen. *PR! A Social History of Spin* (Basic Books, 1996).

Rene A. Henry. *Marketing Public Relations* (Iowa State University Press, 2000).

Ray Eldon Hiebert. *Courtier to the Crowd: The Story of Ivy Lee and the Development of Public Relations* (Iowa State University Press, 1966).

Robert Jackall and Janice M. Hirota. *Image Makers: Advertising, Public Relations and the Ethos of Advocacy* (University of Chicago Press, 2000).

Michael L. Kent and Maureen Taylor. "Toward a Dialogic Theory of Public Relations." *Public Relations Review* (February 2002).

Bruce Livesey. "PR Wars: How the PR Industry Flacks for Big Business." *Canadian Dimension* (November–December 1996).

George S. McGovern and Leonard F. Guttridge. *The Great Coalfield War* (Houghton Mifflin, 1972).

Kevin McManus. "Video Coaches." *Forbes* 129 (June 7, 1982).

Lael M. Moynihan. "Horrendous PR Crises: What They Did When the Unthinkable Happened." *Media History Digest* 8 (Spring–Summer 1988): 1, 19–25.

Joyce Nelson. *The Sultans of Sleaze: Public Relations and the Media* (Between the Lines, 1989).

Barbara Pollock. "A Profession for Tomorrow." Canadian Public Relations Society. Available online at http://www.cprs.ca/cprsprof_tom.html.

"The Rankings." *Marketing Magazine* (June 21, 2004).

Sally J. Ray. *Strategic Communication in Crisis Management: Lessons from the Airline Industry* (Quorum, 1999).

Herbert Schmertz and William Novak. *Good-bye to the Low Profile: The Art of Creative Confrontation* (Little, Brown, 1986).

Michael S. Sweeney. *Secrets of Victory: The Office of Censorship and the American Press and Radio in World War II* (University of North Carolina Press, 2001).

Ray Truchansky. "In Today's Business World, Good PR is Priceless." *Edmonton Journal* (April 7, 2001).

Larry Tye. *The Father of Spin: Edward L. Bernays and the Birth of Public Relations* (Crown, 1998).

Jean Valin. "Truth Pays Dividends with Public." Canadian Public Relations Society. Available online at http://www.cprs.ca/cprstruth.htm.

Perry Dean Young. *God's Bullies: Power Politics and Religious Tyranny* (Henry Holt, 1982).

Chapter 12

Dave Balter and John Butman. *Grapevine: The New Art of Word-of-Mouth Marketing* (Portfolio, 2005).

Mary Billard. "Heavy Metal Goes on Trial." *Rolling Stone* 582–583 double issue (July 12–26, 1990): 83–88, 132.

Competition Bureau. "Law and Litigation: About the Acts." Available online at http://www.competitionbureau.gc.ca.

CRTC. *Navigating Convergence: Charting Canadian Communications Change and Regulatory Implications* (February 2010).

Bruce DeMara. "Now Playing: Corporate Sponsorship." *Toronto Star* (January 24, 2007).

Stephen Fox. *The Mirror Makers: A History of American Advertising and Its Creators* (Morrow, 1984).

John Kenneth Galbraith. *The Affluent Society* (Mariner Books, 1998).

Interbrand. *Interbrand's Best Canadian Brands, 2008*. Available online at http://www.interbrand.ca.

Helen Katz. *Media Handbook: A Complete Guide to Advertising, Media Selection, Planning, Research and Buying*, Third edition (Erlbaum, 2006).

Wilson Bryan Key. *Subliminal Seduction: Ad Media's Manipulation of a Not So Innocent America* (New American Library, 1972).

Otto Kleppner, Thomas Russell and Glenn Verrill. *Advertising Procedure*, Eighth edition (Prentice Hall, 1990).

Bob Levenson. *Bill Bernbach's Book: A History of the Advertising That Changed the History of Advertising* (Random House, 1987).

Jay Conrad Levinson and Charles Rubin. *Guerrilla Advertising* (Mariner Books, 1998).

Nancy Millman. *Emperors of Adland: Inside the Advertising Revolution* (Warner Books, 1988).

David Ogilvy. *Ogilvy on Advertising* (Vintage, 1985).

David Ogilvy. *Confessions of an Advertising Man* (Atheneum, 1963).

Andrew Potter. "Galbraith's Theory of Advertising Had Us All Fooled." *Maclean's* (May 15, 2006).

Anthony Pratkanis and Elliot Aronson. *Age of Propaganda: The Everyday Use and Abuse of Persuasion* (W.H. Freeman, 1992).

Brenda Pritchard and Susan Vogt. *Advertising and Marketing Law in Canada*, Second edition (Butterworth, 2006).

Tom Reichert and Jacqueline Lamblase, editors. *Sex in Consumer Culture: The Erotic Content of Media and Advertising* (Erlbaum, 2006).

Ronald H. Rotenberg. *Advertising: A Canadian Perspective* (Allyn and Bacon, 1986).

Paul Rutherford. *The New Icons? The Art of Television Advertising* (University of Toronto Press, 1994).

Michael Schudson. *Advertising, the Uneasy Persuasion: Its Dubious Impact on American Society* (Basic Books, 1984).

Television Bureau of Canada (TVB). *Canadian Net Advertising Revenue by Medium* (2009).

Keith J. Tuckwell. *Canadian Advertising in Action*, Eighth edition (Prentice Hall, 2009).

Robbin Lee Zeff and Brad Aronson. *Advertising on the Internet*, Second edition (John Wiley, 1999).

Chapter 13

James Atlas. "Beyond Demographics: How Madison Avenue Knows Who You Are and What You Want." *Atlantic* 254 (October 1984): 4, 49–58.

Charles O. Bennett. *Facts without Opinion: First Fifty Years of the Audit Bureau of Circulations* (Audit Bureau of Circulations, 1965).

David Bray. *The Truth about Portable People Meters*. Available online at http://hennessyandbray.com/content/truth-about-portable-people-meters.

Keith Damsell. "Magazine Numbers Unravelled." *The Globe and Mail* (July 6, 2001).

Tom Dickson. *Mass Media Education in Transition: Preparing for the 21st Century* (Erlbaum, 2000).

Dan Fleming, editor. *Formations: 21st Century Media Studies* (Manchester University Press, 2001).

George Gallup. *The Sophisticated Poll Watcher's Guide* (Princeton Opinion Press, 1972).

Michelle Gaulin. "Measuring Readership." *Ryerson Review of Journalism* (Spring 2004).

Shearson A. Lowery and Melvin L. DeFleur. *Milestones in Mass Communication Research: Media Effects* (Longman, 1983).

Philip Meyer. *Precision Journalism*, Second edition (Indiana University Press, 1979).

David W. Moore. *The Superpollsters: How They Measure and Manipulate Public Opinion in America* (Four Walls Eight Windows, 1992).

Paula M. Poindexter and Maxwell E. McCombs. *Research in Mass Communication: A Practical Guide* (St. Martin's Press, 2000).

Alan Prendergast. "Wendy Bergin's Exclusive Hoax." *Washington Journalism Review* 13 (October 1991): 8, 30–34.

Philip Preville. "Do We Have a Sweeps Week?" *Saturday Night* (March 10, 2001).

William S. Rubens. "A Personal History of TV Ratings, 1929 to 1989 and Beyond." *Feedback* 30 (Fall 1989): 4, 3–15.

Robert Strauss. "The Man without a Dog in the Fight." *Trust* 1(2) (Fall 1998): 2–7.

Kenneth F. Warren. *In Defense of Public Opinion Polling* (Westview, 2001).

James G. Webster, Patricia F. Phalen and Lawrence W. Lichty. *Ratings Analysis: The Theory and Practice of Audience Research*, Third edition (Erlbaum, 2006).

Michael J. Weiss. *The Clustering of America* (Harper & Row, 1988).

Roger D. Wimmer and Joseph R. Dominick. *Mass Media Research: An Introduction*, Fifth edition (Wadsworth, 1997).

Richard Saul Wurman. *Information Anxiety* (Doubleday, 1989).

Chapter 14

Ellen Alderman and Caroline Kennedy. *The Right to Privacy* (Knopf, 1995).

Erin Anderssen. "Illegal Downloading: How Do You Explain It to the Kids?" *Globe and Mail* (May 16, 2010).

Paul Benedetti, Tim Currie and Kim Kierans. *The New Journalist* (Emond Montgomery Publications, 2010).

Brian Bergman. "The Battle over Censorship." *Maclean's* (October 24, 1994).

Thomas Bivins. *Mixed Media: Moral Distinctions in Advertising, Public Relations and Journalism* (Erlbaum, 2004).

Richard J. Brennan. "Copyright: Consumer vs. Artists." *Toronto Star* (May 30, 2010).

Steven Chase. "Ottawa to Make Cracking Digital Encryption Illegal." *The Globe and Mail* (June 1, 2010).

Clifford G. Christians, Kim B. Rotzoll and Mark Fackler. *Media Ethics*, Sixth edition (Longman, 2002).

Roy Peter Clark. "The Original Sin: How Plagiarism Poisons the Press." *Washington Journalism Review* (March 1983): 43–47.

Tony Clement and James Moore. "Time to Transform Our Laws." *National Post* (June 2, 2010).

Michael G. Crawford. *The Journalist's Legal Guide* (Carswell, 1996).

Robert E. Denton Jr., editor. *Political Communication Ethics: An Oxymoron?* (Praeger, 2000).

Timothy Findley. "Point–Counterpoint: Ethics in the Media." *Journal of Canadian Studies* 27 (1992–1993): 4, 198.

Matthew Fraser. "Time to Change Channels." *National Post* (March 7, 2001).

Michael Gartner. "Fair Comment." *American Heritage* (October–November 1982): 28–31.

Bernard Goldberg. *Bias* (Regnery, 2002).

Brian Green. *Broadcast News Essentials* (Harcourt Brace, 2001).

Sally Harris and David Potts. "Important Elements of the Internet Applicable to Cyber Libel" (July 31, 2001). Available online at http://www.cyberlibel.com/elements.html.

Carl Hausman. *The Decision-Making Process in Journalism* (Nelson-Hall, 1990).

Matthew Ingram. "Media Stardom is Pricey." *The Globe and Mail* (June 15, 2007).

Walter B. Jaehnig. "Harrison Cochran—The Publisher with a Past." *Journal of Mass Media Ethics* 2 (Fall/Winter 1986–87): 1, 80–88.

Dean Jobb. *Media Law for Canadian Journalists* (Emond Montgomery Publications, 2006).

Paul Kaihla. "Sex and the Law." *Maclean's* (October 24, 1994).

Donna Soble Kaufman. *Broadcasting Law in Canada: Fairness in the Administrative Process* (Carswell, 1987).

Wilfred H. Kesterton. *The Law and the Press in Canada* (McClelland & Stewart, 1976).

Janet Malcolm. *The Journalist and the Murderer* (Knopf, 1990).

John C. Merrill. *The Dialectic in Journalism: Toward a Responsible Use of Press Freedom* (Louisiana State University Press, 1990).

Clark R. Mollenhoff. "25 Years of *Times* v. *Sullivan*." *Quill* (March 1989): 27–31.

Ralph B. Potter. "The Structure of Certain American Christian Responses to the Nuclear Dilemma, 1958–1963" (Ph.D. Diss., Harvard University, 1965).

Lori Robertson. "Ethically Challenged." *American Journalism Review* (March 2001): 20–29.

Stuart Robertson. *Pocket Guide to Media Law* (Hallion Press, 1994).

Stuart Robertson. *The Media Law Handbook* (Self-Counsel Press, 1983).

Nick Russell. *Morals and the Media: Ethics in Canadian Journalism*, Second edition (University of British Columbia Press, 2006).

Ron F. Smith. *Groping for Ethics in Journalism*, Fourth edition (Iowa State University Press, 1999).

Colin Sparks and John Tulloch, editors. *Tabloid Tales: Global Debates over Media Standards* (Rowman & Littlefield, 2000).

Joe Strupp. "Policing Plagiarism." *Editor & Publisher* (August 7, 2000): 19–22.

Philip Weiss. "Bad Rap for TV Tabs." *Columbia Journalism Review* 28 (May/June 1989): 1, 39–42.

Marie Dunn White. "Plagiarism and the News Media." *Journal of Mass Media Ethics* 4 (1989): 2, 265–280.

Chapter 15

Lisa Blackman and Valerie Walkerdine. *Mass Hysteria: Critical Psychology and Media Studies* (Palgrave, 2001).

Donald Bogle. *Primetime Blues: African Americans on Network Television* (Straus & Giroux, 2001).

Jane D. Brown, Jeanne R. Steele and Kim Walsh-Childers, editors. *Sexual Teens, Sexual Media: Investigating Media's Influence of Adolescent Sexuality* (Erlbaum, 2001).

Carolyn Byerly and Karen Ross. *Women and Media: A Critical Introduction* (Blackwell, 2005).

Margaret Gallagher. *Gender Setting: New Media Agenda for Monitoring and Advocacy* (Palgrave, 2001).

Gabriele Griffin. *Representations of HIV and AIDS: Visibility Blues* (Manchester University Press, 2001).

Carolyn Kitch. *The Girl on the Magazine Cover* (University of North Carolina Press, 2002).

Lewis H. Lapham. *Gag Rule: On the Suppression of Dissent and the Stifling of Democracy* (Penguin, 2004).

Paul Lazarsfeld, Bernard Berelson and Hazel Gaudet. *The People's Choice: How the Voter Makes Up His Mind in a Presidential Campaign*, Second edition (Bureau of Applied Social Research, 1948).

Joshua Meyrowitz. *No Sense of Place: The Impact of Electronic Media on Social Behavior* (Oxford University Press, 1985).

Elizabeth M. Peers. *Media Effects and Society* (Erlbaum, 2001).

Michael Pickering. *Stereotyping: The Politics of Representation* (Palgrave, 2001).

Antonia Zerbisias. "What You Can Restrict: Children." *Toronto Star* (January 18, 2007).

Chapter 16

Herbert J. Altschull. *Agents of Power* (Longman, 1984).

J. Augment, P. Bross, R. Hiebert, O.V. Johnson and D. Mills. *Eastern European Journalism Before, During and After Communism* (Hampton, 1999).

Ben Bagdikian. *The Media Monopoly*, Fifth edition (Beacon, 1997).

Stephen P. Banks. *Multicultural Public Relations: A Social-Interpretive Approach*, Second edition (Iowa State University Press, 2000).

Chris Barker. *Television, Globalization and Cultural Identities* (Open Universities, 1999).

Eric Barnouw and S. Krishnaswamy. *Indian Film* (Columbia University Press, 1963).

Carl L. Becker. *Freedom and Responsibility in the American Way of Life* (Vintage, 1945).

Isaiah Berlin. *Karl Marx: His Life and Environment* (Oxford University Press, 1939).

David Buckingham, Hannah Davies, Ken Jones and Peter Kelley. *Children's Television in Britain: History, Discourse and Policy* (British Film Institute, 1999).

Bernard Cohen. *The Press and Foreign Policy* (Princeton University Press, 1963).

Commission on Freedom of the Press. *A Free and Responsible Press* (University of Chicago Press, 1947).

James Curran, editor. *Media Organizations in Society* (Oxford University Press, 2000).

Frank Ellis. *From Glasnost to the Internet: Russia's New Infosphere* (St. Martin's Press, 1999).

Donna Evleth. *The Authorized Press in Vichy and German-Occupied France, 1940–1944: A Bibliography* (Greenwood, 1999).

Howard H. Frederick. *Global Communication and International Relations* (Wadsworth, 1993).

Thomas L. Friedman. *The World Is Flat: A Brief History of the 21st Century* (Farrar, Straus and Giroux, 2005).

Micah Garen and Marie-Hélène Carleton. *American Hostage: A Memoir of a Journalist Kidnapped in Iraq and the Remarkable Battle to Win His Release* (Simon & Schuster, 2005).

Urs E. Gattiker. *The Internet as a Diverse Community: Cultural, Organizational and Political Issues* (Earlbaum, 2001).

Leo A. Gher and Hussein Y. Amin, editors. *Civic Discourse and Digital Age Communication in the Middle East* (Greenwood, 2000).

Joseph Gibbs. *The Soviet Media in the First Phase of Perestroika* (Texas A&M University Press, 1999).

"Global Views on U.S. Media." *Media Studies Journal* (Fall 1995).

Emma Gray. "Glasnost Betrayed." *Media Studies Journal* (Spring-Summer 2000): 94–99.

Shelton A. Gunaratne, editor. *Handbook of the Media in Asia* (Sage, 2000).

William A. Hachten and Harva Hachten. *The World News Prism*, Fifth edition (Iowa State University Press, 1999).

Edward S. Herman and Robert W. McChesney. *The Global Media: The New Missionaries of Global Capitalism* (Cassell, 1997).

William E. Hocking. *Freedom of the Press: A Framework of Principle* (University of Chicago Press, 1947).

Wolfgang Hoffmann-Riem. *Regulating Media: The Licensing and Supervision of Broadcasting in Six Countries* (Guilford, 1996).

Frank Hughes. *Prejudice and the Press* (Devin-Adair, 1950).

L. Martin John and Anju Grover Chaudhary. *Comparative Mass Media Systems* (Longman, 1983).

Carla Brooks Johnston. *Winning the Global TV News Game* (Focal Press, 1995).

Jason Kirby. "Blood Splats and Bean Counters." *Maclean's* (January 29, 2007).

Jerry W. Knudson. "Licensing Journalists in Latin America: An Appraisal." *Journalism and Mass Communication Quarterly* (Winter 1996): 878–889.

Abbas Malek and Anandam P. Kavoori, editors. *The Global Dynamics of News: Studies in International News Coverage and News Agenda* (Ablex, 2000).

Marilyn Matelski. *Vatican Radio* (Praeger, 1995).

Robert W. McChesney. *Corporate Media and the Threat to Democracy* (Seven Stories Press, 1997).

John C. Merrill. *Global Journalism: Survey of International Communication* (Longman, 1995).

John C. Merrill. *The Imperative of Freedom: A Philosophy of Journalistic Autonomy* (Hastings House, 1974).

Ellen Mickiewicz. *Changing Channels: Television and the Struggle for Power in Russia*, Second edition (Duke University Press, 1999).

John C. Nerone, editor. *Last Rites: Revisiting Four Theories of the Press* (University of Illinois Press, 1995).

David D. Perlmutter. *Photojournalism and Foreign Policy: Icons of Outrage in International Crises* (Praeger, 1998).

Frank Rose. "Vivendi's High Wireless Act." *Wired* (December 2000): 318–333.

Herbert Schiller. *Mass Communications and American Empire* (Kelley, 1969).

Fred Siebert, Theodore Peterson and Wilbur Schramm. *Four Theories of the Press* (University of Illinois Press, 1956).

Tony Silvia, editor. *Global News: Perspectives on the Information Age* (Iowa State University Press, 2001).

Frank Smyth. "Danger Zone: When the Press Becomes the Target." *Quill* (December 2000): 58–59.

Colin Sparks, with Anna Reading. *Communism, Capitalism and the Mass Media* (Sage, 1999).

Michael S. Sweeney. *Secrets of Victory: The Office of Censorship and the American Press and Radio in World War II* (University of North Carolina Press, 2001).

Joseph Robson Tanner. *English Constitutional Conflicts of the Seventeenth Century, 1603–1689* (Cambridge University Press, 1928).

Daya Kishan Thussu. *International Communication: Continuity and Change* (Arnold, 2000).

Daya Kishan Thussu, editor. *Electronic Empires: Global Media and Local Resistance* (Arnold, 1999).

Sun Xupei. *An Orchestra of Voices: Making the Argument for Greater Speech and Press Freedom in the People's Republic of China* (Greenwood, 2000).

Chapter 17

Eric Alterman. *When Presidents Lie: A History of Official Deception and Its Consequences* (Viking, 2004).

Ken Auletta. "Vox Fox." *The New Yorker* (May 26, 2003): 58–73.

David Brock. *The Republican Noise Machine: Right-Wing Media and How It Corrupts Democracy* (Crown, 2004).

Noam Chomsky and Edward Herman. *Manufacturing Consent: The Political Economy of the Mass Media* (Pantheon, 1988).

Craig Crawford. *Attack the Messenger: How Politicians Turn You Against the Messenger* (Littlefield, 2005).

David Dadge. *Casualty of War: The Bush Administration's Assault on a Free Press* (Prometheus, 2004).

Claes H. de Vreese. "The Effects of Frames in Political Television News on Issue Interpretations and Frame Salience." *Journalism and Mass Communication Quarterly* (Spring 2004): 36–52.

Shanda Deziel. "Parliament Hill and the Press Gallery: One Big Unhappy Family." *Maclean's* (June 6, 2006).

Dave Eaves. "The Skinny on Stephen Harper's YouTube Moment." *The Globe and Mail* (March 17, 2010).

James Fallows. *Breaking the News: How the Media Undermine American Democracy* (Vintage Books, 1997).

Augie Fleras. *Mass Communication in Canada* (Thomson Nelson, 2003).

Jürgen Habermas. *An Inquiry into a Category of Bourgeois Society* (MIT Press, 1991).

Dean Jobb. *Media Law for Canadian Journalists* (Emond Montgomery, 2006).

Pierre Killeen. *Facebook and Prorogation.* Rideau Institute (January 21, 2010).

Allan Levine. *Scrum Wars: The Prime Ministers and the Media* (Dundurn Press, 1993).

Anne McGrath. "Media and Politics." In *Mediascapes* (Thomson Nelson, 2002).

Elizabeth M. Perse. *Media Effects and Society* (Erlbaum, 2001).

David D. Perlmutter. "Political Blogs: The New Iowa?" *Chronicle of Higher Education* (May 26, 2006): B6–B8.

Michael Pfau, Michel Haigh, Mitchell Gettle, Michael Donnelly, Gregory Scott, Dana Warr and Elaine Wittenberg. "Embedding Journalists in Military Combat Units: Impact on Newspaper Story Frames and Tone." *Journalism and Mass Communication Quarterly* (Spring 2004): 74–88.

Stephen D. Reese, Oscar H. Grady Jr. and August E. Grant, editors. *Framing Public Life: Perspectives on Media and Our Understanding of the Social World* (Erlbaum, 2001).

Nick Russell. *Morals and the Media* (UBC Press, 2006).

Danny Schecter. *Embedded: Weapons of Mass Deception* (Prometheus, 2003).

Jane Taber. "Will Stephen Harper's YouTube Video Go to Pot?" *Globe and Mail* (March 16, 2010).

David Taras. *The Newsmakers: The Media's Influence on Canadian Politics* (Nelson Canada, 1990).

Helen Thomas. *Watchdogs of Democracy? The Waning Washington Press Corps and How It Has Failed the Public* (Scribner/Lisa Dew, 2006).

Ivor Tossell. "Stephen Harper Online! But Don't Call It Social Media." *The Globe and Mail* (March 14, 2010).

Mary Vipond. *The Mass Media in Canada* (James Lorimer and Company, 2000).

Stephen J. Wayne. *The Road to the White House, 2000* (Palgrave, 2001).

Paul Wells. "Without Enemies, Harper Is Looking for Trouble." *Maclean's* (July 20, 2006).

Photo Credits

t/c/b/l/r: top/centre/bottom/left/right

Chapter 1

p. 1 Norman James/GetStock.com; **p. 2** Norman James/GetStock.com; **p. 3** © Andy Sacks/Getty Images; **p. 4** Courtesy Library of Congress; **p. 9** friends.ca; **p. 11** CBS-TV/THE KOBAL COLLECTION

Chapter 2

p. 14 THE CANADIAN PRESS/Sean Kilpatrick; **p. 16** © Hilde Vanstraelen; **p. 17** THE CANADIAN PRESS/Andrew Vaughan; **p. 18/l** © AP Images/Mathew B. Brady; **p. 18/r** © L.C. Handy/CORBIS; **p. 20** © Bettmann/CORBIS; **p. 23** © Yale Joel/Time Life Pictures/Getty Images; **p. 25** © 2007 Linden Research, Inc; **p. 27** © Liz Hafalia/*San Francisco Chronicle*/CORBIS

Chapter 3

p. 33 © FRANCIS SPECKER/Landov; **p. 35** © Robert Voets/CBS/Courtesy Everett Collection; **p. 38** Ben Kaller © TNT/Courtesy Everett Collection; **p. 42** Courtesy of the author; **p. 44** © Andreas Rentz/Getty Images; **p. 46** © Andreas Rentz/Getty Images

Chapter 4

p. 51 © Jeff Cook of the *Quad Times*; **p. 53** Reprinted with courtesy of Canadian Newspaper Association 1998 ad; **p. 54** Used by permission of the *Chicago Tribune*; **p. 57** *National Post*; **p. 58** Courtesy of Metro Valley Newspaper Group; **p. 59** © Lonnie Busch; **p. 60** CP PHOTO/Nathan Denette; **p. 62** Cover/hologram photo illustration by Tom Schaefges. © National Geographic Society. Used with permission; **p. 63/l** Margaret Bourke-White/Time Life Pictures/Getty Images; **p. 63/r** © George Strock//Time Life Pictures/Getty Images; **p. 64/t** Reprinted by permission of *Maclean's* magazine; **p. 64/b** Courtesy of *Chatelaine* magazine; **p. 67** Copyright © 1992 Watterson. Reprinted with permission of Universal Press Syndicate. All rights reserved; **p. 69** © Andrew H. Walker/Getty Images; Courtesy Isobel McKenzie-Price

Chapter 5

p. 71 © Vicki Beaver/Alamy; **p. 72** © AP Images/Dima Gavrysh; **p. 74** © Kim Kulish/CORBIS; **p. 77** Courtesy of author; **p. 80** Photo by Jeff Chalmers; **p. 83** © Reuters/CORBIS

Chapter 6

p. 85 © AP Images/Gregory Bull; **p. 88** © AP Images; **p. 91** © AP Images/Gregory Bull; **p. 93** Courtesy of author; **p. 94** Courtesy XM Satellite Radio

Chapter 7

p. 97 Johnnie Eisen; **p. 99** © Buena Vista/Courtesy Everett Collection; **p. 102** *The Big Snit*, directed by Richard Condie, copyright 1985 National Film Board of Canada; **p. 105/l** © AP Images; **p. 105/r** © Hulton Archive/Getty Images

Chapter 8

p. 116 Phillip MacCallum/Getty Images; **p. 118** © Jonathan Nourok/PhotoEdit; **p. 120/t** Courtesy CBC; **p. 120/c** Courtesy CTV; **p. 120/b** Courtesy Global Television Network; **p. 122** © & ™ Fox/Photofest; **p. 125/t/l** Courtesy LG Electronics MobileComm; **p. 125/t/r** Copyright 2008, Tribune Media Services. Reprinted with permission; **p. 125/c** Cliff Lipson/© CBS/Courtesy Everett Collection; **p. 125/c/r** John Filo/CBS, copyright 2005 CBS Broadcasting, Inc. All Rights Reserved

Chapter 9

p. 130 © Justin Sullivan/Getty Images; **p. 135** © AP Images; **p. 139** © Copyright 2007 Strategic Forecasting Inc. All rights reserved

Chapter 10

p. 144 © M. Kaia Sand, Courtesy Jules and Maxwell Boykoff; **p. 146** Copyright © North Wind Picture Archives. All rights reserved; **p. 147/r** © Bettmann/CORBIS; **p. 147/c** Copyright © North Wind Picture Archives. All rights reserved; **p. 149/t** © Culver Pictures, Inc.; **p. 149/b** © Culver Pictures, Inc.; **p. 150** © Public Domain. *The Halifax Gazette*. March 23, 1752, Cover page and page 2, nic-2638; **p. 156** Courtesy Lori Santarpio/Boston Herald

Chapter 11

p. 164 © TIM SLOAN/AFP/Getty Images; **p. 168/l** Courtesy Colorado Historical Society; **p. 168/r** © AP Images; **p. 172** Used with permission from McDonald's Corporation; **p. 174/l** © Kevin Horan; **p. 174/r** © Abe Frajndlich; **p. 175** Courtesy Dawn Bridges; **p. 176** © NICHOLAS KAMM/AFP/Getty Images; **p. 179** © Bettmann/CORBIS

Chapter 12

p. 181 Chris Wattie/Reuters/Landov; **p. 186** © AP Images/Pat Sullivan; **p. 189** DaimlerChrysler/Screenshot from Tony Hawk's Pro Skater 2, Courtesy Activision Publishing, Inc. © 2000 Activision Publishing, Inc. All Rights Reserved; **p. 191/t** Rick Eglinton/*The Toronto Star*; **p. 191/b** © AP Images/Brian Kersey; **p. 194** Courtesy Ogilvy & Mather, London and Ford of Europe; **p. 195** Courtesy Bamboo, Inc.; **p. 196** © Dick Hemingway; **p. 197** © www.adbusters.org

Chapter 13

p. 199 Courtesy Nielsen Media Research; **p. 202** Courtesy The Gallup Organization; **p. 203** Courtesy The Gallup Organization; **p. 209** © AP Images/The Free Press, Mankato/John Cross; **p. 211** © Dennis Kitchen/Getty Images

Chapter 14

p. 217 © AP Images/Wilfredo Lee; **p. 221** © State Historical Society of Iowa, Iowa City; **p. 224** CP PHOTO/Tobin Grimshaw; **p. 231** © Erich Lessing/Art Resource, NY; **p. 232/t** Copyright © North Wind Picture Archives; **p. 232/c** Copyright © North Wind Picture Archives; **p. 232/b** © Bettmann/CORBIS; **p. 233** © Fritz Goro/Time Life Pictures/Getty Images; **p. 235** Courtesy Office of Communications Arts at Harvard Divinity School; **p. 236** © David M. Grossman; **p. 238** Getty Images

Chapter 15

p. 242 © Culver Pictures, Inc.; **p. 248** A BAND APART/MIRAMAX/THE KOBAL COLLECTION; **p. 250** © J. Emilio Flores/Getty Images; **p. 253/t** © SIO Archives, UCSD; **p. 253/b** Provided by Virgin Comics, LLC. © 2006 DEVI, All rights reserved; **p. 258** © Kyle Cassidy, ASC

Chapter 16

p. 263 Copyright © North Wind Picture Archives. All rights reserved; **p. 265** © PhotoEdit/Alamy; **p. 267** © RABIH MOGHRABI/AFP/Getty Images; **p. 276** © China Photos/Getty Images; **p. 278** Courtesy Video Sound, Inc., NJ; **p. 279** © Reuters/CORBIS

Chapter 17

p. 281 © John G. Mabanglo/epa/Corbis; **p. 284** © CNN. All rights reserved; **p. 285** © PAUL J. RICHARDS/AFP/Getty Images; **p. 291/l** © BRIAN SNYDER/REUTERS/Landov; **p. 291/r** © CHRISTOPHE MORIN/Maxpp/Landov

Name Index

Subject Index

S

T

U

V

W

X

Y